CONGRESS VOLUME

VIENNA 1980

SUPPLEMENTS

TO

VETUS TESTAMENTUM

EDITED BY
THE BOARD OF THE QUARTERLY

J. A. EMERTON - W. L. HOLLADAY - A. LEMAIRE
R. E. MURPHY - E. NIELSEN - R. SMEND
J. A. SOGGIN - M. WEINFELD

VOLUME XXXII

LEIDEN
E. J. BRILL
1981

CONGRESS VOLUME

VIENNA
1980

EDITED BY

J. A. EMERTON

LEIDEN
E. J. BRILL
1981

ISBN 90 04 06514 8

PRINTED IN THE NETHERLANDS

CONTENTS

PREFACE

The Tenth Congress of the International Organization for the Study of the Old Testament was held from 24 to 29 August 1980 in Vienna under the Presidency of Professor W. J. Kornfeld, of the Catholic Faculty of Theology in the University of Vienna. The present volume bears witness that the primary purpose of such meetings was attained: to bring together scholars from different parts of the world and from different religious traditions to study the Old Testament and to discuss its problems. In accordance with their purpose of encouraging international co-operation among scholars, Congresses are also occasions when friendships are made and renewed, and there are welcome opportunities to meet informally and to visit places of interest. The excursion in 1980 was a visit to the Abbey of Melk, followed by a drive along the Danube valley and a stop at Dürnstein. There were also two memorable receptions. One was given in a setting of great splendour at Klosterneuburg by the Cardinal Archbishop of Vienna, Dr Franz König, and the Protestant Bishop, Dr Oskar Sakrausky. The other reception, at the invitation of the Bürgermeister, was at the city Rathaus, where we were given both a good meal and the opportunity to dance—dancing is an innovation at Congresses of the IOSOT, but what could be more appropriate in the city of Johann Strauss? Another innovation, which doubtless brought the Congress to the attention of many who would otherwise have been unaware of its existence, was the issue of special Austrian postage stamps to mark the occasion.

The present volume includes, as usual, all the papers read by invitation at the Congress. I am grateful to Dr André Lemaire and Professor Rudolf Smend, two of my colleagues on the Editorial Board, for suggestions concerning some of the papers in French and German, respectively. It is also a pleasure to record my thanks to Professor G. P. Braulik, the Secretary of the Congress, for his help in ensuring that the papers were ready for me in good time—and it is appropriate to record at the same time the gratitude of all who were present for all that he did to make the Congress a success.

J. A. Emerton

The President, Professor W. J. Kornfeld,
addressing the opening session of the Congress

THE PRESIDENT'S WELCOME TO THE MEMBERS OF THE CONGRESS AT THE OPENING SESSION

J'ai le plaisir et l'honneur de vous souhaiter la bienvenue, à vous, Mesdames et Messieurs les participants au Xe Congrès IOSOT qui êtes venus conformément aux inscriptions de 28 pays. Comme vous savez, après Copenhague, Strasbourg, Oxford, Bonn, Genève, Rome, Upsal, Edimbourg et Goettingen c'est Vienne qui a été choisie comme ville de congrès pour sa jubilée ce qui est une très vive satisfaction pour nous; cette satisfaction s'exprime dans le fait que le Président de la République fédérale d'Autriche a bien voulu se charger du patronage de ce congrès et que la Direction générale des Télécommunications autrichiennes a profité de l'occasion pour éditer un timbre spécial. En raison de son statut de neutralité et de sa position géographique entre l'est et l'ouest l'image de l'Autriche se dessine de plus en plus comme lieu de rencontre pour les étudiants et les représentants des disciplines scientifiques les plus diverses. 11% de tous les étudiants en Autriche sont étrangers et à vrai dire, ils viennent de plus de 100 états différents, 50 % d'Europe, 40 % des pays en voie de développement. Depuis 1960 460 professeurs venant de l'étranger ont été nommés dans une université autrichienne. Environ 100.000 chercheurs participent chaque année à des congrès scientifiques qui ont dépassé depuis longtemps le nombre des 800. Comme c'est le cas de notre congrès, c'est un gain partculièrement important que les collègues venant de l'est et de l'ouest — c'est à dire du monde entier — puissent avoir un échange de vues et d'informations tout à fait libre.

* *
*

May I once more welcome you to our exchange of information and let me make a few remarks on the invitations for reports to be held here in Vienna. In accordance with the wish expressed recurrently that scholars who have not yet given reports at a Congress ought to get a chance to do so, I decided to take up this suggestion for our Congress here in Vienna, as the list of names in the programme indicates.

Moreover, I tried to consider the equal distribution of denominational and linguistic aspects. Under these circumstances no main theme was to be found, yet the choice of topics offered by the highly esteemed participants of this Congress permitted a sub-division into smaller sections.

As all my predecessors in the office of the president of Congresses past can certify, a highly essential task in the preparation and actual performance of our meeting has been the supply of the funds necessary. On behalf of all of us let me therefore express my special gratitude for the subsidies granted by the Austrian Federal Ministry of Science and Research, the City Council of Vienna, the Catholic and Protestant Churches of Austria and the Federal Republic of Germany; with the utmost cordiality I want at the same time to thank all banks, insurance companies and those entrepreneurs whose generous donations greatly contributed to the success of this Congress—they are listed in the *Tabula gratulatoria* of our programme.

This very circumstance permitted the invitation of 55 scholars from the states of Eastern Europe—regrettably not all of them got their authorities' permission to follow this invitation. We are happy to welcome 37 scholars now among us.

* *
*

Gestatten Sie mir nun ein paar Worte über die Beziehung Wiens zu unserer Wissenschaft. Die Wiener Universität wurde 1365 gegründet und ist daher nach dem Ausscheiden der Carolina Prag die älteste Universität des deutschen Sprachraumes. In den Akten der Theologischen Fakultät 1420 findet sich die folgende Eintragung: "Commissum fuit per facultatem magistris Nicolao de Dinkelspühel et Petro de Pulka, ut laborarent pro aliquibus libris Ebraicae linguae saltem melioribus et magis correctis . . .". Die Studiengesetze Kaiser Ferdinands I, aus 1537 und 1554 kennen die Fächer Altes Testament, Neues Testament und Systematische Theologie und bezeichnen den Vertreter unserer Disziplin als "professor primarius", der das Biblicum auf Grund der Vulgata unter ständiger Berücksichtigung des Masoretentextes vorzutragen hatte.

Kaiserin Maria Theresia, deren 200. Todestag wir heuer begehen, errichtete nicht nur die Orientalische Akademie in Wien, sondern erließ 1752 eine neue Studienordnung, nach der täglich 1 Stunde Altes Testament vorzutragen war um in einem vierjährigen Zyklus sämtliche Texte darlegen zu können und für das zweistündige Rigorosum wurde verordnet: "Das Alte Testament Hebraicum muß er fertig, wo es ihm nur aufgemacht wird, interpretiren. In Sacra Scriptura mus er die Antilogien und höheren Sensus Literarios Behändig zu heben wissen." Seit Kaiser Leopold II 1790 gehörten Hebräisch, Aramäisch, Syrisch, Arabisch, die hebräischen Altertümer und Introductio zu den obligaten Fächern der alttestamentlichen Studien.

Stellvertretend für viele Ordinarien unseres Faches an der kath. -theol. Fakultät seien genannt:

1) Johann Jahn, der an der Wende des 18. zum 19. Jhdt hier lehrte und u.a. eine 5-bändige *Biblische Archäologie*, eine 4-bändige *Biblische Hermeneutik* und je eine hebräische, syrische, chaldäische und arabische Sprachlehre samt Chrestomatien herausbrachte und 1806 eine kritische Ausgabe des Masoretentextes publizierte—allerdings mit seiner Auffassung, Job, Tobias und Judith wären Lehrgedichte, in kirchlichen Kreisen Anstoß erregte.

2) Alois Musil (1868-1944) war hier ordentlicher Professor 1909-1920. Seine mehrbändigen Werke *Arabia Petrea* und *Arabia Deserta* sind noch heute grundlegend für die historische Geographie, Topographie und Kartographie des Nahen Ostens.

3) Nivard Schlögl, der mit seinem Werk *De re metrica Hebraeorum veterum* (Wien, 1899) einen Markstein für die Konjekturalkritik und biblische Metrik setzte.

Die hiesige ev.-theol. Fakultät wurde 1821 als Lehranstalt gegründet und 1850 zur Fakultät erhoben, die 1861 das Promotionsrecht erhielt. 1922 wurde sie in die Alma Mater Rudolphina als mit den übrigen Fakultäten gleichberechtigt aufgenommen. Als Ordinarien wirkten hier vor dem jetzigen Professor Georg Sauer (seit 1969): Werner H. Schmidt (1966-69), Ernst Kutsch (1963-66), Georg Fohrer (1954-62), Fritz Wilke (1909-54) und Ernst Sellin (1897-1908).

Schließlich darf nicht vergessen werden, daß die Orientalistik und damit oft indirekt unsere Wissenschaft bereichert wurde in der Vergangenheit durch den innigen Kontakt zwischen Österreich und dem Osmanischen Reich. 1886 wurde hier das Institut für Orientalistik gegründet, welches seit 1887 die *WZKM* herausbrachte, eine Zeitschrift, die auch heute noch erscheint, nachdem das ehem. Institut für Orientalistik in die neuen Institute für Ägyptologie, Judaistik, Altsemitische Philologie, Arabistik, Turkologie und Iranistik aufgegliedert werden mußte.

Es ist wohl selbstverständlich, daß Wien als Metropole eines ehemaligen großen Reiches auch heute noch beachtliche Sammlungen besitzt, die für die alttestamentliche Bibelwissenschaft nutzbringend herangezogen wurden und werden. Aus dem reichen Material des diplomatischen Verkehrs zwischen Wien und der Hohen Pforte konnten die einschlägigen Universitätsinstitute wertvolle Forschungsergebnisse vorlegen. Vor allem möchte ich hier an die über 100.000 griechische, arabische, koptische, hebräische und aramäische Papyri zählende Sammlung Erzherzog Rainer erinnern, aus Faijûm bzw. Alt-Kairo stammend. Aus Anlaß unseres Kongresses habe ich die nichtpublizierten Bibelfragmente dieser Sammlung soeben veröffentlicht und Ihnen je ein Exemplar dediziert, das Sie in Ihrer Kongreßmappe vorfinden.

QDŠ UND GOTTESRECHT IM ALTEN TESTAMENT

VON

WALTER KORNFELD

Wien

Wir sind Zeugen einer weltweiten Bedrohung des Menschen – atomare Vernichtungsmittel, Wettrüsten, Terrorismus, Totalitarismus, Imperialismus, Flüchtlingsströme und Umweltzerstörung seien nur stellvertretend für viele andere Fakten und Symptome genannt. Die im 19. Jahrhundert verkündete Zielvorstellung eines *progressus ad infinitum* hin zu einem Paradies auf Erden erweist sich als Utopie. Forderungen nach Überdenken begangener Wege, nach Veränderung soziologischer Strukturen werden laut. Unübersehbar ist der Schwund naiver Wissenschaftsgläubigkeit. Natur- und Geisteswissenschaften sind gekennzeichnet durch stets zunehmende Spezialisierung, deren Forschungsergebnisse oft faszinieren, aber man vermißt Synthesen und bezweifelt die Möglichkeit, gesamtmenschliche Probleme lösen zu können. Das gleiche Phänomen fortschreitender Gliederung und Unterteilung in stets enger werdende Fachgebiete ist auch in unserer Wissenschaft eine nur allzu bekannte Tatsache. Durch Anwendung der historisch-kritischen Methode werden kleine und kleinste Texteinheiten analysiert, wobei die Resultate naturgemäß nur Detailfragen beantworten. Wissenschaftliche Forschung im Dienste der Wahrheitsfindung muß frei sein und niemand wird Legitimität und Berechtigung unserer Bemühungen zur Lösung auftretender Fragen in Abrede stellen. Darüber hinaus aber darf nicht verabsäumt werden, das Alte Testament, dem wir die Zeit und Kraft unseres Lebens widmen, zur Klärung gegenwärtiger, unsere Existenz berührende Fragen heranzuziehen und bei der Bewältigung akuter Aufgaben zu berücksichtigen. In diesem Zusammenhang erlaube ich mir, in dem mir zur Verfügung stehenden zeitlichen Rahmen einige Gedanken über den Konnex der Begriffsinhalte von *qdš* und Gottesrecht vorzulegen.

Das Begriffsfeld der Radix *qdš* gehört zum unabdingbaren Bestand jeder Religion. Seinem Stellenwert entsprechen Umfang und Bedeutung der einschlägigen religionswissenschaftlichen Publikationen, die aber auch die Änderung in der Beurteilung des Phänomens *heilig* erkennen lassen. Die seit F. Max Müller [1] und James Frazer [2] bevorzugte Ableitung von Machtvorstellungen im Sinne von *mana* und *tabu* erwies sich als wirklichkeitsfremde Konstruktion eines im vorigen Jahrhundert beheimateten evolutionistischen Denkens. Dies gilt, obwohl H. P. Müller noch 1976 für das Alte Testament eine Aufeinanderfolge zweier unterschiedlicher Religiositäten postulierte: "Für eine dynamistisch-magische Religiosität ist *qdš* zunächst mit dem Begriff des Machthaften verbunden. . . Eine persönliche Religiosität gegenüber dem Heiligen kommt erst da auf, wo die heilige Macht in der Gottheit Gestalt findet und dadurch zugleich willenhaft und für den Menschen anrufbar wird".[3] Rudolf Otto [4] setzte mit den Termini *tremendum et fascinosum* insofern eine religionsphilosophische Weichenstellung, als er das Heilige als gegebenes Objekt bestimmte, das dem Menschen als religiösem Subjekt gegenübertritt. Unabhängig von der auf Rudolf Otto folgenden Debatte über das Wie eines religiösen Apriori, eines intuitiven begrifflichen Erkennens besteht heute weitgehendst darin Übereinstimmung, daß das Heilige erfahren wird als Realität, die den Menschen unmittelbar betrifft, als höchste Wertmodalität, als Wertwirklichkeit.[5]

Nun ist im biblischen Bereich – und um diesen geht es uns hier ja ausschließlich – "das Heilige nicht zu denken ohne den Heiligen. . . Das Heilige ist da, wo Gott selber gegenwärtig ist".[6] Ähnlich stellt M. Gilbert in seiner Untersuchung "Le sacré dans l'Ancien Testament" [7] abschließend fest: "Le sacré est toujours en rapport avec le Dieu d'Israël, Yahvé, qu'il s'agisse directement de lui, ou de son culte, ou de son peuple, ou de sa parole" und verweist angesichts der verschiedenen mit *qdš* verbundenen Bedeutungsnuancen auf die Unmöglichkeit, "de montrer un authentique développement chronologique du thème", denn "certains auteurs bibliques insistaient

---

[1] *Natural Religion* (London, 1889).

[2] *Der goldene Zweig* (*The Golden Bough*, Deutsch). *Eine Studie über Magie und Religion* (Köln-Berlin, 1968- Nachdruck).

[3] Art. *qdš*, in E. Jenni - Cl. Westermann, *Theologisches Handwörterbuch zum Alten Testament* 2 (München-Zürich, 1976), Sp. 589-609, bes. 594 und 597.

[4] *Das Heilige. Über das Irrationale in der Idee des Göttlichen und sein Verhältnis zum Rationalen* (München, [40]1973).

[5] J. Splett, *Die Rede vom Heiligen. Über ein religionsphilosophisches Grundwort* (Freiburg-München, 1971); C. Colpe (Hg.), *Die Diskussion um das Heilige* (Darmstadt, 1977).

[6] W. Zimmerli, *Ezechiel* (Neukirchen-Vluyn, [2]1979), S. 1069.

[7] In J. Ries, H. Sauren, G. Kestemont, R. Lebrun, M. Gilbert, *L'expression du sacré dans les grandes Religions* (Louvain-la-Neuve, 1978), S. 205-89.

plus que d'autres sur tel ou tel aspect: la portée de *qdš* n'est pas la même pour tous" (S. 280 f.).

Die Gotteserkenntnis und die mit ihr gegebene Erfahrung des Begriffes "heilig" ist als gesamtmenschliches Phänomen durch die Religionsethnologie erwiesen. Eine semantische Untersuchung der Wurzel *qdš* im Hinblick auf die beiden postulierten ursemitischen Grundformen **qadiš* im ost- und nordwestsemitischen und **qaduš* im westsemitischen Bereich ergäbe im wesentlichen jenen Befund, den H. Cazelles für Ugarit erhob: "*qdš* ... désignant ... des dieux individualisés, puis les lieux ou les personnes qui ont une dépendance vis-à-vis de ces dieux".[8] Daher ist *qādōš* als Attribut Jahwes nicht erstaunlich. Zum erstenmal belegt in der Ladeerzählung "Wer kann bestehen vor Jahwe *hā'aelōhīm haqqādōš*" (1 Sm. vi 20), vergleichbar mit der präexilischen Hapaxform *'aelōhīm qedōšīm hū' 'el qannō' hū'* (Jos. xxiv 19) und der Anrufung "du Jahwe *'aelōhe qodšī*" (Hab. i 12) oder "Jahwe *qādōš hū*'" und "*kī qādōš yhwh 'aelōhenū*" (Ps. xcix 3, 5, 9). Ebenso bedeutet die Eidesleistung Jahwes "bei seiner Heiligkeit" (Am. iv 2; Ps. lxxxix 36) noch nichts außergewöhnliches. Hingegen beginnt der Bereich des religionswissenschaftlichen Sondergutes mit den Textstellen, die die besondere Bindung Jahwes an Israel und umgekehrt voraussetzen. Hier ist vor allem in Anschluß an das Trishagion (Jes. vi 3) das Gottesappellativ *qādōš yiśrā'el* für die gesamte jesajanische Tradition charakteristisch (13 x Protojesaja, 12 x Deuterojesaja, 2 x Tritojesaja und überdies noch Jer. l 29, li 5; Ps. lxxi 22, lxxviii 41, lxxxix 19 und Sir. l 17), an dessen Seite noch *qādōš ya'aqōb* (Jes. xxix 23) zu stellen ist. Ohne außerbiblische Parallele ist, wie H. J. Kraus[9] überzeugend darlegte, die Bezeichnung *'am qādōš*, die zwar nur im Deuteronomium belegt ist (Dt. vii 6, xiv 2, 21, xxvi 19, xxviii 9), aber durch Formulierungen wie "Ihr seid für mich *'anše qōdaeš*" (Ex. xxii 30) oder "Ihr sollt für mich sein *mamlaekaet kōhanīm wegōy qādōš* (Ex. xix 6) vorbereitet wird. Obwohl im Deuteronomium *qādōš* als Gottesattribut nicht vorkommt, wird in ihm doch die Heiligkeit Israels vorausgesetzt, d.h. Israel hat wegen seiner Erwählung zum persönlichen Eigentum Jahwes von selbst die Gebote zu achten und die Fortdauer der Erwählung im Ablauf der

[8] "Impur et sacré à Ugarit", in *Fs. J. Henninger*, *Al Bahit* (*Studia Instituti Anthropos* 28) (St. Augustin bei Bonn 1976), S. 37-47, bes. 39.

[9] "Das heilige Volk. Zur alttestamentlichen Bezeichung *'am qādōš*", in H. J. Kraus, *Biblisch-theologische Aufsätze* (Neukirchen, 1972), S. 37-49 (Erstdruck in *Fs. A. de Quervain*, *Freude am Evangelium* [München, 1966], S. 50-61).

Geschichte hängt von Israels freier Entscheidung ab. In der Priesterschrift hingegen wird die Hauptforderung mit der Heiligkeit Jahwes begründet: *qᵉdōšīm tihyū kī qādōš ʾᵃnī yhwh ʾᵃᵉlōhekaem* (Lev. xix 2), bzw. wird in den Selbstvorstellungstexten Jahwe als der "heiligende" genannt, heiligend Israel *ʾᵃnī yhwh mᵉqaddeš ʾaet-yiśrāʾel* (Ez. xxxvii 28) oder die Priester und die Opfergaben *kī ʾᵃnī yhwh mᵉqaddᵉšām* (Lev. xxi 23, xxii 9, 16).

Durch die Heiligkeit entsteht eine besondere Beziehung zu Gott, sodaß *qdš* etymologisch als "getrennt sein", scilicet vom Nichtheiligen oder Profanen, erklärt werden kann. Primär jedoch ist Jahwe der "Nahe", "Proexistente" (Ex. iii 14), durch dessen Initiative die Schöpfung zur Gemeinschaft mit ihm bestimmt ist. Diese Nähe Gottes bedeutet für den schuldig Gewordenen allerdings ein Strafgericht (Am. ix 1-6; Zef. i 14-18) welches auch unter dem Bild des Weggehens des *kābōd* Jahwes gezeichnet werden kann (Ez. x 18 ff.). Das Naheverhältnis Jahwe-Israel zeigt bereits deutlich die Formulierung *kī ʾel ʾānōkī wᵉlōʾ ʾīš bᵉqirbᵉkā qādōš* (Hos. xi 9; cf. Jes. lv 6; Ps. cxix 151) und setzen die besonders in der Priesterschrift häufigen Stellen voraus, die vom Wohnen Jahwes inmitten seines Volkes handeln (Ex. xxv 8; Lev. xxvi 11 f; Num. v 3; cf. Sach. ii 14). Die Verwendung von *qdš* für das gesamte Land (erstmals Sach. ii 16) und schließlich sogar für die alltäglichen Gebrauchsgegenstände (Sach. xiv 20 f.) verdeutlicht die kommunikative Wirkung.

Mit der Ausweitung des Heiligkeitsbereiches ist auch die Universalisierung des Heiles gegeben, die u.a. in den Texten von der Völkerwallfahrt zum Zion deutlich wird: z.B. *kī betī bet-tᵉpillāh yiqqāreʾ lᵉkol-hāʿammīm* (Jes. lvi 7; cf. Mi. iv 2; Jes. xix 22, xxv 6). Daraus folgt, daß Sünde verstanden werden kann als Weigerung, die Relation der Gottzugehörigkeit und Gottbezogenheit der Schöpfung anzunehmen.

Entgegen der eben vorausgesetzten Erfahrung des Heiligen versucht R. Girard,[10] dieses mit dem Phänomen der Gewalt in Zusammenhang zu bringen. Alle zwischenmenschlichen Beziehungen tendierten zu gegenseitiger Gewalttat. Primitive würden sich daher vor gegenseitiger Vernichtung bewahren, indem sie die diffusen Aggressionen auf ein zufälliges Opfer übertragen und sie auf diese Weise entladen, wodurch das Opfer als "Sündenbock" bis zum Ausbruch einer neuen Krise als Heilbringer empfunden wird. R.

[10] *La violence et le sacré* (Paris, 1972).

Schwager [11] versucht, diese Theorie auf die Bibeltexte anzuwenden und erntete im allgemeinen zustimmenden Beifall.[12] Gewalt wäre das zentralste Thema des Alten Testaments (S. 76), die Handauflegung aller auf den jüdischen Sündenbock veranschauliche die kollektive Entladung einmütiger Gewalt gegen ein stellvertretendes Opfer (S. 33), "ein Übel oder die ansteckende Wirkung des Übels wird übertragen auf jemanden oder etwas und dadurch aus der Gemeinschaft ausgeschlossen... das gleiche dürfte angedeutet sein, wenn in zahlreichen anderen Opfertexten gefordert wird, der Priester oder der Opfernde habe seine Hand auf den Kopf des Tieres zu legen, um eine Entsühnung zu bewirken", wobei es sich bei den Sünden laut Jes. 11-15 nur um Blutschuld handeln könne (S. 97). Die Propheten würden in ihrer Kritik die Untauglichkeit der Opfer aufzeigen, durch die nur eine Vermehrung der Schuld eintrete (S. 100). Rachegebete demonstrierten, daß auch Gerechte in aggressiven Projektionen verfangen blieben (S. 115) und der Ansatz zur Überwindung von Gewalt durch Gewaltlosigkeit würde im Alten Testament durch den *'aebaed* verdeutliche (Jes. lii 13-liii 12), den Gott befähigte, fremde Untaten zu tragen ohne mit gleicher Münze heimzuzahlen (S. 141).

Zunächst erscheint es prinzipiell bedenklich, die von Girard für primitive Gesellschaftsformen erstellte Theorie für das alte Israel mit seiner bäuerlichen und städtischen Kultur anzuwenden, was übrigens Schwager selbst in Erwägung zog (S. 54). Was die nicht in Frage zu stellende Heiligkeit Gottes betrifft, so ist diese sicher nicht als Wirkung eines Opfertodes zu erklären, da Jahwe im Gegensatz zu den Vegetationsgöttern Baal, Osiris, Tammuz etc. nicht stirbt. Völlig unhaltbar ist der Versuch, blutige Opfer und Übertragung kollektiver Gewalt miteinander in Verbindung zu setzen. Das Brandopfer wurde primär dargebracht zur Huldigung (Gen. xxii), Danksagung (1 Sam. vi 14 f.), Bitte (1 Sam. vii 9), ohne daß eine Sühnewirkung erwartet wurde (Gen. viii 20; Ri. vi 19 ff.; 1 Kg. xviii 15 ff. u.ö.). Erst im nachexilischen Kult wurde das Brandopfer vor allem zur Sühne für Sünden gegen Bundespflichten vollzogen. Dabei erfolgte aber weder eine Sündenabladung noch eine

[11] *Brauchen wir einen Sünderbock? Gewalt-Erlösung in den biblischen Schriften*, (München, 1978).

[12] Cf. O. Keel, in *Orientierung* 42 (1978), S. 43-6; N. Lohfink, "Was hat Jesus genutzt?", in *Bibel und Kirche* 34 (1979), S. 39-43; F. J. Stendebach in *Bibel und Kirche* 35 (1980), S. 76.

Straftötung des Opfertieres als Sündenträger – in diesem Fall wäre ja die Opfergabe nicht besonders geheiligt, sondern extrem unrein geworden –, vielmehr war die Handauflegung ein Symbol der Stellvertretung, d.h. das Tier wurde zur Wiederherstellung der Gemeinschaft mit Gott stellvertretend für die Opfernden dargebracht und mit der Lebenshingabe im Blut Sühne geleistet (Lev. xvii 11, 14).[13]

Im übrigen wurde das Sündopfer nur für unabsichtliche Übertretungen der Gottesgebote dargebracht (Lev. iv 1-v 13), während vorsätzliche Sünden als Revolte gegen Jahwe verstanden und mit der Todesstrafe bzw. mit dem göttlichen Strafgericht gesühnt wurden (cf. Num. xv 30 f.; Lev. xx 4 f.).

Im Ritual des großen Versöhnungstages (Lev. xvi), der in vorexilischer Zeit nicht genannt wird und in den erst später dem Heiligkeitsgesetz beigefügten Versen als *yōm hakkippūrīm* – allerdings ohne Sündenbock – erwähnt wird (Lev. xxiii 27 f., xxv 9), werden bekanntlich zwei ursprünglich voneinander unabhängige Kulthandlungen vereinigt. Zur Sühne für das Heiligtum *qōdaeš yiśrā'el*, Unreinheiten *ṭum'ōt*, ihre Freveltaten *piš'ehaem* und ihre Verfehlungen *ḥaṭṭō'tām* werden als Sündopfer ein Stier und ein Bock, und zwar ohne vorherige Handauflegung dargebracht (Lev. xvi 16). Nachdem laut Ritualtext die Sünden vergeben sind, legt nun der Hohepriester – nur er und nicht die ganze Gemeinde! – seine Hände und damit symbolisch die Sünden des Volkes auf den Kopf des Bockes, der daraufhin in die Wüste geführt wird. Das heißt – entgegen der These Girard's – erfolgt weder beim Sündopfer noch beim Rituale des Versöhnungstages eine kollektive Aggressionsentladung auf ein unschuldiges Ersatzopfer, welches überdies an keiner Stelle für das Entstehen alttestamentlicher Heiligkeitsvorstellungen herangezogen werden kann.

Angeregt durch Girard hat auch N. Lohfink das Phänomen der Gewalt aufgegriffen und eine dreiteilige These vorgelegt, nämlich Israels Teilhabe an der Welt der Gewalt, seine Entlarvung der Gewalt und schließlich Israels Verheißung der Gewaltüberwindung.[14]

---

[13] Cf. H. Gese, "Die Sühne", in H. Gese, *Zur biblischen Theologie. Alttestamentliche Vorträge* (München, 1977), S. 85-106, bes. 97; W. Kornfeld, *Das Buch Leviticus* (Düsseldorf, 1972), S. 20 f.

[14] N. Lohfink, R. Pesch, *Weltgestaltung und Gewaltlosigkeit. Ethische Aspekte des Alten und Neuen Testaments in ihrer Einheit und in ihrem Gegensatz* (Düsseldorf, 1978), S. 45-61.

Dabei erhebt sich doch die Frage, ob es nicht zu simplifizierend ist, in gleicher Weise von menschlicher Gewalttätigkeit und Gewalttätigkeit im Gottesbild des Alten Testaments zu sprechen.[15] *ḥāmās* wird nirgends als von Jahwe gewirkt verstanden, was auch vom Begriffsinhalt her ausgeschlossen wäre, denn dabei handelt es sich um die Verletzung einer von Gott gesetzten bezw. garantierten Ordnung.[16] Deshalb ist dieser Ausdruck synonym für Unheil, Schlechtigkeit, Bosheit u.ä. verwendet und bildet das Gegenstück zu *b^erākōt*, *y^ešūʿāh*, *šālōm* etc.[17] Auf einer völlig anderen Ebene liegen jedoch die Anthropomorphismen, die als Bilder für Sanktionen Gottes verwendet werden,[18] welcher Achtung oder Mißachtung seines Willens und seiner Ordnung belohnt oder bestraft – eine Grundwahrheit, die nicht nur im Alten und Neuen Testament (Lev. xxvi 3 ff.; Dt. xxviii 1 ff.; Mt. xxv 31-46) begründet ist, sondern zu der man sich auch nahezu in allen Religionen bekennt. Schließlich wird bekanntlich im menschlichen Verhalten der "Zusammenhang von Tat und Tatfolge" aus theologischer Reflexion "dem richterlichen Walten Jahwes eingeordnet".[19]

In den alttestamentlichen Heiligkeitsaussagen und Heiligkeitsforderungen geht es sicherlich auch um das Problem der Gewalttätigkeit, doch wird es neben anderen Fehlhandlungen gesehen, die in Widerspruch zum zentralen Heilsthema "Gottesgemeinschaft" stehen, deren Voraussetzung und Folge *mišpāṭ* und *ṣ^edāqāh* als Gottesrecht sind. Nach der jüngsten Untersuchung Zimmerli's kann das eigentliche Gottesrecht als das verstanden werden, was Jahwe von seinem Volk erwartet,[20] d.i. die rechte Ordnung und das rechte Verhalten, welche die Gemeinschaft mit Gott und der Menschen untereinander erhält.[21]

---

[15] N. Lohfink, R. Pesch, S. 51[6]: "Es bleibt dabei, daß auf dieser Stufe Gott als einer gesehen wird, der das Recht nur durch Gewalttätigkeit herstellt".

[16] G. von Rad, *Theologie des Alten Testaments* 1 (München, [6]1969), S. 170.

[17] Cf. H. Haag, Art. *ḥāmās*, in G. J. Botterweck, H. Ringgren, *Theologisches Wörterbuch zum Alten Testament* 2 (Stuttgart-Berlin-Köln-Mainz, 1977), S. 1050-61, bes. 1053 f.

[18] Cf. F. Michaeli, *Dieu à l'image de l'homme*, (Neuchâtel-Paris, 1950).

[19] H. D. Preuß, "Das Gottesbild der älteren Weisheit Israel", in *SVT* 23 (1972), S. 117-45, bes. 121; cf. K. Koch, "Der Spruch 'Sein Blut bleibe auf seinem Haupt' und die israelitische Auffassung vom vergossenen Blut", *VT* 12 (1962), S. 396-416.

[20] W. Zimmerli, "Das Gottesrecht bei den Propheten Amos, Hosea und Jesaja", in *Fs. C. Westermann, Werden und Wirken des Alten Testaments* (Göttingen-Neukirchen-Vluyn, 1980), S. 216-35.

[21] H. H. Schmid, *Gerechtigkeit als Weltordnung* (Tübingen, 1968), S. 111-13.

In der 54x, vorwiegend in Jes., Jer. und Ez. belegten Parallelverwendung von *mišpāṭ* und *ṣaedaeq/ṣᵉdāqāh* als von Jahwe selbst gewirkt [22] und gewollt,[32] vom Sproß Davids erhofft [24] und vom König erwartet,[25] den Vorbildern David und Salomo entsprechend.[26] Mit *mišpāṭ-ṣᵉdāqāh* ist nicht nur *ḥāmās* unvereinbar – *ḥāmās wāšōd hāsīrū ūmišpāṭ ūṣᵉdāqāh ʿᵃśū* (Ez. xlv 9) –, sondern überhaupt jedes sich gegen die menschliche Gemeinschaft richtende Verhalten: [27] Unterdrückung, Ausbeutung, Rechtsbeugung, Vergießen von *dām nāqī*, unschuldigen Blutes (Jes. lix 7; Jer. xxii 3, 17) – letzteres offensichtlich in deutlicher Abgrenzung zur legitimen Tötung in Kriegen oder durch strafrechtliche Exekution – ; dem entspricht positiv die dringliche Forderung, dem Notleidenden beizustehen (Jes. lviii 6-10). Da aber in *mišpāṭ-ṣᵉdāqāh* nicht nur die Gemeinschaft der Menschen untereinander, sondern auch jene mit Gott wurzelt, die aufgehoben wird durch Götzendienst (Ex. xviii 5), Sabbatschändung (Jes. lvi 2), kurz durch Verleugnung Jahwes und Abkehr von Gott: *pāšōaʿ wᵉkaḥeš bayhwh wᵉnāsōg meʾaḥar ʾᵃᵉlōhenū* (Jes. lix 13). Da im Alten Testament Recht und Moral nicht differenziert werden,[28] ist es verständlich, daß die in Prophetentexten in Verbindung zu *mišpāṭ-ṣᵉdāqāh* erhobenen Forderungen zwar keine sprachlichen Übereinstimmungen, jedoch zahlreiche Sachparallelen zu den Gesetzen erkennen lassen.[29]

Nun zurück zum eingangs genannten Anliegen. Unsere moderne Gesellschaft ist geprägt von der fortschreitenden Säkularisation unter gleichzeitiger Verdrängung der Religion aus dem Bereich des öffentlichem Lebens. Ebenso breitet sich für jedermann spürbar eine Rechtsunsicherheit aus, da sowohl internationale Vereinbarungen als auch die nationalen Gesetzgebungen von zufälligen Machtverhältnissen oder parlamentarischen Mehrheitsgruppierungen abhän-

---

[22] Jes. xxvi 9, xxviii 17, xxxiii 5, li 4 f.; Jer. ix 23; Hi. xxxvii 23; Ps. xxxvi 7, xcvii 2, xcix 4.

[23] Ps. xxxiii 5, cvi 3.

[24] Jes. ix 6, xvi 5; Jer. xxiii 5, xxxiii 15.

[25] Ps. lxxii 2, lxxxix 15.

[26] 2 Sam. viii 15 = 1 Ch. xviii 14; 1 Kg. x 9 = 2 Ch. ix 8.

[27] cf. Am. v 7, 10-12; Ez. xviii 6.

[28] O. Kaiser, "Gerechtigkeit und Heil bei den israelitischen Propheten und griechischen Denkern des 8.-6. Jhdts", *NZSystThRel* 11 (1969), S. 312-28, bes. 320.

[29] cf. W. Zimmerli, *Das Gesetz und die Propheten* (Göttingen, 1963); W. Kornfeld, "Die Gesellschafts- und Kultkritik alttestamentlicher Propheten", in R. Schulte (ed.), *Leiturgia—Koinonia—Diakonia. Fs. Kard. König zum 75. Geburtstag* (Wien, 1980), S. 181-200, bes. 192-5.

gen. Nun sind alle wesentlichen, unsere menschliche Existenz betreffenden Probleme ethisch-sittlicher Natur und können, wie gerade die Erfahrungen unseres Jahrhunderts lehren, durch ein innerweltliches Profandenken allein nicht gelöst werden. Sobald Gott nicht als irreale menschliche Projektion gesehen, sondern als personale heilige Realität erfaßt wird, kann Recht und Unrecht nicht nach rechtspositivistischen Prinzipien unterschieden werden, sondern einzig und allein nach Möglichkeit oder Unmöglichkeit ihrer metaphysischen Begründbarkeit.

WISDOM AND AUTHORITY: SAPIENTIAL RHETORIC AND ITS WARRANTS

BY

JAMES L. CRENSHAW

Nashville

I

In a recent analysis of classical rhetoric George A. Kennedy writes that "the rhetoric of the Old Testament is preconceptual . . . Indeed, rhetorical consciousness is entirely foreign to the nature of biblical Judaism". [1] Kennedy isolates the essential rhetorical feature in the Hebrew Bible as the "assertion of authority", which leads him to conclude that Old Testament rhetoric "is the simple enunciation of God's truth, uncontaminated by adornment, flattery, or sophistic argumentation" (p. 121). Since divine message-bearers function only as vehicles for God's work, in Kennedy's view, they need no practice in the art of persuasion, for when the time is right, the spirit will move to action those whom God chooses to persuade (p. 122).

One can readily dismiss this misunderstanding of the nature of biblical literature as the inevitable distortion which occurs when specialists attempt to describe the situation outside their respective disciplines.[2] Kennedy's fundamental mistake arises from an assumption that the claim to speak with authority excludes rhetoric. In actual fact, the Hebrew Bible places the two, authority and rhetoric, in uneasy tension in all three canonical divisions, Kennedy's examples notwithstanding.[3] The task of this essay is to throw some light on this strange situation in which persons speak with authority but self-consciously endeavor to master the art of suasion at the same

---

[1] *Classical Rhetoric and its Christian and Secular Tradition from Ancient to Modern Times* (Chapel Hill, 1980), p. 120.

[2] R. Alter, "A Literary Approach to the Bible", *Commentary* 60 (December 1975), pp. 71-2, has rightly faulted the profound analysis of Gen. xxii by E. Auerbach, *Mimesis* (Princeton, 1953), pp. 3-23, for its sweeping character, since many Hebrew narratives are fraught with foreground (e.g. the David story or Esther).

[3] His choice of covenant speeches by Moses and Joshua, adaptation of the form in prophetic literature, and Dame Wisdom's address as representative of the rhetoric in torah, prophecy, and wisdom inevitably led to superficial treatment.

time. For obvious reasons, I shall limit my remarks to the wisdom literature.[4]

It has long been recognized that authority and rhetoric join hands when personified wisdom emerges to take her place upon the Israelite stage.[5] On the one hand, she speaks with an authority approaching the divine, whether inviting persons to life through her or threatening them with abandonment. On the other, she demonstrates rare skill at persuasion, weaving together an argument that is only slightly less appealing, even on the sensual level, than Dame Folly's invitation. The authority which Dame Wisdom assumes flows from at least three different streams: the divine prototypes for personified wisdom,[6] particularly the Egyptian *maat*,[7] the role of teacher which she adopts,[8] and the reliance upon prophetic language.[9] Similarly, her rhetoric

---

[4] For earlier observations on prophetic authority, see *Prophetic Conflict: Its Effect upon Israelite Religion* (*BZAW* 124; Berlin and New York, 1971), pp. 116-23. J. Hempel, "Pathos und Humor in der israelitischen Erziehung", *Von Ugarit nach Qumran* (*BZAW* 77; Berlin, 1958), p. 78, observes that the prophetic claim to divine inspiration resulted in an intimate association between accuracy of prediction and honor; "die Ehre des Weisen aber ist nicht in dem gleichen Ausmass an den pädagogischen Erfolg seines Unterrichtes gebunden". Similarly J. Schmidt singles out wisdom as wholly different from prophecy, poetry, and historical narrative (*Studien zur Stilistik der alttestamentlichen Spruchliteratur* [Munster i. W., 1936], p. 67).

[5] This union of rhetoric and authority is recognized best in two recent works: Phyllis Trible, "Wisdom Builds a Poem: The Architecture of Proverbs 1:20-33", *JBL* 94 (1975), pp. 509-18 [a chiasmus of four concentric circles converging on the center of the poem], and Maurice Gilbert, "Le discours de la Sagesse en Proverbs, 8. Structure et cohérence", *La Sagesse de l'Ancien Testament* (Gembloux and Leuven, 1979), pp. 202-18.

[6] On the phenomenon of personification of wisdom and its impact upon the New Testament, see P. E. Bonnard, "De la Sagesse personifiée dans l'Ancien Testament à la Sagesse en personne dans le Nouveau", *La Sagesse de l'A. T.*, pp. 117-49.

[7] C. Kayatz, *Studien zu Proverbien 1-9* (Neukirchen, 1966), and H. H. Schmid, *Wesen und Geschichte der Weisheit* (*BZAW* 101; Berlin, 1966), pp. 17-22 and *passim*.

[8] B. Lang, *Frau Weisheit: Deutung einer biblischen Gestalt* (Düsseldorf, 1975), discovers the key to understanding personified wisdom in the Israelite scribal school. The teacher serves as a model for Dame Wisdom's activity.

[9] "Wisdom is not such an empirical teacher, resting her case on her personal authority; she promulgates wisdom, advice and admonishment with the authority of Yahweh, and the fear of Yahweh is a new *mūsār*. This is the discipline to which she would have her audience submit, and in introducing this direct claim to divine authority for what she teaches she emerges almost as a prophet, except that she still tends to speak the language of a wisdom teacher" (W. McKane, *Proverbs: A New Approach* [London and Philadelphia, 1970], p. 275). Whether she continues to speak the language of a wisdom teacher is debatable; I would argue that prophetic modes of expression set the distinctive tone here.

combines appeals to ethos, pathos, and logos; stated differently, persuasive technique oscillates among three different poles: the speaker, the audience, and the speech.[10]

The eventual equation of wisdom and torah in Sirach xxiv greatly enhances the presumed authority with which Dame Wisdom addresses her clientele, but this transition is accompanied by no diminution of the necessity for skill at persuasion.[11] Ironically, the subsequent relegation of wisdom to Solomon's bride altogether escapes the notion of bridal subservience, for she is portrayed in regal terminology approaching the divine.[12]

At best, then, we can say that a certain uneasy tension exists in those texts which treat personified wisdom. Does that tension extend beyond this minimal corpus to infuse the entire initial collection of Proverbs? A consensus seems to have formed with regard to this question: Prov. i-ix comprises *instruction* literature, which by its very nature makes authoritative claims. Both the setting for these instructions, the school,[13] and the content, theological wisdom, are said to reinforce the heavy hand of authority present in this collection.[14] Rejection of the school hypothesis[15] in favor of a family context alters the situation little, if any, with respect to authoritative teaching for parents spoke to their children with authority comparable

---

[10] These three categories correspond to the three goals in rhetoric: to charm, to move, and to persuade.

[11] J. Marböck's penetrating analysis of this shifting emphasis, *Weisheit im Wandel: Untersuchungen zur Weisheitstheologie bei Ben Sira* (Bonn, 1971), pp. 34-96, has now been supplemented from the standpoint of canonical criticism, with special attention to anthological composition, by G. T. Sheppard, *Wisdom as a Hermeneutical Construct: A Study in the Sapientializing of the Old Testament* [*BZAW* 151; Berlin and New York, 1980], pp. 19-71.

[12] "Our author is saying in effect that Wisdom is essentially synonymous with the Divine Mind, and thus represents the creative agent of the Deity" (D. Winston, *The Wisdom of Solomon* [Garden City, N.Y., 1979], p. 194).

[13] H.-J. Hermisson, *Studien zur israelitischen Spruchweisheit* (Neukirchen, 1968), pp. 113-36, has endeavored to demonstrate the existence of a temple school in Israel. Further discussion of this vexing problem comes from B. Lang (*Frau Weisheit*, *passim*, and "Schule und Unterricht im alten Israel", *La Sagesse de l'A. T.*, pp. 186-201).

[14] G. von Rad, *Theologie des Alten Testaments* 1 (Munich, 1957), pp. 439-51, E. tr. *Old Testament Theology* 1 (Edinburgh, London and New York, 1962), pp. 441-53; C. Bauer-Kayatz, *Einführung in die alttestamentlichen Weisheit* (Neukirchen, 1969), pp. 36-92.

[15] R. N. Whybray, *The Intellectual Tradition in the Old Testament* (*BZAW* 135; Berlin and New York, 1974), pp. 33-43, and "Yahweh Sayings and their Context in Proverbs, 10, 1-22, 15", *La Sagesse de l'A. T.*, p. 155, n. 8.

to that of teachers who addressed their students. Both parents and teachers recognized the necessity of presenting their message in an attractive form.[16] That is why these brief instructions are rich in persuasive style and vocabulary.

What happens, however, when we move beyond Prov. i-ix and begin to assess the other collections where *sentences* rather than instructions are involved? Does the formal distinction carry in its train a qualitative difference as well? It would seem that the two literary types represent wholly different approaches to reality. Whereas sentences state what is immediately obvious to one and all, once the insight has dawned and achieved verbal articulation, instructions depend upon certain types of legitimating arguments for their cogency.[17] What could be more natural, therefore, than to conclude that the literary types should be distinguished sharply from one another? [18]

The matter is much more complex than this, for in at least four places within Prov. i-ix the two literary types appear hand-in-glove. In each instance a sentence reinforces the argument within an in-

[16] W. Bühlmann, *Vom Rechten Reden und Schweigen*: *Studien zu Proverbien 10-31* (Freiburg, Schweiz and Göttingen, 1976), p. 52, writes: "Die schöne Form verleiht einem gesprochene Wort Authorität und Macht". On the beauty of speech alluded to in Prov. xvi 21, he observes that "solche Worte nicht nur erfreuen, sondern auch andere zu überzeugen vermögen" (p. 59). Hempel describes the art of persuasion in Proverbs and Qoheleth as rich in the following features: (1) ironic metaphors; (2) question and answer; (3) animal similes and numerical proverbs; (4) animal and human imagery; (5) mythical language; (6) better sayings; and (7) other media such as alliteration, rhyme, appeal to special authority (e.g., the royal testament), and irony ("Pathos und Humor", pp. 71-8).

[17] "The most important formal distinction between Instruction and the wisdom sentence is that the imperative is proper to the first and the indicative to the second. The Instruction commands and exhorts and gives reasons why its directives should be obeyed . . . its aim is to command and persuade. The wisdom sentence is an observation with an impersonal form which states a truth but neither exhorts nor persuades" (McKane, *Proverbs*, p. 3). But see his recent perceptive analysis of "Functions of Language and Objectives of Discourse according to Proverbs 10-31", *La Sagesse de l'A. T.*, pp. 166-85. Here McKane distinguishes between transitive and executive language on the one hand and passive speech on the other. On persuasive discourse in Prov. x-xxxi, see also Hermisson, *Studien zur israelitischen Spruchweisheit*, pp. 137-92, and Schmidt, *Studien zur Stilistik der alttestamentlichen Spruchliteratur*, pp. 37-66 (for the entire wisdom corpus).

[18] McKane, *Proverbs*, *passim*, and C. Westermann, "Weisheit im Sprichwort", in K. H. Bernhardt (ed.), *Schalom*: *Studien zu Glaube und Geschichte Israels* (Stuttgart, 1971), pp. 73-85. Note the following claim: "Der Aussagespruch sagt, wie es ist. Zu wissen dass es so ist, ist Weisheit . . . Die Wurde der Weisheit liegt darin, dass sie *nicht* mahnt, *nicht* anstösst, *nicht* auffordert; sie erwartet das Handeln vielmehr als Folge des Erkennens" (p. 76).

struction as if to provide irrefutable proof of the position being defended.

We turn first to Prov. i 6-19, an instruction which warns against highway robbery. The threefold address to the student underlines the heinous nature of the crime as well as its special lure. Although the initial address derives from a family setting, nothing else suggests the context of a home, which seems to have been replaced by a school in this instance. The quotation of the robbers' invitation to villainy contains certain elements that bespeak the attitude of a teacher rather than criminals, suggesting that the speech is an imagined one. To illustrate the folly of such plans, the teacher cites a proverb: "For in vain is a net spread in the sight of any bird". The point seems to be that just as birds watch while a net is being prepared and baited but heedlessly proceed to their capture, so those who scheme violence walk resolutely to their own death.[19] Regardless of the actual sense of this difficult proverb, its presence within an instruction suggests that it functions as a warrant for the teacher's specific message.

The second instruction also begins with an address derived from the family setting, but that context seems to persist throughout (vi 20-35).[20] The legal tradition furnishes the symbolism for the initial verses, which apply torah attributes to Dame Wisdom. The entire instruction juxtaposes two different kinds of fire: the light of parental instruction and seething passion for another man's wife. The first lamp stands as a powerful antidote to the second fire, which threatens to consume those lacking sense. Rhetoric abounds in this endeavor to frustrate the seductive power of the adulteress, but the crowning argument consists of two impossible questions.[21]

> Can a man carry fire in his bosom and his clothes not be burned?
> Or can one walk upon hot coals and his feet not be scorched?
> (vi 27-28) RSV.[22]

These questions function as strong statements which none would dare challenge; as such they constitute an argument from consensus.

---

[19] D. Winton Thomas, "Textual and Philological Notes on some Passages in the Book of Proverbs", *Wisdom in Israel and in the Ancient Near East* (*SVT* 3; Leiden, 1960), pp. 281-2, and McKane, *Proverbs*, pp. 270-1.

[20] For analysis of the structure of this text, see my essay "Questions, dictons et épreuves impossibles", *La Sagesse de l'A. T.*, pp. 100-5.

[21]) On this literary category, see my "Impossible Questions, Sayings, and Tasks in Israelite Wisdom", in Dominic Crossan (ed.), *Gnomic Wisdom* (Missoula, 1980), pp. 19-34.

[22] Scripture translations are taken from the Revised Standard Version.

The third passage differs from the first two in that it lacks the so-called teacher's call for a hearing; here we stand at a transition from instruction to imaginative discourse or anecdote (Prov. ix 13-18). In one sense this description of Madam Folly is derivative, for it clearly serves as a foil to the earlier allusion to Dame Wisdom (Prov. ix 1-6). Both women make elaborate use of erotic language,[23] but only one actually invites her guests to sexual pleasures. In all likelihood, Dame Wisdom's vocabulary echoes her origins as a goddess,[24] but the sensual aspects have been largely transferred to her antagonist who actively solicits at the center of daily activity. Her invitation is remarkably appealing: "Stolen water is sweet, and bread eaten in secret is pleasant" (ix 17).[25] Once again we encounter a proverb at the heart of the argument, confirming our suspicion that teachers reinforced their words with acknowledged authoritative maxims. In this instance the aphorism recalls other sayings, especially the allegorical reference to sexual relations in v 15-20 and the amusing description of an adulteress as one who "eats, and wipes her mouth, and says, 'I have done no wrong' " (xxx 20).

Another instruction which cites a sentence as the decisive proof is found in vi 6-11, which advises sluggards to learn a lesson from the ant and warns against the dreadful consequences of laziness.

> A little sleep, a little slumber,
>   a little folding of the hands to rest,
> and poverty will come upon you like a vagabond,
>   and want like an armed man (vi 10-11).

In xxiv 30-34, this sentence is quoted yet again, this time within an anecdote and prefaced by the self-reflective comment of a teacher who has learned a valuable lesson from experience. The presence of copious imagery precisely when the clinching argument occurs in another anecdote, Prov. xii 6-23, should occasion little surprise.

---

[23] The Dead Sea Psalms Scroll preserves a portion of the original concluding poem to Sirach in which *double entendre* abounds, suggesting that such thinking was equally at home among earlier sages.

[24] B. L. Mack, *Logos und Sophia: Untersuchungen zur Weisheitstheologie im hellenistischen Judentum* (Göttingen, 1973), offers a thoroughgoing analysis from the standpoint of the history of religions. For a recent treatment, see M. Küchler, *Frühjüdische Weisheitstraditionen: Zum Fortgang weisheitlichen Denkens im Bereich des frühjüdischen Jahweglaubens* (Freiburg, Schweiz, and Göttingen, 1979), pp. 33-53.

[25] On this euphemistic language, see my *Samson: A Secret Betrayed, a Vow Ignored* (Atlanta and London, 1978 and 1979), pp. 114-17.

Indeed, the metaphors for self-destruction suggest that a lost sentence may lie behind xii 22-23.

> . . .As an ox goes to the slaughter,
> or as a stag is caught fast
> till an arrow pierces its entrails;
> as a bird rushes into a snare. . .

Nevertheless, the absence of such a sentence in canonical proverbs precludes convincing proof on this point.

The phenomenon of reinforcing an instruction or anecdote by means of a sentence partially explains the peculiar situation in sapiential research where instruction literature is ordinarily distinguished from the remaining proverbs, which are thought to lack an authoritative base. Walther Zimmerli's fundamental analysis of the structure of Israelite wisdom [26] lost sight of the fact that sentences spoke with amazing force; indeed, much later, to be sure, Gerhard von Rad went so far as to exalt proverbs over torah in respect to the power they exercised in the daily lives of ancient Israelites.[27] Even those critics who see clearly the authority residing within sentences rarely take the further step toward awareness that the appeal to authority in instructions bears witness to a sense that they lack inner cogency. Thus a peculiar irony persists: precisely where authority is most lacking, i.e., in instructions, critics assume its prevading presence, and in sentences, which compel assent without the slightest reinforcement, interpreters emphasize their advisory character. It follows that previous discussions of wisdom and authority stand in need of revision. What follows is only a modest effort from a projected volume on the art of persuasion in Israelite wisdom.

---

[26] "Zur Struktur der alttestamentlichen Weisheit", *ZAW* 51 (1933), pp. 177-204 (E. tr. in J. L. Crenshaw (ed.), *Studies in Ancient Israelite Wisdom* [New York, 1976], pp. 175-207). To be sure, Zimmerli later modified his position, but the difference is hardly discernible in *Grundriss der alttestamentlichen Theologie* (Stuttgart, Berlin, Köln, Mainz, 1972), pp. 92-3, 136-46. For a corrective, see B. Gemser, "The Spiritual Structure of Biblical Aphoristic Wisdom", in A. van Selms and A. S. van der Woude (ed.), *Adhuc Loquitur: Collected Essays of Dr. B. Gemser*, (Leiden, 1968), pp. 138-49 (also in *Studies in Ancient Israelite Wisdom*, pp. 208-19). On the meaning of the root *ʿāṣāh*, see now J. A. Emerton, "The root *ʿaṣah* and some uses of *ʿeṣah* and *moʿeṣan* in Hebrew", in W. C. van Wyk (ed.), *Studies in Wisdom Literature*, (*OTWSA* 15 and 16), pp. 13-26.

[27] *Wisdom in Israel* (London, 1972), p. 26 = *Weisheit in Israel* (Neukirchen, 1970), p. 41.

II

In characterizing Dame Wisdom's message I used the categories ethos, pathos, and logos with reference to the speaker, audience, and speech respectively. Now the authority inherent within a spoken or written word derives from one of these three, or any combination of them.[28] For the moment, I shall concentrate on these three warrants for authority in the book of Job.

1. *ethos*[29]

Job's friends are not sufficiently differentiated to permit one to draw a composite sketch of each one's faith claims. Nevertheless, I shall avoid the tendency to treat their arguments as a single attack on Job. In viii 8-10, Bildad appeals to ethos.

> For inquire, I pray you, of bygone ages,
>   and consider what the fathers have found;
> for we are but of yesterday, and know nothing,
>   for our days on earth are a shadow.
> Will they not teach you, and tell you,
>   and utter words out of their understanding?

Here the speaker lays claim to a valuable legacy, the tradition acquired and passed on again and again by earlier generations. Indeed, he perceives the fleeting character of existence that forces dependence on accumulated knowledge. That complex system of beliefs, values, and customs was as natural as breathing itself. Upon this solid foundation wise persons took a stand and whatever authority they may have possessed derived from this base. Naturally, those who managed to linger long enough to acquite gray hairs could lay claim to a lion's share of accumulated lore. Accordingly, Eliphaz reminds Job of this fact.

> Are you the first man that was born?
>   Or were you brought forth before the hills?
> Both the gray haired and the aged are among us,
>   older than your father (xv 7, 10).

But traditional knowledge was useless unless confirmed in one's personal experience, and so Eliphaz insists that he has seen "what

[28] The sources of authority include birth, accomplishment, character, and sanction.

[29] Here I am using ethos in a broader sense than nobility of character. It thus combines the essential meaning of ἔθος and ἦθος (custom and character).

wise men have told, and their fathers have not hidden" (xv 18). Both Bildad and Eliphaz counsel personal appropriation of the inherited tradition, a theme that surfaces in the latter's speeches more than once.

As I have seen, those who plow iniquity
and sow trouble reap the same (iv 8; cf. v 3).
Lo, this we have searched out; it is true.
Hear,[30] and know it for your good (v 27).

Job's arguments also fall within the category of ethos, although he turns the one about age upon its head.

Wisdom is with the aged,
and understanding in length of days...
He (God) deprives of speech those who are trusted
and takes away the discernment of the elders (xii 12, 20).

Job, too has kept his eyes open, ever ready to test cherished beliefs.

Lo, my eye has seen all this,
my ear has heard and understood it.
What you know, I also know;
I am not inferior to you (xiii 1-2).[31]

He has also incorporated lessons from afar into those arising in the home.

Have you not asked those who travel the roads,
and do not you accept their testimony
that the wicked man is spared in the day of calamity,
that he is rescued in the day of wrath (xii 25)?

---

[30] The importance of hearing was highlighted in Egyptian instructions (cf. Ptah-hotep) in a manner not found in Israel, but the latter sages recognized the necessity of appropriating inherited traditions. Thus Hempel writes: "Demgemass ist auch das wichtigste Erziehungsmittel kein anderes als in den anderen altorientalischen Pädagogien: das 'Horen' . . . ." ("Pathos und Humor in der israelitischen Erziehung", p. 68). H. Brunner, *Altägyptische Erziehung* (Wiesbaden, 1957), pp. 131-6, and H. H. Schmid, *Wesen and Geschichte der Weisheit*, pp. 31-3, discuss the significance of hearing to Egyptian sages. C. F. Whitley understands the difficult *we'izzēn* in Qoh. xii 9 as a reference to listening ("*and he listened* and considered the arrangement of many proverbs", *Koheleth: His Language and Thought* [*BZAW* 148; Berlin and New York, 1979], p. 102).

[31] Note the fundamental difference between Job's bold claim to knowledge and the rhetorician's self-effacement, which functions ironically. Qoheleth's response to sapiential claims (viii 17) suggests that the rhetorical effect of putting oneself down arose to counter adverse results of boasting.

Here the two essential ingredients of ethos, inherited tradition and individual appropriation, stand out with impressive clarity.

This bipolarity of ethos provides an important corrective to the oft-mentioned individualism which characterizes wisdom thinking. In a sense, personal authority depends upon something which comes as a legacy from the past; this valuable gift must be appropriated in a given situation by those who wish to lay claim upon it. In this way individuals point beyond themselves to a greater authority, the collective experience of the community.

2. *pathos*

Not every appeal to authority concentrates on ethos; another significant warrant for teaching is pathos. Whereas ethos refers to the person of the speaker, pathos focuses upon the audience. Specifically, it consists of the many ways by which the speaker can sway belief or move an audience to action. Often this type of persuasion implies the heightening of certain emotions, such as fear or awe.

Eliphaz waxes eloquent about an experience of the holy which taught him the folly of presumed righteousness.

Now a word was brought to me stealthily,
  my ear received the whisper of it. . .
A spirit glided past my face;
  the hair of my flesh stood up.
It stood still,
  but I could not discern its appearance.
A form was before my eyes;
  there was silence, then I heard a voice:
Can mortal man be righteous before God?
Can a man be pure before his Maker? (iv 12-17).[32]

Similarly, Elihu argues from pathos in this remarkable account of divine action upon passive subjects.

For God speaks in one way,
  and in two, though man does not perceive it.

---

[32] In the light of xl 2 and xxv 4, on the one hand, and xxxii 2, on the other, a translation such as "Can mortal man be more just than God? Can a man be purer than his Maker?" is attractive. The former two texts use a different construction (*ʿim-ʾēl* rather than *mēʾĕlōah*), one that presents no ambiguity. The sense of *mēʾĕlōhīm* in xxxii 2 is clearly that Job considered himself more just than God. The context of iv 17 *encourages* this understanding, in my view, and the argument from greater to lesser in iv 18-19 becomes all the more forceful. Still, this literal sense is not demanded, for Num. xxxii 22 and Jer. li 5 indicate that the expression does not *require* a comparison.

In a dream, in a vision of the night,
  when deep sleep falls upon men,
  while they slumber on their beds,
then he opens the ears of men,
  and terrifies them with warnings... (xxxiii 14-18)

Such observations are calculated to instill dread in the hearts of hearers, thus transferring their thoughts from human to divine authority. Occasionally, it is difficult to ascertain whether the allusion points beyond the individual or not, for the reference contains just enough ambiguity to function as personal reinforcement.

But it is the spirit in a man,
  the breath of the Almighty, that makes him understand (xxii 8).

This, not age, assures Elihu that his voice should not be stilled while others spout off nonsense. Sometimes this inner voice approximates the modern concept of conscience, for example, when Zophar remarks:

I hear censure which insults me,
  and out of my understanding a spirit answers me (xx 3).

3. *logos*

A third level on which appeals to authority function is logos, by which I mean the cogency of the speech itself. Such warrants for one's message rely neither on the office of the speaker nor on the emotions of the listeners, but endeavor to persuade through logical force alone.[33] Indeed, the actual source of the message may be unknown, and nothing beyond rational clarity may occur, but the authoritative base is present nonetheless.

Perhaps the most obvious appeal to logos takes place when the speaker quotes a saying that compels universal assent, particularly rhetorical questions. In justifying his intemperate outcry against a god who has become a personal antagonist, Job resorts to just such an argument.

Does the wild ass bray when he has grass,
  or the ox low over his fodder?
Can that which is tasteless be eaten without salt,
  or is there any taste in the slime of the purslane? (vi 5-6) [34]

[33] To be sure, we must make allowances for Israelite fondness for emotion-laden language, hyperbole, and generally extravagant speech.

[34] The difficulty of translating verse 6 is illustrated by recent commentaries: "Can flat food be eaten unsalted? Is there flavor in slimy cream cheese?" (M. H.

Bildad counters with a comparable appeal to consensus.

> Can papyrus grow where there is no marsh?
> Can reeds flourish where there is no water? (vii 8-10)

Zophar, too, takes up the argument from consensus, and thus emphasizes the unlikelihood of acquiring wisdom.

> But a stupid man will get understanding,
> when a wild ass's colt is born a man (xi 12).[35]

Yet another appeal to logos is the maxim drawn from nature, the so-called nature wisdom.[36] A remarkably powerful example occurs in one of Job's speeches.

> But ask the beasts, and they will teach you;
> the birds of the air, and they will tell you;
> or the plants of the earth, and they will teach you;
> and the fish of the sea will declare to you.
> Who among all these does not know
> that the hand of the Lord has done this? (xii 7-9)

One can even argue that the choice of rhetorical questions as the mode of divine address derives from a knowledge that God needs no warrants for his speech, but poses a kind of teacher's examination for Job.[37] To be sure, this is no ordinary test, for the impossible questions heighten the distance between creature and creator, a chasm fragilely spanned by renewed discourse.[38]

Pope); "Can tasteless food be eaten without salt, or is there any savor in the juice of mallows?" (R. Gordis); "Can one eat spittle, without salt? or is there any taste in the saliva of the dreams?" (N. H. Tur Sinai).

[35] On the basis of Gen. xvi 12, E. Dhorme understands this *proverb* to mean that a wild ass's colt becomes a master ass, i.e., it acquires the full nature of its breed (*Le livre de Job* [Paris, 1926], pp. 147-8, E. tr. *A Commentary on the Book of Job* [London, 1967], p. 163). M. Pope rejects the rendering "wild ass's colt" in favor of male wild ass, and interprets *ʾādām* as equivalent to *ʾădāmāh*. Hence he translates: "The inane man will get sense, when a wild ass is born tame" (*Job* [Garden City, N.Y., 1973], pp. 83, 86).

[36] H. Richter, "Die Naturweisheit des Alten Testaments in Buch Hiob", *ZAW* 70-71 (1958-1959), pp. 1-19.

[37] von Rad, "Hiob xxxviii und die altägyptische Weisheit", *Wisdom in Israel and in the Ancient Near East*, pp. 293-301, E. tr., *Studies in Ancient Israelite Wisdom*, pp. 267-91, and *The Problem of the Hexateuch and Other Essays* (Edinburgh and London, 1966), pp. 281-91.

[38] "Es ist das demutsvolle Schweigen des Menschen, dessen Existenz in der Begegnung mit Gott erschüttert und in Frage gestellt worden ist für den solches Schweigen einen neue Weg eröffnet... Doch es ist nicht das Schweigen des sich seiner Nichtigkeit bewussten Menschen, sondern das Schweigen des zu Gott hingekehrten Menschen, der in der Gemeinschaft mit ihm zur Ruhe findet" (G. Fohrer, "Dialog und Kommunikation im Buch Hiob", *La Sagesse de l'A. T.*, pp. 229-30).

III

The preceding analysis of warrants for authority has concentrated on the Book of Job, but it could easily be extended to the entire wisdom corpus.[39] For the moment, I wish instead to shift the attention to the other issue being considered in this essay, namely persuasion. Rather than discussing the general features of biblical rhetoric, I prefer to illustrate that phenomenon through analysis of the contest of Darius' guards in 1 Esd. iii 1-v 3. Since I have studied that text in another setting [40] I shall limit my remarks to rhetorical features: choice of material, arrangement of the discussion, vocabulary, and style.

We begin with a look at the conventional material which provided the source for the argument about the strongest thing in the world. I shall isolate two features for discussion: the missing fourth answer and the polarities from Qoheleth concerning a time for everything. As everyone knows, four answers appear in the speeches despite the stipulation that each of the three guards is to give a single response to the question, "What is strongest?" To the answers wine, the king, and woman has been added the victorious response, truth. But certain bits of evidence within the contest point to a further attempt to answer the question in terms of the human capacity for responding to the divine command to subdue the earth.

Echoes of this missing answer persist in iv 2, 14 and 37, where it inserts itself repeatedly. To be sure, the first instance can be explained as a transitional device, but the other two seem to imply that one guard had defended the answer "men". For example, the third speaker begins by referring to the answer defended by the second speaker, then moves to two previous answers: men and wine.

---

[39] Fohrer *Einleitung in das Alte Testament* (revised edn, Heidelberg, 1969), pp. 368-9, E. tr. *Introduction to the Old Testament* (Nashville and New York, 1968), pp. 339-40, perceives a significant transformation of a simple aphorism into a progressive structure in Qoheleth. For example, he notes three steps in Qoh. i 16-18, specifically observation, conclusion, and proof in a proverb. Similarly, iii 1-15 yields theme, conclusion, and proverb cited as motivation. "We see here a structural change in wisdom instruction, brought about by a change in the psychological milieu. The individual, the ego, takes on a certain distance from the events or circumstances with which it appears to be linked. The observing subject confronts his observations as an independent personality. In addition, in order to reinforce or justify his views, Qoheleth goes back to earlier proverbs" (p. 340).

[40] The publication of my extensive analysis of this text ("The Contest of Darius' Guards"), has appeared in B. O. Long (ed.), *Images of Man and God: Old Testament Short Stories in Literary Focus* (Sheffield, 1981), pp. 74-88.

In like manner, the summary statement alludes to these three answers but this time in a different order (wine, king, women, men), the latter of which has been expanded to include "all their works". Perhaps this vying for attention on the part of an answer that underwent harsh handling can alert readers to the possibility that the author has adapted conventional material to a new purpose.

This suspicion that older material underlies the contest gains support from another puzzling aspect of the text, this time in the final speech on truth. The crowning argument against wine, king, woman, and men is their unrighteousness, which signals eventual perishing. Now what prompted the reference to the sun in this context? I suggest that two brief hymn-like passages in Sirach provide that fountain from which this stream flows.

In Sir. xvii 1-3 one reads that God endowed his human creatures with strength like his own, whereas xvii 19 likens all their works to the sun, and xvii 14 introduces the concept of unrighteousness. Furthermore, Sir. xliii 1-4 praises the sun but moves beyond the marvelous work to its creator: "Great is the Lord who made it". It would therefore seem probable that a standard literary convention lies behind the text in 1 Esd. iv 34-41.[41]

A similar adaptation of traditional material takes place within the praise of king as strongest. In iv 7-9, the phrase "if he tells" (ἐὰν εἴπῃ; εἶπεν or εἶπε) occurs seven times; both the sevenfold usage and content recall Qoh. iii 1-9. To be sure, formal differences exist, most notably the parallelism in Qoheleth, but striking resemblances suggest a close relationship (the opposites kill and heal, build and cut down, references to making war, attacking, laying waste, and planting). Of Qoheleth's fourteen opposites,[42] only those appropriate to royal command have commended themselves to the author. The others concern emotional responses and relationships not subject even to a king's wishes. Weeping and laughter, love making and

---

[41] Certain themes would naturally appear in any hymn about the sun, but the stress upon its unrighteousness (*adikon*) must surely exceed normal expectancy. The attempt to discover Semitic parallels to this entire narrative strikes me as essentially on target (K. F. Pohlmann, *Studien zum Dritten Esra*: *Ein Beitrag zur Frage nach dem ursprünglichen Schluss des Chronistischen Geschichtswerkes* [Göttingen, 1970], pp. 42-6). It follows that I do not think the praise of truth is of Greek origin.

[42] J. A. Loader, *Polar Structures in the Book of Qohelet* (*BZAW* 152; Berlin and New York, 1979), exaggerates the significance of opposites in Qoheleth, although he correctly perceives evidence of conscious design in the book.

continence, abstemious saving and wreckless squandering, silence and speech, loving and despising cannot easily be brought under royal supervision.

Now if adaptation of conventional material [43] best describes the author's choice of subject matter, what characterizes the way he or she endeavors to present the data? A distinct broadening of focus is discernible in the arrangement of the discussion. The initial speaker sticks to the subject and shows considerable powers of logical coherence; the second introduces a new idea about human beings as strong, thus providing a decisive clue about a further speech, now missing; and the third has "two arrows in his bow" to begin with, and proceeds to reminisce about the earth's vastness, the height of heaven, and the swiftness of the sun. Furthermore, the dialogue begins by celebrating material and morally inferior wine and proceeds to a higher level, the king, and finally comes to rest in God.[44] Within the argument about woman, the sequence shifts noticeably. "Here he ranges . . . from the noblest (mother love and wifely devotion) to the lowest (selfish whims and silly fancies of coquettes bringing ruin to their lovers) . . ." [45]

The contest achieves a broadening of focus without resort to extravagant language. Indeed, the vocabulary is particularly suited to logical persuasion. Two features stand out as noteworthy in this regard: the use of ironic understatement and exercise in juxtaposition. A single instance of understatement proclaims the authority of a king more eloquently than hyperbole could ever have done. I refer to the choice of the word "tell" (εἶπεν) in describing royal commands (iv 4, 7-9); others may have to raise their voices to attract attention and to insist that certain actions be undertaken, but a king merely tells his subjects the slightest whim and they hasten to turn royal desire into tangible reality.

The second example of restraint in vocabulary appropriate to logical suasion concerns the use of the phrase "look upon with open mouth". It first occurs with reference to a man who holds his most precious possessions in his hands, only to let them go when a beautiful woman passes by, and to stare at her with mouth agape (χάσκοντες

---

[43] On literary conventions, see Alter, "Biblical Type-Scenes and the Uses of Convention", *Critical Inquiry* (Winter, 1978), pp. 355-68.

[44] R. H. Pfeiffer, *History of New Testament Times with an Introduction to the Apocrypha* (New York, 1949), p. 256.

[45] Ibid.

τὸ στόμα θεωροῦσιν αὐτήν, iv 18-19). The other example of this phrase brings the king down to the level of ordinary subjects, for it pictures him as a supplicant pleading with a favorite mistress. This beautiful Apame placed the king's crown upon her own head and slapped the king, who gazed at her with mouth agape (χάσκων τὸ στόμα ἐθεώρει αὐτήν, iv 31). No wonder the final decision about the winner in the contest is made by public acclamation, since the democratization of kingship has resulted.

So far I have discussed noteworthy aspects of theme, arrangement, and vocabulary. But what about style? I shall limit myself to observations about introductory and concluding formulae, rhetorical questions, transition, and irony, since these stylistic features seem to be highly significant in this text. Each speech opens and closes with common formulae. The opening formula states: "Then the first (or the second/third) who had spoken of . . . began and said". Likewise each concludes with a statement that the speaker stopped speaking.

By far the most characteristic feature of the speeches is the free use of rhetorical questions. The first speaker sets the tone of the discussion by means of a question ("Gentlemen, how is wine the strongest?") and uses yet another to invoke assent ("Gentlemen, is not wine the strongest, since it forces men to do these things?"). The second speaker opens with a false answer in question form, only to correct it immediately ("Gentlemen, are not men strongest who rule over land and sea and all that is in them?"). A more appropriate introduction to a discussion of the supreme monarch is difficult to imagine. This speaker also appeals for favorable response ("Gentlemen, why is not the king strongest, since he is to be obeyed in this fashion?"). The third speaker is not content with an introductory and final rhetorical question, but punctuates the speech throughout with such questions.

> Gentlemen, is not the king great, and are not men many, and is not wine strong? Who then is their master, or who is their lord? Is it not women?. . . Do you not labor and toil, and bring everything and give it to women? . . . And now do you not believe me? Is not the king great in his power? Do not all lands fear to touch him? . . . Gentlemen, why are not women strong, since they do such things? . . . Gentlemen, are not women strong . . . Is he not great who does these things?

The impact of these questions is signaled by the bold declaration

("Hence you must realize that women rule over you"), together with the substitution of a doxology for the concluding rhetorical question ("Blessed be the God of truth!").

Transition from one speech to another is wholly natural so long as the answers correspond to the number of speakers. What happens, however, when an additional answer intrudes? Here transition is achieved in outstanding fashion, for it hints that victory has already come for the third speaker. The brief anecdote about the king's love play and the persuasive defense of woman as strongest allow the speaker to shift attention momentarily to the audience. At that decisive point the transition takes place: "Then the king and the nobles looked at one another; and he began to speak about truth" (iv 38). From here on the speaker's thoughts escalate, beginning with the strongest among human beings and soaring from earth to heaven and finally pausing to rest before the God of truth.

Like the Book of Job, this contest consists of a framing narrative and a dialogue. Considerable tension results from this uneasy combination, for the framework pictures the king acting in his capacity as supreme dispenser of favors whereas the speeches challenge that authority with devastating force. On the one hand, the king grants privileges of friendship and fortune, and regal language is applied to truth. On the other, the story portrays a king who falls asleep, and the people themselves usurp royal prerogative in declaring the winner. Furthermore, the dialogue exposes a king's true vulnerability: his might falters before appetite and sleep, when a lone individual could easily be disposed of by others less privileged but at the moment more alert.

These features of theme, arrangement, vocabulary, and style combine to make these speeches truly persuasive.[46] I wish to illustrate the unusual power of the text by reflecting for a moment on the argument concerning wine. The knowledge that men and women are rational creatures was not limited to ancient Greeks. While Plato's students may have made fun of his definition of man as a thinking animal without feathers by attaching to a cock the label "philosophical man", the metaphor of human beings as rational has always seemed appropriate in discussions of their essence. *Cogito*

[46] For textual analysis of this story, see the unpublished Ph.D. Dissertation by William Goodman, Jr. ("A Study of 1 Esdras 3:1-5:6," Duke University, 1971).

ergo sum removes men and women from their environment and exalts them over all other creatures. Yet this distinctive mark succumbs to the power of the vine, whose product leads astray the keenest mind.

Besides this rational essence, an artificial distinction according to sociological status emerges early. Hence class differences surface, men and women being fitted into appropriate niches on the basis of things over which they have no control (birth) or which have nothing to do with their real selves (possessions). The latter make it possible for one person to subject others to servile obedience, for the rich can enslave those indebted to them. And, of course, there must be someone at the very top of artificial distinctions among people; this person of power and privilege acclaims himself king. Such differences pass away when wine wields its strange power, and now at long last king and lowliest subject stand equal, as do master and slave, rich and poor.

Inasmuch as women and men are thinking creatures upon whom class distinctions have been imposed, above and beyond the ordinary causes for anxiety and remorse, they are ever and again victimized by fear, pain, and sorrow. The sentence of death hangs over their heads, and fertile imagination conjures up all sorts of dangers both real and supposed. Actual pain, both their own and that of those dear to them, increases anxiety about approaching death and heightens agony caused by disappointment, intensifying to the breaking point all psychically based consternation. When wine enters the bodies of men and women, frequently the worry-prone victims of death's messengers, they forget for the moment the power of pain. In place of sorrow and financial woe come a glad heart and freedom from care, so powerful is the blood of the grape. Those who under ordinary circumstances and beset by problems of daily existence can muster minimal self-esteem find limitless resources lurking within the cup, which loosen the tongue so that newfound confidence proclaims itself with complete abandon.

Rich experience has taught the value of friendship and the indispensability of fraternal loyalty; without friends or brother, one is vulnerable from every side. Consequently, friendship ties and kinship bonds came to occupy a high position in the order of priorities, for nothing was too great a price to pay to assure the perpetuity of those relationships. Even a grievous offence could be overlooked lest the bond with another be severed, and great care was taken to avoid injury to a friend or brother. But persons who have their fill of wine treat such valuable relationships like ordinary refuse, and with reckless abandon pick a quarrel that leads to blows between friends and brothers.

The seasons come, and the seasons go, and with them birth and death. The strange capacity for remembering, that ability to recall selected events, thoughts, and sensations from the shadowy past, survives the powerful sway of time's monotony. Often cause for wonder and astonishment, this memory enables men and women to relive those cherished moments when time and eternity coalesced and the joyous soul cried out, "Stay, thou art so fair." Furthermore, such remembrance of sacral events opens up new possibilities for those to whom primeval event stands as both summons and demand; from its power they receive renewed redemption and ethical motivation. Still, even this astonishing memory bows in submission to the greater power of wine, and individuals recall nothing that transpired during the drunken stupor. Wine, then, functions as the great leveler: its mighty floodwaters sweep in the swirling maelstrom all human rationality, memory, psychic states, distinctions both real and artificial, and bonds of friendship and brotherhood. From the murky waters left by the subsiding flood one can pull their corpses, newly transformed into perverted thought, forgetfulness, joviality, boasting, comradery and bellicosity. "Gentlemen, is not wine the strongest, since it forces people to do these things?" Such was the brief, but truly cogent, argument of Darius' first guard.

IV

What has this brief consideration of authority and persuasion yielded that will enable us to understand the wisdom literature more fully? Minimally, we can say that formal literary distinctions often ignore other factors like subject and function which link together such unlikely candidates as sentence and instruction. The latter, by virtue of the necessity for authoritative claims, possesses less inherent power of persuasion than do sentences. It follows that interpreters need to distinguish between the authority that a teacher endeavors to impose upon students and that bestowed upon texts by their form or intrinsic nature. Still, we must beware of going too far in the opposite direction and asserting that all sentences possessed full authority, for the presence of motivations in a few sentences [47] warns

[47] Prov xvi 12, 26, xix 19, xxi 7, 25, xxii 9, xxix 19 (cf. xxiii 16b).

against this extreme position. Furthermore, the multiplication of vivid imagery in sentences easily lends itself to the desire to achieve additional authority.

The sanctions for authority which I have applied to the Book of Job are sufficiently broad, it seems to me, to permit application throughout the sapiential corpus, as are the remarks concerning rhetoric in the contest of Darius' guards. At the same time, the concepts of ethos, pathos, and logos are sufficiently specific to illuminate almost any warrant for one's teaching, just as choice of subject, treatment of the material, vocabulary, and style permit entry into the thought of individual sages. Similar forays into other wisdom texts,[48] which I hope to make in the near future, should reveal extensive mastery of rhetorical technique even where the hand of authority weighs heavily upon the material. In a word, Israel's teachers spoke with authority, but they also developed and refined persuasion to an art.

---

[48] Qoheleth is characterized by the same ambiguity between claim to authority (the royal fiction) and striving for persuasive power (xii 9-10). As is well known, the literary fiction of royal authorship fades away after the second chapter, to return again in the epilogue (one Shepherd). The first colophon stresses the sage's great desire to share insights with the populace; to achieve this goal he gave considerable attention to the external form of his words. The emphasis is clearly aesthetic, as well as ethical (Aarre Lauha, *Kohelet* [Neukirchen, 1978], p. 218).

ÉTUDE PHILOLOGIQUE DE *MALʾĀK*

PERSPECTIVES SUR LE *MALʾĀK* DE LA DIVINITÉ DANS LA BIBLE HEBRAÏQUE

par

JESUS-LUIS CUNCHILLOS

Paris

Introduction

Le *malʾak YHWH/ʾĕlōhîm* [1] jouit d'une popularité non négligeable parmi les exégètes de tous les temps. Il a attiré les théologiens qui

---

[1] *malʾāk* apparait 213 fois dans la Bible hébraïque; *malʾākūt* 1 fois (Ag. i 13); *m*^{e}*lāʾkā* 167 fois. Voir concordances. Du *malʾak YHWH/ʾĕlōhîm*, il est question dans les textes suivants: Gen. xvi 7 (*m. YHWH*), 9 (*m. YHWH*), 10 (*m. YHWH*), 11 (*m. YHWH*), xix 1 (*hammalʾākîm*), 15 (*hammalʾākîm*), xxi 17 (*m. ʾĕlōhîm*), xxii 11 (*m. YHWH*), 15 (*m. YHWH*), xxiv 7 (*malʾākô* pour *m. YHWH*), 40 (*malʾākô* pour *m. YHWH*), xxviii 12 (*malʾăkê ʾĕlōhîm*), xxxi 11 (*m. hāʾĕlōhîm*), xxxii 2 (*malʾăkê ʾĕlōhîm*), xlviii 16 (*hammalʾāk haggōʾēl ʾōtî//hāʾĕlōhîm*); Ex. iii 2 (*m. YHWH*), xiv 19 (*m. hāʾĕlōhîm*), xxiii 20 (*ʾānōkî šōlēaḥ malʾāk l*^{e}*pānekā*), 23 (*malʾākî*), xxxii 34 (*malʾākî*), xxxiii 2 (*malʾāk*); Nb. xx 16 (*malʾāk//YHWH*), xxii 22 (*m. YHWH*), 23 (*m. YHWH*), 24 (*m. YHWH*), 25 (*m. YHWH*), 26 (*m. YHWH*), 27 (*m. YHWH*), 31 (*m. YHWH*), 32 (*m. YHWH*), 34 (*m. YHWH*), 35 (*m. YHWH*); Jg. ii 1 (*m. YHWH*), 4 (*m. YHWH*), v 23 (*m. YHWH*), vi 11 (*m. YHWH*), 12 (*m. YHWH*), 20 (*m. hāʾĕlōhîm*), 21 (*m. YHWH* 2 fois), 22 (*m. YHWH* 2 fois), xiii 3 (*m. YHWH*), 6 (*m. hāʾĕlōhîm*), 9 (*m. hāʾĕlōhîm*), 13 (*m. YHWH*), 15 (*m. YHWH*), 16 (*m. YHWH* 2 fois), 17 (*m. YHWH*), 18 (*m. YHWH*), 20 (*m. YHWH*), 21 (*m. YHWH* 2 fois); 1 Sam. xxix 9 (*m. ʾĕlōhîm*); 2 Sam. xiv 17 (*kî k*^{e}*malʾak hāʾĕlōhîm*), 20 (*k*^{e}*ḥokmat m. hāʾĕlōhîm*), xix 28 (*hammelek k*^{e}*malʾak hāʾĕlōhîm*), xxiv 16 (*m. YHWH* + 2 fois *hammalʾāk*), 17 (*hammalʾāk*); 1 R. xiii 18 (*malʾāk*), xix 5 (*malʾāk*), 7 (*m. YHWH*); 2 R. i 3 (*m. YHWH*), 15 (*m. YHWH*), xix 35 (*m. YHWH*); 1 Ch. xxi 12 (*m. YHWH mašḥît*), 15 (*malʾāk, lammalʾāk hammašḥît, m. YHWH*), 16 (*m. YHWH*), 18 (*m. YHWH*), 27 (*malʾāk*), 30 (*m. YHWH*); 2 Ch. xxxii 21 (*wayyišlaḥ YHWH malʾāk*); Es. xxxvii 36 (*m. YHWH*), xlii 19 (*malʾākî*) (?), xliv 26 (*malʾākāw*), lxiii 9 (*malʾak*) (?); Os. xii 5 (*malʾāk*); Ag. i 13 (*m. YHWH*); Zach. i 9 (*hammalʾāk haddōbēr bî*), 11 (*m. YHWH*), 12 (*m. YHWH*), 13 (*hammalʾāk haddōbēr bî*), 14 (*hammalʾāk haddōbēr bî*), ii 2 (*hammalʾāk haddōbēr bî*), 7 (*hammalʾāk haddōbēr bî, malʾāk ʾaḥēr*), iii 1 (*m. YHWH*), 3 (*hammalʾāk*), 5 (*m. YHWH*), 6 (*m. YHWH*), iv 1 (*hammalʾāk haddōbēr bî*), 4 (*hammalʾāk haddōbēr bî*), 5 (*hammalʾāk haddōbēr bî*), v 5 (*hammalʾāk haddōbēr bî*), 10 (*hammalʾāk haddōbēr bî*), vi 4 (*hammalʾāk haddōbēr bî*), 5 (*hammalʾāk*), xii 8 (*m. YHWH*); Mal. i 1 (*malʾākî*) (?), ii 7 (*m. YHWH ṣ*^{e}*bāʾôt*), iii 1 (*malʾākî, m. habb*^{e}*rît*); Ps. xxxiv 8 (*m. YHWH*), xxxv 5 (*m. YHWH*), 6 (*m. YHWH*), lxxviii 49 (*malʾăkê rāʿîm*), xci 11 (*malʾākāw*), ciii 20 (*malʾākāw*), cxlviii 2 (*malʾākāw*); Job iv 18 (*malʾākāw*), xxxiii 23 (*malʾāk*); Qoh. v 5 (*hammalʾāk*).

essaient de percevoir la différence fondamentale entre ce *mal'ak YHWH* et Dieu lui-même. Il a attiré les historiens des religions et même les psychanalystes. C'était justifié et le nombre des travaux le prouve. Pour ne citer que les plus importants: M. J. Lagrange [2] Ad. Lods,[3] H. Gunkel,[4] J. Touzard,[5] J. Rybinski,[6] F. Stier,[7] W. Baumgartner,[8] R. Schärf,[9] A. Caquot,[10] H. Cazelles,[11] Parmi les dictionnaires et les théologies de l'Ancien Testament, on signalera G. Kittel,[12] H. Ringgren,[13] F. Brown — S. R. Driver — Ch. A. Briggs,[14] F. Zorell,[15] L. Koehler — W. Baumgartner,[16] et surtout E. Jenni — C. Westermann.[17] Parmi les ouvrages consacrés à la théologie, nous citerons W. Eichrodt,[18] et le plus réputé d'entre eux

---

[2] "L'Ange de Yahvé", *RB* 12 (1903), pp. 212-25.

[3] "L'Ange de Yahvé et l'âme extérieure", dans K. Marti (éd.), *Studien zur semitischen Philologie und Religionsgeschichte Julius Wellhausen zum 70. Geburtstag gewidmet*, *BZAW* 27 (Giessen, 1914), pp. 263-78.

[4] *Genesis übersetzt und erklärt* (3. Aufl., Göttingen, 1910, et suivantes), p. 187.

[5] "Ange de Yahvé", *SDB* I, col. 242-5.

[6] *Der Mal'ak Jahwe* (Paderborn, 1930).

[7] *Gott und sein Engel im A.T.* (Münster, 1934).

[8] "Zum Problem des Yahwe-Engels", *Schweizerische Theologische Umschau* 14 (1944), pp. 97-102; réédité dans *Vom A.T. und seiner Umwelt* (Leiden, 1959), pp. 240-6.

[9] R. Schärf, "La Figura de Satanás en el A.T.", dans C. G. Jung, *Simbología del Espíritu* (México, 1962; édition allemande *Symbolik des Geistes* [Zürich, 1951]), pp. 111-225, mais spécialement pp. 149 ss. ou il parle du *mal'ak* Jahwe.

[10] "L'Angélologie biblique I: l'Ancien Testament", dans G. Tavard, *Histoire des Dogmes. Les Anges* (Paris, 1971), pp. 11-28.

[11] "Essai sur le pouvoir de la divinité à Ugarit et en Israel", *Ugaritica VI* (Paris, 1969), pp. 25-44. Le thème du *mal'āk* est traité aux pp. 32-6. Notons aussi que Cazelles a publié un autre article rédigé probablement à peu près à la même époque que celui que nous venons de citer, où les exposés sont pratiquement les mêmes: "Les fondements de la Théologie des Anges selon l'Ancien Testament", *Actualités Bibliques, Miscellanea en memoria de Frei Jao Pedreira de Castro* (Petropolis, Rio de Janeiro, Sao Paolo, etc., 1971), pp. 55-68. Il parle du *mal'ak YHWH* (Anjo de Deus) aux pp. 59-61.

[12] Art. ἄγγελος dans *ThWNT* I, pp. 72-87.

[13] *RGG* (3ème éd.) III, col. 1301-3.

[14] *A Hebrew and English Lexicon of the Old Testament* (Oxford, 1907; reprinted with corrections 1953, 1957, 1959, 1962, 1966, 1968), pp. 521-2.

[15] *Lexicon hebraicum et aramaicum* (Rome, sans date mais édité dans les années 50), pp. 438-9.

[16] *Lexicon in Veteris Testamenti Libros* (Leiden, 1953), pp. 525-6, sur *mal'āk*, et 526-7 sur *m*e*lā'kāh*.

[17] *Theologisches Handwörterbuch zum Alten Testament* I (München, 1971; 3ème éd., 1978), col. 900-8, ou l'article *mal'āk* est écrit par R. Ficker dont le plan (celui caractéristique du traitement de chaque mot) et la façon d'étudier le *mal'āk* nous satisfont sur beaucoup de points. Cependant, étant donné la nature du dictionnaire, il y a des lacunes plus ou moins justifiées.

[18] *Theologie des Alten Testaments* Teil 2/3 (5. Aufl., Stuttgart, 1964), pp. 7-11,

G. von Rad.[19] D'autres auteurs de théologies de l'Ancien Testament font de la théologie tout court comme c'est le cas pour P. Van Imschoot [20] ou bien traitent le thème en passant, ainsi, par exemple, Th. C. Vriezen [21] et L. Köhler.[22] La dernière monographie datant de 1979 est de F. Guggisberg.[23]

Devant l'attrayante personnalité du *mal'ak YHWH*, le simple *mal'āk* n'attire l'attention que de rédacteurs de dictionnaires bien obligés de traiter ce mot comme tant d'autres. Voilà pourquoi, nous nous arrêterons davantage sur le *mal'āk* sachant que l'étude du *mal'āk* débouche sur le *mal'āk* de la divinité.

Notre démarche a été la suivante. Nous voulions étudier le *mal'ak YHWH/'ĕlōhîm* de la Bible hébraïque. Nous avons constaté que *mal'āk* est un dérivé de *l'k* non attesté en hébreu ni en aucune autre langue sémitique nord-occidentale, sauf l'ugaritique, mais attesté en arabe et en ethiopien. L'étude de *la'ika* en ugaritique le fait apparaître comme un verbe intransitif dont le champ sémantique est "envoyer un messager avec un message".

Puis nous avons étudié le rôle du *mal'āk* qui est celui d'un intermédiaire entre l'envoyeur et le destinataire. Son rôle d'intermédiaire apparait dans sa morphologie comme dans l'usage littéraire et dans la réalité culturelle.

Le rapprochement de *mal'āk/mᵉlā'kāh* avec *mâr šipri/šiprum* permet de voir les rapports existant entre les deux sens fondamentaux de *mᵉlā'kāh* "ambassade", d'une part, et "travail, ouvrage", d'autre part, ainsi que la liaison entre le *mal'āk* qui parle et le *mal'āk* qui agit. Cela conduira à de nombreux élargissements théologiques.

I. *mal'āk* et *l'k*. Philologie

mal'āk existe dans presque toutes les langues sémitiques nord-occidentales.[24] Il dérive du verbe *l'k* qui n'existe qu'en ugaritique.

qui traite du *mal'ak YHWH* à l'intérieur du chapitre 12 "Erscheinungsformen der Gottheit II. Vergeistigung der Theophanie".

[19] *Theologie des Alten Testaments* (München, 1957-60) 1 (4. Aufl., 1962), pp. 298-300; éd. française: *Théologie de l'Ancien Testament* 1 (Genève, 1963), pp. 250-2. Il consacre à notre thème deux pages tres denses.

[20] *Théologie de l'Ancien Testament* (Paris-Tournai, 1954-6).

[21] *Theologie des Alten Testaments in Grundzügen* (Neukirchen, date présumée 1957), pp. 193, 210, 212 et 301.

[22] *Theologie des Alten Testaments* (4. Aufl., Tübingen, 1966), p. 147.

[23] *Die Gestalt des Mal'ak Jahwe im Alten Testament*, Inaugural-Dissertation zur Erlangung der Würde eines Doctor theologiae der Evangelisch-theologischen Fakultät der Universität Neuenburg (1979).

[24] Cf. Koehler-Baumgartner, l.c., et plus bas les notes 58 et 59.

Quelle aubaine donc que l'ugaritique pour qui veut saisir la sémantique de *l'k* et par conséquent celle de son dérivé *mal'āk*! Mais quelle surprise quand on s'aperçoit qu'on s'est limité à résoudre par comparatisme avec l'arabe et l'éthiopien le sens de *l'k* oubliant d'étudier l'usage de *l'k* en ugaritique. On est arrivé ainsi au résultat *l'k* = "envoyer".[25]

Je n'ai pas à redire ici que l'étymologie toujours nécessaire ne suffit pas pour établir le sens exact d'un mot ou d'une racine dans une langue quelle qu'elle soit. L'analyse de l'usage précis et concret que la langue fait dans les mille et un contextes est le meilleur instrument pour cerner le champ sémantique dans lequel se situe le mot, les nuances de son champ d'expression ainsi que la meilleure garantie de tout évolution sémantique toujours possible.

Nous nous sommes donc penchés sur tous les textes ugaritiques où apparaît le verbe *l'k*, 41 en tout,[26] et nous les avons étudiés minutieusement. Trois séries de textes se dégagent de l'analyse syntaxique des phrases où intervient *l'k*:

1a. *l'k* est pleinement intransitif. Il apparait complètement seul ou avec son sujet. Eventuellement une préposition indique la direction vers laquelle doit s'exercer l'action indiquée par le verbe. Aucune trace de complément d'objet direct. La valeur sémantique de *l'k* est: "envoyer un messager avec un message". A ce groupe appartiennent les textes *KTU* 1.2.I:11; 1.4.V:41; 1.13.26-7(?); 1.14.III:19 (si l'on lit: *w ylak mlakm. lk*); 1.24.16-17; 2.10:10; 2.21:11-12; 2.26.3-5; 2.30:19-20; 2.42:20-22; 2.50:7(?); 2.63:7,10-11,13-14; 2.70:13; *RIH* 78/12:3.

Ainsi l'auteur de la lettre *KTU* 2.10 écrit à partir de la ligne 5: *l trǵds w. l. klby šmʿt. ḫti nḫtu. ht hm. in mm nḫtu. w. lak ʿmy. w. yd ilm. p. k. mtm ʿẓ mid* ... que nous traduisons: "De/par TRǴDS et de/par KLBY j'ai entendu que nous aurions été complètement frappés/vaincus. Or si nous n'avons pas été frappés/vaincus complètement, alors envoie-moi un messager avec un message. La main de(s) dieu(x) est/sera plus puissante que la mort/les mortels..."

[25] Cf. *UT* Glossary n° 1344 et *WUS* n° 1432 pour ne citer que les dictionnaires.

[26] *KTU* 1.2.I:11; 1.4.V:41, 42-3; 1.4.VII:45; 1.5.IV:23, 24; 1.13:27; 1.14. III:19-20; 1.24:16-17; 1.108:24-5(?); 2.10:10; 2.14:7; 2.17:4; 2.21:11; 2.26:4; 2.30:17, 19-20; 2.31:43; 2.32:3; 2.33:36; 2.34:5; 2.36:5, 11, 14; 2.38:11; 2.39:18; 2.42:12, 21, 22, 27; 2.46:9; 2.50:7; 2.53:1; 2.63:7, 10-11, 13; 2.70:13; 2.72:7, 20; *RS* 34.148:9-10; *RIH* 78/12:3.

Laissant de coté un certain nombre de difficultés que nous avons exposés ailleurs [27] on remarquera que *w lak ʿmy* n'a pas de complément d'objet direct. On ne peut pas traduire "envoie-moi!" mais "envoie-moi quelque chose ou quelqu'un". Le contexte montre que l'auteur de la lettre veut être informé d'une situation qui ne lui apparait pas claire. Il demande qu'on lui envoie un messager avec une information sur la situation précise nouvellement crée. La protase *hm in mm nḫtu* trouve son apodose dans *w lak ʿmy*: "Si nous n'avons pas été frappés/vaincus complètement, alors envoie-moi un messager avec l'information".

Un autre exemple qui servira d'argument est *KTU* 2.30:16-20. Il s'agit de la lettre d'un fils à sa mère la reine d'Ugarit. Le fils semble se trouver auprès d'un roi.[28] Tant la mère que le fils semblent craindre le danger de la montée des Hittites à l'endroit où se trouve l'auteur de la lettre. Et celui-ci écrit: *w hm. ḫt. ʿl w. likt ʿmk.w.hm. l. ʿl.w. lakm ilak*: "Et si le Hittite monte, alors je t'enverrai un messager (avec un message), et s'il ne monte pas, je te l'enverrai de toute façon". Encore un cas où *laʾika* n'a pas de complément d'objet direct, sa fonction intransitive est indiscutable. Le sens ne peut être que celui que nous avons indiqué.

Notre exposé ne serait pas complet si nous ne proposions pas un exemple tiré des textes poétiques. Dans *KTU* 1.4.V:41 après toute une série de verbes avec complément, nous lisons: *ylak l kṯr w ḫss*: "Il (Baʿal) envoie un messager avec un message à Kothar-Ḫasis". Pourrait-on traduire "il envoie à Kothar-Ḫasis"?

2a. Dans une deuxième série de textes, *lʾk* a, au moins en apparence, un complément d'objet direct: une personne au sens grammatical. *lʾk* est en effet accompagné de *ġlmm*, *dll*, *ʿdd*, etc. bref d'un nom en partie équivalent de *mlak*. Dans deux cas (*KTU* 1.2.I:11 et 1.14. III:19-20) *ylak* pourrait avoir *mlakm* comme complément d'objet direct mais ces deux cas nous semblent devoir être expliqués autrement (voir plus loin, pp. 37-8).

Ces deux textes mis à part, les noms que l'on retrouve à la place du complément d'objet, font référence à une qualité du personnage. Ces noms ne recouvrent qu'une partie de la signification de *mlak*.

---

[27] A paraître dans les Actes du Congrès d'études ugaritiques de Lattakié (octobre 1979).

[28] Nous avons commenté ce texte dans *Anuario de Filología* (Universidad de Barcelona) 5 (1979), pp. 73-6.

C'est le cas de *ġlmm* [29] "jeunes" dans *KTU* 1.4.V:42 qui fait référence à la jeunesse des "messagers",[30] c'est le cas également de *dll* ("courrier") et *'dd* ("témoin"?) dans *KTU* 1.4.VII:45. Mais le sens de la phrase et peut-être du verbe est celui d'envoyer les *ġlmm/dll/'dd* comme messagers avec un message".

Dans un texte (*RS* 34.148:9-10) *ilak* pourrait avoir *mlakt* comme complément d'objet direct mais la lecture du mot qui précède *l'k* est peu sûre, ce qui incline à la prudence.

3a. Une troisième série de textes présente *l'k* avec, au moins en apparence, un complément d'objet direct. A la différence du groupe précédent, il ne s'agit pas d'un complément de personne mais de chose. Parmi ceux-ci, on trouve: *lḥt spr* (*KTU* 2.14:6-7),[31] *lḥt šlm* (*KTU* 2.34:5-6), *lḥt akl* (*KTU* 2.39:17-18 et 2.46:9-10), *tḥmk* (*KTU* 2.36:5). La valeur sémantique de *l'k* semble être: "envoyer un messager avec un message" que l'on explicite. A cette série appartiennent les textes *KTU* 2.14:6 ss.; 2.34:5-6; 2.36:5; 2.39:17-18; 2.46:9-10; 2.72:7; 2.72:19 ss.[32] Il faut avouer que dans ces cas, la valeur sémantique de *l'k* est plus difficile à cerner et à démontrer. Ces phrases, à mon avis, ont donné le change aux philologues. Elles leur ont permis de conclure que *l'k* signifiait simplement "envoyer". Nous reconnaissons aussi la difficulté. Mais on remarquera que l'auteur de la phrase *lkt lḥt akl* n'a pas reçu une "liste d'aliments" mais une cargaison. Pour cela il fallait bien un *mlak*, voir même une *mlakt*. A notre avis, et si l'on veut tenir compte de tous les faits précédents énumérés dans les deux premières séries de textes, il faut interpréter ces nouveaux faits de la façon suivante: le complément d'objet (par ex. *lḥt akl*) ne clarifie pas directement un aspect laissé obscur par le verbe. Plutôt, l'auteur de la lettre insiste sur le type de "message" envoyé par un messager. Pour bien reproduire le sens de la phrase *likt lḥt akl* il faudrait traduire: "Tu m'as envoyé un messager avec un message consistant en une liste (et cargaison) d'aliments".

---

[29] En fait *ġlmm* dans ce texte est sujet mais d'une forme passive Gp ou passive interne.

[30] La jeunesse semble d'être une des caractéristiques de certains messagers. A Mari aussi, voir par ex. *ARM I*, 17:5 s. et 19 s.

[31]) Nous avons traduit et commenté ce texte dans *UF* 12 (1980), pp. 147-51.

[32] A part les textes en mauvais état de conservation et de lecture, nous estimons que trois textes sont d'attribution difficile et incertaine à l'une ou l'autre des trois séries de textes que nous avons signalées. Nous pensons à *KTU* 2.38:10; 2.70:11 ss.; 2.33:36.

Comment expliquer ces trois séries de textes? Il y a, à notre avis trois explications possibles:

1a. *l'k* a la valeur sémantique "envoyer". Le reste "messager" et "message" que l'on perçoit parfois dans la phrase est à attribuer au contexte littéraire ou à l'ambiance (sociale) de l'auteur et du lecteur. Le contexte littéraire ou l'ambiance sociale lui permettent de comprendre "messager" ou "message" quand il faut, même s'ils ne sont pas contenus dans le verbe.

2a. *l'k* a la valeur sémantique tantôt "envoyer un messager avec un message" (1ère série) tantôt "envoyer un message" (2ème série), tantôt "envoyer un messager" (3ème série).

3a. *l'k* a la valeur sémantique "envoyer un messager avec un message" comme le prouve la première série de textes, la plus nombreuse. La 2ème et la 3ème séries montrent que l'auteur de la phrase veut insister soit sur le type (nature ou qualité) du messager (2ème série) soit sur le type (nature) du message (3ème série). Les compléments d'objet direct n'en seraient pas, à proprement parler, mais seraient plutôt des appositions explicatives d'une partie de la signification de *l'k*. Bref, *l'k* est un verbe intransitif.

Le caractère intransitif de *l'k* est confirmé par la morphologie. Qu'il nous suffise de citer S. Moscati dans ses *Lezioni di linguistica semitica* (Rome, 1960), n° 328, pp. 119-20: "Tema semplice. Questo tema presenta le tre radicali semplici. Si notano in esso delle oscillazioni dello schema vocalico, connesse alla distinzione tra il transitivo e l'intransitivo . . . tali oscillazioni sono meglio perspicue, quanto alla loro connessione semantica, nell'area occidentale del semitico, dove si hanno al perfetto i tre schemi a-a-a per il transitivo, a-i-a per l'intransitivo in stati o condizioni transitorie, a-u-a per l'intransitivo in stati o condizioni durevoli . . . All'imperfetto, la variazione della seconda vocale è conservata . . . avendosi u, i in corrispondenza di a del perfetto *ed a in corrispondenza di i*, mentre per u del perfetto la vocale dell'imperfetto è generalment u." [33] *l'k* qui présente les formes *l'ik* et *l'ikt* au *qtl* et *yl'ak* et *'il'ak* (première personne du singulier) au *yqtl* est bel et bien, d'un point de vue morphologique, un "verbe intransitif en état ou condition transitoire". Ce qui confirme l'analyse faite d'un point de vue sémantique. Il faut donc parler du

[33] Voir aussi C. Brockelmann, *Grundriss der vergleichenden Grammatik der semitischen Sprachen* 1 (Berlin, 1908), § 257 c (p. 505).

verbe *la'ika* et non de *la'ak* ou *la'aka*. Au *yqtl* il faut vocaliser *yil'aku*.

Voici donc la représentation graphique de la valeur sémantique de *la'ika*:

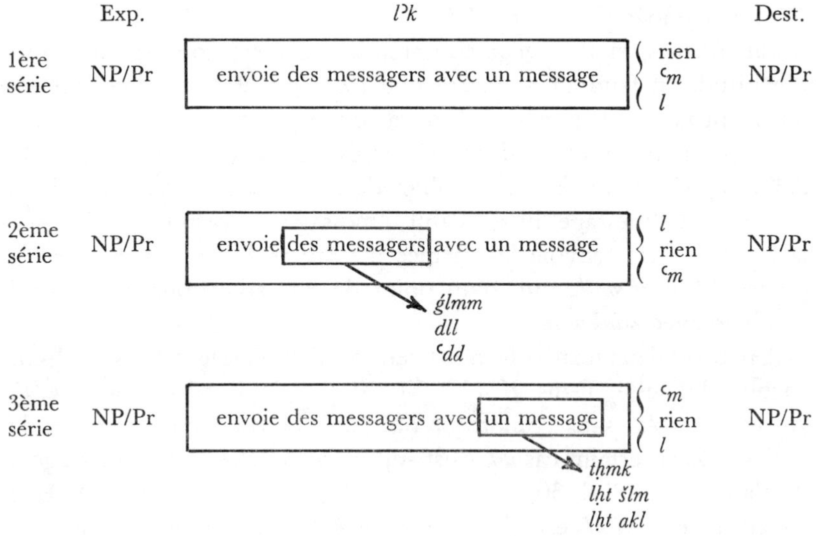

Une "contre-expertise" de la valeur sémantique de *la'ika* peut être établie par l'étude des verbes qui accompagnent *ml'ak* en ugaritique. Deux textes [34] à première vue renversent notre argumentation: *KTU* 1.2.I: 11 où l'on lit *m̊lakm ylak ym* et *KTU* 1.14.III: 19-20: *w ylak mlakm lk ʿm krt mswnh*. Dans le premier cas, on traduit "Yam envoie des messagers" et dans le deuxième "Alors il t'enverra des messagers auprès de Keret au Camp".[35] Sur *KTU* 1.2.I: 11, il faut noter que le *m* de *mlakm* n'est pas sûr et que l'expression *lakm ylak* est celle d'un infinitif avec mimation + *yqtl* que l'on retrouve également et sans doute possible, dans *KTU* 2.30: 19-20 (*lakm ilak*). En ce qui concerne *KTU* 1.14.III: 19-20, l'explication est plus laborieuse. Le passage cité fait partie du cycle de Krt et la phrase est adressée à Krt lui-même. Les commentateurs sont embarrassés par le passage de la deuxième à la troisième personne: "Alors il t'enverra (*lk* deuxième personne) des messagers, auprès de Keret (3ème personne) au camp". A notre avis *w ylak* à la fin de la l. 19 est également la fin psychologique de tout ce qui précède: le roi Pabil ne peut pas

[34] Nous y avons fait allusion plus haut p. 34.

[35] A. Caquot, M. Sznycer, et A. Herdner, *Textes ougaritiques* I, *Mythes et Légendes* (Paris, 1974), p. 523.

dormir à cause de différents bruits et cris d'animaux. Alors il se décide: "et il enverra/il envoie des messagers". La suite (l. 20) reproduit l'ordre que Pabil donne à ses messagers: *mlakm lk ʿm krt mswnh* "Messagers, allez auprès de Keret... !" J'interprète donc *lk* comme impératif du verbe *hlk*.

Par ailleurs, si l'on veut comprendre ce texte comme on le fait d'habitude, il faudrait admettre que *lʾk* régit et *l* et *ʿm* ce qui est tellement rare que ce serait le seul cas que l'on pourrait citer [36] tandis que dans notre interprétation *hlk ʿm* existe par exemple dans *KTU* 2.39:15-16.[37] Après la phrase objet de discussion, le texte continue *tḥm pbl mlk* "message du roi Pabil", message qui se poursuit jusqu'à la l. 32 où Krt renvoie les mêmes messagers à leur maitre avec la phrase *ṯṯb mlakm lh*, qui, d'un point de vue stylistique correspond très bien avec *mlakm lk*.

A part ces deux textes que nous venons d'étudier, les autres n'offrent aucune difficulté. Dans *KTU* 1.2.I (Mythe de Baʿal et Yam) *mlak* apparait 7 fois (sans compter *KTU* 1.2.I:11 dont nous venons de parler). Dans certains cas *mlak* est sujet: *tmǵyn mlak ym* "les messagers de Yam arrivent" (l. 30) et *mlak mṭ* (l. 41) si *mṭ* est un verbe.[38] Dans les autres cas *mlʾak* est objet: *tphn mlak* (l. 22) "ils aperçoivent les messagers"; *aḥd ilm tʿny lḥt mlak ym* (l. 25-6) "*L'un des* dieux doit répondre à la tablette des messagers de Yam" (Caquot-Sznycer-Herdner, p. 130: "aux tablettes"), et *ank ʿny mlak ym* (l. 28) "Moi même je répondrai aux messagers de Yam". Dans *KTU* 1.14, Légende de Krt, on voit apparaître *mlak* 3 fois dans *KTU* 1.14.III lignes 20 et 33 dont nous avons parlé plus haut et dans la colonne VI, ligne 35: *ttbʿ mlakm lyṭb idk* ... "s'en vont les messagers, ils se tournent. . ." Dans ce cas, *mlakm* est sujet du verbe *tbʿ* et dans *KTU* 1.14.III:33 objet du verbe *ṯb*. *KTU* 1.62:6, encore un texte où apparait *mlak*, est fragmentaire. Dans *KTU* 1.124:11 (un oracle) apparait le verbe *mǵy* = "venir" dont l'objet est *mlakk*. Reste le texte non encore publié *RS* 36.1 ou *RS* 1975 ou *RS* 34.356 où l'on lit:... *m*] *ǵy nʾamy*

[36] D. Pardee, "The preposition in Ugaritic", *UF* 7 (1975), p. 354.

[37] Comme signale Pardee, p. 345.

[38] Le texte est difficile à cause de *mlak . mṭ ḥr*. *CTA* 2.I:41 lit *mṭḥr* mais *KTU* voit une séparation entre *mṭ* et *ḥr*. Sans rentrer dans toute la problématique du texte et du contexte, on peut suggérer de voir dans *mṭ* un verbe "chanceler" comme Caquot-Sznycer-Herdner l'indiquent pour la ligne 9 de la même colonne (p. 128, note g). Pour notre ligne 41, les mêmes Caquot-Sznycer-Herdner proposent de lire *mlak mṭḥr yḥb*[*š*], "un messager at[tache] ... son fardeau". Dans ce cas, *mlak* est le sujet de *yḥbš*, ce qui pour l'objet de notre exposé revient au même.

ml'ak où, à part quelques difficultés dont nous ne ferons pas état ici, *ml'ak* serait l'objet de *mǵy*. Bref les *mlakm* "partent" ou "ils arrivent", "ils se tournent" ou "on leur répond", on les "aperçoit". A part ce dernier verbe (ainsi que *mṭ* "chancelant" de *KTU* 1.2.I:41) qui est plus épisodique, les autres ont trait à la fonction des *ml'akm*: ils reçoivent l'ordre de s'en aller, ils s'en vont, ils arrivent et on leur répond (dans ce dernier cas d'ailleurs, on répond plutôt à la tablette qu'aux messagers. Voir *KTU* 1.2.I:26 texte dont dépend évidemment la ligne 28 avec *ank ʿny mlak ym*).

II. *La morphologie de mlak. Le rôle littéraire du malāk et sa fonction sociale*

Nous venons de parler des verbes qui accompagnent *mlak* en ugaritique. Revenons de la main des messagers à la forme *mlak* dont nous sommes partis pour mieux préciser sa morphologie et sa signification.

Le maître J. Barth écrivait: "Mit dem Präfix *ma* und *mi* bildet das Semitische Nomina, welche sowohl die reine Handlung, als auch das concrete Sachwort in seinen verschiedenen Ausstrahlungen, wie die Person, den Ort (im Arab. auch die Zeit, seltener dies in andern Sprachen), das Werkzeug der Handlung bezeichnen können. Diese Mannigfaltigkeit der Bedeutungen hängt mit eben diesem m-Präfix zusammen, dessen Verwandtschaft mit dem Pronomen der Person: *măn*, *mî* 'wer' und der Sache: *mā* 'was' längstschon vermuthet ist".[39]

Une forme *maqtal* signifie donc l'action ou le résultat de l'action (cf. Meyer, p. 33) ou son rayonnement, la personne, le lieu ou l'instrument de l'action. Le *mlak* ne peut pas être la personne qui envoie, mais la personne qui exécute l'action signifiée par la racine *l'k*. Le *mlak* est donc d'un point de vue grammatical, l'instrument de l'action signifiée par *la'ika*. Le caractère instrumental, ou plus exactement intermédiaire, de *mlak* ressortait bien déjà de la lecture des textes où il apparait, ainsi que des verbes qui l'accompagnent en ugaritique. Et nous verrons plus loin que les *mlakm* remplissent, d'un point de vue littéraire, le même rôle d'intermédiaire.

Si les philologues qui attribuaient à *la'ika* la valeur sémantique "envoyer" ont traduit *mlak* par "messager" cela prouve bien qu'ils voyaient dans *l'k* plus qu'une simple action d'envoyer. Ils sous-entendaient "envoyer un message" ou "envoyer un messager"

[39] *Die Nominalbildung in den semitischen Sprachen* (2. Aufl., Leipzig, 1894), p. 233. Voir aussi R. Meyer, *Hebräische Grammatik* II (3. Aufl., Berlin, 1969), p. 33.

sinon, comment expliquer le passage sémantique d'"envoyer" à "messager"? La liaison entre les deux est claire si *la'ika* signifie "envoyer un message" ou "envoyer un messager" ou "envoyer un messager avec un message". Dans ces circonlocutions sémantiques, "message" et "messager" jouent un rôle au moins aussi important que l'élément "envoyer" qui pouvait être exprimé par *šlḥ* (cf. *UT* Glossary 2419). Les Ugaritains l'ont compris ainsi, comme nous l'avons vu plus haut; les Hébreux, Phéniciens et Araméens aussi. Voilà pourquoi ils ont pu emprunter ou tout simplement utiliser *mal'āk* avec une référence claire au message et n'ont pas utilisé, ou ignoré, *l'k*. Pour "envoyer un messager", ils pouvaient dire *šlḥ mal'āk*. Il est également vrai que l'absence de *la'ika* en hébreu et dans les autres langues sémitiques nord-occidentales peut être l'indice d'une perte de valeur sémantique de la part de *la'ika* et que, dans la nouvelle signification, *la'ika* ne différait pas de *šalaḥ*. S'il y a une évolution sémantique du verbe *la'ika*, l'absence de ce verbe en hébreu, en phénicien et en araméen (ainsi que certains faits présents à Ugarit mais difficiles à utiliser) tout cela ne permet pas de penser que *la'ika* a évolué d'"envoyer" vers "envoyer un messager" mais plutôt partant d'"envoyer des messagers avec un message" vers le simple "envoyer" sens qu'il pouvait avoir quand les hébreux, comme les phéniciens ou les araméens n'ont plus senti le besoin de ce verbe. *mlak* par contre sera plus persistant et conservera sa valeur sémantique d'origine.

La sémantique *mlak* = "messager" peut s'appuyer sur la signification de *la'ika* selon ce que nous avons vu. Mais elle reste à préciser. Reste à préciser également le rôle du *mlak*. La morphologie grammaticale le présente comme un instrument de l'action, la littérature comme un intermédiaire.

Instrument de l'action, mais quelle action? Celle indiquée par le verbe, bien entendu. C'est à dire l'action par laquelle l'envoyeur envoie un message au destinataire. Le *mlak* est donc un "porteur de messages". On peut ajouter "lecteur des messages" puisque son rôle ne s'arrêtait pas au simple transport comme c'est le cas de nos postiers, mais il les lisait au destinataire. Pour s'en convaincre, il suffit de lire les textes littéraires, plusieurs fois cités, où il est question des *mlakm*. Quand nous disons "lecteur de messages", il faut voir dans "lecteur" la touche sémantique de "témoignage" ou de "témoin" que semblent y mettre *'dd* et *t'dt*. Le rapprochement avec *KTU* 1.4.VII:45:

dll ("courrier") *al ilak lbn ilm mt*
ʿdd ("témoin") *l ydd il ǵẓr*

vient immédiatement à l'esprit. Le vétérotestamentaire verra avec plaisir dans la nuance "témoin" un rapprochement avec les Prophètes.

Si la morphologie grammaticale présente le *mlak* comme un instrument, la littérature complète sa vision le présentant comme un intermédiaire. Sans nous y attarder, nous donnerons un exemple tiré des formules maintes fois répétées dans les textes littéraires et qui caractérisent le départ des messagers. Je m'y arrête d'autant plus volontiers qu'ils s'agit d'une formule que l'on n'a pas toujours bien expliquée et qui projette un singulier faisceau de lumière sur nos *mlakm*. Je pense à: *ttbʿ mlʾakm l yṯb idk pnm lytn* (par ex. dans *KTU* 1.14.VI:35 s.) "Les messagers partent, *ils se tournent*. Alors ils se dirigent vers. . ." à comparer avec: *ttbʿ btlt ʿnt idk l ttn pnm* (par ex. dans *KTU* 1.6.IV:6) "La vierge Anat part. Alors elle se dirige vers. . ." On remarquera l'absence de *lyṯb* dans la deuxième phrase où le sujet est la déesse Anat. Cette formule a beaucoup préoccupé L. Delekat, *UF* 4 (1972), pp. 13-14, qui se demande, non sans humour, si les *mlakm* "s'orientaient comme les pigeons voyageurs seulement après avoir quitté les lieux". L'absence de *lyṯb* dans la deuxième phrase prouve toujours selon Delekat, que la formule complète et la construction avec l'infinitif absolu (pour Delekat *yṯb* ainsi que *tbʿ* et *ytn* sont des infinitifs absolus) était réservée aux messagers. Un bon messager quitte les lieux dès qu'il a reçu une commission (un message), immédiatement, sans tarder.

A mon avis, les textes ugaritiques qu'il cite ont été écrits pour être entendus par de nombreux auditeurs (et non pour être lus par un seul lecteur) ce qui explique qu'au moment où l'on va changer de scène le narrateur est obligé de la souligner par des formules, d'ailleurs courantes, ce qui permet aux auditeurs de quitter psychologiquement la place où se situait la scène qui vient de finir pour se préparer et se situer dans la scène suivante, à l'endroit (village, temple, etc. . .) où la nouvelle scène est située. La première partie de la formule *tbʿ* souligne donc qu'ils quittent les lieux: "ils se dirigent vers" *idk pnm lytn* etc. souligne qu'ils se dirigent (et l'auditeur doit commencer à se diriger psychologiquement) vers . . . la nouvelle scène.

ltṯb souligne, comme le dit Delekat, que les *mlʾakm* mettent en œuvre immédiatement l'action, mais aussi, et c'est la différence avec le cas d'Anat cité par Delekat, qu'ils ne sont que des personnages intermédiaires, des personnages qui, du point de vue du style et de la technique narrative, ne sont que des "liaisons" entre deux scènes ou deux tableaux, tandis que Anat est le même personnage qui passe d'un tableau à l'autre. La propre action de cette dernière (Anat) justifie d'un point de vue technique le prochain tableau, tandis que dans le cas des messagers, c'est le message d'un tel (qui lui ne bouge pas) qui justifie la scène ou le tableau suivant. *lṯb* sert de charnière (toujours d'un point de vue de la technique narrative) entre le *terminus a quo* (tableau précédent) et le *terminus ad quem* (tableau suivant).

Ces considérations stylistiques nous permettent du même coup de voir quel était le rôle des messagers: des personnages de deuxième ordre dont la personnalité consiste à servir d'intermédiaire entre deux personnages principaux qui, eux, ont une personnalité propre.

La remarque est d'autant plus amusante que la formule se répète normalement avec *l yṯb* quand il s'agit de Gapan et Ugar qui sont appelés *ilm* mais sont et remplissent le rôle de messagers (cf. *KTU* 1.5.I:9 et II:13). On devrait donc être très prudent quand la Bible parle du *malā'k* ou *mal'ak YHWH*. Il ne joue pas un rôle principal, il est toujours un personnage secondaire et joue le role d'intermédiaire.

Par la morphologie grammaticale les *mlakm* sont des instruments; pour la littérature, des charnières du récit, des intermédiaires. Leur fonction sociale est celle de représenter l'envoyeur auprès du destinataire, de faire la connexion entre les deux. De là, découle une certaine assimilation sociale des *mlakm* avec la classe ou le groupe auxquels appartiennent l'envoyeur et le destinataire. De là vient aussi, que les dieux envoient des dieux, même si les dieux *mlakm* sont des dieux de deuxième rang.

Le rôle et la représentativité des *mlakm* sont particulièrement mis en valeur dans la littérature épistolaire. Le *mlak* est l'intermédiaire qui parle au destinataire au nom de l'expéditeur. La littérature epistolaire qu'elle soit en langue akkadienne ou en langue ugaritique, montre par ses formules: 1) l'existence de trois personnes: celle de l'expéditeur, celle du destinataire et celle du *malk*; 2) Ces mêmes formules montrent, à mon avis, que le *mlak* parle au nom de l'expéditeur. En quelque sorte, le *mlak* remplace l'envoyeur pendant les quelques instants que durent sa mission de donner lecture du message dont il est le porteur. Ceci est d'autant plus important à notre avis, que nous découvrons une structure triangulaire là où de nos jours existe [40] une structure linéaire ou binaire. De nos jours, l'auteur d'une lettre s'addresse directement au destinataire sans intermédiaire, le préposé des postes ne jouant dans ce sens aucun rôle. Cé n'était pas le cas au deuxième millénaire avant J. C. et les formules épistolaires auxquelles nous faisions allusion plus haut le montrent bien. En effet, la formule akkadienne des lettres est celle-ci:

	ana NP	à NP
	qibima	dis!:
	umma NP	Ainsi (parle) NP
La formule ugaritique est:	*l* NP	à NP
	rgm	dis!:
	tḥm NP	Message de NP

On remarquera que par l'impératif akkadien *qibima* et par l'impératif ugaritique *rgm*, l'expéditeur s'adresse directement au *mlak* qui reçoit ainsi l'ordre d'aller "dire" au destinataire le message qui suit dans le corps de la lettre. Quand le *mlak* arrive à sa destination, ce même impératif lui sert de "lettre de créance" auprès du destinataire. Ce qui suit, le *mlak* le dit au nom de l'envoyeur, au nom duquel il parle.

Bien entendu, on a interprété autrement la formule d'adresse des lettres. On a pensé à un pur ornement ou à une survivance rhétorique de l'époque où l'on transmettait les messages oralement.[41] Sans nier que la formule ait pu perdre à l'usage une partie de sa valeur sémantique originelle, c'est trop affirmer que de réduire la formule à un reste de la tradition orale sans signification aucune. En effet, il ne faut pas oublier le rôle du *mlak* et du *mâr šipri*. Par ailleurs, la suite du texte des lettres plaide en faveur d'une valeur significative pour cette formule. Ainsi dans les lettres qu'un vassal envoie à son roi (ou à la reine) on trouve 8 fois la formule: [42]

---

[40] On pourrait discuter si de nos jours la structure est linéaire ou triangulaire. Il va de soi que dans la communication social des mass media, la structure n'est pas linéaire mais triangulaire sinon polyangulaire. Mais nous limitons notre affirmation aux lettres et nous ne voulons pas rentrer dans la discussion sociologique, fort intéressante d'ailleurs, de la polyvalence et des intermédiares dans la communication sociale. Nous attirons tout de même l'attention du lecteur sur l'habileté qu'on déploie dans les mass media pour faire croire qu'il y a une ligne droite là où il existe en fait un polyèdre.

[41] Cf. par ex. A. L. Kristensen, "Ugaritic epistolary formulas", *UF* 9 (1977), p. 144, qui l'affirme explicitement. Le nombre de ceux qui semblent donner la même interprétation peut être considérable.

[42] Ajouter aux textes indiqués par Kristensen, p. 157, les suivants: *KTU* 2.51; 2.68 et 2.70 et 2.52 pour la formule incomplète.

lpʿn bʿly/adty šbʿd w šbʿid mrḥqtm qlt: "aux pieds de mon seigneur/madame sept et sept fois de loin je suis tombé/je tombe".

Quel est le sens de *mrḥqtm* "de loin"? Peut-on imaginer l'envoyeur en train de se prosterner à l'endroit où il écrit la lettre? Il semble plus normal de penser au protocole royal selon lequel celui qui avait accès à la présence du roi, au moment d'entrer dans la salle, exprimait son respect par des gestes convenus. Aucune raison de douter de l'existence de ce rituel qui, sous des formes différentes, fait partie de toutes les cultures et arrive jusqu'à nos sociétés démocratiques. Le sens de *mrḥqtm* "de loin" [43] désigne, à notre avis, les quelques mètres qui séparent le roi de celui qui parle: le *mlak* (représentant l'expéditeur). Voilà aussi la raison, peut-être inconsciente, de l'hésitation des traducteurs devant *qlt* (akkadien *amqut*): "Je tombe" [44] ou "Je suis tombé" [45] Les deux traductions sont possibles d'après l'idée que l'on se fait du rituel. A notre avis, il s'agit d'une action immédiate qui vient d'avoir lieu. C'est le *mlak* qui a fait les gestes protocolaires, c'est le *mlak* qui parle au nom de son maître l'expéditeur.

III. *mal'āk et meläʾkāh. mār šipri et šiprum*

La littérature akkadienne d'Ugarit a plusieurs mots qui, à première vue au moins, pourraient désigner le *mlak*. J. Nougayrol l'éditeur de ces tablettes en cite plusieurs: *kallû* = "courrier",[46] *guzalû* = "porte-parole, messager",[47] *nâgiru*,[48] *ḫaššasu*(?) = "coursier" (?),[49] *âlik pâni* = "leader d'un groupe de marchands",[50] mais surtout *mār šipri* = "messager",[51] C'est celui-ci qui correspond le mieux à notre *mlak*, et par l'usage qu'on en fait dans la littérature akkadiene [52] et par la signification de base.

šipru(m) signifie en akkadien "Sendung, Botschaft; Arbeit, Werk"

---

[43] A. Caquot me suggère comme traduction en bon français: "à distance (respectueuse)".

[44] Kristensen, p. 148; Nougayrol, "Je m'effondre": *PRU IV*, p. 221 et passim.

[45] A. Caquot par ex. dans *Annuaire du Collège de France* 79 (1978-9), p. 484.

[46] Voir références dans *PRU III*, p. 233.

[47] Voir références dans *PRU IV*, p. 260.

[48] Voir références dans *PRU III*, p. 234.

[49] Voir références dans *Ugaritica V* (Paris, 1968), p. 349.

[50] Voir références dans *PRU IV*, p. 259.

[51] Voir références dans *Ugaritica V*, p. 340, et *PRU VI*, p. 151.

[52] Cf. *AHW*, p. 616; *CAD* 10, pp. 260-5, qui traduit "messenger, envoy, agent, deputy".

(*AHW*, p. 1245). E. Ebeling donne cet ordre: "Auftrag, Sendung" ("Arbeit").[53] Remarquons que l'usage de *šipru* dans le sens de "travail" "œuvre" "ouvrage" est quatre fois supérieur en nombre à celui de *šipru*: "envoi, ambassade" (cf. *AHW*, p. 1245).

L'existence de ces deux sens de *šipru* ("Sendung" et "Botschaft" d'un côté et "Arbeit" et "Werk" de l'autre) enlève toute "anomalie" à la complexité des tâches du *mal'āk* "messager" et aux significations de "Botschaft, Sendung > Auftrag > Unternehmung, Geschäft > Arbeit, Dienst > Sache, Ware, etwas",[54] prises par *m^elā'kāh* en hébreu, même si la connexion entre les deux significations de base "Sendung" et "Arbeit" n'est plus perceptible en hébreu. Le dernier article paru sur *m^elā'kāh* essaie de resoudre les deux significations de base par d'autres biais. E. L. Greenstein, l'auteur de l'article, se demande comment un mot qui signifie "travail" peut être dérivé d'un verbe signifiant "envoyer".[55] A notre avis *šiprum* avec ses deux valeurs sémantiques "*Sendung*" et "*Arbeit*" est à la base des valeurs sémantiques de *m^elā'kāh*. Les rapports entre *šipru* et *m^elā'kāh* pourraient être une preuve de l'influence mésopotamienne sur la langue et la culture hébraïque. Il va de soi que notre explication nous semble valable également pour le phénicien *ml'kt* "travail".[56] Mais si *šipru(m)* fait mieux percevoir l'origine sémantique de *m^elā'kāh* (et *ml'kt* en phénicien), il nous fait mieux comprendre également les fonctions du *mal'āk* hébreu (et par élargissement du *ml'k* phénicien[57] et du *mal'āk* araméen)[58] ainsi que les rapports entre *mal'āk* et *m^elā'kāh*.

---

[53] *Glossar zu den neubabylonischen Briefen* (München, 1955), p. 235.

[54] Koehler-Baumgartner, p. 526.

[55] "Trans-Semitic idiomatic equivalency and the derivation of Hebrew *ml'kh*", *UF* 11 (1979), pp. 329-36. A la page 332 il écrit: "At first blush one may puzzle over the derivation of a word meaning 'work' from a verb meaning 'to send'".

[56] *KAI* 10:11, 13, 14. Et sur *mlkt* avec le même sens cf. *KAI* 37 A:7. Voir références dans *KAI* III, p. 14. Moins complet cf. R. S. Tomback, *A Comparative Semitic Lexicon of the Phoenician and Punic Languages* (Missoula, 1978), pp. 178-9, Z. S. Harris, *A Grammar of the Phoenician Language* (New Haven, Conn., 1936), p. 114.

[57] *KAI* 19:2. Voir aussi A. Caquot, "Le dieu Milkʿashtart et les inscriptions de 'Umm el ʿAmed", *Semitica* 15 (1965), pp. 29-33 mais surtout 31-2. Dans l'inscription 13, on trouve aussi un *ml'k*, l'ange ou le messager de *mlk ʿštrt* qui participe selon l'inscription à la construction de l'ouvrage sacré. On serait tenté de faire le rapprochement de ce *ml'k* et de son travail (*ml'kt* en phénicien) avec le sens de *mār šipri* dont nous avons parlé. L'interprétation du Prof. Caquot trouve dans ce contexte un argument supplémentaire. Par ailleurs, en ce qui concerne les noms puniques *bʿlml'k* cf. F. L. Benz, *Personal Names in Phoenician and Punic Inscriptions* (Rome, 1972), p. 96.

[58] Cf. par ex. *KAI* 224:8; J. A. Fitzmyer et D. J. Harrington, *A Manual of*

En effet, il a été remarqué depuis longtemps que le *mal'āk* non seulement transmettait des nouvelles ou des informations de son envoyeur mais aussi qu'un *mal'āk* pouvait agir et réaliser des œuvres et des actions très différentes. Ainsi Saül envoie des *mal'ākîm* pour surveiller David (1 Sam. xix 11 ss.), les *mal'ākîm* de Joab tirent Abner de la citerne (2 Sam. iii 26); David envoie les *mal'ākîm* chercher Bethsabée (2 Sam. xi 4); et la fonction du *mal'ak YHWH/Elohim* consiste souvent à accomplir une action (par ex. dans Gen. xix 16; xxix 7, 40; Ex. xiv 19; Nomb. xx 16; 2 Sam. xxiv 16 s.; 2 R. xix 35 = Is. xxxvii 36; 1 Chr. xxi 12 ss.).

De la lecture des textes akkadiens semble se dégager l'image suivante: les rois, les chefs ont besoin de transmettre leurs ordres, de se faire présents à des endroits différents, de commander certains ouvrages, certains travaux. C'est le *Sitz im Leben* des "porteurs de message" qui transmettent des ordres. On appelera *šiprum* le travail et l'œuvre commandés, l'ouvrage réalisé par ordre d'un tel. La valeur sémantique de *šiprum* est très vaste. Commençant à celui qui envoie ou donne des ordres, elle s'élargit jusqu'à la réalisation non seulement de la mission mais de l'œuvre commandée elle-même, objet de la mission, en passant par la transmission de l'ordre, l'exécution du travail, le travail, l'action commandée et le fruit de cette action et du travail. En rapprochant *m^e^lā'kāh* de *šiprum*, on comprend beaucoup mieux la valeur sémantique de l'hébreu *m^e^lā'kāh*, et on voit la pauvreté de notre expression quand nous traduisons *mal'āk* par "messager". En effet, la plupart des éléments de *m^e^lā'kāh*, sinon tous, se retrouvent chez *mal'āk*: le transmetteur de messages, l'espion, l'auteur d'actions aussi disparates que la destruction d'une armée, le fait d'amener une femme ou de tirer quelqu'un d'une citerne. Le *mal'āk* occupe-t-il le même champ sémantique que *mār šipri* en akkadien? En fait il est difficile de dire si *mal'āk* (ug. *ml'ak*) traduit *mār šipri* ou tout simplement *šiprum*. C'est *šiprum* qui a toutes les valeurs sémantiques dont nous avons parlé (voir *AHW*, pp. 1245-6; pour *mār šipri* cf. p. 616), et *šiprum* remplace parfois *mār šipri* (cf. p. 1245: *šiprum* sous 4).

šiprum est un dérivé du verbe *šapāru(m)* "schicken, schreiben" selon l'*Akkadisches Handwörterbuch* (p. 1170). A, Mari, selon O. Rouault il a le sens de: "envoyer (un message), mandater, ordonner

Palestinian Aramaic Texts (Rome, 1978), 5.30:5; 21.2:18; E. Vogt, *Lexicon Linguae Aramaicae Veteris Testamenti documentis antiquis illustratum* (Rome, 1971), p. 100.

(par écrit)".[59] A Tell-el-Amarna, selon A. F. Rainey: "to send, to send in writing".[60] On aurait tort de traduire *mār šipri* par "fils ou homme de l'écrit" comme on aurait tendance à le faire par influence sémitique nord-occidentale. "Ecrire" n'est pas le premier sens de *šapāru(m)* comme nous venons de voir. A part le fait qu'il faudrait approfondir l'étude de *šapāru(m)*, on remarquera que si l'on tient compte de la valeur sémantique de *šiprum* en akkadien et de *m^elā'kāh* en hébreu ainsi que des fonctions attribuées au *mal'āk* dans la Bible hébraïque, le mot "messager" comme traduction de *mal'āk* est très court. Il faudrait soit trouver d'autres mots, soit avoir toujours présent à l'esprit le champ sémantique occupé par ce mot hébreu.

On voit donc que le sens de *šapāru(m)* est celui d'envoyer quelqu'un avec un ordre ou message. Le *mār šipri* est celui qui transmet l'ordre ou le message. Ces deux constatations, d'une part, confirment notre analyse sémantique de *la'ika* et *mlak*, d'autre part, montrent les rapports entre l'akkadien et l'ugaritique. Le *mār šipri* est donc en quelque sorte "l'homme à message(s)" ou plutôt "l'Auftragsmann" (Ebeling, p. 235), le "chargé de mission".

Si notre rapprochement entre *šiprum* et *m^elā'kāh*, *mār šipri* et *mal'āk* est exact une étude approfondie de *māri (meš) šiprim* est non seulement justifiée mais souhaitable. A ce qui a été fait [61] il faudrait ajouter les nouvelles perspectives pour l'étude de l'Ancien Testament. Nous avons réalisé cette étude mais nous ne l'exposerons pas ici pour des raisons d'espace. En résumé, nous avons pu constater que toutes les situations (pour ne pas dire contextes) dans lesquelles le mot *mal'āk* apparait dans le texte hébraïque, trouvent leur pendant en akkadien avec *mār šipri* à l'exclusion, bien entendu, de ce qui est propre à la théologie de l'Ancien Testament. Les perspectives linguistiques donnaient d'énormes possibilités d'élargissement théologique ce que la Bible n'a pas manqué de mener à bon terme.

---

[59] "Mukannišum, L'Administration et l'économie palatiale à Mari", *ARM XVIII*, p. 280, avec de nombreuses références.

[60] *El Amarna Tablets 359-379* (Kevelaer et Neukirchen-Vluyn, 1970), p. 93.

[61] Cf. J. M. Munn-Rankin, *Iraq* 18 (1956), pp. 68-110; J. Bottéro, *ARM VII*, pp. 333-4, 233-6, et 211 sous 3° (chargés d'affaires, ambassadeurs ou diplomates); M. S. Luker, *The Figure of Moses in the Plague Traditions* (diss., Drew University, Madison, 1968), ch. II, "The Messenger Figure in Sumerian and Akkadian Literature"; Y. L. Holmes, "The messengers of the Amarna Letters", *JAOS* 95 (1975), pp. 376-81; R. W. Fisher, "Messengers at Mari", paper read at the Canadian Society of Biblical Studies, London, Ontario (26-28 May 1978) auquel je n'ai pas encore eu accès.

Si notre analyse est correcte:

1. On voit que le champ sémantique occupé en akkadien par *šiprum* et *mār šipri* est occupé en hébreu par *m^elā'kāh* et *mal'āk*. On comprend mieux les deux sens fondamentaux de l'hébreu *m^elā'kāh* "ambassade" et "travail, ouvrage" et le rapprochement avec l'akkadien jette beaucoup de lumière sur le *mal'āk* qui parle et le *mal'āk* qui agit. En effet *mal'āk* est la traduction nord-occidentale de l'oriental *mār šipri*: "le fils ou l'homme du *šiprum*" c'est à dire aussi bien du "message, commision" que de l'"ouvrage". Dans l'état actuel de la documentation, nous pouvons affirmer le rapprochement entre l'akkadien et l'hébreu (entre *mār šipri* ou *šiprum* et *mal'āk* et *m^elā'kāh*) plus facilement qu'entre l'akkadien et l'ugaritique puisque les nuances sémantiques de l'"action" pour le *mlak* et de "ouvrage" "travail" pour *mlakt* ne sont pas décelables dans notre documentation ugaritique tandis qu'elles sont évidentes en hébreu. (Cf. pour l'hébreu *ThHW* I sous *mal'āk*).

2. Ce que nous venons de constater pour l'hébreu semble pouvoir être élargi à tout le sémitique nord-occidental mais avec précaution. En effet, la documentation en phénicien, en araméen et même en ugaritique nous permet d'affirmer que tous les textes connus trouvent leur explication sémantique dans l'une ou l'autre des variantes sémantiques de l'akkadien.

Le phénicien *ml'kt* "travail" est mieux perçu ainsi que le sens de *ml'k* de l'inscription 13 d'Umm-el-'Ahmed de 220 av. J.-C. où l'on voit la connexion entre le *ml'k* et son ouvrage.

L'ugaritique connait également deux mots dérivés de *l'k*: *mlak* et *mlakt*.[62] Tous les deux font partie du champ sémantique qui commence à l'envoyeur et va jusqu'à la délivrance du message et des objets apportés.[63] Mais dans la documentation existant actuellement en ugaritique, manquent les valeurs sémantiques: "ouvrage", "travail", courantes en akkadien, que l'on trouve aussi en hébreu et en phénicien.

---

[62] *mlakt* apparait en ugaritique dans *KTU* 2.17:4(?), 7; 2.23:3; 2.31:49; 2.33:35; et *RS* 34.148:10, et il est traduit par "délégation" (Ch. Virolleaud, *PRU II*, p. 211) ou "ambassade", "mission" (C. H. Gordon, *UT* Glossary n° 1344) "Botschaft" (J. Aistleitner-O. Eissfeldt, *WUS* n° 1432); et même "economic mission" (W. F. Albright, *BASOR* 150 [1958], p. 38), n. 14; M. Dahood, *CBQ* 22 (1960), pp. 403-4, et *Psalms III* (Garden City, New York, 1970), p. 86.

[63] Se rappeler que la *mlakt* même comprise comme "ambassade" ou "mission" apportait des objets, cadeaux. Cela est explicité en akkadien (par ex. à Mari; voir par ex. *ARM I*, 15:6 ss. et passim) et à Ugarit, une phrase comme *lḥt akl dt likt* le laisse penser.

Si ces attestations manquent dans la documentation ugaritique actuelle, on est en droit d'attendre qu'elles paraissent un jour ou l'autre. Dans le cas contraire, il faudrait tirer les conclusions qui s'imposent sur les rapports entre les langues sémitiques nord-occidentales entre elles et avec l'akkadien.

Sans pouvoir affirmer de *šapāru(m)* tout ce que nous avons dit de l'ugaritique *la'ika*, on a la certitude qu'ils occupent le même champ sémantique. *šapāru(m)*: envoyer quelqu'un avec un message; les messages peuvent être des ordres (très souvent) [64] qui doivent être exécutés (cf. *AHW*, p. 1170) d'où le sens de "travail" d'"exécution" et d'"ouvrage exécuté" exprimé par *šiprum*. Mais on peut se demander: pourquoi l'ugaritique et l'hébreu, ainsi que le phénicien et l'araméen, ont choisi la racine *l'k* à la place de *spr* (il faut remarquer que la racine *l'k* existe en akkadien).[65] Le vaste champ sémantique de *l'k* en ugaritique: "envoyer un messager avec un message" semble trouver ainsi sinon une explication au moins une meilleure compréhension. Le vaste champ sémantique de *šiprum* et *mār šipri* commençant à l'envoyeur et s'élargissant jusqu'à l'œuvre réalisée, permet de comprendre que l'ugaritique ait un verbe dont la valeur sémantique commence à l'envoyeur (l'envoyeur est le sujet de *l'k*) et s'étend à la délivrance du message au destinataire.

Résumé et conclusion

Notre démarche a été la suivante. Nous voulions étudier le *mal'ak YHWH/'ĕlōhîm* de la Bible hébraïque. Nous avons constaté que *mal'āk* est un dérivé de *l'k* non attesté en hébreu ni en aucune autre langue sémitique nord-occidentale (mais attestée en arabe et en éthiopien) sauf en ugaritique. Nous avons donc étudié *la'ika* en ugaritique et nous sommes arrivés à la conclusion que *la'ika* était un verbe intransitif avec comme signification "envoyer un messager avec un message", signification qui est exprimée soit complètement soit partiellement, soit que, étant toujours exprimée complètement, celui qui l'utilise sente le besoin d'expliciter un aspect de cette valeur sémantique (l'aspect "courrier" qu'a le messager ou son aspect de "témoin", ou bien le genre du message: *lḥt šlm*, *lḥt akl*).

Puis nous avons étudié le rôle du *mlak* qui est celui d'un intermédiaire entre l'envoyeur et le destinataire. Son rôle d'intermédiaire

---

[64] Cf. par ex. *ARM XIII*, 22:15: *ú-ul ša-ap-ra-ku*, "je n'ai reçu aucun ordre".

[65] Cf. *AHW*, pp. 520 et 542 sous *lêku(m)*, "lécher"; et p. 593 *malāku(m)* I, "une partie de la langue".

apparait dans la morphologie du morphème comme dans l'usage littéraire et dans la réalité culturelle. Il nous a semblé pouvoir indiquer un fait de civilisation ou de culture. La documentation dont nous disposons tant en akkadien qu'en ugaritique, provient en grande partie des lettres. Or si dans notre civilisation moderne la lettre est un moyen de communication directe entre l'expéditeur et le destinataire, ce n'est pas du tout le cas dans l'antiquité où le *mlak/mār šipri* jouait un rôle indispendable d'intermédiaire. Bref, nous sommes, en ce qui concerne les lettres, dans une structure binaire, tandis que les Akkadiens, les Ugaritains et les Hébreux vivaient dans une structure trinaire. Cette structure trinaire chez les anciens, binaire chez nous, explique, à mon avis, que pour exprimer le sens de *laʾika* nous soyons obligés de dire "envoyer un messager avec un message", précision sur l'intermédiaire qui, pour eux, allait de soi. Dans notre civilisation, la structure trinaire existe dans le monde diplomatique et dans les mass media. Il nous faut donc être vigilants sur le concept de "messager" beaucoup plus necessaire et beaucoup plus présent dans l'antiquité que de nos jours.

Cet intermédiaire appelé *mlak*, *malʾāk* ou *mār šipri*, jouait auprès du destinataire un rôle indispensable. Il représentait l'envoyeur, parlait et agissait en son nom. Il parlait au nom de l'envoyeur [66] et on lui répondait en conséquence. Le rôle des prophètes de la Bible est ainsi mis en évidence. La meilleure illustration en est le nom même Malachie (i 1).

Mais s'il parlait au nom de l'envoyeur, il agissait aussi en son nom quand la mission consistait justement dans une action ou un ordre à exécuter. On comprend très bien tous les textes biblique qui font allusion à cette action [67] et quand celui qui agit est le *malʾāk* au sens profane [68] et quand celui qui agit est le *malʾak YHWH/ʾĕlōhîm*.[69]

Essayant d'ouvrir le champ de notre recherche, nous avons eu recours aux autres "messagers" du monde akkadien et cela nous l'avons fait en partant d'Ugarit. Cela nous a conduit à constater avec

---

[66] Confirmation sumérienne, cf. S. N. Kramer, *Enmerkar and the Lord of Aratta* (Philadelphia, 1952), p. 25; voir Luker, p. 59. Le même usage dans la Bible: Jg. xi 13; 2 Sam. iii 12 ss.; 1 R. xx 2 ss., etc.

[67] Gen. xxiv 7, 40; Ex. xiv 19, etc.; 1 Sam. xix 11 ss., etc. Et voir par ex. R. Ficker, *ThHW* I, col. 903 sous b, et col. 904 sous a, et col. 905 sous b.

[68] Cf. par ex. 1 Sam. xix 11 ss.; 2 Sam. iii 26, xi 4, etc. Et voir Ficker, col. 903 sous b.

[69] Gen. xix 16, xxiv 7, 40; Nomb. xx 16; 2 Sam. xxiv 16 s.; 2 R. xix 35, etc.; et voir Ficker, col. 904 sous a, et col. 905 sous b.

beaucoup d'autres que la désignation la plus courante de "messager" en akkadien est celle de *mār šipri*. Mais nous sommes allés un peu plus loin que nos devanciers en constatant les rapports existants entre *šiprum/mār šipri* et *mlakt/mlak* (*m^elā'kāh* et *mal'āk* en hébreu, *ml'kt* et *ml'k* en phénicien et *ml'k* en araméen).

Les élargissement théologiques sont multiples: tout d'abord la connexion entre parole et action fait penser à *dābār* et à la théologie de la parole. Ensuite l'aspect de "témoin" qu'a le *mal'āk* suggère un élargissement dans le sens de la théologie du témoignage. Enfin la même connexion entre message et action suggère l'action du *mal'āk* dans l'histoire du salut. Le *mal'ak YHWH/'ĕlōhîm* joue en effet un rôle très important dans l'histoire du salut (voir par ex. *Th.HW* I, col. 904 ss.). Il agit pour sauver ou pour chatier ou détruire (voir col. 904 ss. sous b, et col. 906 sous b.)

Par ailleurs, on remarquera que l'identification indiscutable à nos yeux, entre l'envoyeur et le *mlak* est une identification fonctionnelle et pas du tout métaphysique, ce qui oblige à poser le problème de l'identification entre YHWH et son *mal'āk* sur le terrain de la fonctionnalité et non de la métaphysique.

Dans un exposé systématique et chronologique, il faudrait commencer par la Mésopotamie, *mār šipri* et *šapārum* et continuer par l'ugaritique *la'ika* et *mlak*, poursuivre en hébreu avec *mal'āk* et *m^elā'kāh* et finir avec l'araméen et le phénicien où en 220 av. J.C., dans l'inscription d''Umm el ʿAmed, on voit la connexion entre le *ml'k* et son ouvrage. On ajoutera que *mal'āk* comme nous l'avons déjà indiqué plus haut, est la traduction de *mār šipri* ce qui prouve que l'institution du *mal'āk* est très ancienne, aussi ancienne que les textes akkadiens. Elle n'est pas d'origine occidentale mais mésopotamienne. L'institution du "messager" *mār šipri* nait en Mésopotamie et passe au monde sémitique nord-occidental sous le nom de *mal'āk*. L'institution du *mal'āk* devient-elle un argument sur l'origine mésopotamienne médiate ou immédiate de certaines institutions de la Bible hébraïque? Notre connaissance des rapports entre le monde sémitique nord-occidental et notamment de la Bible avec la Mésopotamie recevrait ainsi un nouvel éclairage.

LE TEXTE DE DEIR ʿALLA ET LES ORACLES BIBLIQUES DE BALAʿAM

par

M. DELCOR

Paris

En 1967 une expédition hollandaise découvrit à Deir ʿAlla [1] à la sortie du Jabbok, une inscription en araméen en mauvais état de conservation. Parce qu'elle comprend divers fragments, il est souvent difficile de reconstituer le discours primitif, ce qui rend assez problématique l'interprétation de l'ensemble du document.

Dans la première partie de cet exposé, je voudrais marquer les points qui me semblent acquis dans la lecture du texte araméen, puis ce qui reste hypothétique. Dans un second temps, je voudrais examiner si le texte de Deir ʿAlla permet de résoudre certains problèmes posés par les oracles bibliques de Balaʿam.

I. *L'inscription de Deir ʿAlla*

L'édition princeps des textes araméens de Deir ʿAlla est due à J. Hoftijzer et à G. van der Kooij.[2] Ce dernier est l'auteur d'une très longue et minutieuse analyse paléographique. La transcription, la traduction et le commentaire philologique des textes sont l'œuvre de Hoftijzer. Ce dernier n'a pas ménagé sa peine pour élucider le texte araméen grâce à de très abondantes remarques philologiques; aussi lui sera t-on très reconnaissant d'avoir mis à la disposition des exégètes de l'Ancien Testament ce très riche matériel. Par la suite, A. Caquot et A. Lemaire ont de leur côté proposé de notables améliorations au texte araméen, notamment dans le regroupement de certains fragments.[3] H. Ringgren, dans une conférence donnée à Paris au Collège de France, accepta la disposition préconisée par ces derniers auteurs du groupement I des fragments.[4] Les spécialistes de l'épigraphie

[1] Selon F.-M. Abel, *Géographie de la Palestine* (Paris, 1933) 1, p. 309, Deir ʿAlla serait Beth Succoth.

[2] *Aramaic Texts from Deir ʿAlla* with contributions by H. J. Franken, V. R. Mehra, J. Voskuil, J. A. Mosk, Preface by P. A. H. de Boer (Leyde, 1976).

[3] "Les textes araméens de Deir ʿAlla", *Syria* 54 (1977), pp. 189-208.

[4] "Balaam et l'inscription de Deir ʿAlla". Je le remercie d'avoir bien voulu me communiquer le texte de sa conférence au Collège de France. Il doit la publier

montrent quelque hésitation sur la datation exacte de l'inscription faite avec de l'encre, à partir de critères purement paléographiques. A la suite d'une très sérieuse comparaison de chacun des caractères de Deir ʿAlla avec ceux de 17 documents allant de l'ostrakon A de Nimrud publié par J. B. Segal en 1957 [5] jusqu'au sceau ammonite d'Adonipelet étudié par Ch. Clermont-Ganneau [6] et par Ch. C. Torrey [7], G. van der Kooij (p. 96) date l'inscription de Deir ʿAlla vers 700 av. J. C. avec un écart possible de + ou - 25 ans. Cette date diffère de celle proposée par J. Naveh [8] et F. M. Cross.[9] Le premier préfère la deuxième moitié du VIIIème siècle, date aussi retenue par Caquot et Lemaire (p. 192). Le second propose de la dater du milieu du VIIIème siècle. G. Garbini, de son côté, la situe entre le VIIIème et le VIème siècle av. J. C.[10].

Ce texte met en scène un personnage du nom de Balaam bar Beor dont la mention, soit partielle, soit plus complète, apparaît notamment aux lignes 2 et 3 du premier regroupement. Ce personnage est l'objet pendant la nuit (*blylh*) de visions émanant des dieux (*ʾlhn*) qui sont venus à lui. Ils lui annoncent quelque chose qui semble concerner sa postérité ou "ce qui viendra après lui". En effet on ne peut préciser davantage le sens de *ʾḥrʾh* étant donné la fragmentarité du texte que l'on peut traduire: "selon ces paroles (*kml(y)ʾ ʾl*), ils parlèrent à Balaam fils de Beor: ainsi fera de sa postérité un homme destiné à [11] ou fera de son avenir un feu (*ʾš*) pour. . .". On ne sait donc pas exactement le contenu du message adressé à Balaam par les dieux, pendant la nuit (lignes 1 et 2). On sait seulement que Balaam se leva le lendemain: *wyqm blʿm mn mḥr* et pleura (*ybkh*), ce qui semblerait indiquer que le contenu du message délivré par les dieux annonce des événements malheureux. Un certain ʾEliqah se présente alors à lui et lui demande: [*lm*]*h tbk* "Pourquoi pleures-tu?" (lignes 3-4). Les éditeurs ont rapproché cet Eliqah du héros de

---

sous le titre "Balaam and the Deir ʿAlla Inscription" dans la Festschrift I. L. Seeligmann à Jérusalem.

[5] "An Aramaic Ostracon from Nimrud", *Iraq* 19 (1957), pp. 139-45.

[6] *Etudes d'archéologie orientale* (Paris, 1895), I, pp. 85-90.

[7] "A Few Ancient Seals", *AASOR* 1-2 (1923), pp. 103 et sq.

[8] "The Date of the Deir ʿAlla Inscription in Aramaic Script", *IEJ* 17 (1967) pp. 156-8; du même auteur, *The Development of the Aramaic Script* (Jerusalem, 1970), p. 67, n. 14.

[9] "Epigraphic Notes on the Amman Citadel Inscriptions", *BASOR* 193 (1969), pp. 13-19, spécialement p. 14, n. 2.

[10] "L'iscrizione di Balaam Bar-Beor", *Henoch* 1 (1979), p. 168.

[11] C'est la traduction de Caquot et Lemaire, p. 194.

David *'ĕlîqā'* portant un nom apparemment semblable en 2 Sam. xxiii 25, bien qu'ils n'aient rien de commun. Ce dernier était originaire de Harod situé aux environs de Bethléhem et identifié par Abel au Khirbet Khareidan,[12] dans une région bien éloignée de la vallée du Jabbok. Ce nom biblique est formé comme *'lb'* mais on ne sait quel sens lui donner. Au cas où il ne s'agirait pas d'un diminutif de Eliqam, M. Noth a proposé la traduction: El hat ausgespeien " 'El a vomi", sens qui paraît peu vraisemblable.[13] Mais le nom de l'inscription porte un *he* final et non un *aleph* comme dans le T. M. On discute pour savoir quelle relation avait Eliqah avec Bala'am. Le texte araméen porte: *wẙ'l. 'mh. 'lqh.* Certains, dont Caquot-Lemaire et Ringgren ont traduit: "Et Eliqah entra chez lui" (littéralement: "avec lui"). Mais G. Garbini a fait observer que parmi les nombreuses constructions que le verbe *'ll* est susceptible d'avoir, on ne rencontre pas à sa suite la préposition *'m* (p. 17). De fait on aurait plutôt un *'al* ou un *beth* si on avait voulu traduire qu'Eliqah entra dans la maison de Bala'am.[14] Il faut donc revenir à la traduction initiale proposée par Hoftijzer: "et son oncle paternel entra". La réponse de Bala'am qui emploie des verbes au pluriel semble indiquer que d'autres personnes sont venues avec lui auprès du visionnaire. Après avoir invité ses visiteurs à s'asseoir (*šbw*), Bala'am leur délivre, à la première personne, sans doute le message transmis par les dieux: "Je vous montrerai combien sont grandes" (*'ḥwkm mh sgy'*) — il manque ici le mot essentiel — sans doute s'agit-il des décisions ou desseins divins ou de quelque chose d'approchant (ligne 5). "Venez et voyez, dit-il, l'œuvre des dieux" *lkw r'w p'[l]t '[lh]n̊.* On notera que l'expression "œuvre des dieux" a un relent tout à fait biblique et qu'elle est à rapprocher, par exemple, de *pĕ'ullōt yhwh*, "les œuvres de Yahvé", en Ps. xxviii 5 ou mieux encore du Ps. lxvi 5 où l'on trouve, presque mot pour mot, les mêmes termes: *lĕkû ûrĕ'û mip'ălôt 'ĕlōhîm*. Voir aussi Ps. xlvi 9: *lĕkû-ḥăzû mip'ălôt yhwh*, qui contient d'ailleurs un verbe d'origine araméenne (*ḥāzāh*) alors que dans l'inscription *r'w* est un hébraïsme. Dans le dernier passage cité, "les œuvres de Yahvé" sont mises en parallèle avec les dévastations (*šammôt*) opérées par lui sur la terre et visent des faits de guerre: il a fait cesser les combats

[12] cf. F. M. Abel, *Géographie de la Palestine* (Paris, 1938) 2, p. 343.

[13] *Die israelitischen Personennamen im Rahmen der gemeinsemitischen Namengebung* (Stuttgart, 1928; réimpression, Hildesheim, 1966), p. 40, n. 1.

[14] Cf. C. F. Jean-J. Hoftijzer, *Dictionnaire des Inscriptions sémitiques de l'Ouest, sub verbo, 'el.*

jusqu'au bout de la terre, il a brisé l'arc, il a rompu la lance, il a consumé par le feu les chars de guerre. Par contre, dans le premier psaume, "les œuvres de Dieu" se réfèrent à sa geste salvifique lors de l'Exode: "il a changé la mer en terre sèche, on a passé le fleuve à pied", sont autant d'allusions au franchissement miraculeux de la Mer Rouge et du Jourdain. "Les œuvres des dieux" de l'inscription araméenne, à en juger par la description qui suit, visent toutes sortes de bouleversements de l'ordre naturel des choses. Ces "œuvres des dieux" concernent donc plutôt, semble-t-il, un temps de malheur qu'un temps de bonheur.

Les dieux *šdyn* se sont réunis et se sont rassemblés, peut-être pour délibérer entre eux, mais surtout pour s'adresser à une déesse dont nous savons seulement que la première lettre commençait par *š*. A cette divinité féminine, que certains, à la suite de Caquot-Lemaire, pensent être *Šmš* le soleil plutôt que *Šegar* [15]—à Ugarit il s'agit d'une déesse—les *Šdyn* "les puissants" demandent de provoquer l'obscurité et les ténèbres en fermant le ciel avec des nuages noirs (*ʿāb*):

tpry skry šmyn bʿbky
šm ḥšk wʾl ngh

"Couds, ferme le ciel par tes nuages; que là soient les ténèbres et non point la splendeur ..." (lignes 6, 7). La Bible combine aussi les nuages et l'obscurité, par exemple en Ez. xxxiv 12 et en Joël ii 2. L'expression "le jour de nuages et de ténèbres" apparaît chez les prophètes pour décrire, comme on le sait, le jour du jugement. Selon toute vraisemblance, c'est dans le même sens qu'il faut comprendre l'inscription araméenne.

A partir de la ligne 7, le texte mentionne toute une liste de noms d'animaux dont certains ne sont pas toujours faciles à identifier. Les interprétations des auteurs diffèrent notamment sur la lecture et le sens de la fin de la ligne 7 et du début de la ligne 8. La phrase commence par *kî* introduisant la proposition explicative de la grave injonction des dieux au Soleil (?) lui demandant de fermer le ciel: *ky ssʿgr ḥrpt nšr*: "car l'hirondelle a réprimandé le vautour", ce qui

[15] Ringgren observe toutefois qu'il serait plus logique d'adresser la demande non pas au soleil mais à un dieu qui commande les nuages. Il ajoute: "Si nous savions le caractère de la déesse Shegar, il serait plus facile de faire un choix entre les deux possibilités. Or si elle est une déesse de la fécondité, la pluie et les nuages relevaient sans doute de sa compétence". En l'absence d'arguments décisifs, Ringgren laisse la question ouverte sur le choix de la déesse.

est aussi la traduction de Ringgren et de Garbini. L'editio princeps a lu *ss'gr* qui est apparemment un mot composé de deux noms différents que l'on rencontre en Is. xxxviii 14 sous la forme *sûs 'āgûr*. Mais en Jer. viii 7 on trouve *sîs* dans une liste d'oiseaux migrateurs (*sîs wĕ'āgûr*) comprenant *tōr*, la tourterelle. Dans son *Hierozoicon*, Samuel Bochart consacre tout un chapitre fort savant à cet oiseau et démontre qu'il s'agit de l'hirondelle et non de la grue (Symmaque) ou de la cigale (St Jérôme). Cet oiseau tire son nom de son chant: il s'agit d'une onomatopée tout comme en Italie, dans la région de Venise, où, dit-il, zizilla est l'hirondelle qui chante de façon spéciale (zizillare).[16] D'après Bochart, *'gr* désignerait la grue.[17] En effet St Jérôme traduisait par "ciconia" et le Targum et la version syriaque par *kurkĕyā'*. En traduisant "swift", "martinet" (Hoftijzer) ou "passereau" (Ringgren) ou "hirondelle" (Garbini), on ne prête, semble t-il, attention qu'à la première partie de ce nom double. Quoiqu'il en soit du sens précis du mot dans le monde ornithologique, il est probable, comme l'a bien compris Hoftijzer que les oiseaux ont ici une valeur symbolique (*Aramaic Texts*, p. 201). L'hirondelle ou le passereau ainsi que le *nešer*, "l'aigle" ou "le vautour" représentent d'autres réalités, selon un procédé bien connu de la Bible.[18] De petits oiseaux, sans doute les hommes, prétendent insulter d'énormes oiseaux de proie plus puissants symbolisant probablement les dieux, ce qui est contraire à l'ordre des choses établi par les dieux mêmes. Pour ce motif Garbini comprend dans les mêmes perspectives la suite du texte qu'il lit ainsi: *wq*[*n*] *r*[*ḥp*]*n y'nh*, et non comme le font les éditeurs *wql rḥmn y'nh*, que l'on traduit habituellement "et la voix des vautours répondra". En effet Garbini se refuse à comprendre *y'nh* comme un verbe à l'imparfait "il répondra", qui, dit-il, n'a aucun sens dans la succession d'explications introduites par *kî* "parce que". Aussi propose t-il de voir dans *y'nh* (*ya'ănāh*) l'autruche et il traduit la phrase: "la nichée (*qn*) qui couve l'autruche (*rḥpn*)", ce qui donne un sens tout à fait satisfaisant dans la ligne même de la phrase précédente. Les petits oiseaux qui vivent encore dans le nid et qui sont encore dégarnis de plumes prétendent, explique t-il, couver des œufs d'autruche. L'objection que l'on pourrait faire à

---

[16] *Hierozoicon sive Bipartitum opus de animalibus S. Scripturae* (Leyde, 1712) II, cap. X, col. 59-68.

[17] *Hierozoicon* II, cap. XI, col. 68-80; cf. aussi G. R. Driver, "Birds in the Old Testament, II. Birds in Life", *PEQ* 37 (1955), pp. 129-40, et spécialement p. 132.

[18] cf. les rééferences dans Hoftijzer, *Aramaic Texts*, p. 201.

cette explication est que dans le texte araméen il n'y a pas en fait mention des "œufs de l'autruche" mais seulement des autruches. Mais on pourrait supposer que l'on est en présence d'une sorte de proverbe dont l'écriture très ramassée est destinée à piquer la curiosité des auditeurs. Nous aurions à faire alors à une sorte de brachylogie: "l'autruche" pour "les œufs de l'autruche", l'allusion aux œufs étant suggérée par le verbe *rḥpn* participe pluriel du verbe *rḥp* "couver" documenté en Gen. i 2 et en Dt. xxxii 11. De fait, la lecture *rḥmn* préconisée par Hoftijzer n'est pas sûre et lui-même a précisé que la troisième lettre pouvait être *k*, *p*, *n* ou *m*. La lecture *ql* de l'édition princeps n'est pas davantage assurée pour la deuxième lettre. Aux lignes 8 et 9, on énumère une liste d'oiseaux dont on ne sait pas le rôle qu'ils jouent, en raison des lacunes du texte araméen.

On peut, par contre, donner un sens cohérent pour une partie de la ligne 9 si on suit la distribution des mots dans la phrase que donnent Caquot-Lemaire: *b'šr rḥln yybl ḥtr 'rnbn 'klw*: "dans le lieu où la houlette (du berger)[19] conduisait les brebis, les lièvres brouteront (litt.: mangeront)". Si nous comprenons bien, le verbe *'ākal* est à entendre comme un parfait prophétique décrivant un châtiment. Dans les pâturages des bergers il n'y aura plus de brebis mais des lièvres, ce qui semble indiquer que l'herbe deviendra rare en signe de malédiction. On sait que dans l'A.T. *'arnebet* "le lièvre" est compté parmi les animaux impurs (Lev. ix 6; Dt. xiv 7). Mais ces considérations de pur ou d'impur n'ont sans doute rien à faire dans l'inscription araméenne. Le lièvre représente plutôt ici l'animal sauvage qui sur les pâturages prendra la place des brebis, ce qui est considéré comme un châtiment. Ce passage se rattache donc au thème des animaux sauvages dévoreurs d'un pays sur lequel s'est abattue la malédiction, selon les formules prévues dans les traités de vassalité.[20] Dans les inscriptions araméennes de Sfiré, parmi les animaux sauvages qui gîteront dans Arpad transformé en ruine au cas où son roi violerait le traité qu'il a conclu avec le roi de KTK, on nomme précisément le lièvre: "Et qu'Arpad soit un monceau de ruines servant de gîte à l'animal du désert et à la gazelle et au chacalet au lièvre et au chat sauvage et

[19] En syriaque *ḥuṭrā'* désigne le bâton que porte le berger Jacob (Gen. xxxii 21). En araméen *ḥōṭer*, *ḥuṭrā'* peut également désigner le bâton du berger, sa houlette (cf. Jastrow, *Dictionary*). Pour ce motif je ne pense pas que dans l'inscription araméenne *ḥtr* puisse signifier le bâton du châtiment comme le soutient Hoftijzer, *Aramaic Texts*, p. 205.

[20] Cf. Delbert H. Hillers, *Treaty-Curses and the Old Testament Prophets* (Rome, 1964), pp. 54 et sq.

au hibou. . ." (I 33).[21] Il faut aussi mentionner les châtiments prédits par Isaïe contre Edom: "D'âge en âge, elle (la terre) sera désolée, personne n'y passera plus jamais. Le pélican et le hérisson la posséderont, la chouette et le corbeau y habiteront . . . ce sera un repaire de chacals et un parc pour les autruches. Les chats et les chiens sauvages s'y rencontreront et les satyres s'y appelleront les uns les autres" (Is. xxxiv 10-14). A la ligne 10 le thème du châtiment continue, à condition toutefois de bien traduire *štyw ḥmr*. En effet *ḥmr* dans le contexte ne peut guère signifier "colère" (Hoftijzer) et pas davantage "vin". Car si la traduction "ils boiront du vin" est philologiquement possible, le fait de boire du vin, notamment dans la tradition biblique est lié plutôt à des perspectives de bonheur. On sait, par exemple que, chez le prophète Osée, le fait pour Israël de ne plus avoir de vin nouveau est lié au malheur de l'exil (Os. ix 2). En sens contraire, le banquet eschatologique décrit dans l'apocalypse d'Isaïe comprendra, outre les viandes grasses, un festin de vin clarifié. (Is. xxv 6) Dans ces conditions, la traduction proposée par Garbini qui recourt à l'hébreu *ḥōmer* "boue" nous paraît devoir être retenue "ils boiront de la boue", sans qu'on sache pour autant quel est le sujet de cette phrase. Dans les lambeaux d'inscription subsistant aux lignes 9 et suivantes, il n'est plus semble-t-il, question de châtiment proprement dit mais de phénomènes insolites, contraires à l'ordre normal des choses de ce monde. On peut en effet comprendre, à la suite de Caquot-Lemaire suivis par Garbini et Ringgren les phrases suivantes: *wqbʿn šmʿw mwsr gry š*[*ʿl*] (ligne 10): "et les hyènes écouteront l'enseignement des petits renards". *lḥkmn yqḥk wʿnyh rqḥt mr* (ligne 11) *wkhnh*: "et on rira des sages et une pauvresse se parfumera de myrrhe et une prêtresse. . .".

wšmʿw ḥršn mn rḥq: "et les sourds entendront de loin". A la ligne 14 on se retrouve, semble t-il, à nouveau dans un contexte de malédiction. Mais les traductions de la ligne 14 diffèrent sensiblement d'un auteur à l'autre selon qu'on reconnaisse ou ne reconnaisse pas dans les derniers mots deux noms de divinités: *wkl ḥzw qqn šgr wʿštr l.* Ringgren et Garbini, suivant en partie les éditeurs, proposent: "Et tous verront l'oppression de Shegar et de ʿAštart". Caquot-Lemaire: "Et tous voient restreint le croît des bovins et des ovins". Mais peu importent au fond ces divergences de traductions, si l'on observe

[21] Cf. A. Dupont-Sommer et J. Starcky, *Les inscriptions araméennes de Sfiré* (*Stèles I et II*) (Paris, 1958), p. 20; J. A. Fitzmyer, *The Aramaic Inscriptions of Sefîre* (Rome, 1967), pp. 14-15.

que les déesses Šegar et ʿAštart étaient de fait liées à la fécondité des troupeaux bovins et ovins (cf. Dt. vii 13, xxviii 4, 18, 51).[22] Dire que ce sont les divinités Šegar et ʿAštart qui seront opprimées ou comprendre que le croît des bovins et des ovins sera diminué revient finalement au même. En tout cas, c'est bien de la description d'un malheur survenu aux troupeaux qu'il s'agit, si l'on se souvient que dans l'ancien Orient la stérilité des hommes et des animaux apparaît comme un malheur dans les malédictions contenues dans les traités de vassalité, par exemple dans les inscriptions araméennes de Sfiré: "[Que sept béliers] couvrent une brebis et qu'elle ne conçoive pas]" [23] De même dans le traité de vassalité d'Assarhadon on lit:

435 [May Sarpanitu who gives] name and seed
436 destroy your name and your seed [from the land].[24]

A la ligne 15, l'inscription araméenne de Deir ʿAlla continue, semble-t-il, par un oracle de malheur au parfait prophétique (*hqrqt*) qui se réfère à la destruction des animaux domestiques, ici le goret, par les bêtes sauvages (la panthère): *nmr hnyṣ hqrqt* que l'on peut traduire avec tous les auteurs: "la panthère fera fuir le goret".

Avant de passer au deuxième regroupement de textes, résumons nos observations. Si nous comprenons bien le premier regroupement de l'inscription, nous avons affaire à un oracle de malheur prononcé par Balaʿam à la suite d'une vision qu'il a eue peut-être dans un sanctuaire où il aurait passé la nuit. Il s'agirait alors d'une incubation. Des malédictions sont décidées à la suite d'une assemblée des dieux. Ces derniers enjoignent à une divinité féminine dont nous ignorons le nom d'obscurcir le ciel par des nuages. Comme dans les prophéties bibliques, les ténèbres règneront. Balaʿam communique à un certain ʾEliqah et à d'autres personnes ce qu'il appelle "l'œuvre des dieux". Dans un langage imagé, une proposition introduite par *kî* "parce que" explique les motifs des malédictions. Les hommes symbolisés sans doute par les petits oiseaux (hirondelle ou nichée) ont osé réprimander les dieux symbolisés peut-être par de grands oiseaux (aigle, autruche). Si cette exégèse est recevable, il s'agit, si nous comprenons bien, d'une sorte de révolte des humains contre les dieux, d'une faute

[22] Cf. M. Delcor, "Astarté et la fécondité des troupeaux en Deut. 7, 13 et parallèles". *Ugarit-Forschungen* 6 (1974), pp. 7-14. Cet article est repris dans M. Delcor, *Religion d'Israël et Proche-Orient ancien* (Leyde, 1976), pp. 86-93.
[23] Cf. Dupont-Sommer et Starcky, p. 19; Fitzmyer, p. 15.
[24] Cf. D. J. Wiseman, *The Vassal-Treaties of Esarhaddon* (Londres, 1958), p. 62.

qu'on pourrait qualifier d'hybris et qui rappelle maints passages bibliques, tels, par exemple, Is. xiv 13-14. Les malédictions décidées par les dieux atteindront la nature et les animaux domestiques frappés de stérilité ou décimés par les animaux sauvages. Parallèlement à ces malédictions Bala'am annonce un certain nombre de faits insolites, un bouleversement de l'ordre des choses.

Le deuxième regroupement n'est pas sans présenter de sérieux problèmes d'interprétation en raison de l'état du texte dont souvent on ne peut lire que le début des lignes. Essayons d'établir quelques données fermes susceptibles de permettre une exégèse d'ensemble. A la ligne 4 on lit sans difficulté: *ʿlmh rwy ddn k*. A la fin de la ligne précédente, on lit *wʿyn* "et l'œil", qu'on peut joindre au premier mot de la ligne 4, d'où la traduction: "le regard de la jeune fille enivrera les amants", en comprenant avec Garbini *rwy* comme un parfait plutôt que comme un impératif. Mais on pourrait aussi comprendre: "le regard de la jeune fille enivrera d'amour", en pensant au complexe de mots *nirweh dōdîm* bien connu de Prov. vii 18. A la ligne suivante, il est question d'un rejeton *nqr* comme l'ont bien compris les traducteurs à la suite de Caquot-Lemaire. Par la suite, le mot se rencontre trois fois (lignes 5, 12, 14). Ringgren a attiré l'attention sur l'importance de ce terme qui peut donner la clef de tout l'ensemble de la deuxième partie. La première fois qu'il apparaît, dit-il, il pourrait avoir le sens propre de rejeton poussant sur un sol fertile. On peut en effet traduire la ligne 5: "à elle (?) le rejeton et la terre tout à fait fertile" (*lh lm nqr wmdr kl rṭ̊b*). Ailleurs, comme Caquot et Lemaire l'ont bien souligné, le mot est pris au sens figuré, ainsi que le prouvent les termes qui l'accompagnent: *blbb mn̊ nʾnḥ blbh nʾnḥ* (ligne 12): "dans quel cœur soupire le rejeton? C'est dans son cœur qu'il soupire" (Caquot-Lemaire), A la ligne 14 ces mêmes auteurs proposent de traduire ainsi: *yk̊n̊ lbb nqr šhh ky ʾth l*: "le cœur hésitant du rejeton deviendra ferme car il est venu pour ré[pondre]. ." On a rapproché à juste titre le sens figuré de *nqr* "rejeton" de l'hébreu *ṣemaḥ* en Zach. iii 8 et du phénicien *šrš* dans les inscriptions de Larnaka II 16 et III 3 qui ont une signification analogue. Il faut ajouter le *nēṣer* d'Is. xi 1 qui est l'équivalent de l'araméen *nqr*. Dans les exemples bibliques et phéniciens certes, il s'agit toujours d'une descendance humaine, de progéniture et plus spécialement de l'héritier royal. Le texte en son état actuel ne nous dit pas de qui est issu le *nqr* "le rejeton". Est-ce de la *ʿalmāh* "la jeune fille"? A la ligne 6, *yrwy ʾl wyʿbd ʾl byt ʿlmn by*[*t*], on ferait allusion, semble-t-il au rôle joué par le dieu ʾEl dans l'acte sexuel, si l'on comprend l'imparfait *yrwy* au sens de "il arrosera abondamment, il fécondera", ou "il envirera (d'amour)".[25] La phrase pourrait se traduire: "El fécondera, El fera de la maison des jeunes une maison de. . ." C'est le sens que donnent à ʾEl Hoftijzer et Garbini. Mais Caquot-Lemaire et Ringgren sont plus hésitants; le dernier écrit notamment: "Quel-qu'un — peut-être un dieu — va enivrer d'amour la jeune femme . . . et l'endroit où cela se passe est appelé 'maison de la jeunesse' et maison pour le fiancé (*ḥtn*). Cela évoque l'idée d'un mariage sacré." Les traducteurs, en tout cas, écartent avec raison le sens de "tombeau" (litt.: "maison d'éternité") pour *byt ʿlm* proposé par Hoftijzer, car cette expression apparaît dans des documents postérieurs de plusieurs siècles (Palmyre, Eccl. xii 5, etc.) par rapport à l'inscription araméenne.

Le sens des lignes qui suivent demeure bien mystérieux. La traduction de la ligne 8: *byt lyʿl hlk wlyʿl ḥtn šm byt* "maison pour l'utilité du voyageur et pour l'utilité du fiancé", offre en elle-même un sens acceptable. Mais on ne sait quelle signification lui attribuer par rapport au contexte global. La ligne 8 est à peu près inintelligible, tandis que la ligne 9 demeure hermétique. En effet quel est le sujet de la phrase: *ly hlʿṣh bk lytʿṣ ʾwlmlkh lytmlk yšbr* que Caquot et Lemaire traduisent: ". . .ne prendra t-il pas vraiment conseil à ton sujet (ou auprès de toi) ou (ne) délibèrera t-il (pas) vraiment? Il brisera. . .". S'agit-il du peuple ou s'agit-il d'un vassal ou d'une tout autre personne qui vient prendre conseil auprès du rejeton royal? On ne sait et tout essai de réponse à cette question court le risque d'être erronné, car il est impossible de combler les lacunes du texte. A la ligne 15 en tout cas, c'est le roi qui présente une requête: *šʾlt mlk ssh wšʾlt* ". . .la requête du roi c'est son cheval et la requête de . . .". A la ligne 10: *mtksn lbš ḥd* "ceux qui sont couverts d'un seul vêtement" pourraient désigner les pauvres. La partie de la phrase qui est perdue parlait-elle d'un sort meilleur réservé à cette catégorie sociale? Mais on n'ose pas spéculer sur tant d'incertitudes. Et si à la fin de la même ligne il y a vraiment opposition entre la haine (*tšnʾn*) et l'amitié (*yʾnš*), on peut imaginer que l'oracle annonce des temps meilleurs que ceux qui ont précédé.

A la ligne 24 on décrit vraisemblablement l'acte sexuel. Garbini lit *rʾš* (tête) à la fin de la ligne 23 qu'il relie à la ligne 24: *rʾš ʾšt*[*k*] *tḥt rʾšk*. On peut traduire: "la tête de ta femme (sera) sous ta tête".

[25] L'usage de *rwh* avec le sens sexuel au piel est documenté en hébreu en Prov. v 29.

La suite *tškb mškby ʿlmk* peut se comprendre "tu coucheras à la manière dont tu couchais en ta jeunesse", en tenant compte du parallèlisme de Lev. xvii 22 et xx 13, où l'hébreu *miškĕbê ʾiššāh* signifie "l'action de coucher avec une femme". Mais il est plus difficile de savoir ce à quoi fait allusion au juste à la ligne 13 *lyš bmy rḥmwt* "pétri avec les eaux de tendresse" (traduction Caquot-Lemaire) suivi par Garbini et Ringgren. Il n'est pas impossible de penser à un gâteau comme dans 2 Sam. xiii 6-10 où Amnon se fait préparer des gâteaux par Thamar. Mais les deux mots qui suivent *ʿl rḥm* "sur le sein" ne suggèrent-ils pas plutôt qu'il s'agit de l'acte de procréation, l'eau désignant le semen virile? C'est ce sens qu'il aurait à Qumrân, par exemple, où on emploie il est vrai le substantif *mgbl* suivi de *hmym* (1QH I 21) ou de *bmym* (1QH III 25): "Que suis-je, moi, pétri avec de l'eau?",[26] Mais à notre explication on pourrait objecter que l'emploi du verbe *lûš* en hébreu biblique au sens de "pétrir" est toujours lié à l'action du pâtissier ou du boulanger (Gen. xviii 6; Jer. vii 18; Os. vii 4; 1 Sam. xxviii 24) et jamais à celui de l'acte de procréation. Mais en toute hypothèse on pourrait envisager que l'oracle emploie ici un langage imagé, comme on en trouve plusieurs exemples dans notre inscription. En raison du but que nous nous proposons ici, mieux vaut ne pas nous attarder sur le sens de la ligne 17 tant sont divergentes les lectures proposées par les auteurs et aussi leurs interprétations. Si nous avions un choix à faire nous opterions pour la lecture et l'interprétation de Garbini qui nous paraît cohérente: *ldʿt spr dbr lʿnh ʿl lšn l̊k m̊špt wmlq[y] ʾmr*: "Pour la connaissance. Ecris le mot qu'il faut répondre; sur ta langue il y a le jugement et la punition. A dit. . .". Hoftijzer commente qu'il s'agit de la réponse des dieux à une question de Balaʿam, ce qui paraît tout à fait vraisemblable.

Telles sont les quelques bribes lisibles, les quelques lambeaux de phrases, presque toujours incomplètes que nous livre le deuxième groupement de textes. Aussi est-il bien difficile d'y lire un discours cohérent et continu. Il y est question d'une jeune fille amoureuse, la *ʿalmāh*, de relations sexuelles avec une épouse, d'un rejeton probablement d'origine royale et, semble-t-il, de l'annonce ce temps heureux. Peut-être le dieu ʾEl intervient-il comme partenaire d'une union qui, à ce titre, deviendrait un hieros gamos. Malgré l'absence matérielle

[26] Selon P. Wernberg-Møller, *The Manual of Discipline* (Leyde, 1957), p. 155, *mayim* désignerait le "semen virile"; cf. M. Delcor, *Les Hymnes de Qumrân* (*Hodayot*) *Texte hébreu — Introduction — Traduction — Commentaire* (Paris, 1962), p. 86.

de liens entre les bribes de phrases que l'on a pu sauver de la destruction, Ringgren a conclu que le groupement II "parle d'un nouveau roi, sorti d'un mariage sacré et de qui on attendait qu'il introduise une époque nouvelle, un temps de succès et de bonheur. Il est à remarquer, ajoute t-il, que selon la théorie de la royauté sacrale, l'avènement d'un roi nouveau est souvent précédé d'une période de chaos, où toutes les conditions normales sont bouleversées". Cela correspond bien, dit-il, à la description du groupement I telle que nous l'avons comprise ici. Malgré la part réelle d'hypothèse que comporte l'interprétation globale proposée par Ringgren, sa théorie me paraît dans l'ensemble recevable. Elle a d'ailleurs pris comme point de départ les améliorations certaines apportées par Caquot-Lemaire à l'édition princeps.

Il nous reste maintenant à nous demander s'il y a quelque relation entre cette inscription araméenne et les oracles bibliques de Balaʿam et si du moins elle peut apporter quelque solution aux problèmes divers que le texte hébreu pose toujours aux exégètes.

II. *Les oracles bibliques de Balaʿam à la lumière du texte de Deir ʿAlla*

Ces oracles ont suscité ces dernières années une abondante littérature.[27] Mais ils posent toujours un certain nombre de problèmes, soit d'ordre littéraire, soit d'ordre historique. On s'est interrogé notamment pour savoir l'origine des oracles de Balaʿam: il n'est que de rappeler par exemple les titres de trois études, l'une déjà ancienne de A. von Gall (*Zusammensetzung und Herkunft der Bileam-Perikope in Num. 22-24* [Giessen, 1900]) et les deux autres plus récentes de S. Mowinckel ("Der Ursprung der Bilʿāmsage", *ZAW* 48 [1930], pp. 233-71) et de J. Coppens ("Les oracles de Biléam: leur origine littéraire et leur portée prophétique").[28] On s'accorde généralement à reconnaître dans les chapitres xxii-xxiv du livre des Nombres l'aboutissement de deux ensembles littéraires d'origine différente que l'on attribue à l'Elohiste et au Yahviste. Mais les auteurs sont loin de s'entendre sur la répartition des deux sources ou traditions, notamment pour le récit du chapitre xxii. L. M. von Pákozdy a mis en garde les critiques à propos de l'utilisation du changement des noms

[27] Bibliographie. Pour la littérature antérieure à 1960, cf. Otto Eissfeldt, *Einleitung in das Alte Test.* 3ème édition, (Tübingen, 1964), p. 251; et dans l'édition anglaise *The Old Testament. An Introduction* (Oxford 1965), p. 189, n. 9. Les études plus récentes seront citées au fur et à mesure en note.

[28] Dans *Mélanges Eugène Tisserant* (Cité du Vatican, 1964) I, pp. 67-80.

divins Elohim Yahvé comme critère décisif pour l'analyse des sources. Il rappelle le jugement porté par B. Baentsch sur Num. xxii 7-21 qui soulignait l'impression d'unité que laisse ce récit. L'emploi des noms divins correspond, rappelle-t-il, à un plan précis. Le nom de Yahvé est toujours mis dans la bouche de Bala'am qui est présenté comme son prophète (xxii 8, 13, 18, 19), tandis que le nom d'Elohim est employé quand on parle de Bala'am à la troisième personne (xxii 9, 10, 12, 20). Selon Pákozdy, il faut attribuer sans aucun doute tout le morceau à E alors qu'il est impossible de reconstruire le récit yahviste parallèle.[29] Pour le même auteur, 'Elohim dans certains passages des oracles de Bala'am ne désigne pas 'Elohim le dieu d'Israël selon l'emploi qu'en fait l'Elohiste mais le *daimon* du devin et du magicien Bala'am, un 'Elohim, un *numen*.[30]

Ces considérations nous amènent à nous poser une double question: 1°) le texte biblique conserve t-il les traces d'une source païenne? 2°) quelles sont les relations entre les oracles de Bala'am et l'inscription araméenne? Ces deux questions sont d'ailleurs étroitement liées. Il faut d'abord dire qu'il s'agit de part et d'autre d'un même personnage: Bala'am fils de Béor est nommément désigné dans l'inscription avec le nom de son père. C'est un visionnaire qui entre en communication avec les dieux pendant la nuit pour en recevoir un message qu'il doit communiquer à des hommes. Or les faits rapportés à son sujet sont en accord avec la Bible. D'après certaines traditions bibliques, Bala'am fils de Be'or appartient au monde païen, c'est un devin, *qōsēm* (Josué xiii 22) et un magicien: il va à la rencontre de signes magiques: *hlk* ... *lqr't nḥšym* (Num. xxiv 1). Le Targum Neofiti va dans le même sens lorsque interprétant le *pětôrāh* (Num. xxii 5) du texte massorétique, où l'on voit assez communément un nom de lieu, il dit de Bala'am qu'il est "l'interprète des songes" (*ptwrh ḥlmyyh*) qui se trouvait sur la rive du Fleuve dans le pays des fils de son peuple". Cette exégèse du Targum appuyée par la Vulgate (*ariolus*) et la Peschitta (*pāšōrā'*) paraît être la vraie interprétation du terme hébreu *pět(ô)rāh* qui ne peut pas correspondre à nom de lieu pour des motifs divers que nous examinerons plus loin. Il faut en effet supposer que le texte primitif portait comme dans le Penta-

---

[29] "Theologische Redaktionsarbeit in der Bileam-Perikope", *Von Ugarit nach Qumran* (Festschrift O. Eissfeldt), *BZAW* 77 (1958), pp. 161-76.

[30] P. 169. Pákozdy a étudié avec attention le sens que peut prendre le mot *'ĕlōhîm* qui ne désigne pas seulement Dieu mais par exemple l'esprit des morts (1 Sam. xxviii 13), des hommes puissants (Ex. iv 16), etc., pp. 165 et sq.

teuque samaritain *ptrh* vocalisé *pātĕrāh* "l'interprète", "le devin"; il s'agirait du participe kal araméen du verbe *pĕtar* "interprèter" à l'état emphatique. Ailleurs dans le Targum, le même verbe *pĕtar* signifie "interprèter des songes", notamment en Gen. xl 12 où ce don est prêté à Joseph. On peut donc comprendre Num. xxii 5: "Il envoya des messagers auprès de Balaʿam fils de Beor le devin qui se trouvait auprès de la rivière du pays des fils d'Ammon". Dans notre hypothèse, il faudrait donc supposer que le texte hébreu avait conservé sous sa forme araméenne le nom de la fonction de Balaʿam qui, par la suite a été compris comme un nom de lieu suivi du-*āh* final de direction. Le syntagme araméen *blʿm pt(w)rāh*, "Balaʿam le devin" est tout à fait régulier et parallèle par exemple à *šimšay sāpĕrāʾ* "Šimšai le scribe" d'Esdras iv 8. Si cette hypothèse était recevable, le texte hébreu ferait indirectement allusion à une source araméenne connue maintenant par l'inscription de Deir ʿAlla et d'ailleurs soupçonnée par les exègètes bien avant sa découverte: Mowinckel écrivait déjà il y a une cinquantaine d'années que les légendes relatives à Balaʿam étaient d'origine extra-israëlite ("ausser-israelitischen Ursprungs") et qu'elles étaient parvenues aux Israélites d'Edom ou de Nordarabie.[31] Comme nous le verrons plus loin, c'est tout simplement dans le territoire ammonite qu'il faut chercher l'origine de ces traditions, si on lit dans le texte hébreu *bĕnê ʿammôn* "les fils d'Ammon" à la suite de certains manuscrits hébreux, du texte samaritain, de la Vulgate et de la Peschitta.

Quoiqu'il en soit de notre explication, il y a quelques rares contacts de vocabulaire ou de phraséologie entre les oracles bibliques et l'inscription araméenne, dont il importe d'apprécier la portée.

Dans le texte araméen on lit: *hʾwyʾtw ʾlwh ʾlhn blylh*: "Vers lui venaient les dieux pendant la nuit", ce qui correspond presque à la lettre au texte hébreu: *wayyābōʾ ʾĕlōhîm ʾel-bilʿām laylāh* (Num. xxii 20). Mais cette même phraséologie apparaît ailleurs dans la Bible pour décrire l'entrée en communication de Dieu avec un individu au moyen de songes (Gen. xx 3, xxxi 24). Il faut aussi mettre en parallèle la phrase araméenne: *wyqm blʿm mn mḥr* "Et Balaʿam se leva le matin" et le texte biblique *wayyāqom bilʿām babbōqer* de Num. xxii 13, 21. On doit aussi signaler la présence dans le texte araméen, dans les

[31] P. 237; selon J. Lindblom, *Prophecy in Ancient Israel* (Oxford, 1963), p. 91, Balaam nous est présenté comme un *kahin*, tel qu'il existait dans l'ancienne Arabie; dans le même sens, cf. G. Hölscher, *Die Profeten. Untersuchungen zur Religionsgeschichte Israels* (Leipzig, 1914), p. 118.

oracles bibliques du verbe *qābab* "maudire" (Num. xxii 11, 17, xxiii 8, 11, 13, 25, 27, xxiv 10). Dans le T.M. il est employé avec les verbes de sens voisin *'ārar* et *zā'am* (Num. xxiii 7). Cette diversification du vocabulaire de malédiction permet d'ailleurs à certains critiques de distinguer les sources. Selon von Gall (p. 7) et H. Holzinger [32] par exemple, *'ārar* appartiendrait à l'Elohiste tandis que *qābab* ferait partie du vocabulaire yahviste, mais B. Bæntsch se refuse à partir de l'alternance de ces verbes pour établir la distinction des sources,[33] opinion partagée d'ailleurs par plusieurs auteurs tels W. Rudolph,[34] Mowinckel, etc.[35] En réalité il s'agirait seulement de variantes d'ordre stylistique. Les contacts littéraires entre le texte biblique et l'inscription araméenne sont trop rares et trop peu significatifs—il s'agit notamment d'une phrase stéréotypée pour décrire l'entrée en relation d'un dieu avec un individu grâce aux songes—pour qu'ils nous permettent d'établir une quelconque relation littéraire entre les deux groupes d'écrits. Mais s'il n'y a pas de contact littéraire, on constate l'existence de traditions communes relatives au devin Bala'am, au moins sur certains points:

1°) Ce dernier, d'après l'inscription araméenne est lié à la région nord du pays d'Ammon, puisque Deir 'Alla est situé près du fleuve Jabbok qui constituait la frontière nord du royaume ammonite. Il semble que le bâtiment dans lequel a été trouvée l'inscription était un sanctuaire ou en tout cas un bâtiment auquel le public pouvait avoir accès. Bala'am y exerçait sa fonction de devin, probablement au service du roi. A l'époque où fut rédigée l'inscription, probablement vers le milieu du VIIIème siècle, Ammon n'était peut-être pas encore le vassal de l'Assyrie mais elle le deviendra après 732. Au septième et au sixième siècle, Ammon devint le plus important état de Transjordanie.[36] La nouvelle position d'Ammon est illustrée par des tombes collectives,[37] des statues et des sceaux datant du VIIème siècle-

---

[32] *Numeri* (Tübingen et Leipzig, 1903).

[33] *Exodus-Leviticus-Numeri* (Göttingen, 1903).

[34] *Der "Elohist" von Exodus bis Josua, BZAW* 68 (Berlin, 1938), p. 107.

[35] On trouvera l'exposé des diverses opinions dans W. Gross, *Bileam Literar- und formkritische Untersuchung der Prosa in Num. XXII-XXIV* (Munich, 1974), pp. 81 et sq.

[36] Cf. W. F. Albright, "Notes on Ammonite History", dans *Miscellanea Biblica B. Ubach* (Montserrat, 1953), p. 135.

[37] Sur la civilisation ammonite, cf. G. M. Landes, "The material civilization of the Ammonites", dans D. N. Freedman et E. F. Cambell (éd.), *The Biblical Archaeologist Reader* 2 (Garden City, New York), pp. 69-88.

VIème siècle av. J.C.[38] La langue employée est l'ammonite,[39] mais on a trouvé aussi des inscriptions en araméen. L'une d'entre elles qui porte le nom de *Yaraḥ ʿazar* (le dieu lune a aidé) *rb rkšn* "chef des chevaux" est datée du VIIème siècle. Parce que le nom n'est pas araméen mais cananéen Albright y a vu une indication de la diffusion de l'araméen comme langue de culture au VIIème siècle plutôt qu'une pièce importée. L'inscription araméenne de Deir ʿAlla montre que l'on employait déjà l'araméen en pays ammonite au VIIIème siècle av. J. C. La figure de Bala ʿam, enracinée d'après le texte araméen dans le pays des *bĕnê ʿammôn*, aurait été mieux située dans le temps si l'inscription qui s'intéresse à un rejeton royal (*nqr*) nous avait donné le nom du roi sans doute ammonite règnant dans cette région. D'après les listes royales dressées par Albright, il y a malheureusement un trou entre Ba ʿaša (853 av. J. C.) et Sanîp (assyrien Sanipu) (733 av. J. C.) (p. 136, n. 26).

2°) D'après certaines traditions bibliques, on voit également Bala ʿam évoluer autour de sanctuaires tels Bamot-Ba ʿal (Num. xxii 41) et Ba ʿal Pe ʿor situé près de Nébo qui sont aussi en territoire ammonite (cf. Num. xiii 28, xxxi 16). C'est d'ailleurs à ce lieu de culte que des auteurs ont voulu rattacher certaines traditions relatives à Bala ʿam conservées dans Num. xxii-xxiv, et qui auraient été à l'origine indépendantes de celles de Balaq.[40] Le passage de Num. xxiii 28 appartenant au Yahviste qui rattache Bala ʿam à Ba ʿal Pe ʿor s'accorde d'ailleurs avec ce qui est rapporté en Num. xxxi 16 où "les femmes, sur la parole de Bala ʿam, ont entraîné les enfants d'Israël à l'infidélité avec Yahvé dans l'affaire de Pe ʿor". La scène de Bala ʿam sur le Pisga, qui appartient à l'Elohiste, serait secondaire (Num. xxiii 14) par rapport à celle contenue en Num. xxiii

---

[38] Sur l'épigraphie ammonite cf. G. Garbini, "Ammonite Inscriptions", *JSS* 29 (1974), pp. 159-68; P. Bordreuil, "Inscriptions sigillaires ouest-sémitiques. I. Epigraphie ammonite", *Syria* 50 (1973), pp. 181-95; cf. L. G. Herr, *The Scripts of Ancient Northwest Semitic Seals* (Missoula, 1978), pp. 55-75, qui catalogue jusqu'à 46 sceaux ammonites datant du VIIIe-VIIe siècle; N. Avigad, "Ammonite and Moabite Seals", dans J. A. Sanders (éd.), *Essays in Honor of Nelson Glueck. Near Eastern Archaeology in the Twentieth Century* (New York, 1970), pp. 284-9. P. E. Dion, "Notes d'épigraphie ammonite", *RB* 82 (1975), pp. 24-34; E. Puech-A. Rofé, "L'inscription de la citadelle d'Amman", *RB* 84 (1973), pp, 531-46, et la bibliographie citée dans cette étude.

[39] Sur la langue ammonite, cf. G. Garbini, "La lingua degli Ammoniti", *AION* NS. 30 (1970), pp. 249-58.

[40] Cf. M. Noth, *Uberlieferungsgeschichte des Pentateuch* (Stuttgart, 1948), p. 82; Mowinckel, pp. 238-41; J. de Vaulx, *Les Nombres* (Paris, 1972), p. 257.

28. Martin Noth se demande d'ailleurs si le nom même de Bala'am ben Be'or ne serait pas une altération d'un nom primitif Bala'am ben Pe'or, ce qui signifierait que Bala'am était l'homme du sanctuaire de Beth Pe'or ou de Ba'al Pe'or (p. 83, n. 217). Ces considérations sont intéressantes mais le texte de Deir 'Alla met d'une part en relation Bala'am avec un sanctuaire du nord du pays d'Ammon éloigné de celui de Ba'al Pe'or et, d'autre part, nous donne le même nom du père de Bala'am que la tradition biblique: il s'agit de Be'or et non de Pe'or. Pour ces motifs, il y a donc lieu d'être réservé à l'égard de l'hypothèse de Noth sur le nom primitif de Bala'am. En effet, on pourrait tout aussi bien imaginer que Bala'am ben Be'or a été mis en relation avec le sanctuaire de Ba'al Pe'or en raison de la ressemblance des noms.

3°) La tradition biblique connaissait sans doute le sanctuaire de Deir 'Alla où Bala'am était en service. C'est là que Balaq roi de Moab envoie des messagers pour aller quérir le devin Bala'am qui, précise Num. xxii 5 "était sur le bord du fleuve du pays des fils d'Ammon". En effet "le fleuve du pays des fils d'Ammon" ne peut être que le Jabbok. Cette précision géographique sert à le distinguer du Fleuve par excellence, qui dans l'A.T. désignait l'Euphrate (Gen. xxx 21; Ex. xxiii 2; Jos. xxiv 2).

La patrie de Bala'am

L'interprétation que nous donnons de Num. xxii 5 nous conduit à réexaminer brièvement le problème de la patrie de Bala'am qui a suscité une abondante littérature.[41] Une des thèses les plus répandues situe Petor sur le Moyen Euphrate.[42] Ses tenants comprennent d'une part le Petorah du T. M. comme un nom de lieu suivi de la finale *-āh* marquant la direction. Ils invoquent d'autre part le témoignage de Dt. xxiii 5 qui situe Petor en Mésopotamie, littéralement en Aram Naharaïm. Petor est en effet identifiée à Pitru, cité située dans le Moyen Euphrate approximativement au confluent du Sadjur qui vient sur la rive droite se jeter dans le fleuve à une vingtaine de kilomètres en aval de Karkémish au gué de la route de Harran à Alep.[43]

[41] Gross, pp. 96-115, consacre un long excursus à ce problème, et l'on y trouvera exposées les diverses thèses en présence.

[42] Cf. par exemple R. T. O'Callaghan, *Aram Naharaim* (Rome, 1948), p. 104.

[43] Cf. René Largement, "Les oracles de Bile'am et la mantique suméro-akkadienne", *Mémorial du Cinquantenaire de l'Ecole des langues orientales anciennes de l'Institut Catholique de Paris* (Paris, 1964), p. 38.

Cette ville est de fait mentionnée dans les Annales de Salmanasar III qui précisent sa situation géographique: *Pi-it-ru ša ʾili nahar Sa-gu-ra.* Mais Eberhard Schrader qui, au siècle dernier, faisait déjà le rapprochement entre Pitru et Petor dont la Bible semblerait dire (Num. xxii 5) qu'elle était située sur l'Euphrate (*ʿal-hannāhār*) fait l'observation suivante: les inscriptions assyriennes ne disent rien à ce sujet puisque la ville était située immédiatement sur le Saschûr lui-même (Sadjur cité plus haut).[44] Le même savant ajoute que le Pitru de l'Euphrate ne doit pas être confondu avec un autre lieu portant le même nom Pitu-ru (ra) mentionné dans les Annales d'Assurbanipal II, 104, 112 et situé dans la région du Haut-Tigre. L'obélisque de Salmanasar III (858-824) rapporte que sous Assur-rabi II, roi d'Assyrie (1010-970), les Araméens s'emparèrent de Pitru sur la rivière Sadjur de l'autre côté de l'Euphrate et de la ville de Mut-kînu, sur la rive orientale du fleuve. Salmanasar III réoccupe les villes de Pitru et de Mutkînu où son ancêtre Téglath-Phalasar Ier avait installé des garnisons balayées ensuite par les Araméens.[45] Ces villes devaient faire partie de l'état de Bît-Adini. La ville de Pitru — c'est le nom que lui donnaient les habitants de Hatti—précise l'obélisque noir de Salmanasar conservée au British Museum—était appelée Ana-Ašur-utêr-aṣ-bat par les Assyriens. La ville est aussi mentionnée parmi les conquêtes de Thoutmès III, sur les listes de Karnak, sous le nom de Pe-d-ru[î?].[46] Avant de montrer que l'identification de Petorah à Pitru se heurte à de graves difficultés, il nous faut dire un mot de la thèse qui identifie les *běnê ʿammô* de Num. xxii 5 aux ʾAmʾau ou aux ʾAmaw que l'on situe dans la région d'Alalaḫ.

Le pays des Amaʾu

Le T.M. *ʾereṣ běnê ʿammô* peut être traduit "le pays des fils de son peuple", expression qui a été rapprochée parfois de "terre de sa naissance" (Gen. xxiv 7, xxxi 13) pour désigner la patrie de Balaʿam. Mais on a remarqué à juste titre que cette expression est insolite

---

[44] *Keilinschriften und Geschichtsforschung. Ein Beitrag zur monumentalen Geographie, Geschichte und Chronologie der Assyrer* (Giessen, 1878), pp. 220-1, note et p. 141.

[45] Cf. la traduction anglaise dans D. D. Luckenbill, *Ancient Records of Assyria and Babylonia* (Chicago, 1926) I, nº 603, p. 218. Pour l'histoire assyrienne de Pitru cf. J. R. Kupper, *Les nomades en Mésopotamie au temps des rois de Mari* (Paris, 1957), pp. 117-27.

[46] Cf. S. Schiffer, *Die Aramäer. Historisch-Geographische Untersuchungen* (Leipzig, 1911), p. 69, note 1; W. M. Müller, *Asien und Europa nach altägyptischen Denkmälern* (Leipzig, 1893), p. 98, nº 1, 267.

et en tout cas unique. Aussi certains [47] ont-ils proposé d'identifier les *bĕnê ʿammô* avec un nom de peuple connu par divers textes égyptiens [48] et aussi par l'inscription de la statue d'Idrimi, trouvée à Atshana-Alalaḫ au printemps de 1939. Cette inscription met dans la bouche du roi Idrimi, roi d'Alalaḫ, le récit d'une rébellion qui a eu lieu à Alep et de disputes familiales qui l'obligent à fuir à *Ammia* [49] en Canaan où "demeuraient des fils de la cité d'Alep, des fils des pays de Mukišḫi et de Ni' et des guerriers du pays d'*Amau*: [*ṣabe*] *ma-at amaeki*" (lignes 20-23).[50] Sidney Smith, l'éditeur de l'inscription d'Idrimi, situe le pays d'*Ama'u* entre Alalaḫ et Sfiré et identifie la ville avec *Imma* ou *Emma* connue sous ce nom à l'époque romaine, notamment par la défaite que les troupes d'Aurélien infligèrent à la reine de Palmyre, Zénobie. C'est la moderne Yenishehir dont la forteresse protègeait le défilé sur la route d'Antioche à Alep (p. 57). Sous la forme *Am*, elle est mentionnée par Naram-Sin sur la statue provenant de Nippur (p. 57). Mais on ne voit pas sur quoi on se fonde pour situer *Ama'u* entre Alep et Karchemish (de Vaulx, p. 267). Si cette identification était exacte on ne voit pas comment Pitru ferait partie du pays des Am'au, car ce dernier est distant en ligne droite d'au moins 150 km de Karkemish sur l'Euphrate. Mais là n'est pas l'objection la plus grave que l'on peut faire à la thèse identifiant Petor à Pitru dans la règion de l'Euphrate. Cette identification a contre elle l'immense distance qui sépare le royaume de Moab de la région de Pitru. Dillmann, par exemple, compte jusqu'à vingt jours de voyage. Comment imaginer que les messagers de Balaq aillent chercher Balaʿam si loin et qu'ils fassent jusqu'à deux voyages auprès du devin afin d'obtenir sa coopération (cf. Num. xxii 7, 15)? Lorsque Balaʿam se met en route, pourquoi utilise-t-il en guise de monture une ânesse et non un chameau qui conviendrait mieux pour parcourir de si grandes distances? Certains critiques, tels par exemple Holzinger (p. 105), ont bien senti la difficulté et nombreux ont été ceux qui ont cherché à situer la patrie de Balaʿam

---

[47] Cf. par exemple H. Cazelles, *Les Nombres* (Paris, 1952), p. 106, qui suit Albright, "The oracles of Balaam", *JBL* 63 (1944), pp. 207-33.

[48] On trouvera rassemblés ces divers textes dans Gross, pp. 107 et sq.

[49] Ammia est connue par la correspondance de El Amarna 88, 74, etc. Certains l'ont identifiée avec Ambi, la moderne Anfa. R. Dussaud, *Topographie historique de la Syrie* (Paris, 1926), p. 117, note 1, avec Amyun sur la côte syrienne mais l'éditeur de l'inscription d'Idrimi propose une autre identification (cf. infra).

[50] Cf. Sidney Smith, *The statue of Idri-mi, with an Introduction by Sir Leonard Woolley* (Londres, 1949), p. 14.

plus près du royaume de Balaq, soit chez les Ammonites, soit même chez les Edomites. Dans ce dernier cas, certains ont identifié Balaʿam avec le roi édomite Belaʿ fils de Beʿor (Gen. xxxvi 32),[51] lu ʾEdom au lieu deʾAram en Num. xxiii 7 et identifié Petor avec la ville de Fathour.[52] Les partisans de la thèse mésopotamienne ont essayé de l'étayer en montrant que Balaʿam était un *bāru* babylonien. En 1909, Samuel Daiches s'y est essayé,[53] et, il y a quelques années, R. Largement a voulu trouver dans "les grandes séries mantiques suméro-akkadiennes la source de l'inspiration de Bileʿam et dans les rituels de même provenance la raison de la manière d'agir du devin". Tout récemment, Leonhard Rost s'est élevé contre cette thèse en raison du rituel sacrificiel utilisé par Balaʿam ("Fragen um Bileam", pp. 377-87). En effet, par deux fois (Num. xxiii 3, 15) le devin offre avec Balaq un holocauste (*ʿōlāh*) comprenant sept taureaux et sept béliers sur sept autels. Or Rost observe que le monde assyro-babylonien connaissait toutes sortes de sacrifices mais non le sacrifice par le feu, l'holocauste.[54] En Mésopotamie on immolait des animaux dont les morceaux de choix étaient offerts aux dieux. Seul le foie des moutons et des chèvres était utilisé pour l'hépatoscopie. Les sacrifices mentionnés en Num. xxiii 3, 15 manifestent, dit-il, une influence israélite, car c'est en Israël que l'on connaissait l'holocauste. Cela montre clairement, conclut-il, que Balaʿam ne peut pas appartenir au milieu de culture de la Mésopotamie ("Bileam nicht dem mesopotamischen Kulturkreis angehören kann: "Fragen um Bileam", pp. 379-80). Aussi revient-il à la vieille thèse de l'origine édomite de Balaʿam qui n'est pas davantage satisfaisante.

A notre sens Balaʿam était d'origine ammonite,[55] ce qui est en accord avec la trouvaille de l'inscription araméenne à Deir ʿAlla et avec Num. xxii 5 dans le sens où nous l'avons interprété plus haut.

---

[51] Cf. en dernier lieu L. Rost, "Fragen um Bileam", *Beiträge zur alttestamentlichen Theologie* (Festschrift W. Zimmerli) (Göttingen, 1977), p. 386.

[52] Pour le résumé des positions, cf. Gross, pp. 96 et sq.

[53] "Balaam a Babylonian bārū", dans *Hilprecht Anniversary volume* (Leipzig, 1909), pp. 60-70.

[54] "Erwägungen zum israelitischen Brandopfer", dans *Von Ugarit nach Qumran* (*Festschrift O. Eissfeldt*) (Berlin, 1958), pp. 178-9, qui montre que l'holocauste n'est pas connu de tous les Sémites. Il est absent de la religion mésopotamienne et du monde arabe. On le trouve par contre chez les Sémites de l'Ouest en Phénicie et en Israël, et d'après l'A.T. chez les Moabites, les Ammonites et vraisemblablement chez les Edomites. Il est aussi inconnu du monde hittite et du monde égyptien.

[55] Dans le même sens cf. J. Lust, "Balaam an Ammonite", *Ephemerides Theologicae Lovanienses* 54 (1978), pp. 60-1.

La réinterprétation de Petorah comme un nom de ville de Mésopotamie est ancienne puisque Dt. xxiii 5 situe Petor en Aram Naharaïm. Plusieurs siècles après on lit dans la LXX: ἀπέστειλεν πρέσβεις πρὸς βαλααμ υἱὸν βεὼρ φαθουρα (Num. xxii 5). Le traducteur s'est contenté de transcrire le mot hébreu φαθουρα qu'il n'a pas fait précéder d'une préposition. Il en a fait sans doute une apposition à Βαλααμ υἱὸν Βεώρ. En effet certains manuscrits portent ὅ ἐστι ἐπὶ τοῦ ποταμοῦ γῆς . . . qui semblerait se référer à φαθουρα pris comme nom de lieu;[56] mais d'autres (AF) lisent ὅς . . . ce qui indiquerait que φαθουρα n'est pas senti comme un nom de lieu mais bien comme un nom de fonction qui n'était plus compris du traducteur grec. Celui-ci l'a trouvé dans le texte hébreu sous sa forme primitive araméenne et l'a tout simplement transcrit. Ce fait est à lui seul révélateur de l'existence d'une tradition en langue araméenne qui a transmis aux Israélites la figure de Bala'am.[57] Or nous connaissons maintenant un texte en langue araméenne qui nous a transmis son souvenir. Même s'il ne contient pas le mot technique *pāṭĕrāh* ou *pāṭôrāh*, interprète des songes, il nous apprend la même chose de manière équivalente puisqu'il nous dit de lui: c'était un homme qui voyait les dieux (*'š ḥzh 'lhn*); les dieux venaient à lui pendant la nuit (*blylh*). Par ailleurs la tradition biblique (Num. xxiii 7) fait venir Bala'am d'Aram, des montagnes de l'Orient (*mhrry qdm*) qui aux yeux du rédacteur hébreu ne pouvaient désigner que les montagnes de Transjordanie.[58]

Il faut ajouter enfin que l'onomastique elle-même favorise l'origine ammonite de Bile'am. Le nom de *bil'ām* est, semble t-il, composé du nom de *ba'al* (Bel) et de *'am*, "oncle paternel": "Ba'al est mon oncle", comme dans *Bel-am-ma* = *Amma Ba'li*.[59] Or l'onomastique ammonite, à commencer par le nom du peuple des *bĕnē 'ammôn* révèle l'existence d'un dieu *'am*. On retrouve ce dernier dans *Ammi-nadbî*, nom du roi de Bît-Ammani au temps d'Assurbanipal [60] et dans *'mndb* = *'m* + *ndb*

[56] Cf. G. Vermes, *Scripture and Tradition in Judaism* (Leyde, 1961), p. 129, qui comprend le Phatoura de la LXX comme un nom de lieu.

[57] Cf. dans le même sens L. Yauré, "Elymas-Nehelamite-Pethor", *JBL* 79 (1960), pp. 311 et sq.

[58] Pour la discussion du problème cf. Gross, pp. 98-101.

[59] Cf. K. L. Tallqvist, *Assyrian Personal Names* (Helsingfors et Leipzig, 1914; réimression, Hildesheim, 1966). C'est l'explication que retient le *Hebrew and English Lexicon* de F. Brown-S. R. Driver-C. A. Briggs. Pour d'autres étymologies, cf. L. Koehler-W. Baumgartner, *Hebräisches und aramäisches Lexikon*, sub verbo.

[60] Cf. E. Dhorme, *Recueil Edouard Dhorme. Etudes bibliques et orientales* (Paris, 1951), p. 254.

des deux sceaux trouvés à Amman.[61] Comme on le voit, le Balaʿam d'une certaine tradition biblique s'enracine parfaitement bien dans la terre, l'onomastique, et sans doute aussi la religion ammonite dont l'inscription araméenne nous livre quelques noms de dieux: ʾEl, Šegar, ʿAštart, Šaddin.[62] Ajoutons que le texte de Deir ʿAlla permet de situer dans le temps la personne de Balaʿam, c'est à dire vers le milieu du VIIIème siècle avant J.C. Cette constatation rend donc caduques les hypothèses de certains savants tels Albright qui faisait remonter Balaʿam au XIIIème siècle av. J.C. et la mise par écrit des oracles au Xème et au plus tard au IXème siècle av. J.C. A plus forte raison est-il impossible de souscrire aux vues de von Gall qui situait la composition des chap. xxii-xxiv de Nb. à l'époque post-exilienne, voire maccabéenne (pp. 46-7). La date fournie par l'inscription, compte tenu d'une certaine marge d'évaluation toujours possible en épigraphie, fournit donc l'époque à laquelle il faut situer Balaʿam; elle ne semble pas trop éloignée de celle que l'on donne habituellement à l'Elohiste que l'on date du VIIIème siècle, en tout cas avant la chute de Samarie et du royaume du Nord en 722.[63] Le prophète Michée, contemporain d'Isaïe connaissait la consultation que fit Balaq à Balaʿam (Mich. vi 5), ce qui prouve que cette tradition avait déjà pénétré en Juda au VIIIème siècle. Si nos déductions étaient recevables, l'attribution au Yahviste, que l'on date habituellement vers le Xème siècle av. J.C. à l'époque salomonienne,[64] de certaines traditions concernant Balaʿam serait donc à reconsidérer sérieusement. Mais il faudrait alors reprendre tout le problème des sources littéraires de l'oracle de Balaʿam si discuté parmi les critiques.[65] Cela nous conduirait trop loin des questions envisagées ici.

[Depuis la rédaction de cet article, J. C. Greenfield a soutenu que l'inscription n'était pas écrite en araméen dans le compte rendu de l'édition princeps. Faute de pouvoir tenir compte de la recension du *JSS* 25 (1980), pp. 248-52, nous renvoyons à cette critique.]

---

[61] Garbini, "Ammonite Inscriptions", p. 165.

[62] Cf. à ce sujet Hans-Peter Müller, "Einige alttestamentliche Probleme zur aramäischen Inschrift von Deir ʿAlla", *ZDPV* 94 (1978), pp. 62-7.

[63] Cf. H. Cazelles, *Introduction critique à l'Ancien Testament* (Paris, 1973), p. 215.

[64] Cf. par exemple Cazelles. pp. 203-4, et les opinions citées en note.

[65] Cf. par exemple le résumé que donne du problème Coppens, pp. 72-6.

KOMPOSITION BEI AMOS

VON

H. GESE

Tübingen

Es ist keine Frage, daß für die Interpretation geformter Texte die Komposition, der bewußt durchgeführte Aufbau des Textes, eine Bedeutung ersten Ranges hat. Wie Wortwahl und Stil dient die Komposition dem unmittelbaren Ausdruck des Inhalts und ist mehr als bloß eine Äußerlichkeit. Und doch hatte in der alttestamentlichen Exegese bis vor kurzem die Komposition nicht die Beachtung gefunden, die sie verdient. Vielleicht war es die Art der Vers-für-Vers-Interpretation, die den Blick sofort auf die einzelnen inhaltlichen Aussagen sich richten ließ, während das Interesse an der Form fast ganz von den Fragen nach den Gattungseigentümlichkeiten bestimmt war. In neuerer Zeit begegnet man kompositionellen Betrachtungen häufiger, eine moderne Empfänglichkeit für strukturale Phänomene mag dabei im Hintergrund stehen. Aber hier ist wieder die Gefahr, daß bloß formale Beobachtungen gesammelt werden, ohne den unmittelbaren Zusammenhang mit der inhaltlichen Bedeutung herauszustellen: die Form ist jedoch als Bedeutungsträger wesentlich.

Im Folgenden soll eine bestimmte Kompositionsform bei Amos beschrieben werden, nicht um sie an sich vorzuführen, sondern um sie im Zusammenhang mit dem Textinhalt, in ihrer Bedeutung für die Textaussage zu betrachten. Es gibt hier drei größere Stücke, die durch Aneinanderreihung gleicher oder sehr ähnlicher Elemente bewußte Komposition zeigen: 1. das Völkergedicht i 3-ii 16 mit seinen acht jeweils gleich eingeleiteten Strophen, deren letzte, die Israelstrophe, zwar umfangmäßig und dann auch inhaltlich stark abweicht, aber doch die gleiche Einführung zeigt, während die sechs Fremdvölkerstrophen und die Judastrophe sich auch über die Einführung hinaus in der Struktur höchst ähnlich sehen, 2. das Gedicht von den göttlichen Unheilstaten iv 6 ff. mit seinem fünffachen Kehrvers "Doch ihr kehrtet nicht zu mir um, Ausspruch JHWHs", 3. der Komplex der fünf Visionen in c. vii-ix, die nicht nur redaktionell einfach gesammelt und am Ende des Buches zusammengestellt sein können, sondern die, wie die gleiche Einführung in vii 1, 4, 7, viii 1 mit charakteristischer Abweichung in ix 1, die Strukturähnlichkeiten im Fall der ersten vier Visionen und vor allem der Hinweis von vii 8 und viii 2, "ich (JHWH) werde nicht mehr an ihm (meinem Volk Israel) (straflos) vorbeigehen", auf die ersten beiden Visionen zeigen, schon in ihrer ganzen Anlage von vornherein aufeinander bezogen sind.

Neben diesen drei großen Stücken i 3-ii 16, iv 6 ff. und den Visionen in c. vii-ix gibt es innerhalb der einzelnen Sprüche zwar noch gewisse Reihungen, z.B. iii (3) 4-8, die aber doch, weil sie nur das Aufbaugefüge einer in sich geschlossenen Einheit bestimmen, auf einer anderen Ebene liegen als die Komposition großer, gleichberechtigter Einheiten in den drei genannten Fällen. Es ist darum gerechtfertigt, die Komposition dieser drei Stücke, sozusagen die Großkompositionen bei Amos, herauszugreifen und sie in Hinsicht auf Form und Bedeutung zu untersuchen und zu vergleichen.

Es empfiehlt sich, die Untersuchung mit den Visionen zu beginnen, weil wir deutlich Bezüge zwischen den einzelnen Visionen erkennen können. Auf den ersten Blick ordnen sich hier die beiden ersten Visionen zu einem Paar zusammen, und zumindest der Form nach gilt das entsprechend für die dritte und vierte Vision. Nach der Einführung "So ließ mich der Herr JHWH sehen" (vii 1aα = 4aα) wird die Vision selbst mit *w^ehinnē* eingeleitet, innerhalb derer der Prophet redend eingreift: "und ich sprach" (2aγ = 5aα), und fast gleichlautend wechselt die prophetische Fürbitte mit der göttlichen Gewährung: "Herr JHWH, vergib doch (*s^elăḥ-na'*), wie (als wer) kann Jakob bestehen, er ist ja (zu) klein!" (2aδεb: erste Vision) bzw. "Herr JHWH, laß doch ab (*ḥ^adăl-na'*), wie kann Jakob bestehen, er ist ja (zu) klein!" (5aβγb: zweite Vision) und "JHWH ließ sich dessen gereuen, 'Es wird nicht geschehen', sprach JHWH" (3: erste Vision) bzw. "JHWH ließ sich dessen gereuen, 'Auch das wird nicht geschhehen', sprach der Herr JHWH" (6: zweite Vision). Die Unterschiede in den Formulierungen sind ohne weiteres verständlich: die Bitte "vergib doch" im Fall der ersten Vision erbittet noch die Schuldvergebung, die Bitte "laß doch ab" im Fall der zweiten Vision erbittet nur die Straflosigkeit; und die göttliche Gewährung wird im zweiten Fall unter Bezugnahme auf den ersten Fall formuliert: "Auch das wird nicht geschehen". Es wird nicht Zufall sein, daß selbst die Abschlußformel *'amăr YHWH* (3) im zweiten Fall in einer Steigerungsform *'amăr 'adonay YHWH* (6) erscheint, als sollte nach der zweiten Vision ein gewisser Trennungsstrich gez -n-über dem Folgenden gezogen werden, und diese Beobachtung wird sich später bestätigen.[1]

Eine solche formale Parallelität und gegenseitige Zuordnung der ersten beiden Visionen ist schon immer beobachtet worden, und sie bestätigt sich auch im Inhaltlichen: Die erste Vision stellt das Unheil eines Heuschreckenfraßes zur kritischen Zeit des Spätsaataufgangs dar, so daß in jenem Jahr kein Neuanbau mehr möglich wäre und eine Hungersnot durch totalen Ernteausfall [2] bevorsteht.[3] Die zweite Vision ist eine Steigerung dieser Vegetationsbedrohung; sie kündigt das Verzehren der großen *t^e^hôm*, gleichsam der Basis aller Fruchtbarkeit (vgl. Gen. xlix 25; Dtn. xxxiii 13), durch die Feuerflamme an.[4] Wird in der ersten Vision die Vegetation nur von außen ge-

---

[1] Vgl. Anm. 41 zu i 8.

[2] Es ist bei *läqäš* natürlich an Spätsaat, also an Getreide gedacht, vgl. *KAI* 182, 2 (Bd. II, S. 182) und besonders W. Rudolph, *Joel-Amos-Obadja-Jona* (*KAT* XIII 2, 1971), S. 132.

[3] Die Glosse V. 1b macht sich durch die Aufnahme des *w^e^hinnē* selbst als solche kenntlich.- Der Text in V. 2 bedarf keiner Änderung. Zu *ʾim* + pf. im temporalen Sinn "wann, als, da" vgl. Jes xxiv 13 und auch iv 4. Anstelle eines *wäy^e^hî* dient in einem Satzgefüge mit impf. cs. -Fortführung das *w^e^hayā* zum betonten Ausdruck der Gleichzeitigkeit der mit den Verben bezeichneten Vorgänge (Andauer des ersten Vorgangs), wie sich aus 1 Sam i 12 f. ergibt (*w^e^hayā* + *kî* pf. . . ., impf. cs. . . .): Eli dachte nicht, Hanna sei trunken, nachdem sie lange gebetet hatte, sondern als sie lange betete. Entsprechend hier: "Und als der Heuschreckenschwarm dabei war, das Kraut des Landes zu Ende zu fressen / mit dem Fressen fertig wurde, da sprach ich. . ." Die Konstruktion, die Spannung aufs äußerste treibend, will offensichtlich hervorheben, daß der Prophet im letzten Moment eingreift, in dem nämlich die durch die Vision dargestellte geistige Wirklichkeit noch in statu nascendi und damit als Realität noch nicht völlig festgelegt ist; vgl. die folgende Anm.

[4] Die eigentliche Visionsbeschreibung V. 4aβb ist wie V. 1 ursprünglich ohne Explikation des Subjekts formuliert, es wird aber *ʾ^a^donay YHWH* aus theologischen Gründen nachgetragen (bei den mythischen Größen von Feuer und *t^e^hôm* soll die Verursachung allein durch Gott nicht im Dunkel bleiben), doch gibt diese Glosse sich als solche durch ihre Stellung bewußt zu erkennen und sollte darum auch nicht anders als appositionell übersetzt werden. Schwierigkeiten bereitet aber das *lrb bʾš*. Der bestechende, auf M. Krenkel, "Zur Kritik und Exegese der kleinen Propheten", *ZwTh* 14 (1866), S. 271, zurückgehende Vorschlag von D. R. Hillers, "Amos 7, 4 and Ancient Parallels", *CBQ* 26 (1964), S. 221-5. (vgl. H. W. Wolff, *Dodekapropheton 2, Joel und Amos* [*BK* XIV 2, 1969], S. 338), *lirbîb ʾeš* zu lesen, was den überlieferten Konsonantentext ziemlich unberührt läßt, hat leider gegen sich, daß *r^e^bîb*, wenn es auch im Ugaritischen ein singularisches Pendant gibt, im A.T. nur pluralisch vorkommt (6 mal, also nicht ein so seltenes Wort, das man leicht verlesen könnte), und vor allem, daß ein Feuerregen von oben kommt und zuerst das Land, dann das Grundwasser verzehrt, also umgekehrt, als im Text ausgeführt, worauf mit Recht Rudolph, S. 232, hinweist. Die übliche Konjektur *lăhăb* hat gegen sich, daß man ein vom Kontext her so naheliegendes Wort in der Texttradition verloren haben soll. Der Vorschlag

schädigt, so in der zweiten Vision von ihrer Voraussetzung her unmöglich gemacht. Beide Visionen bilden ein Paar; in dieser sich steigernden Abfolge eines umfassenden äußeren und inneren Unheilsgeschehens wird nach dem Formgesetz der Duplik [5] die Totalität des Unheils angedroht, das sich an der Vegetation, an der lebendig-fruchtbaren Erde des von Israel bewohnten Landes, vollziehen soll. Es wäre verkehrt zu fragen, warum erst die dritte und nicht schon die zweite Vision die Unabänderlichkeit des Unheils ansagt; die ersten beiden Visionen bilden zusammen eine höhere Einheit, ebenso wie die dritte und vierte, die beidemal diese Unabänderlichkeit zum Ausdruck bringen, die logisch gesehen doch nur einmal ausgesagt werden dürfte.[6]

Wenn auch die dritte und vierte Vision (vii 7 ff. und viii 1 ff.) durch den Fremdbericht (Er-Stil) in vii 10-17 getrennt sind, so ist doch ihre Zusammengehörigkeit zunächst wenigstens formal nicht zu bezweifeln. Nach der gleichen Einführung (vii 7aα, viii 1a) und der Einleitung *w^ehinnē* mit der folgenden Visionsbeschreibung erscheint im Gegensatz zu den ersten beiden Gottes Frage an Amos mit der Antwort des Propheten: "Und er (JHWH) sprach (zu mir): 'Was siehst du, Amos?', und ich sprach:. . ." – danach die Angabe des Visionsgegenstandes (vii 8a, viii 2a). Diese Antwort wird zumThemawort der anschließenden an "mein Volk Israel" gerichteten Unheilsverkündigung, die mit der Aussage endet: "Ich werde nicht mehr an ihm (straflos) vorübergehen" (vii 8b, viii 2b).[7] Ob das unmittelbar fol-

von O. Procksch in *BHK* z.St., *lišbîb ʾeš* zu lesen, würde nur die Änderung von *š* in *r* voraussetzen. *šebîb* erscheint im A.T. abgesehen von Sir. viii 10, xlv 19 nur in Hi. xviii 5; interessant ist das Vorkommen in 1QH iii 30 (neben vi 18); hier erinnert die Aussage *wtʾwkl ʿd thwm rbh* (31 f.) geradezu an die Amosstelle. TM "Jemand rief zum (Rechts-) Streit das Feuer an" gibt zwar einen (gekünstelten) Sinn, aber *b^e* müßte über *larib* hinweg auf *qoreʾ* bezogen werden. Ob mit *larib baʾeš* "a judgement with fire" gemeint sein kann (J. Limburg, "Amos 7:4", *CBQ* 35 [1973], S. 346-9), bleibt fraglich.- Wie in der ersten Vision greift der Prophet erst im letzten Moment ein: "Und als es (schon) das Feld fraß, da sprach ich. . ." (wie das *w^ehayā* in V. 2 dient das pf. cs. im Zusammenhang mit dem impf. cs. zum Ausdruck der Gleichzeitigkeit der Verbalvorgänge).

[5] Vgl. "Der Dekalog als Ganzheit betrachtet", *ZThK*, N.F. 64 (1967), S. 137 f. (= *Vom Sinai zum Zion* [München, 1974], S. 79 f.).

[6] Man vgl. zur Duplik bei Visionen auch Jer. i 11 ff., wo sich beide Visionen auf das eine Geschehen der Berufung beziehen, oder die Struktur der jeweils paarweisen Visionen Sach. ii 1-4, 5-9 und v 1-4, 5-11, s. "Anfang und Ende der Apokalyptik", *ZThK*, N.F. 65 (1968), S. 35 f. (= *Vom Sinai zum Zion*, S. 217 f.).

[7] Die kleinen stilistischen Differenzen zwischen den beiden Visionen lassen sich leicht verständlich machen. Sie haben ihren Grund darin, daß im Gegensatz zur vierten Vision Gott in der dritten Vision selbst erscheint. Deswegen kann

gende zweite Drohwort vii 9 bzw. viii 3 noch zu den Visionen gehört, ist umstritten.[8] Das formale Argument, daß die Vision kein weiteres Drohwort enthalten dürfe, ist angesichts der letzten Vision – vgl. ix 2 ff. – hinfällig, und auch die poetische Form kann, wie die letzte Vision zeigt, keinen Gegensatz bilden, zumal sich die an die Vision unmittelbar anschließenden Drohworte vii 8bβγδ und viii 2bβγ durchaus auch als Poesie (2 + 2 + 2) auffassen lassen. Es käme auf die Frage an, ob diese zusätzlichen Drohworte vii 9 und viii 3 *inhaltlich* ganz zu den Visionen passen und ob redaktionsgeschichtlich nichts gegen diese Stücke spricht. Sehen wir zunächst von diesen umstrittenen Stücken ab und wenden uns den Visionsinhalten zu!

Die vierte Vision ist nicht schwer zu verstehen. Der Korb mit dem abgeernteten Sommerobst (*qăyiṣ*) – es wird in erster Linie an Feigen zu denken sein, vielleicht auch zusätzlich an Weintrauben [9] – führt zu dem berühmten [10] Wort *ba' hăqqeṣ* "Das Ende ist gekommen". Für gewöhnlich nimmt man an, daß ein reines Wortspiel den Zusammenhang bilde, daß eine reine Assonanzvision vorliege.[11] Die schöne Parallele Jer. i 11 ff., wo der visionäre Mandelstock (*măqqel šaqed*) zur Verheißung "Ich wache (*šoqed 'anî*) über mein Wort, es zu tun" führt, zeigt aber schon, daß abgesehen vom etymologischen Zusammenhang auch ein sachlicher besteht. So wie der Mandelstock die Blüten unmittelbar, ohne Blätter, aus dem tot erscheinenden Holz treibt, wenn er zur frühesten Jahreszeit "erwacht" – man vergleiche Num. xvii 16 ff., um den Symbolwert zu fassen –, so geht die Wirklichkeit aus dem "bloßen" Wort hervor, über das Gott "wacht" und aus dem die göttlichen Kräfte hervorbrechen. Das ist nicht nur eine Assonanz-, sondern auch eine Symbolvision. Ebenso hier: Der für das Visionsbild so wichtige Korb weist auf die Aberntung, und der

---

die Explikation des göttlichen Subjekts in der Einführungsformel vii 8aα unterbleiben, während bei der Einleitung der Frage an den Propheten nach dem Visionsinhalt eine solche Explikation im Fall der dritten Vision vii 8aα gerade nötig wird; denn nicht der in der Vision Geschaute spricht. Um dann nicht dieselbe Formulierung gleich zu wiederholen (vgl. viii 2bα), wird darauf in vii 8bα *wăyyo'mär 'ᵃdonay* gebraucht.

[8] Vgl. z.B. die Polemik Rudolphs, S. 237, bzw. S. 239 Anm. 7, gegen Wolff, S. 340 f. bzw. S. 367.

[9] Tos. Ned. iv 1: nur Feigen, 2: daneben auch Weintrauben.

[10] Vgl. Ez. vii 2 (3), 6 bis; Gen. vi 13 (P).

[11] Vgl. z.B. Rudolph, S. 239: "Beide Wörter in der Amosvision haben weder etymologisch noch sachlich etwas miteinander zu tun, sondern der springende Punkt ist lediglich der Gleichklang".

symbolische Zusammenhang von Ernte und Gericht, Ernte und Tod (vgl. z.B. Am. ii 13) ist unverkennbar, wobei hier die Frucht des im Lande eingegründeten Fruchtbaumes, insbesondere des Feigenbaumes (vgl. Jer. xxiv) den symbolischen Charakter mit prägt. Daß die Assonanz *qăyiṣ – qeṣ* darüber hinaus für den Visionär einen sozusagen "volksetymologischen" Zusammenhang darstellt, kann und sollte man nicht ausschließen, zumal einerseits die Aussprache *qeṣ* statt *qăyiṣ* belegt ist (*KAI* 182, 7) und andererseits die Orthographie des von *qeṣ* abgeleiteten Adjektivs *qyṣwn* (Ex. xxvi 4, 10, xxxvi 10, 17) auf die im späteren Hebräisch dann häufiger belegbare Ausdehnung der Wurzel *qṣṣ* auf die Nebenform *qwṣ* hindeutet. Zwischen der Vision eines Korbes abgeernteter Feigen und dem Unheilswort "Das Ende ist zu meinem Volk Israel gekommen" besteht also ein innerer sachlich-symbolischer und ein äußerer verbal-assonantischer Zusammenhang. Das Ende Israels ist als "Aberntung", als endgültiges, absolutes Ende, eben als Tod verstanden. Und dem entspricht dann inhaltlich das angeschlossene Unheilswort viii 3, das konkret die Todessituation mit einer Qina ausmalt:

Und es heulen (selbst) die Palastsängerinnen [12]
an jenem Tage: [13] (3 + 2)
"Viel sind der Leichen!
Überall hat man (sie) hingeworfen! Still!" (2 + 3)

Die entsetzliche Ernte des Todes ist bis aufs äußerste gezeichnet, bis hin zum Ausruf *hăs*, der strenges Schweigen im Angesicht des Todes fordert (vgl. vi 10) und mit dem die kurze Qina erstirbt.

Viel schwieriger ist das Verständnis der dritten Vision. Nach Landsbergers Aufsatz über das akkadische *anaku* = Zinn [14] dürfte die seit dem Mittelalter beliebte Senkblei-Deutung ad acta gelegt sein.[15] und es braucht hier garnicht erst auf die schon immer schwerwiegen-

---

[12] Da Lieder eigentlich nicht heulen und der Plural *šîrôt* nicht belegt ist, wird wie üblich *šarôt* zu lesen sein. Man hat es wohl als störend empfunden, daß überhaupt noch Palastsängerinnen da sein sollen.

[13] Die erweiterte Gottesspruchformel *n*^{e}*ʾum ʾ*^{a}*donay YHWH*, hier vielleicht als nötig empfunden, da V. 3b Zitat ist, gliedert c. viii, vgl. V. 9, 11, und ist der Redaktion zuzuschreiben, nicht aber *băyyôm hăhûʾ* (so K. Marti, *Das Dodekapropheton* [*KHC* XIII, 1904], S. 215, Rudolph, S. 238 u.a.), das sonst in Anfangsposition erscheinen müßte, vgl. V. 9, 13, außerdem ist es für den Qinarhythmus nötig.

[14] B. Landsberger, "Tin and Lead: The Adventures of Two Vocables", *JNES* 24 (1965), S. 285-96.

[15] Folgen werden bleiben, z.B. daß im Ivrit *ʾ*^{a}*nakî* lotrecht heißt und *ʾ*^{a}*nak* die Bleilot-Bedeutung behält.

den Argumente gegen diese Deutung eingegangen zu werden, daß im A.T. die Setzwaage *mišqālāt* heißt, daß es ein Baugerät und nicht ein nachträgliches Prüfungsgerät für umzustürzende Mauern ist, und vor allem, daß in der dritten Vision eine Prüfung viel zu spät kommt, weil die Straffälligkeit längst feststeht, abgesehen davon, daß diese Deutung zur Streichung des ersten *ʾanak* in V. 7 führte. Die Darlegung Landsbergers, daß es sich bei Amos um eine Zinnvision handeln muß (S. 287), ist von Brunet, Holladay, Ouellette und van Leeuwen aufgenommen,[16] und doch bestehen in der Deutung die größten Unterschiede. Landsberger und Ouellette deuten die Zinnmauer negativ; ersterer betont die Weichheit des Metalls, seine Nutzlosigkeit im nichtlegierten Zustand und seine Vergänglichkeit, letzterer denkt an den in mesopotamischen Ritualen greifbaren negativen magischen Sinn des Metalls. Die anderen interpretieren die Zinnmauer positiv, indem sie auf die Bedeutung des Zinns zur Herstellung der für Waffen hochwichtigen Bronze verweisen, während die Mauer die Masse des Gott zur Verfügung stehenden Zinns symbolisiere. Wir müssen aber davon ausgehen, daß die in den Visionen erscheinenden Phänomene den ihnen eigentümlichen, *spezifischen* Sinn haben, der die geistige Wirklichkeit kennzeichnet, die hier aufscheint. Der Erntekorb ist nichts Gleichgültiges, er zeigt, daß die Feigen geerntet, eingesammelt sind; die Mauer ist nicht bloße Masse, sie zeigt die Wehrkraft, und im Fall einer Metallmauer statt einer normalen Stein-, Holz- oder Erdmauer die Unüberwindlichkeit dieser Wehrkraft.[17] Das beweist deutlich die eherne Mauer von Jer. i 18, xv 20 oder die Eisenmauer von Ez. iv 3, 2 Mac. xi 9, um nur bei den alttestamentlichen Beispielen zu bleiben.[18] Wenn der Prophet

---

[16] G. Brunet, "La vision de l'étain", *VT* 16 (1966), S. 387-95, W. L. Holladay, "Once more *ʾanak* = 'tin', Amos vii 7-8", *VT* 20 (1970), S. 492-4, J. Ouellette, "Le mur d'étain dans Amos VII, 7-9", *RB* 80 (1973), S. 321-31, C. van Leeuwen, "Quelques problèmes de traduction dans les visions d'Amos chapitre 7", *Übersetzung und Deutung* (Nijkerk, 1977), S. 103-12.

[17] Man sollte weder mit Brunet (S. 394 f.) an eine Mauer aus Zinnerzen denken noch mit Ouellette (S. 324 ff.) bloß an einen Metallüberzug, wie es "realistisch" wäre; Mythos, Vision und Idee kennen eine solche Einschränkung nicht. Wenn Gott Jeremia zur ehernen Mauer macht (i 18, xv 20) oder Ezechiel bei einer Zeichenhandlung mit einer eisernen Platte eine Eisenmauer symbolisiert (iv 3), dann ist nicht bloß an eine solche mit Metallüberzug gedacht. Daß die Amosvisionen sehr wohl den "Realismus" hinter sich lassen, zeigt jedenfalls die zweite Vision.

[18] Andere Beispiele besonders bei Ouellette. Nicht erwähnt sind leider die klassischen Beispiele: die eherne Mauer des Tartaros, Hesiod, Theogonie 726, seine eisernen Tore und eherne Schwelle, Homer, Ilias viii 15, vgl. auch Theokrit

Gott auf einer solchen Mauer stehen sieht, so sieht er diese natürlich von vorn, also nicht als schützende, bergende Macht, sondern als Zwingburg.[19] Würde das eine Gold- oder eine Silbermauer sein, so hätte dieser überreiche Strahlenglanz kaum etwas Feindliches an sich und die Symbolik würde in die Richtung äußerster Pracht weisen. In der Reihe der Metalle folgt dem Silber das Zinn, das nach der Faustregel wohl zehnmal weniger wert ist als Silber, aber zehnmal mehr als Kupfer (Landsberger, S. 287), und das zur Bronzeherstellung unentbehrlich war, und zwar bei der üblichen harten Bronze im Verhältnis 1:6. Sanherib rühmt sich, den Zinnanteil noch erhöht zu haben (Landsberger, S. 292 [Luckenbill 141, 9]). Die durch diese Metallmauer symbolisierte Wehrkraft läßt also eine ungeheure Rüstungspotenz erkennen, und dies wird durch das Zinn in der göttlichen Hand, mag es als Waffe oder als bloßes Metall gemeint sein,[20] noch unterstrichen. Nicht ohne Grund wird das Zinn mit dem im assyrischen Einflußbereich üblichen Wort bezeichnet und nicht wie sonst (Num. xxxi 22; Ez. xxvii 14 u.a.St.) *b^edîl* genannt. Um so wichtiger ist es, daß in dieser Vision Gott selbst als der eigentlich Handelnde erscheint, der hinter dieser Macht steht und ohne den sie nichts wäre.

Weist somit das Visionsbild auf die militärische Überwältigung, so greift die Unheilsverkündigung das Stichwort *ʾ^anak* auf, das mit aller Wahrscheinlichkeit hier wie das auf *qāyiṣ* sich beziehende *qeṣ* in der vierten Vision unter stärkster Assonanz an das (assyrische) Wort für Zinn doch einen neuen Sinn hat: Das onomatopoetische Wort für seufzen, stöhnen ist im A.T. sowohl *ʾanăḥ* wie *ʾanăq* (neben *naʾăq*). Schon F. Horst schlug vor, hier *ʾ^anaḥā* zu lesen,[21] und Ouellette

ii 34 und die von Ph.-E. Legrand, *Bucoliques grecs I* 6. Aufl., Paris, 1967), S. 99 f. Anm. 4, angegebene Parallele, die zeigen, daß die Vorstellung der Tartarosmauern aus ἀδάμας durchaus üblich war (in diesem Zusammenhang ist die Septuagintaübersetzung von *ʾ^anak* mit ἀδάμας besonders einleuchtend), und die eindrücklichste Stelle ist gewiß Vergil, Aeneis vi 548 ff.:

"Respicit Aeneas: subito et sub rupe sinistra
moenia lata videt, triplici circumdata muro,
quae rapidus flammis ambit torrentibus amnis,
Tartareus Phlegethon, torquetque sonantia saxa.
porta adversa ingens, solidoque *adamante* columnae,
vis ut nulla virum, non ipsi excindere bello
caelicolae valeant; stat *ferrea* turris ad auras. . . ."

[19] Vielleicht auch als Belagerungsmauer (vgl. Ez. iv 3)?

[20] Zu ersterem vgl. den Sprachgebrauch Koh. x 10, Sir. xlviii 17; eine nähere Beschreibung könnte Gott götterbildhaft festlegen.

[21] "Die Visionsschilderungen der alttestamentlichen Propheten", *EvTh* 20 (1960), S. 193-205: S. 201.

greift auf diesen Vorschlag zurück (S. 329 f.), doch mit dem richtigen Hinweis, daß die Schreibung eines solchen onomatopoetischen Wortes, das ohnehin zwischen *'nḥ* und *'nq* steht, im vorliegenden Fall als *'nk* plausibel wäre,[22] wenn auch dadurch das Verständnis später eher erschwert wurde.[23]

Auf jeden Fall kann am Sinn der dritten Vision kein Zweifel sein: es geht hier um die drohende militärische Überwältigung Israels, während die gesteigerte vierte Vision das Ende, den Tod selbst aussagt, so daß beide Visionen auch inhaltlich ein Steigerungspaar bilden. Diesem Sinn der dritten Vision entspricht nun auch das zweite Unheilswort vii 9 vorzüglich, das wie viii 3 im Fall der vierten Vision das angedrohte Unheil konkretisiert:

> Die heiligen Höhe Isaaks veröden,
> die Heiligtümer Israels werden verwüstet,
> und ich stehe auf gegen Jerobeams Haus mit dem Schwert.

Der Zusammenhang des Volkes mit dem Land, der in den Heiligtümern kultische Gestalt annimmt, wird ebenso zerstört wie die staatliche Macht des Königshauses; d.h. durch kriegerische Überwältigung wird der Großteil des Volkes exiliert und der Staat zerstört während nach der vierten Vision das leibliche Leben selbst vernichtet wird.

Das Drohwort vii 9 war die Anknüpfung für die "Biographie" im Er-Stil vii 10-17, die als Amos' Prophetie ein Wort gegen den Konig Jerobeam ebenso nennt (V. 11) wie es ihn die Zerstörung von Bethel ankündigen läßt (V. 17), und vii 9 ist somit Voraussetzung für diese Anfügung. Die umgekehrte Ansicht,[24] vii 9 wolle das unerfüllte Wort vii 11 gegen Jerobeam selbst durch die Verschiebung

---

[22] Wie im Fall von *qăyiṣ/qeṣ* wird auch hier eine "volksetymologische" Verbindung zwischen dem Wort für Zinn und dem für ächzen, stöhnen vorausgesetzt sein, die in der Eigenart dieses Metalls, daß beim Biegen das knirschende "Zinngeschrei" auftritt, begründet sein könnte.

[23] Immerhin hat der Midrasch (LevR xxxiii 2, BabM 59a) noch von einer zweiten Bedeutung von *'ᵃnak* in Am. vii 7 f. gewußt, die mit *'ôna'ûta'* bzw. *'ôna'ā* ("Bedrückung") angegeben wird. Die Rückschlüsse von M. Jastrow, *A Dictionary of the Targumim, the Talmud Babli*... (New York-London 1903), S. 85b, und J. J. Slotki, *Midrash Rabbah, Leviticus* (zus. m. J. Israelstam, London, 1939), S. 419 Anm. 2, auf eine besondere Wurzel *'nk* lassen sich jedoch nicht halten.

[24] S. oben Anm. 8. Man vgl. auch den eigentümlichen Gebrauch von *yiśḥaq*, der beide Stücke verbindet. Daß dabei vii 9 aus vii 10 ff. herausgebildet ist, ist angesichts der Differenzen zu V. 16 (Umkehrung der Reihenfolge Israel—Haus Issak, Wegfall von "Haus" in letzterem Ausdruck, Ausdehnung auf die Heiligtümer überhaupt) nur schwer zu begründen.

auf die Familie korrigieren und sei somit sekundär, erklärt nicht, wieso es überhaupt zu der Trennung der so eng zusammengehörigen dritten und vierten Vision kommt. Außerdem ist der Sinn, Jerobeam selbst sei mit dem "Haus Jerobeams" nicht gemeint, in V. 9b erst hineingelegt.

Nach den beiden besprochenen Visionspaaren erreicht die Komposition auf einer dritten Stufe in ix 1-4 ihren Höhepunkt. Formal unterscheidet sich diese letzte Vision von den vorhergehenden zunächst durch die andere Einführung "Ich sah" anstelle des "So ließ mich der Herr JHWH sehen, siehe. . .", womit zum Ausdruck kommt, daß Amos in die Vision selbst nicht mehr hineingezogen wird, sei es daß er selbst fürbittend eingreift, sei es daß er durch eine Frage in die schlimme Bedeutung der Vision eingeführt wird, die unabänderlich gilt und jede Fürbitte verbietet. Auf dieser dritten Stufe kann es nicht mehr um die Frage der Geltung gehen.

Dem Inhalt nach handelt es sich um die Aufhebung des heiligen Zentrums Israels, Bethel, der hierin beschlossenen Verbindung zu Gott und der damit gesetzten Asylie. Gott erscheint auf dem Zentralpunkt des Heiligtums von Bethel, dem Altar,[25] und befiehlt einem ungenannten "Engel" – Amos ist ja in diese Vision nicht hineingezogen, und die Aufgabe ist ohnehin übermenschlich –, die Fassadenspitze [26] des Tempels zu zerschlagen,[27] daß die Schwellen, die festen Eingründungspunkte des Tempels, erbeben. Es ist verständlich, daß dieser Akt, der die totale,[28] von oben bis in die Tiefe reichende Zerstörung bezeichnet, nicht der Herr des Hauses selbst vollzieht,

---

[25] Man beachte den Artikel; vgl. 1 Reg. xii 32 f. und die aus 1 Reg. xiii und 2 Reg. xxiii 15-18 hervorgehende Bedeutung des Altars von Bethel.

[26] Daß *kaptôr* das Säulenkapitäl meint, ist in Anbetracht des anderen Wortgebrauchs in all den Fällen, in denen dies zweifellos gemeint ist (*kotärät* 1 Reg. vii 16 ff.; 2 Reg. xxv 17, Jer. lii 22, 2 Chr. iv 12; *ro'š* Ex. xxxvi 38, xxxviii 17 ff.; *ṣäpät* 2 Chr. iii 15) wenig wahrscheinlich; Zeph. ii 14 kann man nur entnehmen, daß es sich um etwas Hochgelegenes handelt, während es sonst den knaufartigen Zierrat bei der Menora bezeichnet. In Am. 1 ist nur von *einem kaptôr* die Rede, und offensichtlich handelt es sich um die Spitze des Tempels, sozusagen um das Akroterion, den obersten Teil der Tempelfassade. Man vgl. als Beispiel etwa das aus dem 10./9. Jahrh. v. Chr. stammende Heiligtumsmodell aus Tell Fara (Samaria) im Palestine Archaeological Museum Jerusalem; s. A. Jirku, *Die Welt der Bibel* (4. Aufl., Stuttgart, 1962), Tafel 87.

[27] Zur Bedeutung von *hăk* vgl. iii 15, vi 11.

[28] Daß der Text meint, Gott verschaffe sich auf diese Weise Zutritt zu seinem Tempel, um die hier Versteckten zu töten oder töten zu lassen (J. Ouellette, "The Shaking of the Thresholds in Amos 9:1", *HUCA* 43 [1972], S. 23-7), setzt einen für das A.T. ungewöhnlichen Anthropomorphismus voraus.

sondern hoheitsvoll seinem "Engel" überträgt. Der Befehl lautet weiter – und zeigt damit die Konsequenz des totalen Gerichts für Israel an – :

> und brich sie ab [29] an ihrer aller Haupt [30] -
> und ihren Rest töte ich mit dem Schwert;
> nicht wird ihnen ein Flüchtender flüchten
> und ein Entrinnender sich retten.

Das Bethelheiligtum wird also als das Haupt und "Kopfende", als die Spitze Israels verstanden, durch dessen Zerstörung oder Aufhebung sie von ihrem Heiligkeitszentrum, ihrer kultischen Gottesverbindung und damit von jeder Asylie abgeschnitten sind. So von ihrem Haupt abgeschnitten trifft ihren Rest (ihr "Hinterende". Vgl. iv 2) das Schwert (Verbum *hrg*), so daß das Gericht ein totales ist, dem niemand entflieht.[31] Diese Unentrinnbarkeit wird in einem zweiten Unheilswort konkretisiert in fünf *ʾim*-Sätzen (V. 2-4), die nun dieselbe Fünferstruktur zeigen, wie die Visionsreihung überhaupt, indem als Zuflucht abgewiesen werden: 1. Hölle und Himmel als absolutes Extrempaar, 2. Karmelgipfel und Meeresgrund als irdisches Extrempaar und 3. in einer großartigen Hyperbel ganz auf die historische Gegenwart treffend selbst die Gefangenschaft, wobei als Inclusio das verbum *hrg* wieder erscheint [32] und die Aufzählung in einer verallgemeinernden Zusammenfassung V. 4b ausklingt.

Die fünfte Vision stellt als dritte Stufe der Visionsfolge mit ihrem Inhalt der Aufhebung jeglicher kultischen Heilsverbindung mit

---

[29] Die masoretische Punktation für normales *ûbṣaʿem* schließt das Suffix ausnahmsweise ohne Bindevokal an, um den Ton auf der vorletzten Silbe zu halten, vgl. *BL* § 13r und 51a'.

[30] Neben dem suffigierten Verbum kann *kullam* nur auf das vorhergehende Wort bezogen werden, so daß Textänderungen wie *răʿăš* unwahrscheinlich sind, und *roʾš* kann auch nicht direktes Objekt zu *bṣʿ* sein, so daß für *beroʾš kullam* nur die Bedeutung "an ihrer aller Spitze" (Dtn. xx 9: 2 Chr. xiii 12) in Frage kommt.

[31] Zur Veranschaulichung sei an ein berühmtes Beispiel aus Athen um 636 v. Chr. erinnert: "Der Archon Megakles hatte die Mitverschworenen des Kylon, die im Athenatempel Asyl gesucht hatten, überredet, herabzukommen und sich vor Gericht zu stellen. Diese banden nun einen gezwirnten Faden an das Götterbild und hielten daran fest, und als sie bei ihrem Abstieg (von der Burg) am Eumenidentempel vorbeikamen, riß der Faden von selbst. Da ließen Megakles und die Mitarchonten sie sofort ergreifen, weil ja die Göttin ihnen das Asylrecht verweigert hätte" (Plutarch, Solon xii 1). Vgl. auch für diese Anschauung des Kontaktes mit dem Heiligen Ps cxviii 27: "Bindet die Prozession mit Stricken an die Hörner des Altars!"

[32] Man beachte auch die Verknüpfungen der drei Teile: *lqḥ* V. 2 + V. 3, *ṣwḥ* V. 3 + V. 4.

Gott und der damit gesetzten Totalität des Unheilsgeschehens ein nicht mehr zu steigerndes Äußerstes dar. Es wäre sinnlos, hieran aus Gründen der Duplik ein Pendant anzuschließen. Und diese Fünferstruktur der drei Stufen bestätigt sich uns als Kleinform noch einmal im Rahmen des Unheilswortes von der Unentrinnbarkeit in der letzten Vision selbst.

Es ist voll verständlich, daß die Redaktion Hinzufügungen negativen Inhalts, Schelt- und Drohworte, an die letzte Vision nicht mehr angehängt hat.[33] Hier war nur noch ein anderer Ton anzuschlagen. Statt dessen konnte vor der letzten Vision in viii 4-14 eine Sammlung von Ergänzungen ihren Platz finden, die ganz unter dem Stichwort *qeṣ* zusammengeordnet ist, hier aber nicht mehr untersucht werden kann.

Für den zweiten Komplex, das Unheilsgedicht mit dem Kehrvers "Doch ihr kehrtet nicht zu mir um, Ausspruch JHWHs" genügen ein paar Bemerkungen. Es wurde hier öfters auf gewisse Erweiterungen hingewiesen,[34] daß aber das Korpus aus einer fünfgliedrigen Plagenaufzählung besteht, ist unbestritten. Doch wie ist diese Fünferstruktur zu beurteilen? Ist es so, wie ein neuerer Kommentar schreibt: "There is no perceptible development in the sections, no heightening of the disasters' intensity. Each is terrible in its own right, no worse than the previous one. The sequence gains its effect from repetition, the recollection of one disaster after another as though the narrative meant to exhaust the catalogue of human misery" (Mays, S. 78)? Die erste Strophe (V. 6) hat es mit dem Mangel an Nahrungsmitteln zu tun, die zweite (V. 7 f.) mit dem Mangel an Wasser. Von Krankheiten oder Zerstörungen u.ä. ist nicht die Rede, es ist nur der Mangel das Thema, der Mangel an Eß- und Trinkbarem. Daß beide Strophen ein Paar bilden und ein solcher Mangel noch die einfachste Erscheinungsform der Katastrophe ist, liegt auf der Hand, mag Durst auch noch viel schlimmer als Hunger sein, so daß eine gewisse Steigerung vorliegt. Die dritte Strophe (V. 9) hat Erkrankung und Zerstörung der Vegetation zum Thema, Getreidebrand und- gilbe, Heuschreckenfraß, die vierte (V. 10) Krankheit und gewaltsamen Tod des Volks. Beides entspricht sich wieder, wenn auch eine Steigerung von der

---

33 Zu ix 7 (f.) vgl. "Das Problem von Amos 9, 7", *Textgemäß* (Göttingen, 1979), S. 33-8.

34 Vgl. die Kommentare, zuletzt z.B. Rudolph, S. 169 ff., J. L. Mays, *Amos* (3. Aufl., London, 1976), S. 76 ff. Daß die ganze Komposition sekundär sein könnte, wofür einiges spricht (vgl. Wolff, S. 250 ff.), tut hier nichts zı r Sache.

Vegetation zum Menschen unverkennbar ist: hier geht es um aktive Eingriffe von außen, nicht mehr bloß um Mangel. Nach diesem zweiten Paar wird das Äußerste in der fünften Strophe (V. 11) erreicht, die von der "Katastrophe" im eigentlichen und extremen Sinn spricht, der *mähpekät ʾälohîm*, dem Untergang wie von Sodom und Gomorrha. Dies läßt sich nicht mehr steigern, und so kommt der Text in V. 12 zum Abschluß, indem er diese Totalität, diese klimaktische Gesamtheit menschlicher Katastrophenerfahrung für die Zukunft androht [35] (V. 12a) und deswegen zur Umkehr, zur Gottesbegegnung im positiven Sinn mahnt (V. 12b).[36] Auf die viel diskutierten Fragen nach Gattung(shintergrund) und Authentizität kann hier nicht eingegangen werden, wo es nur auf den Aufbau selbst ankommt. Dieser ist jedenfalls in eben dem Schema, das auch die Visionen zeigen, gehalten.[37]

Wenden wir uns schließlich der großen Komposition des Völkergedichtes i 3-ii 16 zu! Man sollte hier eigentlich von der fast eine opinio communis zu nennenden [38] Erkenntnis ausgehen können, daß unter den Völkerstrophen die über Tyrus i 9 f., Edom i 11 f. und Juda ii 4 f. sekundär sind. Dem wurde in neuester Zeit zwar öfter widersprochen,[39] aber die starken Unterschiede zu den übrigen

[35] Man sollte nicht bezweifeln (vgl. E. Sellin, *Das Zwölfprophetenbuch* [*KAT* XII, 1922], S. 182, unter Berufung auf Meinhold und Procksch,) daß der Text in V. 6-11 geschehene Ereignisse meint, wenn er gelegentlich bei der dramatischen Ausmalung zum Praesens historicum *übergeht* (wenn nicht an ein iterativum zu denken ist), nie aber so einsetzt.

[36] Zur positiven Bedeutung von *hikkôn* in diesem Zusammenhang vgl. Ex. xix 11, 15, xxxiv 2, auch Ez. xxxviii 7, zu der von *liqrät ʾälohäka* Ex. xix 19, und man beachte schließlich die positive Formulierung "*dein* Gott" mit der Anrede "Israel".

[37] An der poetischen Gestaltung der einzelnen Strophen gibt es manches auszusetzen, doch sind die Strophen bemüht, immer je zwei Erscheinungsformen der jeweiligen Plage zusammenzustellen; V. 6 Hunger: in den Städten nichts, Mangel überall, V. 7 f. Regen: zu frühes Ende, Mangel auch wo es geregnet hat, V. 9 Vegetation: Krankheit und Zerstörung, V. 10 Volk: Krankheit und Tötung, selbst V. 11 bemüht sich mit dem berühmt gewordenen (Sach. iii 2) *ʾûd muṣṣal* eine Parallele zu Sodom und Gomorrha zu bilden.

[38] Vgl. Sh. M. Paul, "Amos 1:3-2:3: A Concatenous Literary Pattern", *JBL* 90 (1971), S. 397-403: S. 397 Anm. 4 in Verbindung mit Anm. 1.

[39] Es seien hier nur genannt neben W. Rudolph, "Die angefochtenen Völkersprüche in Amos 1 und 2", *Schalom* (Berlin, 1971), S. 45-9, und in seinem Kommentar, S. 118 ff.: M. Haran, "The Rise and Decline of the Empire of Jerobeam ben Joash", *VT* 17 (1967), S. 266-97; S. 272 ff., "Observations on the Historical Background of Am. 1:2-2:6", *IEJ* 18 (1968), S. 201-12, M. Weiss, "The Pattern of Numerical Sequence in Amos 1-2", *JBL* 86 (1967), S. 416-23, E. Hammershaimb, *The Book of Amos* (Oxford, 1970), S. 14 f., 21, 26, 35, K. N. Schoville, "A Note

Strophen bedürfen einer Erklärung, und es ist nicht damit getan, sie *möglicherweise* auch für authentisch zu halten: Neben *ʿal* + inf. werden noch weitere Schuldangaben gemacht (i 9bβ, 11b ab *wᵉšiḥet*, ii 4bβγδ), während in der Strafankündigung nur das stereotype [40] "Ich sende Feuer in/nach. . ., und es frißt die Wohnburgen von . . ." erscheint (i 10, 12, ii 5), zu dem jedoch in den echten Fremdvölkersprüchen zwei weitere poetische Verse treten. Der Eindruck, daß das nicht mangelhafte Anpassungen, sondern bewußte Differenzen sind, bestätigt sich durch die eigenartige Tatsache, daß bei der Tyrus-, Edom- und Judastrophe die Botenspruchabschlußformel *ʾamăr YHWH* fehlt; die Redaktion hebt also ausdrücklich diese Strophen ab.[41] Es sind in erster Linie diese auffälligen formalen Differenzierungen,[42] die zur Unterscheidung zweier Überlieferungsebenen führen und eben auch im Sinne der Redaktion führen sollen. Daß aber auch die inhaltliche Deutung der historischen Anspielungen bei Tyrus und Edom *leichter* an eine spätere Zeit als die des Amos und seiner jüngeren Vergangenheit denken läßt, werden selbst diejenigen nicht leugnen, die sich bemühen, zum Nachweis möglicher Echtheit doch nur die Ereignisse vor Amos zum Vergleich heranzuziehen. Ebenso ist der deuteronomische Charakter der Judastrophe eigentlich unbestritten; man versucht höchstens, solche Ausdrucksweise weit zurückzudatieren.

Die beiden neueren Versuche, die formale Geschlossenheit aller Fremdvölkerstrophen zu erweisen – die Judastrophe wird dabei

---

on the Oracles of Amos against Gaza, Tyre, and Edom", *Studies in Prophecy* (*SVT* 26 [1974]), S. 55-63, "The Sins of Aram in Amos 1", *Proceedings of the Sixth World Congress of Jewish Studies* I (Jerusalem, 1977), S. 363-75: S. 364. Zu den formalen Argumenten von Paul und Christensen s.u.

[40] Die auffällige Variation *wᵉhiṣṣăttî ʾeš* statt *wᵉšillăḥtî ʾeš* im Fall der Ammoniterstrophe i 14 erklärt sich aus dem (sekundären) Einfluß von Jer. xlix 2, man vgl. dort die Formulierung *tᵉrûʿăt milḥamā* und vor allem die Identität von Am. i 15 mit Jer. xlix 3b. Daß die Bezüge zwischen Jer. xlix und Am. i betont werden sollen, ergibt sich obendrein aus dem Zusatz Jer. xlix 27.

[41] Die erweiterte Form *ʾamăr ʾadonay YHWH* V. 8 will die Grenzziehung gegenüber den nun folgenden Strophen und damit die engere Zusammengehörigkeit mit der ersten Strophe offensichtlich unterstreichen. Jedenfalls liegt in vii 6bβ der entsprechende Fall vor, die Trennung zwischen der zweiten und dritten Vision gegenüber der Unterscheidung zwischen der ersten und zweiten Vision (nur *ʾamăr YHWH* vii 3) zu betonen (s.o.S. 75 f.).

[42] Der Mangel an Konkretheit, den G. Pfeifer, "Denkformenanalyse als exegetische Methode, erläutert an Amos 1_2-2_{16}", *ZAW* 88 (1976), S. 56-71: S. 62, als Grund für die Unechterklärung der Philisterstrophe angibt, ist zu sehr dem Ermessen überlassen, als daß damit sicher argumentiert werden könnte; sowohl V. 6b als auch die Untergangsdrohung in V. 8bβ sind deutlich genug.

ausgenommen –, können die Abtrennung der Tyrus- und Edomstrophe nicht ausschließen. D. L. Christensen möchte drei Paare von Strophen unterscheiden und muß dann doch zugeben, daß zwischen dem letzten und dem ersten Paar mehr Beziehungen bestehen als zu dem mittleren der Tyrus- und Edomstrophe,[43] und Pauls These einer kettenartigen Stichwortanreihung kann zwar auf die bekannte Nachahmung der vorhergehenden Philisterstrophe durch die Tyrusstrophe (vgl. i 9bα mit i 6b) verweisen, muß aber im Fall einer Verbindung der Edom- zur Ammoniterstrophe eigentlich passen; denn seine Auskunft, *răḥamîm* in V. 11 bedeute nicht "Erbarmen", sondern nach Jdc. v 30 "Mädchen", "Frauen" und verbinde sich so mit den "Schwangeren" in V. 13, ist nicht nur gänzlich unwahrscheinlich (fehlender Parallelismus, in Jdc. v 30 wird die fem. Form *răḥmā* vorausgesetzt), sondern hebt auch das angebliche Prinzip *wörtlicher* Anspielungen auf.[44]

So können wir also im Völkergedicht nach wie vor von einer primären Überlieferung ausgehen, die die Tyrus-, Edom- und Judastrophe noch nicht enthält, und in dieser finden wir wieder das bekannte Fünferschema, d.h. die ersten beiden Fremdvölkerstrophen Aram und Philistäa bilden ein Paar, ein zweites die Ammoniter- und Moabstrophe, und daran schließt sich die Israelstrophe als fünftes Glied, das den entscheidenden Abschluß bildet. Die paarweise Struktur der Fremdvölkersprüche läßt sich zunächst an den Angesprochenen selbst zeigen: Das aramäische Königreich von Damaskus und Philistäa sind die eigentlich existenzbedrohenden Nachbarn Israels, letzteres vor allem in der Frühzeit – und überhaupt erst zur Staatenbildung Israels führend –, aber auch im Zusammenhang mit den furchtbaren Aramäerkriegen der jüngeren Vergangenheit, wie 2 Reg. xii 18, xiii 22 (LXX) zeigen, und jede Situation politischer Schwäche ausnützend. So erscheinen sie in Jes. ix 11 vereint: "Aram von vorn und die Philister von hinten; und sie fraßen Israel mit vollem Maul". Die Ammoniter und Moab sind dagegen geographisch und genealogisch so miteinander verbunden, daß dies keiner weiteren Begründung bedarf. Bei der Ammoniter- und Moabstrophe treten in der Strafankündigung nach der Aussage der Stadtverbrennung die Epiphaniemotive aus der Tradition des heiligen Krieges auf (i 14b, ii 2b) und geben damit diesem Völkerspruchpaar ein besonderes

[43] "The Prosodic Structure of Amos 1-2", *HThR* 67 (1974), S. 427-36: S. 435 f.

[44] Sh. M. Paul, "Amos 1:3-2:3: A Concatenous Literary Pattern", *JBL* 90 (1971), S. 367-403.

Gepräge. Sind auch die angeklagten Vergehen entsprechend zu unterscheiden? Im Fall Arams und Philistäas handelt es sich um kriegsrechtliche Frevel, im Fall der Ammoniter und Moabs offensichtlich um sakralrechtliche. Das Dreschen Gileads mit eisernen Dreschschlitten (i 3b) ist, wie u.a. 2 Reg. xiii 7 zeigt, Metapher für grausame Kriegshandlungen. Die Exilierung ganzer Ortschaften durch die Philister und der Verkauf an Edom (i 6b) ist ebenso als grausame Kriegspraxis zu beurteilen, wird aber sicher noch als gesteigerter Frevel angesehen: Es handelt sich hier nicht um die unmittelbaren Folgen eines äußerst harten gegenseitigen kriegerischen Ringens, sondern um die Ausnützung der Schwäche des anderen, um sich durch Verkauf der versklavten Bevölkerung an Dritte zu bereichern. Jedenfalls wird in der Strafankündigung Arams am Höhepunkt und Ende nur von einer Wegführung gesprochen (i 5b), im Falle der Philister jedoch vom Untergang (i 8bβ). Der Frevel der Ammoniter ist das Aufschlitzen der Schwangeren (i 13b). Mit der Tötung des werdenden Lebens ist die Grenze zum menschlich unverfügbaren sakralen Bereich überschritten ebenso wie beim Frevel am Toten, der vernichtenden Verbrennung der Gebeine des edomitischen Königs durch Moab (ii 1b). Daß hier nicht nur eine polare Zusammenordnung vorgeburtlich – nachtodlich, sondern – ganz gegen unser Empfinden – auch eine Steigerung des Frevels vorausgesetzt wird, kann man an der Strafankündigung ablesen: während bei den Ammonitern nur von einer Wegführung gesprochen wird (i 15), ist im Falle Moabs vom Tod die Rede (ii 2b, 3).

Wie haben es also bei den ursprünglichen Fremdvolkersprüchen deutlich mit zwei Paaren zu tun. Diese Struktur hat sich selbst noch auf die Ergänzung Tyrus – Edom ausgewirkt, die als Paar angefügt wurde, wie der Hinweis auf die jeweils bestehende "Bruderschaft" zeigt. Auf das ursprüngliche Doppelpaar der Fremdvölkersprüche folgt die Israelstrophe, und allein hier finden wir die Vierzahl der Frevel ausgeführt, auf die die stereotype zahlenspruchartige Eingangsformulierung hinweist. Daß der Satz "Wegen dreier Frevel von X und wegen vier nehme ich es [45] nicht zurück" nach den Gesetzen des Zahlenspruchs eine Vierheit meint, sollte man nicht bestrei-

[45] Daß der "Zorn Gottes" in i 3-ii 16 nie ausdrücklich genannt wird, macht die These von R. P. Knierim, " 'I will not cause it to return' in Amos 1 and 2", *Canon and Authority* (Philadelphia, 1977), S. 163-75, das Suffix bezöge sich auf ein *'ăppî*, doch schwierig. Gerade die Unbestimmtheit des "es" bringt das unheimlich Drohende zum Ausdruck.

ten,[46] und tatsächlich werden im Falle Israels vier Frevel aufgezählt: Das sind 1. (V. 6b) die unbillige Härte in der Anwendung der Schuldknechtschaft, 2. (V. 7a) die wirtschaftlich-soziale und rechtliche Bedrückung der Armen, 3. (V. 7b) ein inzestartiges Sexualvergehen mit sozialem Hintergrund, 4. (V. 8) Opfervergehen durch Benutzung von Gepfändetem und von Strafleistungen. Die Tatsache, daß bedingt durch den Parallelismus membrorum in drei Fällen das jeweilige Vergehen in einer doppelten Erscheinungsform vorgeführt wird, darf nicht zu der Ansicht führen, hier seien vielmehr sieben Vergehen genannt; die durch den Parallelismus notwendige Betrachtung eines Vergehens unter doppeltem Aspekt ist etwas völlig anderes als eine Aufzählung zweier verschiedener Vergehen. Schuldknechtschaft ist eine unbillige Härte und nicht anzuwenden in den Fällen, daß der Schuldner sonst als zuverlässig bekannt ist (*ṣaddîq* ii 6bα) oder die Schuld ganz geringfügig ist ("wegen [47] ein paar Sandalen" ii 6bβ; vgl. die ähnliche Ausdruckweise 1 Sam. xii 3 [LXX], Sir. xlvi 19); beide Fälle sind die zwei Aspekte, die die Unbilligkeit bestimmen. Ebenso gehören zusammen die Formen der Bedrückung des Armen als wirtschaftlich-soziale und rechtliche Bedrückung, die in der metaphorischen Ausdrucksweise [48] von V. 7a gemeint sein müssen, dem Treten gegen den Kopf der Armen [49] und der Beugung ihres Weges (vgl. Beugung im Sinne der Rechtsbeugung in Ex. xxiii 2, 6; Dtn. xxiv 17, xxvii 19; Prov. xvii 23, xviii 5; Jes. x 2 u.a.St.). Und daß das Opfervergehen durch gepfändete Gegenstände und durch solche, die man als Bußleistung erhalten hat, herbeigeführt wird, kann schließlich auch nicht dazu führen, in

---

[46] M. Weiss, "The Pattern of Numerical Sequence in Amos 1-2", *JBL* 86 (1967), S. 416-23 (vgl. *Tarbiz* 36 [1966/67], S. 307-18), möchte in dieser Ausdrucksweise sieben (als Ausdruck für Gesamtheit) Frevel gemeint sehen, weil hier erst im zweiten Teil der Satzkern "nehme ich es nicht zurück" erscheint. Es ist aber leicht einzusehen, daß bei der vorliegenden strophischen Aufreihung schon im ersten Teil der Volksname erscheinen muß, so daß für den Satzkern im 3 + 3-Vers kein anderer Platz bleibt. Jedenfalls wäre dieser Fall einer additiven Auffassung des Zahlenspruchs ohne jedes Beispiel.

[47] Das *bă*ʿ*ᵃbûr* ist vom *bᵉ* pretii in V. 6bα zu unterscheiden.

[48] Ein wörtliches Verständnis, wie es Rudolph, S. 138 f., vertritt, würde weder einen klaren Rechtsfall (schlechte Behandlung?) ergeben noch in die Reihe der Vergehen passen.

[49] Die beliebte Ausscheidung von *ʿăl ʿᵃpăr ʾäräṣ* hat eigentlich nur metrische Gründe hinter sich. Wir haben aber in dieser Komposition der Anklagen deutlich eine Metrumssteigerung vor uns: Während V. 6b noch ein Sechser ist, findet sich in V. 7b ein Achter, in V. 8 5 + 5; es wäre also für V. 7a ein Siebener (4 + 3) ganz plausibel.

diesem Parallelismus zwei besonders zu zählende Einzelvergehen zu finden.

Es ist deutlich, daß bei allen vier Vergehensarten im Hintergrund eine Ausnutzung der wirtschaftlichen und äußerlich-rechtlichen Machtposition gegenüber den Armen steht, und doch sind die Vergehen sehr verschiedener Art. Die ersten beiden sind profanrechtlicher Natur, die zweiten sakralrechtlicher Natur. Beide Paare stellen eine sich steigernde Abfolge dar. Die unbillige Härte der Schuldknechtschaft (V. 6b) setzt wenigstens noch einen zu Recht bestehenden Anspruch voraus, ist eben nur eine Unbilligkeit, während bei der wirtschaftlichen und rechtlichen Bedrückung (V. 7a) eindeutiges Unrecht geschieht. Die Anklage, daß "ein Mann und sein Vater zu ein und demselben Mädchen (das will der Artikel sagen [50]) gehen", ist sehr verschieden gedeutet worden.[51] Die Formulierung "ein Mann und sein Vater" zeigt, daß der entscheidende Punkt im Inzestuösen liegt. R. Bach [52] hat auf die Inzestverbote des Verkehrs des Sohnes mit der Frau des Vaters (Lev. xviii 8, xx 11) und des Verkehrs des Vaters mit seiner Schwiegertochter (Lev. xviii 15, xx 12) verwiesen. Und wenn auch der Verkehr eines Mannes mit einer Frau und deren Tochter verboten wird (Lev. xviii 17, xx 14), ist die hier zugrundeliegende sakralrechtliche Vorstellung deutlich: die Konkurrenz zweier sich ausschließender sexueller und familiärer Bezüge, indem die Verbindung mit der einen Frau die anders verbundenen Personen Vater und Sohn [53] unter sexuellem Aspekt vereint.[54] Bei aller sozialen Repression, die bei der *nă῾arā* im Hintergrund steht, ist doch das sakralrechtliche Vergehen als solches im Vordergrund. Das wird durch V. 7bγ "um meinen heiligen Namen zu

---

[50] Auf diesen Artikel im poetischen Kontext (!) wird von manchen Erklärern nicht eingegangen, auch wenn sie gegen die Meinung Stellung nehmen, es handele sich um ein und dasselbe Mädchen, z.B. L. Markert, *Struktur und Bezeichnung des Scheltworts* (*BZAW* 140, 1977), S. 79 Anm. 187.

[51] Wie der Ausdruck *nă῾arā* zeigt, zielt die Aussage höchstwahrscheinlich nicht auf die sakrale Prostitution, und auch ein Abhängigkeitsverhältnis im Sinne der *'amā* von Ex. xxi 7 ff. ist hier nicht *ausdrücklich* vorausgesetzt.

[52] "Gottesrecht und weltliches Recht in der Verkündigung des Propheten Amos", *Festschrift für Günther Dehn* (Neukirchen, 1957), S. 23-34: S. 30 ff.

[53] Die obige Deutung erklärt auch die eigentümliche Formulierung "ein Mann und sein Vater" statt "ein Mann und sein Sohn"; denn das Vergehen gegen den Vater (Mutter/Stiefmutter-Sphäre) ist noch frevelhafter als das gegen den Sohn (Schwiegertochter-Sphäre).

[54] Die Meinung von Wolff, S. 203, hier sei der Fall einer "werdenden Ehe" vorausgesetzt, bei der "der alte, verheiratete Vater das Liebesverhältnis des Sohnes stört", hat gegen sich, daß dann nur der Vater angeklagt werden sollte.

entweihen" eigens hervorgehoben.[55] Sakralrechtlichen Charakter hat auch das letzte der vier angeprangerten Vergehen. Wird das übersehen, so kommt die Auslegung in Schwierigkeiten. Weder kann es sich hier am Ende und Höhepunkt des klimaktisch aufgebauten Komplexes von Anklagen bloß um Taktlosigkeiten handeln, noch greift Amos die Rechtsinstitute der Pfändung und Bußzahlung an sich an, und daß es sich um unrechtmäßige Pfändung oder Bußzahlung handelt, davon – das wäre dann das Entscheidende – wird nichts gesagt. Vielmehr ist die Verwendung des gepfändeten oder als Strafe abgeführten Fremdgutes im Opferkult das Thema. Wir haben keine alttestamentlichen Sakralrechtssätze, die die Verwendung von Fremdgut im Kult untersagen, und es könnte sein, daß die eigene Anschauung des Propheten von dem vor Gott erscheinenden Menschen das damals sakralrechtlich Definierte erheblich überschreitet. Wir können aber sagen, daß das Wesentliche dieser letzten Anklage ist, daß wirtschaftliche Ansprüche gegenüber anderen (Pfändung) und rechtliche Ansprüche (Bußleistung), die noch dazu in der gegebenen sozialen Situation allesamt zweifelhaft sind, zur Veranstaltung eines Gottesdienstes ausgenützt werden, bei dem es doch um die Darbringung des göttlichen Segensgutes und die Teilhabe daran geht; [56] d.h. trotz des sozialen Hintergrundes handelt es sich um ein sakralrechtliches Vergehen, um die innere Verfälschung des Opferkultes.

Wir haben in ii 6-8 eine wohlaufgebaute Vierheit von Vergehen vor uns, zwei sich steigernde zivilrechtliche, unbillige Härte bei bestehenden Schuldansprüchen und wirtschaftlich-rechtliche Unterdrückung, zwei sakralrechtliche, die Sphäre des geschlechtlichen Verkehrs und des Gottesdienstes betreffend. Es legt sich nahe bei

---

[55] Man darf weder V. 7bγ (Wolff, S. 163, Markert, S. 72) noch V. 8aβ (dieselben, aber schon Marti, S. 168 u.a.) streichen. Zum Metrum s. oben Anm. 49. Daß sich die Wendung V. 7bγ erst bei Ezechiel und im Heiligkeitsgesetz findet, ist nur ein relatives Argument, da wir wenig altes sakralrechtliches Material haben; immerhin dürfte der technische Begriff der Heiligkeit des Namens schon in vordeuteronomischer Zeit vorausgesetzt werden können (vgl. Wendungen wie *hizkîr ʾät šem YHWH*, *qaraʾ bešem YHWH*), zu dem *ḥillel* den einfachen Gegensatz bildet. Dieser Terminus des Profanierens ist vordeuteronomisch natürlich auch vorauszusetzen, vgl. Gen. xlix 4, wohl auch Ex. xx 25. Vor allem würde bei einer Streichung der Parallelstichos fehlen. Man könnte höchstens annehmen, daß V. 7bγ die korrekte spätere Ausdrucksweise eines ursprünglich anders formulierten Textes darstelle.- Bei den Streichungen in V. 8 wird übersehen, daß hier tatsächlich sakralrechtliche Vergehen vorliegen.

[56] Beim transitiven Hiphil *yăṭṭû* sind die Objekte, die ausgebreitet werden, nicht genannt. Zu dieser Ausbreitung neben dem Altar werden die gepfändeten Kleider benützt, so daß auch sie zur Opferzeremonie gehören.

der durch die Zahlenspruchform betonten inneren Systematik und Totalität dieser Vierheit, dies mit den vier genannten Vergehen der Fremdvölker zu vergleichen. Den zwei zivilrechtlichen Vergehen entsprechen zwei kriegsrechtliche Frevel, auch hier in sich steigernder Abfolge in dem Sinn, daß im ersten Fall die grausame Härte das Entscheidende ist bei einer gegenseitigen Auseinandersetzung, im zweiten Fall der direkte räuberische Eingriff von sich aus, bloß zum eigenen Vorteil. Die dritte und vierte Freveltat ist sakralrechtlicher Art wie die entsprechenden Vergehen Israels. Der Frevel am werdenden Leben gehört dabei derselben geschlechtlichen Sphäre an, der das menschliche Leben entstammt, wie das Inzestvergehen in Israel, während irgendeine Korrespondenz im vierten Fall ausgeschlossen zu sein scheint. In der Tat, was könnte der Sphäre des Gottesdienstes nun bei den Fremdvölkern anderes entsprechen als ein Götzendienst, an dem man keinen Frevel exemplifizieren kann. Und doch findet sich in Hinsicht auf das Letzte menschlicher Erfahrung eine Entsprechung: der Bereich der Ehrfurcht vor dem Tod kann bei den Völkern als letzte Kategorie die Aufzählung so beschließen wie der Bereich des Gottesdienstes im Falle Israels. Diese erstaunliche Entsprechung der Freveltaten der Völker und der Israels, begründet in der Feindschaft der Völker untereinander wie in der der Einzelmenschen in Israel, wirft ein besonderes Licht auf die Sünde Israels, die durchaus in Korrespondenz steht mit jenen schauderhaften Freveln der Völker, vor denen jeder Israelit zurückschreckt. Die Korrespondenz läßt auch erkennen, daß das unter Gottes Autorität stehende Gesetz in Israel eine Entsprechung hat in dem allgemeinen Rechtsverständnis, das sich menschlicher Einsicht erschließt.

Wir verstehen endlich auch, warum nicht bei jedem Volk, wie die Zahlenspruchformulierung anzukündigen scheint, eine Vierheit von Freveln aufgezählt wird, sondern nur jeweils *ein* Verbrechen. Die Zahlenspruchform deutet eine Totalität von Sünde bei jedem Volk an, bereitet aber wegen der Nennung von je einer Sünde bei vier Völkern auf eine entsprechende Vierheit des Völkerfrevels vor. So wird die fünfte, die Israelstrophe, auch inhaltlich mit den Fremdvölkersprüchen verknüpft. Ebenso wenig wie diese nur die Funktion eines Vorspanns haben und bloß auf Einverständnis der Hörer aus sind, so ist andererseits die Israelstrophe nie ein selbständiges Stück gewesen. Das Ganze bildet ein geschlossenes Fünferschema, und dies wird durch das zahlenspruchartige System der Frevelaufzählungen besonders zusammengehalten.

Wir beobachteten, daß am Ende der fünften Vision in der Reihung der *'im*-Sätze (ix 2-4) die Fünferstruktur noch einmal auftritt. Das ist auch im Fall von i 3-ii 16 so, wo am Ende in ii 14-16 sich eine solche Reihung von Sätzen findet, die ein sich steigerndes Unheilsgeschehen malen. Man hat längst erkannt, daß hier V. 14b und V. 15aβ Hinzufügungen sind;[57] sie wiederholen das stärkste negative Prädikat mit der Todesaussage von V. 15b und sind auch Wiederholungen in der Subjektwahl, wobei die erste Hinzufügung den letzten Satz aufnimmt, die zweite dagegen den ersten. Sehen wir von diesen eindeutig vervollständigenden Additionen ab, so ergibt sich erstens ein Paar die Fußtruppe betreffend: der Schnelle, der nicht fliehen, der Starke, der nicht kraftvoll sein kann, zweitens ein Paar die Wagentruppe betreffend: der Bogenschütze, der nicht standhalten, der Wagenlenker, der sein Leben nicht retten kann, und, schließlich in der Klimax die stärkste und allgemeinste Aussage, jetzt rein positiv formuliert: der beherzte Vorkämpfer, der nur nackt, ohne Waffen, zu fliehen versucht—also unsere bekannte Fünferstruktur. Man könnte darüber spekulieren, ob die auffällige Ergänzung zu einer Siebeneraufzählung wohl zusammenhängt mit der Ergänzung der Fremdvölkersprüche zu einer Siebenergruppe; die allerdings nur äußerlich siebenteilige Aufzählung der Vergehen Israels mag diese Umkomposition zur Siebenerstruktur befördert haben. Es wäre ja auch seltsam, wenn redaktionelle Ergänzungen und Überarbeitungen, die notwendigerweise die alte Komposition überdecken, nicht ihrerseits eine neue Strukturierung versuchen.

Wir haben in der Untersuchung der Großkompositionen im Amosbuch überall eine Fünferstruktur gefunden, die im Grunde eine Dreistufigkeit zeigt, wobei die ersten beiden Stufen eben als Paare erscheinen. Wir konnten dieses Schema als Steigerungssystem verstehen, dessen höchste und letzte Stufe, Höhepunkt und Ziel des Ganzen, für sich allein stehen mußte. Daß diese Kompositionsform allgemein verbreitet und nicht auf das Amosbuch beschränkt ist, bedarf keines Beweises; es mag nur auf ein bekanntes Beispiel hingewiesen werden, die Gestaltung der Erzählung von den ägyptischen Plagen bei P:

I. Das Wasser. a. Die Verwandlung von Wasser in Blut (Ex vii

---

[57] H. Greßmann, *Die älteste Geschichtsschreibung und Prophetie Israels* (*SAT* II 1, 2. Aufl. 1921), S. 335 bzw. Textkritische Anmerkungen S. 12, Wolff, S. 164, zuletzt Markert, S. 73.

19-20aα, 21b-22); b. Die Verwandlung von Wasser in Frösche (viii 1-3, 11aγδb)

II. Das Trockene. a. Staub wird zu Mücken (viii 12-15); b. Ruß wird zu Beulen (ix 8-12)

III. Die Tötung der Erstgeburt.

Das System ist nach dem Ausgeführten ohne weiteres zu verstehen, und auch hier sind es wie bei Amos die göttlichen Gerichtsakte, die in diesem System erscheinen. Doch soll das nicht heißen, daß die Fünferstruktur speziell für einen solchen Inhalt verwendet worden sei. Es bedürfte weiterer Untersuchungen, um die traditionelle Verwendung einer solchen Kompositionsform für bestimmte Inhalte – natürlich höchstens im Sinne einer gewissen Affinität – wahrscheinlich zu machen.

LA DESCRIPTION DE LA VIEILLESSE EN QOHELET XII 1-7 EST-ELLE ALLÉGORIQUE?

par

MAURICE GILBERT

Rome

C'est in lieu commun de l'exégèse de considérer Qoh. xii 1-7 comme une allégorie du grand âge. Mais c'est aussi une banalité de redire ce qu'observait déjà Jérôme au sujet de ce texte: *tot paene sententiae quot homines*! L'exégèse ancienne, au moins jusqu'à la Renaissance, a connu et défendu plusieurs interprétations du même texte, et si la lecture allégorique s'est imposée à beaucoup jusqu'aujourd'hui, elle le doit surtout à Jérôme, qui, on le sait, la tenait du judaïsme. Mais, outre que les commentateurs ne s'entendent pas sur le détail des interprétations allégoriques ni même sur les versets où, à leurs yeux, elle devrait s'imposer, il faut redire que la lecture allégorique n'est pas la seule qui, de ce texte, se soit maintenue pendant des siècles: Hippolyte de Rome, Grégoire le Thaumaturge et Didyme l'Aveugle ont défendu une interprétation de type eschatologique. Même si cette dernière ne reçoit plus d'écho aujourd'hui, pas plus d'ailleurs qu'une interprétation juive ancienne qui lisait le texte à la lumière de l'histoire d'Israël, il paraît difficile de dire que la lecture allégorique s'impose: voici plus d'un siècle déjà, en 1874, C. Taylor l'avait contestée vigoureusement, et d'autres l'ont suivi.[1]

Mais qu'entend-on par allégorie? Je prends la définition de D. Buzy: "Une allégorie est une suite de métaphores coordonnées qui possèdent toutes une signification propre... et le tout constitue un tableau".[2]

J'ajouterai que l'allégorie, aux dires des commentateurs qui l'acceptent, ne se trouve pas dans l'ensemble de Qoh. xii 1-7. Si l'on précise qu'il y a allégorie physiologique dans ces versets, — et c'est ce qu'entendent les commentateurs depuis Jérôme, — alors la majorité d'entre eux ne la trouvent qu'aux versets 3, 4 et 5b; mais, je le répète, leur accord est loin d'être parfait.

---

[1] Cf. J. F. A. Sawyer, "The Ruined House in Ecclesiastes 12: A Reconstruction of the Original Parable", *JBL* 94 (1975), p. 520, n. 5.

[2] "Le portrait de la vieillesse (*Ecclésiaste*, xii, 1-7)", *RB* 41 (1932), p. 340.

Ceci dit, il faut, me semble-t-il, dans l'analyse du texte, le prendre tel qu'il est. Je ne crois pas que retirer certains passages, comme le propose encore récemment A. Lauha pour xii 1, 3-5, 7,[3] ou modifier le texte hébreu, au moins consonantique, comme le fait J. F. A. Sawyer (pp. 519-31) pour xii 3-5, soit la meilleure voie à suivre. Le texte est certes difficile, et au moins aux versets 4-5 à la limite de l' intelligibilité, sinon au-delà. Il vaut cependant la peine de l'accepter au maximum.

Enfin, pour aborder le texte correctement, il convient de le situer dans son contexte, ce que je ferai immédiatement en en soulignant la structure littéraire.

La structure littéraire d'ensemble de Qoh. xi 7-xii 8

Malgré la division traditionnelle en chapitre, la majorité des commentateurs modernes font débuter l'ultime grande péricope de l'œuvre de Qohelet en xi 7 et voient son terme en xii 8. Un certain nombre d'indices littéraires, souvent méconnus, confirment ces limites généralement acceptées.

Un premier indice permettant de structurer Qoh. xi 7-xii 8 se trouve dans le triple emploi du mot fondamental *hèbèl*: on le trouve en effet, toujours en conclusion, à la fin de xi 8, de xi 10 et en xii 8. Ce dernier emploi en xii 8 sert de conclusion finale aux dits de Qohelet et forme, on le sait, la grande inclusion du livre avec i 2. En Qoh. xi 8 et 10, *hèbèl* conclut simplement un élément du discours. Le cas est fréquent dans le livre, où *hèbèl* apparaît le plus souvent en conclusion d'une observation ou d'une réflexion de l'auteur. Les derniers cas se trouvent en viii 10 et 14. Quant au sens de *hèbèl* en xi 8, 10, l'auteur pense, semble-t-il, à la vie humaine, ou plus précisément à l'une de ses étapes, la vieillesse en xi 8, mais aussi la jeunesse selon xi 10, tandis que, comme en vi 12; vii 15 et ix 9, il vise en xii 8 l'ensemble de la vie humaine. Ce premier indice conduit à distinguer trois parties: xi 7-8, xi 9-10, xxii 1-8.

Un second indice confirme les conclusions tirées du premier. En xi 7-8, tous les verbes sont à la troisième personne, mais surtout on trouve deux jussifs placés curieusement à la jointure centrale de xi 8: *yiśmâḥ wᵉyizkôr*, "qu'il se réjouisse et qu'il se souvienne". Or les deux mêmes verbes reviendront, mais séparément, et comme impératifs, en tête des deux parties suivantes: *śᵉmaḥ*, "réjouis-toi",

[3] *Kohelet* (Neukirchen-Vluyn, 1978), pp. 204 ss.

au début de xi 9, et *ûz^ekôr*, "et souviens-toi", au commencement de xii 1. Le *waw* initial de *ûzekôr* souligne bien que le verbe doit être lié à celui qui ouvre xi 9, *ś^emaḥ*. On ne peut guère échapper à l'impression que les deux verbes centraux de xi 8, "se réjouir" et "se souvenir", sont en fait des indices d'une annonce de thème.[4] De nouveau, la division xi 7-8, xi 9-10, xii 1-8 se trouve soulignée.

Mais il faut observer que la deuxième partie, xi 9-10, présente une structure complexe. Elle me paraît concentrique, et ce point mérite attention. Après les encouragements très positifs à se réjouir en xi 9a, vient une phrase qui apparaît comme une antithèse: "mais sache que sur tout cela Dieu te fera venir en jugement" (xi 9b). Toutefois xi 10a reprend le même thème que xi 9a, mais sur un ton négatif: écarte toute peine et de ton cœur et de ta chair. Le rapport entre xi 9a et 10 est encore souligné par la reprise de quelques termes: *yaldût*, "jeunesse", en xi 9a et 10b, et *libbekâ*, "ton cœur", deux fois en xi 9a et une fois en xi 10a. Ainsi, xi 9b apparaît isolé, central même. Certes naguère beaucoup de commentateurs considéraient cette phrase de xi 9b comme une addition. Il me semble que la position centrale de cette phrase en souligne l'importance et prépare le développement de xii 1. En effet les deux verbes clés, "se réjouir" et "se souvenir", de xi 9a et xii 1 sont en quelque sorte doublés; le premier négativement avec les verbes de xi 10a: "éloigne", et le second par le verbe de xi 9b: *wedâʿ*. La pensée de l'auteur semble se déployer en deux temps: réjouis-toi, mais sache; écarte la peine, mais souviens-toi. Pourtant ce dernier impératif *ûzekôr* ouvre certainement le développement de xii 1-8, et le *hèbèl* de xi 10b clôt si nettement, je crois, la deuxième partie, xi 9-10, qu'il semble préférable de souligner la complémentarité de xi 9a ("réjouis-toi") et de xi 10a ("écarte la peine"), et de considérer xi 9b comme une amorce en contrepoint du "mais souviens-toi" de xii 1.

Dès lors, la mention de *hâʾĕlôhîm* en xi 9b s'explique et se révèle significative: la référence à Dieu, centrale dans la deuxième partie (xi 9-10), se retrouvera, plus marquée encore, aux extrêmes de la troisième: "ton Créateur" (xx 1) et *hâʾĕlôhîm* (xii 7).

Quelques indices complémentaires montrent encore d'autres liens entre les trois parties ainsi délimitées: 1) le thème de la lumière et du soleil en xi 7 reviendra en xii 2, mais dans l'ordre inverse, de même que le thème de l'obscurité qui vient en xi 8 revient en xii 2, 3; 2) le thème

---

[4] Avec E. Glasser, *Le procès du bonheur par Qohelet* (Paris, 1970), p. 167.

des années et des jours qui est fondamental en xi 8 reparaît en xi 9 pour les jours et en xii 1 pour les années comme pour les jours; 3) l'expression *bîmé — b^{e}ḥurôtèkâ*, "aux jours de ton adolescence", qui se lit en xi 9 et en xii 1, met un certain parallélisme entre le début de la deuxième partie et celui de la troisième.

Toutes ces observations permettent de mieux voir comment xii 1-8 se rattache à ce qui précède et, en particulier, comment le début et la fin de cette péricope qui nous interéresse ici, xii 1-2, 7-8, sont littérairement lies à xi 9-10 et plus encore à xi 7-8. En outre, il est curieux de constater que les versets 3-6, les plus énigmatiques, échappent à ces rapports verbaux avec xi 7-8, 9-10, hormis des récurrences secondaires en xii 3 (*ḥšk*) et 5 (*hâ'âdâm*).

La structure de Qoh. xii 1-7

Quelques éléments peuvent souligner la structure des versets xii 1-7. Le principal est sans conteste la reprise de *'ad 'ašèr lô'* en xii 1b, 2a, 6a. Cette conjonction composée signifie littéralement "jusqu'à ce que... ne pas", et ici "avant que..."; mais à l'exception de 1 R. xvii 17 où la nuance est simplement "jusqu'à ce que... ne pas", de même qu'en 1 S. xxx 4 (avec *'ad 'ăšèr 'én*), l'Ancien Testament connaît surtout la forme positive *'ad 'ăšèr*, "jusqu'à ce que", et plusieurs fois elle est suivie du verbe *bw'*, "venir" (Gn. xxxiii 14; 2 Chr. ix 6; Neh. ii 7, iv 5) qu'on trouve en Qoh. xii 1b. Cela revient à dire que l'usage de cette conjonction composée en Qoh. xii est en partie original. Il développe l'idée contenue dans l'expression clé "aux jours de ton adolescence" (xii 1; cf. xi 9): il y aura un contraste fondamental entre le temps de la jeunesse, vécu "avant que vienne" l'autre, et celui de la vieillesse, celui des jours d'obscurité (xi 8b).

Mais la série des trois subordonnées introduites par *'ad 'ăšèr lô'* présente des variations stylistiques importantes. La première subordonnée (xii 1bc) conserve une référence explicite au disciple (*tô'mar*, "tu diras"). La deuxième (xii 2-5), qui est centrale, ne se réfère plus explicitement au disciple, pas plus d'ailleurs que la troisième (xii 6-7), mais elle comporte une longue insertion (xii 3-5) où généralement les commentateurs trouvent l'allégorie physiologique. Cependant dans cette insertion, on notera l'unité de xii 3-4a: en plus de l'unité thématique, dont nous reparlerons, il y a le fait que les verbes extrêmes ("au jour où tremblent" et "tandis que baisse") ont une tournure temporelle explicite, tandis que les autres verbes sont tous au parfait inversif avec *waw*;[5] par contre, en xii 4b-5b, les verbes sont à l'imparfait avec *waw* de simple coordination. En outre, en xii 3-4a l'ordre des éléments des propositions est toujours le même, verbe suivi du sujet, et six propositions se succèdent, avec une légère expansion à la fin de la troisième, c'est-à-dire au centre. Mais en xii 4b-5b, une telle symétrie disparaît pour reparaître en xii 6-7, comme nous le dirons.

Qoh. xii 1

"Souviens-toi de ton Créateur aux jours de ton adolescence": tel est le sens traditionnel de ce stique, et je voudrais montrer que *bôr'èkâ* malgré le *yod* doit se comprendre au sens de "ton Créateur". Le *yod* donne alors une forme majestative, analogue à la forme plurielle *'ělôhîm*.

Que nous apprend le contexte? En xi 8, l'auteur invite le disciple non seulement à jouir des années qu'il lui est donné de vivre, mais à se souvenir des jours d'obscurité, à se mettre bien en tête qu'ils viendront. En xi 9, Qohelet encourage le jeune homme à profiter du temps de sa jeunesse, mais aussi à savoir que Dieu le fera venir en jugement "sur tout cela". Qoh. xii 1 invite alors ce disciple à garder présent à la mémoire son "Créateur"; au terme de la péricope, Qohelet évoquera la mort proprement dite: "et la poussière retourne à la terre selon ce qu'elle était, et le souffle retourne à Dieu qui l'a donné" (xii 7). Or si ce verset xii 7 s'inspire de l'anthropologie simple utilisée en Gn. ii 7 et iii 19, le terme *rûaḥ* ne vient pas de Gn., mais il se trouve en contexte analogue en Ps. civ 29bc-30, cxlvi 4a; Job xxxiv 14-15; Qoh. iii 20-21 (cf. Sir. xl 11 hébreu): le contexte est toujours en relation avec l'acte créateur. Au reste la *rûaḥ* a été donnée précisément à la création.

Ainsi, pour évoquer la mort, Qohelet se réfère à la création; le cercle s'achève: la fin est liée au début. C'est pourquoi il ne faut pas s'étonner de voir en xii 1 une mention explicite du Créateur: se souvenir de lui ne signifie pas un retour au passé originel, mais une attention portée sur la fin où la *rûaḥ* donnée aux origines retournera à celui qui l'a donnée.

L'invitation à se souvenir, adressée ici au disciple, est surtout d'allure sapientielle: il s'agit de se mettre en tête un fait d'avenir, et non pas du passé. On trouve principalement de tels emplois du

---

[5] Notée par Sawyer, p. 524.

verbe "se souvenir" dans des textes plus récents que Qohelet. Quelques-uns sont particulièrement proches de Qoh. xii 1. On lit dans la sagesse de Ben Sira:

Ne te range pas parmi les pécheurs:
souviens-toi que la Colère ne tardera pas.
Abaisse grandement l'orgueil,
car l'espoir de l'homme, c'est la vermine! (Sir. vii 16 hb. corr.)
En toutes tes œuvres, souviens-toi de la fin,
et pour toujours tu ne pécheras pas. (Sir. vii 36 hb.)
Souviens-toi que tous nous devons être réunis. (Sir. viii 7b hb.)

Un passage de Tobie mérite aussi d'être cité: avant de mourir, le vieux Tobit donne à son fils Tobie des conseils de sagesse, parmi lequels on trouve celui-ci, qui ne dépend pas de la Sagesse d'Ahiqar:

Tous tes jours, souviens-toi de "ton Créateur"
et tu ne pécheras pas devant lui. (Tob. iv 5)

Nous avons donné le texte hébreu de Münster, alors que, pour la LXX, le Sinaiticus donne "Seigneur" et le Vaticanus "notre Dieu".[6]

Dans le Testament de Job, qui date du Ier siècle de notre ère, on lit encore:

Et maintenant, mes enfants, voici que je vais mourir. Seulement n'oubliez pas le Seigneur; faites du bien aux pauvres...(45)

Toutes ces observations incitent à penser qu'en Qoh. xii 1 le conseil du sage au jeune disciple implique la référence à la mort (xii 7), au jugement de Dieu (xi 9), et qu'il constitue une invitation discrète à ne pas pécher.

Le dit d'Aqabia ben Mahalalel, antérieur à 70 de notre ère, confirme cette interprétation, tout en laissant entendre que le texte consonantique de Qoh. xii 1a était déjà soumis à diverses lectures:

Considère trois choses
et tu tomberas pas au pouvoir du péché:
sache ta source (*beʾérekâ*),
où tu vas (*bôrekâ*, "ta fosse")
et à qui tu auras à rendre compte, le Roi des rois des rois (Pirqè Abot iii 1).

[6] Ce verset existe dans les fragments inédits araméens et hébreux trouvés dans la grotte 4 de Qumrân: cf. J. T. Milik, *RB* 73 (1966), p. 522, n. 3.

Ce dernier texte confirme la lecture "ton Créateur", connue également de la version grecque conservée dans la LXX et due probablement à Aquila.[7]

Un ultime texte de Ben Sira montre que le participe de *bârâ'*, utilisé pour désigner Dieu, était employé par les sages dans leur enseignement à propos du péché:

> Il irrite son Créateur celui méprise sa mère (iii 16b hb).

Le jeune homme est invité à se souvenir de son Créateur aux jours de son adolescence, c'est-à-dire aux jours heureux dont xi 9-10 l'a invité à profiter. Mais Qohelet commence ici de nouvelles précisions qui occuperont xii 1-7. Les jours de l'adolescence précèdent les jours mauvais, les années dont on dit: "je ne les aime pas!". En raison de l'opposition, ce ne peut être que les vieux jours, le temps de la décrépitude.

Qoh. xii 2

Le verset xii 2 précise une nouvelle fois, mais en reprenant en son début les termes de xi 7-8: "avant que s'obscurcissent le soleil et la lumière", c'est-à-dire qu'en ces jours, la douceur et le plaisir auront disparu (xi 7). Mais en ajoutant "la lune et les étoiles", une addition aux yeux de beaucoup, le texte fournit une expression polaire: ni de jour ni de nuit, il n'y aura de bonheur. En poursuivant: "et que reviennent les nuages après la pluie", Qohelet insiste encore: point de bonheur, sans cesse le ciel bouché comme en hiver. C'est l'hiver de l'homme, avec les moments les plus pénibles comparables aux averses hivernales. Aucun espoir de voir se réaliser le dicton: "après la pluie le beau temps": les améliorations ne sont même pas encourageantes, puisque le ciel reste bouché. L'homme ne sortira pas de son hiver!

Ainsi jusqu'à présent, tout peut s'expliquer parfaitement par de simples métaphores générales, sans aucun recours à une allégorie physiologique poussée. Mais qu'en est-il dans les versets suivants?

Qoh. xii 3-4a

On l'a dit, xii 3-4a forme une unité. Faut-il voir dans l'expression "au jour où" une précision de l'image précédente de l'hiver? Rien dans les versets 3-4a ne permet de le dire. Il s'agit plutôt d'une nouvelle image qui poursuit, non le symbole, mais ce qui est symbolisé: l'homme perd ses forces. De nouveaux symboles interviennent, et

[7] Cf. D. Barthélemy, *Les devanciers d'Aquila*, *SVT* 10 (Leiden, 1963), pp. 21-30.

ce fait est courant dans la poésie biblique. R. Gordis l'a dit;[8] j'ajouterai un seul autre cas: pour inviter son disciple à rechercher la Sagesse, Ben Sira, en vi 23-31, se sert successivement des images de l'esclavage, de la chasse, de la possession amoureuse et du sacerdoce. Ici en Qoh. xii 3-4a, l'image est celle de la maison bourgeoise, ou plus exactement de ses habitants. En xii 3, Qohelet décrit successivement les serviteurs et les maîtres (les "nobles", cf. 2 R. xxiv 16; Sir. xliv 6 hb, plutôt que des "hommes de guerre"), les servantes (ce sont elles qui normalement moulent: Ex. xi 5; Job xxxi 10; Is. xlvii 2) et leurs maîtresses. Cette succession est une nouvelle série d'expressions polaires qui signifie que tous sont atteints, hommes et femmes, maîtres et serviteurs; tous deviennent incapables de tenir leur rôle.

Le résultat est indiqué en xii 4a: "les portes sont fermées sur la rue, tandis que baisse le son du moulin". Si l'on moud le soir, comme on le reconnaît souvent, le vers est cohérent: l'homme atteint le soir de sa vie, comme on dit aujourd'hui, le temps de l'obscurité; l'isolement et l'abandon le tiennent.

Faut-il voir en xii 3-4a l'image du corps humain comparé à la maison? Sawyer a repris cette idée. Pourtant on peut redire avec E. Podechard[9] que le texte de Qohelet insiste plus sur les habitants que sur la maison elle-même.

Faut-il allégoriser tous les éléments de ces versets 3-4a et y voir la mention de différentes parties du corps humain qui dépérit? Outre que ce serait méconnaître le caractère polaire des expressions, il me semble que le texte ne l'impose pas clairement.

Certes, si les gardes tremblent, c'est en raison de leur grand âge, et cela se remarquera surtout aux mains, voire à la tête; si les nobles se courbent, se voûtent, disons-nous (et cela vaut pour tous, puisqu'il s'agit d'expressions polaires), cela se voit à leur dos et à leurs épaules. Pas d'allégorie physiologique ici, mais de simples images qui se comprennent d'elles-mêmes. Si ces dames "s'obscurcissent" aux treillis des fenêtres, c'est qu'elles perdent la vue; certes, le verbe "s'obscurcir" est surtout utilisé pour les yeux, dans la Bible (Lam. v 17; Ps. lxix 24; la Bible signale évidemment, mais avec d'autres verbes, qu'avec le grand âge les yeux s'affaiblissent: Gn. xxvii 1, xlviii 10; 1 S. iii 2; 1 R. xiv 4), mais le poète peut donner un raccourci saisissant, sans qu'il requiert un décodage par l'allégorie physiologique.

[8] *Koheleth—The Man and his World* (New York, ²1955), p. 339.

[9] *L'Ecclésiaste* (Paris, 1912), p. 457.

Reste la difficulté à propos de celles qui moulent: "elles cessent" *kî miʿeṭû*, "car elles sont trop peu nombreuses", traduit-on habituellement. En général, les partisans de l'allégorie physiologique triomphent ici, car, disent-ils, faute de dents, le vieillard ne peut plus mâcher sa nourriture. Si au contraire on cherche à prendre la phrase au sens littéral, comme le fait par exemple Buzy (pp. 354-5), on s'explique mal la raison donnée: "car elles sont trop peu nombreuses". Mais est-il sûr que le sujet de *miʿeṭû* soit celles qui moulent? J'observe que l'explication donnée par Qohelet vient exactement au centre des versets 3-4a et que c'est la seule explication fournie dans ce petit passage. D'autre part, être trop peu nombreux peut difficilement être le fait des seules vieilles servantes chargées de moudre la farine pour le pain de tous les habitants de la maison. Dans l'antiquité peu de gens arrivaient à un âge avancé: ce sont les personnes âgées qui sont trop peu nombreuses. Dès lors pourquoi ne pas voir dans *miʿeṭû* un impersonnel? Un autre pluriel impersonnel se retrouvera au début du verset 5. Je propose donc de traduire: "car on est trop peu nombreux". Dans ce cas, il n'y a plus nécessité de recourir à l'allégorie physiologique.

Qoh. xii 4b-5

Si la fin du passage xii 3-4a faisait allusion à la soirée, le passage suivant, xii 4b-5 débute par une allusion au matin. C'est du moins ainsi que se lit le texte massorétique qui de nouveau peut être compris comme un impersonnel: "on se lève au son de l'oiseau". Le mélange de singulier et de pluriel pour exprimer l'impersonnel se lit ailleurs dans la Bible (1 R. xxii 37-38). De la sorte, aucun changement textuel ne s'impose, malgré Symmaque (que Podechard, p. 461, lui-même avoue ne pas être "ordinairement un des témoins les plus sûrs"). On se lève tôt; c'est le sort de nombreux vieillards, au sommeil court et léger.

"Mais toute chanson s'affaiblit". C'est le contraste souligné aussi par le jeu de mots entre *qôl* et *kol*. Les filles du chant sont plus normalement chansons;[10] elles s'affaiblissent;[11] elles se font rares et chevrotantes sur les lèvres du vieillard. S'il se lève tôt, ce n'est pas un lever

[10] Cf. L. Di Fonzo, *Ecclesiaste* (Rome, 1967), p. 320; F. Piotti, "Osservazioni su alcuni paralleli extrabiblici nell' 'allegoria della vecchiaia' (*Qohelet* 12, 1-7)", *Bibbia e Oriente* 19 (1977), p. 125.

[11] Même verbe, en contexte analogue, en Is. xxix 4.

joyeux; il se lève tôt, au son de l'oiseau, mais lui, le vieillard, il ne chante plus guère.

Il se lève, mais sa marche est bien limitée. Le verset 5a le souligne: on craint même de monter sur la terrasse ou de se tenir sur le toit de la maison, le lieu privilégié lors de la chaleur de l'été; en rue, ce sont les frayeurs pour un homme à la démarche pénible. Le voilà confiné à la chambre.

Jusqu'ici tout peut se lire sans allégorie physiologique et sans modifier le texte massorétique. Mais en xii 5b, comment lire le premier verbe? Le *qéré* propose *yânéṣ*, hifil imparfait de *nṣṣ*, et le sens est: "fleurit l'amandier". C'est la leçon des versions anciennes et c'est sur elle que plusieurs auteurs s'appuyent pour parler d'un contraste entre le déclin du vieillard et le renouveau printanier de la nature.[12] Pourtant le *ketib* introduit un *aleph*, qui suppose le verbe *n'ṣ*, "dédaigner, mépriser". Dans le *qéré*, il est difficile d'expliquer le *aleph*; on a parlé de *scriptio plena* et l'on renvoie à Os. x 14 et Prov. xiii 23.[13] Mais l'explication vaut-elle vraiment? Podechard (p. 463) considère que la seule explication plausible de ce *aleph* est de voir ici le verbe *n'ṣ*; C. D. Ginsburg [14] était du même avis au siècle dernier et il rappelait qu'Ibn Esra avait noté la chose. Ginsberg vocalisait simplement *yan'éṣ*, comme forme apocopée du hifil au sens de "causer du dégoût". Cette interprétation, que Podechard acceptait, même s'il préférait le pual (p. 463), me paraît toujours valable, le sujet étant, comme dans les deux stiques suivants, le substantif qui suit le verbe, ici l'amande (cf. Gn. xliii 11).

Le stique suivant peut se traduire: "et la sauterelle se fait lourde". Le hithpael ayant parfois la valeur d'un passif, comme le note encore Podechard (p. 463), le verbe peut se comprendre dans ce sens que la sauterelle devient lourde pour l'estomac du vieillard.

Quant au troisième stique, nous le comprenons ainsi: "le câpre cesse d'avoir de l'effet";[15] ce condiment toujours apprécié n'excite plus l'appétit. Cette interprétation conserve le texte massorétique.

Bref, Qohelet signifierait que le vieillard n'est plus sensible aux mets recherchés. Il perd le goût de manger. On sait que des

---

[12] Cf. Buzy, pp. 337-8; Glasser, p. 166; Sawyer, pp. 528-9, qui cependant ne signale pas la difficulté du verbe.

[13] Depuis Fr. Delitzsch; cf. Gordis, p. 345; Di Fonzo, p. 322.

[14] *Coheleth, commonly called The Book of Ecclesiastes* (London, 1861), p. 462.

[15] Avec le hifil: cf. Ginsburg, p. 464; Gordis, p. 346; Di Fonzo, p. 322; Piotti, p. 126.

commentateurs juifs du moyen âge, suivis par quelques auteurs du XIXe siècle et récemment par Gordis donnaient à ce verset 5b une interprétation sexuelle;[16] mais celle-ci exigerait de laisser de côté le sens littéral pour passer à l'allégorie physiologique que rien n'impose ici pas plus qu'auparavant.

Ainsi le vieillard se replie sur lui-même, il perd ses forces, il n'ose plus sortir; même renfermé chez lui, il n'y a plus rien qui provoque son appétit. Dès lors l'explication de Qohelet tombe on ne peut plus clair: "car l'homme s'en va vers sa demeure éternelle et les pleureurs tournent dans la rue".

L'homme, c'est celui que Qohelet invitait en xi 8 à jouir de toutes les années qu'il aurait à vivre, mais le voici arrivé aux jours obscurs. Enfermé chez lui, il s'approche de son départ de cette vie, il s'en va doucement vers la tombe, tandis que dans la rue, ce monde séparé par la porte close, ce monde qu'il craint, les officiels du deuil attendent déjà que tout soit fini.

Qoh. xii 6

Le verset 6 marque une nouvelle étape, la dernière. Ce verset est lié au suivant, puisqu'en xii 6ab-7 chaque vers est composé de deux parties; en outre chacune de ces parties est normalement jointe à l'autre: le fil d'argent à la coupe d'or, la jarre à la poulie, la poussière au souffle; mais xii 6ab-7 indiquent la séparation et donc la ruine de l'unité que les deux parties formaient. L'idée de mort est donc présente dès xii 6a, et c'est normal après xii 5. De plus les trois distiques de xii 6-7 ont des liens de vocabulaire ou de grammaire. Le verbe *rṣṣ* apparaît en 6ab, toujours dans le second stique, de même que les mots apparentés *gullâh* et *galgal*; 6b ajoute dans chacun de ses stiques une précision de lieu: *'al* et *'èl*, qui reparaissent en 7, dans le même ordre, mais en plus avec une subordonnée dans chaque stique: "selon ce qu'elle était" et "qui l'a donnée". On observera encore que la structure des propositions est toujours la même: le verbe suivi du sujet, auquel on joint une précision, sauf en 7b où le sujet vient en tête, marquant une insistance qui convient bien à cette finale. Enfin, en xii 6-7, il y a une alternance continue de masculin et de féminin: 6a: masculin-féminin; 6b: féminin-masculin; 7: masculin-féminin.

Comme 5c dans l'ensemble de 4b-5, le verset 7 donne la clé des vers précédents de 6, et les faits littéraires que je viens de relever

---

[16] Ginsburg, pp. 462-4, et Gordis, pp. 345-6, citent ces auteurs.

excluent déjà l'hypothèse qui veut considérer 7b comme une addition.

Quant au sens des deux vers de xii 6, malgré la parenté de vocabulaire entre leurs deuxièmes stiques, je ne crois pas qu'ils désignent une seule et même image, comme le pensent Gordis et Lauha, à la suite d'auteurs juifs du moyen âge, en commençant par Rashi et Ibn Esra. Le vers 6aβ me semble être à la base de toute la difficulté avec le mot *gullâh*. Quel sens lui donner? Ou bien on le réfère à 1 R. vii 41-42 et 2 Chr. iv 12-13, et l'on traduit par "boule", ou bien on le réfère à Zach. iv 2-3 où *gullâh* a le sens de "réservoir" pour une lampe à huile. Dans la première hypothèse, *gullâh* est le contrepoids de la chaîne à la poulie du puits (Gordis, p. 348); et dans ce cas 6ab énumère les quatre éléments: chaîne, contrepoids, jarre et poulie, qui permettent de prendre de l'eau au puits. Dans la seconde hypothèse, 6a se lit pour lui-même, sans rapport à 6b, et il parle de la lampe suspendue par un fil; le fil se détache, se sépare de la lampe (et l'on garde ainsi le texte consonnantique traditionnel).[17] Le fait que *gl ḫrṣ* se lise en ougaritique avec le sens clair de "coupe d'or" rend plus plausible le même sens en Qoh. xii 6a.[18] En outre on ne voit pas pourquoi *gullâh* aurait ici le sens précis de boule de contrepoids; ce sens ne semble pas pas pouvoir être justifié par 1 R. vii 41-42. Enfin, les deux stiques de 6a ont des déterminations cohérentes et complémentaires que rien ne permet de lier à 6b, qui a ses précisions propres, tout comme le verset 7.

Bref, Qoh. xii 6a doit être interprété, me semble-t-il, indépendamment de xii 6b.[19] Depuis Fr. Delitzsch et Ginsburg, en passant par Podechard et Di Fonzo, beaucoup de commentateurs voient en xii 6a l'image de la lampe qui se brise parce que le fil par laquelle elle est suspendue s'en détache. Gordis et Lauha, qui se montrent partisans de l'autre interprétation liant 6a à 6b, reconnaissant toutefois que voir en 6a l'image de la lampe demeure une hypothèse défendable. J'ai dit pourquoi je la préfère.

En xii 6b, on est au bord du puits, sur la margelle. Au fond du puits, l'eau courante. La jarre dans laquelle on puise l'eau se brise (ce stique est clair) et la poulie ou le moulinet s'en va se fracasser au

---

[17] Ginsburg, p. 466, a signalé que les voyelles du texte massorétique étaient celles du *qéré*.

[18] Keret, CTA 14 (I K), IV, 165: cf. M. Dahood, "Canaanite-Phoenician Influence in Qoheleth", *Bib* 33 (1952), p. 216.

[19] La proposition de J. E. Burns, "The Imagery of Eccles 12 6[a]", *JBL* 84 (1965), pp. 428-30, qui s'appuie sur les versions, est trop hypothétique.

fond du puits: la préposition *'èl* suppose un mouvement. Mais le verbe *nârôṣ* fait problème. Ou bien on le conserve comme nifal parfait de *rṣṣ* et l'on traduit: "se fracasse"; mais même dans ce cas, on préfère lire l'imparfait (en s'appuyant indirectement sur les versions — Podechard, pp. 467-8) et on lit *yérôṣ*. Ou bien on s'appuie sur les versions (G. S^{h}. S. Targ.) et on lit *yârûṣ*, au sens de "s'encourt". Je me demande si cette dernière hypothèse ne mérite pas attention, bien qu'elle change le texte consonantique (*n* devient *y*), car est-il normal de garder deux emplois aussi rapprochés du même verbe *rṣṣ*? D'autre part, ce sont les récipients qui se brisent, tandis que ce sont les moyens de les utiliser qui cèdent et se séparent. Enfin le chiasme souligné plus haut apparaîtrait encore plus clairement: le fil de la lampe se détache et la poulie du puits s'encourt.

Plusieurs images sont ici évoqueés, celle de la lampe (et les commentateurs ont dit qu'elle symbolise la vie), celle de l'eau, également symbole de vie; mais aussi celle de la jarre ou de la coupe brisée, qui évoque le vase fragile qui, pour s. Paul, symbolise l'être humain dans sa chair; enfin l'idée de séparation violente. Le récipient se brise, tandis que ce qui permet de l'utiliser s'échappe: le verset 7 est alors tout à fait préparé.

Ainsi compris, le verset 6 apporte de nouvelles métaphores, et l'allégorie physiologique n'y reçoit aucune place. D'ailleurs les auteurs récents renoncent clairement à la faire intervenir en xii 6.[20]

Conclusion

Que conclure, sinon que le texte de Qoh. xii 1-7 peut s'expliquer sans cette allégorie physiologique. Celle-ci exige une cohérence des images que le texte ne présente pas. Aussi on comprend pourquoi la majorité des auteurs a retenu tout d'abord l'explication littérale. C'est elle que nous avons tenté à notre tour d'éclairer en respectant au maximum le texte massorétique. Le texte de Qohelet se montre à la fois ferme et souple. Une attention spéciale à sa structure le révèle. Et ses descriptions poétiques ont un seul but: servir d'ultime enseignement au jeune.

Reste une dernière question: pourquoi l'interprétation allégorique de Qoh. xii 1-7 s'est-elle si largement répandue au cours des siècles? Tout d'abord parce que si l'on veut décrire la décrépitude du vieillard, il faut bien penser au délabrement de son physique; si l'on dit que

---

[20] Podechard, p. 469: Gordis, p. 348; Di Fonzo, p. 326; Lauha, p. 211.

les gardiens en viennent à trembler, on entend qu'un tremblement de vieillard agite les bras etc.; si l'on dit que les nobles se courbent, on entend qu'avec l'âge, l'homme se voûte, sa colonne vertébrale s'incurve; et ainsi de suite pour plusieurs images de la péricope. Deuxièmement, il y a le verbe central de xii 3b *miʿéṭû* qu'on a toujours lu en référence à celles qui moulent; comment alors ne pas penser aux dents, aux molaires? mais j'ai proposé de lire ce verbe comme un impersonnel. Enfin, sur la lancée de l'interprétation allégorique, on a vu un détail physiologique à chaque pas de la description; on en est arrivé ainsi à une interprétation apparemment cohérente dans son principe, mais qui abusait du texte, puisque celui-ci multiple les images sans y mettre la cohérence qu'on croit y voir et malgré le fait que quelques vers de cette description ne peuvent avoir qu'un sens littéral.

ARAMAIC STUDIES AND THE BIBLE

by

JONAS C. GREENFIELD

Jerusalem

Although there has been a quickening of Aramaic studies in recent years because of discoveries in various areas, it still remains a dormant field to some extent and has not attracted the number of scholars that it deserves. This article will deal with material both published and discovered in the last thirty years. This will enable me to cover the important discoveries and publications and also to match my own years of study. The material will be dealt with, on the whole, from a chronological rather than a typlogical point of view. I have set the end of the Persian perod as the limit of this article and therefore have not deal with either the Aramaic material from Qumran or Targumic studies. Including these two important fields would require a much longer article than the space allotted.

The rather sparse corpus of Early Aramaic received an important addition in 1965 with the publication of the third Sfire inscription by A. Dupont-Sommer and then in 1960 with his republication of Sfire I and II.[1] These inscriptions from the middle of the eighth century essentially doubled the number of lines of Early Aramaic available to scholars. It supplied them with a sizeable block of text that could be studied from the vantage point of literary, religious and political history on the one side, and from the morphological, lexicographical and syntactic point of view on the other. It was clear that the vocabulary of literary Early Aramaic in the West was closer to Canaanite than had been previously thought. This might have been adduced from the Zakkur inscription, but that inscription was considered by some,

---

[1] A bibliography of the Sfire inscriptions up to 1967 will be found in J. A. Fitzmyer, *The Aramaic Inscriptions of Sefire* (Rome, 1967). See also E. Lipiński, *Studies in Aramaic Inscriptions and Onomastics* I (Leuven, 1975), pp. 24-57 (henceforth *Studies*). For the "phases of the Aramaic language" see a study by that name in J. A. Fitzmyer, *A Wandering Aramean* (Missoula, 1979), pp. 57-84. My view of the "phases" can be seen in "Aramaic", *IDB Supplement Volume*, pp. 39-44. Historical orientation for the periods under discusssion in this article may be found in the articles of A. Malamat, "The Aramaeans", and G. Widengren, "The Persians", in D. J. Wiseman (ed.), *Peoples of Old Testament Times* (Oxford, 1973), pp. 123-65, 312-57.

wrongly in my eyes, to suffer from Canaanite admixtures.[2] One is therefore not surprised to find in the Sfire inscriptions a number of verbs and nouns, idioms and expressions shared with Hebrew.[3] Since these have been listed in detail elsewhere, I will choose only a few examples here: *ngd-pqd* (II, 10), *nāgīd pāqīd* (Jer. xx 1); *šqr b* (III, 9), *šqr l* (III, 16) for treaty violation, cf. Ps. xliv 18 for the first and Gen. xxi 23 for the second; *nqm dm mn yd* (III, 11), cf. 2 Kings ix 7; and *nś' ʿl śptyn*, cf. Ps. xvi 4. As noted above, the inscriptions are important for a variety of reasons. Since they contain a treaty and are arranged in treaty form, they should affect the discussion of the dating of the covernant form in the Hebrew Bible. Terminology and clauses are from the sphere of covenants and international relations; thus the use of *ʿdn*, *ʿdy'* and *ʿdy* for treaty stipulations has cast new light on the use of the Hebrew *ʿēdūt* and has restored to Hebrew the word *ʿādīm* "treaty" in Isa. xxx 8 (in agreement with the reading of 1QIs a).[4]

These inscriptions contain a series of treaty curses which relate to those in the Hebrew bible and elsewhere.[5] These are important from another point of view for they are framed in poetic form Thus Sfire I, 27-28 can be set out as:

šbʿ šnn y'kl 'rbh
wšbʿ šnn t'kl twlʿh
wšbʿ [šnn y.]q twy ʿl 'py 'rqh

"For seven years may the locust devour, and for seven years may the worm devour and for seven years may . . . upon the land", which has been compared with Deut. xxviii 38-39. Indeed, even some of the treaty stipulations in Sfire III are set out in parallelism: *ltmšl ly bz'* || *wltršh ly ʿlyh* "you shall not control me in this matter, nor have any authority over me about it" (III, 9) which may be compared to *hămālōk timlōk ʿālēnū* || *'im-māšōl timšōl bānū* (Gen. xxxvii 8). Various types of word repetition, parallelism and set forms are found in the text. These are to remain the characteristics of Aramaic poetry through

[2] For the reading of *ZKR* as *Zakkur* see A. R. Millard, *PEQ* 110 (1978), p. 23, on the basis of a stele of Adad-Nirari III in the Antakya Museum. I am indebted to the authorities of that museum for allowing me to examine the stele in July 1977.

[3] J. C. Greenfield, "Stylistic Aspects of the Sefire Treaty Inscriptions", *Acta Orientalia* (Copenhagen) 29 (1965), pp. 1-18; "Three Notes on the Sefire Inscriptions", *JSS* 11 (1966), pp. 98-105.

[4] For *ʿēdūt* see M. Parnas, "*ʿEdūt*, *Edōt*, *ʿEdwōt* in the Bible, Against the Background of Ancient Near Eastern documents" (in Hebrew), *Shnaton* 1 (1975), pp. 235-46; for *ʿādīm* see D. R. Hillers, *HTR* 64 (1971), pp. 257-9.

[5] See D. R. Hillers, *Treaty-Curses and the Old Testament Prophets* (Rome, 1964).

the Words of Ahiqar, the Book of Daniel, the Genesis Apocryphon and Qumran Enoch into classical Syraic poetry and prose.[6] Although, as can be seen from the examples quoted, the technique comes close to that of the various types of parallelism known biblical poetry, it is nevertheless different in type with a strong emphasis on repetition and on the use of synonomous expressions, e.g.: *hn tʾmr bnbšk wtʿšt blbbk* "if you will plan and plot" (II B 5) or *wlḥbzt wlʾbdt ʾšmhm* "to smite and destroy them" (II B 7). There can be no doubt that in turn this sort of poetic style influenced late Biblical Hebrew poetry, e.g.: Isa. lxiii 9 *bĕʾahăbātō ūbḥemlātō hūʾ gĕʾālām || waynaṭ-ṭĕlēm waynaśśĕʾēm kol-yĕmē ʿōlām* "in his love and compassion he redeemed them, and bore and sustained them for all the days". The use of two virtually synonymous nouns in the first part of the verse and of two synonymous verbs in the second are signs of this influence.

The inscription with its list of gods called upon to open their eyes and witness the treaty (*pqḥw ʿynkm lḥzyh* I A 13) is an additional source for the history of Aramean religion if used carefully. The student of Hebrew scripture should find the remark at the end of Sfire III (line 24)—that when the gods smote his father's house certain territory came to belong to another (*hwt lʾḥrn*) but now *hšbw ʾlhn šybt by*[*t ʾby*] "the gods have restored my father's house"—of interest. This usage is of importance in determining the exact connotation of the frequent idiom (*h*)*šb šbwt*/*šbyt*.[7] The role of the gods in history as envisaged by the Aramaeans may also be discerned in this inscription.

Before we go on to other material, mention should be made of an important inscription that is as yet unpublished. At Tell Fakhariya, ancient Sikanu, a life-size statue of a king with a Neo-Assyrian inscription on its front and a long 23-line Aramaic inscription on its back was found in the winter of 1979. The statue is on exhibition in the Damascus Museum. It is to be published soon by Dr Rainer Degen who dates it on paleographic grounds to the 10th century. It is a dedicatory inscription of King Haddayišʿī of Sikanu and Guzanu set up in gratitude to his god Hadad of Sikanu. Hadad is praised in Aramaic in the manner that Adad is often praised in Akkadian; thus he is called *ʾlh rḥmn* = *ilu rēmēnu* "merciful god". Although

[6]) See J. C. Greenfield, "Early Aramaic Poetry", in the M. Bravmann Memorial Volume *JANES* 11 (1979), pp. 45-51.

[7] The spelling *šybt* is found once in the Hebrew Bible in Ps. cxxxvi and the versions treat as *šĕbūt*. Cf. W. L. Holladay, *The Root ŠÛBH in the Old Testament* (Leiden, 1958), pp. 107-8, 110-15. The Sfire form would favor the theory that the original idiom in Hebrew was *šāb šābūt* "render a restoration".

the Aramaic is on the whole straightforward there are some passages that can be understood only in the light of Akkadian idioms and there are some otherwise unknown loan-words. Therefore lines 1-16 give the impression of being translated from Akkadian. The Aramaic is close to Samallian from the morphological point of view. It shares such words as *lwd* "remove" and *mrq* "illness" (< *mrḍ*, later Aramaic *mĕraʿ*) with the Sfire inscription. The second part of the inscription (lines 16-23), which does not have direct Akkadian parallels, consists of a curse threatening famine to the land of anyone who would remove the name of King Haddayišʿī from the vessels (*m'ny'*) of the temple. The main part of the curse is shared to some extent with the first curse of Sfire I (*KAI* 222) in which we read that (lines 21-24) "seven women will nurse a lad (*ʿlym*) and he will not be sated (*yśbʿ*) and seven mares will nurse a colt (*ʿl*) and he will not be sated and seven cows will nurse a calf (*ʿgl*) and he will not be sated and seven ewes will nurse a lamb (*'mr*) and he will not be sated". The words that follow in the Sfire inscription (line 24) are difficult but I would agree with the proposal that they have to do with searching for food (*lḥm*) unsuccesfully. The Tell Fakhariya inscription has 100 ewes, cows and women suckling a lamb, a calf and a boy, but the thirst of the sucklings is not quenched, the verb being *yrwy* rather than *yśbʿ*. The following line continues the theme: one hundred women will bake bread *lḥm* in a single oven and not fill it. This is indeed close to Lev. xxvi 26 "ten women will bake your bread in a single oven, they shall dole out your bread by weight, and though you eat, you shall not be satisfied". These curses as well as the others in this last portion of the text do not have any known predecessors in the Mesopotamian area. Their appearance on a statue divorced from any treaty context should raise doubts concerning certain curses being "treaty curses" as such and should also lead to a revision of certain ideas as to the necessary dependance of the series of maledictions in Deuteronomy upon Neo-Assyrian models.[8]

I referred to the Zakkur inscription briefly above. This important inscription, known for over seventy years, has been the object of renewed interest in recent years since it bears essentially our only clear testimony to the presence of seers *ḥzyn wʿddn* among the Ara-

[8] This idea is forcefully stated by M. Weinfeld, *Deuteronomy and the Deuteronomic School* (Oxford, 1972), pp. 116-26. However, one must consider the strong possibility that the Neo-Assyrian curses also drew from an earlier source which they shared with the Aramaeans and others in the West.

maeans of Syria. The attention paid to pre-Israelite prophecy because of the presence of prophetic elements in the texts from Mari and the discussion of revelation dreams in Mesopotamia made the Zakkur inscription a natural focus for attention.[9] The use of phraseology which is associated with certain types of biblical hymns was noted and the antecedents of certain of these phrases were traced.[10] Our growing knowledge of certain cultic practices widespread throughout the ancient Near East has elucidated references to these in some well known Aramaic inscriptions.

An outstanding lacuna among the Early Aramaic material until recently was legal material. The only items that could be considered as belonging to this category were the few Aramaic dockets on Neo-Assyrian tablets and the Aramaic documents on clay found at Assur and at Tell Halaf.[11] These have recently been re-examined in detail and their understanding considerably advanced.[12] An important addition is the clay tablets published by Pierre Bordreuil which has been commented on by various scholars.[13] Its exact meaning is still open to dispute and only the future discovery and publication of similar texts will enable us to determine this meaning. There is an as yet unpublished group of clay tablets in the possession of the Musées Royaux d'Art et d'Histoire (Brussels) to be published by Edward Lipiński, who has provided in a series of articles and lectures important information about these texts.[14] They deal primarily with loans and bonds and have helped to clarify the terminology used in

[9] James F. Ross, "Prophecy in Hamath, Israel and Mari", *HTR* 63 (1969), pp. 1-28.

[10] H.-J. Zobel, "Das Gebet um Abwendung der Not und seine Erhörung in den Klagliedern des A.T. und in der Inschrift des Königs Zakir von Hamath", *VT* 21 (1971), pp. 91-9; J. C. Greenfield, "The Zakir Inscription and the Danklied", *Proceedings of the Fifth World Congress of Jewish Studies* I (Jerusalem, 1969), pp. 174-91.

[11] A. R. Millard, "Some Aramaic Epigraphs", *Iraq* 34 (1972), pp. 131-7.

[12] Lipiński, *Studies*, pp. 83-142.

[13] P. Bordreuil, "Une tablette araméenne inédite de 635 av. J.C.", *Semitica* 23 (1973), pp. 96-102; E. Lipiński, "Textes juridiques et économiques araméens de l'époque sargonide", *Acta Antiqua* 22 (1974), pp. 373-84; M. Fales, "Sulla tavoletta aramaica A.O. 25.341", *AION* 36 (1976), pp. 541-7; S. Kaufman, "An Assyro-Aramaic *egirtu ša šulmu*", *Essays on the Ancient Near East in Memory of J. J. Finkelstein* (Hamden, Conn., 1977), pp. 119-27; J. Teixidor, *Syria* 56 (1979), pp. 390-2.

[14] ibid.; "*Nešek* and *Tarbīt* in the Light of Epigraphic Evidence", *Orientalia Lovaniensia Periodica* 10 (1979), pp. 133-41; "Les temples néo-assyriens et les origines du monnayage", in E. Lipiński (ed.), *State and Temple Economy in the Ancient Near East* (Leuven, 1979), pp. 565-88.

the Hebrew Bible. According to Lipiński, terms like *nešek* and *tarbīt* may now be properly understood. These documents from the seventh century BCE provide a glimpse into the preoccupations of daily life and provide the background which we lack from Palestine proper, for certain legislation dealing with interest and usury. They also indicate the sort of short legal texts which were in use in biblical times written on perishable materials.

One of the important conclusions to be drawn from the new material published during the last thirty years, when studied in conjunction with that previously known, is that Aramaic was not a single dialect as it is usually described.[15] At an early period, as anyone with linguistic training might assume, there were already a variety of dialects in use. Under the Assyrians, Aramaic had become a *lingua franca* in the West, and possibly also in the East. It was in all likelihood this type of Aramaic that was in use among the Aramaic-speaking tribes of Mesopotamia, in the area that had long since been absorbed by Assyria. Assyria itself had become highly Aramaicized, especially during the Sargonid era.[16] There are no other major early Aramaic inscriptions to report on. The recently published Deir ʿAlla inscription has purposely been omiited from this survey, since I do not believe that this inscription may truly be classified as Aramaic. A disservice was done to scholarship when it was called Aramaic in the first releases that appeared. There is, in my opinion, nothing *in the inscription proper* that qualifies the language in which it is written as Aramaic. Both my colleague Joseph Naveh and I have expressed this view in detailed reviews.[17] Suffice it to say here that the features that the editors considered as Aramaic are either chimeric or can be otherwise interpreted. The inscription is in all likelihood in a "Transjordanian" dialect akin to Ammonite and Moabite and sharing certain features (such as the masculine plural in *-n*) with Aramaic. The attentive reader may find some isoglosses with the language of some chapters of Job.

During the period in which the Babylonians had hegemony over the Near East the role of Aramaic was increased. It is indeed plausible that Neo-Babylonian was on the whole a written rather than a spoken

---

[15] J. C. Greenfield, "The Dialects of Ancient Aramaic", *JNES* 37 (1978), pp. 93-9.

[16] For the penetration of Aramaic by Akkadian and a discussion of the Assyrian-Aramaic symbiosis see S. A. Kaufman, *The Akkadian Influences in Aramaic* (Chicago, 1964). H. Tadmor discusses the Aramaicization of Assyria in the forthcoming proceedings of the Berlin, 1978 *Rencontre Assyriologique*.

[17] See Naveh, *IEJ* 29 (1979), pp. 133-6; Greenfield, *JSS* 25 (1980), pp. 248-52.

language during this period. The dialect of Aramaic used in Babylon (an Eastern one) became dominant. The so-called Adon letter discovered in Sakkara and written by a kinglet of the Philistine coast to the Pharaoh (c. 600) is written in Aramaic.[18] The plaque published by A. Caquot is also to be dated to the Neo-Babylonian period.[19] Despite the efforts of various scholars, it has not yet yielded all its secrets. An expression, at the beginning of the text, commented on by Lipiński, deserves our attention: *'yš zy y*... "any one who would... This sort of phrase has been known to us from the area of cuneiform law from the Old Babylonian period on (*awīlum ša* ...). In Hebrew texts its equivalent is *'īš 'ăšer y*... found primarily in late texts.

Official Aramaic

Official Aramaic, in the real sense of the term, begins with the Achaemenid period. In my view it was based on the Aramaic in use in Babylon which had during the period of Babylonian hegemony achieved a wide-spread use in the Near East. From references in contemporary texts from Babylon it may be inferred that various *sēpiru* who had functioned under Nabonidus continued in their positions under Cyrus and Cambyses.[20] It is important to stress two pertinent linguistic observations here: 1) that official languages are conservative by nature and therefore innovative features of Eastern Aramaic are not prominent in Official Aramaic; and 2) that other dialects of Aramaic were in use, in writing, at the same time. This can best be seen from the many texts found in Egypt.[21] It would also not be amiss to note the important role of the easily-written cursive Aramaic in the spread of the Aramaic language. There is a constant and consistent development of the Aramaic script throughout the Persian Empire, with various types, such as the more monumental lapidary and formal cursive developing.[22] Despite the widespread use of the Aramaic script from the Indus Valley to Upper Egypt, literally

---

[18] Most recently B. Porten, "The Identity of King Adon", *BA* 44 (1981), pp. 33-52, with an extensive bibliography.

[19] "Une inscription araméenne d'époque assyrienne", *Hommages à André Dupont-Sommer* (Paris, 1971), pp. 9-16; Lipiński, *Studies*, pp. 77-82; P. E. Dion, *Biblica* 55 (1974), pp. 399-403; F. M. Falks, *AION* 38 (1978), pp. 273-82. The dating to the Neo-Babylonian period on palaeographic grounds has been demonstrated by Naveh in an unpublished paper.

[20] J. Lewy, *HUCA* 25 (1954), pp. 198-9.

[21] J. C. Greenfield, above n. 15.

mēHōddū wĕʿad Kūš, national scripts were not entirely overwhelmed; the Early Hebrew and Phoenician scripts, as well as the various scripts in use in Asiar Minor (including Greek), continued to develop. The remark in Esther (i 22) that the decree was sent out to every province in its script and to every nation in its language has some basis in reality.

The use of more than one script in an area is also typical of this period, and this is at times notable in a concrete manner even in a relatively minor matter. Thus a seal of this period reads *YHWYŠMʿ BT ŠWŠŠRʾṢR*, Yehoyishma, the daughter of Shawash-shar-uṣur, with the Hebrew name in early Hebrew script and the Babylonian name in Aramaic script.[23] By the end of the Persian period the influence of Aramaic will be dominant even in areas where Aramaic was never a spoken language and the script of the area will for centuries to come be a derivative of the Aramaic script, and many of the elements of chancery style in the formulation of decress, letters and business documents will pass from culture to culture together with the script in which they were written. With the break-up of the Achaemenian empire and the replacement of Aramaic by Greek as the language of officialdom, national Aramaic scripts develop; thus the Jewish variey of the Aramaic script will replace the early Hebrew script almost entirely,[24] and Nabatean and Palmyrence scripts will develop in the West as well as various scripts in the East.[25]

Alongside many inscriptions of varied size and content, five major groups of texts have added greatly to the growth of our knowledge of the period.[26] They are, in approximate chronological order: 1) the Hermopolis letters; 2) the Brooklyn Museum papyri; 3) the Arsham letters; 4) the Saqqara papyri; 5) the Wadi Daliyah papyri. The first four were discovered in Egypt, the last in Palestine. They

---

[22] J. Naveh, *The Development of the Aramaic Script* (Jerusalem, 1970).

[23] N. Avigad, *IEJ* 15 (1965), pp. 228-30.

[24] N. Avigad, "The Palaeography of the Dead Sea Scrolls and Related Documents", *Scripta Hierosolymitana* 4 (Jerusalem, 1958), p. 56-87; F. M. Cross, "The Devlopment of the Jewish Scripts", *The Bible and the Ancient Near East* (Garden City, N.Y., 1961), pp. 133-202.

[25] J. Naveh, *BASOR* 198 (1970), pp. 32-7; *IOS* 2 (1972), pp. 293-304; *IEJ* 25 (1975), pp. 117-23.

[26] Over a hundred Aramaic ostraca have been found in Palestine of the Persian period but they are limited in interest, being primarily lists or dealing with administrative matters. It is a great loss that the many documents on which the bullae that were published by N. Avigad, "Bullae and Seals from a Post-Exilic Judean Archive", *Qedem* 4 (Jerusalem, 1976), were sealed had totally disintegrated.

offer the biblical scholar rich fare, only part of which can be indicated here.

The Hermopolis letters are, according to palaeographic considerations, to be dated to the late sixth century and are contem porary with the Bauer-Meissner papyrus and like it they come from an Aramaean rather than a Jewish background.[27] The letters form an archive in which the preoccupations of daily life and the cares and needs of an Aramaean family emerge. They are also instructive as to the assimilation of these Aramaeans with the local Egyptian environment and their intermarriage with Egyptians and others. I will concentrate on the religious information that may be derived from the letters. Although reference to religious matter is limited to the opening formulae of the letters, they do tell us something about the religious affiliation of the common people and their essentially syncretistic cult. Thus in the greeting formulae the names of the temples that existed in Syene are mentioned; *šlm byt nbw*, or *byt bnt*, *byt bt'l* and *byt mlkt šmyn*. After that greeting the writer declares *brktk lptḥ zy yḥwny/yḥzny 'pyk bšlm* "I have invoked Ptah's blessings on you that he may show me your face in well-being". (The same sort of greeting with *byt yhw* and *yḥzny yhw* is found in one of the Padua letters.) From these and other letters it is clear that the Aramaeans of Egypt had absorbed the Mesopotamian Nabu and Banitu and adopted the Egyptian cult of Ptah along with their own gods such as *mlkt šmyn* and *bt'l*, Hadad, Eshem, Attar, etc.

The reference to *mlkt šmyn*, the "queen of heaven", as worshipped on Egyptian soil takes us naturally to Jer. vii 18 where the familial nature of this cult is stressed and also to Jer. xliv 44 where there is a long peroration on the continued worship of this goddess in Egypt. The Aramaeans were syncretistic; there are indications that some of the Jews at Elephantine were also syncretistic. This should not be surprising and in this writer's opinion much of the apologetics on this score is wasted. On the other hand there is no need to exaggerate this point.

---

[27] For the date cf. J. Naveh, "The Palaeography of the Hermopolis Papyri", *IOS* 1 (1971), pp. 120-2; F. M. Cross, *AUSS* 7 (1969), pp. 223-9. A bibliography of these letters may be found in *IOS* 4 (1974), p. 14, to which may be added J. C. L. Gibson, *Textbook of Syrian Semitic Inscriptions* 2, *Aramaic Inscriptions* (Oxford, 1975), pp. 125-43; D.R. Hillers, "Redemption in Letters 6 and 2 from Hermopolis", *UF* 11 (1979), pp. 379-82. A convenient edition of these texts may be found in B. Porten and J. C. Greenfield, *Jews of Elephantine and Arameans of Syene: Fifty Aramaic Texts with Translation* (Jerusalem, 1974), pp. 151-65.

It should be noted that since these are personal letters the language is idiomatic and at times colorful: *w'nh nktny ḥwyh whwt myt wlh šlḥtn hn ḥy 'nh whn mt 'nh* "and as for me, I was bitten by a snake and I was dying; and you didn't inquire if I am dead or alive" (V, 8-9). The Aramaic of the Hermopolis letters contain certain orthographic and morphological features that connect it with Western Aramaic and with the dialect in which the "Proverbs of Ahiqar" were written.[28]

The Brooklyn Museum Aramaic papyri (*BMAP*) published in 1953 aroused renewed interest in Elephantine and in the many questions that had been raised on the basis of earlier material and remained essentially dormant for many years.[29] In the two decades following its publication, important articles and books appeared dealing among other things with the terminology of the legal documents, with the Egyptian and Iranian loan-words and with the law of the papyri. The names of Benveniste, Couroyer, Ginsberg, Grelot, Kraeling, Kutscher, de Menasce, Muffs, Rabinowitz, Verger, Volterra and Yaron should be mentioned, as well as the cumulative work of Porten, *Archives from Elephantine* (Berkeley, 1968).[30] Of the many possible topics that reference to Elephantine can elicit I shall deal with some questions in two areas—religion and family law.

In dealing with religious questions one should mention that the *BMAP* have added a dimension to our appreciation of the existence of the *BYT YHW* at Yeb and have enabled scholars to attempt once again to place its physical location in relation to other building there. Jews resident elsewhere in Egypt headed their letters, as mentioned above, with a greeting to the *BYT YHW* at Yeb. Beside the *khny'*, the *kōhănīm*, (known to us from *CAP* 30 and elsewhere), from *BMAP* we have gotten to know a member of the lesser clergy, *'Ănanyā bar 'Ăzaryā lāḥēn zī YHW 'ĕlāhā zī bĕYēb bīrtā* "Ananya the son of Azarya, the *lḥn* of YHW the god who is in Yeb the fortress" (*BMAP* 2, 2). Our acquaintance with him stretches for almost 50 years, from 451 BCE (*BMAP* 2) to 402 (*BMAP* 12). The exact function of the *lḥn* is not known to us, the term being a loan-word

[28] B. Porten and J. C. Greenfield, "The Aramaic Papyri from Hermopolis", *ZAW* 80 (1968), 216-31.

[29] E. G. Kraeling, *The Brooklyn Museum Aramaic Papyri* (New Haven, 1953). All the texts are incorporated in Porten and Greenfield (above n. 27) with improved readings and translations

[30] Porten provides en extensive bibliography, where the works of the above-mentioned scholars may be found.

from Akkadian where it is used for a type of temple functionary in the neo-Assyrian period. 'Ananya was married to an Egyptian slave girl, Tapmut, who bore him a daughter, who was given the good Yahwistic name Yehoyishmaʿ (and a son Pilṭai who disappears from the records). Both mother and daughter were manumitted (*BMAP* 5); Yehoyishmaʿ was married off (*BMAP* 7) and eventually fulfilled her filial duties by supporting her father (and, we may assume, her mother), in his old age (*BMAP* 9).[31] Tapmut, when manumitted, was described as "released to god", a term which when used in the case of freed slave indicates joining a religious communion. In a later text (*BMAP* 12) she is called *lĕḥēnā zī YHW ʾĕlāhā šākēn Yēb bīrtā* "the *leḥena* of *YHW* the god who dwells in Yeb the fortress". Was this title bestowed on Tapmut simply as the wife of a *lāḥēn* or did it entail a role, cultic or not? From her full title it should be clear that to the Jews of Elephant their sanctuary was more than a *miqdāš mĕʿaṭ* (where prayers and incense were offered) but that it should have the status of a temple with the right to burnt offerings as well as meal oblations and incense. However, as we know from *CAP* 32/33 Bagoas, with the advice of Daliya of Samaria, would allow only meal offerings and incense. This limited service would follow the description of Mal. i 11: "For from where the sun rises to where it sets, my name is honored among the nations, and everywhere incense and pure oblation are offered to my name". The Elephantine ostraca mention the Sabbath (*šbh*) and its eve (*ʿrwbh*), but the texts are somewhat obscure and after all these years have still not been properly published. As we know from the Passover papyrus (*CAP* 21) the Passover was observed according to prescription; and an ostracon contains a question as to the date of the Passover.[32] I would add that some of the practices *possibly* indicated by the Passover papyrus go beyond biblical prescription and may point to the type of piety that is usually associated with Judaism at a slightly later stage. The same may be said for the type of mourning practiced, according to *CAP* 30/31, by the Elephantine Jews during the period when their sanctuary was destroyed: fasting—which means not eating meat; not drinking wine; not anointing themselves; and abstaining from sexual intercourse. This is reminiscent of the sort of asceticism that typified a person like Judith (cf. too Dan. x 3).

---

[31] For a discussion of the many problems of the Ananiah archive see Porten, *Archives*, pp. 200-34.

[32] For the Passover papyrus see Porten and Greenfield, *Jews of...*, pp. 78-9; Porten, *Archives*, pp. 130-3, 311-14.

The second item that I would like to deal with is legal procedure among the Jews of Yeb. Although various aspects were discussed in detail by the scholars mentioned above, I nevertheless believe that these texts have not been adequately used as a source of Jewish law. It has recently become the usual procedure to describe the law that emerges from the Elephantine texts as if it were a branch of Aramaic law and in turn to see it, following Y. Muffs, as being influenced by Mesopotamian models and particularly influenced by developments within the Neo-Assyrian sphere.[33] Without entering into polemical detail at this point of view, there is no doubt that the documents reveal strong connections with other Western—that is "peripheral" from the Mesopotamian point of view—legal material and that the terminology is in many cases influenced by Mesopotamian models. However, the legal procedure, especially in matters of family law, should be considered Jewish. We do not know to what extent Egyptian legal procedure was followed in such matters as buying, selling and land tenure.[34] Thus the formal matters that emerge such as the groom's "asking" the bride of her father or guardian; the use of the *mōhar* by the groom; the right of both parties to initiate divorce (dealt with below); the right of the divorced woman to go where she wants (and eventually to marry whomsoever she wants); the role of the *ʿēdāh* in the divorce procedure; [35] the right of the woman to control her own property and of her sons to inherit it—all these items should be seen as elements of Jewish legal practise during this period. Aspects of manumission and adoption as they emerge in the archive of Tapmut and Yehoyishmaʿ must also be examined

[33] R. Yaron, *Introduction to the Law of the Aramaic Papyri* (Oxford, 1961), pp. 99-128, was extremely doubtful about the influence of Mesopotamian law; Y. Muffs, *Studies in the Aramaic Legal Papyri from Elephantine* (Leiden, 1969), pp. 179-93, stressed the Neo-Assyrian connection. This was rigorously challenged by R. Yaron, *RB* 77 (1970), pp. 408-16; cf. too B.A. Levine, "On the Origins of the Aramaic Legal Formulary at Elephantine", in J. Neusner (ed.), *Christianity, Judaism and other Greco-Roman Cults, Studies for Morton Smith at Sixty* III (Leiden, 1975), pp. 37-54. It is this writer's opinion that the source of much of Neo-Assyrian legal terminology should be sought in Aramaic usage.

[34] Yaron, *Introduction*, tends toward strong Egyptian influence. Porten, *Archives*, pp. 334-43, has presented a comparison of the schema of Aramaic and Demotic legal documents but notes (p. 342) that "the points of dissimilarity in both form and substance outweigh those of similarity".

[35] Yaron, *Introduction*, p. 55, believes that the role of the congregation was granting certainty and publicity and had no judicial function. However, examination of ancient Near Eastern divorce texts shows that they record the appearance of the parties before a court or witnesses as is clear from the texts studied by J. J. Finkelstein, *WdO* 8 (1976), pp. 236-40, and other texts.

in this light. There can be no doubt that there are parallel developments in Mesopotamian law in this period, but these institutions are shared with, rather than borrowed from, Jewish legal practice. I will deal with three items from this group.

The first item is adoption—was there such an institution in ancient Israel? Later Jewish law is not of help here since adoption as an institution was unknown in classical Jewish law.[36] Adoption, however, was widespread throughout the ancient Near East, and it would be truly surprising if only Israel lacked this institution. The standard handbooks are vague on this point and some writers insist that the biblical verses in which adoption terminology is used are to be taken figuratively rather than literally (such as in Ps. ii 7 or Ps. lxxxix 26-27).[37] It is my contention that Elephantine material sheds light on this subject. For the positive statement of the marriage formula *hy ʾntty wʾnh bʿlh* "she is my wife and I am her husband", found at Elephantine (*CAP* 15 5; *BMAP* 2, 3-4; 7, 4), has made two items clear: the first, that the negative formulation known from Hosea ii 4: *kī-hīʾ lōʾ ʾištī wĕʾānōkī lōʾ ʾīšāh* "she is not my wife and I am not her husband" was the divorce formula; and the second, that the positive version had in all likelihood been used (in its Hebrew or Aramaic version) as the *verba solemnia* among the Israelites.[59] The same is

[36] As Dr A. Skaist of Bar Ilan University has reminded me, early Israelite society was tribal and lineal in descent and therefore adoption would be unlikely, but with the breakdown of tribal structure the normal Near Eastern situation would prevail. Note that the rabbinic formulation *kol-hamĕgaddēl yātōm* ... *kĕʾillū yĕlādō* "he who raises his friend's son is considered as if he gave birth to him" uses the terminology *giddēl*, *yālad* familar from biblical contexts of child rearing and bearing (*BT* Meg. 11a; Sanh. 19b).

[37] S. M. Paul, "Adoption Formulae", *Maarav* 2 (1980), pp. 173-86, has gathered the extensive material on the subject and elucidated it. Note the important article of M. Weinfeld, "The Covenant of Grant in the Old Testament and the Ancient Near East", *JAOS* 90 (1970), pp. 184-203.

[38] For the use of *verba solemnia* see S. Greengus, "The Old Babylonian Marriage Contract", *JAOS* 89 (1969), pp. 505-32; and M. Friedman, "Israel's Response in Hosea 2, 17b 'You are my husband'", *JBL* 99 (1980), pp. 199-204. My approach ot the use of *verba solemnia* at Elephantine and in Israel is less hesitant than that of Friedman.

[39] It is the contention of many writers that this formula is one of legitimization of the ruler rather than adoption. This passage was studied in detail by G. Brin, "The History of the Formula 'He Shall Be to Me a Son and I will Be to Him a Father'", in B. Uffenheimer (ed.), *Bible and Jewish History, Studies in Bible and Jewish History Dedicated to the Memory of Jacob Liver* (Tel Aviv, 1971), pp. 57-62 (in Hebrew). It was also discussed by T. Ishida, *The Royal Dynasties in Ancient Israel* (*BZAW* 142, Berlin and New York, 1977), pp. 62-3, 90, 108. Most recently A. Malamat has discussed 2 Sam. vii 1-17 in "A Mari Prophecy and Nathan's

true of the formula found in 2 Sam. vii 14: *'ănī 'ehyeh-lō lĕ'āb wĕhū' yihyeh-lī lĕbēn* "I will be a father to him, and he will be a son to me"; this was not a theoretical formulation, invented by the writer, but was based on the actual statement of adoption.[39] This is confirmed by *BMAP* 8 where in the clear case of adoption of Yedoniah bar Tahwa by Uriah bar Mahseiah the latter declares: *bry yhwh* "he will be my son" (lines 5, 8). With this declaration Uriah precludes the possibility of Yedoniah being enslaved again.[40] In contemporary Neo-Babylonian texts the formula for adoption is *māruya šū* "he is my son".[41] Another term used for adoption occurs in Esther ii 7 *ūbĕmōt 'ābīhā wĕ'immāh lĕqāḥāh Mordokay lō lĕbat* "and at the death of her (Esther's father and mother), Mordechai took her as his daughter". As is well known *lāqaḥ lĕbat* matches the standard Akkadian term for adoption, *ana mārūti leqû*. There can be no doubt that the institution of adoption was not foreign to Jewish law in the biblical period.

The second item concerns divorce or, more precisely, a woman's right to divorce her husband. This right was not unknown, under certain conditions, in the ancient Near East, especially in what may be termed the peripheral areas of cuneiform law.[42] Did it exist, even in a limited manner, in ancient Israel? All handbooks offer a negative reply and admittedly the biblical evidence would seem to point in that direction. Let us review the evidence. The Hebrew Bible

---

Dynastic Oracle", in J. A. Emerton (ed.), *Prophecy, Essays Presented to Georg Fohrer on his 65th Birthday, 6 September 1980* (*BZAW* 150, Berlin and New York, 1980), pp. 68-82. These writers have not taken into consideration the fact that the oblique, third person formulation is the late mode of the formula in both marriage and adoption *verba solemnia*. In its present form it could not have served as a model for the first person formulation found in Ps. ii and in Ps. lxxxix. In addition, the "legitimization" act in the Mari text discussed by Malamat, putting a person between one's legs (or on one's lap or bosom), is in actuality an adoption act. From the practical standpoint there is little difference between adoption and legitimization of a person as the performer of the duties incumbent on a son or daughter and as inheritor. The subsequent disappearance of adoption in Judaism may be due to the emergence of certain religious trends.

[40] As J. J. Rabinowitz, *Jewish Law* (New York, 1956), p. 29, n. 24, has suggested, it may be a case of manumission by adoption. The same phrase occurs, it would seem, in one of the Saqqara texts to be published by J. B. Segal (see n. 57 below).

[41] The phrase occurs in a variety of texts from the Neo-Babylonian period and has been discussed by M. San Nicolò, *Archiv Orientální* 7 (1935), pp. 16-18. San Nicolò considers this the *verba solemnia* for adoption, comparing it with *lū aššati ši* "she is my wife" used as the Neo-Babylonian marriage formula.

[42] A. Skaist has dealt with these in "Studies in Ancient Near Eastern Marriage and Divorce Law" (University of Pennsylvania, Ph.D. dissertation, 1963).

speaks only of man divorcing his wife, and legislates purely in terms of a man not taking back his wife if she had meanwhile been married to another man (Deut. xxiv 1-4). Yet at Elephantine it is quite clear from the existent marriage contracts that both men and women could introduce divorce procedures before the *ʿēdāh*. The term used for divorce in these texts, or for the formal statement of request for for divorce, is *śnʾ* "hate". Is this seeming departure from the accepted norm to be attributed to external (Egyptian) influence, or can this possibly be an internal Jewish development? As is well known, this right may be shown to exist at a later period.[43] One may point to the Palestinian *kĕtubbōt* as quoted in a fragmentary manner in the Palestinian Talmud where the formula is" *ʾin sĕnēʾ ʾin sĕnēʾt* "if he hated, if she hated" (*PT* Ket. 5, 10; 30b, etc.). This had long since been noted in connection with the Elephantine material. Although such *kĕtubbōt* were rare and perhaps irregular they were still valid.[44] The fact that there was a hiatus in documentation is not sufficient reason to believe that the formulation recorded in the Palestinian Talmud is not the continuation of a tradition but rather a separate link in the ancient Near Eastern tradition from which the Elephantine practice had developed. A clause similar to the one noted in the Palestinian Talmud reappears some 700 years later in the Palestinian *kĕtubbōt* discovered in the Cairo Geniza (10th through 12th centuries). Was this the revival of an ancient clause, or is the time-gap due to the lack of material for the intervening period?[45] In any case these *kĕtubbōt* testify to the possibility that under certain circumstances a woman could initiate divorce proceedings. The divorce itself was granted by the court. At Elephantine, as noted above, the declaration of divorce took in the *ʿdh* (the Hebrew *ʿēdāh*). This assembly in all likelihood gave an official stamp to the act. It is to be noted that the *qāhāl* or *ʿēdāh* is involved in biblical texts in matters of family law.[46]

---

[43] The subject is discussed thoroughly by M. A. Friedman, *Jewish Marriage in Palestine, A Cairo Geniza Study* I (Tel Aviv and New York, 1980), pp. 312-46.

[44] Mark x 12 in distinction from Matthew v 32 and Luke xvi 18 assumes that a woman can divorce her husband. Without entering into detailed discussion of this subject and its constantly-growing literature it may be suggested that the Gospel of Mark was not influenced by its supposed foreign background but that in this case it reflects a possible, rather than the usual, procedure.

[45] M. A. Friedman (p. 319), is inclined to see these as separate links but in my view this is the survival of an ancient legal tradition.

[46] See Prov. v 14 (*qāhāl wĕʿēdāh*) and Ezek. xvi 40 and xxiii 46-47 (*qāhāl*). Note that according to the Palestinian Targum to Deut. xxiv 1 the divorce document is written before the *bēt dīn*.

The third matter of legal interest is the woman's right to own property. It is assumed by the handbooks that since women did not inherit in ancient Israel they also did not own property. This is in accord with the legislation in Num. xxxvi 1-9 and the attendant narrative. Therefore, when a woman does have property the handbooks and the commentators are constrained to assume extenuating circumstances in each case. At Elephantine, however, it is quite clear that a woman did achieve control over her property and after the death of her husband also over his property.[47] It is true that the texts carefully limit the use of *yrt* "to inherit" (which equals the Hebrew *yrš*) to males, but a childless woman inherited her husband's property if this was stipulated in the documents drawn up at the time of marriage. This may be inferred from the use of the word *šlyṭh* "having control, possession" and from the statement that she can convey the possessions to whomsoever she wishes. It was pointed out some years ago that this terminology is used in the Book of Daniel to point out God's omnipotence and his ability to grant power to whomsoever he wishes.[48]

Mibtahya, a thrice married lady who managed to gain control of quite a lot of personal property, even lent money to her father at one point (for which he paid dearly it would seem), and left slaves, among other property, to her sons after she died. In *CAP* 28, written c. 50 years after the first document in which she is named (*CAP* 8), her sons divide these slaves among themselves. Yehoyishmaʿ, mentioned above, received property as a gift from her father for looking after him (*BMAP* 9). Was this control of property by women limited only to Elephantine or the result perhaps of Egyptian influence? I believe that the biblical record when properly read would say "no". There is no need to provide special interpretation for the three biblical cases: Mikiyahu's mother having funds of her own (Judg. xvii 1-4); the property of the Shunammite, which had been confiscated while she was abroad (2 Kings viii 3-6); and the case of Naomi (Ruth iv 3, 9). This may not have been the simple ownership that was usual for men, yet this was control over possessions. Finally, to judge by the Book of Judith (viii 7, xvi 24), Judith inherited both

---

[47] At a later period the archive of Babatha, known from the as yet unpublished documents from Nahal Ḥever, shows that women had control over extensive holdings. For the present see Y. Yadin, *IEJ* 12 (1962), pp. 241-8.

[48] For the use of *šlyṭ* (with literature) see *Studies in Hebrew and Semitic Languages in Memory of E. Y. Kutscher* (Ramat Gan, 1980), pp. xxxii-xxxiv.

landed property and moveable goods from her husband and was able to dispose of them as she wished. The term *šallīṭā* used in the papyri is matched by the word *šalleṭet* used in Ezek. xvi 30 to describe a whoring wife who owns property of which she can dispose freely, and who needs no help from her lovers.[49]

The Arsham Letters

These letters, sent by Arsham, the governor of Egypt from Susa and/or Babylon, to his assistants in Egypt while he was away at the Court, are written in official Aramaic on leather. It may be assumed that neither Arsham nor the Egyptian recipients of his letters were speakers of Aramaic. These documents were found in their original leather pouch and after some vicisitudes found their way to the Bodleian Library, where they are now housed, They were published in 1954 by G. R. Driver.[50] Arsham looked after his affairs from afar, gave diverse orders and urged his underlings to be more assiduous in pursuing their master's good and welfare. In the file there was also a sort of "passport" listing the stations and ordering that provisions be given to the travellers and their animals (*DL* 5).[51]

A great deal of historical, cultural and linguistic information was provided by the letters and one may learn a great deal from them concerning epistolary style during the Persian period.[52] Alongside the usual *ʿl X mn Y* "to X from Y", which derives from the earlier widespread "to X says Y" and remains in use during the period, we find in the Arsham correspondence and in the one Arsham letter from Elephantine (*CAP* 26) the form *mn X ʿl Y* "from X to Y". This indicated, on the whole, that the communication was from a superior to an inferior. This form continued in use for centuries; it

[49] See a forthcoming study of Ezek. xvi 30 in *Eretz-Israel* 16, the H. M. Orlinsky *Festschrift*.

[50] *Aramaic Documents of the Fifth Century B.C.* (Oxford, 1954); an abridged and revised edition appeared in 1957 which was reprinted with further additions and corrections in 1963. J. D. Whitehead's dissertation, *Early Aramaic Epistolography: The Arsames Correspondence* (University of Chicago, 1974), has, as far as I know, not been published; see his study, J. D. Whitehead, "Some Distinctive Features of the Language of the Arsames Correspondence", *JNES* 37 (1978), pp. 119-40.

[51] This text serves as an example of the "sealed document" or "authorization" that is mentioned in the Elamite travel-ration texts discussed by R. T. Hallock, *Persepolis Fortification Tablets* (Chicago, 1969), pp. 6-7. It also casts light on the messenger system reported in Esther viii 10.

[52] For a survey of Aramaic epistolary style during the Achaemenid period see J. A. Fitzmyer, "Aramaic Epistolography", *A Wandering Aramean* (Missoula, 1979), pp. 183-204.

was prevalent at the Achaemenid chancelleries, where in all likelihood it came into being, and is found in use in the later successor Iranian chancelleries and also remained in use during the Chalifate. The Bar Koseba (Kokeba) letters from Murabbaʿat and Naḥal Ḥever as well as letters quoted in Talmudic literature attest to its popularity.[53]

Although the introductory formula does not have a parallel in biblical material, the Arsham letters in conjunction with other Aramaic epistolary material discovered in Egypt, provide the needed background to the structure of various letters and royal orders found in Ezra and alluded to in Esther and Nehemiah. It is not a question of authentification but rather of comparative typology.[54] Thus in the letters quoted in Ezra there is continual reference to various officials *wakĕnāwāthōn* "and their colleagues"; this is well-documented in the Yedoniah archive from Elephantine and in the Arsham letters. The letters in Ezra were executed by a *bĕʿēl ṭĕʿēm* and a *sāprā* while those in the Arsham archive are executed by a *ydʿ ṭʿm* and a *sāpar*. One example of a phrase that has its counterpart in later biblical material will suffice—*hn ʿl mrʾy lm kwt ṭb ʾgrt yšṭlḥ* "if it please my lord, may a letter be written that..." (*DL* X, 2) comparable to Esther *ʾim ʿal hammelek ṭōb yikkātēb lĕ*... "if it pleases the king may it be written that ..." The peremptory tone of the letters in Ezra are matched by that of the Arsham correspondence.[55]

The two remaining items are the Daliya Papyri and the Sakkara Documents. Neither of these has been published yet, but the information about them given in various sources has been helpful. The Daliya papyri, to be published by F. M. Cross, are on the whole slave sale documents written in the fourth century BCE which were taken along by the fleeing inhabitants of Samaria who hoped to return one day to their holdings and regain possession of them.[56] The documents are of interest in that their terminology is different from that of the

---

[53] I have discussed this in "Some Notes on the Arsham Letters", in S. Shaked (ed.), *Irano-Judaica* (Jerusalem, 1981), pp. 4-11.

[54] See B. Porten, "The Documents of the Book of Ezra" (in Hebrew), *Shnaton* 3 (1978-9), pp. 174-96.

[55] The Aramaic religious text in Demotic script reported on by R. A. Bowman, *JNES* 3 (1944), pp. 219-31, is now being prepared for publication by scholars at the Oriental Institute, Chicago. Since it is a literary text it will be of importance for the study of Aramaic language and literature.

[56] For the present cf. F. M. Cross, "Papyri of the Fourth Century B.C. from Daliyeh", in D. N. Freedman and J. C. Greenfield (ed.), *New Directions in Biblical Archaeology* (New York, 1969), pp. 45-69. I am grateful to Professor Cross for discussing these texts with me

Elephantine documents and shows some contacts with what is known from the legal documents of the Bar Kokeba finds and those recorded in Talmudic literature. The term for oath or obligation is *ʾsr* with *hqym ʾsr* and *hšnh bʾsr* for taking and breaking an oath. In Biblical Hebrew the term *ʾissār* is limited to one chapter—Numbers xxx—considered as belonging to P. Should the use of *ʾsr* in this Persian period have more than a passing relationship to the dating of P? For the marking of slaves *rwšm* is used in the Daliya texts instead of *šntʾ* (a loanword from Akkadian) used in the Elephantine texts. It is known from Mishnaic Hebrew, Babylonian Aramaic and Syriac usage.

The Saqqara archive, to be published by J. B. Segal, contains over two hundred texts, but only about thirty of these yield a satisfactory context.[57] Of these some deal with legal and judicial matters, some with taxation, some with actual events. (Segal considers an official letter about Ionians and Carians as the most important in this group.) Some deal with commercial matters and the last group is varied in nature. On publication the texts will provide interesting material for the historian, student of religion, and the philologian.

It is in the Persian period that we find a series of bilinguals, particularly in border and multilingual areas. From Asia Minor there are texts in Lydian and Aramaic (Sardis *KAI* 260) and in Greek and Aramaic (Limyra *KAI* 262).[58] But in many ways the most interesting inscription of them all is the trilingual text in Greek, Lycian and Aramaic, discovered in 1973 in the Sanctuary of Leto at Xanthos.[59] It comes from the fourth century BCE and records the building of a temple for the royal god of Kounous and his Companion (Aramaic:

---

57 Professor Segal informs me that these texts are scheduled for publication in *Aramaic Texts from North Saqqara* in 1981. For the present cf. his remarks in the report on the Saqqara Papyri in the *Proceedings of the XIV International Congress of Papyrologists* (London, 1975), pp. 252-5, and "New Aramaic Texts from Saqqara: An Introduction", in the forthcoming *Proceedings of the Conference of Aramaic Studies* (Bar Ilan University, January, 1980).

58 For the Sardis inscription see most recently Lipiński, *Studies*, pp. 153-61, and for the Limyra inscription, pp. 162-70.

59 The preliminary publication was H. Metzger, E. Laroche, A. Dupont-Sommer, "La stèle trilingue récemment découverte en Létôon de Xanthos", *CRAI* 1974, pp. 82-149. The Aramaic text was commented on by J. Teixidor, *Syria* 52 (1975), pp. 287-9; *JNES* 37 (1978), pp. 181-5, and G. Garbini *SMEA* 19 (1977), pp. 173-318. The definitive edition was provided in *Fouilles de Xanthos*, VI: *La stèle trilingue du Létôon* (Paris, 1979). In this edition the Aramaic text is on pp. 133-69. In addition, the Iranian elements are studied by M. Mayrhofer, pp. 181-5. Cf. now J. Teixidor, *Syria* 56 (1979), pp. 393-5.

knwth); the appointment of a priest (*kmr'*) and the grant of an annual sum by the land-holders (*b'ly*) for the sacrifice of a sheep (*nqwh*) every new-moon (*r'š yrḥ'*) and a bull (*twr'*) every year (*šnh bnšh*). The inscription is called a *dt'*, a legal promugation, and comparison with the other two inscriptions which are narrative in manner shows that the Aramaic inscription is undoubtedly the official decree. The inscription ends with a curse against anyone who would remove (*hnṣl*) the property of the priest or the temple. The use of terminology such as *r'š yrḥ'* and *šnh bšnh* taken from the cultic sphere is instructive. It indicates a broader spread for these terms than that usually assumed and again brings us into contact with P.[60]

Finally, I would like to point out some instances where our increased knowledge of Aramaic has enhanced our appreciation of the Aramaic *Vorlage* behind the words put into the mouths of Aramaic speakers or used in conversation with them. For example, the words of Laban contain some strange expressions from the point of view of Biblical Hebrew, as do those of Jacob when speaking to his wives. First Laban to Jacob: (Gen. xxxi 28) *wělō' nĕṭaštanī lĕnaššēq lĕbānay wĕlibnōtāy* "you have not let me kiss my sons and daughters". In this verse the use of *nāṭaš* is exceptional; by common consent it is translated "to let, allow". In Biblical Hebrew, however, where *nāṭaš* ordinarily means "to leave, abandon, forsake", the usual word for "allow" is *nātan*. The use of *nāṭaš* in this verse must be considered a calque on Aramaic *šbq*, which beside "leave, abandon, forsake, release" also means "to allow". Thus in *CAP* 30 23 *bzyl' šbqn ln lmbnyh* "as they do not allow us to (re)build it", and other passages may be quoted. In both Targum Onqelos and the Peshiṭta to this passage *nĕṭaštanī* is naturally translated *šĕbaqtanī*. Jacob to his wives: Gen. xxxi 9 *wayyaṣṣēl 'ĕlōhīm 'et-miqnē 'ăbīkem wayyitten-lī* "God has taken your father's goods and given them to me". The relation of (*h*)*nṣl-ntn* in this passage to the *našû-nadānu* formula known from Ugarit and elsewhere has been noted;[61] it was subsequently pointed out that the phrase *hnṣl-ntn* is found in a legal document from Elephantine (*CAP* 8, 19-19) where the donor asserts that he no longer has the right to convey (literally: take and give) the house to anyone

[60] Note that in the Achaemenid Aramaic inscription from Bahardili (*KAI* 278, l. 5) the expression *'yš zy* ... "anyone who would..." the equivalent of biblical *'yš 'ăšer* ... known from P (as noted above) is found.

[61] C. J. Labuschagne, "The *našû-nadānu* Formula and its Biblical Equivalents", *Travels in the World of the Old Testament, Studies Presented to Professor M. A. Beek at the Occasion of his 65th Birthday* (Assen, 1974), pp. 176-80.

else *wl' 'hnṣl mnky lmntn l'ḥrnn.*[62] In *CAP* 9, the compliment to *CAP* 8, a similar phrase is used, but here the formula is *lqḥ-ntn*: *l' šlyṭh hy lmlqḥh wlmntnh l'ḥrnn* (line 9). That there can be no doubt about this use of *hnṣl* may be seen in the words of Hosea, a prophet whose language is replete with Aramaisms, *lāken 'āšūb wĕlāqaḥtī dĕgānī bĕ'ittō wĕtīrōšī bĕmō'ădō wĕhiṣṣaltī ṣamrī ūpištī lĕkassōt 'et-'erwātāh* "assuredly I will take back my new grain in its time and my new wine in its season, and I will take away my wool and my linen that serve to cover het nakedness" (ii 11). The prophet skillfully uses both verbs, *lāqaḥ* and *(h)nṣl*, together in this verse.

The "Aramaisms" in this and other chapters of the pattriarchal stories are found not only in coversations but also in the course of the narrative. Thus when Laban overtakes Jacob the word used (xxxi 23) is *wayyadbēq* (a *hapax legomenon* usage) while in a later verse (xxxi 25) the more usual *wayyaśśēg* is used. The Targum Onqelos translates *wayyaśśēg* by *'adbēq*.

Was an early author particularly skillful in putting Aramaisms in the mouth of his principal characters? Or were these stories given their final edition at a later period when Aramaic was better known in Judah? It goes without saying that in those portions of the Hebrew Bible where contact with Aramaic may be assumed because of considerations of time and geography, this component will be very strong.

---

[62] J. C. Greenfield, "*našû-nadānu* and its Congeners", in M. de Jong Ellis (ed.), *Essays on the Ancient Near East in Memory of J. J. Finkelstein* (Hamden, Conn., 1977), pp. 87-91, in particular p. 91. The discussion by B. Kienast of the *našû-nadānu* formula, *UF* 11 (1979), pp. 431-52, does not affect the interpretation of the Aramaic usage.

SYNTAKTISCHE ERSCHEINUNGEN AM ANFANG ALTHEBRÄISCHER ERZÄHLUNGEN: HINTERGRUND UND VORDERGRUND

VON

WALTER GROSS

Tübingen

Von der althebräischen Erzähltechnik wissen wir wenig. Um die Ausdrucksseite alttestamentlicher Erzählungen und mit deren Hilfe ihre Aussageabsicht, ihre feineren Gattungsunterschiede und ihre literarische Wirkung präziser zu erfassen, wäre es aber wichtig, die dem Erzähler zu Gebote stehenden formalen Mittel in ihren Oppositionen zu kennen, das sprachliche Relief eines Textes differenzierter beschreiben und von dem eines anderen Textes deutlich abheben zu können.

Der Erzählanfang stellt dem Autor besondere Probleme; der Kontext muß erst aufgebaut werden. Unter Exegeten regt sich hier auch die literarkritische Frage nach der Möglichkeit, an der syntaktischen Gestalt von Texteinsätzen abzulesen, ob ursprüngliche Anfänge bzw. Unteranfänge zumindest vorliegen können oder ob die Texte zum Zweck ihrer Einfügung in umfassendere Kompositionen am Beginn sprachlich verändert wurden.

Solche Untersuchungen sind methodisch kompliziert, denn sie sind zwischen Sprachwissenschaft und Literaturwissenschaft, zwischen der Lehre von den Verbfunktionen, den Sätzen, Satzverbünden und Textsegmenten angesiedelt. Sie operieren auf der Ebene des Satzes und auf der umfassenderen, schwerer abzugrenzenden Ebene des Textes. Man sollte mit Satztypen argumentieren können. Diese sind jedoch im Bereich des AT nicht hinreichend isoliert und beschrieben. Zudem sollte jeder herangezogene Text auch formkritisch analysiert sein, damit sich die Einzelbeobachtungen einem größeren Rahmen einfügen. Ich nenne daher lediglich einige Beobachtungen und Gesichtspunkte in der Hoffnung, weiterführende Diskussionen zu provozieren.[1]

---

[1] Zahlreiche Anregungen verdanke ich den Diskussionen im Münchner Kreis um Prof. Dr W. Richter und in der syntaktischen Arbeitsgruppe mit Prof. Dr A. Denz, München. Als Textbasis dient die Prosa in Gen.-2 Kön. Andere Prosa-Belege werden nur unsystematisch herangezogen.

Nach einer kurzen Einführung wähle ich als Einstieg die Vorstellung einer Person zu Beginn einer erzählenden Einheit und erläutere daran die syntaktische Eigenart der Hintergrundschilderung. Im Hauptteil diskutiere ich die häufig begegnenden Hintergrundschilderungen der Form *w=x-qaṭal*, und zwar vornehmlich die Belege am Erzählanfang; hier interessieren besonders die Beispiele mit *HYY*. Abschließend zeige ich mögliche Konsequenzen für die syntaktische Interpretation der heftig umkämpften Verse Gen. i 1, 2 auf.

I. *Einführung*

Wie fängt man im Althebräischen an, wenn man von Vergangenem sprechen will? Die komplizierte literarische Geschichte der meisten alttestamentlichen Texte, die Tatsache, daß selbst viele Buchgrenzen sekundär sind, erschweren die Suche nach eindeutigen Anfängen. Anders steht es mit der Textsorte Rede. Die Anfänge von Reden sind formal klar gekennzeichnet und in der Regel literarkritisch nicht umstritten. Nach einer Einleitung mit *ʾMR* ist der erste Satz einer Rede Neueinsatz.[2] Welche syntaktische Gestalt haben erste Redesätze, die keine Konjunktionalsätze sind und vergangene Sachverhalte bezeichnen? Von den Stellungsregeln her erwartet und üblich ist *x-qaṭal*[3] sowie im Einwortsatz *qaṭal*.[4] Sehr häufig begegnet die Wortfolge *qaṭal-x*.[5] Dagegen fehlen alle syndetischen Sätze:

[2] Zu Ausnahmen vgl. W. Groß, *Verbform und Funktion. wayyiqṭol für die Gegenwart? Ein Beitrag zur Syntax poetischer althebräischer Texte* (St Ottilien, 1976), S. 35-7. Kein mir bekannter Beleg bezieht sich auf vergangene Sachverhalte.

[3] Weitergeführt durch: *wayyiqṭol* (z.B. Gen. xxvi 28, xlviii 3; Dtn. vi 21; Jos. xxiv 2; Ri. xx 4; 2 Kön. i 6, vi 28, xiv 9), *w= x-qaṭal* (z.B. Ex. ii 19; Num. xxvii 3; 2 Sam. xix 10), *w= qaṭal-x* (z.B. 1 Sam. xvii 34), *whnh+ Partizipialsatz* (z.B. 2 Sam. i 6), *w= Nominalsatz* (z.B. Ri. xiii 6). Charakteristisch für die Textsorte Rede sind solche ersten Sätze, deren *x hn* bzw. *hnh* bzw. eine Partikel wie *ʾmnh* ist (z.B. Gen. xxvii 6; Dtn. v 24; Jos. ii 2, vii 20).

[4] Z.B. Gen. xlvii 25; Num. xxii 34; 1 Sam. xii 10, xiii 13, xv 24.

[5] Vgl. W. Groß, *wayyiqṭol* (wie Anm. 2), S. 32-5. Neuerdings erkennt O. Rößler "Zum althebräischen Tempussystem. Eine morphosyntaktische Untersuchung", in ders. (Hrsg.), *Hebraica, Marburger Studien zur Afrika- und Asienkunde*, Serie B: *Asien*, Bd 4 (Berlin, 1977), S. 53, dies als "Grenzfall ... bei Eröffnung der Rede" an (dieser "Grenzfall" fügt sich Rößlers System kaum widerspruchslos ein). *qaṭal-x* für vergangene Sachverhalte steht jedoch auch in nichtersten Redesätzen (vgl. Dtn. ii 7, v 28d; Jos. vii 11; Ri. vii 14; 1 Sam. xiii 14; 2 Sam. xvi 8; 1 Kön. xvii 18, xxii 19; 2 Kön. xx 5e= Jes. xxxviii 5e; nach Imperativ von *RʾY*: Gen. xxxix 14; Jos. xxiii 4; 1 Sam. xxv 35). Ohne daß syntaktisch relevante Asyndese—z.B. als Explikation oder als Attributsatz—vorläge, ist dies, im Gegensatz zur alle Sachverhalte miteinander verknüpfenden Erzählung,

w = Verbalsatz, *w = Partizipialsatz*, *w = Nominalsatz* und sogar *wayyiqṭol*; dieses ist lediglich sehr selten nach *w*-losem *x* in Pendenskonstruktion belegt.[6]

Ein ganz anderes Bild bieten Textanfänge, die von Vergangenem handeln und keine Redesätze sind: (1) Die Wortfolge *qaṭal-x* fehlt; sie ist in Prosa auf Redesätze beschränkt.[7] (2) Überwiegend treten syndetische Sätze und Verbformen auf: *wayyiqṭol*, *w = x-qaṭal*, *w = Partizipialsatz*, *w = Nominalsatz*. Wegen der literarkritischen Probleme verzichte ich hier auf die Untersuchung der interessanten Frage, ob syndetische Textanfänge auch am absoluten Text- bzw. Buchanfang oder nur bei Anfängen minderen Ranges—z.B. bei einer Erzählung innerhalb eines größeren erzählenden Kontextes, am Beginn eines zweiten Erzählstranges—möglich sind.

---

in Rede möglich, da der Sprecher jederzeit im Lauf seiner Redeäußerung neu einsetzen kann. *qaṭal-x* für vergangene Sachverhalte in ersten Redesätzen begegnet: (1) ohne Subjektslexem: Gen. xxvi 32, xxxii 7, xxxvii 17, xxxviii 26; Ex. ix 27, x 16, xvi 12, xxxii 9, xxxiii 12g; Num. xiii 27; Dtn. i 20, 41, v 28, ix 13; Ri x 10; 1 Sam. v 10, vii 6, xv 2, xviii 8, xxii 9, 22; 2 Sam. xii 13, 27, xvii 20, xviii 29, xxiv 10; 1 Kön. v 22, ix 3, xxi 10, xxii 17; 2 Kön. ii 10, vii 10, viii 14, x 8, xx 5 = Jes. xxxviii 5; morphologisch auch als Partizip deutbar: 2 Kön. ix 20; meist steht das Verb in 1. oder 2. Person (3. Person: Gen. xxxvii 17, xxxviii 26; 1 Sam. v 10, xviii 8; 2 Sam. xvii 20; 2 Kön. ix 20, x 8); (2) mit lexematisch ausgedrücktem Subjekt: Gen. xxx 6, 18, 20, 23, xlii 28, 30, xlv 9; Num. xxii 14; Jos. x 17; Ri. xvi 23, 24; 1 Sam. vi 21, xiii 4, xiv 29, xv 28 (oder Koinzidenz?), xviii 7 = xxi 12 = xxix 5, xxiii 7, xxvi 8; 2 Sam. vi 12, xiii 30, xv 10, 13, xvii 9, xix 3; 1 Kön. xvi 16, xxi 13, 14; 2 Kön. xxii 9; morphologisch auch als Partizip deutbar: Gen. xxxix 17; 1 Sam. iv 17, xv 12; 2 Kön. viii 7, ix 18; das Verb steht in 3. Person; außer dem pronominalen Objekt (Gen. xxx 6, 20, xlv 9; 1 Sam. xxiii 7) tritt kein Element zwischen Verb und das unmittelbar folgende Subjekt (Ausnahme: Gen. xxxix 17). Davon zu unterscheiden sind die gegenüber *x-qaṭal* seltenen Belege von *qaṭal-x* für Koinzidenz: Num. xiv 20; Dtn. xxvi 3; 2 Kön. ii 21, ix 6, 12; nach Imperativ von *R'Y*: Dtn. i 8, iv 5; Jos. vi 2, viii 1; mitten in Rede: Dtn. xxx 19a.

[6] Jes. vi 1; Jer. xxviii 8, xxxiii 24.

[7] Hier scheint sich der von H. Weinrich, *Tempus. Besprochene und erzählte Welt* (Stuttgart, [2]1971), analysierte Unterschied zwischen "besprochener" und "erzählter" Welt auszuwirken. Entgegen W. Schneider, *Grammatik des Biblischen Hebräisch* (München, 1974), S. 182 ff., ist dies jedoch nicht die grundlegende, das gesamte althebräische Verbalsystem organisierende Opposition. Diese Annahme führt Schneider S. 189 Anm. 9 zu der überraschenden These: "Das Perfekt ist also eigentlich gar kein Tempus, weil es gegenüber der grundlegenden Opposition: Erzählen/Besprechen indifferent ist." Da Progresse in Vergangenheit auch in Redesätzen durch *wayyiqṭol* bezeichnet werden (vgl. die Beispiele oben Anm. 3), müßte Schneider seine Behauptung konsequenterweise auch auf *wayyiqṭol* ausdehnen und sie damit ad absurdum führen. Für die Wahl der Verbformen bedeutend einflußreicher scheint im Althebräischen der Gegensatz Vordergrund-Hintergrund zu sein.

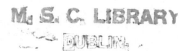

II. *Einführung einer unbekannten Person zu Beginn einer Erzählung*

Die Einführung unbekannter Personen im ersten Satz einer Erzählung geschieht im AT auf vier syntaktisch verschiedene Weisen:
(1) *x-qaṭal* (von *HYY*): Ijob i 1: *ʾyš hyh bʾrṣ ʿwṣ.*[8] Dieser Typ begegnet nur im absoluten Anfang.[9]
(2) *wayyiqṭol* (von *HYY*): Ri. xvii 1: *wyhy ʾyš mhr ʾprym.*[10] Dieses Formmuster ist am häufigsten belegt; es steht auch da, wo eindeutig der Zweitstrang einer Erzählung eröffnet wird; z.B. Ri. xvii 7.[11]
(3) *w = Nominalsatz*: 1 Sam. xxv 2: *wʾyš bmʿwn.*[12]
(4) *w = x-qaṭal* (von *HYY*): 2 Kön. v 1: *w = nʿmn śr ṣbʾ mlk ʾrm hyh ʾyš gdwl lpny ʾdnyw.* Im Gegensatz zu (1)-(3) beginnt dieser Satz nicht mit einem indeterminierten Appellativum, sondern mit dem Eigennamen der einzuführenden Person. Dennoch werden nicht von dem als bekannt vorausgesetzten Naaman Aussagen gemacht, sondern Naaman wird durch die Sätze des Verses v 1 allererst vorgestellt.

Fall (2) ist syntaktisch unauffällig, die übliche Form für Progreß in Vergangenheit. Die Frage, wieso und unter welchen Bedingungen eine Erzählung mit einem Progreß beginnen kann, obgleich die Progreßform die Zweitsetzung eines Sachverhalts bezeichnet, der erste Satz einer Erzählung aber für diese faktisch Erstsetzung bedeutet, ist wohl in der Stilistik hebräischer Erzählkunst zu diskutieren, falls man nicht zu dem literarkritischen Urteil gelangen sollte, so könnten nur Erzählungen beginnen, die nicht ein selbständiges

---

[8] Vgl. auch 2 Sam. xii 1.

[9] In ersten Redesätzen steht für vergangenen Sachverhalt mit indeterminierter Nominalgruppe als Subjekt auch *x-qaṭal* von anderen Verben als *HYY*, z.B. Jos. ii 2; 2 Kön. i 6 (wohl besprechende Kontexte).

[10] Vgl. auch Ri. xiii 2; 1 Sam. i 1, ix 1. Literarkritisch fraglich ist Ri. xix 1; sollten sich die Sätze xix 1ab als redaktionell sekundär von einer ehemals mit 1c beginnenden Erzählung abheben lassen, wäre dies eine Variante mit *wyhy* . . . *Partizip*. Diese Belege wurden von W. Richter, *Traditionsgeschichtliche Untersuchungen zum Richterbuch* (Bonn, ²1966), S. 12 f., 384-6, als "Erzählungs-Eröffnungsformel" diskutiert; dort weitere formale Varianten. Soweit sie nicht im ersten Satz einer Erzählung stehen, werden sie hier nicht aufgeführt.

[11] Erste Sätze von Zweitsträngen können freilich unbekannte Personen auch ganz anders einführen; z.B. (a) *w = hnh + indeterminierte Nominalgruppe* (= *Subjekt*) + *Partizip*: 1 Kön. xiii 25; (b) *w = indeterminierte Nominalgruppe* (= *Subjekt*) + *Partizip*: 1 Kön. xiii 11; (c) *w = Nominalsatz*: Rut ii 1; (d) *wayyiqṭol* von anderen Verben als *HYY*: Ex. ii 1; Num xi 26. Diese Fälle sind besonders schwer zu beurteilen. Hier fehlt jedes syntaktische Signal für den Neueinsatz. (e) *w = x-qaṭal*: 1 Kön. xx 35; 2 Kön. iv 1, 42 (oder als Partizip zu deuten?), vii 3.

[12] Vgl. auch 1 Kön. xi 26; vielleicht ursprünglich ein Erzählbeginn. Bezüglich des Eigennamens vgl. Nr. (4).

Werk eröffnen, bzw. Erzählungen mit *wyhy* im ersten Satz könnten so nicht selbständig einzeln tradiert worden sein.[13]

Fall (1) ist am absoluten Anfang erwartet. *qaṭal-x* ist außerhalb von Rede in Prosa nicht möglich. Nominalsatz ohne *w* ist auch ausgeschlossen: Der unabhängige *w*-lose Nominalsatz enthält kein Formelement, das die zeitliche Einordnung des von ihm bezeichneten Sachverhalts andeutete; er ist dem Gegenwartspunkt des Sprechers zugeordnet, bezeichnet somit die Gegenwart. Eröffnet dagegen *w* den Nominalsatz, so kann das anzeigen, daß der Nominalsatz nicht auf den Gegenwartspunkt des Sprechers, sondern auf den voraufgehenden Satz bezogen ist, d.h. daß der Nominalsatz einen mit dem Sachverhalt dieses vorhergehenden Satzes gleichzeitigen Sachverhalt bezeichnet. Selbständiger Nominalsatz ohne *w* kann also eine Erzählung, die in Vergangenheit spielt, nicht eröffnen, da er eben auf Grund seiner syntaktischen Gestalt nicht einen vergangenen, sondern einen gegenwärtigen Sachverhalt bezeichnen würde. So muß hier die Suffixkonjugation von *HYY* hinzutreten, um die Zeitsphäre des Satzes anzudeuten.[14]

Anders steht es mit Fall (3), dem syndetischen Nominalsatz. Wie in Fall (2) beginnt der Text mit *w*. Dieser syndetische Nominalsatz ähnelt formal einem Umstandssatz (Ḥāl-Satz) der Gleichzeitigkeit, der—entsprechend der Zeitsphäre des voraufgehenden Satzes, dem er syntaktisch zugeordnet ist—einen Sachverhalt der Vergangenheit, Gegenwart oder Zukunft bezeichnen kann. Die syndetische nominale Erzähleröffnung von 1 Sam. xxv 2 hat manches mit dem Ḥāl-Satz gemeinsam, unterscheidet sich aber auch in wesentlichen Punkten.

---

[13] Diese literarkritische These scheint mir angesichts des alttestamentlichen Befunds unwahrscheinlich. Immerhin steht in solchen Sätzen nicht beliebiges *wayyiqṭol*, sondern stets *wyhy*. Die Eröffnung einer selbständigen Erzählung mit *wayyiqṭol* anderer Verben als *HYY* ist meines Wissens im AT nicht belegt. Steht derartiges *wayyiqṭol* an größeren Erzähleinschnitten, so ist eine übergreifende literarische Bearbeitung und Komposition anzunehmen.

[14] Soweit nicht statt dessen *wyhy* gewählt wird. Zu *HYY* im Nominalsatz vgl. mit reicher Literatur N. Kilwing, "*hyh* als Kopula im Nominalsatz", *Biblische Notizen* 7 (1978), S. 36-60. Nominalsatz und Verbalsatz werden nach der Wortart des Prädikats, nicht nach inhaltlichen Merkmalen der durch diesen Satz bezeichneten Aussage unterschieden. Im Gegensatz zu Kilwing und vielen anderen betrachte ich daher alle Sätze mit finiten Formen des Verbs *HYY* als Verbalsätze. Charakteristika des Partizips, die dieses zwischen den Wortarten Nomen (Substantiv, Adjektiv) und Verb ansiedeln (vgl. W. Richter, *Grundlagen einer althebräischen Grammatik 1* [St Ottilien, 1978], S. 171 f.), berechtigen ferner dazu, die Partizipialsätze von den Nominalsätzen zu unterscheiden und als eigene Kategorie von Sätzen zu beschreiben.

Die Gemeinsamkeiten: (1) 1 Sam. xxv 2a ist ein syndetischer Nominalsatz, der (2) Nebenumstände bezeichnet, Zusatzinformationen gibt, (3) bezüglich seiner Zeitsphäre nicht auf den Gegenwartspunkt des Sprechers, sondern auf die Zeitsphäre des Kontextes bezogen ist.[15]

Die Unterschiede: (1) Dem Satz 1 Sam. xxv 2a geht kein weiterer zur selben Kleinen Einheit gehöriger Satz voraus, (2) er enthält daher auch keinen Rückverweis auf einen solchen Satz in Gestalt eines selbständigen oder enklitischen Personalpronomens,[16] (3) er ist infolgedessen auch nicht syntaktisch auf einen vorhergehenden Satz bezogen.[17]

Vor allem die Stellung des Satzes—er folgt nicht dem Satz, dessen Zeitsphäre er zugeordnet ist, sondern geht ihm vorauf—und die Tatsache, daß er von seiner Bedeutung her nicht als "wobei"-, "indem"- oder "während"-Sachverhalt aufgefaßt werden kann, machen es unmöglich, in ihm einen Ḥāl-Satz zu sehen. Die Übereinstimmungen mit den Ḥāl-Sätzen, vor allem das auffällige *w*, obgleich es sich um den ersten Satz einer Einheit handelt, begründen aber die Wahrscheinlichkeit, daß hier eine eigene Satzkategorie mit vergleichbarer Funktion vorliegt. Der Satz läßt sich als syntaktische Gestalt der Schilderung gleichzeitiger Hintergrundsachverhalte bestimmen. Tatsächlich enthalten die Verse 1 Sam. xxv 2, 3 mit

---

[15] Auch die Folge *w + Subjekt + Prädikat* ist charakteristisch (vgl. F. I. Andersen, *The Hebrew Verbless Clause in the Pentateuch* [Nashville und New York, 1970], S. 35, 45 f.), jedoch nicht notwendig; vgl. Sätze, die Besitz anzeigen, des Typs: *w = l = enklitisches Personalpronomen x* (vgl. Andersen, S. 49 f., und S. 82 Nr. 295).

[16] Kataphora mittels enklitischem oder selbständigem Personalpronomen ist in hebräischer Prosa nicht üblich. Pronominalen Rückbezug enthalten die meisten echten Ḥāl-Sätze im Hebräischen. Allerdings ist die Kategorie des Umstandssatzes im Althebräischen nach Form wie Funktion noch sehr unzulänglich analysiert. Vgl. die restriktive Definition von Umstandssatz bei E. König, *Historisch-Kritisches Lehrgebäude der hebräischen Sprache mit comparativer Berücksichtigung des Semitischen überhaupt, Zweite Hälfte 2. (Schluss-) Theil. Syntax* (Leipzig, 1897), S. 498 ff., § 362 a-w, mit dem weiteren Gebrauch von circumstantial clause bei S. R. Driver, *A Treatise on the Use of the Tenses in Hebrew and Some Other Syntactical Questions* (Oxford, [3]1892, Nachdruck: Norwich, 1969), S. 195 ff. (Appendix I), und von proposition circonstantielle bei P. Joüon, *Grammaire de l'Hébreu Biblique* (Rom, 1923; édition photomécanique corrigée: Graz, 1965), S. 487 ff., § 159.

[17] Die syntaktischen Merkmale des Bezugs der Hintergrundsätze auf den jeweils folgenden Vordergrundsatz sind noch nicht befriedigend geklärt, zumal nicht selten mehrere solcher Hintergrundsätze am Beginn von Erzählungen stehen.

Ausnahme eines *wyhy*-Satzes neun derartige syndetische Nominalsätze, die Hintergrundinformationen für die in xxv 4 mit *wayyiqṭol* einsetzende Vordergrundhandlung geben.

Bezeichnet *w = Nominalsatz*, formal dem nominalen Umstandssatz nahestehend, syntaktisch den gleichzeitigen Hintergrundsachverhalt, so ist entsprechend dem verbalen Ḥāl-Satz der Form *w = x-qaṭal* dieses Satzmuster ebenfalls für den Hintergrundsachverhalt erwartet. Fall (4): 2 Kön. v 1 bezeugt diese Form.[18] Auch *w + Nominalgruppe (= Subjekt) + Partizip*, die Form des Ḥāl-Satzes, der nicht gleichzeitige Zustände, sondern gleichzeitige Nebenhandlungen beinhaltet, begegnet als Hintergrundsatz zu Beginn von Erzählungen, die nicht am Anfang eines Werkes stehen; allerdings ist mir kein Beleg mit indeterminierter Nominalgruppe als Subjekt bekannt; vgl. 1 Kön. x 1.[19]

Die Fälle (3) und (4) der Einführung einer unbekannten Person zu Beginn der Erzählung haben somit Beobachtungen und Überlegungen provoziert, die sich in folgender These zusammenfassen lassen: Am Erzählanfang, wo sie auf Grund ihrer Position nicht als Ḥāl-Sätze deutbar sind, dienen folgende syntaktisch von den Satzformen des Erzählvordergrunds unterschiedene Satzformen der Schilderung des Erzählhintergrunds: (1) *w = Nominalsatz*, (2) *w + Nominalgruppe (= Subjekt) + Partizip*, (3) *w + Nominalgruppe (= Subjekt) + qaṭal*.

Da Hintergrundschilderungen nicht auf den ersten Satz oder die ersten Sätze von Erzählungen beschränkt sind, zieht diese These weitere Behauptungen nach sich. (1) Solche Hintergrundschilderungen sind auch am Beginn von Unterabschnitten zu erwarten. (2) Es gibt überhaupt keine Regel, die dem hebräischen Autor vorschriebe, an welchen Stellen seiner Erzählung er Hintergrundinformationen zu geben habe. Infolgedessen ist auch im Kontext bei allen Sätzen der beschriebenen Formen, die—weil nicht oder nur gezwungen als "wobei"-, "indem"-, "während"-Sachverhalte deutbar—nur schwer als Ḥāl-Sätze interpretiert werden können, zu prüfen, ob sie nicht Hintergrundsätze sind, ob sie daher nicht, statt dem Voraufgehenden, vielmehr dem Folgenden zugeordnet sind. Das ist vor allem bei Sätzen ohne selbständigen oder enklitischen pronominalen Rückbezug wahrscheinlich.

---

[18] Zur Funktion dieser Suffixkonjugation von *HYY* vgl. den folgenden Abschnitt III.

[19] Vgl. auch Jos. vi 1; Ri. xviii 1b, falls 1a literarkritisch abzutrennen ist.

Wir erhielten damit ein syntaktisches Instrument, das uns befähigte, die Reliefgebung alttestamentlicher Erzählungen genauer zu erfassen, so zu erkennen, was der hebräische Autor in den Vordergrund, in das Zentrum des Interesses rücken und was er dagegen eher als Hintergrundsinformation erscheinen lassen wollte. Freilich ist dies nur dann ein syntaktisches Instrument, sind die Funktionen solcher Sätze nur dann an der Form ablesbar, wenn die am Erzählanfang dazu in Opposition stehenden Satzformen: *wyhy + Nominalgruppe* (= *Subjekt*), *wyhy. . .Partizip*, *x-hayā*, *x-qaṭal*,[20] *x-yiqṭol Langform*[21] nicht ebenfalls Hintergrund schildern, sondern im Vordergrund erzählen. Mir scheint diese Annahme auf Grund meiner bisherigen Text-Beobachtungen naheliegend und von der Sache her sinnvoll. Daß derselbe Sachverhalt—z.B. die Einführung einer unbekannten Person am Erzählanfang—von einem Erzähler als Vordergrund (Fälle 1 und 2), vom anderen als Hintergrund (Fälle 3 und 4) gestaltet wird, bereitet keine Schwierigkeit. Was Vorder- und was Hintergrund ist, liegt nicht so sehr in der Natur des Sachverhalts als vielmehr in der Erzählstrategie des Autors begründet.[22]

Diese These, Hintergrundsatz sei eine syntaktisch relevante Kategorie im Althebräischen, wurde an syntaktisch eindeutigen und formal unzweifelhaft in Opposition stehenden Belegen erarbeitet.

---

[20] *x* = Zeitbestimmung oder Partikel wie *ʾz*.

[21] Nach *ʾz*. Sätze mit Partikeln wie *ʾz*, *ṭrm* (z.B. Gen. ii 5; hier ist jedoch die ursprüngliche syntaktische Gestalt des Textanfangs unklar, da 4b redaktionell sein dürfte), die das Verb an nicht-erste Position verweisen, sind als eigene Gruppe gesondert auf ihre Oppositionen hin zu untersuchen. Dasselbe gilt für die Konjunktionalsätze.

[22] Weinrich (wie Anm. 7), führt bezüglich europäischer Literatur aus (S. 93 f.): "Was in der Erzählung Hintergrund und was Vordergrund ist, läßt sich nicht ein für allemal sagen . . . Die Erzählung hat . . . normalerweise eine Einleitung. In der Einleitung steht gewöhnlich ein Hintergrundtempus. Viele Erzählungen bezeichnen außerdem den Schluß durch eine ausdrückliche Ausleitung. Auch die Ausleitung liebt das Hintergrundtempus. Das ist nicht notwendig und nicht immer so, aber man trifft doch verhältnismäßig oft eine Ballung der Hintergrundtempora am Anfang und am Ende der Erzählung . . . Im eigentlichen Erzählkern findet man dann die Tempora des Hintergrunds . . . bei Nebenumständen, Beschreibungen, Reflexionen und allen anderen Gegenständen, die der Erzähler in den Hintergrund zu rücken wünscht. Auf der anderen Seite ist ebenfalls nicht a priori zu sagen, was in einer Erzählung Vordergrund ist . . . Vordergrund ist, was der Erzähler als Vordergrund aufgefaßt wissen will." S. 132 ff. zeigt Weinrich an Boccaccio und an mittelalterlichen Novellensammlungen, daß Erzählungen, die in einen Rahmen eingebunden sind, oft ohne Hintergrundschilderungen unmittelbar im Vordergrund beginnen. Z.B. S. 137: Einsatz im Vordergrund: "Fuit quidam comes Imperatoris"; Fortführung im Hintergrund: "qui sedebat in domo sua et habebat quendam parvulum natum. . ."

Sie muß an vielen erzählenden Texten überprüft und verifiziert werden. Sie könnte eine schärfere Erfassung auch des vom Hintergrundsatz unterschiedenen hebräischen Umstandssatzes ermöglichen. Ich wende mich im folgenden der am Anfang bzw. bei Unterabschnitten von Erzählungen häufigsten Form von Hintergrundschilderungen zu: *w = x-qaṭal* und diskutiere einige in solchem Zusammenhang noch nicht beachtete Probleme der Verwendung von *HYY*.

III. *Hintergrundschilderungen der Form w = x-qaṭal*

Vorbemerkung: An beliebiger Position im Text gilt: Wenn *x* eine Konjunktion ist, kann die Suffixkonjugation in Position *x-qaṭal* entweder einen zur vergangenen Handlung des übergeordneten Satzes vorvergangenen Sachverhalt oder einen nur auf den Gegenwartspunkt des Sprechers bezogen vergangenen Sachverhalt bezeichnen, wobei dessen zeitlicher Bezug zum Sachverhalt des übergeordneten Satzes unberücksichtigt bleibt. Im Gegensatz z.B. zum Deutschen, das für auf den vergangenen Sachverhalt des übergeordneten Satzes bezogene Vergangenheit, also Vorvergangenheit, die Form Plusquamperfekt bereithält, vermag das Hebräische hier, soweit *qaṭal* verwendet wird, mit syntaktischen Mitteln nicht zu differenzieren.[23]

Auch wenn *x* keine Konjunktion ist, kann *w = x-qaṭal* im Kontext beide Sachverhaltszuordnungen bezeichnen: bezogene Vergangenheit (= Vorvergangenheit), den sog. Rückgriff,[24] und einfache Vergangenheit; dies zweite vor allem bei Betonung oder Antithese in Satzpaaren der Form *wayyiqṭol-x w = x-qaṭal*.[25] Daher ist zu vermuten, daß für Hintergrundsätze der Form *w = x-qaṭal* dasselbe gilt.

Im folgenden interessiert vor allem die Verwendung der Suffixkonjugation von *HYY* in ersten Hintergrundsätzen, sei es am Beginn einer Einheit, sei es als Eröffnung eines Unterabschnitts. Der Übersicht halber unterscheide ich die Prädikate nach Wortart bzw. Wortgruppe, ohne damit behaupten zu wollen, es handle sich um unterschiedene syntaktisch relevante Satztypen.

---

[23] Das habe ich für *qaṭal* nach *ʾšr* gezeigt; vgl. W. Groß, "Das nicht substantivierte Partizip als Prädikat im Relativsatz hebräischer Prosa", *JNSL* 4 (1976), S. 23-47. Der Hebräer konnte beide Sachverhaltszuordnungen dennoch unterscheiden, da sie bei Ersetzungsproben mit Präfixkonjugation Langform und mit Partizip verschieden reagieren (vgl. ebd. S. 27 ff.). Vgl. zu Suffixkonjugation nach *kī*: Bezug nur zum Gegenwartspunkt des Sprechers: z.B. Gen. xiii 6, xxi 16, xlii 5, xlvii 20; Ex. xii 33; Bezug zum vergangenen Sachverhalt des übergeordneten Satzes: z.B. Gen. xxvi 20, xxviii 11, xli 21.

[24] Z.B. Gen. xxxi 34; 1 Sam. xxviii 3; 2 Sam. xviii 18.

[25] Z.B. Gen. xli 54; Num. xxiv 25.

(a) Prädikat ist ein Adjektiv oder ein Substantiv. Mit *HYY*: Gen. iii 1: *whnḥš hyh ʿrwm mkl ḥyt hśdh.*[26] Mir ist nur ein Kontrastbeispiel ohne *HYY* in dieser Erstposition bekannt: 1 Kön. xi 26.[27] Häufiger finden sich entsprechende Sätze ohne *HYY* mitten im Kontext, oder sie folgen auf andere Hintergrundsätze.[28]

(b) Prädikat ist eine Präpositionalverbindung bzw. ein Nomen in Funktion prädikativer Umstandsbestimmung. Mit *HYY*: 1 Kön. xv 16: *wmlḥmh hyth byn ʾsʾ wbyn bʿšʾ mlk yśrʾl kl ymyhm.*[29] Kontrastbeispiel ohne *HYY* im ersten Hintergrundsatz: 1 Sam. xxv 2.[30]

(c) Prädikat ist ein Partizip. Mit *HYY*: Ex. iii 1: *wmšh hyh rʿh ʾt ṣʾn ytrw ḥtnw khn mdyn.*[31] Gegenbeispiele ohne *HYY* am Erzählanfang überwiegen;[32] in ersten Hintergrundsätzen an Unterabschnitten häufen sie sich.[33]

Der Befund ist somit uneinheitlich.[34] Folgende Feststellungen scheinen mir möglich. (1) Während der *w*-lose Nominalsatz und der *w*-lose Partizipialsatz in Vordergrundschilderung der Suffixkonjugation von *HYY* bedürfen (und damit zu Verbalsätzen werden),[35] um als Sachverhalte der Vergangenheit verstanden zu werden,

[26] Vgl. auch Ri. xi 1; 2 Kön. iii 4, v 1.

[27] Bei Vordergrundformulierungen ohne *w* ist *HYY* unentbehrlich, um die Vergangenheit des durch Nominalsatz ausgedrückten Sachverhalts zu bezeichnen: Gen. vi 9.

[28] Vgl. 1 Sam. xxv 2, 3; 2 Sam. xiii 3, xvii 25; 1 Kön. xi 28. In Gen. xxix 17 ist der Hintergrundsatz 17a ohne *HYY*, der parallele Satz 17b mit *HYY* formuliert. Hier dient *HYY* dazu, das Adversativverhältnis zu signalisieren.

[29] Vgl. 2 Sam. iii 17; 2 Kön. vii 3; Prädikat ist hier *ptḥ hšʿr.*

[30] In Vordergrundformulierungen ohne *w* ist *HYY* notwendig: 2 Sam. xii 1; Ijob i 1; oder der Vordergrund ist mit *wyhy* formuliert; vgl. Ri. xvii 1, 7 und die Belege Anm. 10.

[31] Vgl. 2 Kön. vi 8. Wiederum kann bei Vordergrundformulierungen ohne *w* *HYY* nicht fehlen: Gen. xxxvii 2; Ri. i 7; 1 Sam. xvii 34.

[32] Vgl. Jos. vi 1; Ri. xviii 1 (vgl. Anm. 19); 1 Kön. x 1.

[33] Vgl. 1 Sam. vi 13, xxxi 1; 2 Sam. xviii 24; 1 Kön. i 5, xiii 11, xxii 10; 2 Kön. vi 32.

[34] Er wird noch unübersichtlicher, wenn man solche Hintergrundsätze einbezieht, die entweder auf andere Hintergrundsätze folgen oder als einzelne im Kontext stehen. In diesen Fällen bilden die Sätze mit *HYY* eine unbedeutende Minderheit, ohne daß der Grund für die Setzung des *HYY* einsichtig würde. Ich nenne zwei Beispielgruppen. (a) Mit *HYY*: Gen. xli 56 (ähnlich mit Suffixkonjugation eines anderen Verbs: Gen. xliii 1); ohne *HYY*: 2 Kön iv 38 (Vordergrundformulierungen mit *wyhy*: Gen. xii 10, xxvi 1, xli 54; 2 Sam. xxi 1). (b) Mit *HYY*: Num. xxxii 1; Ri. viii 30; 1 Sam. ix 2; ohne *HYY*:Gen. xxix 16; Ri. xvii 5 (Pendenskonstruktion); 1 Sam. i 2 (im selben Vers Vordergrundformulierung mit *wyhy*); 2 Sam. iv 4, ix 12, xiii 1, 3; 2 Kön. x 1 (dagegen Vordergrundformulierungen mit *wyhy*: Ri. x 4, xii 9, 14; 1 Kön. v 29).

[35] Vgl. Anm. 14.

läßt sich für erste Hintergrundsätze der Gestalt *w = Nominalsatz*, *w = Partizipialsatz* kein syntaktisch zwingender Grund nennen, der erklären könnte, warum *HYY* in einem Fall steht, im anderen fehlt. Es ergibt sich keine Opposition für solche Sätze mit und ohne *HYY*.

(2) Dennoch ist eine Tendenz erkennbar: Eröffnen die ersten Hintergrundsätze mit Substantiv, Adjektiv, Präpositionalverbindung als Prädikat die Erzählung, so überwiegen die Sätze mit *HYY* deutlich. Das ist leicht zu verstehen: Im ersten Satz der Erzählung, dem ja noch keine Zusatzinformationen aus dem Kontext vorgegeben sind, signalisiert *HYY* dem Hörer/Leser sofort, daß es sich um vergangenen Hintergrund handelt.

(3) In allen bisher diskutierten Hintergrundsätzen bezeichnet *HYY* den Sachverhalt lediglich als vergangen bezüglich des Gegenwartspunktes des Sprechers, nicht als vorvergangen, d.h. nicht als vergangen bezüglich des vergangenen Sachverhalts eines folgenden Satzes oder eines anderen vergangenen Relationswerts. *w = Partizipialsatz* und *w + Nominalgruppe (= Subjekt) + hayā + Partizip* bzw. *w = Nominalsatz* und *w + Nominalgruppe (= Subjekt) + hayā + nominales Prädikat* stehen also nicht in Opposition wie Bezeichnung der einfachen Vergangenheit (deutsch: "war") und der Vorvergangenheit (deutsch: "war gewesen").

Daraus ergeben sich zwei Konsequenzen. (a) Ein Hintergrundsatz der Form *w = Partizipialsatz* oder *w = Nominalsatz* bezeichnet in vergangenem Kontext einen vergangenen gleichzeitigen Hintergrund, er drückt die Gleichzeitigkeit des vergangenen Hintergrunds zum vergangenen Vordergrund aus. Ein Hintergrundsatz der Form *w + Nominalgruppe (= Subjekt) + hayā + Partizip* bzw. *w + Nominalgruppe (= Subjekt) + hayā + nominales Prädikat* bezeichnet dagegen in vergangenem Kontext lediglich einen vergangenen Hintergrund, läßt aber unausgedrückt, ob dieser sich zu seinem vergangenen Vordergrundsachverhalt gleich- oder vorzeitig verhält.[36] Die in der Vorbemerkung geäußerte Vermutung hat sich also bestätigt. (b) Dasselbe ist für Hintergrundsätze der Gestalt *w = x-qaṭal* von anderen Verben als *HYY* zu vermuten.[37]

---

[36] Vorzeitig sind z.B. folgende Hintergrundsätze mit *HYY* zu verstehen: Ri. xx 38; 2 Kön. ix 14.

[37] Rückgriffe, also vorzeitige vergangene Hintergrundsachverhalte, bezeichnen z.B. Gen. xxxix 1; 1 Sam. ix 15, xiv 47, xxviii 3; 2 Kön. xiii 14. Dagegen scheint die Annahme lediglich auf den Gegenwartspunkt des Sprechers bezogen vergangener, also faktisch (aber nicht formal als solcher bezeichneter) zum vergangenen Kontext gleichzeitiger Hintergrundsachverhalte wahrscheinlicher bei Sätzen wie Gen. iv 1; 1 Kön. xi 1, xx 23, 35, xxii 34; 2 Kön. ix 1, 11.

Das hat bedeutende Konsequenzen für die Übersetzung und für die zeitliche Einordnung solcher Sätze. Die Kombination sprachwissenschaftlicher (Syntax) und literaturwissenschaftlicher (Hintergrund—Vordergrund) Kategorien hat sich als fruchtbar erwiesen. In abschließenden Überlegungen möchte ich kurz zeigen, was sich aus diesen Beobachtungen zur syntaktischen Gestalt althebräischer Erzählanfänge und Hintergrundschilderungen für die syntaktische Deutung von Gen. i 1, 2 ergibt. Zugleich ist hier noch ein neuer Gesichtspunkt einzuführen.

IV. *Gen. i 1-3*

Die ersten beiden Verse des AT sind sowohl hinsichtlich ihrer inhaltlichen Deutung als auch bezüglich ihrer syntaktischen Analyse heftig umstritten. Ich berücksichtige im folgenden ausschließlich syntaktische Gesichtspunkte. Nur wenn, was häufig geschieht, die syntaktische Erörterung mehrere Interpretationen als möglich erweist, können unter Umständen inhaltliche Erwägungen herangezogen werden, um zu entscheiden, welche syntaktische Auffassung den Vorzug verdient. Da die Hypothese, es gebe eine spezielle Syntax von Schöpfungsaussagen, keine Wahrscheinlichkeit beanspruchen kann, versuche ich von rekurrenten syntaktischen Mustern her zu argumentieren.

Zu den syntaktischen Problemen von Gen. i 1-3 zählen vor allem die Artikellosigkeit von *br'šyt*, der syndetische Anschluß von Vers 2a, die Stellung des Verbs an nicht erster Position in 2a, überhaupt die Anwesenheit von *HYY* in diesem Satz, der doch einen Zustand schildert, und die daraus resultierende Beziehung der Sätze von Vers 2 sei es zu Vers 1, sei es zu Vers 3.

Nicht selten [38] werden i 1-3a als eine umfangreiche Periode gedeutet. Diese Interpretation ist wahrscheinlich syntaktisch annehmbar, stößt aber auf formale Bedenken. (1) Sie vermag das *HYY* in 2a nicht einsichtig zu machen. (2) Soweit sie, um der Schwierigkeit, Vers 2 als Umstandssätze zu Vers 1 (oder Vers 3) ansehen zu müssen, zu entgehen, Vers 2 als Parenthese bezeichnet,[39] arbeitet sie mit

---

[38] Z.B. K. Beyer, "Althebräische Syntax in Prosa und Poesie", in *Tradition und Glaube. Das frühe Christentum in seiner Umwelt, Festschrift K. G. Kuhn* (Göttingen, 1971), S. 76-96. Er verbindet damit die von der masoretischen Punktation ohne zwingenden Grund abweichende Deutung von *br'* als infinitivus constructus.

[39] So auch Beyer, S. 82: "weniger vorangestellte Zustandssätze (temporale Vordersätze) als eine (temporale) Parenthese".

einer unklaren Kategorie. Parenthese ist ein syntaktisch unverbunden eingeschalteter Satz; im Hebräischen werden Parenthesen asyndetisch eingefügt; so bleibt das *w* von 2a unerklärt. Vor allem stört diese syntaktische Hypothese den formelhaften Aufbau der Schöpfungswerke in Gen. i, die jeweils mit *wy'mr 'lhym* beginnen.[40]

Denjenigen Autoren jedoch, die sich durch die Artikellosigkeit von *br'šyt* nicht daran gehindert sehen, Vers 1 als Hauptsatz aufzufassen, könnte das in diesem Vortrag Dargestellte als Argument dienen. 2a hat die Gestalt eines ersten Hintergrundsatzes am Anfang einer Erzählung: ein syndetischer Satz mit Wortfolge Subjekt—Prädikat und mit Substantiv als Prädikat. In einem solchen Satz ist, wie soeben ausgeführt, *HYY* zwar nicht syntaktisch unabdingbar, aber doch üblich.

Versteht man Vers 2 als Kette von Hintergrundsätzen, so entfällt der Anstoß, die drei Sätze dieses Verses als Umstandssätze zu Vers 1 deuten zu müssen. Vielmehr ist Gen. i 1 dann Überschrift des ganzen Textes i 1-ii 4a und gehört noch nicht zur erzählenden Entfaltung des Schöpfungsvorgangs. Die so überschriebene Einheit beginnt mit der Schilderung des gleichzeitigen vergangenen Hintergrunds. *HYY* im ersten Satz dieser Einheit signalisiert dem Hörer, daß Vers 2 vergangene Sachverhalte als Hintergrund zu den in Vers 3 einsetzenden vergangenen Sachverhalten im Vordergrund benennt. Vers 2 ist somit nicht Vers 1, sondern den folgenden Versen zugeordnet, nicht aber in syntaktischer Abhängigkeit als Umstandssatz,[41] so daß Vers 3 in eine umfangreiche Konstruktion eingebunden wäre, sondern so, wie der Hintergrund seinem Vordergrund zugeordnet ist.[42] "Im Anfang hat Gott den Himmel und die Erde

[40] Vgl. mit weiteren Argumenten O. H. Steck, *Der Schöpfungsbericht der Priesterschrift. Studien zur literarkritischen und überlieferungsgeschichtlichen Problematik von Genesis 1, 1-2, 4a* (Göttingen, 1975), S. 223 ff.

[41] Umstandssätze beziehen sich immer auf den voraufgehenden, nicht auf den folgenden Satz; s.o.

[42] Dieser Deutung kommt J. Bjørndalen, "Om syntaks, stil og mening i Gen. 1, 1-3a", in *Deus Creator. Bidrag til skapelsesteologien, Festschrift I. P. Seierstad* (Oslo, 1971), S. 29-52, nahe. Allerdings beharrt er auf der Kategorie des Umstandssatzes. So muß er ohne hinreichende syntaktische Begründung behaupten, Vers 2 könne, obgleich vorausstehend, Umstandssatz zu Vers 3 sein (S. 39). Seine These schließlich, Vers 2a sei Umstandssatz und dennoch Hauptsatz (S. 42), umschreibt das Problem, ohne es zu lösen. Dieser Vortrag versucht mit Hilfe der Kategorie des Hintergrundsatzes, der zwar dem Umstandssatz formal in vielem ähnelt, aber von diesem in mehreren Punkten unterschieden und auf einen weiter unten im Text folgenden Vordergrundsatz bezogen ist, eine syntaktische Antwort.

erschaffen.—Die Erde nun war wüst und wirr . . . Da sprach Gott."

Zwei Probleme freilich vermag auch diese Deutung nicht zu beseitigen: (a) Nach sonstigen Überschriften (Toledot-Formulierungen) beginnt P in Gen. asyndetisch mit Vordergrundsätzen.[43] Die Abweichung in Gen. i könnte durch die inhaltliche Eigenart und die Vorgeschichte des Textes bedingt sein. (b) *br'šyt* hat keinen Artikel. Alle beigebrachten Parallelen für artikellosen Gebrauch von *r'šyt* und vergleichbaren Lexemen entstammen der Poesie.[44] Poetische Texte aber setzen den Artikel anders als Prosa-Texte, nach noch wenig durchschauten Regeln.[45] Somit ist es methodisch unerlaubt, mit poetischen Belegen die Artikellosigkeit von *br'šyt* in Gen. i, einem in Prosa verfaßten Text, zu erklären.

Daher ist eine syntaktische Analyse textnäher, die *br'šyt* als status constructus und den übrigen Wortlaut von Vers 1 als diesen constructus regierenden und determinierenden Attributsatz auffaßt.[46] Wo wird dann der mit *br'šyt* eröffnete Satz weitergeführt? Solche Erwägungen wurden von den Autoren angestellt, die Gen. i 1-3 als Periode, somit 3a als Weiterführung von *br'šyt* ansehen. Ich möchte im folgenden die nur selten[47] vertretene These wahrscheinlich machen, Vers 2a sei diese Weiterführung. Dazu muß ich auf einige syntaktische Muster verweisen.

---

[43] Z.B. Gen. vi 9, xxxvii 2.

[44] Vgl. König, (wie Anm. 16), S. 287 § 294g; Joüon, (wie Anm. 16), S. 424 § 137k. Vgl. hierzu P. Humbert, "Trois notes sur Genèse I", *NTT* 56 (1955), S. 85-96, spez. S. 85-8.

[45] Wo der Konsonantenbestand nicht hinderte, haben die Punktatoren nicht selten den Artikelgebrauch der Prosa in poetische Texte eingetragen. Umso bedeutsamer ist das Fehlen des Artikels in Prosa: *br'šyt* in Gen. i 1. Dagegen scheint A. Angerstorfer, *Der Schöpfergott des Alten Testaments. Herkunft und Bedeutungsentwicklung des hebräischen Terminus br' (bara) "schaffen", Regensburger Studien zur Theologie 20* (Frankfurt, 1979), S. 181, mit Samaritanus und griechischen Transskriptionen die Punktation mit Artikel zu befürworten.

[46] Vgl. zu dieser vor allem bei Zeitbestimmungen nicht ungewöhnlichen syntaktischen Konstellation: E. Kautzsch, *Wilhelm Gesenius' Hebräische Grammatik völlig umgearbeitet* (Leipzig, [28]1909, Nachdruck Hildesheim, 1962), S. 441 f. § 130d; C. Brockelmann, *Hebräische Syntax* (Neukirchen, 1956), S. 140 f. § 144.

[47] C. Westermann, *Genesis. 1. Teilband= Genesis 1-11, BK I, 1* (Neukirchen-Vluyn, 1974), S. 132, nennt Abraham ibn Ezra und H. Grotius; W. H. Schmidt, *Die Schöpfungsgeschichte der Priesterschrift. Zur Überlieferungsgeschichte von Genesis 1, 1-2, 4a und 2, 4b-3, 24* (Neukirchen-Vluyn, [3]1973), S. 74 Anm. 1 nennt K. D. Ilgen, 1798. Jüngster Vertreter: H. G. Stigers, *A Commentary on Genesis* (Grand Rapids, 1976), S. 48. Im Widerspruch hierzu behauptet er allerdings S. 50, grammatisch hingen die drei "circumstantial clauses" in Gen. i 2 von i 1 ab. Vgl. auch die Übersetzung z. St. in *The New English Bible* (Oxford, Cambridge, 1970).

Soweit *wyhy* mit Präpositionalverbindung Zeitangaben einführt, wird dieser Satz weitergeführt durch: (a) *wayyiqṭol*,[48] (b) *qaṭal-x*,[49] (c) *x-qaṭal*,[50] (d) *w* = *x-qaṭal*; hier steht das Subjekt betont vor dem Verb; als *qaṭal* begegnen in dieser syntaktischen Konstellation sowohl *HYY*[51] als auch andere Verben.[52] Die Eröffnung durch *wyhy* ist charakteristisch für Kontextformulierungen, erste Sätze an Unterabschnitten oder zu Beginn von Erzählzweitsträngen, nicht aber für den absoluten Anfang einer Einheit, eines Buches.

Wie nun statt Form (a) am absoluten Anfang ohne *wyhy* gesagt werden kann: *präpositionale Zeitangabe—wayyiqṭol*: Jes. vi 1: *bšnt mwt hmlk ʿzyhw wʾrʾh ʾt ʾdny yšb ʿl ksʾ rm wnśʾ*,[53] so muß entsprechend statt Form (d) am absoluten Anfang ohne *wyhy* gesagt werden können: Gen. i 1+2: *präpositionale Zeitangabe* (*brʾšyt* + *determinierender Attributsatz*) - *w* = *x-qaṭal* (*whʾrṣ hyth thw wbhw*): "Am Anfang, als Gott sich daran machte, den Himmel und die Erde zu erschaffen, war die Erde wüst und wirr".[54] Diese Interpretation weist die Sätze von Vers 2 nicht dem Hintergrund, sondern dem Vordergrund der Darstellung zu, obgleich sie inhaltlich Größen benennen, die dem in Vers 3 einsetzenden Schöpfungswirken vorgegeben sind. Diese Deutung scheint mir syntaktisch die geringsten Probleme zu bieten und Stil wie Aufbau von Gen. i 1-ii 4a am besten zu entsprechen.

---

[48] Vgl. Gen. iv 3, 8 und die überwiegende Zahl der Belege.

[49] Z.B. Gen. viii 13, xl 1; Ex. xvi 22, 27; Dtn. i 3, ix 11; Jos. vi 16, x 27; 1 Kön. xiv 25, xv 29, xvi 11, xvii 17.

[50] Z.B. 1 Sam. xxiii 6; 1 Kön. xi 4.

[51] Gen. vii 10; 1 Kön. xviii 1; Rückgriff: 2 Sam. iii 6.

[52] Gen. xxii 1; Ex. xii 29; Jos. vi 8; 1 Kön. viii 10, xi 29, xxii 32; 2 Kön. ii 9, iv 40. An den folgenden Stellen bezeichnet *w* = *x-qaṭal* dagegen sicher oder möglicherweise einen Rückgriff: 1 Sam. xiii 10 (?), xviii 19 (?), xxx 1; 2 Sam. i 1, xiii 36; 1 Kön. xviii 45.

[53] Auch mitten in einer Erzählung: Gen. xxii 4.

[54] Die Behauptung P. Beauchamps, *Création et séparation. Étude exégétique du chapitre premier de la Genèse*, *BSR* (Bruges, 1969), S. 151, diese Deutung stoße auf ernsthafte syntaktische Bedenken, trifft somit nicht zu. Die obige Übersetzung setzt voraus, daß (1) die Form des perfektiven Aspekts: *qaṭal* auch den Ingressiv bezeichnen kann, daß (2) die Suffixkonjugation des Attributsatzes (wie beim *ʾšr*-Satz; vgl. W. Groß, *Partizip* [wie Anm. 23], S. 29-31) nicht auf den übergeordneten Satz bezogen sein muß ("als Gott erschaffen hatte" bzw. "zu erschaffen begonnen hatte"; gegen Stigers, *Commentary* [wie Anm. 47], S. 48), sondern auch lediglich auf den Gegenwartpunkt des Sprechers bezogen sein kann.

ZUR INTERPRETATION DER BÜCHER ESRA-NEHEMIA

Zugleich ein Beitrag zur Methode der Exegese

von

A. H. J. GUNNEWEG
Bonn

Otto Plöger zum 70. Geburtstag

Wer war zuerst, Esra oder Nehemia, oder wirkten beide doch gleichzeitig? Welches war das Gesetz, das Esra aus dem Exil mitbrachte, um die Heimgekehrten und überhaupt die restaurierte Gemeinde darauf zu verpflichten? Wie sind diese Ereignisse relativ und absolut zu datieren? So lauten meistens die ersten Fragen, deren Beantwortung man von dem erwartet, der sich mit den Büchern Esra-Nehemia beschäftigt. Die historische Fragestellung also hat und hatte vielfach das Gewicht des die Erkenntnis leitenden Interesses, und sei es auch dergestalt, daß erst auf dem Umweg über den rekonstruierten historischen Verlauf die Theologie des Chronisten faßbar zu werden schien.

Aufschlußreich ist, um nur ein Beispiel zu nennen, die forschungsgeschichtliche Skizze, die W. F. Stinespring den *Ezra Studies* von Charles C. Torrey (New York, ^{2}1970 [Chicago, 1910]) vorausschickt: Die Datierungsprobleme stehen am Anfang und lösen die kritischen Bemühungen überhaupt erst aus. In denselben Bereich historischer Fragestellungen gehören auch die Bemühungen um die Historizität bzw. um den unhistorischen Charakter des Erzählten, welche insbesondere von Torrey intensiv vorangetrieben worden sind. Bezeichnend nicht nur für Torrey, sondern für eine ganze Forschungsrichtung ist der Schlußsatz seiner frühen Schrift *The Composition and Historical Value* [!] *of Ezra-Nehemiah*: [1] "But his work, whatever else may be said of it, certainly throws no light on the history of the Jews in the Persian period".

---

[1] *BZAW 2* (1896), S. 65. Wer die gegenteilige These vertritt, wie etwa Ed. Meyer, *Die Entstehung des Judentums* (Halle, 1896), bleibt derselben Fragestellung erst recht verhaftet. Daß sich an diesem Ansatz, trotz aller Meinungsvielfalt, auch gegenwärtig nichts Wesentliches geändert hat, lehrt die Einleitung der *Untersuchungen zur Theologie des chronistischen Geschichtswerkes* (Freiburg, 1973) von R. Mosis, S. 11 ff.

Die historische Zuverlässigkeit oder Unzuverlässigkeit konnte so geradezu zum unbezweifelbaren Kriterium der Bewertung überhaupt werden.[2]

Zum Unterschied von diesem Ansatz soll hier versucht werden, primär die eigene Konzeption und Aussageintention der Bücher Esra-Nehemia in ihrem überlieferten Bestand zu erfassen.

1. Dies ist nur möglich, wenn vorab geklärt wird, ob die Bücher Esra-Nehemia Teil sind des chr Geschichtswerkes oder nicht. Daß die Antwort auf diese Frage für die gesamte Beurteilung von großer Wichtigkeit ist, bedarf keiner Erörterung. Die Infragestellung des "Common Authorship" von Esra-Nehemia einerseits und der beiden Chronikbücher andererseits durch Sara Japhet hat großen Eindruck auf die Forschung gemacht.[3] Freilich hat der erste Eindruck bei näherem und sorgfältigerem Zusehen keinen bleibenden Bestand. Zu bemängeln ist nicht nur, daß die verschiedenen Schichten innerhalb des chr Werkes—Chr, Quellen, Zusätze—nicht genügend gesondert betrachtet werden,[4] sondern es lassen sich auch andere Einwände erheben. Eine Überprüfung der Argumente von Sara Japhet lehrt, daß die wesentlichsten sprachlichen Unterschiede zwischen Esra-Nehemia und den Chronikbüchern auf den bewußten Kompositionswillen des Chr zurückgeführt werden können, oder eben durch die Eigenart der späteren Tradenten bedingt sind: Nachdem die beiden Hauptteile des chr Werkes einmal getrennt worden waren, setzte auch eine getrennte und jeweils spezifische Überlieferung ein. Japhets eigener Verweis auf grammatisch-orthographische Eigentümlichkeiten des Samaritanischen Pentateuch und der Jesaja-Rolle im Vergleich mit den Büchern Esra-Nehemia zeigt bereits, daß spätere spezifische Schreiber- und Schulgewohnheiten

---

[2] Man vergleiche nur die vernichtenden Urteile von J. Wellhausen, *Prolegomena zur Geschichte Israels* (Berlin, [6]1927), S. 165 ff.

[3] "The Supposed Common Authorship of Chronicles and Ezra-Nehemiah Investigated Anew", *VT* 18 (1968), S. 330 ff.; vgl. auch Th. Willi, *Die Chronik als Auslegung* (Göttingen, 1972), S. 180 ff.; P. Welten, *Geschichte und Geschichtsdarstellung in den Chronikbüchern* (Neukirchen-Vluyn 1973), S. 4, Anm. 15; die beiden zuletzt Genannten rechnen mit zwei Werken eines Verfassers. Insbesondere aber H. G. M. Williamson, *Israel in the Books of Chronicles* (Cambridge, 1977), folgt Japhet und versucht ihre linguistisch begründete These inhaltlich abzustützen; vgl. dagegen die ausführlichere Besprechung der Monographie von Williamson durch H. Cazelles in *VT* 29 (1979), S. 375 ff.; die hier geübte Kritik dürfte durchschlagend sein; vgl. auch Mosis (Anm. 1), S. 214, Anm. 23.

[4] So schon mit Recht Welten (s. Anm. 3).

etwas vorschnell von ihr als literarkritische Kriterien gewertet werden. Sodann ist daran zu erinnern, daß die Sprache des Chr überhaupt uneinheitlich ist, so daß literarkritische Sonderungen aufgrund solcher Merkmale mißlich bleiben. Auf einige andere Einzelheiten sei hier etwas näher eingegangen.

Die unterschiedliche Verwendung von Kurz- oder Langformen des Imp. cons. bei Verben *lamed-he* des verlängerten Imp. cons. starker Verben und von Eigennamen *yh-yhw*, die von Japhet als literarkritisches Kriterium verwendet wird, läßt sich einfach daraus erklären, daß der Chr in seinen in vorexilischer Zeit spielenden Abschnitten dem älteren Brauch folgt und hier archaisiert, während er umgekehrt für die nachexilische Geschichte die "authentische" Sprache der späteren Zeit spricht bzw. sprechen läßt. Diese Deutung legt sich nahe, da der Chr ja sogar die aramäische Sprache derer schreiben kann, über die er erzählt.

Andere Unterschiede erklären sich daraus, daß der Chr seine Quellen wiedergibt oder sie nachahmt.[5] Daß bestimmte Termini nur jeweils in einem der beiden Teile vorkommen, kann auch daran liegen, daß die betreffenden Phänomene als solche nur vorexilisch oder nur nachexilisch bestanden. Als Beispiele seien hier genannt *mdynh* = Provinz, von der so nur nachexilisch die Rede sein kann; der Terminus begegnet dementspechend nur in Esra-Nehemia; und *qṭr* = räuchern, das nur in den Chronikbüchern begegnet, weil nur in vorexilischer Zeit ein Räucheraltar vorhanden war.[6]

Die wenigen dann noch verbleibenden sprachlichen Differenzen sind so geringfügig, daß sie gegenüber den altbekannten Gemeinsamkeiten, wie sie schon S. R. Driver registriert hat,[7] kaum noch ins Gewicht fallen können.

Wie die sprachlichen lassen sich auch die insbesondere von H. G. M. Williamson (s. Anm. 3) aufgestellten inhaltlichen Argumente unschwer widerlegen. Da dies vor kurzem erst von H. Cazelles in seiner ausführlichen Besprechung des Buches von Williamson getan

---

[5] So insbes. Willi passim (Anm. 3).

[6] So auch Mosis (Anm. 1 u. 3).

[7] *An Introduction to the Literature of the O.T.* (Edinburgh, [9]1913), übers. und hrsg. v. J. W. Rothstein (Berlin, [5]1896), S. 572 ff.; vgl. E. L. Curtis-A. A. Madsen, *A Critical and Exegetical Commentary of the Books of Chronicles* (Edinburgh, 1910), S. 27 ff. Früher schon L. Zunz, *Die gottesdienstlichen Vorträge der Juden, historisch entwickelt* (Berlin, 1832); F. C. Movers, *Kritische Untersuchungen über die biblische Chronik* (Bonn, 1834). Statt einer ausführlicheren forschungsgeschichtlichen Skizze kann hier auf Willi (Anm. 3), S. 12 ff. verwiesen werden.

worden ist (s. Anm. 3), mögen einige ergänzende Hinweise hier genügen. Der Hauptunterschied zwischen den beiden Teilen des chr Werkes ist vor allem dadurch bedingt, daß der Chr im ersten Teil—auf seine Weise—bereits geschriebener Geschichte folgt, im zweiten Teil jedoch viel selbständiger als Autor tätig wird. Andere scheinbare Differenzen ergeben sich aus der Konzeption des Chr: Da der Chr, wie noch zu erörtern sein wird, von der Erfülltheit der vorexilischen Prophetie mit ihrer Gerichts- und Heilsbotschaft ausgeht, bleibt kein Raum für nachexilische Propheten, es sei denn für sie als eine Art von geistlichen Beratern und Förderern des Tempelbaus, als welche er Haggai und Sacharja darstellt.

2. Der Versuch, die eigene theologische Intention von Esra-Nehemia zu erfassen, kann ferner nur gelingen, wenn zuvor auch die Frage nach der ursprünglichen Reihenfolge der einzelnen Abschnitte bzw. Kapitel und nach dem Bestand von Esra-Nehemia einigermaßen einleuchtend beantwortet ist. Dabei kommt bekanntlich der Beurteilung von 3. Esra besondere Bedeutung zu. Auch hier ist nach der ausführlichen Auseinandersetzung von Williamson mit K.-F. Pohlmann [8] eine Kurzfassung erlaubt. Über den Einzelnachweis, den Williamson durchführte, hinaus ist ergänzend auf folgendes hinzuweisen. Auch wenn 3. Esra ein Fragment ist oder sein kann, ist damit keineswegs bewiesen, daß es Teil einer einst vollständigen und ursprünglicheren Übersetzung des chr Werkes ohne die Nehemia-Denkschrift ist. Mag es immer Fragment sein, die nachweislich hier später aufgenommene Pagenerzählung und die dadurch ausgelösten Umstellungen und Änderungen sind ebensoviele Argumente dafür, daß hier eine selbständige Schrift vorliegt, welche die kanonischen Bücher benutzt, um in gefälliger Weise de templi restitutione zu erzählen. Mit ihrer Hilfe einen vermeintlich ursprünglicheren Bestand von Esra-Nehemia rekonstruieren zu wollen, ist daher abenteuerlich. Dasselbe gilt von dem Versuch, das Werk mit Esra iii 13 enden zu lassen und die ganze Esragestalt für später erfunden zu halten. Was an diesem Charakter mit seiner Mischung von Priestertum und Schriftgelehrtentum auch immer legendarisch sein mag, solche Gestalten pflegen keine bloße Erfindung zu sein. Esras Nichterwähnung im Jesus-Sirach-Buch und 2. Makkabäer besagt nicht, daß Esra diesen Schriften noch unbekannt war. Viel wahrscheinlicher

[8] *Studien zum dritten Esra. Ein Beitrag zur Frage nach dem ursprünglichen Schluß des chron. Geschichtswerkes* (Göttingen, 1970), und Williamson (Anm. 3), S. 12 ff.

ist ja, daß dieser Vertreter einer Theokratie, welche die ausländische Regierung ausdrücklich als Schutzmacht von Gottes Gnaden anerkennt, hier kein Lob zu verdienen schien.[9]

3. Nach diesen Bemerkungen zur Literar- und Textkritik etwas zur Frage der Quellen. Eine der wenigen unumstrittenen Erkenntnisse ist immer noch, daß die Nehemia-Denkschrift, gleichviel wie im einzelnen einzugrenzen und zu beurteilen, eine echte Quelle ist.[10] Dasselbe gilt aber auch von der aramäischen Urkundensammlung. Sie ist gewiß nicht das Erzeugnis des Chr. Dabei kommt dem sprachlichen Argument am wenigsten Gewicht zu, denn auch der Chr kann die aramäische Sprache anwenden. Wichtiger ist, daß die Urkundensammlung mit ihrem Bericht über einen verhinderten Mauerbau doch nicht recht zu der chr Erzählung über die Tempelrestauration paßt.[11] Auch stimmen die hier genannten Namen von persischen Königen schlecht mit dem Erzählungsfaden des Chr überein, dem immerhin bekannt und bewußt war, daß Kyros der Begründer des persischen Imperiums war, als dessen Nachfolger er Darius betrachtete. Auch teilen die aramäischen Stücke die chr Vorliebe für Priester und Leviten nicht, sondern lassen die "Ältesten" als Vertreter des Volkes auftreten (Esra v 5, 9). Diese Eigentümlichkeit begegnet nun aber in der erzählenden Rahmung der "Urkunden"; es liegen somit nicht einfach vom Chr aufgenommene "Urkunden" vor, sondern eine nicht-chronistische Erzählung, welche die "Urkunden" zitiert. Diese berichtet aber eindeutig aus jüdischer Sicht, wie ja auch die verarbeiteten "Urkunden" jüdisch gefärbt sind. Darauf ist seit

---

[9] Gegen J. C. H. Lebram in seiner Besprechung von U. Kellermanns Nehemia-Monographie (Anm. 10) in *VT* 18 (1968), S. 564 ff.; der perserhörige Esra als Idealgestalt im Kampf gegen fremde Herrscher ist ganz unwahrscheinlich. Anders erklärt P. Höffken, "Esras Nichterwähnung in J. Sirach", *ZAW* 87 (1975), S. 184 ff., mit einer antilevitischen Tendenz. Solches mag in der Tat hinzukommen.

[10] Zu ihr vgl. U. Kellermann, *Nehemia. Quellen, Überlieferung, Geschichte*, *BZAW* 102 (1967); vgl. auch die Besprechung durch Lebram (Anm. 9) und die Beurteilung und "Feinanalyse" der Nehemia-Denkschrift in der jüngsten Ausgabe von O. Kaiser, *Einleitung in das AT* (Gütersloh, ^{4}1978), S. 166 f.; 167 Anm. 12.

[11] Die von Torrey, *Ezra Studies* (Anm. 1), S. 199 ff., vertretene Auffassung, tatsächlich handle auch der erste Teil der aramäischen Geschichte vom Tempelbau, dieser werde lediglich von den Gegnern der Juden in verleumderischer Absicht als Stadterneuerung hingestellt, erklärt vorliegende Reihenfolge unter Inrechnungstellung chronologischer Konfusion; sie ist unabhängig von der Beurteilung von Esra iv 24; man sollte den Vers mit u.a. Torrey, *Composition*, S. 7 ff., gegen u.a. Torrey, *Ezra Studies*, S. 159, für eine chr Glosse zur Verdeutlichung halten.

C. C. Torrey über G. Hölscher bis O. Kaiser [12] so häufig hingewiesen worden, daß man hier nur Bekanntes wiederholen könnte. Nur die massivsten Argumente seien genannt: iv 9 f. macht in tendenziöser Absicht die Hintermänner der Petition an die persische Obrigkeit zu einem Völkergemisch; iv 12 teilt die jüdische Auffassung, daß es heimgekehrte Exulanten waren, welche die Restauration betrieben; iv 15, 19 f. rühmt in Form einer Rüge die frühere Herrlichkeit und Macht Israels; vi-vii 8 setzt insgesamt voraus, daß im ersten Jahr des Kyros Heimkehr und Restauration auf persische Anordnung hin begannen; ist dies unhistorisch, dann können die solches zur Voraussetzung habenden Urkunden auch nicht echt sein.

4. Ähnliches gilt von dem Artaxerxes-Reskript in Esra vii 12-26, bei dem sogar E. Meyer, der Verfechter der Echtheit der aramäischen Urkunden, annehmen mußte, daß dieses "Dokument" mit königlicher Erlaubnis von Esra selbst verfaßt worden ist ([Anm. 1] S. 65). Anders als die aramäischen Stücke in Esra iv 5 f. ist dieses Stück nachweislich chr.[13] In diesem Artaxerxes-Reskript spiegelt sich freilich ein durchaus historisches Phänomen, das bis in hellenistische und römische Zeit nachwirkte, nämlich die Anerkennung der jüdischen Religion als religio licita und die Sanktionierung der überlieferten Thora als Staatsgesetz seitens der Obrigkeit (vgl. Esra vii 26). Gegen die Begründung dieses Rechtsstatus in persischer Zeit ist historisch nichts einzuwenden. Dies entspräche ja der auch sonst bekannten persischen Religionspolitik. Daß die tatsächliche Bedeutung des historischen Esra in solchen Zusammenhängen anzusetzen sein wird, mag man annehmen, ohne es zwingend beweisen zu können.

5. Außer der jüdischen, in aramäischer Sprache geschriebenen Erzählung, den Büchern Haggai und Sacharja, der Nehemia-Denkschrift und Listenmaterial hat der Chr über keinerlei schriftliche Quellen verfügt. Die Esra-Memoiren sind eine überbietende Nachahmung der Nehemia-Denkschrift, wie U. Kellermann überzeugend nachgewiesen

---

[12] G. Hölscher, *Die Bücher Esra und Nehemia*, *HSAT* II (Tübingen, ⁴1923), S. 491 ff.; Kaiser (Anm. 10), S. 165. Auch das schon von Torrey, *Ezra Studies*, S. 161 ff., herausgestellte sprachliche Argument verdient Beachtung: Die relative Einheitlichkeit des biblischen Aramäisch dürfte sich am leichtesten erklären, wenn die aramäischen Abschnitte hier und im Danielbuch etwa der gleichen Zeit zuzurechnen sind.

[13] Vgl. schon Torrey, *Ezra Studies*, S. 157 ff.

hat ([Anm. 10] S. 95). Die höchst auffälligen Parallelen und Entsprechnungen—Entsendung durch den Hof, die Rede von der gütigen Hand Gottes, militärische Eskorte—ausdrücklich kein militärisches Geleit, die Rast von drei Tagen, um nur das Auffälligste zu erwähnen—können nicht Zufall, sondern müssen literarische Absicht sein. Diese Überhöhung Esras auf Kosten Nehemias beabsichtigt freilich nicht, wie Kellermann meinte, eine völlige Desavouierung Nehemias—den er ja hätte übergehen können!—, sondern will beider Person und Werk in die rechte—chronistische—Rangordnung bringen. Dabei stellt der Umstand, daß die Nehemia-Denkschrift und die "Esra-Memoiren" auf solche Weise aufeinander bezogen sind, ein überaus starkes Argument dafür dar, daß die Nehemia-Denkschrift ursprünglicher Bestandteil der Bücher Esra-Nehemia ist. Die positiven und negativen Anspielungen innerhalb der Esra-Erzählung auf die Nehemia-Denkschrift wären ja ohne diese letztere völlig beziehungslos. Die durch Nachahmung der Nehemia-Denkschrift entstandene differenzierende Ähnlichkeit beider Erzählkomplexe ist Stilmittel, das die sachliche Zusammengehörigkeit, die Kohärenz des hier und dort, des hier ähnlich wie dort geschilderten Geschehens zur Darstellung bringen soll.

6. Dies wird noch deutlicher, wenn man nunmehr versucht, Struktur und Konzeption des überlieferten Bestandes zu erfassen. Dieser Versuch sieht zunächst aus methodischen Gründen von der Frage nach der Historizität des Berichteten ab und will primär das überlieferte Geschichtsbild als solches deuten. Die verschiedenen Kapitelumstellungen beruhen vielfach auf historischen Überlegungen bezüglich der überlieferten Chronologie. Als eine bis heute wirksam gewordene Hypothese sei hier nur die Ansetzung Nehemias vor Esra durch A. Van Hoonacker genannt.[14] Zumeist auf ähnlichen Erwägungen beruhen auch die vielfach vorgenommenen Umstellungen, welche den ursprünglichen, angeblich nachträglich gestörten Erzählduktus wiederherstellen wollen. Markantes Beispiel hierfür ist der große Kommentar von W. Rudolph *Esra und Nehemia* (Tübingen, 1949). Aber eben dieser Ansatz ist methodisch sehr fragwürdig. Nicht nur sind die Textrekonstruktionen vielfach willkürlich und vermögen

[14] "Néhémie et Esdras", *Le Muséon* 9 (1890), S. 151 ff.; 317 ff.; 389 ff.; ders., *Nouvelles études sur la restauration juive après l'exil de Babylone* (Paris, 1896); eine gute Übersicht über die seitherige Debatte bei U. Kellermann, "Erwägungen zum Problem der Esradatierung", *ZAW* 80 (1968), S. 55 ff.; vgl. S. 62 ff.

nicht plausibel zu erklären, wie es zum vorliegenden Textbestand gekommen sei; schwerer wiegt, daß man auf diesem Wege Gefahr läuft, in einen circulus vitiosus zu geraten, indem man mit Hilfe von Textumstellungen einen unbekannten Geschichtsverlauf rekonstruiert, um dann mittels der rekonstruierten Historie den ebenso rekonstruierten Text auszulegen. Ja, auch hermeneutisch ist dieses Vorgehen ungenügend, weil solche Rekonstruktionen auch dann noch nicht als Auslegung der Texte in ihrem eigenen Anspruch gelten können, wenn mit ihrer Hilfe der Geschichtsverlauf zutreffend nachgezeichnet worden wäre! So hat neuerdings R. Mosis [15] mit vollem Recht moniert, daß es zwar legitim sei, die Bücher Esra-Nehemia für die Rekonstruktion der Geschichte Israels auszuwerten, ein solches Verfahren aber noch nicht als Auslegung dieser Texte selbst aufgefaßt werden dürfe. An eben diesem Punkt wird die methodische und hermeneutische Fragwürdigkeit eines rein historistischen Ansatzes deutlich. Damit sollen Textstörungen nicht a priori für unmöglich und historische Interessen nicht für illegitim erklärt werden. Ehe aber nicht der sorgfältige Versuch gewagt worden ist, die Überlieferung als solche zu interpretieren, und erst wenn sich dieser Versuch als zum Scheitern verurteilt erweist, sind Eingriffe und Umstellungen methodisch erlaubt, und auch dann noch unter striktem Vorbehalt!

7. Solche Umstellungen erübrigen sich, wenn man Esra-Nehemia auf dem Hintergrund und als Abschluß des in 1 und 2 Chr. Erzählten interpretiert. Ist im Pentateuch auf seiner jetzigen priesterschriftlichen Grundlage das Sinaigeschehen mit seiner Kultstiftung, Gesetzgebung und Selbstvergegenwärtigung des Gottes Israels das Zentrum, so in der vorexilischen Geschichtsdarstellung des Chr die

---

[15] Zu erinnern ist hier auch an einen Satz von H.-G. Gadamer, *Wahrheit und Methode* (Tübingen, ²1965), S. 287: "Der Text, der historisch verstanden wird, wird aus dem Anspruch, Wahres zu sagen, förmlich hinausgedrängt. Indem man die Überlieferung vom historischen Standpunkt aus sieht. . ., meint man zu verstehen. In Wahrheit hat man den Anspruch grundsätzlich aufgegeben, in der Überlieferung für einen selber gültige und verständliche Wahrheit zu finden". Ähnlich und mit Bezug auf biblische Texte schon früher (1950) R. Bultmann, "Das Problem der Hermeneutik", *Glauben und Verstehen* II (Tübingen, ⁴1965), S. 211 ff. (213 f.), unter Berufung auf H. Patzer, "Der Humanismus als Methodenproblem der klassischen Philologie". *Studium Generale* 1 (1948), S. 84 ff.; wenn die Texte nur noch dazu dienen, "eine vergangene Zeit zu rekonstruieren", verliere "die Theologie ihren eigentlichen Gegenstand, die Interpretation der Texte um des Verstehens willen".

Kultstiftung durch David und Salomo. Was vorher war, schrumpft zu einem bloßen Vorher zusammen; was nachher geschah, ist nachmaliger Abfall und nachmalige Restauration—bis hin zum Nullpunkt der Tempelzerstörung und Exilierung. Diese Darstellung verlagert das Zentrum Israels nach Jerusalem, und nur vom Jerusalemer Standpunkt aus läßt sich mit dem chr Abia sagen: "Mit uns aber ist Jahwe, unser Gott, den wir nicht verlassen, und die Priester, die Jahwe dienen, die Aaroniden, und die Leviten in ihrem Dienst" (2 Chr. xiii 10). Abfall von Jerusalem ist darum Abfall von Jahwe und Ausscheiden aus der wahren Jahwe-Gemeinde. Schisma ist Häresie—ein Prinzip, das bekanntlich auch sonst geltend gemacht wurde und wird, wo die "wahre" Zugehörigkeit zur "Wahrheit"—welcher Art auch immer—rechtlich fixiert wird.

Zwar mußte auch Jerusalem-Juda ins Gericht des Exils, aber eben "bis die siebzig Jahre voll" waren, von welchen die Prophetie gesprochen hatte, und "bis das Land seine Sabbate erstattet bekam", also bis eine durch das Gericht geläuterte Gemeinde im ersten Jahr des Kyros die Erlaubnis für einen Neuanfang bekam. Zwischen Exil und Restauration, zwischen Gericht und Gnade, zwischen Unheil und Heil gibt es keine Zwischenstufen und darum auch keine Zwischenzeit. Das erste Jahr des Kyros ist ein theologisches Datum. Und wie die katastrophalen Ereignisse seit Josias Tod vom Chr zu einem einzigen Gerichtsgeschehen, das sich Schlag auf Schlag vollzieht, zusammengerafft werden,[16] so ist auch die Restauration ein geschlossener, kohärenter Akt in mehreren Szenen, die engstens miteinander verzahnt sind.

8. Die erste Szene (Esra i-vi) umfaßt die Heimkehr der Exulanten und die Wiederherstellung des Tempels trotz des Widerstandes der "Widersacher Judas und Benjamins" (Esra iv 1). Die hier mitgeteilte aramäische Erzählung ist darum keine bloße Einlage und nicht nur eine wörtlich mitgeteilte Quelle, sondern der Angelpunkt dieses Teiles der chr Erzählung selbst: Der Widerspruch der "Widersacher" richtet sich gegen den Sinn der Rückkehr, ja den Sinn der Existenz der aus dem Exil Heimkehrenden selbst; kehren sie doch heim, einzig um den Tempel zu bauen und sich als die um das Heiligtum des präsenten Gottes gescharte Gemeinde neu zu konstituieren.[17] Diese

[16] Richtig beobachtet von Mosis (Anm. 1), S. 205 ff.
[17] So mit Mosis (Anm. 1), S. 223.

restaurierte Gemeinde repräsentiert das wahre und das ganze Israel, wie durch die (ursprüngliche) Zwölfzahl am Kopf der Liste Esra ii 2 = Neh. vii 7 zum Ausdruck gebracht wird. An kaum einer Stelle wird die Arbeitsweise des Chr, der die Zeitlinie zu kohärenten Akten bzw. Szenen zusammenrafft, deutlicher als hier: neben Scheschbazzar werden Serubbabel (vielleicht sogar mit Scheschbazzar identifiziert?) und auch noch Nehemia als Anführer der Heimkehrer genannt.

Die zweite Szene (Esra vii-x) beginnt abermals mit einem Aufbruch, nämlich der Entsendung Esras. Sie schließt unmittelbar an die erste an. *'ḥr hdbrym h'lh* in vii 1 überbrückt im Sinne des Chr nicht eine chronologische Lücke, über die er nichts zu erzählen wußte, wie die meisten modernen Exegeten, die primär historisch und nicht theologisch denken, annehmen! Dem Chr lag ja nicht wie dem modernen Historiker eine Liste von Jahreszahlen vor, sondern er verfolgte seine eigene Konzeption. *'ḥr* heißt "danach" im Sinne von "gleich danach", "im Anschluß daran". Dieser Anschluß ist nicht schroffer und nicht härter als sonst, wo dieser oder ähnliche Ausdrücke Verwendung finden. So wird also, nachdem der Tempel restauriert worden war, Esra entsandt, und zwar, wie es im Aramäischen heißt, *l^ebaqqārā'* (Esra vii 14), um eine Untersuchung, Überprüfung durchzuführen gemäß dem Gesetz, das hier dem Status einer religio licita gemäß als staatliches Gesetz gelten soll. Dies wird als seine Aufgabe formuliert. Daß er ein neues Gesetz einzuführen habe—den Priesterkodex oder den Pentateuch—, ist eine Vorstellung, die mit der Ausarbeitung der Urkundenhypothese der alttestamentlichen Wissenschaft zusammenhängen dürfte, vom Text jedoch nicht gestützt wird. War vor allem dies Esras Aufgabe, besteht auch kein Anlaß zur Annahme, er habe 12 Jahre untätig zugewartet. Laut Esra x 16 hat er alsbald eine Kommission eingesetzt, die sich mit Erfolg der gestellten Aufgabe widmete und deren Tätigkeit hebräisch mit *yidrōš* bezeichnet wird, was dem aramäischen *l^ebaqqārā'* entspricht! Auch diese zweite Szene wird wie die erste von ihrer Mitte aus zusammengehalten, und wieder sind es Widerstände, die überwunden werden müssen. Wie am Schluß der ersten Szene der Tempel restauriert ist, so ist am Ende der zweiten Szene eine gereinigte und darum wahre Jahwegemeinde da.

Daran schließt sich die dritte Szene an, die mit Hilfe der hier aufgenommenen Nehemia-Denkschrift zur Darstellung gebracht wird. Auch sie setzt wieder mit einer Reise ein, auch sie weiß von Widerständen von Widersachern zu erzählen, und auch sie schließt mit einem endlichen vollen Erfolg: Die reine Gemeinde vollbringt den Bau der Mauer der heiligen Stadt. Auch noch die viel diskutierte Wiederholung der Liste von Esra ii in Neh. vii erscheint von dieser Konzeption aus als durchaus sinnvoll: Die Gemeinde, welche nach dem Wiederaufbau von Tempel und Stadtmauer sich feierlich und festlich konstituiert, wie in Esra viii-x berichtet wird, ist personell keine andere als die durch das Gericht geläuterte und aus dem Exil heimgekehrte, deren Namen in der "Heimkehrerliste" verzeichnet stehen. Man übertreibt nicht, wenn man von der geradezu präsentisch-eschatologischen Bedeutung dieses Verzeichnisses spricht; enthält es doch die Namen, die das wahre Israel in Erfüllung der Prophetie darstellen. Eben dies läßt der Chr von Nehemia konstatieren (Neh. vii 5). Die Liste ist in ihrer Bedeutsamkeit das präsentisch-eschatologische Gegenstück zu dem himmlischen Buch apokalyptischer Erwartung, in dem die Namen der Erretteten verzeichnet stehen (Jes. iv 3; Dan. xii 1; Jub. xix 9; äth. Hen. xlvii 3). Ist das göttliche Heil präsent, so müssen auch die Namen derer, die es erlangten, namhaft gemacht werden können, wohingegen das apokalyptische Buch des Lebens erst "an jenem Tage" geöffnet werden wird. Auch noch die fast gleichlautende erzählerische Fortsetzung der Liste hier und dort, eines der Kernprobleme der Interpretation von Esra-Nehemia, läßt sich mühelos erklären. Sie wurde vom Chr als erzählende Weiterführung des von ihm als Heimkehrerliste und zugleich Heimkehrbericht interpretierten Verzeichnisses komponiert. Und es ist Nehemia, der nach chr Darstellung die Liste mitsamt Erzählung vorfindet und so erfährt, daß und wie das heimkehrende Israel sich niedergelassen hat. Und dadurch erfährt zugleich der Leser, daß sich an dieser Situation und an der Identität von "gänz Israel", das sich nunmehr aufgrund des Gesetzes konstituieren wird, nichts geändert hat. Die Unterschiede der nämlichen Erzählungsstücke hier und dort lassen sich mühelos als spätere Eingriffe hier und dort erklären, die zur differenzierenden Anpassung an die unterschiedlichen historischen Situationen dienen sollen. Es war ein Irrweg, den ursprünglichen Text entweder hier oder dort finden bzw. rekonstruieren zu wollen; vielmehr wurde derselbe Text nachträglich je verschieden bearbeitet. Es war ein Bearbeiter, der theologisch Gemeintes bereits historisch mißverstand.

Ein Beispiel möge dies verdeutlichen: der viel erörterte Vers Esra ii 70 = Neh. vii 72 am Schluß der Liste und der zugehörigen

Erzählung. Der Vergleich zeigt zunächst, daß an beiden Stellen die differenzierende Aufzählung des gegliederten Kultpersonals auf je verschiedene Weise nachgetragen ist. Gerade der verschiedene Ort und die unterschiedliche Reihenfolge beweisen den Zusatzcharakter. Während der Chr von Priestern und Leviten sprach und damit das ganze Kulturpersonal meinte, differenziert der Zusatz in Angleichung an die Liste. Sodann steht ii 70 das *beʿārēhem* zweimal auf engstem Raum; auch das dürfte kaum ursprünglich sein. Wichtiger indessen als dies ist die richtige Interpretation des chr Kernbestands. Vielfach meint man, aus 3 Esra ein "in Jerusalem" nach *hāʿām* einfügen oder in Neh. vii 72 das *min-hāʿām* streichen zu müssen, weil man aus dem Text eine präzise Angabe über die Verteilung der Volksgruppen über Jerusalem und die Landorte herausliest. Das scheint der Text erst recht nahezulegen, wenn er samt Zusatz gelesen wird; aber auch sein ursprünglicher Bestand scheint ja zwischen bestimmten Gruppen und "ganz Israel" zu unterscheiden. Dieses "ganz Israel" pflegen die Ausleger dann als das "ganze übrige Israel" aufzufassen. So versteht es allerdings auch schon 3 Esra. Wer dieser Lesart folgt, mißversteht das wirklich Gemeinte, und zwar gerade die theologische Konzeption gründlich. Auch hier geht es dem Chr nicht um eine genaue Beschreibung tatsächlicher Siedlungsverhältnisse. Das *min-hāʿām* bedeutet auch nicht in dem Sinne einen Teil des Volkes, daß ein anderer Teil sich woanders niederläßt, sondern es ist das übrige Volk zum Unterschied von Priestern und Leviten gemeint. Diese Ausdrucksweise ist dadurch bedingt, daß der Chr einerseits seiner Gewohnheit gemäß Priester, Leviten und Laien unterscheidet, sodann aber an dieser Stelle andererseits gesteigerten Wert auf "ganz Israel", das diese Gruppen umfaßt, legt: Priester, Leviten und die Laien ließen sich nieder, und damit wohnte ganz Israel in seinen Städten, — in eben den Städten, aus denen es als ganz Israel vertrieben worden war und in die es nunmehr zurückgekehrt ist. Das wahre und in der Liste namentlich erfaßte Israel ist zugleich das ganze Israel. So ist es auch das wahre und ganze Israel, das im geheiligten Monat ans Werk des Tempelbaus geht, wie es sich in genauer Entsprechung laut Neh. vii 72b, viii 1 zur konstituierenden Feier sammelt.

Es folgt in Neh. viii-x die Erzählung über die große Gesetzesverlesung, das Laubhüttenfest, die Trennung von allem Fremdländischen überhaupt (*mikkol-benē nēkār*) verbunden mit der Verpflichtung künftiger Reinerhaltung und einer Regelung der Siedlungsverhältnisse (ix 1 f., xi 29-31).

Es ist einzig durch eine Anzahl späterer Wucherungen bedingt, daß die sonst so klaren Konturen der Konzeption gegen Ende des Nehemiabuches verwischt worden sind. Der Streit darüber, welche Teile als Nachträge zu betrachten sind, wird nicht in jedem Falle sicher geschlichtet werden können. Sicher ist immerhin einiges: Das Gebet Neh. ix 6 ff., das arg negative Erfahrungen mit der fremden Obrigkeit widerspiegelt, stammt aus derselben Feder wie das chr Esra-Gebet (Esra ix), das Gott dafür dankt, daß er den Heimgekehrten die Gunst der persischen Obrigkeit zugewandt hat, so daß die Entronnenen den Tempel bauen und darin neues Leben und neuen Halt in Jerusalem finden dürfen (ix 9); die vielfach mit *bywm hhw'* eingeleiteten Einzelmaßnahmen Nehemias (Neh. xii 44 ff.) machen den Eindruck, späteren Datums zu sein; sekundäres Listenmaterial, dessen damalige Aktualität heute nicht mehr zu erfassen ist, läßt die ursprünglichen Konturen verschwimmen. Mit guten Gründen kann aber vermutet werden, daß der Chr am Ende seines Werkes die Nehemia-Denkschrift noch einmal zu Worte kommen ließ und mit einem überarbeiteten Bericht über die Mauerweihe (Neh. xii 27 ff.) seine Erzählung schloß. Aber auch wenn Torrey [18] recht haben sollte, der die Mauerweih-Erzählung für rein chronistisch hält, ändert sich an den obigen Aufstellungen nichts. Wichtiger ist die Beurteilung von Neh. xiii. Die älteren Einwände Torreys haben noch nichts von ihrer Überzeugungskraft eingebüßt, sprechen aber nicht für chr sondern nach-chr Herkunft. Das vom Chr gezeichnete Idealbild wird hier nachträglich der weniger schönen und glatten Wirklichkeit angepaßt. Was an dem hier Erzählten Tatsachenbericht und was Postulat sei, ist kaum mit Sicherheit zu entscheiden. Liegt aber nicht mehr Nehemia-Denkschrift vor und auch schon nicht mehr Chr dann wird auch so noch einmal deutlich, daß Chr keine Herabsetzung Nehemias, sondern nur dessen "rechte" Zuordnung zu Esra beabsichtigte.

Die Verzahnung und Zusammenordnung von Esra- und Nehemia-Geschichten und dieser wiederum mit der Erzählung der Restauration überhaupt ist somit schriftstellerische Absicht. Ihr dienen auch die Datierungen, sofern sie nicht als Veranschaulichung und Verumständung Elemente chr Stils sind: Über die Bedeutung des ersten Jahres des Kyros und der unbestimmten Zeitangabe von Esra vii 1 war schon gesprochen worden; nachdem im 6. Jahr des Darius der Tempel vollendet worden war, findet im 7. Jahr des Artaxerxes Esras Reise

[18] *Composition* (Anm.1), S. 42 ff.; *Ezra Studies*, S. 248 ff.

statt (Esra vii 7-9), was immerhin die Vermutung einer Zahlenkonstruktion nebst Identifikation verschiedener persischer Könige nahegelegt hat.[19] Wie dem auch sei, dieses Datum—7. Jahr des Artaxerxes—und dazu und in Kombination damit die Zeitangabe von Ezra x 17—bis Jahresende nach Esras Ankunft in Jerusalem ist die Ehescheidungsaktion durchgeführt—, Neh. ii 1—Entsendung Nehemias im 20. Jahr des Artaxerxes—, Neh. vi 15—Fertigstellung der Mauer am 25.6.—sowie Neh. viii-x—Gemeindeversammlungen im 7. Monat—ergeben zusammen mit der Mitteilung von Neh. v 14 eine Tätigkeitsdauer von 12 Jahren sowohl für Esra als auch für Nehemia, in dessen Amtszeit der krönende Abschluß von beider Werk innerhalb der restaurierten Mauer der heiligen Stadt stattfindet. Diese Datierungen ordnen beide Gestalten und deren Werk einander zu, wie es der Chr überhaupt durch Nachahmung der Nehemia-Quelle und die Art ihrer Rezeption zu tun bestrebt ist.

Auch hier erübrigen sich Änderungen dieser Angaben und Eingriffe in die Überlieferung, sobald erkannt wird, daß nicht exakt datierte Historie geschrieben, sondern eine geschichtstheologische Konzeption dargeboten werden soll.[20]

9. Diese Konzeption ist primär positiv als geschichtstheologische Legitimierung der nachexilischen Jerusalemer und judäischen Gemeinde und der sich zu ihr haltenden Diaspora als allein berechtigter Erbin des vorexilischen Israel gemeint. Sie impliziert aber eine polemische Abwehrhaltung gegen die Bevölkerung des ehemaligen Nordreichs wie gegen alles Fremdländische, das die reine Gemeinde beflecken könnte. Ist diese Gemeinde aber in Erfüllung prophetischer Verheißung das wahre Israel, das aus dem verbliebenen Stumpf von Jes. vi 13 (vgl. Esra ix 2!) hervorging, so ist für eine nachexilische futurische Prophetie kein Raum mehr. Haggai und Sacharja haben in dieser Sicht keine eschatologische Botschaft, sondern fordern lediglich den Tempelbau. Diese Umdeutung vollzieht bekanntlich auch, wie W. A. M. Beuken nachgewiesen hat, die sekundäre Redaktion der Bücher Haggai und Sach. i-ix.[21]

---

[19] So K. Galling, *Studien zur Geschichte Israels im persischen Zeitalter* (Göttingen, 1964), S. 161; Kellermann (Anm. 10), S. 58 f.; ders., "Erwägungen zum Problem der Esradatierung", *ZAW* 80 (1968), S. 55 ff. (S. 79), hier eine revidierte Ansicht.

[20] Ob der Chr überhaupt zwischen den verschiedenen Königen, die den Namen Artaxerxes tragen, zu unterscheiden wußte, kann man fragen.

[21] Vgl. W. A. M. Beuken "Haggai-Sacharja I-VIII. Studien zur Überlie-

10. Auch darin schon—in diesen Uminterpretationen und deren Motivation—zeigt sich das Problem, das die chr Theologie nicht gelöst hat. Es ist nicht historischer und chronologischer Art und besteht nicht in Datierungsschwierigkeiten. Man kann mit guten Gründen vermuten, daß der Chr historisch zutreffende Erinnerung weitergab und sich an richtige Tradition gebunden wußte, als er die Sendung des Esra derjenigen des Nehemia vorangehen ließ. Esras Werk als leuchtender Abschluß des ganzen chr Geschichtswerkes entspräche seiner Tendenz weit besser und wäre auch schriftstellerisch leichter darstellbar gewesen, und der Chr hätte sich seine mühsame Technik der Verzahnung und Verschränkung, die er anwendet, ersparen können. Auch daß der sakral- und staatsrechtlichen Konsolidierung der nachexilischen Gemeinschaft—Esras Werk—die politische Verselbständigung Judas unter eigener Statthalterschaft—Nehemias Werk—folgte, läßt sich unschwer vorstellen.[22] Man kann sich das vorstellen und man mag es vermuten. Es bleiben freilich Mutmaßungen, bei denen man in Rechnung stellen muß, als heutiger Historiker mehr wissen zu wollen, als dem Chr selbst noch bekannt war. Solche historische Neugierde ist nicht illegitim, aber, wie die lange und breite Diskussion über das "Problem der Esradatierung" (s. Anm. 19) ja zeigt, kaum noch mit Sicherheit lösbar. Aber auch wenn es gelänge, diese Frage zu beantworten, bliebe das eigene und eigentliche Problem des Chr selbst ungelöst.

Ist wirklich, wie es der Chr sagt, mit dem Regierungsantritt des Kyros das göttliche Gericht des Exils beendet, so muß das Heil mit der Heimkehr der geläuterten Gemeinde, dem Wiederaufbau des Tempels und der Restauration des Kultes und der feierlichen Verpflichtung auf das Gesetz angebrochen sein. Was mit Kyros anbricht, ist Erfüllung der prophetischen Verheißung, wie es programmatisch an der Wende von der exilischen hin zur nachexilischen Zeit betont gesagt wird. Und doch stehen zu diesem Heil die tatsächlichen Verhältnisse in einem schmerzlichen Widerspruch. Daß trotz erfüllter Prophetie und angebrochener Gottesherrschaft die fremden Herrscher immer noch nicht entmachtet sind, ist nur das auffälligste Symptom dieses Widerspruchs. Mehr noch als die chr Erzählung prägt er das

---

ferungsgeschichte der frühnachexilischen Prophetie", *StSN* 10 (1967); R. A. Mason, "The Purpose of the Editoral Framework in the Book of Haggai", *VT* 27 (1977), S. 413 ff.

[22] Vgl. A. H. J. Gunneweg, *Geschichte Israels bis Bar Kochba* (Stuttgart, ³1979), S. 146 f.

große Esra-Gebet in Esra ix, das in Wahrheit eine theologische Reflexion und Belehrung in der fiktiven Gestalt eines Gebets ist: Jahwe hat "ein Aufleben geschenkt und die Augen leuchtend gemacht" (Esra ix 8). Gleichwohl ist es nur "ein wenig Aufleben", denn trotz neuer Gnadenzuwendung bleibt die Knechtschaft des Gottesvolkes unter fremder Herrschaft. Das "Schon-jetzt" der Gottesherrschaft, die seit dem 1. Jahr des Kyros, dessen Geist Jahwe erweckte, da ist, ist nicht dialektisch von einem "Noch-nicht" umschlossen und umgekehrt, sondern wird durch die faktische Widrigkeit der waltenden Verhältnisse quantitativ zu "ein wenig Aufleben" eingeschränkt. Die Umstände, wie sie tatsächlich sind, verringern das Heil, das Gott in Erfüllung seiner Verheißung schenkt!

Die alte Frage, ob der Chr eine eschatologische Hoffnung verkündet, ist mit Nein zu beantworten. Er kann sie von seinen eigenen Voraussetzungen her nicht haben und spricht sie auch tatsächlich an keiner Stelle seines Werkes aus. Wer sie dennoch aus seinem Werk indirekt herauszulesen versucht,[23] hat das Problem der chr Konzeption erfaßt und versucht nun zu lösen, was der Chr selbst ungelöst ließ. Es ist das theologische Problem des Verhältnisses von Präsens und Futurum göttlichen Heils—eine Frage von größerem Gewicht nicht nur für die Beurteilung der hier betrachteten Bücher Esra und Nehemia—denn ob Esra früher war als Nehemia oder umgekehrt.[24]

[23] So zuletzt Mosis (Anm. 1), vgl. den Schlußsatz des Werkes auf S. 234.
[24] Zu dieser fundamentalen Problematik s. A. H. J. Gunneweg - W. Schmithals, *Herrschaft* (Stuttgart, 1980), S. 85 ff.; 113 ff.

THE TRANSLATION OF ANTHROPOMORPHISMS AND ANTHROPOPATHISMS IN THE TARGUMIM [1]

BY

MICHAEL L. KLEIN

Jerusalem

I. Introduction: The Old Testament

Anthropomorphic descriptions of the Deity prevail throughout the entire Old Testament—from the earliest Pentateuchal narratives and the classical prophets through the apocalyptical Book of Daniel. The Lord God moves (walks) about noisily in the Garden of Eden (Gen. iii 8); he smells the pleasant odor of sacrifices (Gen. viii 21); just as incense is placed before his nostril (Deut. xxxiii 10). His feet are supported by the likeness of a sapphire pavement (Exod. xxiv 10); and whereas his palm shields his face from being seen, his back may be seen (Exod. xxxiii 20-23); the Lord is seated on a high and lofty throne and the skirts of his robe fill the Temple (Isa. vi 1); the throne appears to be made of sapphire and the enthroned figure has the semblance of a human being (Ezek. i 26); and finally, the One of ancient days is seated, his garb white as snow, and the hair of his head like lamb's wool (Dan. vii 9).

This anthropomorphic God was believed to be visible by man in certain circumstances—even though such an experience was fraught with the danger of death. Thus Manoah says to his wife, "We shall surely die, for we have seen God" (Judg. xiii 22, RSV, JPS; but "a divine being" in new JPS). Indeed the statement "you cannot see my face, for man may not see me and live" (Exod. xxxiii 20) is to be understood in the same manner, i.e., not that God is invisible, but that the one who gazes upon him will surely die.[2]

---

[1] My sincerest thanks to Professor Menahem Haran and Professor Shlomo Morag for their devoted guidance in an earlier stage of this study at the Hebrew University, Jerusalem. The term anthropomorphism is used throughout as an abbreviation for the more cumbersome pair "anthropomorphism and anthropopathism. We shall deal with both human forms and human feelings attributed to the Deity in the O.T.

[2] Cf. J. Barr, "Theophany and Anthropomorphism in the Old Testament", *Congress Volume: Oxford 1959*, *SVT* 7 (1960), p. 34. On the other hand, Barr's

Moreover, in Gen. i 26, 27 God says: "Let us make man in our image after our likeness", and then "God created man in his image, in the image of God he created him"—indicating a similarity of physical form.

II. Rabbinic and Medieval Jewish Literature

The origins of Jewish anti-anthropomorphism remain shrouded in obscurity. What is clear, however, is that by Mishnaic times (1st-2nd century CE), two distinct schools emerged and crystallized. Whereas the school of R. Aqiba interpreted biblical anthropomorphisms quite literally, the anti-anthropomorphic school of R. Ishmael dismissed them as allegory.[3] What is also clear is that the anti-anthropomorphic tendencies reflect an internal development within Judaism, and are not the result of Hellenistic influence, which they antedate.[4] It is only natural that the targumim, being an integral part of Rabbinic literature, and ultimately deriving from the same schools and the same periods,[5] would reflect rabbinic attitudes towards biblical anthropomorphism. This was to be expected especially in view of the fact that all the targumim are paraphrastic and midrashic to varying degrees, even in matters that are not of theological or doctrinal import.[6]

Indeed, great Jewish medieval scholars such as Sa'adiah Gaon (882-942) and Maimonides (1135-1204) were quick to notice that many of the biblical anthropomorphisms are transformed in Onqelos by paraphrase or circumlocution. Sa'adiah, being convinced of the pure spirituality and transcendence of God, takes all the human traits attributed to God to be allegorical. Accordingly, he writes that "*wherever* the 'faithful interpreters of our Torah' [i.e., the ancient targumists—and particularly Onqelos] found any of these expressions,

---

distinction between simple anthropomorphic phrases and theophanies in human form, though valid in itself, is, I believe, not germane to the present discussion.

[3] A. Marmorstein, *Old Rabbinic Doctrine of God* 2, *Essays in Anthropomorphism* (London, 1937; reprinted New York, 1968), pp. 61, 113-22. Marmorstein has collected the characteristic phrases of each school; e.g. "If it were not written in Scripture we would not dare say it" (literalists) versus "The Torah speaks in the language of human beings" (allegorists).

[4] H. A. Wolfson, *Philo* (Cambridge, Mass., 1948) 2, p. 127.

[5] We need not enter here into the problematics of dating particular targumim, nor into the distinction between date of composition and date of final redaction.

[6] Cf. M. L. Klein, "Converse Translation: A Targumic Technique," *Biblica* 57 (1976), pp. 515-37, and references in p. 515, n. 2.

they refrained from translating them literally".[7] Sa'adiah then lists the following examples of avoidance of anthropomorphism in Onqelos.

Exod. ix 3	the *hand* of the Lord (*yd yhwh*)
Onq.	a *plague from before* the Lord (*mḥ' mn qdm ywy*)
Exod. xxiv 10	beneath his *feet* (*wtḥt rglyw*)
Onq.	beneath his *throne of glory* (*tḥwt kwrs' dyqryh*)
Exod. xvii 1	by the *mouth* of the Lord (*'l py yhwh*)
Onq.	by the *word* of the Lord (*'l mymr' dywy*)
Num. xi 13	in the *ears* of the Lord (*b'zny yhwh*)
Onq.	*before* the Lord (*qdm ywy*).

There are however, two serious errors in Sa'adiah's argument, which, as we shall see, were later repeated by 19th and 20th century scholars. First, Sa'adiah ignores all the contradictory examples in which Onqelos transmits anthropomorphisms most literally. Second, some of the targumic passages cited are not anti-anthropomorphisms at all, but rather translational equivalents employed by Onqelos in other contexts as well. For example,

Gen. xlv 21	by the *mouth* of Pharaoh (*'l py pr'h*)
Onq.	by the *word* of Pharaoh (*'l mymr' dpr'h*)
Gen. xxiii 16	in the *ears* of the sons of Heth (*b'zny bny ḥt*)
Onq.	*before* the sons of Heth [8] (*qdm bny ḥt*).

Maimonides was more thorough than Sa'adiah. When speaking of the verb of motion "to descend" (*yrd*) as applied to God, Maimonides notes that in all cases but one it is translated in Onqelos "was revealed".[9] For example,

Exod. xix 11	the Lord will *descend* upon Mount Sinai (*yrd yhwh. . . 'l hr syny*)
Onq.	the Lord will *be revealed* . . . upon Mount Sinai (*ytgly ywy . . . 'l ṭwr' dsyny*)
Gen. xviii 21	I (God) will *go down* and see . . . (*'rdh n' w'r'h*)
Onq.	I will *be revealed* and judge . . . (*'tgly k'n w'dwn*).

---

[7] *The Book of Beliefs and Opinions*, Treatise ii, Ch. 10, (tr. S. Rosenblatt; New Haven, Connecticut, 1948), pp. 115-16. Also in *Three Jewish Philosophers* (ed. H. Lewy, et al., Cleveland and Philadelphia, 1960), Book of Doctrines and Beliefs (tr. A. Altmann), pp. 88-9.

[8] Cf. M. L. Klein, "The Preposition QDM ('Before'), A Pseudo-Anti-Anthropomorphism in the Targums", *JTS*, N.S. 30 (1979), pp. 506-7; and J. Shunary, "Avoidance of Anthropomorphism in the Targum of Psalms", *Textus* 5 (1966), p. 139.

[9] *Guide for the Perplexed*, Part 1, ch. 27, (tr. S. Pines; Chicago, 1963), pp. 57-9; cf. Maimonides *Yad Ha-Ḥazaqah* (Code), Laws of Principles of the Torah, ch. 1, §§ 8-10.

Maimonides, however, notes the exception to the rule:

Gen. xlvi 4 I (God) will *go down* with you to Egypt (*'nky 'rd*)

which is translated literally in Onqelos, by the root *nḥt* (*'n' 'yḥwt 'mk lmṣrym*). He then attempts to explain away this exception with two alternative arguments: 1) this verse is not a description of reality, but rather a dream; or 2) it refers to an angel, and not to God himself.

Elsewhere in his *Guide for the Perplexed*, Maimonides tries to explain why Onqelos always paraphrases the statement "God heard" with the passive indirect "it was heard before God" (*šmy' qdm ywy*) or with "God received (the prayer, etc.)" (*qbl ywy*), whereas the statement "God saw" is only sometimes paraphrased "and it was revealed unto God" (*'tgly qdm ywy*), while at other times it is translated literally (*ḥz' ywy*). Maimonides first proposes a distinction between "hearing", which implies the acquisition of new information through sensory activity, and "seeing", which connotes "understanding of the mind". The first implies a perceptive change at some point in time: the second, a timeless cognition. However, Maimonides himself is not satisfied with this answer, since if the phrase "God saw" is not anthropomorphic, then why does Onqelos ever bother to replace it with "was revealed before God"? Maimonides then proposes the hypothesis that Onqelos avoids only those cases in which the object of God's seeing is sinful or evil. However, here too Maimonides is aware of three exceptions (Gen. vi 5, 12 and xxix 31) which are translated literally. Unable to fit these three verses into the rule, he suggests that perhaps they are scribal errors! [10] Finally, regarding the anthropomorphism perpetuated by Onqelos in Exod. xxxi 18 and Deut. ix 10 that the tablets "were written by the finger of God" (*ktybyn b'ṣb'' dywy*) Maimonides, submits that he is at a loss for any explanation.[11]

III. Several Modern Views

I have dwelt at some length upon Maimonides because this great medieval scholar anticipated two major trends among modern scholars. First, he has retrojected his own sensitivity on the issue to the early Aramaic translators, assuming that they avoided *all* expressions of anthropomorphism. Second, he has tried to systemat-

---

[10] *Guide*. . ., Part 1, ch. 48 (tr. Pines, pp. 106-8).
[11] Ch. 66 (tr. Pines, pp. 160-1).

ize the obvious inconsistencies in the targum, on the assumption that a system does exist. The first of these assumptions has been repeated for centuries right down to our very decade. The generalization that the targumim eliminate or tone down *all* expressions of anthropomorphism is repeated by H. Seligsohn and J. Traub,[12] T. Walker,[13] W. Bacher,[14] E. Schürer,[15] A. Sperber,[16] Y. Komlosh,[17] B. Grossfeld,[18] and M. McNamara,[19] to name only a few. The second somewhat contradictory assumption which recognizes that not all *prima facie* anthropomorphic expressions are avoided, but which assumes a consistent system, has been the underlying premise of three works devoted entirely to the problem of anthropomorphisms in the targumim. I refer to the 19th century dissertations of S. Maybaum [20] and M. Ginsburger,[21] and to the more recent monumental work of Domingo Muñoz Leon.[22] Maybaum sought the "geheimen Fäden eines Systems in der Weise der Umschreibung des Onkelos" (p. 6). For example, he asserts that the verbs "to remember" (*zkr* and *pqd*) are always transformed into the passive participle in Onkelos, because "an ihn tritt kein *neues* Wissen heran". He further asserts that the verb "to see" is translated literally when the object is an event in time, but it is rendered "revealed before the Lord" when the object is an existent state of being. Among the expressions that attribute parts of body to God, Maybaum distinguishes between those that retained their figurative meaning in later times, and those that were no longer in use and might have been misunderstood by the people

---

[12] "Über den Geist der Übersetzung des Jonathan ben Usiel zum Pentateuch. . .," *MGWJ* 6 (1857), p. 107.

[13] "Targum", in J. Hastings (ed.), *A Dictionary of the Bible* 4 (Edinburgh and New York, 1903), p. 679.

[14] "Targum", *Jewish Encyclopedia* 12 (New York and London, 1907), p. 60.

[15] *History of the Jewish People in the Age of Jesus Christ 1* (revised and edited by G. Vermes and F. Millar; Edinburgh, 1973), p. 100.

[16] *The Bible in Aramaic* 4B *The Targum and the Hebrew Bible* (Leiden, 1973), p. 37.

[17] *The Bible in the Light of the Aramaic Translations* (Tel-Aviv, 1973), p. 103 (Hebrew).

[18] "Bible: Translations, Aramaic (Targumim)", *Encyclopaedia Judaica* 4 (Jerusalem, 1971), p. 842.

[19] "Targums", *IDB Supp.* (Nashville, 1976), p. 860.

[20] *Die Anthropomorphien und Anthropopathien bei Onkelos und die spätern Targumim* (Breslau, 1870).

[21] *Die Anthropomorphismen in den Thargumim* (Braunschweig, 1891).

[22] *Dios-Palabra*: *Memra en los Targumim del Pentateuco* (Granada, 1974); and *La Gloria de la Shekiná en los Targumim del Pentateuco* (Madrid, 1977). This latter work was unfortunately not available to the writer.

(p. 14). Only these latter cases were altered by Onqelos. However, upon thorough investigation, it becomes evident that all these rules and distinctions are not without exception in Onqelos, and are totally invalid in the various Palestinian Targumim.

Whereas Maybaum tried to find a system along topical lines, Ginsburger took an Hegelian developmental approach, in three chronological stages. Ginsburger openly admits that no targumim have survived from the earliest period that he posits (p. 8), yet he argues that only the personal substitutes *mēmrāʾ* and *dĕbīrā* were employed in this early stage, in order to avoid attributing direct conversation to God and man. It was not until the later stages that the same substitutes were employed in place of parts of the body attributed to God and other anthropomorphic verbs. Ginsburger's developmental theory is complicated and lacking in textual evidence.

The most recent works by Muñoz argue, once again, for a thematic or topical system among the targumim in their use of certain substitutive surrogates for God. For example, Muñoz argues that there is consistency and theological significance to the use of *mēmrāʾ* in contexts of creation, revelation and salvation. We shall return to this work in our later discussion of the use of the surrogate *mēmrāʾ* in the various targumim.

As opposed to the above mentioned generalizers and systematizers, there is a group of modern scholars who have concluded that there is no consistency in the targumic avoidance of anthropomorphisms. Regarding Onqelos, M. Kadushin has stated the case as follows:

> Since Targum Onkelos is a rabbinic version, it is once more evident that philosophy and rabbinic thought are two distinct and different worlds. To employ any philosophic criterion in an approach to Targum Onkelos leads us nowhere. We cannot speak of Targum Onkelos, therefore, as making a principle either of the incorporeality of God or of the corporeality of God . . . The Targum then is not consistent. But now we are not called upon to account for every deviation and non-deviation, for consistency here is not to be expected. The idea of God's otherness is a very indefinite idea; it permits of exceptions and it ignores inconsistencies.[23]

R. Hayward has argued for a similar situation in Neofiti and its marginal glosses.[24] Other scholars have observed the same inconsis-

[23] *The Rabbinic Mind* (3rd edn, New York, 1972), pp. 330-1.

[24] "The Memra of YHWH and the Development of its Use in Targum Neofiti I", *JJS* 25 (1974), pp. 412-18. See also Hayward's reviews of Muñoz's works *JJS* 27 (1976), pp. 94-6; and *JJS* 30 (1979), pp. 99-102.

tency in the targumim of Psalms [25] and Job,[26] as well as in various parts of the Septuagint.[27]

I shall devote the remainder of this article to the substantiation and elaboration of this latter view, demonstrating in some detail that the issue of anthropomorphism was not of theological import, and that the various targumim are extremely inconsistent in their translation of these expressions. Had the early *mĕturgĕmānīm* truly been concerned about the theological and philosophical implications of anthropomorphisms, they would have avoided them with much greater care and consistency.

IV. Human Parts of the Body Attributed to God

There are instances in which, not only have the targumim not avoided anthropomorphic expressions, but they have even amplified and intensified them. Two cases in point are:

Exod. xv 17	The sanctuary, O Lord, which your hands established (*kwnnw ydyk*)
Neof, Neof gl, P, V, CG [28]	... which your *two hands* perfected (*trtyn ydk šklly ytyh*)

---

[25] J. Shunary, "Avoidance of Anthropomorphism in the Targum of Psalms", *Textus* 5 (1966), pp. 133-44.

[26] R. Weiss, *The Aramaic Targum of Job* (Ph.D. thesis, Hebrew University, Jerusalem, 1974), pp. 273-93; published Tel Aviv, 1979 (= *Tarbiẓ* 44 [1974/75], pp. 54-71 (Hebrew)).

[27] The works of H. M. Orlinsky and his students, e.g., review of C. T. Fritsch, *The Anti-Anthropomorphisms of the Greek Pentateuch* in *Crozer Quarterly* 21 (1944), p. 157; idem, *HUCA* 27 (1956), pp. 193-200; *HUCA* 30 (1959), pp. 153-67; *HUCA* 32 (1961), pp. 239-68; A. Soffer, *HUCA* 28 (1957), 85-107; and M. S. Hurwitz, *HUCA* 28 (1957), pp. 75-83. This has all been reinforced most recently by T. Wittstruck, "The So-called Anti-anthropomorphisms in the Greek Text of Deuteronomy", *CBQ* 38 (1976), pp. 29-34.

[28] The following is a key to the sigla used for targumic texts:

Neof	MS Vatican Neofiti 1, ed. A. Díez Macho, *Neophyti 1* (Madrid, 1968-78).
Neof gl	marginal and interlinear glosses in Neof.
P	MS Paris Bibliothèque nationale Hébr. 110
V	MS Vatican Ebr. 440. Both P and V ed. M. L. Klein, *The Fragment Targums of the Pentateuch* (Rome, 1980).
CG	Cairo Geniza Fragments of Palestinian Targum. A new collection of these MSS is in preparation by the present writer. Part of the collection appears in P. Kahle, *Masoreten des Westens II* (Stuttgart, 1930, and Hildesheim, 1967), and in scattered articles in various journals.
PsJ	Pseudo-Jonathan, ed. D. Rieder, *Pseudo-Jonathan: Targum Jonathan ben Uziel on the Pentateuch...* (Jerusalem, 1974).
O	Onqelos ed. A. Sperber, *The Bible in Aramaic* 1 (Leiden, 1959).

Deut. xxxii 41	And my hand takes hold on judgement (*wt'ḥẓ bmšpṭ ydy*).
Neof, V	And my *right hand* takes hold on (true) judgement (*wttwqp bdynh bqwšṭh yd ymyny*).

This may be compared with the similar translation of a verse in a human context:

Exod. xv 9	my (Pharaoh's) hand shall destroy them (*twryšmw ydy*).
Neof, P, V, CG, PsJ	my *right hand* shall destroy them (*tšyṣy ythwn byd ymyny*).

It is quite clear from these verses, and others, that the targumim felt no embarrassment or compunction when speaking of God's hand or his right hand or both of his hands. The same is true of God's palms:

Exod. xxxiii 22	and I shall shield you with my palm (*kpy*; *RSV*, *Torah*: hand)
Neof, V	I shall spread (V: cast) my palm over you
Neof gl	I shall cast *the palm of my hand* (*kp ydy*) over you.

The single instance of feet attributed to God in the Pentateuch is translated literally in all the extant Palestinian Targumim:

Exod. xxiv 10	and beneath his feet (*wtḥt rglyw*) there was the likeness of a pavement of sapphire
Neof, PsJ	and beneath the *footstool of his feet* (*wtḥwt 'pypwdn drglwy*).

The paraphrase "footstool of his feet", if anything, intensifies the anthropomorphism.[29]

The targumim introduce the anthropomorphic "mouth" even where it is lacking in the original Hebrew.

Deut. xxxiii 9	for they observed your word (*'mrtk*)
Neof, V	for they observed *the word of your mouth* (*mymr pwmk*).

Likewise the expansive introductions to the Ten Commandments in the various Palestinian Targumim follow the pattern: "The first

---

[29] Contrast: 1 Chron. xxviii 2 — the footstool of our God
tg Chron. — the footstool of the *throne of glory* of God.
See also, tg Isa. lxvi 1.

statement as it emerged *from the mouth* of the Holy One, may his name be blessed ..." (*dbyr' qdm'h kd npq mn pwm qwdš'*) (Exod. xx 1 Neof, P, PsJ.). One last example regarding human parts of the body:

Deut. xi 12	the eyes of the Lord your God are always upon it
Neof, V	*the eyes of the Lord* your God are gazing upon it (*ʿyynwy dy'y 'lhkwn bh mstklyn*).

The above examples of hand, palm, feet, mouth and eyes are sufficient, I believe, to prove that the targumim are not consistently anti-anthropomorphic. In fact, we may go one step further: had the early *mĕturgĕmān* been troubled by biblical anthropomorphisms, he might have disposed of these obvious instances with little effort. Apparently he was simply not interested.

V. Pseudo-anti-anthropomorphisms

I have thus far presented examples of anthropomorphisms which are literally transmitted in the targumim. There is another class of expressions which have been altered in the course of their translation, for non-theological reasons, but which have nevertheless been presented in the past as evidence of the anti-anthropomorphic nature of the targumim. (Two of the four examples cited above from Saʿadiah fall into this category.)

It is methodologically essential to determine the cause of a particular paraphrase before it may be applied as proof of the theological and doctrinal motivations of the translator. To reverse the order is to beg the question. The following are some examples:

The biblical expression "crying/complaining in *the ears* of the Lord" (*b'zny yhwh*) is translated "... in *the hearing* of the Lord" (*bmšmʿh dy'y*) in all three cases in Neofiti, and "... *before* the Lord" (*qdm ywy*) in Onqelos and Pseudo-Jonathan.[30] I submit, however, that none of these transformations is in any way related to the philosophic problem of anthropomorphism. The evidence for this assertion lies in the fact that the targumim employ the very same idiomatic paraphrase in the purely human context in no fewer than 14 instances.[31] In fact, the substitution of the Aramaic "in the *hearing* of" for the original Hebrew "in the *ears* of" was so common, that it actually became a fixed translational equivalent for the marginal

[30] Num. xi 1, 18, xiv 28.
[31] E.g., Gen. xx 8, xxiii 10, 13, 16, l 4; Exod. x 2, xi 2, xvii 14.

annotator of MS Neofiti, who then applied it *ad absurdum*. Thus, in Gen. xxxv 4, the phrase "and the rings that were on their *ears*", which is rendered literally in all the targumim, is hyper-corrected in Neof gl to "(the rings) that were in *their hearing*" (*d'yt bmšm'hwn*)!

Another example is the biblical expression "found favor in the *eyes* of the Lord" which is translated in Neofiti in five instances "... *before* the Lord",[32] and in five others "... in the *face* of the Lord".[33] First, the "*face* of the Lord" is no less anthropomorphic than is "the *eyes* of the Lord". Second, the transformation to "*before* the Lord" is not for the purpose of avoiding the anthropomorphism. In the purely human context, in Deut. xxiv 1, the wife who fails "to find favor in his (the husband's) *eyes*" is rendered by Neofiti "if she does not find favor and grace *before* him". We find the same idiomatic paraphrase in a Palestinian Targum (Cambridge, University Library T-S Misc. 27.1.4) to Gen. xlvii 29, where Jacob says to Joseph "If I have found favor in your eyes"; and the targum reads "If, now, I have found favor and grace *before* you".[34]

A third and final example of such pseudo-anti-anthropomorphisms is the Hebrew expression "by the *mouth* of" (*'al pī*), which is translated in both divine and human contexts "by the *word/decree* of". As in the two previous examples, the targumim transmit the intended meaning of the phrase, and not a literal one-for-one translation of its elements. For instance, in Gen. xli 40 Pharaoh says to Joseph "and by your mouth shall all my people be directed". The following are the targumic renderings:

Neof:	And by *the decree of your mouth* (*gzyrt pwmk*) shall all my people be fed
CG:[35]	And (by) the *word* of (your) mouth (*mymr pym*[*k*]) shall all (my people) be fed
PsJ:	And by *the decree of the word of your mouth* (*gzyrt mymr pwmk*)
O:	And by *your word* (*mymrk*).

Clearly, in this human context the substitutions of "your word, the word of your mouth, the decree of your mouth" and the composite "decree of the word of your mouth", have absolutely nothing to do with anthropomorphism. They must rather be compared to the modern renditions "as/at your command" (RSV, Torah), which are simply

[32] Gen. vi 8; Exod. xxxiii 12, 13, 16, xxxiv 9.
[33] Gen. xviii 3; Exod. xxxiii 13, 17; Num. xi 11, 15.
[34] On the preposition *qdm* ("before") see note 8, above.
[35] Cambridge University Library, T-S NS 76.1.

idiomatic. In Gen. xlv 21 the Hebrew "by the mouth of Pharaoh" becomes "by the *decree* of Pharaoh's mouth" (Neof), and "by Pharaoh's *word*" (*mēmrā'*; PsJ, O). Likewise, in Deut. xvii 6 "upon the mouth of two witnesses", becomes "upon the *mouth of the word* (*pem mēmar*) of two witnesses" (Neof) [36] and "upon *the word* (*mēmar*) of two witnesses", (PsJ, O). Here the modern translations use "evidence" (RSV) and "testimony" (Torah).

To sum up, then, it is clear that figurative phrases such as "spoke in the ears of" or "found favor in the eyes of" or "upon the mouth of" which are common in biblical Hebrew, are rendered idiomatically in the targumim. The elimination of ears, eyes and mouth and the introduction of "decree" or "word" (*mēmrā'*) in these cases, are not to be related to the theology of anti-anthropomorphism.

VI. Memra

The present framework does not allow for a full treatment of the uses of *mēmrā'* in the targumim. Nevertheless, in view of the recent works by D. Muñoz Leon, R. Hayward and others,[37] it is impossible to discuss the problem of anthropomorphisms in the targumim without at least touching upon the subject of *mēmrā'*.

It is generally accepted that *mēmrā'* of the targumim is not a personification or a hypostasis, but rather a nominal substitute.[38] Its conceptual origins lie in such biblical verses as Ps. xxxiii 6 "By the *word of the Lord* the heavens were made, by the breath of his mouth all their hosts". The idea is also paralleled in early rabbinic literature in statements such as "with ten statements (*m'mrwt*) the world was created" (M. Abot v 1) [39] and the liturgical benediction

---

[36] The Aramaic *'al pim mēmar tĕrēn sāhădīn*, of course, means "*according to* the word of two witnesses," just as the Hebrew *'al pī haggōrāl* (Num. xxvi 56) means "*according to* the lot" and *'al pī hattōrāh* (Deut. xvii 11) means "according to the instruction". My use of "by the mouth of" has come only to convey the language of the texts, and does not ignore their figurative or idiomatic sense.

[37] See notes 22 and 24, above, and M. McNamara "*Logos* of the Fourth Gospel and *Memra* of the Palestinian Targum", *Expository Times* 79 (1967-8), pp. 115-17; L. Sabourin, "The MEMRA of God in the Targums", *Biblical Theology Bulletin* 6 (1976), pp. 79-85 (review of Muñoz).

[38] E. g., G. F. Moore, *Judaism in the First Centuries of the Christian Era* (Cambridge, Mass., 1923) 1, p. 419: ". . . nowhere in the Targums is *memra* a 'being' of any kind or in any sense, much less a personal being." With many more targumic texts available today, that statement still holds.

[39] The ten statements refer to the ten occurences of the phrase "God said" (same root *'mr* as in *ma'ămār* and *mēmrā'*) in the creation story at the beginning of Genesis.

"Who with his word (*bm'mrw*) created the heavens" (B. Sanhedrin 42a).

In the targumim *mēmrā'* appears as the subject of sentences in place of God's name or pronoun, in almost every type of context. It is found with 46 different verbs, and in sundry possessive phrases.

Applying both deductive and inductive methods, Muñoz and Hayward try to discover the relationship of *mēmrā'* to the Godhead. They also search for a systematic pattern of employment of the term in the targumim (esp. Neofiti and its glosses). There are several verses in Exodus in which the Palestinian targumim seemingly define that relationship:

Exod. iii 12 (MT)	*ky 'hyh ʿmk*
Neof	*'rwm 'hwwy mmry ʿmk'*
Neof gl	*yhwwy bsʿdk*
MT	For I shall be with you
Neof	For I shall be my *memra* with you
Neof gl	(For) it (my *memra*) shall be in your support.

Hayward believes that the targum is defining the term *mēmrā'* and equating it with God's name *'EHYEH*, which represents his past and future "active presence" in creation and history. The difficulty with this theory is that the word in the present verse is no more than the simple verb "to be". It is not until Exod. iii 13-14 that *'EHYEH* serves as a proper name:

> *... w'mrw ly mh šmw mh 'mr 'lhm.*
> *wy'mr 'lhym 'l mšh 'hyh 'šr 'hyh wy'mr kh t'mr lbny yśr'l 'hyh šlḥny 'lykm*
> "... they will ask me "What is his name?' What shall I say to them? And God said to Moses, 'Ehyeh-Asher-Ehyeh'. And he said, thus shall you say to the Israelites, 'Ehyeh sent me to you'."

The variant modern translations for the name are "I Am Who I Am" or "I Will Be Who I Will Be"—both related to the root *hyh*, "to be".

The phrase "God was/will be with someone" is fairly common in the Pentateuch. The following examples represent the various possible translations in the Palestinian targumim:

a) *literal*

Gen. xxxix 2	*wyhy yhwh 't ywsp*
Neof	*whwh y'y yt*(!) *ywsp* [40]
Gen. xxxix 3	*wyr' 'dnyw ky yhwh 'tw*
Neof	*wḥm' rbwnyh 'rwm y'y hwwh ʿmyh*

---

[40] On the mechanical translation of the prepositional *'ēt* by *yāt*, see my note "Deut 31:7, *tavo'* or *tavi'*?", *JBL* 92 (1973), p. 585. Also, cf. Gen. xxxix 21, where Neof uses the preposition *ʿim* in the same phrase.

b) *addition of bmymr'*
Gen. xxvi 3 *w'hyh 'mk*
Neof *w'hwwh bmymrh*(!) *'mk*
Gen. xxxi 3 *w'hyh 'mk*
Neof *w'hwy bmmry 'mk*

c) *translation of 'm/'mdy ("with") by bs'd' ("in support of")*
Gen. xxviii 20 *'m yhyh 'lhym 'mdy*
Neof *'n yhwwy y'y bs'dy*

d) *addition of bmymr' and translation of 'm by bs'd'.*
Deut. xxxi 23 *w'nky 'hyh 'mk*
Neof *w'nh bmmry 'hwy bs'dk.*

This last compound type is the standard rendition in Neof gl and in CG.[41] There is, however, an unusually high incidence of scribal errors in the translation of this phrase. For example:

Gen. xxvi 3 *w'hyh 'mk*
Neof *w'hwwh bmymrh 'mk.*

The third person suffix is used instead of the first person. As already noted, in Gen. xxxix 2 the prepositional *'t* ("with") is translated *yt.*

Exod. iv 15 *w'nky 'hyh 'm pyk*
Neof *w'n' bmymry 'lh 'm mml pmk*
Neof gl_1 *'hwy*
Neof gl_2 *hwwy 'm mll pmk.*

The word *'lh* in Neof is inexplicable; the verb *hwwy* in Neof gl_2 is an error for the 1st person singular imperfect. Even in the Cairo Genizah MSS there are indications of irregularity in the translation of this phrase. For example:

Gen. xxxi 3 *w'hyh 'mk*
CG (E) *wyhy mmry* (*'ṁ*) *bs'dk.*

The scribe apparently began to write *'mk*, stopped short, marked the *mem* with a dot, and continued with the expected *bs'dk*. It is impossible at this point to prove that the manuscript from which the scribe was copying also read *'mk*—but the possibility certainly exists. Another telling example from the same Genizah text is Gen. xxviii 20, 21:

MT (20) *'m yhyh 'lhym 'mdy* . . . (21) *whyh yhwh ly l'lhym*
CG *'n yhwh mmrh dyO bs'dy . . . wyhyy mṁ dyO bs'dy l'lh prwq.*

---

[41] E.g., CG Gen. xxviii 20, xxxix 2, 3 and Neof gl Gen. xxxi 3, xxxix 21.

Here the second *bs'dy* is mechanically inserted, even though the sense of the verse is not "God will be *with me*" but rather "the *mēmrā'* of the Lord will be my redeeming God" (Heb.: "then YHWH will be my God"). Neof and PsJ, which both use *yhwy mmryh dy'y bs'dy* in *v.* 20, correctly refrain from using it in *v.* 21. All these examples of confusion and corruption in the various Palestinian targumim lead me to agree with Muñoz, against Hayward,[42] that *'hwy* in the phrase *'rwm 'hwy mmry 'mk* is but a scribal error for *yhwy*. It cannot be taken as a statement of definition or identification "I shall be my *mēmrā'* with you". It would seem that the scribal error reflected here involved the introduction of the word *mēmrā'* without the required adjustment of the verb from first to third person (or the common interchange of the initial '/*y* in imperfect verbs in Neofiti, as R. Le Déaut suggested at the Congress).

The second verse cited by Hayward is even more confused and corrupt.

Exod. iv 12 *w'nky 'hyh 'm pyk*
Neof *w'n' 'm mmry 'hyh 'm mmll pmk.*

If, as Hayward argues, the targum has intentionally preserved the Hebrew proper name EHYEH, then the sentence remains without the imperfect verb "to be". Furthermore, instead of the phrase *'m mmry* we expect *bmmry*. The verse as it stands is meaningless: "and I, with my *mēmrā'*, EHYEH with the speech of your mouth". This passage can hardly serve as evidence for the meaning of *mēmrā'*.

Regarding the use of *mēmrā'* throughout MS Neofiti 1, I must agree with Hayward as opposed to Muñoz, that it is sporadic or even erratic. Hayward has shown that, among the 46 verbs for which *mēmrā'* serves as the subject, only six verbs have *mēmrā'* more than five times. Regarding the remaining 40 verbs, Hayward notes that the use of *mēmrā'* "appears arbitrary and unmotivated by theological considerations".[43] As to the 72 verbs with which *mēmrā'* appears in Neof gl, Hayward correctly notes that their range of meaning "is so wide as to once again defy any satisfactory classification". I would add that, even after recent works by Clarke, Lund and Foster,[44]

---

[42] *Dios Palabra*, p. 38, n. 56 "Ngl corrige con su variante 'estará' "; cf. Hayward, *JJS* 27 (1976), p. 94.

[43] *JJS* 25 (1974), pp. 413-14.

[44] E. G. Clarke, "The Neofiti I Marginal Glosses and the Fragmentary Targum Witnesses to Gen. VI-IX", *VT* 22 (1972), pp. 257-65; and S. Lund and J. Foster, *Variant Versions of Targumic Traditions Within Codex Neofiti 1* (Missoula, 1977).

the sources of Neof gl remain for the most part shrouded in mystery. As such, one can hardly make statements about the translational tendencies of Neof gl.

It is generally acknowleged that the main body of Neofiti is partially composite, and that at least the beginning of Genesis and the end of Deuteronomy derive from distinct sources. The creation narrative at the beginning of Genesis is of particular interest since, as mentioned above, the repetition of the phrase *wy'mr 'lhym* nine times elicited the Mishnaic comment that the world was created through ten *ma'ămārōt*. It is, therefore, inexplicable that only seven of the nine instances contain *mēmrā'* in Neof, and that only one of the two "missing" *mēmrā'*s is provided by Neof gl.[45] This type of inconsistency (and I have presented only one of many examples) pervades the entire Neofiti, in all its identified underlying sources. I find it difficult to believe that an important theological principle would have been handled so carelessly and inconsistently by the early *mĕturgĕmān*.

VII. Syntactic Peculiarities of Some Anti-anthropomorphisms

There is a preponderance of syntactic irregularities in the targumim, in anti-anthropomorphic contexts. Certain syntactic constructions which are normally avoided or even eliminated by the *mĕturgĕmān* suddenly appear with relative frequency in anti-anthropomorphic translations.

For example, the combination of a passive verb with the *nota accusativi 't* appears in the Hebrew Bible some 28 times.[46] In 15 instances Neofiti removes the particle *'t*, or transforms the verb from passive to active, or makes some other grammatical change. Thus:

Num. xxvi 55	*'k bgwrl yēḥālēq 't h'rṣ*
Neof	*lḥwd b'dywn ttplg 'r'*
Gen. xl 20	*ywm hldt 't pr'h*
Neof	*ywm gnysy' dpr'h.*

The other targumim also tend to avoid the combination of passive verb plus accusative. It is therefore significant that the very construc-

[45] Gen. i 3, 6, 9, 11, 20, 24, 29. The word *mēmrā'* is missing in Neof in *vv.* 1 and 26. It is provided in the gloss to *v.* 26. The verb *'mr* has the highest number of occurrences of *mēmrā'* in Neofiti (19 times).

[46] See P. Joüon, *Grammaire de l'Hébreu Biblique* (2nd edn, Rome, 1947), § 128, "Accusatif avec verbe passif", pp. 383 ff. Cf. A. E. Cowley (ed.), *Gesenius' Hebrew Grammar as edited and enlarged by the late E. Kautzsch* (2nd edn [= 28th German edn], Oxford, 1910) § 121, "Construction of passive verbs", pp. 387 f.

tion that is normally eliminated by the targumim, is introduced into the text in the context of anthropomorphisms. The following cases are typical:

Gen. xli 16	*ʾlhym yʿnh ʾt šlwm prʿh*
Neof	*mn qdm y'y ytʿnh yt šlmʾ dprʿh*
Num. xvii 19	*ʾšr ʾiwwāʿēd lkm šmh*
Neof	*dy ʾzdmm mmry lkwn tmn*
Gen. i 4	*wyrʾ ʾlhym ʾt hʾwr ky ṭwb*
Neof	*wgly qdm y'y yt nhwrʾ ʾrwm ṭb*
Exod. ii 24	*wyšmʿ ʾlhym ʾt nʾqtm*
Neof, O	*wšmyʿ qdm y'y yt qblthwn.*

Another type of syntactical irregularity is found in the targum when it alters verbs in anthropomorphic phrases without paying attention to the remainder of the verse—and especially to the prepositions. A case in point is

Lev. xxvi 31	*wlʾ ʾryḥ bryḥ nyḥḥkm*
Neof	*wlʾ ʾqbl brʿwwh bryḥ qrbnykwm.*

There are two possible explanations that suggest themselves: 1. In his preoccupation with obviating the anthropomorphism, the *mĕturgĕmān* inadvertently violated his normally good sense of grammar. 2. The original text was grammatically correct and some later pious copyist removed the anthropomorphisms from what had been a literal translation. In so doing he introduced only minimal changes, often at the expense of grammar and syntax. In view of the many anthropomorphic phrases that have survived unscathed in the Palestinian targumim, I would tend to accept the second of these two alternatives.

VIII. Conclusion

The long repeated generalization that the targumim avoid or tone down all biblical anthropomorphisms, is no longer acceptable. In fact, the targumim in their present textual state are highly inconsistent on this matter, and the frequency of anti-anthropomorphisms is much smaller than has hitherto been asserted. By systematically comparing certain supposed anti-anthropomorphisms to their counterparts in a non-divine context, we have shown that they are common idiomatic and translational phenomena, and not related at all to theology or philosophy. Finally, it would seem that a goodly number of anti-anthropomorphisms in MS Neofiti 1 are of secondary origin, and do not belong to the original compositional strand of that text.

LE THÈME DE LA CIRCONCISION DU COEUR (DT. XXX 6; JÉR. IV 4) DANS LES VERSIONS ANCIENNES (LXX ET TARGUM) ET À QUMRÂN

par

R. LE DÉAUT

Rome

I

L'usage de la métaphore de la circoncision du coeur dans la tradition biblique et juive revêt un certain intérêt soit en raison de ses connexions avec des thèmes importants, comme celui de la "nouvelle alliance" et du "coeur nouveau", soit à cause du rôle qu'a joué la dialectique circoncision physique/c. spirituelle dans le Judaïsme ancien et le Christianisme primitif.

Si l'interprétation de la c. a beaucoup varié dans la tradition biblique et juive, un point est demeuré fermement établi: son importance essentielle.[1] Un rite primitif d'initiation au mariage a reçu peu à peu une signification religieuse plus haute, au terme d'une évolution qui paraît avoir été lente (cf. Ex. iv 24;[2] Jos. v 2-8). Durant l'exil, au milieu des Babyloniens incirconcis, la c. devint une marque distinctive des Israélites, une sorte de confession de foi en leur Dieu. Le Code sacerdotal (P) intégrera le rite dans sa construction

---

[1] Voir 1 Macc. i 15, 48, 60, ii 46; 2 Macc. vi 10 (cf. 4 Macc. iv 25); Jubilés xv (commentant Gen. xvii): la c. l'emporte sur le sabbat (xv 14); les anges sont créés circoncis (xv 27). La tradition fera naître les Patriarches avec le signe de l'alliance (*LAB* 9, 13 pour Moïse; *ARN* 2; cf. L. Ginzberg, *The Legends of the Jews* [Philadelphia, 1909-1946] V, p. 273; VII, p. 87). L'exclamation "Grande est la c." revient souvent dans les écrits rabbiniques (cf. P. Billerbeck, *Kommentar zum Neuen Testament aus Talmud und Midrasch* [München 1922-1961] IV, p. 38). Philon commence son *De Specialibus legibus* par un préambule sur la c. Sur les controverses dans la première communauté chrétienne, cf. Act. xv. La c. de Gilgal permit l'entrée en Terre promise et sa négligence fut cause de l'exil (cf. Ginzberg, VI, p. 172 et 391). Judaïsme et c. sont parfois identifiés (Esther viii 17: περιετέμοντο καὶ ιουδάιζον). La c. fut imposée aux Ituréens et aux Iduméens (cf. E. Schürer - G. Vermes - F. Millar, *The History of the Jewish People* 1 [Edinburgh, 1973], p. 538) et son interdiction sous Hadrien est l'une des causes retenues de la grande révolte de 132-135 (ibid., p. 536-40). Et l'on pourrait citer bien d'autres faits.

[2] Sur ce texte et ses interprétations anciennes, cf. G. Vermes, *Scripture and Tradition in Judaism* (Leiden, 1961), p. 178-92.

théologique: il scelle l'entrée dans l'alliance, devient le "signe de l'alliance" perpétuelle avec Yhwh (Gen. xvii 11, 13) et de l'agrégation à la communauté d'Israël.[3] L'expression qui désignera la c. sera "alliance d'Abraham", alliance et c. devenant si intimement associées (cf. διαθήκη περιτομῆς: Act. vii 8) que le terme biblique *bĕrît* sera parfois interprété de la circoncision et la désignera souvent directement.[4]

Cette institution reçut, dès l'AT, diverses interprétations métaphoriques.[5] Ex. vi 12 (P) parlera de "lèvres incirconcises" (au sens d'incapacité ou d'incompétence à transmettre le message de Dieu), Jér. vi 10 d' "oreille incirconcise" (au sens d'inaptitude ou d'impuissance à recevoir la parole de Dieu) et Lév. xix 23-25 demande que l'on considère, pendant trois ans, comme "chose incirconcise", les fruits d'un arbre nouvellement planté. Mais la métaphore la plus célèbre est celle de la *circoncision du coeur*.

Rappelons que, pour les Sémites, le coeur est considéré comme étant *réellement* à la fois l'organe de la pensée, du vouloir, de la mémoire et des divers sentiments et qu'ils ne comprendraient rien au tiraillement pascalien entre le coeur et la raison.[6] De lui proviennent et le bien et le mal; [7] point de rencontre de Dieu et de l'homme, l'état du coeur révèle la qualité de leurs rapports. Ainsi un coeur endurci [8] n'entend plus la voix du Seigneur (Ps. xcv 8).

---

[3] Sur la c. en général, cf. R. Meyer, *TWNT* VI, p. 72-83; R. de Vaux, *Les institutions de l'Ancien Testament* I (Paris, 1958), p. 78-82; Billerbeck, IV, p. 23-40; G. F. Moore, *Judaism* (Cambridge, Mass., 1927-1930) II, p. 16-21; O. Kuss, *Der Römerbrief* (Regensburg, 1957), p. 92-8; H. J. Hermisson, *Sprache und Ritus im altisraelitischen Kult* (Neukirchen-Vluyn, 1965), p. 64-76.

[4] Pour Ex. xxiv 8, cf. Billerbeck, IV, p. 38. Noter que *krt* (verbe technique pour "sceller une alliance") est employé à Ex. iv 25 pour "couper le prépuce".

[5] Ici métaphore = transposition sur le plan figuré (ou spirituel) de la signification d'un acte rituel (comparer "lavage de cerveau"). Sur ces emplois, voir Hermisson, p. 70 ss. Ils sont groupés dans Gen. R 46, 4-5 à xvii 2. Pour Qumrân, cf. 1 QH II 7-18 (lèvres), XVIII 20 (oreille).

[6] E. Dhorme, "L'emploi métaphorique des noms de parties du corps", *RB* 31 (1922), p. 489-508; E. Jacob, *Théologie de l'AT*[2] (Neuchâtel, 1968), p. 132-5; J. Behm, in *TWNT* III, p. 609-16; A. Dihle, ibid., IX, p. 623-5; F. Stolz in *Theol. Handw. zum AT* I, col. 861-7. Pour une sorte de concordance des emplois métaphoriques de *lēb*, voir Eccl. R I, 16.

[7] Cf. Matth. xii 34: "La bouche ne verse que le trop-plein du coeur"; dans la version de E. Renan, *Vie de Jésus* XIV (9e éd., Paris, 1864), p. 162.

[8] Sur les divers termes exprimant l'endurcissement du coeur (*kbd, ḥzq, qšh, šrr*), cf. F. Hesse, *Das Verstockungsproblem im AT*, *BZAW* 74, (Berlin, 1955), p. 7-16; A. Hermann, "Das Steinharte Herz", *Jahrb. f. Antike und Christentum* 4 (1961), p. 77-107.

La vraie conversion devra donc toucher l'homme en son coeur, à la source même de son comportement religieux.

La première mention de la circoncision du coeur se lit dans Dt. x 16: "Vous circoncirez donc le prépuce de votre coeur et votre nuque vous ne raidirez plus" (*wmltm 't 'rlt lbbkm w'rpkm l' tqšw 'd*).

On notera le parallélisme (souligné en hébreu par l'allitération *'orlâ/'ōrep*) entre "prépuce du coeur" et "raideur de nuque" (exprimant entêtement et indocilité). L'injonction est immédiatement motivée par le rappel de l'*élection* [9] d'Israël (*v.* 15) et l'infinie majesté et puissance du Seigneur (*v.* 17) qui exige une adhésion totale et sincère à sa Loi: "en aimant et en servant le Seigneur, ton Dieu, de *tout* ton coeur et de *toute* ton âme" (*v.* 12). Cette formule évoque le commentaire du *Shema' Israel* (vi 4-5) et les autres mentions du coeur dans Dt. (iv 29, xi 13, xiii 4, xxvi 16). Ainsi la c. du coeur signifie non seulement le don à Dieu de l'intime de soi-même, mais de tout l'être.[10] Désormais ce thème apparaîtra surtout dans les exhortations à la conversion.

L'image est reprise dans Jér. iv 4: "Soyez circoncis pour Yhwh (ou: pour moi), ôtez le prépuce de votre coeur" (*hmlw lyhwh whsrw 'rlwt lbbkm*).[11]

Cet oracle [12] répond à la confession du peuple de iii 22-25 et

---

[9] Dans Gen. xvii, alliance et c. sont étroitement associées.

[10] St. Lyonnet, "Le 'chrétien anonyme' ou Le païen au 'coeur circoncis' selon Romains 2, 29" (texte ronéotypé, Institut Biblique, Rome, 1973), p. 13 (= *Mélanges Fr. J. Leenhardt* [Genève, 1968], p. 87-97); Hermisson, p. 74. T. Gen. xxii 1 (Ps-Jonathan) interprète la c. comme la consécration de *tout* le corps à Dieu (cf. Yoma 85b; Shab 132a). Dans le commandement de l'amour, le coeur est impliqué en premier (avant l'*âme*). La Loi est dans le coeur (Jér. xxxi 33); Israël est "le peuple de ceux qui ont la Loi dans le coeur", selon Is. li 7, passage marqué d'un signe dans le ms de Qumrân (cf. G. R. Driver, *The Judaean Scrolls* [Oxford, 1965], p. 528-9). Sur le retour à l'Alliance *de tout son coeur*, cf. 2 Chron. xv 12 (passage très proche de 1 QS I 1-2).

[11] Litt.: "les prépuces" (beaucoup de mss ont le sg). Le verbe *sûr* se retrouve dans Éz. xi 19, xxxvi 26 ("*J'enlèverai* le coeur de pierre"). LXX xi 19: ἐκσπάσω; xxxvi 26: ἀφελῶ.

[12] Pour l'établissement et le commentaire du texte, cf. W. Rudolph, *Jeremia*² (Tübingen, 1958), p. 26-9. Il s'agit d'un oracle de jeunesse (G. von Rad, *Théologie de l'AT* II [Genève, 1967], 166-8 = *Theologie des Alten Testaments* II (München, 1960], p. 205-8) de Jérémie qui commence son ministère en 626 (réforme de Josias 622). La question des rapports entre Dt. et Jérémie reste débattue: J. P. Hyatt, "Jeremiah and Deuteronomy", *JNES* 1 (1942), p. 156-73 (la formule "c. du coeur" relèverait de la "terminologie du temps et non de relations entre eux: p. 165); H. Cazelles, "Jérémie et le Deutéronome", *RSR* 38 (1951), p. 5-36 (estime "peu probable qu'une image aussi originale

insiste sur la nécessité d'un changement radical, un défrichement profond avant les semailles (*v.* 3). Les signes extérieurs d'une conversion apparente (iii 10) ne suffisent pas pour être sauvé. Il faut défricher son coeur et aller jusqu'aux racines du mal. La c. du coeur est ici oeuvre de l'homme, mais elle reste, au fond, grâce de Dieu (cf. iii 22). En utilisant cette métaphore, le prophète n'émet bien entendu aucun jugement de valeur sur le rite lui-même de la circoncision.[13] On perçoit cependant une prise de conscience très nette des exigences intérieures de toute action morale: la conversion doit atteindre le centre même du dynamisme spirituel, au fond du coeur où le péché, refus de Dieu, s'enracine. Ainsi le rite antique sert à marquer une étape importante dans l'évolution de la religion d'Israël.

Une nouvelle étape est marquée par Dt. xxx 6 dans un développement qui suppose l'expérience de l'exil. Dieu promet à Israël repentant de ramener les captifs au pays de leurs pères et de parfaire lui-même le processus de conversion:

> YHWH, ton Dieu, circoncira (*wml*) ton coeur [14] et le coeur de ta descendance, pour aimer YHWH, ton Dieu, de *tout* ton coeur et de *toute* ton âme, afin que tu vives.

C'est donc Dieu lui-même qui opère cette rénovation et qui crée en l'homme la capacité d'aimer. Si la formulation rappelle Jér. iv 4 le contenu évoque davantage Jér. xxxi 31-34, xxxii 39-41; Éz. xi 19-20, xxxvi 24-27 où ce qu'il y a de neuf est l'*intériorisation* de la religion.[15] Cette circoncision du coeur permet d'obéir à la voix

---

ait été inventée à la fois par deux auteurs ... Jérémie semble supposer l'image connue": p. 13).

[13] Hermisson, p. 73. Cela vaut aussi de Dt.

[14] *The Torah* (Philadelphia, 1962): "Then the Lord your God will open up your heart". Note: "Others 'circumcise' ". Traitement de la métaphore qui a des modèles fort anciens, comme nous le verrons.

[15] A. Dillmann qualifiait l'annonce de Dt. xxx 6 de "reine messianische Verheissung" (*Die Bücher Numeri, Deuteronomium, und Josua*[2] [Leipzig, 1886], p. 384). Sur la nouvelle alliance, citons seulement P. Buis, *VT* 18 (1968), p. 1-15 (qui cite le beau texte de Baruch ii 30-35, à lire dans notre contexte). La "c. du coeur" n'est qu'une métaphore et le contenu est ce qui importe. On ne s'étonnera donc point de la voir si peu employée dans l'AT et la tradition juive, malgré son expressivité. Ce contenu peut être exprimé en termes explicites (de renovation, de conversion) ou par d'autres images (comme celle du "coeur nouveau"). La même remarque vaudra pour les versions: si parfois le texte hébreu n'est pas traduit littéralement, ce peut être simplement pour donner en clair le contenu de la métaphore. Mais il peut y avoir aussi d'autres motivations.

de Yhwh, de garder ses commandements et de revenir à lui "de *tout* son coeur et de *toute* son âme" (*vv.* 8-10). On doit comprendre la c. du coeur dans Dt. à la lumière de ces formules; [16] elle constitue en quelque sorte l'envers d'autres thèmes (comme la *nouvelle alliance* ou le *coeur nouveau* qui me paraissent aller bien au-delà), la suppression de ce qui empêche d'aimer Dieu. Rien d'étonnant dès lors que cette métaphore soit par la suite souvent interprétée par d'autres formules comme "ôter l'endurcissement du coeur, enlever le penchant mauvais".

On peut rapprocher de ce texte, pour la date et pour le contenu, un passage de la Loi de sainteté (Lév. xxvi 41) qui se situe aussi dans le cadre des perspectives de la conversion d'Israël:

> Alors [17] leur coeur incirconsis s'humiliera (*ykn' lbbm h'rl*), alors ils expieront leur iniquité. Je me rappellerai mon *alliance* ...

Ici encore la conversion du coeur (cf. Sifra ad loc.) est notée comme condition pour le rétablissement de l'alliance.[18]

Mentionnons enfin deux passages où sont juxtaposées circoncision physique et c. du coeur. Jér. ix 24-25 annonce le châtiment de nations voisines et celui d'Israël lui-même parce que "incirconcis de coeur".[19] La c. physique prend donc sa valeur religieuse des dispositions du coeur qu'elle signifie. Éz. xliv 7, 9 (écrit au début de l'exil) exclut du Sanctuaire les étrangers "incirconcis de coeur et incirconcis de chair": la c. dans son sens réel et son sens figuré

---

[16] Dt. vise déjà une obéissance *intérieure*. Ce qu'apporte l'alliance nouvelle de Jér. xxxi, c'est que "Dieu imprime sa volonté directement dans le coeur de l'homme, (le libérant) de tout effort d'obéissance" (G. von Rad, *Théologie* II, p. 184 = *Theol. d. Alten Testaments* II, p. 226).

[17] En lisant *'āz*, au lieu de *'ô 'āz*. Cf. LXX et Pesh. (*whydyn*). LXX: τότε ἐντραπήσεται (= Vulg.: "donec erubescat"; Pesh.: *nttbr*, "se brise") ἡ καρδία αὐτῶν ἡ ἀπερίτμητος. Sifra interprète *ykn'* de la pénitence/conversion (*tšwbh*).

[18] Ce texte est cité (à la 1ère personne, comme étant réalisé) dans 4 QDibHam VI 5: "Et maintenant, en ce jour où *notre coeur s'est humilié*, *nous avons expié notre iniquité*". L'adjectif *h'rl* a été omis! Tout ce document, sans doute préessénien, décrit admirablement la conversion: cf. M. Baillet, "Un recueil liturgique, de Qumrân, Grotte 4: 'Les paroles des luminaires' ", *RB* 68 (1961), p. 210—11, 230, 250.

[19] La fin du *v.* 25 est peut-être une glose adaptant le texte de Jérémie à une époque postérieure où la c. serait tombée en désuétude, sauf en Israël (cf. *TOB*). Ou bien, avec W. Rudolph (p. 65), lire *h'lh* (ces), au lieu de *'rlym* ("incirconcis"): "Toutes ces nations et toute la maison d'Israël sont incirconcis de coeur". LXX: πάντα τὰ ἔθνη ἀπερίτμητα σαρκί (= Syro-Hex.) καὶ πᾶς οἶκος I. ἀπερίτμητοι καρδίας αὐτῶν (Aquila: ἀκρόβυστοι καρδίᾳ): "Tous les peuples sont incirconcis *de chair* et ... *de coeur*".

est une condition préalable à la participation au culte.[20] Si Ézéchiel ne mentionne pas ailleurs la c. du coeur, par contre on notera la place du coeur nouveau dans la description de l'alliance nouvelle (xi 19, xxxvi 26), rénovation qui est don de Dieu (cf. Dt. xxx 6).

En résumé, on peut dire que, selon l'AT, la circoncision signifiait l'incorporation dans l'alliance, la consécration et l'appartenance à Yhwh, après une purification et la libération d'une tare congénitale (Jos. v 9?).[21] Les emplois métaphoriques, somme toute assez rares, précisaient les conditions d'une entrée authentique dans cette alliance par un don total de soi à Dieu dans l'obéissance à ses volontés. Le coeur circoncis est un coeur ouvert à son influence, obéissant à sa voix, malléable à son action. Ainsi le rite, sans jamais être contesté, est transcendé au bénéfice de sa signification.[22] Voyons comment la tradition juive postérieure a repris occasionnellement ces interprétations ou greffé sur ces textes des significations nouvelles, motivées par l'évolution de la pensée religieuse.

II

Dans l'histoire de l'interprétation de l'AT, les premières sources à examiner sont les versions grecques. Nous consulterons aussi les écrits de Philon et de Flavius Josèphe, comme représentants du Judaïsme hellénistique.[23] Il faut donc reprendre les textes essentiels, revus par les traducteurs grecs, et en relever les traits marquants.

---

[20] Is. lii 1: "incirconcis et impur" (*ʿrl wṭmʾ*: cf. 1 QH VI 20) sont exclus de la ville sainte. Mais Ézéchiel ne parle pas directement d'impureté: cf. Hermisson (p. 75) qui conteste W. Eichrodt selon qui "die Begriffe unbeschnitten und unrein immer mehr identisch werden (*Theologie des Alten Testaments* I [Stuttgart et Göttingen, 1957], p. 82). Même si les notions sont voisines, au niveau de l'AT, on ne doit pas concevoir "weder die Beschneidung selbst noch die Beschneidung des Herzens als Reinheitsritus".

[21] Cf. Gen. xvii 1 où *tāmîm* est rendu par ἄμεμπτος dans la LXX: voir Gen. R ad loc., Nedarim 32a et Ginzberg, V, p. 269. Josèphe interprète *Gilgal* (Jos. v 9) par ἐλευθέριον (*Ant.* V § 34).

[22] Hermisson écrit: "Beschneidung ist ja—wesentlich: Beschneidung des Herzens" et remarque que cette spiritualisation du rite pouvait conduire à son abandon; mais il faut attendre le NT pour voir franchir ce pas, à partir d'autres prémisses (p. 76).

[23] Dans la Diaspora, à cause des prosélytes et du milieu païen, on était porté à présenter le précepte de la c. d'une façon plus libérale qu'en Palestine, à en discuter le sens et la portée. Mais on n'aboutit jamais aux conclusions extrêmes de Paul (cf. E. Käsemann, *An die Römer*[3] [Tübingen, 1974], p. 68).

Dt. x 16: LXX: καὶ περιτεμεῖσθε τὴν σκληροκαρδίαν ὑμῶν (Aquila: ἀκροβυστίαν καρδίας ὑμῶν) καὶ τὸν τράχηλον ὑμῶν οὐ σκληρυνεῖτε ἔτι.

Jér. iv 4: LXX: περιτμήθητε τῷ θεῷ ὑμῶν καὶ περιέλεσθε τὴν ἀκροβυστίαν τῆς καρδίας ὑμῶν.[24]

Dt. xxx 6: καὶ περικαθαριεῖ (Aquila: περιτεμεῖται) κύριος τὴν καρδίαν σου.

On observera ces quelques points:

a) Le verbe *mûl* (circoncire) est rendu à Dt. xxx 6, non par περιτέμνω, mais par περικαθαρίζω (purifier, nettoyer complètement),[25] verbe que l'on trouve à Lév. xix 23 à propos des fruits interdits pendant trois ans (*wʿrltm ʿrltw ʾt pryw*) parce qu'ils sont considérés "incirconcis" (*ʿărēlîm*): "Vous purifierez son impureté (περικαθαριεῖτε τὴν ἀκαθαρσίαν); ses fruits seront pour vous impurs (ὁ καρπὸς αὐτοῦ . . . ἀπερικάθαρτος)".[26] Le traducteur grec a donc associé à *ʿorlâ*/*ʿārēl* l'idée d'impureté, trait que nous retrouverons dans Symmaque.

A Jos. v, la LXX emploie une fois seulement περικαθαίρειν (synonyme de περικαθαρίζω) pour traduire *mûl*, alors que περιτέμνω revient constamment dans le passage. Au *v.* 4 le traducteur *interprète* l'action de Josué qui circoncit les Israélites, alors que l'hébreu veut simplement en donner le motif: "*De cette manière*, Josué *purifia* les enfants d'Israël (ὃν δὲ τρόπον περιεκάθαρεν)".[27] A Dt. xviii 10,

---

[24] Selon J. Ziegler, *Jeremias* (Göttingen, 1957). On a donc une version littérale de l'hébreu (sauf τῷ θεῷ ὑμῶν), comme dans Pesh. A. Rahlfs: καὶ περιτέμεσθε τὴν σκληροκαρδίαν ὑμῶν (influence de Dt. x 16).

[25] Seul cas où *mûl* est rendu par περικαθαρίζω. Meyer (p. 73) notait comme un aspect caractéristique de la LXX qu'un seul verbe περιτέμνω traduisait tous les termes hébreux pour "circoncire" (à l'exception de Dt. xxx 6 et Jos. v 4). Cela est inexact si l'on admet le choix de Ziegler pour Jér. iv 4 (περιαιρέω), περιτέμεσθε n'étant pas original, et la version d'Esther viii 17 est clairement interprétative. On ne peut donc insister sur l'uniformité de la LXX. En revanche, il est juste qu'elle parle plus souvent de circoncision que l'hébreu (ibid., p. 74).

[26] H. G. Liddell-R. Scott ne donne que ces deux exemples bibliques du verbe. Le substantif περικάθαρμα signifie "expiation, victime expiatoire" (cf. Prov. xxi 18; 1 Cor. iv 13). Comparer l'usage de περικαθαριεῖ à Is. vi 7 (LXX), lviii 11 (Théod.). A Lév. xix 23 les versions grecques secondaires sont littérales. Noter Vulg.: "Auferetis praeputia eorum: poma . . . *immunda* erunt vobis" (Onqelos: *mrḥq*).

[27] Syro-Hex. donne une version littérale: καὶ οὗτος ὁ λόγος ὃν περιέτεμεν Ἰησους. Selon D. W. Gooding ("Traditions of Interpretation of the Circumcision at Gilgal", in *Proceedings of the Sixth World Congress of Jewish Studies* I

le même verbe περικαθαίρειν substitue l'expression "faire passer son fils par le feu": les traducteurs ne pouvaient admettre que leurs ancêtres se soient adonnés à une telle pratique, à l'instar des Carthaginois, et ils ont compris le passage "comme se référant à un rite de purification par le feu".[28]

b) L'expression "prépuce du coeur" n'apparaît que deux fois dans la Bible (Dt. x 16 au sg. et Jér. iv 4 au pl.). La LXX la traduit une fois littéralement à Jér. iv 4 (τὴν ἀκροβυστίαν τῆς καρδίας); mais à Dt. x 16 on lit σκληροκαρδία (endurcissement du coeur), idée reprise, pour la nuque, dans le verbe σκληρυνεῖτε qui est le terme employé dans le refrain sur l'endurcissement du coeur de Pharaon dans Ex. iv-xiv (ailleurs seulement dans Ps. xciv 8 et Is. lxiii 17). Ainsi est sauvegardée l'allitération de l'hébreu.

Création des LXX, σκληροκαρδία n'est employé dans l'AT grec qu'à Dt. x 16 et à Sir. xvi 10.[29] Le traducteur a donc interprété l'expression hébraïque à l'aide d'une autre image biblique: la circoncision du coeur supprime cette dureté qui le rend imperméable à l'action de Dieu, cette *šĕrīrût* que Jérémie mentionne huit fois [30] et qui commande le comportement d'Israël, s'opposant à sa conversion.[31] La Septante ouvre la voie aux autres versions (surtout ara-

[Jérusalem 1977], p. 149-64), περιεκάθαρεν est synonyme de circoncire et ne signifie pas directement purifier.

[28] E. Bickerman, *Studies in Jewish and Christian History* (Leiden, 1976), p. 194 ("The Septuagint as a Translation"). Le verbe est utilisé dans 4 Macc. i 29 pour la Raison maître-jardinier qui désherbe. Philon emploie καθαίρεσθαι au sujet de l'hygiène corporelle, une des raisons de la c. (*Spec. leg.* I 5).

[29] Hébreu: *zdwn lb* (racine qui reviendra dans le Targum). On trouve σκληροκάρδιος à Éz. iii 7; Prov. xvii 20; Sir. xvi 9 (dans Grec II) et dans Is. xlvi 12 (Symmaque). Cf. J. Behm, *TWNT* III, p. 616. L'Itala a "duricordia/duricordes". Noter la formule de Barnabé ix 5: περιτμήθητε τὴν πονηρίαν ἀπὸ τῆς καρδίας ὑμῶν. Pour 1 Hén. v 4 les fragments grecs donnent σκληροκάρδιοι (M. Black, *Apocalypsis Henochi graece* [Leiden, 1970], p. 20). La formule araméenne correspondante apparaît (mais en piteux état) dans 4 QEn[a] 1 II 1, 14: [*qšy lb*]*bn*, "(vous) durs de coeur" (J. T. Milik, *The Books of Enoch* [Oxford, 1976], p. 146). Éthiopien: *yĕbusān lĕb* (même racine à Jub. i 7, 22 pour "dureté de nuque"), "secs de coeur" (F. Martin, *Le livre d'Hénoch* [Paris, 1906], p. 7) ou "hard of heart" (M. A. Knibb, *The Ethiopic Book of Enoch* [Oxford, 1978] II, p. 65).

[30] iii 17, ix 13, xvi 12, xviii 12, vii 24, xi 8, xiii 10, xxiii 17. Seuls exemples en dehors de Jér: Dt xxix 18 (LXX: ἀποπλάνησις, erreur); Ps. lxxxi 13 (LXX paraphrase: κατὰ τὰ ἐπιτηδεύματα τῶν καρδιῶν αὐτῶν). Jamais LXX ne rend *šerīrût* par σκληροκαρδία, mais paraphrase (désirs, imaginations du coeur) ou omet (xi 8, xiii 10). A Ex. vi 12 "incirconcis des lèvres" devient: ἄλογός ειμι.

[31] Comparer Rom. ii 5: κατὰ τὴν σκληρότητά σου καὶ ἀμετανόητον καρδίαν.

méennes) qui préciseront ces obstacles moraux à l'emprise de Dieu que la métaphore "c. du coeur" désignait de façon imprécise. A Dt. x 16 et Jér. iv 4, la LXX garde encore l'image de la c. du coeur, du transfert du signe de l'alliance dans le coeur. Certaines traductions, au contraire, perdront la force d'expression de l'hébreu ("circoncire le prépuce du coeur") pour décrire les dispositions incompatibles avec l'action divine.

c) Parmi les versions grecques secondaires, le cas d'Aquila ne présente pas de surprise: à son habitude, il retourne à une version littérale de l'hébreu. Par contre, on a relevé chez Symmaque [32] une tendance à lier les notions de pureté/impureté à la circoncision/incirconcision.

Jér. iv 4: Sym.: καθαρίσθητε τῷ κυρίῳ καὶ περιέλεσθε (cf. LXX) τὰς πονηρίας τῶν καρδιῶν ὑμῶν.[33]
Jér. vi 10: Aquila/Sym.: ἀκάθαρτον τὸ οὖς αὐτῶν.
Éz. xliv 9: ἀκάθαρτος καρδίᾳ καὶ ἀκάθαρτος σαρκί (Syro-Hex.: *l' dky' blb' wl' dky' bbśr'*).
Ex. vi 12: Sym.: οὐκ εἰμὶ καθαρὸς τῷ φθέγματι (Aquila: ἀκρόβυστος; Théod.: ἀπερίτμητος).
Lev. xxvi 41: Ἄλλος: ἡ ἀκάθαρτος (marge du *Cod. Vat.* 128).

Si Hermisson [34] a raison de soutenir que, dans la Bible, la circoncision n'implique nullement l'idée de pureté (Reinheit), Symmaque en revanche l'interprète clairement suivant cette catégorie. La LXX pointait déjà dans la même direction (Dt. xxx 6; Lév. xix 23). En outre, Symmaque distingue dans sa version l'emploi de circoncision au sens figuré de sa signification physique: dans tous les exemples cités, il emploie un terme de la racine καθαρ- quand il s'agit de

[32] Judéo-chrétien ébionite, vers la fin du IIe siècle de notre ère, selon H. J. Schoeps. Cf. *Theologie und Geschichte des Judenchristentums* (Tübingen, 1949), p. 33-7, 350-80; *Aus frühchristlicher Zeit* (Tübingen, 1950), p. 82-119; *Jewish Christianity* (Philadelphia, 1969), p. 15; F. Field, *Origenis Hexaplorum quae supersunt* (Oxford, 1875), p. XXVIII-XXXVII; A. Geiger, *Nachgelassene Schriften* IV (Breslau, 1885), p. 88-92.

[33] Jérôme (souvent influencé par Symmaque) écrit: "Symmachus posuit: Purificamini Domino, et auferte malitias cordium vestrorum; circumcisionem *emundationem*, et praeputia *vitium* intelligens" (*PL* 24, 706, comm. ad loc.).

[34] P. 75. W. Zimmerli, *Ezechiel* (Neukirchen-Vluyn, 1969), p. 1125, en revanche, considère la c. du coeur comme un transfert de la c. "als Reinigungszeichen". Meyer (p. 77) donnait pour motivation des c. forcées des Iduméens sous Jean Hyrcan l'idée de "Terre sainte" excluant les Gentils.

métaphores,[35] réservant περιτέμνω à la signification physique.[36] Selon R. Meyer, il rejoindrait ainsi l'attitude du Judaïsme rabbinique qui insistera exclusivement sur la signification physique de la c., en réaction contre l'interprétation apologétique de la c. du coeur par les chrétiens.[37]

Chez Philon d'Alexandrie, nous retrouverons l'éventail des conceptions traditionnelles de la circoncision, avec les développements sur le sens spirituel les plus étendus que nous ait laissés la littérature juive ancienne.

Il ouvre son traité *De specialibus legibus* (I 1-12) par un plaidoyer en faveur de la c. pour laquelle il énumère six justifications.[38] Ce préambule n'a pas seulement un but apologétique: avant de commencer l'exposé des *Lois spéciales*, Philon laisse comprendre qu'à ses yeux la c. "est comme un abrégé de toute la Loi".[39] Dans une exhortation à Israël (ibid. 304-305), il admoneste les "incirconcis de coeur . . . rebelles par dureté de caractère; ils se cabrent, rétifs, et secouent le joug". Citant Dt. x 16, il commente: "Ce qui veut dire (τὸ δέ ἐστι): ces formations superflues de l'élément dirigeant (τοῦ ἡγεμονικοῦ) en vous, que les élans immodérés des passions y ont semées et fait germer, que la folie (ἀφροσύνη), cet exécrable jardinier de l'âme, a cultivées, hâtez-vous de les retrancher!"[40]

Dans les *Quaestiones in Genesim* (III 46), Philon distingue deux

---

[35] Schoeps, *Aus frühchristlicher Zeit*, p. 88. Noter pourtant qu'à Éz. xliv 9 on a ἀκάθαρτος σαρκί (plus précisément οὐ καθαρός, avec Geiger p. 90), mais peut-être entraîné par le parallélisme. A Jér. ix 24 *bʿrlh* est traduit par ἐν ἀκροβυστίᾳ. Voir aussi Lév. xix 23 (si Ἄλλος = Σ). D. Barthélemy, *Les devanciers d'Aquila*, *SVT* 10 (Leiden, 1963), p. 45, a relevé le "caractère peu systématique" de Symmaque.

[36] Comparer Lév. xix 23 (LXX). Geiger (ibid.) note que Symmaque évite d'employer *mûl* pour les païens et d'appliquer *ʿārēl* à Israël (cf. M. Nedarim III 11).

[37] P. 83. Chez les Ébionites la c. l'emportait sur le sabbat (Schoeps, *Jewish Christianity*, p. 113). Noter l'insistance dans la LXX de Gen. xvii 14 sur la c. "le *huitième* jour".

[38] Comparer *Quaestiones in Genesim* III 48. *Spec. leg.* I 6 ne parle pas de la c. du coeur. Commentaire de E. R. Goodenough: "The rite makes the organ by which animate things are generated resemble the heart in which thoughts are engendered" (*An Introduction to Philo Judaeus* [New Haven, Conn., 1940], p. 206).

[39] S. Daniel dans *Les oeuvres de Philon d'Alexandrie* 24, *De Specialibus Legibus* I et II (Paris, 1975), p. XIV.

[40] Trad. Daniel, p. 193. Elle renvoie à *Somn.* II 64 et 4 Macc. i 28-29. "Philo has made circumcision into a mystic rite of abandonment of fleshly desire and confidence, as it is a rite of complete dedication to God" (Goodenough, p. 207).

circoncisions: celle de la chair et celle de l'esprit (νοῦς).[41] Cette dernière est la "seconde circoncision", à savoir celle du coeur dont parle la Torah (Dt. x 16). Elle consiste à éliminer toutes les excroissances superflues, l'orgueil et l'arrogance (47-48). L'expression "c. du coeur" revient plus loin dans son exposé (48).

A propos d'Ex. xxii 20 "Tu ne molesteras pas l'étranger", Philon entend προσήλυτος de la LXX au sens de "prosélyte" et explique que "le prosélyte est non celui qui circoncit le prépuce, mais celui qui (retranche) les désirs, les plaisirs des sens et les autres passions de l'âme (ψυχή)".[42] Les Israélites, en Égypte, n'étaient point circoncis; mais ils se comportaient comme de vrais prosélytes, vivant "circoncis de coeur" dans une attitude qui leur valut d'être libérés.[43]

Malgré ses commentaires spirituels, Philon n'entend pas minimiser le rite de la c. dont la validité reste hors de cause: "S'il est vrai que la circoncision (τὸ περιτέμνεσθαι) représente (le fait de) se couper (ἐκτομήν) du plaisir et de toutes les passions . . . n'allons pas pour autant supprimer la loi concernant la circoncision" (*De migrat.* 92). Il s'en prend ici à ceux qui "se montrent excessivement minutieux dans l'analyse du symbole, mais en prennent à leur aise avec la lettre, qu'ils mépriseraient" (*ibid.* 89).[44] Une spiritualisation extrême

---

[41] Interprétation fondée sur Gen. xvii 10-11 (LXX) qui demande de circoncire πᾶν ἀρσενικόν, puis τὴν σάρκα.

[42] *Quaestiones in Exodum* II 2. Fragment grec dans R. Marcus, *Philo. Supplement* (Loeb classical Library; London et Cambridge, Mass., 1953) II 36, ou dans F. Petit, *Oeuvres de Philon d'Alexandrie* 33, *Quaestiones. Fragmenta graeca* (Paris, 1978), p. 239: ὅτι προσήλυτός ἐστιν . . . τῆς ψυχῆς. Dans *Quest. in Gen.* III 46, 52, Philon parlait de c. de l'esprit (νοῦς). Le changement de terme s'explique par la citation du texte parallèle d'Ex. xxiii 9: "Vous n'opprimerez pas l'étranger, car vous connaissez τὴν ψυχὴν τοῦ προσηλύτου". Le commentaire poursuit: τίς δὲ προσηλύτου διάνοιά ἐστιν; bien qu'il ne fasse pas ici usage de la métaphore, c'est le thème biblique de la c. du coeur qu'il a à l'esprit.

[43] Goodenough (p. 207) signale que Philon n'exige pas la c. des Gentils, mais avant tout les dispositions qu'elle symbolise. (Cf. plus loin Josèphe.) Cette attitude était-elle motivée pour des raisons de tactique missionnaire? Meyer (p. 78) cite aussi Or. Sib. IV 165 où un bain d'eau courante semble seul exigé des pécheurs repentis. Mais le contexte ne semble guère appeler une mention de la circoncision. Philon (*Quaest. in Gen.* III 48) estime sage la loi (Gen. xvii 12) de circoncire les enfants, car la peur ferait hésiter un adulte à s'y soumettre de plein gré.

[44] Tr. J. Cazeaux dans *Les Oeuvres de Philon d'Alexandrie* 14, *De Migratione Abrahami* (Paris, 1965), p. 149. Cf. H. A. Wolfson, *Philo* (Cambridge, Mass., 1962) I, p. 127. Sur les réactions des rabbins devant un allégorisme dangereux (Aboth III 12), voir E. E. Urbach, *The Sages* (Jérusalem, 1975), p. 295-6 (qui pense à une riposte à Rom. ii 28-29). Origène (*Contre Celse* II 3) parle

risquait d'énerver l'observance du précepte, en exaltant la suprématie de la c. du coeur sur l'institution rituelle dont, au reste, Philon développe moins la richesse théologique que ne le feront les rabbins.

Un passage de Josèphe doit être cité dans ce contexte. Izatès, le fils d'Hélène d'Adiabène, est gagné au Judaïsme par un marchand juif, Ananias. Estimant qu'il ne serait "définitivement (βεβαίως) juif qu'une fois circoncis, il était prêt à se faire circoncire". Sa mère ainsi qu'Ananias s'y opposent, à cause des dangers qu'ils courraient l'un et l'autre pour avoir introduit des pratiques étrangères. "Le roi, disait Ananias, pouvait d'ailleurs adorer Dieu (τὸ θεῖον σέβειν), même sans être circoncis, s'il avait décidé d'observer complètement (πάντως . . . ζηλοῦν) les lois ancestrales des Juifs, ce qui importait plus que la circoncision."[45] Plus tard un autre Juif, Éléazar, venu de Galilée, le convainquit de se faire circoncire, car, disait-il, il ne suffit pas de lire la Loi, il faut en accomplir les préceptes.[46]

L'attitude d'Ananias paraît représenter une position d'équilibre des maîtres juifs, convaincus que la signification spirituelle de la c. l'emporte sur le rite matériel, mais qui ne contestent nullement l'importance de ce dernier. Le sens *théologique* de la c. comme condition et signe de l'alliance et de l'appartenance au peuple élu n'est pas mis en question. Cela arrivera avec le NT par le biais du thème biblique de la circoncision du coeur. A Qumrân, il n'en est pas encore ainsi, mais les textes fournissent la preuve qu'une conception spirituelle était bien élaborée dans le Judaïsme palestinien du Ier siècle.

---

de Juifs convertis qui ont délaissé les coutumes juives "sous prétexte d'interprétations et d'allégories".

[45] Τοῦτ' εἶναι κυριώτερον τοῦ περιτέμνεσθαι (*Ant.* XX 38-41). Voir l'allusion à cette histoire dans Gen. R 46, 10 à xvii 11.

[46] Sur les diverses interprétations de cet épisode, cf. L. H. Feldman dans *Josephus* IX (Loeb Library; London et Cambridge, Mass., 1965), p. 410—11 (avec Bibliog.). Il n'y a sans doute pas ici l'écho d'une controverse entre deux écoles rabbiniques, sur la nécessité ou non de la c. des prosélytes. Le principe général qu'un danger grave dispense de certaines lois peut être invoqué ici: mais la motivation religieuse que donne Josèphe de la dispense de la c. reste intéressante. Ailleurs (§ 139 et 145) il mentionne sans commentaire la c. de deux princes étrangers. Dans *Vie* 113, il rappelle avoir empêché des Galiléens de circoncire de force deux sujets du roi de Trachonitide, chacun devant "honorer Dieu selon sa conviction personnelle, non par contrainte" (trad. A. Pelletier). Le Judaïsme hellénistique était avant tout préoccupé de diffuser la croyance en un seul Dieu, avec ses conséquences éthiques, plus que d'imposer la c. et autres prescriptions rituelles (cf. K. G. Kuhn, *TWNT* VI, p. 731).

III

Dans les textes de Qumrân, la circoncision physique tient peu de place.[47] Par contre, les conditions spéciales dans lesquelles vivent les sectaires de la nouvelle alliance (CD VI 19, VIII 21, XIX 34, XX 12; 1 QpHab II 3),[48] en marge du Judaïsme de Jérusalem, expliquent qu'ils aient recours à la métaphore de la c. du coeur, à la fois pour expliciter les conditions morales et spirituelles impliquées par cette alliance *nouvelle* et éventuellement, dans le registre polémique, pour s'opposer à leurs adversaires. On ne peut cependant pas dire que cette image soit typique de Qumrân.

Notre premier exemple appartient au stade III de la Règle qui légifère pour une communauté déjà bien établie et prospère qui se définit "la communauté de l'alliance éternelle" (1 QS V 5).[49] Le titre de la section (V 1) en résume bien le contenu: "Voici la règle ... pour *se convertir* de *tout* mal et pour s'attacher à *tout ce qu'Il a commandé* selon Sa volonté". Après avoir énuméré les vertus qui caractérisent le moine qumrânien (humilité, justice, charité, modestie), l'auteur décrit (V 5-6) les obstacles à surmonter pour qui veut former la communauté des saints (V 13) et "se convertir à la Loi de Moïse de *tout* son coeur et de *toute* son âme" (V 8-9):

Que nul ne marche dans *l'obstination* (*šryrwt*) [50] *de son coeur* (Jér. xi 8)

[47] H. Braun dans "Qumran und das Neue Testament", *Th. Rund.* 29 (1963), p. 251, note: "Die Beschneidung ... in den Qumrantexten überhaupt eine unwesentliche Rolle spielt". K. G. Kuhn (*Konkordanz*, p. 116) cite seulement 3 emplois de *mûl* (1 QS V 5; 1 QpHab XI 13; CD XVI 6) et, dans les textes araméens, *gzr* n'a pas le sens de circoncire. Rappelons pourtant que le Livre des Jubilés qu'on lisait à Qumrân (cf. CD XVI 4) insiste beaucoup sur la c. CD XVI 4-6 établit un parallèle entre la c. d'Abraham (entrée dans l'alliance) et l'engagement à se convertir en adhérent à la secte (cf. Jub. xv 1-34). Mais Ch. Rabin (*The Zadokite Documents* [Oxford, 1958], p. 75) lit *nyṣwl* (fut sauvé), au lieu de *nymwl*.

[48] Sur ce thème à Qumrân, voir la remarquable analyse de A. Jaubert, *La notion d'alliance dans le Judaïsme aux abords de l'ère chrétienne* (Paris, 1963), p. 209-49. Sur la place centrale de Jér. xxxi 31-33 à Qumrân, cf. G. Vermes, *The Dead Sea Scrolls, Qumran in Perspective* (London, 1977), p. 165.

[49] Ce stade remonterait à la fin du règne de Jean Hyrcan (134-104) selon J. Murphy-O'Connor, "La genèse littéraire de la *Règle de la communauté*", *RB* 76 (1969), p. 528-49 (surtout p. 533-7). Le terme *hyḥd* (la communauté) apparaît 12 fois à ce stade (et *berît*, alliance, 16 fois) contre une seule fois à chacun des stades I/II (p. 534). Une rédaction différente de la col. 5 (encore inédite) se trouve dans 4 QS ^{bdg}, "plus courte et plus intelligible" et "sans doute plus primitive" dit J. T. Milik (*RB* 63 [1956], p. 61; 67 [1960], p. 412).

[50] Toujours avec *lēb* (coeur). Expression typique de Jérémie qui se trouve 8 fois dans 1 QS et 8 fois dans CD (1 ex. dans 1 QH IV 15). Obstination qualifiée de *ʾšmh* (coupable) dans 1 QS I 6; parfois opposée à l'observation de la Loi

pour errer après son coeur et ses yeux (Nb. xv 39; Éz. vi 9) et *les pensées de son penchant* (*mḥšbt yṣrw*). Mais *ils circonciront* dans la communauté *le prépuce de l'instinct et la nuque raide* (. . .[51] *lmwl byḥd ʿwrlt yṣr wʿwrp qšh*).

L'allusion à la circoncision du penchant, appuyée sur une prescription de la Torah (Dt. x 16), semble une synthèse de toutes les exigences antérieures.

Le sens de l'expression "pensées de son penchant" (*mḥšbt yṣrw*)[52] est éclairé par le passage parallèle de CD II 16 qui exhorte à ne pas se laisser entraîner par "les pensées du penchant *coupable* et les yeux luxurieux" (*mḥšbwt yṣr ʾšmh wʿny znwt*). Cf. 1 QS I 6.

Si *yēṣer* a, dans l'AT, une signification générale neutre ("produit" du coeur, disposition, qualité), certains contextes lui donnent déjà une coloration péjorative (Gen. vi 5, viii 21).[53] Mais on reste loin de la conception rabbinique du *yēṣer hāraʿ*. Ben Sira connaît encore un usage neutre du terme, mais Qumrân semble amorcer, à l'intérieur de son anthropologie propre et de son dualisme, une tendance

(1 QS IX 9-10; CD XX 9-10), elle désigne aussi la volonté propre (CD III 6, 12). Le rejet de cette obstination étant une condition d'admission, sa réapparition constitue un motif d'exclusion temporaire ou définitive (1 QS VII 19, 24). Cf. H. Bardtke dans *Qumran-Probleme* (Berlin, 1963), p. 38; Hesse, *Das Verstockungsproblem*, p. 16; D. Simeone, *Il "cuore" negli scritti di Qumrân* (Tesi, Univ. di Roma, 1979).

[51] Le ms a *wʾʾm*, diversement interprété. Généralement corrigé en *kî ʾim*: cf. *ky ʾm* (sic) au début de la ligne 14 (seul ex. dans 1 QS). M. Burrows lit *ʾšm* "(penchant) coupable" (cf. CD II 16). D'autres lisent *ʾnšy hʾmt* ("hommes de vérité") ou recourent à un *nôṭārîqôn* (cf. Driver, *Judaean Scrolls*, p. 336). W. H. Brownlee, *The Dead Sea Manual of Discipline* (New Haven, Conn., 1951), p. 19, 49, y voit une abréviation de "Dieu des dieux et Seigneur des seigneurs", formule qui suit immédiatement Dt. x 16 dont le passage s'inspire. Sur ce problème, cf. P. Garnet, *Salvation and Atonement in the Qumran Scrolls* (Tübingen, 1977), p. 60-4.

[52] Sur le *yēṣer*, parmi de nombreux travaux, on pourra consulter: Moore, *Judaism* I, p. 479-86; Billerbeck, IV, p. 466-83; S. Schechter, *Some Aspects of Rabbinic Theology* (London, 1909), p. 242-92; R. Murphy, "*Yēṣer* in the Qumran Literature", *Biblica* 39 (1958) p. 334-44; W. D. Davies, *Paul and Rabbinic Judaism* (London, 1958), p. 16-35; J. Hadot, *Penchant mauvais et volonté libre dans la Sagesse de Ben Sira* (Bruxelles, 1970); Urbach, *The Sages*, p. 471-83. Sur le thème voisin de *bāśār*, voir R. Murphy, "*Bśr* in the Qumrân Literature and *sarks* in the Epistle to the Romans", in *Sacra Pagina* (Gembloux, 1959), p. 60-76; K. G. Kuhn, "New Light on Temptation, Sin, and Flesh in the New Testament", dans K. Stendahl (éd.), *The Scrolls and the NT* (London, 1958), p. 94-113 = *ZThK* 49 (1952), p. 200-22; W. D. Davies, *Christian Origins and Judaism* (London, 1962), p. 145-77.

[53] Accentuée à Dt. xxxi 21 (LXX) par la version πονηρία (Aquila/Symmaque: πλάσμα). A Gen. vi 5 et viii 21 les Targums suivent l'hébreu.

à prendre le *yēṣer* en mauvaise part (CD II 16; 1 QH VI 32, VII 3-4).[54] Toutefois *yēṣer* conserve souvent son sens de tendance ou *caractère* qui prédomine en l'homme suivant l'esprit, du mal ou du bien, dont son coeur subit l'influence. Il n'est pas encore une chose indépendante du coeur comme le sera le *yēṣer* rabbinique ou le *gramen seminis mali* de 4 Esdras (iv 30).[55]

Comme 1 QS V 5 fait allusion à Dt. x 16 (et non à xxx 6), il faut, semble-t-il, comprendre que ce sont les membres de la communauté qui sont les auteurs de la circoncision.[56] Mais une modification du texte biblique est intervenue: on parle ici de "circoncire le prépuce de l'*instinct*" et non plus du *coeur*. Précision importante: ce n'est pas une simple substitution du mot *coeur*, puisque l'on signale ce qui, dans le coeur, doit être émondé. Il s'agit de le débarrasser de cette source du mal agir qui infecte les dispositions(*yēṣer*) du coeur, l'empêchant de suivre la volonté de Dieu "de *tout* son coeur".[57] On notera le parallélisme (et l'allitération reprise de Dt. x 16): "circoncire *le prépuce* de l'instinct et *la raideur* de nuque". Il ne s'agit pas, comme dans le Rabbinisme, de supprimer le *yēṣer* mais ses impulsions mauvaises (*mḥšbt yṣrw*; cf. 1 QH V 6: "les infamies de mon *yēṣer*"—*zmwt yṣry*), les rébellions de l'instinct contre la loi de Dieu.[58] Nous franchissons une nouvelle étape dans l'interprétation du rite biblique de la circoncision: c. physique → c. du coeur → c. du *yēṣer* (du coeur) → destruction du *yēṣer hāraʿ* (dans la tradition rabbinique).

Cette circoncision spirituelle, qui édifie la communauté et a valeur d'expiation (V 5-6), se fait "dans la communauté" (*byḥd*).[59]

[54] A. R. C. Leaney, *The Rule of Qumran and its Meaning* (London, 1966), p. 167. Cf. 11 QPs^{a}Plea 15-16: *yṣr rʿ* ("evil inclination" selon J. A. Sanders, *DJD* IV, p. 78; traduction préférable, en raison du contexte, à l'interprétation de Hadot, *Penchant mauvais*, p. 15); 1 Q18: *yṣr* [*rʿ*] (*DJD* I, p. 83; dans le texte hébreu de Jub. xxxv 8-10); 4 Q280 2: *yṣr ʾšmtkh* (cf. J. T. Milik, *JJS* 23 [1972], p. 127 et 131). Comparer Test. Ruben iv 9 et Test. Lévi xxii 3 (ms *e*).

[55] Murphy (p. 343) fait *yṣr* quasiment synonyme de *lēb*: en fait, il est *dans* le coeur.

[56] P. Wernberg-Møller, *The Manual of Discipline* (Leiden, 1957), p. 93. Brownlee, interprétant *wʾʾm* de Dieu, en fait l'auteur de la c. (comme Dt. xxx 6). De toute façon, la justification reste l'oeuvre de Dieu (1 QS XI 2-15); il revient à l'homme de supprimer l'obstacle à son action. Vermes et d'autres traduisent: "circumcise . . . the foreskin of evil inclination *and of* stiffness of neck" (*The Dead Sea Scrolls in English*², p. 78).

[57] W. D. Davies a compté 73 emplois de "tout" dans la Règle (*Christian Origins and Judaism*, p. 174).

[58] Qui finira par se résumer dans μὴ ἐπιθυμεῖν (4 Macc. ii 6); cf. Rom. vii 7.

[59] Voir le commentaire de Jaubert, *Alliance*, p. 170. Cf. VI 2-3: "en commun

L'insistance sur cet aspect de la purification qui donne accès aux bénéfices de l'alliance nouvelle souligne qu'*en dehors de la secte point de salut*! Une application directe est faite à V 26 au cas de la réprimande fraternelle (cf. CD IX 3-7) qui doit se pratiquer sans haine, "raideur de nuque" et "coeur incirconcis".[60] Allusion nouvelle à Dt. x 16 et reprise des thèmes de V 4-5, comme le montre aussi l'emploi des mêmes termes "vérité, humilité, charité" qui décrivent, dans les deux cas, le comportement de celui qui "marche dans la voie de la perfection" (IX 9). Au fond, l'usage métaphorique de la c. exprime à sa façon la primauté des dispositions intérieures sur lesquelles insistait III 3-12: droiture de coeur, humilité de l'esprit et observation méticuleuse de la Loi garantissent seules l'efficacité des expiations et ablutions. Cela est en pleine conformité avec la théologie biblique.[61]

A Qumrân, le thème de la c. du coeur [62] est donc employé pour illustrer les conditions *morales* d'une vie de perfection [63] dans l'alliance nouvelle. Mais elle est aussi revendiquée comme le privilège des membres de la secte, les distinguant de tous les autres Israélites

---

ils mangeront, en commun ils béniront et en commun ils délibéreront". Sur *yaḥad*, voir: S. Talmon, *VT* 3 (1953), p. 133-40; J. Maier, *ZAW* 72 (1960), p. 148-66; S. H. Siedl, *Qumran. Eine Mönchsgemeinde im alten Bund* (Rome, 1963), p. 7-34; P. Wernberg-Møller, "The Nature of the YAḤAD according to the Manual of Discipline and Related Documents", *ALUOS* 6 (1966-1968), p. 56-81; J. Pouilly, *La Règle de la Communauté de Qumrân* (Paris, 1976), p. 96-101.

[60] "Qu'il ne le haïsse pas (à cause du prépuce) de son coeur" (G. Vermès, *Les manuscrits du désert de Juda*[2] [Paris, 1954], p. 144). Il y a une déchirure: [*b'rlt*] *lbbw*; mais la hampe du *lamed* est très visible. Le texte de 4 QS[d] (recension courte) omet la mention de la "nuque raide", rendant l'allusion à Dt. x 16 plus problématique: cf. J. T. Milik, *RB* 67 (1960), p. 412.

[61] Sur ce texte, voir J. Schmitt, "La pureté sadocite d'après 1 *QS* III, 4-9", *RevSR* 44 (1970), p. 214-24; B. E. Thiering, "Inner and Outer Cleansing at Qumran as a Background to NT Baptism", *NTSt* 26 (1980), p. 266-77.

[62] Bien entendu, celui-ci doit être inséré dans un contexte plus large, englobant, par exemple, la doctrine des deux Esprits, la conception de l'homme et la description des moyens comme des effets de cette conversion intérieure: cf. J. Becker, *Das Heil Gottes* (Göttingen, 1964); W. H. Brownlee, "Anthropology and Soteriology in the DSS and in the NT", in *The Use of the Old Testament in the New and Other Essays* (*Studies . . . W. F. Stinespring*) (Durham, N.C., 1972), p. 210-40. Je préfère me limiter strictement aux mentions explicites de la c. du coeur et n'en pas gonfler l'importance dans la théologie qumrânienne; mais, dans les nombreux fragments inédits, d'autres exemples peuvent se présenter.

[63] A Qumrân, des expressions comme *hlk btmym drk*, *hlk tmym*, *lhthlk lpnyw tmym*, *tmymy drk*, sont fréquentes (cf. Kuhn, *Konkordanz*, p. 234) et évoquent Gen. xvii 1.

(physiquement circoncis!), considérés comme impies, mauvais, voués à la perdition (V 19-20). On s'explique ainsi que les textes parlent pour ainsi dire uniquement de circoncision au sens figuré. D'autres exemples le confirment.

Dans 4 Q184 (frag. 2),[64] un texte très lacunaire contient une série de qualifications péjoratives comme *lb wlb* (coeur double), *rwm ʿynym* (élévation des yeux), *rwm lbb* (élévation du coeur: cf. 1 QS IV 9) et *lb ʿrl* (coeur incirconcis). L'absence de contexte rend l'interprétation incertaine. Mais on peut supposer que ces épithètes visaient les ennemis des sectaires.

Un autre fragment de la grotte 4 (4 Q 177) présente un plus grand intérêt. J. M. Allegro (p. 70) l'intitule Catena (A), mais J. Strugnell le décrit comme "une suite d'observations exégétiques, sur la valeur ou la réalisation *b'ḥryt hymym* de certains passages bibliques",[65] basées sur des passages des seize premiers Psaumes et autres textes bibliques. Le frag. 9, interprété par Strugnell, parle des "hommes qui ont servi (*ʿbdw*) Dieu [. . .] *ôtent les prépuces de leur coeur* de chair à la dernière génération".[66] Nous trouvons donc une allusion à Jér. iv 4 (texte unique, avec Dt. x 16, qui parle de "prépuce du coeur", et le seul au pluriel) et une fusion remarquable du thème de la circoncision du coeur et de celui de l'alliance nouvelle (cf. Jér. xxxi 31). Encore une fois les lacunes du contexte empêchent une interprétation assurée. On pourrait reconnaître ici une conception analogue (quant au contenu) à celle du Targum (cf. plus bas) qui prévoit la destruction du *yēṣer hāraʿ* à la fin des temps. S'il était permis de rapprocher ce texte de 1 QS V 5, ce serait un nouvel exemple de la conscience qu'avaient les sectaires de vivre déjà dans "les derniers temps".[67]

---

[64] Cf. J. M. Allegro, *DJD* V, *Qumrân Cave 4* I (4 Q158-4 Q186) (Oxford, 1968), p. 84; J. Strugnell, "Notes en marge du volume V des *Discoveries in the Judaean Desert of Jordan*", *Revue de Qumran* 7 (1969-71), p. 268 (je cite sa lecture *lb wlb*).

[65] P. 236. Traduction et commentaire, p. 244-5.

[66] [*hs*]*yrw* (lecture probable) *ʿrlwt lb* [*b*]*śrm bdwr h'*[*ḥrwn*]. Le texte paraît un amalgame des formules "circoncire le prépuce du coeur" (Dt. x 16; Jér iv 4) et "c. la chair du prépuce" (Gn. xvii 11, 14, 23, 24, 25). Auparavant, on parle de "purification du coeur des hommes de . . .", de "purs et purifiés" (Strugnell, p. 244).

[67] H. W. Kuhn, *Enderwartung und gegenwärtiges Heil* (Göttingen, 1966). Les "Paroles des luminaires" décrivent aussi la conversion d'Israël en formules qui évoquent l'alliance nouvelle, mais sans rappeler la c. du coeur: ". . . du fond du coeur et du fond de l'âme et pour implanter ta Loi dans nos coeurs . . . Et tu nous délivreras de pécher envers toi" (II 13, 16); cf. M. Baillet, *RB* 67

Le texte de Dt. x 16 est appliqué au Prêtre Impie [68] dans le pesher d'Habaquq (XI 9-14), interprétant ii 16: "*Tu t'es rassasié d'ignominie plus que de gloire. Bois, toi aussi, et titube . . .*"

> Son interprétation concerne le Prêtre dont l'ignominie l'a emporté sur sa gloire, car *il n'a pas circoncis le prépuce de son coeur* (*ky' l' ml 't ʿwrlt lbw*) [69] et il est allé dans les voies de l'ivresse afin d'étancher sa soif.

Le commentateur a tiré profit de deux variantes de l'hébreu,[70] *hērāʿēl* (tituber, chanceler d'ivresse) et *hēʿārēl* (montrer son incirconcision), forme du TM, puisqu'il parle d'incirconcision et des "voies de l'ivresse".[71] La métaphore de la c. du coeur est utilisée contre l'ennemi numéro un de la secte à qui ne s'appliquerait pas l'invective méprisante d'incirconcis (1 Sam. xvii 26; Éz. xxviii 10; Éph. ii 11); c'était le désigner comme faisant partie de cette *massa damnata* des impies qui n'étaient pas entrés dans l'alliance nouvelle par la vraie circoncision, celle du coeur (1 QS V 5) [72] et l'assimiler aux incirconcis qui sont "fils de perdition" et "fils de Béliar" (Jubilés xv 26, 33). Relevons enfin que, dans ce passage, la c. est présentée comme oeuvre de l'homme lui-même (cf. Dt. x 16) et non comme accomplie par Dieu (Dt. xxx 6).[73]

(1961), p. 201, 216. "Il est remarquable que la justification soit considérée à Qumrân comme un don déjà actuel" (A. Jaubert, *Dict. de Spir.* VIII, "Judaïsme", col. 1507).

[68] Très diversement identifié, avec Ménélas, Jonathan ou Simon Maccabée, Alexandre Jannée: cf. J. Carmignac dans *Les Textes de Qumrân* II (Paris, 1963), p. 55-6.

[69] Le mot *ʿwrlt* est coupé en deux dans le ms *ʿwr lt* (Voir la photo de la col. 11 dans Vermès, *Les manuscrits*, p. 128); autre exemple à III 9: *pny hm*). W. H. Brownlee, *BA* 14 (1951), p. 65, 69, propose de comprendre: *ʿwr* = peau (terme attendu dans un tel contexte) et *lt* = *L*(*bw*) *T*(*wʿbh*) = "the skin of his heart is an abomination" (*twʿbh* apparaît dans un contexte analogue à VIII 13).

[70] Sur cette exégèse des variantes dans 1 QpHab, cf. W. H. Brownlee, *The Text of Habakkuk in the Ancient Commentary from Qumran* (Philadelphia, 1959), p. 118-23; K. Stendahl, *The School of St. Matthew* (Lund, 1954), p. 186-9. Le Targum suppose la leçon du TM: *'ytʿrṭl* (dénude-toi), tandis que LXX (διασαλεύθητι καὶ σείσθητι) et Aquila (καὶ καρώθητι: sois pris d'une torpeur d'ivrogne) ont lu *rʿl* comme notre commentaire. Vulg. (*consopire*: somnole) et Pesh. (*'ṭṭrp*: défaillis) favorisent aussi *rʿl*.

[71] Ivrognerie et impudeur vont de pair (Lam. iv 21).

[72] Il s'agit ici de schisme intra-Israël, dans Paul d'opposition païens-Israël, mais on peut comparer Rom. ii 28-29: "Le vrai Juif l'est au dedans et la circoncision dans le coeur". Cf. H. Schlier, *Der Römerbrief* (Freiburg, 1977), p. 89. On pourrait lire une conception analogue dans la LXX de Jér. ix 25 (citée plus haut). Mais les Qumrâniens auraient difficilement admis la possibilité de c. du coeur chez des païens (Braun, p. 193): c'était une exclusivité "nouvelle alliance" (1 QS V 5).

[73] Si les lectures proposées par J. Carmignac, *Rev. de Qumran* 3 (1961-2),

A ces quelques exemples, tirés de la littérature de Qumrân, il convient d'ajouter Jubilés i 22-23.[74] Dieu répond à une prière d'intercession de Moïse pour son peuple: [75]

> Je connais leur *esprit de révolte* et leurs pensées et leur *raideur de nuque* (Dt. xxxi 27); ils ne se soumettront pas jusqu'à ce qu'*ils confessent leur propre péché* (*ḥṭ'*) *et le péché de leurs pères* (Lév. xxvi 40; Néh. ix 2). Et après cela, *ils se retourneront vers moi* en toute droiture, *de tout leur coeur et de toute leur âme* (2 Chron. vi 38); *je circoncirai* (*wqy*) *le prépuce de leur coeur et le prépuce du coeur de leur postérité.* Je créerai en eux un esprit saint et je les purifierai de sorte qu'ils ne se détournent plus de moi depuis ce jour à jamais (*laʿālam*).

Grâce à cette intervention divine, Israël s'attachera à Dieu et à ses commandements (i 24).

Le passage est un centon de textes bibliques à peine modifiés. La fin fait allusion au Ps. li 10, cité plus haut (*v.* 21) dans la prière de Moïse: "Crée en eux un coeur pur et un esprit saint", s'opposant à "l'esprit de Béliar" (*v.* 20), ce qui a une saveur nettement qumrânienne. L'auteur a amalgamé Dt. x 16 ("le prépuce du coeur") et xxx 6 ("Yhwh circoncira ton coeur et le coeur de ta descendance"), en transposant à la première personne. C'est Dt. xxx qui paraît surtout l'avoir inspiré, car l'attribution de la purification du coeur à Dieu lui-même est propre à ce texte. L'affirmation se trouve ici insérée, dans une sorte de préambule à tout l'ouvrage, au centre d'une description de l'histoire future d'Israël (rébellions, conversion, restauration) qui va jusqu'à l'établissement définitif du règne de Dieu parmi son peuple (xv 26-27).[76]

---

p. 505-6, sont justes, on aurait à Qumrân deux autres mentions des "incirconcis de coeur": à 1 QpHab II 6 (*ʿrl*[*y lb wkly*]*wt*) et 1 QH I 37 ([*ʿr*]*wly lb*). Sens qui convient bien aux contextes.

[74] On a retrouvé à Qumrân des fragments hébreux d'au moins 12 manuscrits des Jubilés: cf. A. S. van der Woude, "Fragmente des Buches Jubiläen aus Qumran Höhle XI (11 QJub)", in *Tradition und Glaube* (*Festgabe K. G. Kuhn*) (Göttingen, 1971), p. 141 (avec Bibliog.). Il semblerait "daß das Jubiläenbuch tatsächlich aus Qumrankreisen stammt" (p. 146). Aucun des fragments publiés ne recouvre notre passage, attesté seulement en éthiopien (sans variantes significatives): cf. R. H. Charles, *The Ethiopic Version of the Hebrew Book of Jubilees* (Oxford, 1895), p. 3; *The Book of Jubilees* (London, 1902), p. 6.

[75] Jub. i 4b-26 ferait partie d'une seconde édition: cf. G. L. Davenport, *The Eschatology of the Book of Jubilees* (Leiden 1971), p. 14; analyse de i 19-25, 26-28.

[76] Il n'est pas évident que "ce passage démarque les textes prophétiques sur la nouvelle Alliance (Jaubert, *Alliance*, p. 106), bien que i 24 continue: "Leurs âmes s'attacheront à moi et à tous mes commandements; je serai leur père et ils seront mes enfants". Mais des expressions caractéristiques comme "Loi

On peut encore verser au dossier un passage des Odes de Salomon [77] (conservées en syriaque et datées entre 70-125 de notre ère) dont les affinités avec les textes de Qumrân ont été relevées par divers spécialistes.[78] Le Papyrus Bodmer XI a aussi conservé une recension grecque de la belle Ode du Paradis qui s'ouvre sur l'image de la circoncision du coeur (xi 1-3):

> Mon coeur a été émondé (*gzr*) [79] et sa fleur est apparue. La grâce alors y a germé et il a produit des fruits pour le Seigneur. Car le Très-Haut m'a circoncis (*gzr*) par son Esprit Saint ... et sa circoncision (*gzwrth*) est devenue pour moi le salut (*pwrqn'*).[80]

Il n'y a aucun doute qu'il s'agit bien de la c. du coeur, insinuée ici par une image peut-être empruntée à la taille de la vigne. Comme c'est Dieu lui-même qui circoncit, Dt. xxx 6 semble être encore à

dans le coeur", "coeur nouveau, esprit nouveau" sont absentes. Commentant Jub. i 23, G. Kretschmar écrivait aussi: "Das ist der neue Bund" (*ZK* 67 [1954-55], p. 252). Mais les analogies seraient à chercher, plus que dans la formulation, dans le contenu et l'action propre de Dieu qui crée la possibilité de vivre selon l'alliance nouvelle. L'annonce de la construction du Temple définitif à Jérusalem (i 27, 29) prend un relief tout spécial, parmi les espérances des Ésséniens, après la découverte de 11 QTemple.

[77] Voir J. H. Charlesworth, *The Pseudepigrapha and Modern Research* (Missoula, 1976), p. 189-93 (avec Bibliog.). L'original serait plutôt syriaque que grec, l'oeuvre judéo-chrétienne. En faveur du syriaque (contre Carmignac qui propose l'hébreu), cf. J. A. Emerton, "Some Problems of Text and Language in the Odes of Solomon", *JThSt*, N.S. 18 (1967), p. 372-406, article consacré à l'Ode xi.

[78] Admettent une relation, et peut-être même une influence directe: J. Carmignac, "Les affinités qumrâniennes de la Onzième Ode de Salomon", *Rev. de Qumrân* 3 (1961), p. 71-102; "Un Qumrânien converti au Christianisme: l'auteur des Odes de Salomon", dans *Qumran-Probleme*, p. 75-108; J. H. Charlesworth, "Les Odes de Salomon et les manuscrits de la Mer Morte", *RB* 77 (1970), p. 522-49; "Qumran, John and the Odes of Solomon", dans J. H. Charlesworth (éd.), *John and Qumran* (London, 1972), p. 107-36. Mais, contre Testuz (*Papyrus Bodmer X-XII* [Genève, 1959], p. 58), Charlesworth maintient que les Odes ne sont pas esséniennes (*Pseudepigrapha*, p. 190). Battifol (J. Labourt-P. Battifol, *Les Odes de Salomon* [Paris, 1911], p. 47) classait l'Ode xi parmi les morceaux "incolores", entre les "sûrement juifs" et les "purement chrétiens".

[79] Labourt rend trois fois la racine *gzr* par "couper/coupure", en notant: "Peut-être circoncis", "peut-être circoncision". C'est la racine commune pour "circoncire" dans Targum et Peshitta. Ps-Jonathan l'emploie à Lév. xxv 3, 4 pour "tailler" la vigne. Emerton relève l'importance du jeu de mots que le grec a préservé (p. 374). M. Lattke, *Die Oden Salomos in ihrer Bedeutung für Neues Testament und Gnosis* (Göttingen, 1979), traduit par "beschnitten/Beschneidung" (p. 107).

[80] Grec: περιετμήθη ἡ καρδία μου ... ὁ ὕψιστος περιέτεμέν με ... ἐγένετό μοι εἰς σωτηρίαν ἡ περιτομὴ αὐτοῦ.

l'arrière-plan; on pourrait avoir ici une combinaison du thème deutéronomique et de celui de la nouvelle alliance qui inclut le don d'un coeur nouveau et d'un esprit nouveau. Le rôle prépondérant de l'Esprit à Qumrân dans la conversion et la rénovation de l'homme,[81] exprimée aussi par la c. du coeur, favorise l'hypothèse d'une utilisation heureuse des deux thèmes (cf. Jub. i 23). M. Testuz a d'ailleurs noté la "parenté d'inspiration tout à fait étonnante" entre cette Ode et les écrits de Qumrân et tient même l'auteur pour Essénien (p. 57-8).

Sauf erreur, la métaphore de la c. du coeur n'apparaît pas ailleurs dans les Apocryphes où d'autres expressions et images servent à décrire la conversion du coeur. Ainsi, dans les Testaments des XII Patriarches, les seuls exemples de περιτέμνω/περιτομή (Lévi vi 3, 6) concernent la c. des Sichémites (Gen. xxxiv) et il n'y a aucun exemple de ἀκροβυστία.[82] Il y est souvent fait mention de διαβούλιον en rapport avec le coeur,[83] mais la métaphore de la c. du coeur semble hors d'usage dans le milieu des auteurs des Testaments grecs. On y est déjà proche de la phraséologie rabbinique (cf. le pluriel διαβούλια dans Asher i 3, 5 ou ἐπιθυμία πονηρά dans Ruben iv 9). Il en va de même de l'Apocalypse d'Esdras (vi 26) [84] ou de l'Apocalypse de Moïse (xiii 5) qui annoncent pour la fin des temps un changement des coeurs et la disparition du "coeur mauvais."

IV

Le Targum servira de dernier terme de comparaison, surtout les Targums du Pentateuque qui constituent, quant aux traditions exégétiques, un bloc assez homogène.[85] Ils ont aussi, sur le point qui nous occupe, quelque originalité par rapport à la littérature rabbinique.[86]

---

[81] 1 QS III 6-7, IV 21; 1 QH XVI 12, XVII 26; 4 QDibHam V 15, etc. Cf. Jaubert, *Alliance*, p. 238-45; F. F. Bruce, "Holy Spirit in the Qumran Texts", *ALUOS* 6 (1966-68), p. 49-55. Pour le rapprochement circoncision/Esprit. cf. Rom. ii 29.

[82] D'après l'*Index* de M. de Jonge, *The Testaments of the Twelve Patriarchs* (Leiden, 1978). Test. Siméon vi 2 parle de se débarrasser de la σκληροτραχηλία qu'une partie de la tradition manuscrite remplace par σκληροκαρδία (ibid. 21).

[83] Cf. Hadot, *Penchant mauvais*, p. 58-63; O. Böcher, *Der johanneische Dualismus im Zusammenhang des nachbiblischen Judentums* (Gütersloh, 1965) (passim).

[84] Cf. A. L. Thompson, *Responsibility for Evil in the Theodicy of IV Ezra* (Missoula, 1977).

[85] C'est un des résultats importants acquis par A. Shinan, *The Aggadah in the Aramaic Targums to the Pentateuch* (Jérusalem, 1979).

[86] Sur les diverses recensions, cf. R. Le Déaut, *Targum du Pentateuque* I (Paris, 1978), p. 14-42; *Bibliographie* IV (Paris, 1980), p. 309-20.

Le Targum des Prophètes[87] paraphrase librement à Jér. iv 4 ("Retournez au culte de Yhwh et ôtez la perversité de votre coeur — *twbw lplḥn' dywy w''dw rš' lbkwn*") et à Jér. ix 24-25: "Je vais punir toutes *les nations* incirconcises *ainsi que la maison d'Israël dont les oeuvres sont semblables aux oeuvres des incirconcis* . . .[88] car toutes les nations sont incirconcises *dans leur chair* (cf. LXX) et tous (ceux de) la maison d'Israël sont incirconcis dans leur coeur."[89]

Les Targums du Pentateuque témoignent de deux attitudes divergentes face à l'original hébreu: celle qui opte pour la paraphrase (Onqelos et Ps-Jonathan) et celle qui propose une version littérale (Neofiti 1).

Dt. x 16:

Onqelos (O): "*Ôtez l'endurcissement* de votre coeur (*wt'dwn yt ṭpšwt lbkwn*) et ne raidissez plus (*tqšwn 'wd*) votre nuque."[90]

Ps-Jonathan (Jo) — id — sauf *lybkwn* et *twb* au lieu de *'wd*.

Neofiti 1 (N): "Circoncisez donc le prépuce *de l'endurcissement* de vos coeurs (*wtgzrwn yt 'rlt ṭpšwt lbbykwn*) et ne raidissez plus vos nuques *rétives* (*wqdlykwn qšyy'*[91] *l' ttqpwn twb*)".

Dt. xxx 6:

O: "Et Yhwh, ton Dieu, *ôtera l'endurcissement de* (*wy'dy ṭpšwt*) ton coeur et *l'endurcissement du* coeur de tes *fils* (Pesh.: + à jamais)

---

[87] A. Tal date la compilation des *Prophètes antérieurs* d'avant la seconde révolte de 135 (*The Language of the Targum of the Former Prophets and its Position within the Aramaic Dialects* [Tel-Aviv, 1975]). Son étude devrait être poursuivie pour les autres livres. S. A. Kaufman situe, comme lui, Onqelos et Jonathan entre 70 et 135 (*JAOS* 93 [1973], p. 327), dans leur ultime rédaction palestinienne.

[88] Comparer Rom ii 25.

[89] *'rlyn bbśrhwn . . . 'rlyn blybhwn* (= Pesh.). A Éz. xliv 7, 9, *'rly lb / 'rly bśr* deviennent "pervers de coeur — *ršy'y lb* — et incirconcis de chair". On peut remarquer que Jér. iv 4 n'est jamais cité dans le Midrash Rabbah ou le Talmud Babli et Jér. ix 24, 25 seulement dans une liste des divers "prépuces" dans Gen. R 46, 5 à xvii 2 (reprise dans Lév. R 25, 6 à xix 23) et Nedarim 31b (cf. M Nedarim III 11).

[90] Pesh. traduit littér. l'hébreu. Recension christo-palestinienne: *tygzwrwn qšywt lbkwn dl' tqšwn qdlkwn 'wd* (M. H. Goshen-Gottstein, *The Bible in the Syropalestinian Version*, Part I, Pentateuch and Prophets [Jérusalem, 1973], p. 42). Cette recension est considérée comme une version secondaire de la LXX (ici la parenté saute aux yeux); mais parfois une dépendance des traditions targumiques est possible ("There are resemblances to Jewish Aramaic Targums which cannot be easily pushed aside", p. VIII).

[91] Lecture de la glose interlinéaire. Texte: *qyšyy'*. Ce mot est supprimé par les variantes marginales (fol. 384 a) qui, réunies, donne le texte suivant: (*wtgzrwn yt*) *qšywt lbbkwn* (*wqdlykwn*) *l' tqšwn 'wd*; vocabulaire de la recension christo-palestinienne.

pour aimer (*lmrḥm*) YHWH, ton Dieu, de tout ton coeur et de toute ton âme pour que tu vives".

Jo: — id — sauf pour les formes de pluriel (*votre* Dieu, *vos* coeurs, *vos* fils). Pour la seconde partie du verset, cf. ci-dessous.

N: "Et Yhwh, *votre* Dieu, circoncira (*wygzr*) *vos* coeurs et les coeurs de *vos* descendants (*zrʿykwn*) pour aimer (*lmyrḥm*) *l'enseignement de la Loi* [92] de Yhwh, *votre* Dieu, de tous *vos* coeurs et de toutes *vos* âmes pour *vous* faire subsister (*lmqyymh*)".

Nous sommes manifestement en présence de deux traditions: celle de O (dont Jo dépend directement) qui *oblitère totalement l'image de la circoncision du coeur* et celle de N où elle est maintenue, en dépendance étroite de l'hébreu. La LXX, tout en omettant de traduire le terme *ʿorlâ* conservait la métaphore (περιτεμεῖσθε τὴν σκληροκαρδίαν). Le verbe circoncire n'apparaît que dans N (*gzr*),[93] tandis que O/Jo (pour Dt. x 16) ont le verbe *ʿdy* et *ʿorlâ* est interprété par *ṭpšwt* (empâtement, hébétude, endurcissement).[94] Ce terme se lit aussi dans N (à x 16); mais il s'agit évidemment d'une leçon confluante (le prépuce du/l'endurcissement du coeur) due à la tradition représentée par O/Jo. En l'omettant, on retrouve une version littérale de l'hébreu.[95] N est de la sorte le seul Targum à avoir conservé l'image de la c. du coeur.

---

[92] *ʾwlpn ʾwryth*. Sur cette formule, qui remplace onze fois "aimer Dieu" dans N (vi 5, x 12, 20; xi 1, 13, 22, xiii 4, 5, xxx 6, 16, 20), cf. J. Malfroy, *Semitica* 17 (1967), p. 91.

[93] Même verbe dans Pesh. et Targum sam. qui rendent litt. x 16 et xxx 6. A xxx 6 cependant, Pesh. ajoute "(Le Seigneur, ton Dieu, circoncira) *pour toujours- lʿlm*". C'est *gzr* qui traduit "circoncire" dans Gen. xxxiv des fragments du Caire (P. Kahle, *Masoreten des Westens* [Stuttgart, 1930], p. 11-12) et le seul, sauf erreur, qui apparaisse dans N. Jo, au contraire, connaît la racine *mhl* passée en hébreu mishnique (cf. M. H. Segal, *A Grammar of Mishnaic Hebrew* [Oxford, 1927], p. 53) et en araméen, fréquente dans le Talmud et le Midrash (cf. M. Jastrow, *A Dictionary of the Targumim* . . . [London et New York, 1903], p. 737; J. Levy, *Wörterbuch über die Talmudim und Midraschim*², [Berlin/Wien, 1924] III, p. 37-9): Nombres xv 31: *mhwltʾ* (cf. T. Éz. xvi 6); Gen. xxiv 8, 9, xlv 4; Ex. iv 25; Dt. xxxiv 6: *gzyrt mhwltʾ* (cf. T. Cant. ii 9). Ce pourrait être une autre indication du caractère tardif de Jo.

[94] Cf. O à Lév. xxvi 41: "Leur coeur stupide (*ṭpsʾ*) se brisera (*ytbr*)". N/Jo: *zydnʾ/zdnʾ* (présomptueux, endurci).

[95] Tant que le Targum était une institution vivante, la lecture antécédente de l'hébreu contraignait le meturgeman à ne pas trop s'écarter de l'original (cf. Vermes, *Scripture*, p. 184). O le fait d'ordinaire, quand l'état du texte n'impose pas la paraphrase; quant à Jo, c'est une compilation littéraire (d'un auteur unique sans doute) qui, telle quelle, n'a jamais connu d'usage synagogal (Shinan, p. 63).

La tradition attestée dans O/Jo correspond à une attitude souvent décelable dans la littérature rabbinique. La métaphore de la circoncision du coeur ne se rencontre que rarement (cf. Sifra Lev. 9, 6) en dehors de passages se référant aux textes bibliques qui la mentionnent (comme sont rares les allusions aux prophéties de l'Alliance nouvelle).[96] On préfère employer des images analogues, comme celle du "coeur de chair", ou parler, comme nous le verrons, de la suppression du *yēṣer hāraʿ*.

A partir de la fin du Ier siècle, le Judaïsme rabbinique insiste exclusivement sur une interprétation physique de la c. qui était du reste devenue, en raison des persécutions, comme un signe de la foi juive. Des maîtres, comme R. Ismaël et R. Aqiba, rejettent toute interprétation spirituelle de *ʿorlâ*.[97] G. Vermes a montré (*Scripture*, p. 178-90) que l'interprétation ancienne d'Ex iv voyait la valeur du rite dans son caractère expiatoire et non dans l'accomplissement d'un précepte [98] comme le soutiendront les docteurs du IIe siècle. On chercha, d'autre part, au delà de la signification biblique de la c., à souligner la valeur religieuse de la c. *physique*. Par exemple, en insistant sur le rôle du sang (Billerbeck, IV, p. 34), sa valeur méritoire et rédemptrice ou en la rattachant de quelque manière aux fêtes et au culte.[99]

La fin de Dt. xxx 6, dans le Ps-Jonathan, doit aussi s'expliquer dans le cadre des conceptions rabbiniques, en particulier sur les *deux penchants*.

> (Yhwh enlèvera l'endurcissement de votre coeur) ... car il fera disparaître du monde le penchant mauvais (*ybṭl* [100] *yṣrʾ byšʾ mn ʿlmʾ*) et il créera [101] le bon penchant (*wybry yṣrʾ ṭbʾ*) qui vous exhortera à

---

[96] Cf. Billerbeck, II, p. 683; III, p. 126. Les commentaires d'Éz. xxxvi 25-27 ou du Ps. li 12 ne la mentionnent pas. Le Targum ne l'utilise qu'aux passages bibliques où elle se lit.

[97] Gen. R. 46, 5 à xvii 2. Sur tout ceci, voir R. Meyer, *TWNT* II, p. 79-80.

[98] Cf. T. Nombres xxiii 10 (Jo). Plutôt qu'un rappel de Jos. v 3 que j'avais indiqué dans *Targum du Pentateuque* III (Paris, 1979), p. 221, on pourrait (avec Ginzberg, VI, p. 132) voir dans l'expression "poussière du désert" une allusion à l'emploi de poussière pour cicatricer les plaies.

[99] Cf. l'aggadah sur le *mélange* des sangs, de la Pâque et de la c., dans T. Ex. xii 13; T. Éz. xvi 6; T. Cant. ii 9; Mekhilta Ex. 12, 6 (*La nuit pascale* [Rome, 1963], p. 209-12). Ps-Jonathan situe la c. d'Abraham un 14 *nisan* (cf. *Targum du Pentateuque* I, p. 185) (d'après une conjecture de S. Speier).

[100] L'*editio princeps* (Venise, 1591) vocalise comme un *Peʿal* et Levy (*Chaldaïsches Wörterbuch* I, p. 91) l'interprète ainsi: "es wird aufören der böse Trieb". Comme Dieu est sûrement sujet de *ybry*, mieux vaut lire un *Paʿel* (*yĕbaṭṭēl*= "annihiler, détruire").

[101] Cf. Ps. li 12 et Jub. i 20-23 (éthiopien: *faṭar*, "créer, engendrer").

aimer (*ymlykynkwn lmyrḥm*) Yhwh, votre Dieu, de tout votre coeur et de toute votre âme, afin que votre vie se prolonge à jamais (*ʿd ʿlmyn*) [102].

Cette promesse se réfère à la fin des temps, au terme de "tous les exils" (*v.* 1), quand Dieu rassemblera les dispersés "par l'intermédiaire d'Élie, le grand prêtre et ... par l'intermédiaire du Roi Messie" (*v.* 4).[103]

La tradition rabbinique des deux penchants [104] apparaît, pour le Targum du Pentateuque, dans le *seul* Ps-Jonathan (Gen. ii 7; Dt. vi 5, xii 23, xxx 6); mais l'expression "penchant mauvais" se lit aussi dans N (e.g. à Gen. iv 7). L'annonce pour la fin des temps de la suppression définitive du *yēṣer hāraʿ* substitué par un coeur de chair, est aussi un thème courant;[105] mais la création par Dieu d'un penchant intérieur qui conseille, exhorte (*mlk*) à l'amour parfait de Dieu (cf. Dt. vi 5) ne me paraît pas attestée, sauf erreur, en dehors du Targum. C'est équivalemment l'annonce de la création du coeur nouveau et de l'esprit nouveau; il peut même y avoir une allusion à l'alliance nouvelle, dans l'enseignement intérieur de l'amour de Dieu (Jér. xxxi 31), rôle assigné à l'Esprit [106] dans Éz.

---

[102] Lire ainsi avec *ed. princeps* et *Ms Add.* 27031 (British Library). M. Ginsburger, *Pseudo-Jonathan* (Berlin, 1903), p. 354: *ʿlmʾ*.

[103] Comparer T. Jér. xxxiii 13. Sur Élie, cf. T. Ex. vi 18, xl 10 (seulement dans Jo); Schürer-Vermes-Millar, *The History of the Jewish People* II, p. 515 et 530. Ce n'est pas le lieu d'étudier les traditions complexes de ces versets de Jo.

[104] Gen. R 14, 4 à ii 7; Ber. 61a; Tanḥuma B Gen. 25. Comparer Hermas, *Mand.* 12, 1 (ἐπιθυμία πονηρά/ἐ. ἀγαθή). Cf. Billerbeck, IV, p. 466-8; Urbach, *The Sages*, p. 471-83. Doctrine fondée sur la présence de *deux yod* dans *wayyiṣer* ("il modela") à Gen. ii 7 ou du double *beth* dans le mot *lēbāb* à Gen. xviii 5; Dt. vi 5. En revanche, on découvrait l'annonce de la disparition du mauvais penchant dans des textes comme Is. lxvi 14 ou Ps. xlviii 14 où le mot "coeur" n'a qu' un seul *beth*, *lēb* (cf. Billerbeck, p. 483).

[105] Sukkah 52a; *PRK* 24, 17; Nombres R 17, 6 à xv 40; Ex. R 30, 17 à xxi 19; 41, 7 à xxxii 14; Cant. R 1, 2. Cf. Billerbeck, p. 483 (qui ne cite pas T. Dt. xxx 6 !). Comparer Apocalypse de Moïse xiii, 5; *LAB* (Ps-Philon) 33, 3; 4 Esdras vii 92.

[106] Si l'on remplaçait, dans notre texte, "penchant" par "Esprit", une comparaison s'imposerait avec 1 QS IV 20-24: lutte des deux esprits, de vérité et de perversion (*ʾmt wʿwl*) dans le coeur de chacun (20, 23), jusqu'au jugement décisif (20). Alors les justes, élus par Dieu pour l'alliance éternelle, comprendront et connaîtront le Très-Haut (22). Le Targum, bien sûr, parle un autre langage et sa théologie n'est pas dualiste; mais, dans les deux passages, est décrite l'espérance, en partie analogue, du règne définitif du Bien pour les élus. Patrimoine, sans doute, du Judaïsme "commun". Si la lutte intérieure de Rom. vii 14-20 décrit bien l'affrontement des deux penchants (cf. Billerbeck, III, p. 239; O. Michel, *Der Brief an die Römer*⁴ [Göttingen, 1966], p. 92-3: W. D. Davies, *Christian Origins*, p. 155), le schéma de Rom. vii-viii trouverait

xxxvi 27. Mais l'image biblique de la c. du coeur s'est évanouie. Toutefois il est possible qu'elle ait été présente obscurément à l'esprit des commentateurs anciens, comme le suggère l'exemple suivant.

Le message de Moïse (Lév. ix 6): "Voici ce que Yhwh a commandé de faire pour que sa Gloire vous apparaisse" est paraphrasé par Jo: "Voici ce que vous devez faire: *ôtez le penchant mauvais de votre coeur* (*'ʿbrw yt yṣrʿ byš' mn lybkwn*) et aussitôt se révélera à vous la Gloire de la Shekinah de Yhwh."[107] L'interprétation du Sifra est identique ("Ce penchant mauvais, enlevez-le — *hʿbyrw* — de votre coeur"), mais elle est expliquée par la citation de Dt. x 16: "Circoncisez le prépuce de votre coeur".[108]

V

Nous avons jusqu'ici rencontré des mentions sporadiques, rarement élaborées, de la circoncision du coeur depuis Jér. iv 4 jusqu'au Targum, des îlots dont la continuité, réelle ou non, nous échappe. Les données textuelles sont insuffisantes pour préciser les relations possibles entre les éléments d'une série allant de Jérémie aux Esséniens, pour aboutir à Paul.[109] Il pourrait s'agir de développements analogues, nés de raisons historiques diverses, à partir d'une source commune: la Bible. Par contre, le témoignage du NT sur la circoncision spirituelle est abondant et facile à interpréter dans un cadre historique assez précis. Un simple rappel des textes fondamentaux suffira.

Dans un climat nettement polémique,[110] face à ce qu'il considère comme une surestimation de la c. physique et de sa nécessité pour le salut, Paul, en bon midrashiste, argue de l'Écriture. Il rappelle

---

ici un titre, *in chiave rabbinica*, toujours en lisant "Esprit" au lieu de "penchant". Sur T. Gen. vi 3 ("N'avais-je pas mis en eux mon Esprit de sainteté pour qu'ils accomplissent des oeuvres bonnes?", cf. R. Le Déaut, *BThB* 4 [1974], p. 256-9).

107 Cf. Matth. v 8. Même texte dans une variante de N. Sur le rapport entre elle et Jo, voir S. Lund-J. Foster, *Variant Versions of Targumic Traditions within Codex Neofiti* 1 (Missoula, 1977), p. 56, 92, 81. Ici Jo doit dépendre du Sifra. On peut le considérer comme une compilation de matériaux provenant de O, des Targums palestiniens et des midrashim. Cf. P. Schäfer, *VT* 20 (1970), p. 309.

108 Trad. française du passage dans J. Bonsirven, *Textes rabbiniques* ... (Rome, 1955), p. 39.

109 R. Meyer (*TWNT* VI, p. 82) semble suggérer une ligne continue.

110 Michel insiste sur cet aspect, dans son commentaire de Rom. ii 28-29 (p. 90-3). Exposé récent dans C. E. B. Cranfield, *The Epistle to the Romans* I (Edinburgh, 1975), p. 171-7, 234-8.

le fait de la justification des Patriarches avant leur c. (Rom. iv 9-12) [111] et le thème biblique de la c. spirituelle qui l'emporte sur le rite matériel. La vraie c. est celle du coeur, celle qu'opère l'Esprit, force créatrice de Dieu (ii 29),[112] "où la main de l'homme n'est pour rien" (Col. ii 11: περιτομὴ ἀχειροποίητος). Le baptême dans la mort du Christ est appelé περιτομὴ τοῦ X. (ibid. 11, 12), c'est-à-dire la c. (du coeur) que le Christ opère dans le fidèle.[113] Dans le Christ désormais "ni circoncision, ni incirconcision ne comptent, mais *la foi agissant par l'amour*" (Gal. vi 5), ". . . ce qui importe, c'est *la nouvelle création*" (vi 15), ". . . le tout, c'est d'*observer les commandements de Dieu*" (1 Cor. vii 19): toutes ces formules, qui transcendent le dilemme circoncision/incirconcision, décrivent au fond le *contenu* traditionnel du thème biblique de la c. du coeur. Mais cette transposition va jusqu'à une rupture radicale avec le Judaïsme et son attachement à la c. physique: ἡμεῖς γάρ ἐσμεν ἡ περιτομή (Phil. iii 3), "les (vrais) circoncis c'est nous (qui le sommes de coeur)".[114]

Ce problème divisera l'Église primitive elle-même. L'accord pratique d'Act. xv entre partisans de la c. des Gentils et les opposants menés par Paul (Gal. ii 3) suffit à délimiter tactique et territoire missionnaires (ii 7), *Ecclesia ex circumcisione* et *Ecclesia ex gentibus*.[115] Mais cet arrangement, issu d'un conflit provisoire concernant l'admission des païens dans l'Église (Act. xv 1-7), n'allait pas au fond du problème théologique: [116] qu'en était-il des Juifs eux-mêmes, descendants d'Abraham, pour qui le commandement de Gn. xvii restait toujours en vigueur? Si certains textes (Barnabé ix 4, 7) [117] attaquent la c. physique parce que le précepte divin visait une c.

---

[111] Ils étaient justes, avant la c., "ayant la vertu du Décalogue inscrite dans leurs coeurs" (Irénée, *Adv. Haereses* IV 16. 2, 3). La tradition juive affirmait aussi que les Patriarches avaient observé la Torah (Ginzberg, V, p. 259).

[112] Cf. Jub. i 23; Odes de Salomon xi 1-3. Nous avons vu que les Qumrâniens ne semblent pas avoir commenté Dt. xxx 6 où Dieu est auteur de la circoncision.

[113] Cf. H. Sahlin, "Die Beschneidung Christi. Eine Interpretation von Eph. 2: 11-22", in *Symbolae Biblicae Upsalienses* (1950), p. 5-22. Toute la section Col. 11-23 laisse soupçonner des influences qumrâniennes: cf. H. Braun, *Th. Rund* 29 (1963), p. 248-51; W. D. Davies, *Christian Origins*, p. 156-9.

[114] La c. du coeur apparaîtra désormais le plus souvent dans des invectives contre les Juifs. Cf. Act. vii 51 où Étienne les accuse de prendre le contre-pied de Dt. x 16 (σκληροτράχηλοι καὶ ἀπερίτμητοι καρδίαις) et de résister à l'Esprit saint, l'agent de la c. intérieure qui ouvre le coeur aux appels de Dieu.

[115] Comme le proclame la mosaïque du Ve siècle de Sainte Sabine (Rome). Sur l'arrière-plan historique, voir E. E. Ellis, *Prophecy and Hermeneutic in Early Christianity* (Tübingen, 1978), p. 116-28 ("The circumcision party and the early Christian mission").

[116] Ainsi que le notait justement Meyer, p. 83.

[117] Cf. H. Windisch, *Der Barnabasbrief* (Tübingen, 1920), p. 350-3; P. Pri-

spirituelle, des Judéo-chrétiens resteront fidèles à la pratique juive: n'était-il pas plus parfait d'obéir à la Torah, sans contester pour autant la primauté des dispositions intérieures? [118] Si toute cette controverse fut si vive, c'est qu'au coeur du débat se trouvait la conception de l'*alliance nouvelle* et donc de l'*élection*.[119] On comprend dès lors que sur le problème de la vraie circoncision la polémique prévalut, juifs et chrétiens se retranchant sur des positions durcies et irréductibles.[120]

VI

Ceci n'était qu'un survol et le sujet mériterait une monographie permettant une analyse des diverses étapes et l'examen de leurs contextes, ce qui est primordial pour évaluer la portée des textes. Résumons notre parcours. D'une utilisation pacifique de l'image de la circoncision du coeur sur le plan *moral* (description des dispositions intérieures parfaites), on est aisément passé à une utilisation *théologique* (c. signe de l'alliance et de l'élection) pour se définir face à d'autres groupes, transposition qui suscita des formulations de caractère *polémique* dont l'outrance masque sûrement la véritable portée dans l'ensemble de la tradition religieuse juive ou chrétienne: l'une comme l'autre, après tout, savent bien que l'homme devant Dieu vaut en proportion de la qualité de son coeur.

---

gent, *L'Epître de Barnabé (I-XVI) et ses sources* (Paris, 1961), p. 50-60; *Epître de Barnabé, SC* 175 (Paris, 1971), p. 141-9. A propos de ix 4-5 il écrit: "Ce florilège est une oeuvre chrétienne, mais . . . le Judaïsme en a préparé les voies" p. 145). A. Marmorstein, "L'Épître de Barnabé et la polémique juive", *REJ* 60 (1910), p. 213-20, pense que la position de R. Aqiba dans Gen. R 46, 5 viserait une interprétation spirituelle comme celle de Barnabé.

118 Act. xxi 21 pose délicatement le problème.

119 Et non simple stratégie missionnaire, comme le suggère H. Freedman (*Midrash Rabbah, Genesis* I [London, 1939], p. 390): Paul aurait aboli la c. pour faciliter l'expansion du Christianisme. C'est de théologie de l'alliance qu'il s'agit et Justin (*Dialogue* XI-XII) posait cette question essentielle.

120 Du côté juif, rappelons l'insistance sur la c. physique et Gen. R 46, 5. Mais est-il légitime de parler d'un point de vue juif "accordant à la seule c. corporelle un caractère salvifique en ce monde et dans l'autre"? (Meyer, p. 82). Voir l'article "Circumcision" de H. C. Hahn dans C. Brown (éd.), *The New Intern. Dictionary of NT Theology* (Exeter, 1975) I, p. 307-12. Du côté chrétien, outre Barnabé, on peut mentionner Aphraate, *Demons.* XI, *De circumcisione* (*Patr. syriaca* I, p. 469-503; J. Neusner, *Aphrahat and Judaism* [Leiden, 1971], p. 19-30); Justin, *Dialogue* XIX, XXXIII; Tertullien, *Adv. Marcionem* V. 9 etc. Sur la c. du coeur chez les Pères, cf. K. H. Schelkle, *Paulus Lehrer der Väter*[2] (Düsseldorf, 1959), p. 89-93. Le thème est moins développé chez les pagano-chrétiens, moins familiarisés avec la circoncision. Remarquons que pour Justin (*Dial.* XII 3) la δευτέρα περιτομή est la c. spirituelle, tandis que pour Aphraate (*Dem.* XI 6), commentant le *šēnīt* de Jos. v 2, c'est la c. physique, parce que les Hébreux "étaient déjà circoncis de coeur" (citant Dt. x 16).

LA DATATION DU LIVRE DE JOB

par

JEAN LÉVÊQUE

Paris

La datation du livre de Job pose depuis longtemps aux exégètes des problèmes redoutables,[1] et parmi les auteurs qui se hasardent à proposer une solution tant soit peu précise, la plupart ne le font qu'avec mainte précaution. Cette prudence est amplement justifiée, et il serait illusoire d'attendre pour un avenir proche la fin des débats sur cette question disputée. Mais puisqu'un regain d'intérêt se manifeste depuis quelques années pour la littérature sapientielle, à défaut de pouvoir apporter un thèse inédite ou définitive, le moment semble venu de procéder, plus modestement, à une nouvelle pesée des arguments en présence.

A vrai dire, s'agissant d'un livre qui a connu une histoire littéraire aussi complexe, c'est une série de datations qu'il faut envisager. Autre, en effet, est la période qui a vu la formation puis la mise par écrit de la légende en prose telle que nous la retrouvons dans le Prologue et l'Epilogue, autre l'époque où ont été composés les monologues de Job et ses dialogues avec ses amis et avec Dieu, autres, enfin, les dates assignables aux deux grands ajouts que constituent les discours d'Elihu (ch. xxxii-xxxvii) et le poème de Job xxviii sur la sagesse introuvable.

Le récit en prose, qui se présente avec le schématisme, les refrains et les redondances typiques des contes populaires, remonte très probablement à une légende très ancienne et préisraélite.

Le nom même de Job se rencontre dès le IIe millénaire dans le Croissant fertile sous diverses formes: *Ayyabum* (prince de Šutu) dans un texte d'exécration égyptien, vers 1900-1800 av. J.-C., *A-ya-ab* dans une lettre d'El Amarna, *A-ya-bi* à Alalaḫ, *Hy'abn* à Ugarit et *Ha-a-ya-bu-um* à Mari.

---

[1] On trouvera sur ces problèmes deux panorama commodes dans: C. Kuhl, "Neuere Literarkritik des Buches Hiob", dans *ThRu*, *NF* 21 (1953), p. 163-205 et 257-317; "Vom Hiobbuche und seinen Problemen", ib. 22 (1954), p. 261-316; et dans H.-P. Müller, *Das Hiobproblem. Seine Stellung und Entstehung im Alten Orient und im Alten Testament* (Darmstadt, 1978).

Le thème du juste souffrant remonte encore plus haut. Il fait l'objet du poème sumérien présenté en 1953 par J. J. A. Van Dijk [2] et édité par S. N. Kramer,[3] et dont le prototype pourrait dater de la IIIe dynastie d'Ur, soit 2000 environ avant J.-C. On le retrouve dans le récit et le dialogue de la tablette cunéiforme du Louvre AO 4462, que J. Nougayrol fait remonter à la première dynastie de Babylone, et plus précisément au règne d'Ammiditana, donc à la première moitié du XIXe siècle. Le poème babylonien *ludlul-bēl-nēmeqi*, long monologue d'un juste qui décrit ses souffrances passées et l'action salvatrice de la divinité, provient lui aussi du début du deuxième millénaire, bien que les tablettes qui nous l'ont conservé datent du VIIe siècle. Enfin l'on peut faire remonter à l'époque cassite le Dialogue acrostiche entre un malheureux et son ami publié par E. Ebeling en 1924, où l'homme souffrant se heurte au mystère d'un dieu lointain et d'une destinée ressentie comme arbitraire. Plus récents (environ 1300 av. J.-C.), mais plus proches d'Israël par leur origine géographique, certains textes publiés dans *Ugaritica V* ont prouvé l'intérêt que les lettrés d'Ugarit portaient à l'interprétation sapientielle de la souffrance des humains. C'est le cas surtout dc la tablette RS 25460 où un juste raconte comment, abandonné des dieux et déjà tenu pour mort par son entourage, il est demeuré fidèle à Marduk qui finalement l'a sauvé.

Les données de la littérature comparée [4] rendent donc très probable la haute antiquité du thème du juste souffrant; mais le texte même du Prologue et de l'Epilogue de Job présente des traits certains d'archaïsme. Ainsi Job est présenté comme un fils de l'Orient semi-sédentaire, associant encore à l'agriculture un élevage transhumant. De plus les pillards Sabéens et Chaldéens qui interviennent dans la légende sont encore considérés comme nomadisant dans le désert syro-arabe. Les *b^enē hāʾĕlōhīm* qui dans le Prologue forment la cour céleste ont leurs parallèles cananéens à Arslan Tash (*kl bn ʾlm*) et à Ugarit (*ʿdt ilm*, *pḫr bn ilm*, *mpḫrt bn il*). Enfin la symbolique des nombres 3, 7, 10, telle qu'on la trouve dans la légende de Job, rappelle l'usage qui en est fait à Ugarit.[5] Un autre détail, insignifiant en ap-

---

[2] *La littérature suméro-accadienne* (Leiden, 1953), p. 119-34.

[3] "Man and his God, a Sumerian Variation on the Job Motif", dans *SVT* 3 (1955), p. 170-82.

[4] Pour l'ensemble du dossier, nous nous permettons de renvoyer à notre étude *Job et son Dieu* (Paris, 1970), p. 13-116. Cet ouvrage sera cité ici avec le sigle *JD*.

[5] Voir en particulier G. Sauer, *Die Sprüche Agurs* (Stuttgart, 1963).

parence, permet peut-être de proposer un *terminus a quo* pour la formation de la légende: le cheptel de Job comprend 3000 chameaux; or la domestication du chameau n'a guère commencé au Proche-Orient avant 1200.[6]

Née hors d'Israël et plutôt dans la région du Hauran qu'au pays d'Edom,[7] la légende de Job a été acclimatée très tôt dans la culture hébraïque, et elle a pu recevoir sa première frappe israélite à l'époque où ont pris forme les récits de la geste patriarcale.[8] La yahwisation du vieux conte a fort bien pu intervenir vers la même date. Aussi, quelques siècles plus tard, vers 600, Ezéchiel pourra-t-il utiliser dans une perspective franchement yahwiste l'exemple des justes "Noé, Danel et Job" pour ôter aux habitants de Jérusalem leurs dernières illusions (Ez. xiv 13-23). En revanche l'insertion du personnage de Satan n'a eu lieu qu'après l'exil, comme le suggèrent les parallèles linguistiques assez frappants que l'on relève entre le Prologue de Job et le Proto-Zacharie (520-518): le mot *śāṭān* n'est accompagné de l'article que dans Job et Za. iii 1; l'expression "circuler sur la terre" (*hithallēk bā'āreṣ*) de Job i 7 et ii 2 se retrouve également en Za. i 11, vi 7, et le verbe *šûṭ* ("rôder", Job i 7, ii 2) est employé en Za. iv 10 à propos des yeux de Yahweh.[9] On peut noter aussi que Job et Za. iii sont les seuls textes vétérotestamentaires qui présentent le Satan comme l'un des êtres célestes qui forment la cour de Yahweh. Introduire le Satan dans la légende à titre d'exécuteur des basses œuvres était d'ailleurs une manière d'atténuer la responsabilité de Yahweh dans les malheurs de Job. A plus haute époque les auteurs israélites ne manifestaient pas ce scrupule, et ils rapportaient sans sourciller les épreuves les plus terribles ou les plus étranges à l'intervention directe de Dieu[10] ou à des êtres célestes

---

[6] Cf. R. Walz, "Zum Problem des Zeitpunkts der Domestikation der altweltlichen Cameliden", *ZMDG* 101 (1951), p. 29-51; "Neuere Untersuchungen zum Domestikationsproblem der altweltlichen Cameliden", ib. 104 (1954), p. 45-87.

[7] Cf. *JD*, p. 87-90.

[8] Ce point a éte démontré de manière très convaincante par G. Fohrer dans son étude: "Überlieferung und Wandlung der Hioblegende", *Festschrift Fr. Baumgärtel* (Erlangen, 1959), p. 41-62 = *Studien zum Buche Hiob* (Gütersloh, 1963), p. 44-67.

[9] L'idée de Dieu qui sait tout grâce à ses messagers et à ses "yeux" circulant sur toute la terre a pu être rapprochée des usages de la cour royale de Perse; cf. M. Limbeck, "Les sources de la conception biblique du diable et des démons", *Concilium* 103 (1975), p. 31-44.

[10] Ex. xi 4; Lv. xxvi 26; Dt. xxviii 22.

mandés expressément par Dieu pour apporter la maladie ou la mort.[11]

L'histoire de la vieille légende de Job peut donc être retracée, au moins dans ses grandes lignes. Il est déjà plus difficile de préciser à quelle époque un texte écrit de cette légende a pris en Israël le relais de la tradition orale. Celle-ci suffirait encore à expliquer l'allusion d'Ezéchiel, mais il paraît certain que l'auteur des dialogues poétiques a connu et utilisé une forme écrite de la légende de Job, qu'il a, du reste, respectée au maximum,[12] au risque de laisser subsister quelques disparates mineures entre le conte et le poème.

A quelle époque a travaillé cet Israélite de génie, c'est ce qu'il nous reste maintenant à élucider, et c'est à ce sujet que l'on rencontre la plus grande diversité d'opinions. Depuis la période mosaïque (Talm. Bab., Baba bathra 14b, 15a) jusqu'au IIe siècle av. J.-C. (K. Siegfried), on peut dire que toutes les datations possibles ont été proposées, et il serait fastidieux de les passer en revue.[13] Par souci de clarté, je voudrais indiquer tout de suite la solution qui me paraît la moins fragile, pour revenir ensuite à loisir sur diverses thèses encore récentes et discuter les arguments que l'on avance pour les accréditer.

En laissant provisoirement de côté les problèmes posés par les discours d'Elihu et le poème de Job xxviii, la période la plus probable

---

[11] Ex. xii 23; 1 Sm. xvi 14; 2 Sm. xxiv 16s.; 2 R' xix 35; Ps. lxxviii 49, xci 6. Cf. notre étude: "Le sens de la souffrance dans le livre de Job", *Rev. Th. Louv.* 6 (1975), p. 438-59.

[12] Cf. G. Fohrer, "Zur Vorgeschichte und Komposition des Buches Hiob", dans *Studien zum Buche Hiob*, p. 26-43.

[13] Voici, à titre indicatif, un bref échantillonnage des datations retenues par les auteurs: *époque prémosaïque*: Origène (*PG* 11, 1365), M. Beheim-Schwarzbach; *période mosaïque*: Talm. Bab. (Baba Bath. 14b; 15a), Méthode d'Olympe, Ebrard, Rawlinson, W. T. Davison, G. W. Hazelton, F. A. Lambert, Nichol; *époque de Salomon*: Grég. de Nazianze (PG 35, 1061); *longtemps avant l'exil*: J. P. Free; *VIIIe siècle*: Th. Nöldeke; *VIIIe-VIIe*: W. F. Albright (1968), D. N. Freedman; *VIIe siècle*: H. Ewald, W. M. L. de Wette, E. Reuss,P. Szczygiel, R. H. Pfeiffer, M. H. Pope; *époque de Jérémie*: H. Gunkel, E. König, Pfeiffer, L. H. K. Bleeker; *VIe siècle*: J. C. Matthes, W. H. Kosters, A. Kuenen, A. Dillmann; *époque de l'exil*: Davidson-Lanchester, S. Terrien, A. Guillaume: *début de la période postexilienne*: les rabbis tannaïtes Yoḥanan et Eleazar (Talm. Bab., Baba Bath. 15a; Talm. Yerush., Soṭāh 8; Midr. Rabb. Gn LVII), R. Gordis; *première moitié du Ve siècle*: B. Duhm, E. Dhorme, C. Larcher, C. J. Ball, M. B. Crook: *deuxième moitié du Ve siècle*; W. O. E. Oesterley-T. H. Robinson, H. Rongy, J. J. Weber, H. Gans; *Ve-IVe siècle*: G. Fohrer; *vers 400*: K. Budde, J. A. Bewer, M. Jastrow, H. Junker, I. J. Gerber, M. Buttenwieser, A. Lods, A. S. Peake; *IVe siècle*: O. Eissfeldt, Slotki, P. Volz, N. Peters, L. Bigot, A. T. et M. Hanson, E. G. H. Kræling, G. Hölscher (400-200); *l'époque des Ptolémées*: O. Holtzmann; *le IIe siècle*: K. Siegfried.

pour la composition de la partie dialoguée du livre de Job semble être, dans l'état actuel des recherches, la première moitié du Ve siècle, entre l'époque du Proto-Zacharie et celle de Malachie. Et voici les principales raisons que l'on peut invoquer en ce sens.

1° Le *terminus a quo* est l'œuvre de Jérémie, dont notre poète s'est manifestement inspiré dans son monologue du ch. iii (cf. Jr. xx 14-18). Ce premier point est admis par un grand nombre d'auteurs.[14]

2° Un autre argument permet de descendre plus bas: la légende, telle que le poète l'a reprise, comprenait déjà les deux interventions du Satan comme membre de la cour céleste; or le Satan n'apparaît avec cette fonction qu'au niveau du Proto-Zacharie. Le poète de Job a donc réalisé son œuvre au plus tôt pendant le ministère de ce prophète, ce qui nous amène vers la fin du VIe siècle.[15] On objectera peut-être que le poète lui-même aurait pu introduire le Satan dans la légende; mais cette hypothèse paraît peu vraisemblable. En effet, pour ce poète, l'axe théologique du drame de Job ne passait pas par le Satan, lequel comptait si peu à ses yeux qu'il le négligera totalement par la suite tout au long des dialogues.

3° Un précieux indice est fourni par le poème au ch. xix, puisque ce chapitre se présente comme une anthologie des Lamentations. Le tableau suivant visualise le travail de mosaïste auquel s'est livré ici l'auteur des poèmes de Job:

	Job xix	*Lm.*
— hi. du verbe *yāgāh* (seuls emplois)	*v.* 2	iii 32, i 5, 12
		Is. li 23
— *ʿiwwēt*	*v.* 6	iii 36
ʿiwwāh		iii 9
ʿawwātāh		iii 59 (hapax)
— *šūaʿ/ṣāʿaq* ou *šūaʿ/zāʿaq*	*v.* 7	iii 8
— *gādar . . . w^{e}lōʾ ʾeʿĕbōr*	*v.* 8a	
. . . mēʿăbōr		iii 44
— *n^{e}tībōt*	*v.* 8b	iii 9
— *ḥōšek*	*v.* 8b	iii 2, 6
— (thème du déshonneur)	(*v.* 9)	(iii 14)
— *ʿăṭeret rōʾšī . . . ʿăṭeret rōʾšēnū*	*v.* 9	v 16a
— (thème de l'espoir perdu)	(*v.* 10b)	(iii 18)

---

[14] Cf. S. Terrien, *Job* (Neuchâtel, 1963), p. 24.

[15] La légende, dans son état actuel, trahit aussi, en xlii 16-17, l'influence stylistique de la strate sacerdotale du Pentateuque. Par exemple, l'expression *way^{e}ḥī ʾaḥărē-zōʾt* rappelle Gn. v 7; les 140 ans supplémentaires de xlii 16 et l'expression *zāqēn ūś^{e}baʿ yāmīm* évoquent la longévité des patriarches (Gn. xxv 8, xxxv 29; cf. xlvii 28). Mais on ne peut tirer argument de ces correspondances, car il se peut que les versets xlii 16s., les derniers du livre, soient une addition, postérieure à l'œuvre du poète principal.

	Job xix	*Lm.*		
— *ʾap / ḥrr . . . ḥărōn-ʾap*	*v.* 11a	ii 3		iv 11
cf. *ʾap*		ii 1, 21s et iii 43, 66		
— *ṣār*	*v.* 11b	ii 4b		
— *ʾohŏlī . . . ʾōhel bat-ṣiyyōn*	*v.* 12	ii 4c		
— *ʿōrī . . . ʿaṣmī; ʿōrām . . . ʿaṣmām*	*v.* 20			iv 8
— (thème de la pitié)	(*v.* 21)			i 12, 18
— *rādap*	*v.* 22	i 3, 6,	iii 43, 66	
			iv 19,	v 5

Les correspondances de vocabulaire, spécialement entre Job xix et Lm. iii et ii, sont trop nombreuses et parfois trop précises pour être fortuites.[16] De plus cette synopse révèle que l'unique ch. xix trouve des parallèles linguistiques dans les cinq Lamentations, ce qui tend à prouver que Job est influencé par les Lamentations et non l'inverse.[17] Dans le cas de Job xix, en effet, nous avons affaire manifestement à un seul auteur, tandis que pour les Lamentations, si W. Rudolph maintient encore l'unité d'auteur, d'aussi bons connaisseurs que E. Sellin, O. Eissfeldt, M. Haller, A. Lods, N. K. Gottwald penchent nettement pour la pluralité. Il est a priori peu probable que les deux ou trois auteurs des Lamentations, séparés par quelques décennies, se soient tous inspirés d'un même chapitre de Job; tandis que l'auteur du poème jobien a pu avoir accès à la collection des cinq lamentations; or celle-ci n'a guère pu être constituée avant la fin du VIe, voire le début du Ve siècle.[18]

4° Si la limite haute se situe ainsi au début du Ve siècle, la limite

---

[16] Nous ne partagerions pas, sur ce point, la sévérité de Kuhl: "Aus den Beziehungen des Hiobgedichts zu Psalmen und Threni lässt sich für die Datierung gar nichts entnehmen" (p. 316).

[17] D'autres rapprochements viennent corroborer cette conclusion, et ils intéressent en premier lieu Lm. iii. On peut ainsi comparer Lm. iii 12: *dārak qaštō wayyaṣṣībēnī kammaṭṭārāh laḥēṣ*, et Job xvi 12s.: *way*^{e}*qīmēnī lō l*^{e}*maṭṭārāʾ* (pour *maṭṭārāh*, "cible", cf. 1 Sm. xx 20) or encore Job vii 20: *lāmāh śamtanī l*^{e}*mipgāʿ lāk*. Comparer Lm. iii 15: *hiśbīʿanī bamm*^{e}*rōrīm hirwanī laʿănāh*, avec Job ix 18: *kī yaśbīʿanī mamm*^{e}*rōrīm*; Lm. iii 14: *hāyītī ś*^{e}*ḥoq l*^{e}*kol-ʿammīm n*^{e}*gīnātām kol-hayyōm*, ou iii 63; *ʾănī mangīnātām* avec Job xxx 9: *w*^{e}*ʿattāh n*^{e}*gīnātām hāyītī wāʾěhī lāhem l*^{e}*millāh*, ou Job xii 4: *ś*^{e}*ḥōq l*^{e}*rēʿēhū ʾehyeh . . . ś*^{e}*ḥōq ṣaddīq tammīm* (le mot *ś*^{e}*ḥōq*, au sens de "dérision", ne se retrouve ailleurs qu'en Jr. xx 7 et xlviii 26, 27, 39; le mot *n*^{e}*gīnāh*, au sens de "chanson moqueuse" ne se trouve que dans les textes ci-dessus). On peut encore citer Lm. ii 16: *pāṣū ʿālayik pīhem . . . šār*^{e}*qū wayyaḥar*^{e}*qū-šēn*, ou iii. 46: *pāṣū ʿālēnū pīhem*, en regard de Job xvi 9-10: *ʾappō ṭārap wayyiśṭ*^{e}*mēnī ḥāraq ʿālay b*^{e}*šinnāyw . . . pāʿărū ʿālay b*^{e}*pīhem*. Quant à Job iii 23: *l*^{e}*geber ʾăšer-darkō nistārāh wayyāsek ʾělōah baʿădō*, il rappelle à la fois Is. xl 27: *nist*^{e}*rāh darkī ūmēʾělōhay mišpāṭī yaʿăbōr* (cf. Job xix 8) et Lm. iii 7, 9: *gādar baʿădī w*^{e}*lōʾ ʾēṣēʾ . . . gādar d*^{e}*rākay*.

[18] Cf. *JD*, p. 383.

basse semble pouvoir-être fixée à l'époque de Malachie, c'est-à-dire vers 450 ou vers 430 av. J.-C., selon qu'on place son activité dès avant ou seulement après la première mission de Néhémie (444-432).

Le rapprochement s'impose, en effet, entre des textes comme Mal. ii 17, iii 14-16 et la thématique de certains passages des discours d'Elihu (Job xxxii-xxxvii). Les récriminations vigoureuses des *yir'ē yhwh* contemporains de Malachie rejoignent celles qu'Elihu relève dans les propos de Job, le *y*^{e}*rē' 'ĕlōhīm* par excellence (i 1). Qu'il y ait ou non dépendance littéraire au sens strict,[19] les deux textes reflètent les mêmes préoccupations théologiques et le même état d'esprit.[20] Or il ne fait aucun doute que la rédaction des discours d'Elihu est postérieure à la composition des dialogues de Job et des trois premiers amis. En admettant un intervalle d'au moins une génération, ce qui semble nécessaire pour rendre compte des caractéristiques de la langue d'Elihu, en particulier d'une imprégnation araméenne notablement plus forte, l'œuvre poétique principale devrait être datée de la première moitié du Ve siècle, ce qui corrobore les déductions précédentes.

Examinons maintenant quelques thèses encore récentes qui proposent une datation antérieure au Ve siècle. Leur discussion permettra d'apporter des précisions supplémentaires.

Selon M. H. Pope,[21] le VIIe siècle paraît être la date la plus probable pour la composition des dialogues, et il justifie ce choix par un argument de vraisemblance historique: si l'auteur était un Judéen ou un Juif qui avait vécu le choc du désastre national ou la joie de la restauration, il aurait fait, inévitablement, de l'histoire de Job une parabole du sort de sa nation; or l'auteur nulle part ne laisse deviner un tel propos. De plus, ajoute Pope, le choix d'un Edomite comme héros du récit eût été, après l'exil, un affront aux sentiments nationalistes des Judéens. On peut répondre, au niveau du texte, que le souvenir de la ruine de Jérusalem et de la grande tourmente de l'exil n'est pas totalement absent du poème de Job, puisqu'il affleure, par exemple,[22] dans les passages inspirés des Lamentations et dans la plainte de Job en xvi 12:

[19] On peut comparer Mal. ii 17 et iii 15 avec Job xxxiii 8, xxxiv 5, xxxv 2s., 14; Mal. ii 17b avec Job. xxii 3b; Mal. ii 17c avec Job. xxxiv 5; Mal. iii 14 avec Job xxii 2, 3a, xxxiv 9, xxxv 3; Mal. iii 16 avec Job xxxiii 31.

[20] Voir E. Dhorme, *Le livre de Job* (Paris, 1926), p. CXXXIV.

[21] *Job* (2e éd., Garden City, New York, 1973), p. XXXVII.

[22] Il s'agit d'allusions peu nombreuses et peu appuyées. Même si le souvenir

J'étais tranquille et il m'a rompu,
il m'a *saisi* par la nuque et *m'a mis en pièces*!

Le couple de verbes *'āḥaz/pāṣaṣ* employé ici rappelle le couple équivalent *'āḥaz/nāpaṣ* que l'on trouve dans le Ps. cxxxvii, lequel reprend, après l'exil, une complainte des exilés où la Fille de Babel est prise à partie:

Heureux celui qui *saisira* et *mettra en pièces*
tes enfançons contre le roc!

Job imagine Dieu la saisissant par la nuque et lui martelant la tête contre le roc, tout comme les soudards de Babylone s'étaient acharnés sur des enfants innocents. Quant au ressentiment que pouvait provoquer un héros Edomite, cet argument tombe de lui-même si le pays de ʿUṣ, patrie de Job, doit être cherché non pas vers le sud, en Edom, mais plutôt en Transjordanie, dans la région du Hauran.

Une date un peu moins haute est retenue par S. Terrien. On peut lire, dans l'introduction de son commentaire (p. 23s.) les affirmations suivantes: "La date de la discussion poétique (ch. 3-31) peut être fixée à la première moitié du VIe siècle av. J.-C., quelques années après la destruction de Jérusalem . . . Bien que la majorité des savants propose une date voisine du Ve siècle av. J.-C., celle d'environ 575 semble préférable". Et Terrien tire son argument principal d'une comparaison entre Job et le Deutéro-Isaïe: "Le poète jobien a essayé toutes les solutions possibles afin de trouver des raisons susceptibles d'expliquer la souffrance humaine . . . Serait-il vraiment concevable que le poète, s'il avait vécu au Ve siècle av. J.-C., plusieurs générations après le Second Isaïe, révélât par sa langue et surtout par sa pensée des affinités intimes et multiples avec le grand prophète de l'exil sans jamais souffler mot de l'explication de la souffrance par substitution sacrificielle ou solidarité vicaire, un thème qui précisément est central à la théologie deutéro-ésaïenne? Ce silence s'explique sans difficulté

des souffrances du peuple décimé et exilé habite le poète de Job, c'est le destin de l'individu qui, de toute évidence, demeure sa hantise principale. Depuis quelques décennies, un certain nombre d'auteurs, se plaçant au niveau de l'actualisation du texte biblique, ont aimé lire dans le poème jobien une allégorie de la destinée d'Israël tout au long de son histoire. Cf. C. L. Feinberg, "Job and the Nation Israel", *Bibliotheca Sacra* 96 (1939), p. 405-11; 97 (1940), p. 27-33, 211-16; E. E. Kellett, "Job: An Allegory?" *ET* 51 (1939-40), p. 250s.; M. Susman, *Das Buch Hiob und das Schicksal des jüdischen Volkes* (Zürich, 1948); D. Gonzalo Maeso, "Sentido nacional en el libro de Job", *Estudios Biblicos* 9 (1950), p. 67-81; B. D. Napier, *Song of the Vineyard* (New York et London, 1962), p. 339-43.

si l'on conjecture pour le poème de Job une date antérieure à celle des chants du serviteur."

Nous trouvons là une nouvelle forme de la thèse défendue jadis par R. H. Pfeiffer,[23] et ces relations entre le Deutéro-Isaïe et Job sont depuis longtemps au centre des débats. Il est indéniable que les deux œuvres ont en commun certains mots rares et bon nombre d'expressions ou d'images identiques, spécialement lorsqu'il s'agit, en style hymnique, de souligner la caducité de l'homme et la transcendance de Dieu (cf. Terrien, p. 24s.). La liste en a été dressée à plusieurs reprises.[24] Les correspondances sont même si frappantes qu'elles obligent, en tout état de cause, à maintenir Job, partiellement, dans l'orbite théologique du Deutéro-Isaïe. Il faut reconnaître, également, qu'on ne trouve nulle part dans le livre de Job l'idée que les souffrances d'un juste puissent avoir une valeur de salut pour la multitude. Mais la simple absence de cette perspective n'autorise aucune conclusion, car nous ignorons absolument quelle audience réelle l'interprétation deutéro-isaïenne de la souffrance du juste trouva en Israël dans les décennies qui suivirent le retour de l'exil. Dans l'état actuel de notre documentation, rien ne prouve qu'elle eut un impact immédiat et important sur les mentalités, puisqu'il faut attendre le Deutéro-Zacharie (xii 10) pour trouver, dans le rôle dévolu au mystérieux Transpercé, une réplique possible de la destinée du Serviteur. L'auteur des dialogues de Job aurait fort bien pu connaître la théologie sous-jacente à Is. liii sans la reprendre à son compte. En tout cas des parentés de vocabulaire assez nettes existent [25] entre le livre de Job et les chapitres l et liii d'Isaïe qui décrivent les outrages et les souffrances qui accablent le Serviteur.

Rien n'oblige donc à penser que le poème de Job soit antérieur au Deutéro-Isaïe. L'analyse littéraire fournit même un argument qui tend à prouver l'antériorité du Deutéro-Isaïe, et le force de cet argument vient surtout de ce qu'il prend en compte des ensembles de textes. Il s'agit des passages doxologiques du livre de

---

[23] "The Priority of Job over Is. 40-55", *JBL* 46 (1927), p. 202-6.

[24] Voir les commentaires de Driver-Gray (p. LXVIII), Dhorme (p. CXXIIss.) et Davidson-Lanchester (p. LXXIV).

[25] Rapprocher Job xvi 10: *hikkū l*^{e}*ḥāyāy*, et Is. l 6a; *l*^{e}*makkīm ūl*^{e}*ḥāyāy*; Job xxx 10 et Is. l 6b (*rōq*); Job xiii 19: *mī-hūʾ yārīb ʿimmādī* et Is. l 8: *mī-yārīb ʾittī*; Job xiii 28: *w*^{e}*hūʾ k*^{e}*rāqāb yibleh k*^{e}*beged ʾăkālō ʿāš*, et Is. l 9: *hēn kullām kabbeged yiblū ʿāš yoʾklēm*; Job xix 4a et Is. liii 3a (*ḥdl*); Job xix 21b et Is. liii 4c (*ngʿ*); Job xvi 10b et Is. liii 4d (*hikkū, mukkēh*); et enfin Job xvi 17 et Is. liii 9cd (*ḥāmās*).

Job, pris dans les discours des amis [26] ou ceux de Job lui-même,[27] et de leur comparaison avec les passages hymniques du Deutéro-Isaïe. Dans ce dernier,[28] quelle que soit la force des deux thèmes jumelés de l'action créatrice de Dieu et de son action recréatrice dans l'histoire, l'accent est mis nettement sur un troisième thème: la puissance et la fidélité de Yahweh opposées au néant des idoles, et le dessein de l'auteur reste avant tout parénétique; mais la leçon visée reste toujours homogène à l'ensemble du message et les thèmes hymniques gardent leur fonction originelle de louange. Au contraire, dans les doxologies des amis ou celles de Job, la visée de louange est toujours gauchie. Les trois visiteurs sollicitent les images hymniques traditionnelles pour faire triompher non pas Dieu, mais leur théorie sur la rétribution; et Job, de son côté, par une distorsion audacieuse des images hymniques, retourne en griefs contre Dieu des expressions ordonnées primitivement à la louange. Ainsi, dans les doxologies de Job, les formes restent hymniques, mais la fonction change.[29] Cette manière typiquement jobienne d'ironiser sur la Parole de Dieu serait encore impensable à l'époque et dans le contexte théologique du Deutéro-Isaïe.

La même datation relativement haute (vers 575), que nous venons de discuter à partir de la thèse de Terrien, reparaît dans l'introduction à Job de la *Traduction Œcuménique* française,[30] mais assortie d'une conjecture curieuse sur l'occasion du poème. "Comme les rhapsodies de la Grèce homérique ou les chants épiques des troubadours médiévaux, écrit le présentateur, les plaintes de Job furent vraisemblablement chantées dans les cercles de déportés juifs en mal de fêtes . . . A cette époque trouble et incertaine, on se mit à célébrer le Nouvel An et le Jour du Grand Pardon avant la Fête des Tentes. Le poète de Job profita-t-il de cette occasion pour distraire les foules et leur adresser sous une forme para-rituelle un message concernant le vraie foi?" A une communauté privée de culte et déracinée l'auteur aurait "proposé, sous une forme quasi dramatique, une sorte de divertissement littéraire" (p. 1445s.). Cette série d'hypothèses manque de vraisemblance. On voit mal un déporté raffermir la foi de ses coreligionnaires en insufflant au vieux conte de Job une théologie

---

26 Job v 9-18, xi 7-11, xxii 12, 29s., xxv 1-6, xxvi 5-14.
27 Job vii 12, 17, 20, ix 4-13 et x 8-12, xii 7-10, 11-25.
28 Abstraction faite des chants du Serviteur.
29 Voir, pour une étude plus ample de ce point particulier, *JD*, p. 293-328.
30 *Traduction œcuménique de la Bible. Ancien Testament* (Paris, 1975).

toute nouvelle et relativement corrosive. De plus les longs dialogues de Job et leur poésie concise et raffinée n'offrent rien de vraiment théâtral, encore moins de distrayant pour les foules, et c'eût été courir à un échec que d'articuler de tels textes sur un déroulement liturgique de type populaire.

Plus inattendue est la thèse qui accompagnait, en 1968, la traduction de A. Guillaume,[31] faite du point de vue d'un arabisant. Pour lui le livre de Job dans sa totalité, sans distinction du conte et du poème, a été écrit par un juif domicilié en Arabie, très précisément entre 552 et 542 av. J.-C., c'est-à-dire durant le séjour de Nabonide dans l'oasis de Tēma'. Utilisant les données d'une Chronique babylonienne du règne de Nabonide [32] et le texte inscrit sur deux stèles de Nabonide lui-même trouvées à Ḫarran,[33] Guillaume croit pouvoir retrouver dans le livre de Job mainte trace des événements réels de cette époque. Ainsi les souffrances de Job, et celles des pauvres réduits à vivre dans la steppe (Job xxx 3-6), ont été occasionnées par les troupes (chaldéennes!) de Nabonide (xii 6a). Si Job, en xxxi 26ss., proteste qu'il n'a jamais été idolâtre, c'est que Nabonide a tenté d'imposer à la communauté juive de son oasis le culte du dieu lunaire Sin. Même l'Epilogue de Job cesse d'être le banal happy end d'un conte et trouve son explication rationnelle: quand, au bout de dix ans, en 542, cesse l'occupation babylonienne du pays de Job, la colonie juive du Hidjaz, les "parents et amis de Job", l'aident à restaurer sa fortune.

Cette historicisation un peu forcée des données du conte et du poème ne saurait emporter l'adhésion, d'autant plus que la critique littéraire n'entre à aucun moment en ligne de compte dans cette reconstruction.

Citons enfin un essai de datation tout récent, celui de P. P. Zerafa [34] Selon ce chercheur le livre de Job fut composé vers la fin du VIe siècle comme une parabole du destin de la nation juive et dans un contexte polémique très particulier. Dans l'hypothèse de Zerafa les exilés, revenus de Babylone à Jérusalem, irritaient par leur attitude impérieuse et arrogante ceux qui étaient restés au pays. S'appuyant sur les vieux principes des écoles de sagesse ils se présentaient comme des justes enfin récompensés par Dieu pour leur fidélité. L'auteur

[31] J. Macdonald (ed.), *Studies in the Book of Job, with a new translation* (Leiden, 1968).

[32] A. K. Grayson, *Assyrian and Babylonian Chronicles* (New York, 1975), p. 106-8.

[33] K. Galling, *Textbuch zur Geschichte Israels* (2e éd., Tübingen, 1968), nº 47; ou *ANET*, *Supplement*, p. 126.

[34] *The Wisdom of God in the Book of Job* (Roma, 1978).

de Job, qui n'avait pas été déporté, résolut de réagir contre cette morgue. Pour montrer aux anciens exilés à quel point leur vantardise était déplacée, il les peignit sous les traits d'un étranger, un potentat édomite passablement vaniteux. L'histoire de Job, soudainement puni puis rétabli dans ses biens sans raison apparente, lui servit ainsi à montrer que la sagesse humaine ne peut percer le mystère des voies de Dieu.

En proposant la fin du VIe siècle, Zerafa semble très proche de la datation actuellement la plus sûre. Il est certain, par ailleurs, que l'auteur des dialogues entend régler des comptes avec la sagesse préexilique et ses théories trop mécaniques de la rétribution. Cependant l'hypothèse de Zerafa minimise le changement de perspective opéré par l'auteur des dialogues. Celui-ci polémique, certes, mais non pas avec Job, qu'il présente au contraire avec une sympathie évidente; il s'en prend aux amis et à leur interprétation des souffrances du héros. De plus rien ne prouve, dans le texte, que le poète ait voulu s'en prendre à d'anciens exilés.

Restent à préciser, autant que possible, les dates deux grands ajouts faits à l'œuvre du premier poète.

Pour les discours d'Elihu, les correspondances thématiques et verbales que nous avons décelées avec Malachie invitent à penser à la deuxième moitié du Ve siècle. Quant au poème de Job xxviii sur la sagesse introuvable, on ne peut guère l'attribuer à l'auteur principal. Non pour des raisons stylistiques,[35] mais parce qu'on peut difficilement imaginer le poète stoppant, même pour un instant, la dynamique de son œuvre. Si l'on prête à Job cet aveu d'impuissance de la sagesse humaine et cette méditation résignée, on ne comprend plus le discours autojustificatif qui suit immédiatment (xxix-xxxi) et encore moins le défi lancé à Dieu en xxxi 35ss.; si l'on met ce même poème de Job xxviii dans la bouche de l'un des visiteurs, l'impasse est encore plus complète, car les amis de Job n'ont cessé de revendiquer

---

[35] Certes, Job xxviii ne serait pas indigne du poète principal, et quelques affinités de vocabulaire ont été repérées entre ce chapitre et les discours de Yahweh (Dhorme) ou même les dialogues (Tournay). Plusieurs de ces ressemblances sont frappantes, lorsqu'il s'agit de mots rares, tel *šāzap*, au sens de "remarquer", qui ne se trouve qu'en Job xx 9 et xxviii 7, ou d'une expression comme *b^e^nē šaḥaṣ*, "fils de l'orgueil", pour désigner les fauves (Job xxviii 8 et xli 26). Dhorme cite également *derek laḥăzīz qōlōt*, "un chemin pour le nuage tonnant" (Job xxviii 26b et xxxviii 25b). A vrai dire, l'on retrouverait tout aussi bien *ḥazīz* dans des textes tardifs comme Za. x 1; Si. xxxii 26, et même *ḥazīz qōlōt* en Si. xl 13.

pour eux-mêmes une sagesse irréfutable, voire une révélation venue de Dieu (iv 12, xi 6). Job xxviii se comprend beaucoup mieux comme une addition. Un rédacteur, avec un goût littéraire et théologique très sûr, aura voulu conclure les entretiens de Job et de ses visiteurs en proposant à son tour une réflexion radicale, qui réfute définitivement la sagesse trop courte des trois amis et dénie aux thèses classiques des sages toute valeur d'explication de la souffrance des justes. L'homme ignore le chemin de la sagesse, et elle ne se trouve pas sur la terre des vivants. La méditation de Job xxviii fait ainsi pressentir la grande leon que Dieu donnera à Job quand il lui répondra du sein de l'orage théophanique.

On ne peut fixer de manière trop catégorique la date de cet ajout. Tout porte à croire, cependant qu'il a été utilisé, approximativement vers 200 av. J.-C., par l'auteur du Poème sapientiel sur la Sagesse privilège d'Israël de Bar. iii 9-iv 4. Dans ce cas l'adjonction de Job xxviii serait intervenue au plus tard dans le courant du IIIe siècle. Le traducteur de la Septante l'a trouvé à sa place actuelle, et l'a d'ailleurs passablement malmené pour le plier à ses préférences théologiques, comme l'a souligné récemment Zerafa (p. 133-6). On retrouve également Job xxviii à cette place, mais avec la teneur du texte hébreu, dans le Targum araméen de la grotte 11 de Qumran, au premier siècle avant notre ère.

Tels sont, rapidement décrits, les divers stades par lesquels est passé le livre de Job. En l'absence d'allusions historiques précises,[36] l'étude conjointe des écarts et des contiguïtés littéraires et l'attention portée aux mutations théologiques permettent de situer avec vraisemblance dans la première moitié du Ve siècle la phase essentielle de la composition du livre, celle de la création des dialogues de Job et des discours de Yahweh. Cette solution n'est pas nouvelle, puisqu'elle avait déjà la préférence de B. Duhm bien avant d'être retenue par E. Dhorme.

Un grand nombre des remarques accumulées depuis près d'un siècle sur la langue du livre de Job confirment une datation nettement postexilienne. Il ne pouvait être question ici de reprendre l'ensemble

[36] On a pensé parfois en trouver en vi 19, ix 24, xii 17-19, xv 19, xxxi 26, xxxvi 7-12. Deut allusions paraissent plus intéressantes: en iii 14s. l'énumération "rois . . . conseillers . . . princes" pourrait correspondre aux usages de l'administration perse, cf. Est. vii 28, viii 25; et le type d'inscription décrit en xix 23s. rappelle l'inscription rupestre de Darius Ier.

de ce dossier,[37] aussi bien ne parviendrait-on à circonscrire par ce moyen qu'une période encore relativement large, celle où l'araméen d'empire pénètre en Israël au niveau littéraire. La langue du livre de Job par beaucoup d'aspects reste insaisissable; tantôt le poète, sous la pression de sa vaste culture ou par volonté de varier et donc de créer son langage, accueille largement des mots ou des formes grammaticales que l'on retrouve seulement dans la langue tardive; tantôt c'est l'héritage du passé qui reprend ses droits, véhiculé surtout par les images et les formules des Psaumes et des derniers grands prophètes. Cette oscillation se trouve maîtrisée, dans le texte, par la vigueur même de la poésie et par la rigueur toute classique du cadre rythmique; mais en réalité le livre demeure en tension à tous ses niveaux: carrefour théologique où s'entrechoquent les certitudes traditionnelles et les nouvelles interrogations, creuset littéraire où sont fondus ensemble des genres aussi divers que la légende, l'hymne et la plainte, le livre de Job témoigne en même temps d'une mutation irréversible de la langue hébraïque. Avec ses audaces et ses fidélités, à partir de la première moitié du Ve siècle il prend place dans le patrimoine d'Israël et de tous les croyants comme l'œuvre géniale d'une période de transition.

[37] Voir les commentaires de Fr. Delitzsch (p. 125ss.), E. Dhorme (p. CXL-CXLIII) et Driver-Gray (p. XLIV-XLVIII et LXX).

RELATIONS BETWEEN POETRY AND PROSE IN THE BOOK OF JEREMIAH WITH SPECIAL REFERENCE TO JEREMIAH III 6-11 AND XII 14-17

BY

W. McKANE
St Andrews

I

A consideration of the relation between poetry and prose in the book of Jeremiah may have the form of a general lexicographical enquiry in which an attempt is made to examine the stock of vocabulary which is common to poetry and prose. If this is to be more than a mere cataloguing, in which presumably one would not go very far wrong but would have difficulty in saying anything that commanded attention or awakened interest, certain assumptions have to be incorporated into the enquiry. The assumption that the poetry is a reservoir for the prose is, in general, a reasonable one: it does not commit us to the proposition that all the poetry in the book is attributable to the prophet Jeremiah and that none of the prose is attributable to him, or that the prose is always later than the poetry. If, however, we say that the poetry is a reservoir for the prose, there is an implication that the authors of the prose who use the poetry of the book in this way are distinct from the author(s) of the poetry. There is an assertion that the poetry is a nucleus of the *corpus* and that in the process of enlarging and complicating that *corpus* writers other than the authors of the poetry make use of its vocabulary.

The principal competing assumption would be that the presence of vocabulary common to poetry and prose is an indication that the author of the poetry is also the author of the prose or of some of it. It is doubtful whether lexicographical or linguistic criteria by themselves will enable us to decide these matters: to determine the nature of the relationship between constituent parts of the Jeremianic *corpus*, whether interest is mainly focused on the prose or whether it is more precisely the relation between poetry and prose which is under consideration. This assertion, however, may seem to be contradicted by the pronounced lexicographical orientation of books which deal with the prose of the book of Jeremiah. The objection may be made that the books of W. Thiel [1] and H. Weippert [2] are marked by the attention which they have given to linguistic details and that the conclusions which are reached in them are founded on lexicographical considerations. There is a sense in which this is true, but, perhaps, a more significant and profound sense in which it is untrue. These books are principally concerned with the prose of the book of Jeremiah, but an examination of the lexicographical arguments which are used in them has a bearing on the interpretation of the relation between poetry and prose in that book.

When close attention is given to these books by Thiel and Weippert, it becomes evident that methods so different that they must necessarily lead to contrary conclusions are being encountered. Thiel and Weippert are at cross-purposes, sometimes for obvious reasons, sometimes for reasons which are more subtle, but their disagreement is inevitable and they are set on a collision course. The clearest and simplest expression of this is given where Thiel is evaluating prose vocabulary which does not occur outside the book of Jeremiah, but which he classifies as Deuteronomistic and which he assigns to an editor with the *siglum* D. It will be obvious that this involves arguments different in principle from those which he uses when he is seeking to establish affinities between the prose vocabulary in the book of Jeremiah and the vocabulary of the book of Deuteronomy or the Deuteronomistic historical books. The latter operation may be fairly described as a linguistic one, and we are in a position to set out the alleged parallels, scrutinize them and consider to what extent Thiel's account of the resemblances and the construction which he places on them commends itself to our judgement. It is in this area that the critical engagement of Weippert with Thiel is most interesting and fruitful, and it is here that her methods and interests are most clearly lexicographical and semantic. That this should be so is not surprising, because this comparative activity principally involves lexicographical skills and a range of linguistic judgements.

So far as Weippert is concerned to impose more refined evaluations on crude statistics her efforts are to be applauded. There is a danger in making too much of comparisons between vocabulary in the prose of the book of Jeremiah, on the one hand, and in the book of Deuter-

---

[1] *Die deuteronomistische Redaktion von Jeremia 1-25*, (Neukirchen, 1973).
[2] *Die Prosareden des Jeremiabuches*, *BZAW* 132 (Berlin, 1973).

onomy and the Deuteronomistic historical literature on the other. If these comparisons are too general, they do not have the significance which is sometimes attached to them, and there is a skill involved in deciding when they have a degree of particularity sufficiently striking to require us to raise the question of direct literary connections. For, example, if no more is being done than the cataloguing of isolated items of vocabulary (single words) which are common to the two areas being compared, there is a danger of ending up with statistics which do not have much significance and which are not capable of supporting the arguments into which they are pressed. An extreme statement of this point of view, which is, perhaps, a caricature, but which makes the point forcefully, is that we may be demonstrating no more than that the prose of the book of Jeremiah and the prose of Deuteronomy or the Deuteronomistic historical literature are both written in Hebrew. For the most part, arguments of the kind which are being considered will have a more substantial character, but if they rest on observations which involve only individual words, it is hardly possible to reach conclusions about direct literary relationships on such a foundation. This is so even if the words in question occur only or principally in the prose of the book of Jeremiah, in the book of Deuteronomy and the Deuteronomistic historical literature. It is reasonable to regard this as a significant statistic, but to determine what kind or degree of significance is to be attached to it is a matter of the greatest difficulty. It may indicate affinities which are to be expressed in terms of a cultural or theological consensus—sympathies of a broad kind which are shared but are not necessarily limited to one organized religious party or movement. Certainly connections of this kind may represent a state of affairs which cannot be expressed as direct literary relationships between two bodies of literature.

Identical phrases or word-strings in different *corpora* constitute resemblances with a higher degree of particularity, on the basis of which questions about literary relationships can more reasonably be raised. Thiel's arguments for the Deuteronomic or Deuteronomistic affiliations of the prose in the book of Jeremiah are often occupied with entities of this kind, and the counter-arguments of Weippert seek to establish that the word-strings in the *corpora* which are being compared are significantly different in nuance or function, despite a general appearance of resemblance or even identity. It will be obvious that, when phrases or strings of words are being compared with a view to establishing a literary connection between different Old Testament books, the degree of distinctiveness possessed by these combinations, or the extent to which they have striking idiomatic qualities, enhances the probability that such a special significance should be attached to them. This is something more than simple terminological identity, because equations involving several items of vocabulary in a string do not necessarily, if the vocabulary is ordinary and the nature of the grammatical association pedestrian, enable us to conclude that there is a particular, literary relationship between the *corpora* in which they occur. We may find that we have not transcended the generality and relative insignificance of statistics which consist of the cataloguing of individual items of vocabulary common to different *corpora*. If the manner of combining these items is grammatically ordinary, we are not in a position to go beyond the kind of conclusions which have already been suggested: the combinations may indicate affinities of a cultural and theological kind, but they do not have the striking particularity which is necessary to create a probability that there is a direct literary relationship. As with comparisons of individual words, these word-strings might, at the point where their terminological particularity is minimized and they fade into insignificance, tell us no more than that the language in the two cases being compared is Biblical Hebrew.

The most interesting aspect of Weippert's treatment of parallels which are supposed to demonstrate the terminological dependence of the prose of the book of Jeremiah on Deuteronomy and the Deuteronomistic historical literature is the attention which she gives to the semantic functioning of the same vocabulary in different contexts, and the efforts which she makes on this foundation to establish significant distinctions of nuance which disengage terminology in the prose of the book of Jeremiah from identical terminology in Deuteronomy and the Deuteronomistic historical literature. This is indicative of an exegetical interest and it is in principle a legitimate way of refining statistics which consist of a mere listing of items of vocabulary common to different *corpora*. Exegetical enquiry directed to a context may elicit important lexicographical nuances for the same words in different bodies of literature. To put the matter simply, the same word may not be used in the same way or have precisely the same sense in one *corpus* which it has in another. It may be that Weippert tries too hard on occasions to drive a wedge between the prose of the book of Jeremiah and Deuteronomic or Deuteronomistic prose with the help of these considerations. The concern to separate the prose of the book of Jeremiah from Deuteronomic and Deuteronomistic connections becomes all-consuming and there is a danger of enforcing hair-splitting distinctions. Even where the lexicographical nuances are genuine, it is not necessarily true that an absolute semantic distinction between an item of vocabulary in the prose of the book of Jeremiah and the same item in Deuteronomy or the Deuteronomistic literature has been established, so that all postulated connections have to be severed.

There are thus positive and negative judgements which may be made about this sphere of Weippert's activity. On the negative side it can be said that the methods which she uses are not capable of supporting the conclusions which she wants to reach. Her objective is to show that the *Prosareden* of the book of Jeremiah are, for the most part, nothing less than the prose style of the prophet Jeremiah. It would need arguments of striking particularity and great finesse to achieve this, and it is unlikely that the available evidence, however superbly marshalled, could ever be made to support such a conclusion. The demonstration that hitherto unnoticed differences of nuance exist between lexical items common to different *corpora* is a valuable contribution. Between this and the unbelievably bold assertion that the distinctiveness of the prose-speeches of the book of Jeremiah is the distinctiveness of the prose style of an individual prophet, there is set a gulf as unbridgeable as that which separated the rich man from Lazarus.

The positive aspect of Weippert's approach consists in the possibility which it opens up of wooing us away from a too great pre-occupation with the Deuteronomic and Deuteronomistic affiliations of the prose of the book of Jeremiah. It was said earlier that Thiel and Weippert, given their respective methods, were inevitably at cross-purposes and the reason why this is so may now be clear. Weippert *prima facie* might seem to have the better case, since from her point of view Thiel has a way of arguing which amounts to heads I win and tails you lose. The absence of parallels to prose vocabulary of the book of Jeremiah in Deuteronomy and the Deuteronomistic literature does not deter him from identifying this prose as Deuteronomic or Deuteronomistic. A state of affairs which for her is evidence of a distinctive Jeremianic prose—prose disengaged from Deuteronomic or Deuteronomistic connections—is explained by him as the vocabulary of his Deuteronomistic editor of the book of Jeremiah. If the prose of the book of Jeremiah has external connections, he uses these in order to demonstrate that it is Deuteronomic or Deuteronomistic and is the work of a Deuteronomistic editor. If it does not have these external connections, he still maintains that it is derived from this editor, but the mode of argument is one which is internal to the prose of the book of Jeremiah and might be regarded as an argument in a circle. It depends on the discernment of affinities between different passages of prose, their constitution as a group and the conclusion that they all have the marks of the editor D. This is a case which is built up gradually by proceeding from one passage to the next and it has cumulative force only if one is persuaded of the validity of earlier conclusions all the way through. It leans heavily on the identification of the literary habits of the postulated D editor, on a claim to discern his attitude and objectives which sometimes seems exaggerated, and on the assumption that there is a comprehensive, systematic orientation under which all the passages can be subsumed. If one is unconvinced near the beginning and follows the argument from passage to passage, it takes on the appearance of a superstructure which has been raised on a foundation of sand.

The intention is not to take sides with either Thiel or Weippert, but to suggest that an attempt should be made to overcome the antitheses which arise from the confrontation of their respective methods. It does not seem reasonable to deny that there are affinities between Deuteronomic and Deuteronomistic prose and the prose of the book of Jeremiah, but a precise definition of these affinities will always be difficult to achieve. Even where the prose vocabulary of the book of Jeremiah is not represented in Deuteronomy and the Deuteronomistic literature, the significance of this state of affairs should not be magnified and absolute distinctions should not be imposed on such a foundation. It does not contribute meaningfully to a conclusion that the prose-speeches of the book of Jeremiah represent, for the most part, the prose style of the prophet Jeremiah. The same statement holds good for the vocabulary which is common to the *corpora* in question, but where differences of nuance are discernible from one *corpus* to another.

To Weippert it should be said that it is not surprising that these differences are noticeable, because the lexicographical constituents and the nuances of the prose of the book of Jeremiah are influenced by the *corpus* of which they are part. This does not constitute a demonstration that the prophet Jeremiah wrote the prose, but it is an indication that there is a Jeremianic nucleus which is distinctive, so that the prose which is generated by it, in connection with the processes of growth and aggregation which produce our extant *corpus*, is, in greater or lesser degree, influenced by this distinctiveness. Hence we might expect vocabulary identical with items in Deuteronomy or the Deuteronomistic literature to have different nuances, because it serves the interests of a *corpus* which has its own particular character and orientation. The concept of a *corpus* is, however, introduced with an awareness of the difficulties which cling to it and the false expectations which may be raised by it. There is not an intention to assert that the book of Jeremiah presents an aspect of form and comeliness or that its parts are fitly joined together to make a well-rounded, literary whole. It is introduced along with the caveat that there is a tendency to underestimate the untidy and desultory character of the aggregation of material which comprises the book of Jeremiah, and to invest it with architectonic properties which it does not possess. It is introduced along with what might seem to be a counter-assertion, that the processes which brought about the final product are only partially and imperfectly understood by us and that we make a mistake when we suppose that they are always susceptible of a rational explanation, or that they necessarily contribute in an orderly way to a thoughtful, systematic redaction.

The objection may be made that the notion of a *corpus* which is being invoked is ambiguous, vague and ill-defined, and the only defence which can be offered is that it, nevertheless, serves the end which is in view. We may find that there is no comprehensive framework of literary arrangement or theological system within which the parts of the book of Jeremiah are fitted together; that there is more of accident, arbitrariness and fortuitous twists and turns in the growth of the book than has been generally allowed; that the processes are dark and in a measure irrecoverable, and that we should not readily assume them to possess such rationality that they will yield to a systematic elucidation. The process of generation or triggering which enlarges the pre-existing material of the *corpus* is not necessarily related to a grand theological scheme and, perhaps, does not look beyond the verse or verses which set it in motion. Even so, and even if there is no systematic expression of the term *corpus* on offer, its use is justified in so far as growth is generated and its shape to a greater or lesser degree determined by the pre-existing material which triggers it.

This adds up to something much less than the systematic Deuteronomistic redaction which Thiel discerns in Jer. i-xxv, but it is a different aspect of Thiel's work which claims our attention, since it has a particular relevance to the overcoming of the opposition discerned in the rival methods of Thiel and Weippert. The time has come—and this is a departure which Weippert has made—to concentrate more on the internal relations of the material in the *corpus* constituted by the book of Jeremiah and to be less bothered about comparisons between the prose of the book of Jeremiah and the prose of other *corpora*. It is important, however, that this statement should not be misunderstood. It should not be taken as a denial that there are significant resemblances between the prose of the book of Jeremiah and the prose of Deuteronomy and the Deuteronomistic literature. It does not arise out of an apologetic concern to demonstrate that the prose of the book of Jeremiah is clearly distinct from the prose of other *corpora*. It simply gives expression to a feeling that arguments about which labels are to be attached to the prose of the book of Jeremiah, while they possess historical and critical importance, may have the effect of distracting us from matters which are more intrinsic to the study of the book, namely, the internal relations of its constituent parts. A correct appreciation of the way in which the prose functions within the Jeremianic *corpus* and how it serves the ends of that *corpus* is more important than the attachment of particular labels to it. As matters stand, with continuous cross-references to Deuteronomy and the Deuteronomistic literature the fashion of scholarship, one is always in danger of succumbing to a condition of distraction and disorientation.

The general part of this article is almost complete and the second part will deal with particular cases of the relation between poetry and prose in the book of Jeremiah. There is still, however, a transition to be made and some justification of the relevance of the long, general section to the particular task in hand has to be attempted. It will have been noticed that the argument in its final form was not strictly lexicographical or linguistic. Although it was urged that the lexicographical evidence available to Weippert was incapable of supporting the conclusion that the prophet Jeremiah was the author of the prose-speeches of the book of Jeremiah, it would be disingenuous to represent that this was the only consideration which made her conclusion unpalatable. It is likely that she too had an extra-linguistic concern which commended to her the construction which she put on the lexicographical material which she handled, a concern to attribute the prose-speeches of the book to Jeremiah to the prophet Jeremiah. At any rate the extra-linguistic perception which puts her conclusions out of court is that they imply a view of the inner relations of the constituent parts of the book of Jeremiah and of the processes of growth and composition which is altogether incredible. We are dealing with a long, complicated, untidy accumulation of material extending over a very long period, to which many people have contributed. The supposition that a major part of it, including much of the prose, was already in existence in the lifetime of the prophet Jeremiah is a literary judgement which seems to take no account of the problems which arise when one considers in detail the baffling inconcinnities of the constituents of the book. In this regard the account which Thiel gives of the growth of the Jeremianic *corpus*, with the prominence attached to a Deuteronomistic redaction and the allowance for large post-Deuteronomistic accretions (for example, the oracles against foreign nations), shows a more realistic grasp of the long period of time over which the book was in the process of formation. The question-mark which has been raised against Thiel's account is whether there is a redaction of the far-reaching and systematic kind which he claims to discover in chapters i-xxv. The concern of the foregoing discussion has been to focus attention on the concept of a Jeremianic *corpus* and to ask what kind of internal relationships we should envisage between its constituent parts. One of the most interesting aspects of this is the relations which obtain between the poetry and prose of the book, and the examination of this which follows will, perhaps, compensate for the necessarily general character of the preceding part of the article and illustrate in a less rarified manner some of the views which have been expressed.

II

It has been argued that the prose of the book of Jeremiah should not, for the most part, be attributed to the prophet Jeremiah, because this is not compatible with the long drawn-out processes which we must assume to have attended the formation of the *corpus*. In connection with the relations between poetry and prose different exegetical considerations will be introduced, designed to show that there are cases where the prose is triggered by the poetry and is derivative. First of all, however, it should be observed that when W. L. Holladay [3]

[3] "Prototypes and Copies: A New Approach to the Poetry-Prose Problem in the Book of Jeremiah", *JBL* 79 (1960), pp. 351-67.

speaks of poetic prototypes and prose copies he is making this kind of assumption, and it is in accord with the attitude which has generally prevailed in critical operations directed at prose passages in the book of Jeremiah. These have usually had a particular character and a specific exegetical aim, whereas Holladay's work has the form of a more comprehensive, lexicographical enquiry. In the tradition of critical scholarship the aim has sometimes been to discover a metrical nucleus or core in a prose passage and to show how this has been enlarged and overlaid by subsequent prose elaboration. This is a way of dealing with prose compositions which is still influential in the work of Thiel. He is aware of the considerations raised by Holladay, and in considering the sources of the vocabulary of his editor D he looks not only to Deuteronomic and Deuteronomistic sources, but also to the poetry of the book of Jeremiah. He has, however, a closer accord with earlier critical procedures in that he is always alive to the possibility that a prose composition attributed to D may have been formed around a fragment of poetry, and his tendency is to assign such a fragment to the prophet Jeremiah. There are thus two ways in which a relation between prose and poetry is envisaged by Thiel: in the first case the prose composition is wholly created by D, but he has quarried single words or phrases from the poetry of the book of Jeremiah; in the second case he has formed a composition around a verse or verses of poetry whose metrical structure is identified or restored.

The kind of relation between poetry and prose in the book of Jeremiah of which two examples are now to be given is different from those which have just been described. It does not involve extracting a metrical nucleus from a prose composition; it deals not with a hypothetical core which has been encapsulated in prose, but with a relation of adjacency or contiguity between poetry and prose. The argument is that the prose has been generated by the poetry and has the character of exegesis or comment. The implication is that the enlargement of the Jeremianic *corpus* in these cases has taken place through prose additions which are exegetical, which are limited and particular rather than systematic and general, because they are a specific response to small pieces of text.

The first passage is iii 1-13 and a question is asked about the relation of *vv.* 6-11 (prose) to *vv.* 1-5 and 12-13 (poetry). The reasons why *vv.* 6-11 rather than *vv.* 6-13 are regarded as a unit will appear presently; the latter is normally regarded as the correct delimitation. That *v.* 1 is seminal in relation to *vv.* 6-11 is indisputable, since the model of divorce, interpreted as the exile of the northern kingdom, supplies the author of *vv.* 6-11 with his theme. The treatment of the theme is certainly influenced by the supposition that *vv.* 12-13 are also addressed to the inhabitants of the former northern kingdom, but *vv.* 6-11 are not more intrinsically related to *vv.* 12-13 than they are to *vv.* 1-5, although they have been editorially connected to *vv.* 12-13 with greater deliberation. It is unlikely that the interpretation of *vv.* 1-5 which is assumed by *vv.* 6-11 is the right one, since there is no reason to suppose that *vv.* 1-5 relate so particularly to the former northern kingdom. If *vv.* 1-5 are from the prophet Jeremiah, it would be more natural to conclude that they were spoken to Judah. Nor should it be assumed that the interpretation which has been put on the poetry in *vv.* 12-13 by the connecting piece in *v.* 12 ("Go and proclaim these words to the north, saying"), which associates these verses with *vv.* 6-11, is necessarily a correct indication. The expression *meššûbāh yiśrā'ēl* is common to *v.* 12 and *vv.* 6-11, but it does not follow from this that there is an original literary continuity between *vv.* 6-11 and *vv.* 12-13. Another possible explanation is that *meššûbāh yiśrā'ēl* was appropriated by the author of *vv.* 6-11 from *v.* 12 in the same way as he took the idea of "divorce" from *v.* 1 and developed it.

The logic of what has just been said is that if *vv.* 1-13 are all attributable to the prophet Jeremiah (Graf,[4] Giesebrecht, Cornill, Volz, Rudolph, Weiser), there are no better reasons for making a unit out of *vv.* 6-13 than there are for making a unit out of *vv.* 1-13, because the connection between *vv.* 6-11 and *vv.* 12-13 is no more intrinsic than the connection between *vv.* 1-5 and *vv.* 6-11. Hence, given his assumptions, H. W. Hertzberg [5] is entirely logical in making a unit out of *vv.* 1-13 by embracing *vv.* 1-5 and supposing that these verses too were addressed by Jeremiah to the inhabitants of the former northern kingdom. It might be objected that *v.* 5 connects impressively with *v.* 19, and this has often been said, but it will not stand up to close scrutiny. If, however, we go along with the view that *vv.* 6-13 constitute a unit, we have to suppose that the historical notice in *v.* 6 is to be taken seriously and that we have an indication of Jeremiah's concern for those who were inhabitants of the former northern kingdom, whether expressed before or after Josiah's reform

---

[4] Commentaries to which reference is made are listed below.

[5] "Jeremia und das Nordreich Israel", *ThLZ* 77 (1952), pp. 598 f.

in 621, and perhaps related to the political interest which the king had in this territory. It is then a matter of dispute whether in *vv.* 12-13 we have an address to exiles, as most suppose, or whether *šûbāh* excludes the nuance of "Return" and is to be understood as a call to repentance issued to those who were not deported to Assyria and were still resident in Palestine.[6]

Another view disengages *vv.* 6-11 from the prophet Jeremiah, while maintaining that *vv.* 6-13 constitute a significant unit. In the case of Holladay [7] and Thiel (pp. 85-91) this goes with the assertion that *vv.* 6-13 are the composition of a Deuteronomistic editor. J. P. Hyatt, who also holds that *vv.* 6-13 are a Deuteronomistic composition, takes a different view of *vv.* 12-13, since he doubts whether these verses had an original reference to the inhabitants of the former northern kingdom. Rudolph notes that Hyatt himself has conceded that *vv.* 6-11 have "little D diction", and Thiel, for his part, acknowledges that there is little Deuteronomistic vocabulary in *vv.* 6-12aα. There is an important respect in which Thiel's view of *vv.* 6-11 is the right one. Whoever composed these verses borrowed his ideas and quarried his vocabulary from surrounding passages. Thiel has overdone his demonstration that *vv.* 6-11 are a *pastiche*, but his understanding of their secondary character is essentially correct. Once it has been established that the ideas of divorce and harlotry are derived from *vv.* 1-5 and that the working out of these in a comparison of degrees of guilt attaching to Israel and Judah is suggested by the assumption that *vv.* 12-13 are an offer of reconciliation to Israel, the case has been sufficiently made. Thiel is right to suppose that *mešûbāh yiśrā'ēl* has been derived from *v.* 12, that the "divorce" idea has been developed in *v.* 8 in dependence on Deut. xxiv 3 and that the epithet *bāgôdāh* or *bôgēdāh* (*vv.* 7, 8, 10) has been suggested by iii 20.

Verses 6-11 come into existence as a kind of exegesis of pre-existing texts; we are dealing with an exegetical activity and the primary answer to the question how a passage like this arises must be a literary one. The content of *vv.* 6-11 is determined by a particular interpretation which has been put on *vv.* 1-5 and *vv.* 12-13. Whether one can go any further than this and establish the particular historical circumstances and theological concerns which promoted such exegesis

[6] A. C. Welch, "Jeremiah and Religious Reform", *The Expositor* (1921), p. 467.

[7] *The Root Šûbh in the Old Testament with particular Reference to its Usages in Covenantal Contexts* (Leiden, 1958), pp. 132-4.

is doubtful. Giesebrecht believed that the organization of the argument about Israel and Judah in *vv.* 6-11 implied that the exile of Judah still lay in the future, and Cornill, comparing *vv.* 6-11 with Ezek. xvi 51 f., maintained that the dependence was on the side of Ezekiel. Both these scholars were certainly influenced by their conviction that *vv.* 6-11 were to be assigned to the prophet Jeremiah. Without this premise and the historical anchorage which it affords, one cannot tell from an examination of *vv.* 6-11 whether the exile of Judah is envisaged as in the past or in the future, nor can one pronounce on priority and dependence as between the Jeremiah and Ezekiel passages. The argument that the polemical situation which had developed between Jews and Samaritans rules out the post-exilic period (Thiel, p. 90) depends for its effectiveness on the assumption that the type of exegetical activity represented by *vv.* 6-11 has to be related significantly to a historical moment and a theological climate.

It would be dogmatic to assert that the interest which is reflected here is purely exegetical and that *vv.* 6-11, being no more than an attempt to deal with problems which were thought to inhere in existing texts (What did the "divorce" of Israel signify? Why did Jeremiah address an offer of reconcilation to Israel?), do not require an explanation in terms of appropriate historical circumstances. This having been said, it should be appreciated that it may not be so easy as has been supposed to demonstrate the appropriateness of the exilic period and the inappropriateness of the post-exilic period. The derivative character of *vv.* 6-11, and the circumstance that their interpretation of the texts out of which they arise (*vv.* 1-5, 12-13) is almost certainly wrong, establishes that they are not the work of the prophet Jeremiah and that they are at least as late as the exilic period. It is probable that the "divorce" model and the description of harlotry attached to it (*vv.* 1-5) has been wrongly referred to the apostasy of the northern kingdom and the subsequent exile. It is certain that *m*ᵉ*šûbāh yiśrā*ʾ*ēl* (*v.* 12) has been wrongly identified with the northern kingdom and that *vv.* 12-13, misinterpreted as a gracious offer of reconciliation to those who once constituted that kingdom, has awakened reflections on the comparative culpability of Israel and Judah. A purely exegetical account of *vv.* 6-11 may be inadequate, because the correspondence between these verses and Ezek. xvi 51 f. is close and impressive. Samaria was not half the sinner that Judah was; the sins of Judah are so much greater that her sister, Samaria, by comparison appears almost innocent. It appears that these ideas were abroad among Jews in Babylon consequent on the fall of Jerusalem (according to W. Zimmerli, Ezek. xvi 51 f. is exilic), and it is a reasonable conclusion that behind the particular, exegetical operations of the author of *vv.* 6-11 there is this more general current of speculation and questioning.

The understanding of *vv.* 6-11 which is being recommended is that they represent secondary, exegetical development which arises from *vv.* 1-5 (especially *v.* 1) and *vv.* 12-13. A commentary in prose is generated by these two passages and is inserted between them. It is supposed wrongly by the exegete that *vv.* 1-5 refer to northern Israel and "divorce" is interpreted by him as the exile of the northern kingdom. The invitation to return and repent in *vv.* 12-13 is also thought to have been addressed to the inhabitants of the former northern kingdom in exile, and the exegete develops the idea that the lesser guilt of Israel over against Judah justifies this offer of forgiveness and reconciliation. His primary interest is in understanding texts which are available for interpretation. It is a difficult task to recover the historical circumstances and theological tendencies which might have promoted such exegesis, but the similar ideas which appear in Ezek. xvi 51 f. suggest that there was a more general climate of theological pondering which spurred the particular, exegetical activity.

The other example to be investigated is xii 14-17, and some attention must be paid to *'ettôš mittôkām*, although no attempt will be made to deal with all the complexities of this piece of text. A broad distinction can be made between those who take *'ettôš mittôkām* as a reference to the deliverance of Judah (Kimchi, Calvin, Lowth, Duhm, Ehrlich[8]) and those who suppose that it is an allusion to exile (Hitzig and most of the recent commentators). Kimchi comments, "Those (of my people) who went into exile in their midst I will root out from them, when I restore the fortunes of my people." It is not entirely clear what Kinchi means by this. It could be urged that he envisages Jews exiled in neighbouring lands who are to be repatriated to Judah—this is the exegesis of the passage favoured by Duhm and Volz. It is more probable that Kimchi refers to Jews in exile in Babylonia who are mixed up with Edomites, Moabites and so on. What he is then saying is that after the exile Jews will be effectively separated from their neighbours, and so he has the post-

[8] A. B. Ehrlich, *Randglossen zur hebräischen Bibel* 4 (Leipzig, 1912), pp. 276 f.

exilic Jerusalem community in mind. In connection with *v.* 15 he cites passages in the oracles on foreign nations which refer to the restoration of Moab (xlviii 47) and Ammon (xlix 6). When Judah and Benjamin return from exile, their former neighbours will also be restored. The conditions, however, are those set out in *v.* 16 on which Kimchi comments, "For after the Israelites returned from exile they did not worship idols nor swear by Baal." If the neighbouring nations learn Israel's ways in this regard, it will amount to the abolition of idolatry. On *w^enibnû b^etôk ʿammî* (*v.* 16) he remarks, "For many of them will become *gērîm* when they return from exile and will reside among the Israelites." On *v.* 17 he refers to an exegesis of xlix 6 according to which the promise of restoration is confined to Ammonites who "learn the ways of Israel".

It is interesting and significant that Kimchi interprets *vv.* 14-17 in a post-exilic context. There are, of course, no critical implications in this: he regards these verses as a prophecy about the shape of the future by the prophet Jeremiah and not as an *ex eventu* prophecy composed in the post-exilic period. Apart from this, his perception of the historical setting in which sense can be made of the passage is one to which we should attend carefully, and, in particular, his explanation of the enigmatic *w^eʾet-bêt y^ehûdāh ʾettôš mittôkām* could be the right one. The obvious criticism to be applied to the latter is that *ntš* is used in *vv.* 14 and 15 of "uprooting" (exiling) Judah's neighbours and that a different sense of *ntš* ("separating") is difficult to maintain in *w^eʾet-bêt y^ehûdāh ʾettôš mittôkām*. This is a cogent but perhaps not a fatal objection, because it is possible that *ntš* may have been used to play on the preceding occurrences and to convey the stringency of Jewish separation from neighbouring nations—the "uprooting" of all associations.

According to Thiel (pp. 162-8) *vv.* 14-17 are an *ex eventu* prophecy composed by D. He has latched on to *naḥ^alāh* in *vv.* 7, 8, 9, but he has also undertaken to refer to events which he regards as the sequel of those described in *vv.* 7-13. The "evil neighbours" whose exile is predicted in *v.* 14 are the *rôʿîm rabbîm* of *v.* 10 and the *šôd^edîm* of *v.* 12. D's prophecy is founded on the events of 582 B.C. (cp. Nicholson) when, according to Josephus (Ant. x 181 f.) Nebuchadrezzar marched against Coele-Syria, occupied it, subdued Moab and Ammon, and carried off Jewish captives to Babylon. The last part of this can be correlated with Jer. lii 30, according to which seven hundred and forty-five Judaeans were deported by Nebuzaradan in Nebuchadrezzar's twenty third year (582—this agrees with the date given by Josephus). The assumption that an exilic editor knew about events involving Moab and Ammon in 582 is a vote of confidence in Josephus, and Thiel brushes aside the questions which R. Marcus [9] asks about the sources available to Josephus. He may have used Jer. lii 28-30 for the latter part of his notice, although he does not mention Nebuzaradan. What sources did he have for his references to Moab and Ammon? Marcus says that these are loosely founded on the notices in the foreign oracles about the uprooting of these nations. Since Josephus was writing centuries after 582, we need to know more about his sources before we can found on his statements a conclusion that an exilic editor was alluding to a punitive Babylonian expedition against Moab and Ammon in 582 B.C.

A historical anchorage of this kind should not be sought for *vv.* 14-17: *vv.* 14-15 are a late, artificial prophetic composition to which qualifications have been subsequently added in *vv.* 16-17. It is a composition in the sense that it is composed from pre-existing passages of scripture, especially the definition of Jeremiah's prophetic office in the call narrative (i 10—a prophet to the nations who is to uproot and to build), and the notices about the restoration of Judah's neighbours in the foreign oracles of the book of Jeremiah. This awareness of the connection of *vv.* 14-15 with other Old Testament passages is already present in Kimchi and can be seen also in Lowth. Kimchi notes that the restoration of Moab is prophesied in xlviii 47 and that of Ammon in xlix 6. The expression used in both passages is *w*^{e}*šabtî š*^{e}*bût*, "And I will reverse the exile of" or "And I will restore the fortunes of". This is recorded as a decision of Yahweh without reference to the repentance or conversion of those who are restored, and in that respect it is comparable with *'āšûb w*^{e}*riḥamtîm wah*^{a}*šîbôtîm* in *v.* 15. Cornill, who postulates a saying of the prophet Jeremiah consisting of *vv.* 14-16*, cites xvi 19 f. as another passage where repentance is attributed to *gôyīm*. But *vv.* 14-15 have nothing to say about repentance which is introduced only in the secondary qualification of *v.* 15 in *vv.* 16-17. Lowth too was aware that the oracles on foreign nations prophesied Yahweh's judgement against them. He cited Jer. xlix 1 ff. (Ammon), Ezek. xxv 3, 6 (Ammon), 8 (Moab), 12 (Edom); Zeph. ii 8 (Moab and Ammon). The last mentioned has a special affinity with Jer. xii 14, because it has a reference to encroachment on Judah's territory (*wayyagdîlû 'al-g*^{e}*bûlām*).

[9] *Josephus VI, Loeb Classical Library* (London-Cambridge, Mass., 1937), pp. 258 f.

Verses 14-15 are generated by the poetry in *vv.* 7-13 and *naḥ^a^lāh* (*vv.* 7, 8, 9, 14, 15) serves as a stitch. The invaders who execute Yahweh's judgement on Judah are identified as neighbouring nations and a prophecy is composed on the foundation of the notices about the uprooting and resettlement of these neighbours in the oracles on foreign nations (xlviii 47, xlix 6). The vocabulary is influenced by the account which is given of Jeremiah as a prophet to the nations in i 10. Verses 16-17 are a subsequent qualifying of the promise of restoration, and it is interesting that we know from Kimchi that there was a discussion about the right exegesis of xlix 6: that, according to one interpretation, it was not to be understood as an unconditional promise but as one made to those who would "learn the ways of Israel". We may conclude that *vv.* 16-17 arise out of this kind of interest and concern: *v.* 15 is one exegesis of *w^e^šabtî š^e^bût ʿammôn* (*môʾāb*) and *vv.* 16-17 is another. As Kimchi observed, "learning the ways of my people" (*v.* 16) presupposes a community of Jews purified of idolatry and every other form of disloyalty to Yahweh. *w^e^ʾet-bêt y^e^hûdāh ʾettôš mittôkām*, on the interpretation which has been adopted, is indicative of the effective separation of the Jews from surrounding Gentiles. Such a state of affairs could perhaps be said to exist in a Jewish community in Babylon, enforcing its separation and apartness from its Gentile environment by a stringent interpretation of Yahwism, but the geographical area which is envisaged in *vv.* 14-15 is Judah and its surroundings. Hence we should think in terms of the post-exilic Jerusalem community: *vv.* 14-15 are post-exilic and *vv.* 16-17 are post-exilic *a fortiori*. This is a judgement which differs from Kimchi only in so far as it assumes that *vv.* 14-17 are *ex eventu* prophecy and a post-exilic composition. Otherwise it supposes like Kimchi that *vv.* 14-17 are to be referred to a post-exilic setting. The neighbours who gloated over Judah's misfortunes and took advantage of her weakness when she suffered dismemberment and exile (cp. Obad. 10 ff.; Zeph. ii 8) themselves suffered in turn, as the prophet Jeremiah was believed to have predicted. The post-exilic Jerusalem community, separated from the corrupting influences of her neighbours, has nothing to fear, even when these are restored to their former territories, as scripture predicted that they would be. But, according to *vv.* 16-17, their restoration is to be entertained only so far as they swear allegiance to Yahweh and are integrated in his community.

Wherever the kind of activity uncovered in iii 6-11 and xii 14-17 is present in the book of Jeremiah, the hypothesis that there is a poetic nucleus is justified. Moreover, this is a type of enlargement and elaboration which operates within narrow contextual limits and does not have the comprehensive, systematic theological objectives which it is customary to ascribe to prose redactions of the book of Jeremiah. The general contention of the article is that we should take more account of expansions of such limited scope in our efforts to understand the complicated and untidy processes by which the Jeremianic *corpus* was developed. A type of expansion through commentary or exegesis which attaches itself to pre-existing elements of the *corpus* has been neglected or, at least, underestimated. In so far as the growth of the *corpus* was achieved by processes of this kind we should not expect too much in the way of coherence or artistic unity from the end product. Those who claim a systematic theological activity for a Deuteronomistic editor and identify compositions in which this is realized are perhaps professing to know more of the inner workings of his mind than can be gathered from the text. They are in danger of creating systematic theological aims for the editor whom they postulate rather than extracting these from the text. In general they exaggerate the coherence of the book and underestimate its lack of cohesiveness and obscurities.

Commentaries

J. Calvin, *Praelectiones in Librum Prophetiarum Jeremia et Lamentationes* (Geneva, 1589[3]).
C. H. Cornill, *Das Buch Jeremia* (Leipzig, 1905).
B. Duhm, *Das Buch Jeremia* (Tübingen and Leipzig, 1901).
F. Giesebrecht, *Das Buch Jeremia* (Göttingen, 1894, 1907[2]).
K. H. Graf, *Der Prophet Jeremia* (Leipzig, 1862).
F. Hitzig, *Der Prophet Jeremia* (Leipzig, 1866[2]).
J. P. Hyatt, "The Book of Jeremiah", *IB* 5 (New York and Nashville, 1956).
W. Lowth, *A Commentary upon the Prophecy and Lamentations of Jeremiah* (London, 1728).
W. Rudolph, *Jeremia* (Tübingen, 1968[3]).
P. Volz, *Der Prophet Jeremia* (Leipzig, 1928[2]).
A. Weiser, *Das Buch Jeremia* (Göttingen, 1969[6]).
W. Zimmerli, *Ezechiel* i (Neukirchen, 1969).
Kimchi is cited from *Miqrā'ôt G^edôlôt*.

ESAIE LIV ET LA NOUVELLE JERUSALEM [1]

par

ROBERT MARTIN-ACHARD

Genève

Dans l'important étude qu'il a consacrée à "Jerusalem als Urbild und Abbild" (p. 224), K.-L. Schmidt déclare que la racine de la tradition juive, aussi bien apocalyptique que rabbinique, sur la Jérusalem céleste se lit dans Esaïe liv 10-13; [2] il attire ainsi notre attention sur ces quelques versets, et même sur l'ensemble d'un chapitre qui traite, comme nous le verrons, du nouveau statut de la cité de David.

C'est à dessein que j'ai évité d'utiliser l'expression aujourd'hui couramment employée de "la nouvelle Jérusalem" qui n'apparaît que rarement dans les textes anciens et jamais dans l'Ancien Testament. On ne la lit en effet que dans Test. Dan. v 12—un passage qui pourrait être glosé—, en Hen. éth. xc 29—sous la forme d'une "nouvelle maison"—et à deux reprises dans l'Apocalypse johannique: ἡ καινὴ Ἰερουσαλήμ (iii 12, xxi 2). Il existe sans doute d'autres manières de désigner la future Sion, comme la Jérusalem d'en haut ἡ ἄνω Ἰερουσαλήμ (Gal. iv 26; cf. aussi Hen. sl. lv 2; Restes des Paroles de Baruch v 33, etc.),[3] mais le silence des documents vétérotestamentaires sur ce point est d'autant plus remarquable que le prophète anonyme, responsable d'Esaïe lxv, annonce une triple activité créatrice ou recréatrice de YHWH—avec l'emploi de *bārā'*—(*vv.* 17s.), mais n'utilise l'adjectif "nouveau" (*ḥādāš*) que pour qualifier les cieux et la terre (*v.* 17), et non pour Jérusalem (*v.* 18). Il suggère peut-être de cette manière que s'il peut surgir, par l'intervention divine, un univers nouveau, il ne saurait y avoir une autre Jérusalem! De toutes

---

[1] Une bibliographie se trouve à la fin de l'article.

[2] Le même auteur signale encore d'autres passages qui font écho a Es. liv, ainsi Es. lx-lxii notamment, Ag. ii 1 ss.; Zac. i 7, 12 ss., etc.

[3] On se reportera à ce propos à la présentation de P. Volz, *Die Eschatologie der jüdischen Gemeinde im neutestamentlichen Zeitalter* (Tübingen, [2]1934; réimpression, Hildesheim, 1966), pp. 371-6 (375); E. Schürer, *The History of the Jewish People in the Age of Jesus Christ* (Revised Edition by G. Vermes, F. Miller and M. Black, avec une bibliographie mise à jour) 2 (Edinburgh, 1979), pp. 529-30.

façons le prophète n'insiste pas sur l'apparition d'une nouvelle Sion, mais sur la transformation de sa situation, caractérisée par la joie et l'enthousiasme (*v.* 18), et de celle de ses habitants (*vv.* 19ss.).

L'expression "la nouvelle Jérusalem" est d'ailleurs ambiguë, car il s'agit de préciser en quoi consiste cette nouveauté que l'on attribue à la future cité de Dieu, ce qui la distingue de la Jérusalem actuelle, faut-il dire de la première ou de l'ancienne Jérusalem? [4] Or les textes intertestamentaires et autres qui traitent de l'avenir de la ville de David révèlent des vues différentes, voire opposées à cet égard; le judaïsme de l'époque gréco-romaine est loin d'être unanime sur ce point comme sur tant d'autres, et d'un auteur à l'autre les perspectives varient. Certains textes, comme 4 Esd. x, se bornent à envisager une transformation de la cité terrestre, ainsi son agrandissement et son épanouissement, mais sa grandeur future, si importante soit-elle, reste dans les normes de ce monde, alors que d'autres passages insistent sur le caractère transcendant de la nouvelle Jérusalem, voire sur sa préexistence dans les lieux célestes où elle se confond plus ou moins avec le paradis, c'est ce que suggèrent 4 Esd. xiii 36; Hen. eth. xc 29; Test. Dan. v; Apo. syr. Bar. iv; 4 Esd. viii 52 etc.: ici la relation entre l'ancienne capitale du royaume de Juda et la métropole céleste et bienheureuse est à la fois distendue et contrastée; la Sion à venir n'a que peu de points communs avec le centre urbain où s'est dressé jadis le Temple de YHWH.[5]

Cette diversité de vues s'est prolongée par la suite et sans doute jusqu'à aujourd'hui; elle n'est pas sans conséquence religieuse, voire politique. On peut dire que d'une façon générale la tradition juive, avec le courant rabbinique, s'est efforcée de maintenir un contact entre la Jérusalem future ou "d'en haut" et celle d'aujourd'hui ou "d'en bas", comme l'illustre la belle parole attribuée à R. Joḥanan

[4] Le même problème se pose au sujet de l'expression "la nouvelle alliance" en Jer. xxxi 31-34.

[5] Sur le développement de la tradition relative à Jérusalem, on consultera en particulier A. Causse, "Le mythe de la nouvelle Jérusalem du Deutéro-Esaïe à la IIIe Sibylle", *RHPhR* 18 (1938), pp. 377-414; "La vision de la Nouvelle Jérusalem (Esaïe LX) et la signification sociologique des assemblées de fête et des pèlerinages dans l'Orient sémitique", *Mélanges R. Dussaud* (Paris, 1939), pp. 739-50; "De la Jérusalem terrestre à la Jérusalem céleste", *RHPhR* 27 (1947), pp. 12-36; cf. aussi N. W. Porteous, "Jerusalem-Zion: The Growth of a Symbol", *FS. W. Rudolph* (Tübingen, 1961), pp. 235-52; G. Fohrer-E. Lohse, "Σιών", *ThWNT* 7 (1964), pp. 291-338 (324 ss.) (bibliographie); R. Martin-Achard, "De la Jérusalem terrestre à la Jérusalem céleste", *Colloque sur la Ville* (Cartigny-Genève, 1979), à paraître.

(mort en 279) selon laquelle Dieu aurait dit ne pas vouloir entrer dans la Jérusalem d'en haut tant qu'il ne pourra le faire dans la Jérusalem d'en bas,—qui reste précisément à rebâtir—, subordonnant ainsi l'apothéose qui doit marquer la fin des temps à la reconstruction concrète de la cité terrestre,[6] alors que la tradition chrétienne, à la suite de l'apocalyptique juive, insistera surtout sur la spécificité de la future Sion, sur son originalité par rapport à l'actuelle métropole juive, et accentuera ainsi la distance entre l'ancienne ville de David et la Jérusalem de Dieu qui descendra du ciel toute parée de gloire à la fin des temps (Ap. Jn. xxi); dans cette perspective il n'est pas étonnant que la nouvelle Jérusalem soit destinée à remplacer l'ancienne et qu'elle se soit souvent plus ou moins confondue avec l'Eglise du Christ.[7]

Les textes vétérotestamentaires ne vont pas jusque là; les déclarations exiliques et postexiliques envisagent essentiellement le renouveau de Jérusalem à la suite des malheurs que celle-ci a connus et non sa transformation en quelque réalité céleste.[8] En des termes variés, mais convergents, ils annoncent que Sion sera reconstruite, repeuplée et réintégrée dans le plan de YHWH; Esaïe liv ne fait pas exception à cet égard. La cité détruite sera rebâtie; la ville désertée doit être à nouveau occupée par ses enfants revenus de toutes parts; la métropole humiliée connaîtra sa réhabilitation, et sa gloire à venir sera à la dimension de son abaissement actuel, la Jérusalem coupable sera pardonnée et purifiée de ses péchés, sa sainteté lui sera rendue . . . Ce retournement dans la situation de Sion est précisément le thème d'Esaïe liv qui est bâti sur cinq contrastes, comme Bonnard (pp. 288ss.)

[6] Cf. H. L. Strack-P. Billerbeck, *Kommentar zum NT aus Talmud und Midrasch* (München, 1926) 3, p. 573. La tradition s'inspire particulièrement à ce sujet d'Es. xlix 16 et de Ps. cxxii 3 (cf. Targum s. Ps. cxxii 3; Taʿan. 5a, etc.); cf. tout dernièrement, E. Starobinski-Safran, "Aspects de Jérusalem dans les écrits rabbiniques", *RThPh* 112 (1980), pp. 151-61. Sur un point de vue juif actuel à propos de Jérusalem, cf. A. Safran, *Israël dans le temps et dans l'espace* (Paris, 1980), pp. 125 ss., 177 ss.

[7] Un exemple de cette équivalence entre la Nouvelle Jérusalem et l'Eglise se rencontre dans l'étude récente de P. Harnoncourt, "'Jerusalem' in den Liedern des neuen Gesangbuches", *Memoria Jerusalem, Freundesgabe F. Sauer* (Graz, 1977), pp. 205-22. Comme l'indique son titre, la plupart des contributions à cet intéressant volume sont consacrées à Jérusalem. Cf. aussi E. Lamirande, art. "Jérusalem céleste", *Dict. de Spiritualité* 8 (Paris, 1974), col. 944-58 (bibliographie).

[8] Cf. en plus des oracles du 2e Esaïe, les déclarations d'Ezéchiel (Ez. xvi, xl ss.), celles d'un auteur anonyme qui prolonge le message du 2e Esaïe (Es. lx ss., où sont longuement évoqués la reconstruction de Sion, son repeuplement, sa réhabilitation, sa glorification) et les propos, plus brefs, de Zacharie (i 14 ss., ii 5 ss., 16), etc.

l'a bien mis en évidence: la cité stérile devient la mère d'une postérité innombrable (1-3); celle qui était comme veuve est à nouveau épousée par le Seigneur (4-6); l'abandonnée est rétablie dans l'alliance indéfectible de son Dieu (7-10); la ville en ruines verra une éblouissante reconstruction (11-13); l'opprimée sera désormais à l'abri de tout danger (14-17). Mais malgré la description enthousiaste du 2e Esaïe, celui-ci ne dépasse pas l'horizon terrestre, et la Jérusalem dont il parle n'est pas—pas encore—d'essence différente de celle dont il mesure aujourd'hui la misère et la déchéance. Il conviendrait donc, en tous les cas au niveau de l'Ancien Testament, de parler *du nouveau statut* que YHWH réserve à sa cité plutôt que de la nouvelle Jérusalem.

Traduction

v. 1 Crie de joie, stérile, (toi) qui n'as pas enfanté[a],
éclate en cris de joie[b], jubile, (toi) qui n'as pas mis au monde,
car plus nombreux seront les fils de la délaissée
que les fils de l'épousée, dit YHWH.
v. 2 Elargis l'espace de ta tente,
que les toiles de tes demeures soient distendues[c],
sans restriction[d],
allonge tes cordages et affermis tes piquets,
v. 3 car à droite et à gauche tu te répandras[e];
ta descendance prendra possession des nations[f],
ils peupleront des villes désolées.

*

v. 4 Ne crains pas, car tu ne seras pas honteuse,
ne te sens pas confuse, car tu n'auras pas à rougir,
car la honte de ton adolescence, tu l'oublieras,
et l'opprobre de ton veuvage, tu ne t'en souviendras plus,
v. 5 car celui qui t'a fait est ton époux[g],
YHWH Ṣebaot est son nom;
le Saint d'Israël est ton rédempteur,
on l'appelle le Dieu de toute la terre.
v. 6 Car comme une femme délaissée,
à l'esprit accablé, YHWH t'a (r)appelée;
"La femme de la jeunesse serait-elle répudiée?"[h]
dit ton Dieu.

*

v. 7 Un bref instant[i], je t'ai délaissée,
mais dans de grandes compassions, je te recueillerai;
v. 8 dans un débordement[j] d'indignation, j'ai caché
ma face, un instant, loin de toi,
mais avec une amitié indéfectible[k], j'ai compassion de toi,
dit ton rédempteur, YHWH,
v. 9 Il en sera comme aux jours de Noé[l] pour moi,
quand j'ai juré
que les eaux de Noé[m] ne déferleraient plus sur la terre,
ainsi je jure
de ne pas m'indigner contre toi, ni de te menacer.
v. 10 Car les montagnes peuvent chanceller,
les collines vaciller,
mon amitié, loin de toi, ne chancellera pas,
mon alliance de paix ne vacillera pas,
dit YHWH, qui a compassion de toi.

*

v. 11 Humiliée, secouée, inconsolée,
Voici que moi je vais cerner de fard[n] tes pierres,
je te fonderai[o] sur des saphirs;
v. 12 je ferai tes créneaux[p] en rubis,
tes portes en escarboucles[q],
et toute ton enceinte en pierres ornementales[r];
v. 13 tous tes fils seront les disciples de YHWH,
grande sera la prospérité de tes bâtisseurs[s],
v. 14 par la justice tu seras affermie[t].

*

Loin de toi[u] l'oppression, que tu n'auras pas à craindre,
et la terreur, car elle ne t'approchera pas!
v. 15 Voici qu'on assaille, sans que cela vienne de moi,
qui t'assaille, contre toi tombera![v]
v. 16 Voici[w] que moi j'ai créé l'artisan
qui souffle sur un feu de braises,
et en extrait un instrument[x] pour un usage déterminé,
mais c'est moi (aussi) qui ai créé le destructeur pour ruiner.
v. 17 Tout instrument (de guerre) façonné contre toi sera inefficace,
et toute langue qui s'élèvera en justice contre toi,
tu la convaincras de culpabilité.

Telle est la part des serviteurs de YHWH,
leur justice (vient) de moi, oracle de YHWH.

Notes sur la traduction

[a] Ou plutôt, avec Lack, p. 192, "la stérile, celle qui n'a pas enfanté ... celle qui n'a pas eu les douleurs" qui sont autant de sobriquets donnés à Jérusalem par ses voisins malveillants à la suite de 587.

[b] *rinnā* manque dans la LXX et est parfois supprimé, ainsi par Marti, Köhler, etc. pour des raisons de rythme, mais ce substantif se trouve généralement associé à *pṣḥ* (Es. xliv 23, xlix 13, lv 12).

[c] Certaines versions comme la LXX, Syr., Vulg. ont lu l'impératif, soit *haṭṭī*, "distends", en accord avec les autres impératifs du *v*. 2; d'autres versions, comme Aq., Sym., Th. ont lu *yuṭṭū*, "soient distendues", traduction que nous adoptons avec divers exégètes, dont North (1964), p. 246. Le texte massorétique a *yaṭṭū*, "qu'on les distende", ainsi Bonnard. Dernièrement Dahood, pp. 383-4, propose de voir dans *yṭy*, attesté par 1 Q Is^{a}, un impératif yiphil. Williams, pp. 93-8 (96 s.), veut expliquer l'expression "élargis l'espace de ta tente" par un recours à l'égyptien; l'expression évoquerait la liberté.

[d] litt. "ne retiens pas". Pour Chouraqui, "ne lésine pas".

[e] *prṣ*, faire une brèche, d'où s'étendre, se répandre (cf. Gen. xxviii 14; Ex. i 12; Os. iv 10, etc.).

[f] *yrš*, soumettre, prendre possession, hériter—1 Q Is^{a} a le pluriel—(cf. Gen. xv 3 s., etc.). Les exégètes s'interrogent sur le caractère militaire ou pacifique de cette occupation comme la variété des traductions proposées en témoignent; ainsi pour ne donner que quelques exemples en français, on lit "ta race va déposséder des nations" (*BJ*); "ta descendance prendra possession des nations" (Segond); "ta race évincera des nations" (*BP*); "ta semence déshérite des nations" (Chouraqui); "ta descendance héritera des nations" (*TOB*). Sur *v*. 3b, cf. Beuken, p. 39.

[g] Les désinences du pluriel (*-ayik*) étonnent; on l'explique généralement par un pluriel de majesté, puisqu'il s'agit de YHWH. On pense parfois que le *yod* originel est réapparu dans *ʿōśayik* et que *bō*^{ʿa}*layik* a été construit par assonance avec lui, ce qui pouvait permettre aussi d'éviter la formule *ba*^{ʿa}*lēk* qui aurait amené la confusion entre YHWH et le dieu Baal! (cf. par exemple, Bonnard, p. 287; North, p. 246, etc.) 1 Q Is^{a} a ajouté le *yod* au-dessus de *ʿśwk*.

[h] Cette "question-réponse" mise dans la bouche de YHWH suppose une réponse évidente, qui ne peut être que négative. A propos de *q*^{e}*rā'āk*, Beuken (pp. 36 s., n. 1) estime que YHWH envisage le rappel de la femme, alors que North (p. 250) pense que le prophète fait allusion au fait que l'élection d'Israël (Os. ii; Jer. ii), dans le passé, demeure toujours valable.

[i] Au lieu de *brgʿ* "un (bref) instant", Targ. et Syr. ont lu *brgẓ* "dans une (brève) excitation", en accord avec l'indignation de 8a.

[j] *šeṣep* est un hapax, qu'on rapproche de la racine *šṭp* qui évoque l'idée de débordement; il annonce le motif des "eaux du déluge" (*v*. 9), selon Bonnard. On explique parfois ce substantif, choisi sans doute en fonction du mot suivant, par *šsp* qui signifie couper, détacher; on pourrait alors traduire "dans un coup d'exaspération" ce que la LXX (ἐν θυμῷ μικρῷ) et Aq. (ἐν ἀτομῷ ὀργῆς) semblent avoir compris. La Syr. a lu *b*^{e}*šēpeṣ* (akk. *šipṣu*). Cf. Whybray, p. 186, qui cite North, p. 247.

[k] Je préfère "amitié indéfectible" (Bonnard: "amitié sans fin") à "un amour éternel" (*BJ*); "une bienveillance durable" (*BP*); "la grâce de perpétuité" (Chouraqui), etc. 1 Q Is^{a} lit *ḥsdy*, c.à.d., "mon amitié" (cf. *v*. 10).

[l] Lire *kīmē-nōaḥ* "comme les jours de Noé" avec Targ., Syr., Aq., Th., Vulg. plutôt que *k*^{e}*mē-nōaḥ* "comme les eaux de Noé", avec la plupart des manuscrits hébreux et la LXX.

[m] *mē-nōaḥ*, "les eaux de Noé" manque dans la LXX.

[n] *pūk* poudre fine, fard pour les yeux: cf. 2 R. ix 30; Jer. iv 30; Job xlii 14; (1 Chr. xxix 2?;) on comprend parfois ce terme dans le sens de "mortier" (1 Chr. xxix 2) ou on le corrige en *bannōpek*, pierre précieuse, comme la turquoise du Sinaï. On obtient ainsi des traductions différentes: "Je garnirai tes pierres de stuc" (Segond); "je vais poser tes pierres sur des escarboucles" (*BJ*); "je mettrai un cerne de fard autour de tes pierres" (*TOB*).

[o] On lit parfois, au lieu de *wīsadtīk* "je te fonderai sur des saphirs" (*TM*), *wīsōdōtayik* "et tes fondations sur des saphirs" (ainsi *BJ*) en accord avec 1 Q Is[a] et la LXX.

[p] *šimšōtayik* litt. "tes soleils", en fait tes créneaux en forme de soleil.

[q] *kadkōd*, probablement rubis, cf. aussi Ez. xxvii 16; *ʾeqdāḥ*, peut-être escarboucle ou béryl.

[r] *ʾabnē-ḥēpeṣ* litt. "pierres de plaisir", c.à.d. pierres précieuses, pierres ornementales; la même expression se trouve en Sir. xlv 11, l 9; 1 Q M v, 6, 9, 14, xii 13.

[s] *šālōm* dans le sens de prospérité, plénitude. Avec 1 Q Is[a] (*bwnyky*), lire *bōnayık* "tes bâtisseurs" plutôt que *bānayık* "tes fils", déjà attesté en 13a; il existe d'ailleurs un lien entre ces deux termes (cf. Es. xlix 17).

[t] *ṣ*^{e}*dāqā* est parallèle à *šālōm* (*v.* 13b) et comme souvent dans 2 Esaïe équivaut à "salut" (cf. par exemple Bonnard, pp. 65 s.).

[u] *raḥ*^{a}*qī* litt. "tiens-toi loin de l'oppression", un ordre qui équivaut à une promesse d'avenir sûr!

[v] *ʾepes* manque dans la LXX et la Syr.; il faut lire avec 1 Q Is[a] *mēʾittī* et non *mēʾōtī*; plus loin les mots *mī-gārʾittāk* ne se trouvent pas davantage dans la LXX; la tradition textuelle de ce verset paraît mal conservée.

[w] Lire *hinnē* avec Q et 1 Q IS[a].

[x] Sans doute un instrument de guerre, forgé pour détruire, mais à son tour anéanti! Schwarz, pp. 254-5, propose de lire *b*^{e}*lī*, corruption, au lieu de *k*^{e}*lī*, qui s'accorderait, selon lui, mieux avec *lāšōn*.

L'aspect formel d'Esaïe liv

Esaïe liv témoigne, sauf peut-être dans ses dernières lignes où le texte, notamment au *v.* 15, paraît avoir été mal conservé, des qualités esthétiques de son auteur. Avec le brio qu'on lui connaît, le prophète, comme au chapitre xlvii qui lui répond, utilise ici les diverses ressources de la poésie hébraïque: interpellations, répétitions, redondances, jeux de mots, assonances, . . . et les met au service d'une idée qui lui tient particulièrement à coeur: le retour en grâce de Jérusalem auprès de son Dieu dont l'amitié lui est garantie à jamais.

Le 2e Esaïe ouvre son poème par une interpellation insistante (*v.* 1) sur laquelle il reviendra encore au *v.* 11; les impératifs joyeux dont il se sert à trois reprises (*ronnī*; *piṣ*^{e}*ḥī*; *ṣah*^{a}*lī*) donnent le ton à l'ensemble de son intervention[9] et anticipent sur d'autres impératifs où se retrouvent une des formules les plus familières du prophète: "Ne crains pas, car ..." (Es. xli 10, 13s., xliii 1, 5, xliv 2, li 7, 12, etc.; cf. aussi *v.* 14.[10] Il use aussi fréquemment de l'assonance, et c'est doute sans pour cette raison qu'il choisit l'hapax *šeṣep* pour accompagner *qeṣep* pour évoquer le débordement d'indignation qui a, un instant, saisi YHWH contre les siens (*v.* 8). Au *v.* 4a, comme le remarque Lack (1973), on entend à deux reprises "*altī ... kīlōt*" et une ligne plus loin *ʿᵃlūmayik* répond à *ʾalmᵉnūtayik*. Certains pensent qu'au *v.* 5, *bōʿᵃlayik* est dû à *ʿōśayik* et tout lecteur du *v.* 6 a noté que la femme *ʿᵃzūbā* est aussi qualifiée de *ʿᵃṣūbat rūaḥ*. Ces quelques exemples suffisent pour donner une idée de la maîtrise avec laquelle le 2e Esaïe use de sa langue, mais Lack, qui continue son analyse, aussi minutieuse que subtile, découvre encore parmi d'autres indices de l'art du prophète le fait qu'au *v.* 11c *marbîṣ* est l'exacte inversion de *sappīrīm* (*rbṣ/spr*) ou encore que *mōṣīʾ* (*v.* 16b) "commande dans le stique suivant *yûṣar* et *yiṣlāḥ*" et que le "*š* de *mašḥît* se prolonge au *v.* 17 dans *lāšôn-mišpāṭ-taršîʿî*"; il voit même dans la frequence de la consonne *m*, attestée 14 fois dans les *vv.* 9s., comme une référence prolongée aux eaux (*mē*) du déluge, tandis que le triple *ḥ* de 16a, complété par un double *ḥ* à la fin de 16b, lui semble évoquer le "travail du forgeron soufflant sur le feu".[11]

Le Second Esaïe affectionne les répétitions de termes qui suggèrent que les diverses strophes d'Esaïe liv constituent un ensemble solidement coordonné; des mots ou des expressions-crochets ou des renvois sont répartis dans les 17 versets qui composent son poème: le radical *ʿāzab* se lit au *v.* 6 comme au *v.* 7; *ʾal-tīrᵉʾī* au *v.* 4 devient *lōʾ tīrāʾī* au *v.* 14; *gōʾᵃlēk* est répété (*vv.* 5 et 8) de même que la formule *hinnē ʾānōkī* (*vv.* 11b et 16). La particule *kī* accompagne toute la première partie de la déclaration du prophète (*vv.* 1-10) et se retrouve à deux reprises au *v.* 14 alors que l'expression *ʾāmar YHWH*, d'ailleurs soigneusement développée, se lit aux *vv.* 1, 6, 8 et 10 et que les derniers mots du chapitre *nᵉʾūm YHWH* lui font écho.[12]

---

[9] On notera la fréquence des sons *a/i* dans cette ouverture du poème (v. 1a) auxquels répondent les sons *o/u/a* en 11a.

[10] Pour l'analyse des genres littéraires dans les *vv.* 1 ss., cf. en particulier Melugin, pp. 169-71, qui renvoie souvent aux travaux de Westermann.

[11] Pour toute cette analyse, cf. notamment Lack, pp. 190-7.

[12] On remarquera le soin avec lequel les termes qui qualifient le Dieu YHWH sont choisis: YHWH (*v.* 1) devient "ton Dieu" (*v.* 6), "ton rédempteur" (*v.* 8) et pour conclure "qui a compassion de toi" (*v.* 10); plus le prophète parle, plus

Le rythme sert à sa façon l'intention du poète, mais sur ce point délicat l'accord est loin d'être fait. Pour ne citer que deux exemples, si en 1923, Köhler, moyennant quelques légères modifications de la tradition massorétique, retrouvait dans Es. liv le plus généralement des vers de 3 + 3 accents (et parfois 2 + 2 + 2) jusqu'au *v.* 14a et pour la fin uniquement des stiques de 2 + 2 accents, un demi-siècle plus tard, en 1973, Lack estime que la rythmique d'Es. liv est plus diversifiée dans sa première partie, mais qu'une ligne de 3 + 4 accents y est relativement fréquente (ainsi dans les *vv.* 1-2a et 4b); [13] il remarque que le rythme utilisé par le prophète épouse parfois de façon rigoureuse sa pensée, ainsi "L'élargissement de la tente (2a) s'accompagne d'un mètre allongé (3 + 4). Par contre, le renforcement des piquets (2b) est marqué par un rythme bref (2 + 2)" et aussi "par une structure syntaxique d'une symétrie chiastique parfaite ... et par une séquence vocalique extrêmement voisine d'un hémistiche à l'autre" (p. 193). Le 2e Esaïe a mis ainsi tout son art au service du message qu'il désire communiquer à ses contemporains en exil.[14]

La composition d'Esaïe liv

Pour des raisons de commodité, vu la longueur du chapitre, ou à la suite d'une analyse d'Esaïe liv, les critiques divisent parfois la déclaration du prophète de l'exil en deux parties qu'ils traitent séparément: 1-10 et 11ss., et seuls ces derniers versets évoqueraient "la nouvelle Jérusalem",[15] comme la remarque de K. L. Schmidt, citée plus haut, nous y invite d'ailleurs. Récemment Westermann s'est demandé, sans se prononcer définitivement, si on pouvait défendre l'unité d'Esaïe liv, comme Elliger l'a proposé et comme dernièrement encore Beuken a cherché à le démontrer.[16]

---

il insiste sur la sollicitude quasi maternelle de YHWH à l'égard de celle qu'il interpelle.

[13] Köhler, pp. 51-5; Lack, p. 191, qui remarque un certain flottement au *v.* 9 (style narratif!); pour les *vv.* 11-17, Lack, p. 196, s'en tient aux propositions de Köhler: 3 + 3 accents à la base des *vv.* 11-14 et 2 + 2 pour les *vv.* 14-17.

[14] Avec d'autres auteurs, Westermann, p. 218, insiste sur la corrélation entre l'aspect formel d'Es. liv et son contenu.

[15] Cf. les titres donnés au commentaire des *vv.* 11 ss. chez North, 1956; Muilenburg, 1956; Fohrer, 1964; Schoors, 1973; Herbert, 1975; etc.

[16] Elliger, pp. 135 ss.; Westermann, p. 223; Beuken, pp. 29-70, qui a soutenu la thèse qu'à travers Es. liv l'auteur vise la même réalité, évoquée à trois moments de son existence, et qui n'est autre que le peuple d'Israël lui-même, représenté et personnalisé par la femme-cité; il s'appuie notamment sur la notion de "personnalité corporative" (cf. ses conclusions pp. 63 et 70).

A lire ce poème attentivement on peut reconnaître qu'il se partage en plusieurs péricopes ou strophes dont il s'agit d'établir les limites respectives et les relations profondes. Les exégètes sont loin d'être unanimes à cet égard comme l'examen de quelques commentaires en témoigne: Fohrer subdivise Es. liv en 5 morceaux: 1-3, 4-6, 7-8, 9-10 et 11-17; Westermann admet que les *vv.* 1 à 10 forment un ensemble, mais il voit par contre en 11-13a et 13bss. (précédé de 14a) deux péricopes indépendantes; Melugin estime que le chapitre liv (avec le suivant) est constitué d'une série d'unités indépendantes, comme l'examen des genres littéraires utilisés en témoigne, mais rassemblées par la suite, et de façon plus ou moins lâche, autour du thème de l'alliance.[17]

Pour ma part, je défendrai l'opinion qu'Esaïe liv est pour l'essentiel une œuvre d'un seul tenant qui a pour auteur le Second Esaïe, comme déjà les remarques sur l'aspect formel de ce chapitre nous conduisent à le penser. Cette unité fondamentale n'exclut nullement que le prophète ait utilisé des formes littéraires différentes pour transmettre son message—le contraire serait étonnant—et que sa pensée tout au long des 17 versets que compte ce texte progresse au lieu de se répéter! La diversité que chacun peut constater dans la forme comme dans le contenu d'Esaïe liv ne met pas en question son unité.[18]

En fait, le 2e Esaïe ne cesse de s'adresser à une même personne ou réalité, sans jamais la nommer explicitement,[19] qu'il évoque successivement en tant que mère, femme et cité.[20] Si son poème peut se subdiviser en 5 parties distinctes: 1-3, 4-6, 7-10, 11-14a, 14b-17, son auteur a soin de marquer par des mots-renvois les liens qui existent entre les diverses strophes et d'utiliser certaines formules comme d'un refrain pour souligner la continuité de son développement: la formule lapidaire, contestée à tort, par laquelle il conclut

[17] Cf. les commentaires ad loc. Melugin, p. 169, présente encore d'autres variantes sur la division du chapitre.

[18] Certains exégètes traitent d'Es. liv comme d'un tout, ainsi Kissane, 1943; McKenzie, 1968, qui suggère cependant que les derniers versets (15-17) pourraient être une glose en prose; Bonnard, 1972, etc.

[19] Le Targum précisera à cinq reprises (*vv.* 1 [2x], 10, 15, 17) que le prophète s'adresse à Jérusalem. Cf. aussi Gal. iv 26 s. qui se réfère au *v.* 1.

[20] Cf. à ce propos l'intéressante étude de Beuken, citée plus haut. Il me semble cependant que ce chapitre liv d'Esaïe concerne bien la cité de Jérusalem, tout en se rappelant que celle-ci porte en elle le destin du peuple de YHWH, son avenir en particulier, comme son passé; elle a pour lui une signification quasi sacramentelle.

(*v.* 17c),[21] résume enfin son point de vue, qu'il a présenté avec autant de chaleur que de rigueur.[22]

On notera précisément l'insistance du prophète: il prononce une sorte de plaidoyer, avec des répétitions et des redondances qui sont tout à fait dans son style: les *vv.* 4-6 reprennent et complètent la strophe précédente; les *vv.* 7-8 se prolongent en 9s.; les *vv.* 11s. et 14ss. se conjuguent pour évoquer le statut final de celle à qui YHWH s'adresse. Esaïe liv s'ouvre ainsi par une double invitation à la joie et à la sérénité dont le prophète donne immédiatement les motifs (1-3 et 4-6); il se poursuit avec les *vv.* 7 à 10 qui constituent la charnière, le cœur de la déclaration prophétique en révélant sur quoi ou mieux sur qui repose la destinée passée, présente et future de l'interpellée: YHWH lui-même prend la parole pour se référer d'abord à l'histoire des relations entre sa partenaire et lui (*vv.* 7s.), il affirme ensuite que la décision qu'il a prise en sa faveur est irrévocable (*vv.* 9s.) si bien que ce que le 2e Esaïe a déclaré jusqu'ici et ce qu'il pourra ajouter par la suite se fonde sur cette prise de position du Dieu d'Israël. Les deux dernières strophes (*vv.* 11-14a et 14b-17) tirent les conséquences de la volonté que YHWH vient d'exprimer dans deux domaines particuliers; elles évoquent l'une la splendeur à laquelle la cité (de Dieu) est promise, l'autre la sécurité totale qui lui est garantie.

Le prophète a ainsi admirablement organisé les divers éléments qui forment le contenu de ce chapitre de telle sorte qu'il n'est pas possible d'en lire les premières lignes sans tenir compte des dernières, ni de se référer au statut futur de Jérusalem (*vv.* 11ss.) en ignorant les déclarations qui inaugurent Esaïe liv (*vv.* 1-10).

Le contenu d'Esaïe liv

La 1ère strophe (*1-3*) s'ouvre par une formule hymnique familière au prophète de l'exil (cf. Es. xliv 23, xlix 13, lii 9) qui implique pour celle qui est ainsi interpellée un changement radical dans sa situation.[23] Jérusalem n'est pas explicitement désignée, mais il ne

---

[21] Ainsi la succession des *kī* dans les *vv.* 1 ss., la formule répétée *ʾāmar YHWH* (*vv.* 1-10), l'interpellation en la à laquelle 11a fait écho . . .

[22] Le pluriel *ʿabdē* a fait problème (cf. par ex. Whybray, p. 190) mais il est déjà motivé par le pluriel de *limmūd* au *v.* 13a; les disciples de YHWH sont en même temps ses serviteurs, ils sont les fils et les bâtisseurs de Sion selon le plan divin. Cf. l'étude récente de B. Keller-R. Voeltzel, "Les 'Serviteurs' dans le Livre d'Esaïe", *Mélanges E. Jacob*, *RHPhR* 59 (1979), pp. 413-26 (423).

[23] Sur les genres littéraires attestés en Es. liv, cf. notamment Westermann,

fait pas de doute, comme le Targum l'a précisé, que le 2e Esaïe pense à l'ancienne capitale du royaume de Juda qui apparaît comme la mère de tous ceux qui se réclament de YHWH. A la suite du désastre qui a marqué la chute de Sion, celle-ci est comme une femme qui a perdu ses enfants ou, ce qui revient au même, qui n'en a jamais eus. Le *v.* 1a fait écho aux quolibets dont les voisins de Juda ont accablé la ville vaincue ("stérile, incapable d'enfanter" Lack) en même temps qu'à la plainte des survivants qui s'exprime notamment dans les Lamentations (cf. Lam. i 1, 13, 16). Ici encore le message du prophète se présente comme une réponse aux doléances et aux questions de ses contemporains.[24] A la situation actuelle, le Second Esaïe oppose l'avenir et la transformation totale que connaîtra Jérusalem, grâce à l'intervention divine (*v.* 1b); le *v.* 2 appelle la cité à accueillir ses enfants qui reviendront à elle en masse; comme une femme nomade, responsable de l'installation du campement, il lui faut faire de la place en allongeant les cordages et en consolidant les pieux; ses fils doivent se répandre dans toute la région (Gen. xxviii 14, xiii 14-17) et en (re)prendre possession d'une manière ou de l'autre (*v.* 3). La Terre Sainte est comme ré-occupée par ses légitimes propriétaires (Dt.).[25]

On notera que le prophète, pour décrire le sort futur de la cité de David, fait appel ici comme en d'autres occasions à la tradition patriarcale, il évoque le motif de la naissance quasi miraculeuse si familier aux récits de la Genèse et semble s'intéresser tout spécialement à Sara;[26] il inaugure par ailleurs un thème qui fera fortune dans la tradition juive, celui de l'extension de Jérusalem (cf. aussi Jer. xxxi 37-39).[27]

---

pp. 217 ss.; du même auteur, "Sprache und Struktur der Prophetie Deuterojesaja", *Forschung am Alten Testament* (München, 1964), pp. 92-170; Melugin, pp. 169 ss., etc.

[24] Ce point mis en évidence par H. E. von Waldow, *Anlass und Hintergrund des Verkündigung des Deuterojesaja*, a été dès lors souvent souligné.

[25] Sur le v. 3b, cf. Beuken, pp. 38 s., qui évoque à ce propos des textes comme Gen. xv 7 s., xxviii 4, xxii 17, xxiv 60 et comme Num. xxxiii 52; Deut. iv 38, ix 1, xi 23, etc. La tradition patriarcale semble être comme relayée par la théologie du Deutéronome (cf. aussi Whybray, pp. 184 s.).

[26] Le terme *ʿaqārā* se retrouve précisément dans la Genèse (Gen. xi 30, xxv 21, xxix 31; cf. aussi 1 Sam. ii 5; Ps. cxiii 9) et le rapprochement avec Gen. xi 30 est significatif. Beuken, pp. 30, 37 ss., qui renvoie à ce sujet à l'étude de J. van der Merwe, *Pentateuchtradities in die prediking van Deuterojesaja* (Groningen, 1956), rappelle qu'en Es. li 1 ss. il est aussi question de Sara. La mention de la tente serait-elle encore une allusion à l'époque patriarcale? (cf. aussi le thème de l'installation de la tente, Es. xxxiii 20 et Jer. x 20).

[27] Cf. à ce sujet, Volz, p. 372, qui cite Hen. éth. xc 29, 36; Pesikta K. 12

La 2e strophe (*4-6*) offre une certaine analogie avec la précédente, mais elle a la forme caractéristique d'un oracle de salut, ici redoublé. Elle traite un autre aspect de la détresse de la ville de David et de ses habitants, l'humiliation.[28] Ainsi que dans d'autres déclarations où il utilise le même genre littéraire (Es. xl 9, xli 10, 13s., xliii 1, 5, etc.), le 2e Esaïe indique que YHWH a pris au sérieux la prière de ses frères et l'exauce. La honte que Jérusalem connaît du fait de sa défaite—l'échec s'accompagne quasi-automatiquement de déshonneur—doit disparaître (*v.* 4). On remarquera l'insistance du prophète sur ce point, pas moins de cinq expressions se réfèrent à la confusion de la cité, qui est comme une femme stérile, abandonnée ou violée (cf. Gen. xxx 23; 2 Sam. xiii 13). Le 2e Esaïe fait allusion à deux moments où Jérusalem a été abaissée; on pense parfois que le temps de l'adolescence vise la servitude en Egypte et celui du veuvage l'occupation babylonienne (par exemple Bonnard), mais la question reste ouverte.[29]

Cette double humiliation sera à jamais oubliée,[30] et les *vv.* 5s. justifient cette promesse en rappelant les liens qui ont uni et qui ne cessent d'unir Jérusalem et YHWH. La première, qui se substitue ainsi à Israël dans son ensemble, en qui le prophète Osée a salué l'épouse de YHWH, n'est autre en effet que la partenaire du second; elle lui doit l'existence (*ʿāśā*), l'amour et la protection (*bāʿal*), la défense de ses intérêts (*gāʾal*) (*v.* 5).[31] YHWH appelle (à nouveau) sa cité, il ne saurait mettre en cause la relation conjugale qui depuis des temps lointains le lie à elle, il ne se conduit pas envers elle comme

---

(108 ab); 20 (143b); v Sib. 251 s., etc. qui se réfèrent à des textes comme Es. xlix 2 s., liv 2; Zac. ii 5 ss., ix 1, etc.

[28] Westermann, p. 220, insiste sur ce point.

[29] Cf. Bonnard, p. 291. Selon Fohrer, p. 170, l'époque de l'adolescence concernerait le temps de la royauté et la confrontation avec l'Egypte et l'Assyrie; pour Schoors, p. 82, *ʿalūmayik* signifierait l'esclavage et serait l'équivalent du veuvage; pour Muilenburg, p. 635, le prophète penserait à l'ensemble de la période préexilique . . . Mais le 2e Esaïe ne pourrait-il pas faire allusion, comme Ezéchiel, en Ez. xvi, à l'origine douteuse de Jérusalem?

[30] "oublier, se souvenir" sont des verbes importants dans Es. xlss. Cf. à ce propos Bonnard, p. 533.

[31] Cf. le lien entre Jérusalem et Israël mis en évidence par l'étude de Beuken (note 20). Le même auteur s'interroge sur la façon de comprendre les expressions des *vv.* 5b et 5c (quel est le sujet et quel est le prédicat?), il adopte finalement la même construction que Köhler, que j'ai aussi retenue, et conclut que, *parce* qu'il est le créateur d'Israël, YHWH sera son époux, *parce* qu'il est le Saint d'Israël, il se conduira envers son peuple comme un *gōʾēl* (pp. 43-5).

un homme qui renie sa parole donnée à la femme de sa jeunesse.[32] Chacune des expressions utilisées par le prophète veut assurer ses contemporains qu'ils peuvent compter absolument, et Jérusalem avec eux, sur la fidélité de YHWH à la cause de son peuple. Cette 2e strophe, qui annonce que le temps de la honte est dépassé et anticipe sur les *vv.* 11ss., prépare les affirmations décisives, placées dans la bouche même du Dieu d'Israël, des *vv.* 7 à 10.

La 3e strophe (*7-10*). Cependant la prise de Jérusalem reste un fait qui ne peut être simplement passé sous silence et pas davantage les événements qui l'ont précédé et suivi. Le prophète répond à cette objection que ne pouvaient manquer de lui faire les exilés, ce qui l'amène à esquisser une réflexion théologique pour situer 587 par rapport à l'ensemble de la destinée de sa cité et surtout en fonction de son avenir (*v.* 7s.). On retrouve de pareilles réflexions de théologie de l'histoire ailleurs dans son message, ainsi en xliii 22-28 et en xlvii 6 (xlii 24, l 1). On remarquera, avec Lack (p. 192), la construction rigoureuse de la première partie de cette 3e strophe: 7a est repris en 8a et 7b en 8b; ce que le 2e Esaïe veut surtout mettre en évidence, c'est le contraste—le double contraste—entre la colère divine, qui se réfère à la chute de Jérusalem—qui ne dure qu'un instant (*regaʿ* est employé à deux reprises) et est qualifié de *qāṭōn* en 7a),[33] et l'ampleur illimitée de sa compassion (le radical *rḥm* est utilisé deux fois, il est accompagné des qualificatifs de *gādōl*—le pluriel est significatif—et de *ḥesed ʿōlām*). Il n'y a donc aucune mesure entre le drame de 587, malgré la détresse et la honte qu'il a provoquées, et l'attention pleine de tendresse et d'affection que YHWH porte à sa cité et qui sous-tend l'existence entière de celle-ci et donc commande son avenir.

Ainsi le 2e Esaïe ne nie pas qu'il y ait entre Dieu et Jérusalem une déchirure, mais il situe celle-ci dans le cadre de l'amitié indéfectible de YHWH: pour lui Sion est déjà recueillie, elle voit ses enfants se rassembler autour d'elle (*qbṣ*, *v.* 7b).

---

[32] *ʾēšet neʿūrīm* peut avoir, selon Schoors, p. 84, le sens de "femme légitime" (cf. Mal ii. 14 s.; Prov. v 10).

[33] Selon Driver, "Studies . . .", pp. 298-9, pour qui *regaʿ* a quelques fois le sens d'"émotion", un *qāṭōn regaʿ* aurait le sens d'"une brève émotion", c.à.d. "d'un coeur léger"! Rignell traduit, ad loc. "un moment insignifiant", mais le prophète peut-il aller jusqu'à prétendre que 587 était un fait sans importance? Pour Westermann, p. 220, le 2e Esaïe utilise ici un motif emprunté aux Psaumes (Ps. xxx 6).

La seconde partie de la strophe confirme et prolonge cette perspective. YHWH en effet n'hésite pas, selon le prophète de l'exil, à s'engager par serment à ne plus s'irriter contre celle qu'il considère comme son épouse (cf. *vv.* 5-6). Il fonde sa déclaration solennelle sur un élément de la tradition du déluge: de même que YHWH a alors promis de ne plus se déchaîner contre la terre, il jure maintenant que les événements qui ont conduit Jérusalem à la ruine et au déshonneur ne se reproduiront plus. On notera qu'une fois encore, le 2e Esaïe fait appel à la narration de la Genèse, qu'il interprète d'ailleurs librement.[34]

Cette volonté inébranlable de YHWH en faveur de Sion est confirmée par la déclaration du *v.* 10: même si ce qui paraît le plus stable aux yeux de ses contemporains, les montagnes et les collines, venait à être ébranlé—ce qui est quasi hors de question—, le lien *ḥesed* établi entre YHWH et sa cité ne saurait être rompu.[35] L'avenir de Jérusalem repose sur une *b^erīt šālōm* qui qualifie "l'état de salut" (Westermann) dans lequel l'ancienne capitale de Juda est instituée.[36]

Le prophète ne pouvait pas mieux répondre à une question angoissante que se posaient ses frères: YHWH se mettra-t-il une nouvelle fois en colère contre les siens au cas où ceux-ci viendraient à lui être encore infidèles? L'alliance rétablie ne peut-elle être à son tour rompue, si bien qu'il ne reste plus à Sion qu'à vivre dans la hantise d'une seconde catastrophe plus grave que la première? YHWH s'engage ici, de manière particulièrement émouvante, à ne plus jamais revenir sur ce qu'il a décidé, dans sa compassion pour Jérusalem (*rḥm* se retrouve en conclusion de la 3e strophe) en sa faveur. L'avenir de celle-ci repose définitivement sur la fidélité de son Dieu à sa parole.

---

[34] Le prophète se réfère en particulier à Gen. viii 21-2 (J) et à Gen. ix 11-17 (P); pourtant aucune de ces deux versions, même la tradition sacerdotale, ne mentionne à proprement parler un serment de Dieu, quoique celui-ci soit plus ou moins implicite dans les déclarations solennelles divines au lendemain du déluge (cf. Muilenburg, p. 637). Selon Whybray, pp. 186-7, il y aurait encore une allusion au déluge au *v.* 10 (cf. Gen. vii 19-20).

[35] Même référence aux réalités de la nature en Jer. xxxi 35 ss. pour exprimer l'idée de la stabilité du statut du peuple de YHWH; en Es. xlix 15 par contre il est fait appel à l'amour maternel pour indiquer que Dieu ne saurait changer à égard des siens.

[36] *b^erīt šālōm* est attesté également en Ez. xxxiv 25 (Os. ii 20) et xxxviii 26; ici l'alliance-de-paix est mise en parallèle avec *ḥesed*, elle est irrévocable. Pour Muilenburg, p. 637, *b^erīt* et *šālōm* sont quasi interchangeables. Westermann, pp. 223 ss., insiste sur le fait qu'ici le 2e Esaïe décrit une nouvelle situation que connaîtra Jérusalem (Heilzeit, Heilzustand) plutôt que de parler d'une intervention salvatrice (Heilsereignis) de YHWH.

La 4e strophe (*11-14a*) montre, avec la dernière, les effets concrets de ce que YHWH projette pour Sion. Ces versets qui reçoivent généralement le titre de "la nouvelle Jérusalem", mais qui ne doivent pas être séparés de leur contexte, malgré les développements auxquels ils ont donné lieu (ainsi Tob. xiii 15-18; Apo. Jn. xxi 18-21) s'ouvrent par une triple interpellation qui renvoie au *v.* 1a, mais cette fois la compassion s'exprime et non l'ironie: "humiliée, secouée, inconsolée". Chacun de ces qualificatifs se retrouve dans le message du 2e Esaïe: l'humiliation rappelle Es. li 21 (cf. aussi xli 17, xlviii 10, xlix 13, liii 4, 7); la cité qui "n'a pas été consolée" [37] fait écho à Lam. i 2, 9, 16s., 21 comme aux paroles consolantes du prophète de l'exil (Es. xl 1 [2 ×], xlix 13, li 3 [2 ×], 12, lii 9); la ville "secouée" fait songer à la Jérusalem "enivrée" d'Es. li 17ss. (21).

Les *vv.* 11bss. constituent une sorte de réponse à la plainte implicite contenue en 11a. YHWH lui-même annonce ses intentions: il veut (re)construire une cité, puisqu'il est question de pierres et de fondations (selon 1 Q Isa), de créneaux et d'enceintes; fait surprenant, le texte n'insiste ni sur la hauteur des tours, ni sur l'ampleur des fortifications,[38] mais sur la beauté de la ville dont Dieu apparaît plus l'orfèvre que l'architecte. Jérusalem sera couverte de bijoux; elle apparaît toute chatoyants sous ses parures multiples: saphirs, rubis, escarboucles,[39] autant de pierres précieuses qui en font une cité somptueuse (*vv.* 11bs.).

Les exégètes cherchent à expliquer ce trait original en recourant soit à l'histoire, soit au mythe. Certains voient dans cette description des *vv.* 11-12 une référence aux inscriptions royales mésopotamiennes dont les souverains avaient l'habitude de doter leurs constructions; en 1926 déjà Stummer avait fait ce rapprochement, et dernièrement Beuken a comparé la déclaration du prophète à une sorte d'oracle de fondation.[40] Le Second Esaïe aurait simplement voulu souligner

---

[37] *lōʾ nūḥāmā* évoque non sans pertinence le nom de la fille d'Osée: *lōʾ rūḥāmā* Os. i 6 (ii 3); 1 Q Is[a] a lu, pour *sōʿarā*, *sḥwrh*, qui serait un synonyme, selon de Boer, p. 77.

[38] Les commentateurs remarquent également qu'à l'inverse des perspectives d'Ezéchiel sur l'avenir de Jérusalem, il n'est pas question ici du temple.

[39] La signification précise de certains termes utilisés ici (Es. liv) comme ailleurs (Ex. xxviii; Ez. xxviii) reste incertaine; cf. P. L. Garber, R. W. Funk, "Jewels", *IDB* II (1962), pp. 898-905.

[40] Stummer, pp. 188-9, Beuken, pp. 57-8. Volz a rapproché les déclarations des *vv.* 11-12 de la description d'un palais royal égyptien ... et du dôme du Rocher à Jérusalem! (p. 136); pour Fohrer, le prophète s'inspire de listes cananéennes (p. 174). Les modèles n'ont pas dû manquer au 2e Esaïe.

la magnificence de la future cité de Dieu en la comparant aux plus beaux édifices de la région; peut-être même y aurait-il une pointe polémique dans ses propos, il aurait insinué que la Jérusalem que YHWH a en vue sera plus grandiose que la capitale que Nébucadnesar se vante d'avoir bâtie! [41]

D'autres commentateurs songent aux traditions mythiques selon lesquelles le paradis était non seulement un lieu à la végétation inouïe, mais aussi un jardin orné de pierreries les plus éclatantes. Un texte comme Ez. xxviii 13-14 fait écho à cette conception que Gen. ii 11-12 évoque à sa manière et que connaît déjà l'épopée de Gilgamesh (IX, V 48ss., VI).[42] Le 2e Esaïe aurait repris ce motif en Es. liv, il songerait non à une ville ordinaire, mais à une cité idéale, aux caractéristiques paradisiaques, et sa vision aurait stimulé les rêves les plus fantastiques sur la Jérusalem céleste, dont l'Apocalypse johannique est un des témoins.

A ces deux interprétations qui ne s'excluent pas nécessairement, Lack vient d'en proposer une troisième qu'on peut qualifier de symbolique (p. 195 et plus loin pp. 220ss.). Il existe, selon lui, une relation étroite entre Es. liv 1-10 et les versets qui suivent: "Sion, écrit-il avec raison, est, à la fois, une ville construite de pierres precieuses et une femme qui s'épanouit en ses fils." On ne doit donc pas traiter ce chapitre comme s'il était fait de deux parties autonomes parce qu'à l'image de la femme succède celle de la cité; en réalité la première se prolonge à travers tout le poème et la seconde est déjà présente dans la déclaration initiale du prophète (*vv.* 1ss.). La

---

[41] Déjà souligné par Stummer (cf. note 40) et repris par ex. par Westermann, p. 224, qui insiste cependant sur l'originalité du prophète.

[42] On lit dans l'épopée de Gilgamesh, selon la traduction de R. Labat:

"Il se dirigea (alors) vers [le Jardin] pour voir les arbres de [pierre]:
la cornaline y porte des fruits,
une grappe pendait, brillante à contempler.
La lazulite y portait du feuillage,
et portait aussi des fruits, riants à regarder . . ."

in *Les religions du proche-orient. Textes babyloniens, ougaritiques, hittites*, présentés et traduits par R. Labat, A. Caquot, M. Sznycer, M. Vieyra (Paris, 1970), p. 201 s. (cf. aussi *ANET*^{3} [1969], p. 89—le P. R. Tournay me signale qu'il étudie précisément ce texte difficile—; pour la version sumérienne de Gilgamesh et Agga, ligne 74, p. 46); sur les parures de Inanna (lors de la Descente en Enfer) cf. *ANET*^{3}, p. 53 (lignes 18 ss.), p. 54 (lignes 48 ss., 103 ss.), etc. Ici encore les témoignages relatifs aux déesses ou grandes dames parées d'or, de lapis-lazuli et d'autres brillants ne manquent pas. (cf. par ex. "Textes Ougaritiques", *LAPO* [1974], p. 525, ou encore à propos du Bien-aimé du Cantique, Cant. v 14-15, et plus tard Dan. x 5-6, etc.).

ville renvoie à la femme et réciproquement; "ville et mère symbolisant entre elles, il s'établit une certaine communication des idiomes" ajoute Lack (p. 221), qui, à la suite de I. Blythin [43] attire l'attention sur un texte ancien, Gen. xxx 3, qui établit, comme Es. liv, une interrelation entre le motif de la maternité et celui de la construction. Il s'agit de Rachel qui est restée jusqu'ici stérile et qui souhaite que Jacob lui donne des enfants par l'intermédaire de sa servante; "alors, dit-elle, je serai *construite* (*w*^{e}*'ibbāneh*)"; avoir un fils, c'est être bâtie! Ainsi la femme s'édifie comme une cité, dont les enfants constituent les pierres, alors que la ville est une mère pour ses habitants, elle les accueille en son sein et en un sens les enfante, elle est, comme Jérusalem, une métro-pole! (cf. Ps. lxxxvii, surtout dans la LXX). "La cité est un des symboles de la mère sous le double aspect de protection et de limite, écrit P. Grison—ou plutôt M. McDavy—,[44] cité par Lack qui remarque qu' "en Es. liv 3 les enfants de Sion sont, au sens fort du terme, mis au monde . . ." (p. 221). Le 2e Esaïe semble tenir compte de cette association entre ville/pierres d'une part et femme (ou mère)/fils de l'autre aux *vv.* 12-13 où il est successivement question de pierres (*v.* 12 [2 ×]) et de fils (*v.* 13 [2 ×], ou si l'on suit 1 Q Isa de fils (13a) et de bâtisseurs (13b); cf. encore Lam. iv 1-2 qui atteste cette connexion entre fils [*v.* 2] et pierres [*v.* 1]).

On peut dès lors se demander avec Lack si la mention des pierres précieuses des *vv.* 11s. ne doit pas se comprendre à partir du même symbolisme; en fait, tout en parlant de la ville, le prophète continuerait à penser à la femme. Lack écrit: "L'image de Sion couverte de pierres précieuses jusqu'en ses fondations invisibles est la représentation symbolique du mystère de sa maternité. Dans l'univers de la femme, bijoux et enfants sont le signe et le gage, les premiers de l'amour reçu, les seconds l'amour échangé. Voilà pourquoi Sion est visée imaginativement comme une femme embellie de brillants et d'enfants. La meilleure manière de lire Is. 54, 11ss. est donc de se laisser enchanter par le sens littéral et d'y percevoir, non pas l'expression de l'utopie, mais le support imaginatif d'un symbole" (p. 195).

La déclaration prophétique, plutôt que d'évoquer une cité de rêve fêterait donc Sion comme une femme comblée par son époux, fière de ses parures et dont les bijoux démontrent l'entière réhabilitation (*v.* 4).

---

[43] "A Note on Isaiah xlix 16-17", *VT* 16 (1966), pp. 229-30.
[44] "ville", J. Chevallier (ed.), *Dictionnaire des symboles* (Paris, 1969), p. 804.

La 5e strophe (*14b-17*) se présente, selon Westermann,[45] sous la forme d'une bénédiction dont on trouve des formules analogues en Ps. xci, cxxi; Job v 17-26, sa thématique n'est par ailleurs pas étrangère à la tradition sapientiale: celui qui médite le mal (contre Sion) connaîtra l'échec et le malheur! (*vv.* 15bss.). Le fidèle que YHWH bénit peut être assuré d'être conduit et soutenu par lui; ce sera le cas de Jérusalem qui se sait accompagnée et protégée par son Dieu. Si la cité de David et des fils, c.à.d. les vrais disciples de YHWH (*v.* 13a)[46] sont promis au bonheur (*šālōm* [13b]; *ṣ^edāqā* [14a]), c'est parce qu'ils sont gardés par Dieu lui-même: Sion a le droit—et même le devoir—de vivre sans souci de l'oppresseur; elle ne verra plus l'angoisse, ni la terreur (*v.* 14b), puisque YHWH fera échouer tout assaut contre elle (*v.* 15), lui, qui contrôle tout: le forgeron qui façonne l'outil (de mort) et le destructeur qui l'anéantit (*v.* 16). Dans le nouveau statut accordé à Jérusalem, l'assaillant court à sa perte, et le plaideur à sa confusion (*v.* 17a). Par ces exemples, le prophète veut convaincre ses frères, les exilés, à la fois inquiets et culpabilisés, que la cité de Dieu qui les attend est vraiment un lieu où s'épanouissent la justice et la paix, il conclut par une déclaration brève, mais solennelle (*v.* 17b) où est rappelé, de façon quasi juridique (*naḥ^alā*),[47] le sort futur des serviteurs de YHWH.

Trois remarques en guise de conclusion

a) *Es. liv et le message du Deutréro-Esaïe*: ce poème s'inscrit parfaitement dans l'ensemble de l'intervention du prophète de l'exil, qui revient sans cesse sur l'avenir de Jérusalem.[48] Le 2e Esaïe inaugure son ministère par une parole de consolation adressée à Sion (Es. xl 1ss.), il lui annonce qu'elle sera rebâtie (Es. xliv 24ss. [28a]) et que YHWH hâte pour elle l'heure du salut (Es. xliv 13). La chute de

---

[45] pp. 224-5, qui attire l'attention sur Ps. xci 5a, 10, Job v 9b à propos de 14b, et Job v 25 pour 13b.

[46] Il s'agit de ceux qui écoutent l'enseignement c.à.d. qui obéissent à la Loi (cf. Es. l 4; cf. aussi Es. viii 16): la Sion future ne comptera que des Yahvistes fidèles (cf. Jer. xxxi 34). Le passage du singulier (Es. l 4) au pluriel (Es. liv 13a) est caractéristique de la période postexilique; le pluriel de ce verset entraîne le pluriel du *v.* 17c.

[47] Cf. l'importance de ce terme dans la théologie d'inspiration deutéronomiste. Westermann, p. 225, en particulier, insiste sur le fait que, dans tout ce passage, il n'est pas tellement question d'intervention salvatrice (Heilsereignis) que de l'instauration d'une ère de bonheur (Heilszustand).

[48] Selon Bonnard, pp. 514-15, le nom de Jérusalem se retrouve 10x dans Es. xl-lv et celui de Sion 11x.

Babylone (Es. xlvii) ouvre pour Jérusalem une nouvelle période, aussi dès le chapitre xlix le prophète va-t-il insister sur la restauration de l'ancienne capitale de Juda et sur sa réhabilitation. Es. xlix 14-21 contient une série de motifs qui seront repris et développés dans le chapitre liv [49]); Es. l 1ss. utilise le symbole de la relation conjugale qu'on retrouvera en Es. liv; Es. li-lii confirme l'intention de YHWH de venir en aide à Sion (*v.* 1) et invite Jérusalem à se lever (li 17-18) et à se vêtir d'habits de fête (lii 1-2) pour aller à la rencontre de son Dieu qui vient à elle (*vv.* 6ss.); bref la pensée de Jérusalem et de son destin futur est au cœur du message du 2e Esaïe dans la seconde partie de son livre et Es. liv apparaît comme le point culminant de ses déclarations à ce sujet.[50]

b) *Es. liv et la tradition sur le statut à venir de Jérusalem*: comme K.-L. Schmidt l'a fort bien remarqué, la description enthousiaste du prophète de l'exil sur la Jérusalem de demain n'est pas restée sans écho et des textes comme Tob. xiii et Apo. Jn. xxi, qu'il faudrait avoir le temps d'étudier, en sont la preuve.[51] Plus récemment les découvertes de Qumrân ont fait apparaître quelques fragments d'un commentaire d'Es. liv 11s. (4 Qp Isa^{d} [4 Q 164]) qui a retenu l'attention des spécialistes du NT parce qu'il y est question d'un groupe de "douze" qui dispose d'une autorité particulière! Voici ce texte tel que l'a reconstitué M. P. Horgan: [52]

1. "... tout Israël comme un fard autour des yeux. *Je te fonderai sur des saphi*[*rs* (Es. liv 11c) l'interprétation de ce passage est]
2. [qu]e le conseil de la communauté a été fondé [parmi les/au milieu de] prêtres et le peu[ple]
3. la congrégation de ses Elus, comme une pierre de saphir au milieu des pierres [*je ferai* (*en*) *rubis*]

---

[49] Par ex. la plainte de Sion (*v.* 14), la tendresse de YHWH plus constante que celle d'une mère (*v.* 15), l'afflux des fils (bâtisseurs, selon les versions) (*vv.* 17 ss.), l'espace nécessaire pour les accueillir tous (*vv.* 20-1) ...; dans la tradition juive, Es. xlix 16 fut interprété en relation avec la Jérusalem céleste!

[50] Le lien entre Es. lii et Es. liv est évident, par contre le 4e "Cantique" du Serviteur semble constituer un morceau à part.

[51] Cf. à ce propos pp. 238-40 et les notes 2 à 6.

[52] *Pesharim*: *Qumran Interpretations of Biblical Books* (Fordham University, Theology, microfilm, New York, 1977), pp. 248-59 (bibliographie); on consultera aussi J. M. Baumgarten, "The Duodecimal Courts of Qumran", *JBL* 95 (1976), pp. 59-78. Le texte de 4 QpIsa^{d} publié d'abord par J. M. Allegro in *JBL* 77 (1958), pp. 215-21, se lit aussi dans *DJD* 5 (Oxford, 1958), pp. 27 s. (cf. aussi Y. Yadin, in *IEJ* 9 [1959], pp. 39-42, etc.).

4. *tous tes créneaux* (Es. liv 12a). Son interprétation concerne les douze [hommes du conseil de la communauté qui]
5. éclairent par la décision de l'Urim et Tummim [ ]
6. celles qui manquent d'entre eux, comme le soleil . . . avec toute sa lumière *et tou*[*tes tes portes en escarboucles*] (Es. liv 12b)
7. son interprétation concerne les chefs des tribus d'Israël à la f[in des temps]
8. son lot, les offices de [ ]

De ce passage malheureusement bien mutilé, retenons que l'auteur fait de la parole du 2e Esaïe une lecture allégorique, comme l'apôtre Paul, mais dans la ligne traditionnelle des *p^e^šārīm* de Qumrân. Il s'appuie non seulement sur Es. liv, mais encore sur Ez. xlviii 30-34, où la cité de Dieu apparaît avec ses douze rues portant les noms des douze tribus d'Israël, et sur Ex. xxviii 15-30, qui décrit le pectoral du Grand Prêtre, avec ses douze pierres précieuses, sur lesquelles se trouvent également les noms des tribus d'Israël, et l'Urim et Tummim. Il identifie les pierres précieuses d'Es. liv avec les diverses catégories de personnes qui constituent la communauté de Qumrân: ainsi les saphirs (Es. liv 11c) sont mis en relation avec la fondation (du conseil) de la communauté et (parmi/par?) les prêtres; les rubis (Es. liv 12a) semblent désigner les douze (prêtres?) munis de l'Urim et Tummim, et les portes en escarboucles, les chefs d'Israël.[53] L'intérêt de ce document est de montrer, malgré ses obscurités, que la déclaration prophétique n'a pas donné lieu ici à une description fantastique d'une Jérusalem quasi céleste, mais à une interprétation de type plutôt "ecclésiologique": c'est d'Israël, c.à.d. de la communauté des Elus de Dieu et de son organisation, qu'il serait question en Es. liv! [54]

Si le poème du 2e Esaïe est à l'origine de diverses relectures, il faut se demander si, à l'autre bout de la chaîne, le prophète de l'exil n'est pas tributaire de son prédécesseur Esaïe. Il semble que la péricope d'Es. i 21-26 pourrait être l'une des sources de la proclamation du

[53] La lecture du document comme son interprétation restent encore incertaines et varient d'un commentateur à l'autre. On lira avec intérêt de J. M. Ford, "The Jewel of Discernment (A study of stone symbolism)", *BZ*, N.F. 11 (1967), pp. 109-16.

[54] Un autre texte biblique, celui d'Ez. xl ss., semble avoir retenu l'attention des membres de la communauté de Qumrân à propos de la Jérusalem de demain (cf. 1 Q 32, *DJD* 1 (1955), pp. 134-5; 2 Q 24, *DJD* 3 (1962), pp. 84 ss.; 5 Q 15, ibid., pp. 184 ss.

Deutéro-Esaïe sur le sort futur de Jérusalem. Ce texte, qui est ordinairement qualifié de complainte et dont l'authenticité ne doit pas être mise en doute à quelques détails près,[55] malgré une longue et impressionnante étude de Vermeylen qui situe ces versets "à l'époque de l'exil, dans un milieu influencé par la théologie deutéronomienne" (pp. 71-105 [104]), décrit l'histoire de la cité de David c.à.d. en clair, sa déchéance, son châtiment et sa rénovation: la ville fondée sur le droit et la justice (*v.* 21) est devenue le repaire des assassins et des voleurs, l'iniquité y triomphe (*vv.* 21ss.). YHWH prend des mesures pour éliminer les coupables, purifier Sion (*vv.* 24-5) et la rendre à sa vocation première d'être la Cité-de-la-Justice (*v.* 26)! [56] Comme le prophète du VIIIe siècle, le 2e Esaïe évoque le destin de Jérusalem, son passé, son présent, son avenir, mais alors qu'Esaïe intervient avant le jugement divin et que sa mission consiste avant tout à dénoncer le mal qui sévit dans les murs de la ville de Dieu, le prophète de l'exil doit insister après 587 sur les nouvelles possibilités que YHWH offre à Sion; son message est essentiellement une parole de salut. Mais l'un et l'autre se rencontrent dans une réflexion théologique sur l'histoire de Jérusalem; ils s'accordent aussi pour confirmer celle-ci dans sa vocation initiale.

c) *Caractéristiques théologiques d'Es. liv*: Ce qui frappe d'emblée dans ce chapitre, c'est la place qu'y tient YHWH. Son nom revient sans cesse, accompagné de qualificatifs éloquents; Saint d'Israël, époux, rédempteur, Dieu de toute la terre . . . Tout au long du poème, directement ou par l'intermédiaire de son prophète, Dieu s'adresse à Jérusalem pour lui rappeler qui il est et ce qu'il représente pour elle; il promet d'agir en faveur de Sion, il s'engage solennellement à assurer son bonheur, et paraphe son intervention par une ultime déclaration à l'intention de ses serviteurs (*v.* 17c). Il n'est pas nécessaire d'insister sur le caractère théocentrique de cette page qui s'accorde avec tout ce que nous savons par ailleurs du message du Deutéro-Esaïe.

La spécificité d'Es. liv se trouve sans doute dans son contenu qui est essentiellement sotériologique, ou mieux encore dans le ton que le 2e Esaïe adopte. En d'autres occasions, le prophète polémique,

---

[55] Sur ce texte, cf. les commentaires; bibliographie dans J. Vermeylen, *Du Prophete Isaïe à l'Apocalyptique* I (Paris, 1977), pp. 71 ss.

[56] Dans son étude, Porteous insiste sur la relation entre Jérusalem et les notions de *ṣedeq* et de *šālōm* qu'attestent les textes bibliques (pp. 239 ss.).

il s'en prend aux nations et à leurs idoles, il fait le procès d'Israël et dénonce son aveuglement (Es. xli 1-5, 21-29, xlii 18-25, xliii 9-13, etc.); ailleurs il souligne l'aspect doxologique de l'action divine au profit des exilés: par respect pour son Nom, YHWH suspend sa colère (Es. xliii 25, xlviii 9, 11), car le salut d'Israël doit manifester sa gloire et la terre entière célébrera alors sa grandeur (Es. xlix 26, lii 10, lv 13, etc.). Israël en effet a été créé pour démontrer aux yeux du monde la suprématie de son Dieu (Es. xliii 7, 21), il est l'instrument de la révélation de YHWH et son destin permet à l'univers dans son ensemble, cieux, terre, abîmes, montagnes, forêts et humains, de rendre au Dieu d'Abraham l'hommage que lui valent ses exploits (Es. xliv 23, xlix 13); la finalité de l'intervention salvatrice en faveur d'Israël est clairement indiquée par le prophète.

En Es. liv le 2e Esaïe évoque un Dieu avant tout soucieux de réconforter celle qu'il aime et à qui il demeure fidèle. YHWH laisse ici parler son cœur, il révèle sa tendresse, il proclame son attachement envers la cité de son choix. Il parle pour consoler Sion, la soutenir; il lui annonce que son sort va définitivement changer et dans son attachement pour elle il se voit déjà la comblant de parures les plus précieuses. Les versets 7 à 10 constituent bien le cœur de ce poème tout entier consacré à dire l'amour immuable et efficace de YHWH pour Jérusalem.

BIBLIOGRAPHIE

1. *Commentaires et travaux consultés*

Baltzer, D., *Ezechiel und Deuterojesaja*, *BZAW* 121 (Berlin, 1971).

Beuken, W. A. M., "Isaiah LIV: the multiple identity of the person addressed", *OTS* 19 (Leiden, 1974), pp. 29-70.

Boer, P. A. H. de, *Second Isaiah's Message*, *OTS* 11 (Leiden, 1956).

Bonnard, P. E., *Le second Isaïe. Son disciple et leurs éditeurs (Isaïe 40-66)* (Paris, 1972).

Cohen, C., "The 'widowed' city", *The Gaster Festschrift*, *JANES* 5 (1973), pp. 75-81.

Dahood, M., "Yiphil imperative *yaṭṭi* in Isaiah 54, 2", *Or.*, N.S. 43 (1977), pp. 383-4.

Dennefeld, L., *PC* 7 (Paris, 1947).

Driver, G. R., "Studies in the vocabulary of the Old Testament. VIII", *JThS* 36 (1935), pp. 293-301 (298-9).

Duhm, B., *HK* 3/1 (Göttingen, 1892, 1914[3], 1968[5]).

Elliger, K., *Deuterojesaja in seinem Verhältnis zu Tritojesaja* (Stuttgart, 1933).

Fischer, J., *HSAT* 7, 2 (Bonn, 1939).

Fohrer, G., *Das Buch Jesaja* 3, *ZBK* (Zürich et Stuttgart, 1964).

Golebiewski, M., *Analyse littéraire et théologique d'Is 54-55. Une alliance éternelle avec la nouvelle Jérusalem* (diss., Pont. Inst. Bib., Rome, 1975; *résumé* [Rome, 1976]).

Herbert, A. S., *Isaiah 40-66* (Cambridge, 1975).
Jones, D. R., "Isaiah II and III', *Peake's Commentary on the Bible* (London et Edinburgh, 1963[2]).
Kissane, E. J., *The Book of Isaiah* 2 (Dublin, 1943).
Köhler, L., *Deuterojesaja (Jesaja 40-55) stilkritisch untersucht*, *BZAW* 37 (Giessen, 1923).
König, E., *Das Buch Jesaja* (Gütersloh, 1926).
Lack, R., "Dans un amour éternel j'ai pitié de toi", *Ass. du Seigneur* 22 (1972), pp. 13-19.
——, *La Symbolique du Livre d'Isaïe* (Rome, 1973).
McKenzie, J. L., *Second Isaiah*, *AB* (Garden City, N.Y., 1968).
Marti, K., *KHC* 10 (Tübingen, Freiburg i. B. et Leipzig, 1900).
Melugin, R. F., *The Formation of Isaiah 40-55*, *BZAW* 141 (Berlin, 1976).
Muilenburg, J., *IB* 5 (New York et Nashville, 1956).
North, C. R., *TBC* (London, 1952).
——, *The Second Isaiah* (Oxford, 1964).
Porúbčan, Št., *Il Patto Nuovo in Is 40-66* (Rome, 1958), pp. 139-43.
Preuss, H.-D., *Deuterojesaja. Eine Einführung in seine Botschaft* (Neukirchen-Vluyn, 1976).
Rignell, L. G., *A Study of Isaiah Ch. 40-55* (Lund, 1956).
Rohland, E., *Die Bedeutung der Erwählungstraditionen Israels für die Eschatologie der alttestamentlichen Propheten* (diss., Heidelberg, 1956), pp. 200 ss.
Schoors, A., *I am God your Saviour. A Form-Critical Study of the Main Genres in Is. XL-LV*, *SVT* 24 (1973).
Schwarz, G., "'Keine Waffe . . .' (Jes. 54, 17a)?", *BZ*, N.F· 15 (1971), pp. 254-5.
Smart, J. D., *History and Theology in Second Isaiah. A Commentary on Isaiah 35; 40-66* (London, 1967).
Steinmann, J., "Le livre de la consolation d'Israël et les prophètes du retour de l'exil", *LD* 28 (1960), pp. 177ss.
Stuhlmueller, C., *Creative Redemption in Deutero-Isaiah* (Rome, 1970), pp. 115-22.
Stummer, F., "Einige keilschriftliche Parallelen zu Jes. 40-66", *JBL* 45 (1926), pp. 171-89 (188-9).
Volz, P., *KAT* 9/2 (Leipzig, 1932).
Waldow, H. E. von, *Anlass und Hintergrund der Verkündigung Deuterojesajas* (diss., Bonn, 1953).
Westermann, C., *ATD* (Göttingen, 1964) = *Isaiah 40-66* (London, 1969).
Whybray, R. N., *NCB* (London, 1975).
Williams, R. J., "Some Egyptianisms in the Old Testament", *Studies in Honor of John A. Wilson* (Chicago, 1969), pp. 93-8.

2. *Varia*

Bietenhard, H., *Die himmlische Welt im Urchristentum und Spätjudentum* (Tübingen, 1950), pp. 207-48.
Bruschweiler, F., (éd.), *Les Actes du Colloque sur la Ville dans le Proche-Orient ancien* (Cartigny-Genève, 1979), à paraître.
Donfried, K. P., *The Setting of Second Clement in Early Christianity* (Leiden, 1974), pp. 107 ss., 192 ss.
Ellul, J., *Sans feu, ni lieu* (Paris, 1975).
Müller, W., *Die heilige Stadt. Roma quadrata, himmlisches Jerusalem und die Mythe vom Weltnabel* (Stuttgart, 1961).
No. spécial de *La Vie Spirituelle* 36 (Paris, avril 1952).
Schmidt, K.-L., "Jerusalem als Urbild und Abbild", *Eranos-Jahrbuch* 18 (1950), pp. 207-48.

Stolz, F., "Ṣijjōn", *THAT* 2 (1976), col. 543-51.
Talmon, S., "Die Bedeutung Jerusalems in der Bibel", dans W. T. Eckert, N. P. Levinson et M. Stöhr (éd.), *Jüdisches Volk-Gelobtesland* (München, 1970), pp. 135-52.
Vriezen, T. C., *Jahwe en zijn Stad* (Amsterdam, 1962).
Zimmer, S., *Zion als Tochter, Frau und Mutter. Personifikation von Land, Stadt und Volk* (diss., München, 1959)—inaccessible.

On trouvera d'autres indications et notamment sur la tradition relative à Jérusalem dans les notes; cf. aussi la bibliographie dans *ThWNT* 10/2 (1979), pp. 124-5.

LA PROBLÉMATIQUE DE L'ANCIENNE ET DE LA NOUVELLE ALLIANCE DANS JÉRÉMIE XXXI 31-34 ET QUELQUES AUTRES TEXTES

par

JORGE MEJÍA

Rome

Il faudrait, je crois, commencer la présentation de ce sujet par la justification du fait qu'on a cru opportun de l'aborder à nouveau. On pourrait, en effet, penser qu'après les études de Mgr J. Coppens [1] (1963), de P. Buis [2] (1968), de Helga Weippert [3] (1979), les importants devéloppements de Gerhard von Rad dans sa *Theologie des Alten Testaments*,[4] et encore des commentaires plus ou moins classiques sur Jérémie, comme celui de W. Rudolph [5] et autres,[6] il ne resterait vraiment pas grande chose à en dire qui soit à la fois original et utile. Si j'ose encore le faire c'est pour deux raisons spéciales, l'une plutôt technique ou académique, l'autre plutôt théologique. Je m'explique. Du point de vue technique (ou exégétique, si l'on préfère), il y a eu récemment deux études, qui, s'ils ne se limitent certes pas au texte cité de Jérémie, en font une partie importante de leurs réflexions et donnent ainsi à la fois un contexte plus large et un nouveau *status quæstionis* a la problématique de la Nouvelle Alliance. Je parle de l'étude du Professeur Winfried Thiel, d'un coté,[7] en rapport avec sa thèse,[8] et de celle du Professeur Moshe Weinfeld,[9] de l'autre, qui se

[1] "La nouvelle alliance en Jér 31, 31-34", *CBQ* 25 (1963), pp. 12-21.

[2] "La Nouvelle Alliance", *VT* 18 (1968), pp. 1-15.

[3] "Das Wort vom neuen Bund in Jeremia xxxi 31-34", *VT* 29 (1979), pp. 336-51.

[4] II, *Die Theologie der prophetischen Überlieferungen Israels* (München, 1962³), pp. 274ss., 281ss., 334s., 413.

[5] *Jeremia* (Tübingen, 1968³), pp. 201-7.

[6] Vgr. J. Bright, *Jeremiah* (Garden City, N.Y., 1965), p. 287 (extrêmement concis); L. Alonso Schökel/J. L. Sicre Díaz, *Profetas, Comentario* I (Madrid, 1980), pp. 564-6. C'est, si je ne me trompe, le dernier commentaire paru et un des très rares en langue espagnole.

[7] "Die Rede vom 'Bund' in den Prophetenbüchern", *Theologische Versuche* 9 (1977), pp. 11-36.

[8] L'auteur a traité le même sujet dans une partie de sa dissertation, *Die deuteronomistische Redaktion des Buches Jeremia* (Berlin, 1970), qui n'est pas accessible.

[9] "Jeremiah and the Spiritual Metamorphosis of Israel", *ZAW* 88 (1976), pp. 17-56.

suivent à un an de distance. La question est ainsi relancée au plan même de l'analyse exégétique.

Du point de vue théologique aussi, le livre récent du Professeur F. Mussner, *Traktat über die Juden* (München, 1979), mais aussi plusieurs autres publications, de valeur inégale il est vrai, prolongent et spécifient la problématique de la Nouvelle Alliance, d'une façon assez inattendue, du moins si l'on se place dans la perspective des commentaires et des analyses classiques. Il s'agit surtout d'examiner si les textes de Jérémie et des autres nous aident à mieux comprendre, dans une perspective chrétienne, la place du Judaïsme postbiblique dans l'économie divine; c'est-à-dire, de façon plus précise encore, si la Nouvelle Alliance, ou l'Alliance éternelle, est *exclusivement* l'Alliance dans le Christ (cf. Luc. xxii 20; 1 Cor. xi 25, et surtout Hébr. viii 7-13), ou si l'on peut parler avec une certaine légitimité théologique, d'une permanence de l'Alliance avec le peuple juif. Cette question est évidemment centrale pour une théologie chrétienne du Judaïsme, comme celle que Mussner veut faire (et d'autres), et on ne peut plus l'éviter quand on étudie la portée théologique du texte cité et des textes parallèles. On y reviendra.

Pour ces raisons, donc, je crois opportun d'entamer à nouveau l'analyse de Jér. xxxi 31-34, et d'autres textes semblables. Seulement, il ne faut pas refaire évidemment le chemin déjà fait. Je me limiterai ainsi, dans la mesure du possible, au *status quæstionis* offert pas les deux études suscitées, tout en tenant compte de la nouvelle problématique théologique dont je viens d'esquisser le sens fondamental.

Il y a quand même une question que l'on pourrait qualifier de *méthodologique*, dont je voudrais m'occuper brièvement au préalable. Elle pourrait être formulée ainsi: comment aborder l'analyse du texte de Jérémie? C'est bien, je crois, cette façon précise de l'aborder qui détermine à sa suite les conclusions habituelles sur l'authenticité du texte en question, sur son *Sitz im Leben*, sur l'origine de la tradition que l'on y trouve exprimée et finalement sur sa perspective théologique.

On peut l'aborder, premièrement, dans le contexte d'une théorie générale sur le *Bund*. C'est ce que fait l'étude citée de Thiel (pp. 11-12), en s'inspirant à son tour des positions bien connues de E. Kutsch et de L. Perlitt. Ses conclusions sont, comme on pouvait s'y attendre, assez négatives. Non seulement l'Alliance est en elle même étrangère à Jérémie lui-même, mais elle est aussi etrangère à tous les prophètes, au moins dans leurs textes "authentiques" (pp. 25-7). C'est la thèse du *Bundesschweigen* des prophètes, dont la raison serait, parmi d'autres, que ce thème théologique est bien "der prophetischen Botschaft wurzelfreund" (p. 26). Même les prophètes vivant "in der Zeit nach der Proklamation des Dtn . . . sich ihrer nicht bedienten"(p. 26). Les textes qui en parlent seraient tous tardifs, plus ou moins occasionels et, de plus marginaux.[10] Du point de vue littéraire, ils ressortiraient à l'école (ou à la tradition) dtr, ou post-dtr (p. 18, nn. 2 et 3). Il est légitime de se demander si cette vision si négative répond vraiment aux faits théologiques et littéraires tel qu'ils se présentent dans les livres examinés, surtout Jérémie et Ezéchiel.

Si l'on prend, d'autre part, le livre même de Jérémie comme point de départ, on arrive a des conclusions différentes, ou même radicalement opposées, comme le sont celles de Weinfeld, dans l'article cité (supra, n. 9). Qu'il me soit permis de noter ici, en passant, que l'article de Thiel, publié en 1977, mais préparé auparavant (puisqu'il reprend une partie de sa thèse), ignore complètement celui de Weinfeld, publié l'année précédente. Celui-ci croit pouvoir isoler, dans le livre de Jérémie, un certain type d'oracles ("utterances", "statements"), construits selon un schéma de thèse et antithèse (pp. 17-19): *non comme* on disait/faisait/les choses se passaient auparavant . . . *mais*, dans les jours à venir, même les institutions fondamentales d'Israël seront changées. En mettant ensemble ces divers oracles, Weinfeld conclut que Jérémie annonce ce qu'il appelle "the Spiritual Metamorphosis of Israel". Il serait très intéressant de suivre le professeur israélien dans le détail de sa démonstration. Je ne le ferai pas maintenant. Mais je voudrais noter deux choses à cet égard. *Primo*, l'étude que Buis a dédiée à la structure de l'annonce d'une nouvelle alliance et que j'ai citée en commençant cet article (supra, n. 2) suit une voie différente. Weinfeld ne mentionne pas cet article de Buis. On peut se demander dans quelle mesure les conclusions de Buis sont modifiées par les analyses de Weinfeld et les nouvelles perspectives qu'elles ouvrent. *Secundo*, Weinfeld inclut, bien entendu, dans cette série d'oracles antithètiques, identifiés par lui, celui qui fait l'objet central de notre étude. On en tiendra compte dans ce qui suit.

Je voudrais quand même prendre un point de départ quelque peu différent. Je commence par constater que les chapitres xxxi à xxxiv

[10] P. 18 "am Rande des Buches (Jeremias)"; p. 22 "am Rande des Buches (Ezechiel)"; pp. 25ss. (les conclusions).

de Jérémie traitent tous, d'une façon ou de l'autre, de l'alliance. Sans entrer ici dans la problématique difficile et compliquée de l'histoire rédactionelle du livre, certains auteurs, dont Rudolph (pp. XIX, 225) voient dans ces chapitres une unité littéraire.[11] Je crois que l'on peut trouver un nouvel argument pour l'existence de cette unité dans cette thématique commune de l'alliance. Ceci tendrait à situer cette thématique, non en marge et comme en appendice, plus ou moins adventice, de l'œuvre jérémienne,[12] mais au cœur de son message, même si l'on admet que quelques uns de ces textes, dans les chapitres cités, ont été remaniés par la suite. Ce serait notamment le cas des chapitres xxxii et xxxiii que l'on accepte ou non les conclusions de l'analyse littéraire de Mowinckel. Il est, en effet, difficile (pour ne pas dire arbitraire) de croire que cette notion d'alliance, quantitativement et qualitativement si importante, soit seulement le fruit d'un ajout plus ou moins étranger au livre lui même et à son message.[13]

On pourrait dire, d'ailleurs, en retournant l'argument de Thiel,[14] que le contexte historique expliquerait suffisamment la présence, chez Jérémie (et peut-être aussi chez Ezéchiel), de la thématique du pacte. Je pense évidemment à 2 Rois xxiii 3, qui pourrait trouver un écho (le fait en lui-même, pas le texte, bien entendu) en Jér. xi, quoiqu'il en soit des remaniements dtn. que ce texte aurait subi.[15] Il ne faudrait pas oublier non plus le pacte qui forme le sujet de la deuxième partie du chapitre xxxiv (8-21), dont il n'y a aucune raison de nier l'historicité, bien que l'on puisse différer dans son interprétation théologique (cf. vgr. Thiel, pp. 15s.) et son rapport avec le Deutéronome (xv 12-13) (cf. ib. et encore Rudolph, p. 223). C'est toujours un pacte que Dieu peut appeler "sien" (*v.* 18 *b^erîtî*) et qui, en tout cas, est célébré "en ma présence" (*l^epānāy*).

C'est ici que l'on peut trouver le vrai contexte de l'oracle qui nous occupe. Il y aurait, en effet, comme un *terminus a quo* et un *terminus*

---

[11] L'unité commencerait pour Rudolph soit avec le ch. xxvi (p. XIX), soit avec le ch. xxxii (p. 225), mais ces deux affirmations ne s'opposent nécessairement pas. Rudolph y inclut aussi le ch. xxxv, ce qui est digne d'attention.

[12] C'est la thèse de Thiel; cf. supra.

[13] Je laisse ici entièrement de côté l'argument strictement statistique, si difficile à manier. Weinfeld a démontré, à mon avis, la cohérence interne des différentes annonces jérémiennes (passim).

[14] P. 26: "Das [la radicale Fremdheit] wird eindrücklich dadurch belegt, dass selbst die Propheten, die in der Zeit nach der Proklamation des Dtn. lebten und dessen Bundestheologie kennen mussten (Jeremia, Ezechiel) sich ihrer nicht bedienten."

[15] Cf. à ce propos, Weinfeld, pp. 29s. et les nn. 45, 46.

ad quem, c'est-à-dire, l'alliance de Josias et la ruine de Jérusalem. Je ne crois pas qu'il faille descendre plus bas, quand la situation change du tout au tout. Personellement, je pense que le texte en question se situe assez tôt dans cette période et que, dans ce sens, il peut avoir été originellement destiné à l'Israël du Nord, comme c'est l'opinion de plusieurs auteurs.[16] Mais cela n'est pas nécessaire. Il suffit d'affirmer l'authenticité jérémienne, encore récemment soutenue par Weippert (p. 348).

Si, d'autre part, on considère le contenu spécifique de l'oracle, on arrive à la même conclusion. Le thème de l'intériorisation, si typique de l'annonce de la Nouvelle Alliance, est bien un thème jérémien, et ceci sous la double forme (assez spéciale) de l'écriture sur le cœur et de la connaissance intérieure de Dieu. Le premier élément (l'écriture du cœur), repris par St Paul dans un contexte similaire (cf. 2 Cor. iii 2ss.), est déja présent dans le texte xvii 1, étudié par Weippert (pp. 345s.), en rapport avec d'autres textes semblables, toujours en fonction d'une intériorisation: celle du péché dans ces textes. Mais c'est comme le négatif d'une photo, dont le positif se trouve dans l'oracle du chapitre xxxi 31-34. La rémission totale du péché, dont on parle à la fin de l'oracle (*v.* 34), comme la raison de ce qui précède,[17] suppose l'inscription à sa place, dans la même dimension intérieure et secrète de l'homme, de la loi divine.

Mais il y a aussi la connaissance, intérieure et personnelle. C'est, en effet, le cœur qui connait, d'après l'oracle destiné à expliquer l'aspect positif de la vision des figues (xxiv 7): "Je leur donnerai un cœur (*TOB*, p. 945: "une intelligence") pour me connaître". La mouvance de cet oracle (5-7) est, d'ailleurs, assez semblable à celle de l'oracle que nous étudions maintenant: ce sont toujours des déportés, que l'on pourrait considérer abandonnés à cause de leurs péchés, et qui, au contraire, deviennent l'objet de la providence amoureuse de Dieu, qui ne se contente pas de les ramener chez eux, mais les transforme aussi de l'intérieur.

C'est précisément dans ce contexte que Weinfeld mentionne, très justement à mon avis, le thème de la circoncision du cœur (cf. iv 4),[18]

---

[16] Cf. vgr. Rudolph, "(die Verse) nur Efraim gelten" (p. 201); Alonso Schökel/ Sicre, p. 564 (cf. p. 405); von Rad hésite: cf. d'une part, p. 224, et de l'autre, la n. 28; Bright (p. 285) affirme qu'il ne faut pas descendre "after approximately the middle of the Exilic period". Il est inutile de rappeler toute la gamme des opinions exprimées.

[17] Cf. Alonso Schökel/Sicre (p. 505).

[18] Cf. Weinfeld, pp. 33-4. Le texte de ix 25 est plus difficile. On connait la

dont je ne vais pas parler maintenant. Qu'il suffise de noter ici que, dans cet oracle de conversion (iv 1-4), ce sont les auditeurs eux-mêmes qui sont invités à transformer leurs cœurs (il s'agit des Judéens et des Jérusalémites), sans doute par association avec la circoncision corporelle. Mais c'est toujours Dieu qui inspire, anime et, au fond, pratique lui-même cette transformation radicale.

Tout ce qui précède nous ramène à Ezéchiel, d'un côté, au Deutéronome, de l'autre. On sait bien, en effet, que cette thématique de l'intériorisation et la transformation par le dedans sont propres à l'un et l'autre, n'en déplaise à Thiel (pour ce qui se réfère à Ezéchiel). Comme ces deux points ont été, je crois, suffisamment élucidés par Weinfeld [19] en tenant compte des particularités de chacun, je n'y insisterai pas. Ce qui frappe le plus, c'est peut-être l'absence de la référence à l'esprit, chez Jérémie (p. 32). Notons encore que, à cette référence près, les deux textes (Jér. xxxi 33a, beta; Ez. xxxvi 27a) sont identiques. On se meut dans la même ambiance littéraire et religieuse, sans nier pour autant les différences personelles et historico-traditionelles.

Le texte Jér. xxxii 37-41 appartient sans doute à la même coulée. J'ai déjà noté la parenté redactionelle qui associe ces textes jérémiens, quoi qu'il en soit de leur authenticité de détail. On trouve ici fondamentalement le même vocabulaire: le cœur (un, changé ou nouveau)[20] et le don (*'ettēn*) intérieur de la "crainte", à la place de la loi (*vv.* 39, 40),[21] et, bien entendu, le pacte éternel (*v.* 40). On sait que plusieurs auteurs considèrent 29b-41 comme "interpolés".[22] Mais d'autres sont moins négatifs.[23] Il ne faut pas descendre en tout cas jusqu'à une deuxième rédaction dtn. (comme le fait Thiel, p. 27). Je dirais, au contraire, que tous ces textes se tiennent et appartien-

correction proposée par Rudolph (p. 69) et acceptée par la *Biblia Hebraica Stuttgartensia*. On se demande si elle est strictement nécessaire. Le thème de la circoncision du cœur est ignoré par Thiel et aussi, si je ne m'abuse pas, par Weippert.

[19] Pp. 30ss. Weinfeld note très justement que le thème de la connaissance est assez diversement présenté par Ezéchiel (p. 33).

[20] Respectivement le TM, les LXX et le syriaque.

[21] C'est toujours, en effet, d'un côté et de l'autre, la même phraséologie. Cf. Weinfeld, pp. 30s., n. 49. Mais je crois que la "crainte" est plus proche de la "loi" (c.à.d., de son observance) que de la "connaissance".

[22] Cf. vgr. Rudolph, p. 215. Mais il reconnait en même temps que xxxi 31-34 y est "approfondi". Cf. aussi Alonso Schökel/Sicre (p. 569).

[23] Cf. vgr. Bright, p. 298: "Although there is nothing in these verses that is foreign to Jeremiah's thought. . .". Même Alonso Schökel/Sicre (ubi supra) se contentent de dire: "Es fácil que el texto primitivo haya sido sometido a amplificaciones posteriores".

nent à une intuition très profonde d'un certain courant prophétique.

Il est vrai, et il faut le souligner très nettement, que le texte jérémien xxxi 31-34 s'en détache avec une valeur propre, d'une audace extraordinaire. Il se permet, en effet, au nom de l'auteur du pacte lui-même, une comparaison entre un pacte "antérieur", conclu "avec leurs pères quand je les ai pris par la main pour les faire du sortir du pays d'Egypte" (*v.* 32, traduction *TOB*) et un "pacte nouveau". On sait que cette expression est un hapax VT. Elle ne se retrouve que dans la partie chrétienne de la Bible (et à Qumran). On ne se tromperait pas beaucoup si l'on voyait dans cette affirmation de Jérémie un des éléments les plus personnels et les plus distinctifs de son eschatologie.[24]

On sait que le Deutéronome ne parle pas de pacte "nouveau", mais de pacte "renouvelé", ce qui n'est pas tout à fait la même chose. Von Rad a souligné ce point.[25] Buis (pp. 9, 11) arrive même à dire que la tradition dont ce texte pourrait dépendre "n'est pas celle qui s'exprime dans les textes élohistes et dans le Deutéronome; c'est une tradition originale, sans doute propre à Jérusalem".

Je serais plutôt tenté de suivre Weinfeld (pp. 43ss.) et de trouver chez Osée les origines de cette conception de l'alliance nouvelle. L'expression, il est vrai, ne s'y trouve pas. Mais il y a le même rythme de pensée et plus d'un contact littéraire et théologique. Il y a, par exemple, une étape qui finit (cf. Os. i 9, ii, 4) et une autre qui commence (cf. ii 16 et surtout *v.* 20), précisément sous le signe de la *b^erît*. Il y aussi la notion de la connaissance de YHWH, si typique du livre d'Osée.[26] Et l'on sait les rapports qui existent, de l'avis de beaucoup d'exégètes, entre les deux prophètes, surtout aux débuts du deuxième. Je crois donc que la position de Thiel (pp. 12-13) est par trop négative.

Il reste à préciser, dans la mesure du possible, en quel sens cette alliance est "nouvelle". S'il est vrai, comme je viens de le dire, que l'alliance de Jér. xxxi est la seule à être ainsi qualifiée, il ne faut

---

[24] Cf. encore Bright, p. 287: "Although the passage may not preserve the prophet's *ipsissima verba*, it represents what might well be considered the high point of his theology. It is certainly one of the profoundest and most moving passages in the entire Bible."

[25] II, p. 282: "Nur in einem Punkt besteht ein Unterschied: darin nämlich, dass Jeremia von einem neuen Bund spricht, während das Deuteronomium an dem alten Bund festhält, indem es dessen Gültigkeit bis an die Grenze des theologisch Möglichen hin . . . ausdehnt." Une idée qu'il serait fécond d'explorer.

[26] S'il m'est permis de me citer moi-même, j'ai voulu expliquer ces textes à cette lumière, dans *Amor, Pecado, Alianza* (*Una lectura del Profeta Oseas*) (Buenos Aires, 1977), pp. 21, 41, etc. Le langage nuptial répond au langage du pacte.

pas perdre de vue le fait qu'il y a plusieurs alliances "nouvelles" dans l'histoire religieuse d'Israël. Celle avec Abraham (Gen. xv, xvii) n'est-elle pas "nouvelle" par rapport à celle avec Noé (Gen. ix 8-17)? Et celle du Sinaï (quoiqu'il en soit de la critique historico-littéraire des textes) n'est-elle pas aussi "nouvelle" par rapport avec celle d'Abraham (cf. Ex. xxiv)? Et n'oublions pas le pacte avec David (cf. 2 Sam. xxiii 5; Ps. lxxxix 4, 35, 40, cxxxii 12), si difficile que soit son interprétation. On pourrait donc dire, au moins dans un certain sens et en prenant les textes tels quels, que cette histoire est présentée comme une succession d'alliances.[27] C'est un contexte à ne pas ignorer quand on fait l'exégèse d'une alliance qui est spécifiquement proclamée comme "nouvelle".

De fait, celle-ci est qualifiée de telle par rapport à celle conclue "à la sortie d'Egypte". La formule est encore répétée trois fois: xi 4, 7, xxxiv 13, toujours, semble-t-il, à propos du Deutéronome. Mais ce n'est pas à l'alliance de Moab que Jérémie fait allusion. Celle-ci n'est d'ailleurs qu'un renouvellement de celle du Sinaï-Horeb. C'est de cette dernière que le texte parle (*v*. 32),[28] avec même une référence à ce que l'on tient à appeler le "prologue historique". Elle a été "rompue" (*prr*) par "eux", plutôt la "maison d'Israël" (et dans la relecture, celle de Juda: *v*. 31) que les "pères". Ils en étaient donc partie prenante et avaient ce redoutable pouvoir. On reconnait, sans l'imagerie matrimoniale (laquelle, d'ailleurs, n'est pas absente: cf. ii 1-2, iii 1-5), le mouvement de pensée d'Osée. Mais, précisement, une alliance de ce genre n'est jamais totalement rompue. C'est ici qu'intervient la question de l'inégalité des partenaires, dont on a fait tant de cas récemment.[29] Le partenaire divin, qui prend l'initiative, n'est pas nécessairement affecté par l'infidélité de l'autre. C'était déjà le message d'Osée, soit sous l'imagerie matrimoniale (ch. i-iii), qui rend compréhensible en elle-même cette perséverance, soit sans elle (cf. xi 8-9). Le présent chapitre de Jérémie commence par affirmer la valeur éternelle de l'amour et de la *ḥesed* de YHWH (xxxi 3). La "nouveauté", si elle suppose la rupture du pacte précédent, est toujours en continuité avec ce qui l'inspirait et sur quoi il a été fondé. On n'en tient pas suffisamment compte quand on veut l'expliquer.[30]

---

[27] Et pas seulement par les deutéronomistes. Cf. Thiel, p. 16.

[28] Cf. vgr. Rudolph, p. 201; Weippert, p. 337, etc. D'autres auteurs ne se posent même pas le problème (cf. vgr. Bright).

[29] Cf. Thiel, p. 11, en se réclamant de Kutsch.

[30] Ainsi vgr. von Rad (II, p. 283s.): "denn es wurde von ihm [Jeremia] die

Cependant il est clair que la "nouveauté" est en rapport avec la fragilité du pacte ancien, du côté humain, et est destinée à rémédier ce qui la rendait possible. La loi n'est certainement pas laissée de côté. Au contraire, elle est toujours là (cf. *tôrātî*, *v.* 33). Seulement, elle devient désormais aussi un principe intérieur d'action, qui donne la possibilité de l'observer fidèlement. On voit que, en un certain sens, Jérémie fait face au problème qui, plusieurs siècles après, angoissera Paul (cf., par ex., Gal. iii), et qui, de son temps, ou peu après, est aussi considéré par Ezéchiel (xxxvi 26-27). C'est parce que les Israélites reçoivent un cœur nouveau et un esprit nouveau qu'ils deviennent capables d'observer les commandements. Ce problème théologique n'est donc pas propre au Nouveau Testament, comme on le dit fréquemment, mais est déja perçu, dans toute sa gravité, au sein même de l'Ancien.

Il y a encore le thème de l'enseignement, ou plutôt de la connaissance de Dieu, propre à chacun (*v.* 34a), et qui rendrait celui-là superflu. Au fond, et si l'on considère les choses dans leur dimension la plus vraie, ce thème ne diffère pas radicalement du précédent, étant donné que la "connaissance" dont il s'agit n'est que l'adhésion au vrai Dieu et à sa volonté.[31] Ce qui est annoncé c'est donc, encore une fois, la possibilité de rester fidèle à cette adhésion et d'en traduire les conséquences dans la vie. On pourrait même dire que Jérémie envisage ici surtout le dépassement de l'idolâtrie et de la fausse religion qu'il a si vivement condamnées (cf. vgr. vii 1-11).[32] Dans cette même ligne, je voudrais souligner ici l'importance de la "formule d'appartenance" (aussi appelée "formule d'alliance") du *v.* 33b. On sait les discussions que suscite l'interprétation de cette formule.[33] Je n'y entre pas. Je me rallie aux conclusions de Weinfeld.[34] Le contexte original de la formule serait celui du mariage et de l'adoption

---

Gültigkeit des Heilgrundes, auf den sich das damalige Israel berief, auf den ganzen Linie bestritten" (mais cf. les limitations suggérées, p. 285: "das Neue wird sich . . . ganz nach dem Modell des Alten ereignen"). C'est aussi la position de Buis (p. 5) et, si je l'ai bien comprise, aussi celle de Weinfeld (p. 34, etc.).

[31] Cf., dans mon livre cité supra n. 26, le commentaire à Os. vi 6 (pp. 67-8).

[32] Sur les problèmes littéraires posés par ce texte (et qu'il ne faut pas exagérer) cf. vgr. Rudolph, pp. 50-1.

[33] Cf. déja Buis, p. 4, qui se réclame de R. Smend, dont il reprend la curieuse affirmation: "Une telle expression (la formule en question) ne peut s'employer qu'avant l'alliance—quand il faut la présenter—ou quand elle a disparue, et non tant qu'elle est vécue." On se demande pourquoi. Cf. encore Thiel, pp. 21, 22 avec la note 67a, où il enregistre sa bibliographie.

[34] Pp. 27 ss., n. 41, et les articles qu'il y cite, notamment *JAOS* 90 (1970), p. 90, et *Bib* 56 (1975), p. 125, avec les notes.

(cf. ici même xxxi 9b).[35] Elle est donc très apte à exprimer le rapport de l'alliance, qui tend à établir un lien libre, exclusif et aimant entre les deux partenaires. Je note encore que cette formule forme ici le centre d'un espèce de chiasme, dont les éléments parallèles sont précisément les conditions de "nouveauté" de l'alliance, expliquées plus haut. Or, si je ne me trompe pas, l'usage même de la formule confirme ce que je viens de dire sur l'horizon religieux qui dominerait ici la pensée de Jérémie: il s'agirait surtout de la suppression définitive de l'idolâtrie et du vrai rapport avec Dieu. Israël n'aura plus d'autre Dieu que Dieu et lui obéira du fond du cœur.

Est-ce cela que signifie, comme le suggére (entre autres) Weinfeld, si je comprends bien sa pensée, que le pacte nouveau ne sera plus "based on formal statutes" (p. 32) et qu'il sera plutôt associé "with a circumcision of the heart than with a circumcision of the flesh" (p. 34)? [36] Il y a sans doute du vrai en tout cela. On pourrait ainsi se demander, comme le font plusieurs auteurs, si la "nouveauté" du pacte ne consiste dans l'instauration d'une religion purement intérieure, sans loi écrite et en marge d'un enseignement extérieur.[37] On s'est aussi demandé si la critique prophétique du culte impliquait la suppression de toute religiosité extérieure.[38] Mais la pensée jérémienne ne va pas précisément dans cette direction. Les "formal statutes" ne disparaîtront pas, ni (au moins pour le moment) la circoncision de la chair, ni la nécessité d'une catéchèse, ou d'un enseignement. Il s'en faut encore de beaucoup pour que la Loi soit mise en question comme telle. Et on peut argumenter qu'il y a toujours des "lois" et des affirmations dogmatiques, pour ne pas parler de magistère, même dans les versions les plus spiritualisées du christianisme.

Jérémie, dirai-je, se préoccupe surtout de la possibilité finalement

[35] C'est la conclusion de Weinfeld, au moins pour ce qui regarde le mariage. C'est ici, je crois, qu'il faut trouver l'explication de *bāʿaltî* au *v.* 32, où résonne le *baʿal* d'Os. ii 18. On sait que précisément Osée hésite entre rapport nuptial et filial comme expression (toujours insuffisante) de celui qui intercède entre Israël et son Dieu (cf. xi 1ss.).

[36] Weinfeld pense aussi que Jérémie laisse de côté l'arche (pp. 19-26) et relativise considérablement les sacrifices (pp. 52-5). Ce sont deux des antinomies qu'il croit découvrir dans le livre. Je n'entre pas dans le détail.

[37] Cf. à ce propos von Rad (II, p. 227): "Infolge dieser schöpferischen Einpflanzung des Gottenwillens in das menschliche Herz wird also jegliches theologische Lehramt in Wegfall kommen und alles Mahnen und Zurechtbringen überflüssig werden."

[38] Cette problématique me semble aujourd'hui dépassée. Cf. vgr. R. de Vaux, *Les Institutions de l'Ancien Testament* II (Paris, 1960) pp. 344-7.

octroyée à l'israélite (et au fond, à l'homme tout court) de faire sien cet enseignement au sens le plus fort du mot et d'adhérer ainsi de tout son être personnel à son Dieu, sans dissimulation et sans défaillance. L'alliance qui "obligeait" [39] et qui "oblige" toujours, donne aussi la faculté d'y obéir pleinement "de tout son cœur, de tout son être, de toute sa force", comme le dit la formule deutéronomique bien connue (cf. vi 5 et passim, avec des modifications diverses). C'est la "nouveauté" de cette alliance. Ce thème de la "nouveauté" sera repris ensuite de façon diverse et dans des contextes différents, dont je n'ai pas à m'occuper. Qu'il suffise ici de noter qu'il est destiné à incorporer la création entière (cf. Is. lxv 17, lxvi 22) [40] et qu'il domine le Nouveau Testament, soit dans la tradition évangélique (cf. déjà les deux petites paraboles de Marc ii 21-22 par), soit dans la pensée paulinienne (cf. par ex. Gal. vi 15), soit dans l'apocalyptique (cf. Ap. xxi 5).

Etant donné le caractère exceptionnel de cette alliance, il n'y a pas à s'étonner si elle est, par la suite, qualifiée d'"éternelle". On retrouve déjà ce terme dans le texte du chapitre xxxii (*v.* 40), dont on a parlé auparavant et qui donne comme un commentaire de l'oracle du chapitre précédent.[41] Mais il devient surtout fréquent dans Ezéchiel et le Deutéro-Isaïe. Les textes d'Ezéchiel (xvi 60, xxxiv 25,[42] xxxvii 26 avec *b^e^rît šālôm*) sont généralement considérés comme postérieurs au prophète lui-même.[43] Cela ne veut pas dire cependant qu'ils soient étrangers à sa pensée authentique, laquelle n'aurait connue aucune *Bundestheologie* (selon Thiel, p. 22). Pour le deuxième Isaïe on est moins négatif (Thiel, pp. 22-3). Ici, on a le terme (lv 3, lxi 8) [44] et la chose (liv 9-10, lix 21).[45] La *b^e^rît ʿōlām* réapparait encore chez Baruch (ii 35), dans un développement qui dépend de sources antérieures.

Ce serait sans doute une erreur de réduire des textes si différents, par leur origine et leur contexte, à un dénominateur commun.

---

[39] Cf. la *Verpflichtung* de Kutsch, dont Thiel fait état (pp. 11, etc.) et l'article (déjà cité) de Weinfeld, "*B^e^rît*-Covenant vs. Obligation", *Bib* 56 (1975), pp. 120-8.

[40] On sait que la "nouveauté" est un des thèmes majeurs du Deutéro-Isaïe.

[41] On a déja mentionné les problèmes d'authenticité que ce texte suscite et qui encore une fois ne doivent pas être majorés.

[42] Ce texte parle de *b^e^rît šālôm*, mais avec le même caractère de pérennité.

[43] Ainsi dans le commentaire de W. Zimmerli, *Ezechiel* (Neukirchen-Vluyn, 1969), pp. 369s., 847, 913. Cf. aussi Weinfeld, pp. 45ss., moins préoccupé de questions d'authenticité littéraire.

[44] Ce texte se rattache plutôt au troisième Isaïe.

[45] Même observation.

Mais il faut quand même retenir la pénétrante observation de von Rad, dans sa *Theologie des Alten Testaments* (II, p. 283), sur le fait que pendant une certaine période de l'histoire religieuse d'Israël "das Bundesproblem die Menschen beschäftigt hat". Ce serait, selon lui, le temps du deuxième Isaïe et de la révision rédactionnelle d'Ezéchiel (p. 283). C'est peut-être un peu trop court. Quoiqu'il en soit, on comprend bien que, quand tout semble remis en question (pour ne pas dire complètement fini), après la ruine de Jérusalem (mais il y a ici et là des lueurs d'espoir), le sens et la valeur de l'engagement de Dieu avec son peuple soient réaffirmés avec une force éclatante. Dans une certaine mesure, c'est le *Sitz im Leben* de l'affirmation originelle de Jérémie. Et j'ajouterai que l'histoire deutéronomique (ou sa dernière rédaction, si elle en a plus d'une) se meut dans le même climat, puisque, comme j'ai essayé de le montrer ailleurs,[46] un des grands dilemmes de cet ouvrage est l'apparente opposition entre l'indignité de la monarchie davidique et la fermeté de la promesse faite à David, antinomie que l'historien dtn résout dans le sens positif, ou, pour mieux dire, pour laquelle certains indices révèlent de quel côté il voit la solution.[47]

Il faut noter encore, puisque nous parlons de David et de la promesse davidique, que plus d'un texte cité rattachent l'alliance définitive à la restauration du "prince David" (cf. Ez. xxxiv 23-24 avec la formule d'appartenance rattachée à celui-ci; xxxvii 24), tandis que Is. lv 3 est lui-même un texte "davidique". La critique littéraire croit trouver une césure entre les mentions de l'alliance et l'annonce du nouveau David.[48] C'est peut-être vrai. Mais il se trouve que la même association existe déja dans les textes jérémiens (cf. xxx 8-9 et surtout dans le commentaire de xxxiii 15 // xxiii 5, qui se trouve dans les *vv.* 12-26 du même chapitre) et leurs prolongations.[49] D'autre part, la première référence au *b^e^rît ʿōlām* se trouve dans les *novissima verba Davidis* (2 Sam. xxiii 5). Le texte d'Is. lv 3 témoigne de la même association, même s'il s'agit de l'extension à tout Israël du privilège

[46] Dans ma communication au VI Congrès d'Etudes juives à Jérusalem.

[47] C'est, je crois, le sens de la conclusion de tout l'ouvrage, tel qu'il nous est parvenu (2 Rois xxv 27-30).

[48] C'est l'opinion de Zimmerli, pp. 844ss., 911ss.

[49] Jer. xxxiii 12-26 est considéré postérieur, surtout à cause de la mention des lévites. Cf. Rudolph, p. 217. On sait qu'il manque dans les LXX. Weinfeld, (pp. 43ss.) suit l'histoire de cette "dimension" davidique de ce qu'il appelle "the redemption by David" (p. 43), à la place de la "redemption by Moses". Cette nouvelle rédemption serait en rapport soit avec le nouvel Exode soit avec la nouvelle alliance.

davidique.[50] L'alliance "éternelle" aurait donc été vue, au moins par quelques uns, en rapport étroit avec le *Davidbund*.

On sait, d'ailleurs, que cette alliance indéfectible est, selon P, celle conclue avec Noé (Gen. ix 16) et surtout avec Abraham (Gen. xvii 7, 13, 19). Sans entrer ici dans la question de plus en plus discutée de la date de P, on constate que, à un certain moment aussi, la réflexion sacerdotale a projeté sur la vieille alliance abrahamique et sur sa propre conception d'une alliance noachique, le même caractère d'indéfectibilité. Est-ce que cela répond au même besoin de garantie divine contre toute rupture? [51] Il est clair, en tout cas, que, dans toute cette série de textes, le problème de l'obéissance intérieure à la volonté divine et de la transformation requise pour le faire n'est pas posé (sauf, bien entendu, en Ez. xxxvi). La solution à la question de l'infidélité est cherchée ailleurs, à savoir, dans un acte souverain (et unilatéral) du partenaire divin. [52]

L'alliance aurait donc changé de structure et, de bilatérale, elle se serait transformée en unilatérale? C'est le problème que Buis soulève (pp. 11s.) à propos de la forme littéraire qu'il croit avoir discernée dans les textes étudiés (et dans plusieurs autres). On sait que d'autres auteurs sont allés beaucoup plus loin: il n'y aurait jamais eu une "auf Gegenseitigkeit beruhendes, wechselseitig einklagbares Verhältnis" (Thiel, p. 11, d'apres Kutsch). Sans entrer dans le vif du débat, on peut se demander s'il n'y a pas ici un équivoque de base. Le rapport de Dieu avec l'homme, et particulièrement avec un peuple, ne peut jamais être exprimé de façon adéquate. Si une certaine tradition biblique (il y en a d'autres) a choisi la notion de pacte ou d'alliance pour l'exprimer, en s'inspirant de modèles contemporains, ce n'était pas pour l'assumer telle quelle. On n'a jamais conçu ce rapport d'alliance comme un rapport synallagmatique, ou comme un *do ut des*.[53] Il n'y a jamais eu notamment de "Rechtsanspruch Israels gegen YHWH" (Thiel). Mais il peut y avoir eu la libre acceptation d'un service et d'une obéissance exclusive (comme on la retrouve, par exemple, dans Jos. xxiv). Celle-ci est, de son côté, caractéristique du

[50] Cf. Thiel, n. 76, et les auteurs cités.

[51] Cf. Cl. Westermann, *Genesis* Lief. 14 (Neukirchen-Vluyn, 1979), pp. 315s.

[52] C'est ici, je pense, qu'il faudrait tenir compte de l'observation proposée par H. Cazelles, dans sa recension du livre de J.Van Seters (*VT* 28 [1978], p. 248), sur l'usage de *hēqîm* comme verbe régissant *b*ᵉ*rît*. Mais l'on constate que, dans Ez. et le Dt.-Is., le verbe est toujours *kārat*, sauf (si je ne me trompe pas) en Ez. xvi 60.

[53] C'est ce que semble supposer la présentation de Thiel.

Dieu d'Israël. Et c'est précisément cette prétention à l'exclusivité et au don total qui est présentée sous forme de pacte, quelle que soit la date de son apparition. Personellement, je crois qu'elle est assez ancienne.

C'est l'expérience répétée de l'échec qui a conduit à la recherche d'une nouvelle solution. Cette nouvelle solution n'exclut pas la libre acceptation du partenaire humain, qui ne reste pas (et ne peut pas rester) totalement passif. Mais elle peut suivre un double chemin. Elle peut envisager la transformation intérieure du partenaire humain de façon que son acceptation et sa réponse ne soient plus mises en question. C'est la solution de Jér. xxxi 31-34 et d'Ez. xxxvi 26ss. Elle peut aussi insister sur l'absolue gratuité du don divin et mettre l'accent sur le caractère non conditionnel de ce don. C'est ce que nous trouvons chez les autres textes d'Ezéchiel, chez le deuxième et le troisième Isaïe (et chez Baruch), et plus particulièrement chez P.[54] A ce niveau, comme l'a très bien vu le cantique hébraïque de Luc i 68-79, que nous connaissons sous le nom de cantique de Zacharie, l'alliance est aussi un serment (cf. *v.* 72-73).[55] Paul parlera d'une "promesse" ou des "promesses" (cf. vgr. Gal. iii 16 (ἐπαγγελίαι), mais c'est toujours le pacte avec Abraham (*v.* 17 διαθήκη). L'alliance est tout cela à la fois, et même plus.

Il reste un mot à dire sur la question posée au commencement de cet article, c'est-à-dire, le rapport de la problématique esquissée dans cette brève présentation et l'un des aspects sans doute fondamentaux d'un théologie chrétienne du Judaïsme. L'alliance "nouvelle et éternelle" [56] est-elle exclusivement "dans le Christ", l'autre étant

[54] C'est ce que Weinfeld appelle "the covenant of grace" (p. 50) et "the covenant of grant" (*Bib* 56 [1975], p. 125, où il cite son article de *JAOS* 90 [1970], pp. 184-203, qui s'intitule précisément "The Covenant of Grant in the Old Testament and in the Ancient Near East"). Weinfeld a très bien vu qu'il ne s'agit que d'un type de *b^e^rît*. Il y en a au moins un autre. Cf. *Bib* 56, pp. 124s.: "One cannot escape the conclusion therefore that though *b^e^rît* as such denotes 'Verpflichtung' its general understanding was that of an agreement. Our translation of *b^e^rît* with 'covenant' and 'Bund' is therefore not far from the truth. The same applies to the theological aspect of *b^e^rît*. Though the *b^e^rît* sworn for the Patriarchs or for David is a unilateral pledge of God, while the *b^e^rît* of Sinai constitutes the pledge of the people for the purpose of keeping the law, the very existence of mutual commitments created a kind of reciprocity which no doubt fertilized theological thinking in ancient Israel." Je trouve ces vues assez justes.

[55] Il n'est pas sans importance que le cantique souligne (*v.* 69) le rapport avec David. Cf. supra et R. E. Brown, *The Birth of the Messiah* (Garden City, New York, 1977), p. 383.

[56] Les deux termes ont été finalement associés dans la formule de consécration du vin eucharistique de la liturgie romaine.

irrémédiablement vieillie et caduque? C'est bien ce que semble affirmer le fameux passage de l'épître aux Hébreux viii 7-13. Mais ici encore, il faut se méfier des solutions trop hâtives et unilatérales. Il est vrai que, pour les chrétiens, le double caractère de nouveauté et d'indéfectibilité de l'alliance se réalise d'une façon tout à fait unique dans le Christ, sa mort et sa résurrection, le Nouvel Exode dont parle Luc ix 31. Mais il y a eu autre nouvel exode avant celui-ci: celui dont parlent plusieurs des textes éxaminés ici et d'autres encore.[57] Je crois que H. Cazelles a raison de rattacher le "commencement" de la nouvelle alliance à ce nouvel exode, quitte à affirmer tout de suite qu'elle n'est "pas encore 'achevée' à la fin de la Bible hébraïque".[58] Si l'on ne peut parler, comme on le fait parfois, de deux alliances également "nouvelles" et "indéfectibles",[59] on pourrait quand même dire (toujours du point de vue d'une théologie chrétienne) que l'alliance, ou les alliances, conclues avec le peuple élu n'ont pas perdu toute leur valeur, mais qu'elles restent inachevées tant que l'union des deux peuples, juif et gentil, n'est pas consumée "dans le Christ". "Car, comme le dit l'épître aux Romains, les dons et l'appel de Dieu sont irrévocables" (ii 29).[60]

---

[57] Ces textes ont été bien étudiés par Buis (pp. 2ss.) et aussi, d'un point de vue plus théologique, par Weinfeld (pp. 48ss.).

[58] Cf. la récension citée supra (note 52) p. 248.

[59] L'une, dit-on dans certaines présentations, celle conclue dans le Christ, serait reservée aux Gentils, l'autre propre aux Juifs. Mais on pourrait ainsi contredire un texte aussi explicite que Eph. ii 11-22, qui, s'il souligne le privilège des Juifs, insiste sur l'unité, dans le Christ, des deux peuples.

[60] L'alliance "près de disparaître" d'Hébr. viii 13 (ἐγγὺς ἀφανισμοῦ) ne représenterait ainsi qu'une étape entre autres, en attendant la consommation définitive.

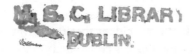

SANCTA CONTAGION AND ALTAR/CITY ASYLUM

BY

JACOB MILGROM

Berkeley, California

§1. *The formula.* The formula for sancta contagion is *kol-hannōgēaʿ b-yiqdāš*. It occurs four times in the Priestly Code, twice in connection with sacred furniture of the Tabernacle (Exod. xxix 37, xxx 26-29) and twice with sacred offerings (Lev. vi 11, 20). These objects of *nōgēaʿ b-* merit closer examination.

The first instance singles out the sacrificial altar (*bammizbēaḥ*, Exod. xxix 37).[1] In the second, the antecedent of *bāhem* (Exod. xxx 29) is all the previously enumerated sancta: "With it (the sacred anointing oil) anoint the Tent of Meeting, the Ark of the Pact, the table and all its utensils, the lampstand and all its fittings, the altar of incense, the altar of whole offering and all its utensils, and the laver and its stand" (*vv*. 26-28). Thus not just the outer altar but the Tabernacle and all its furniture—all anointed with the sacred oil—come under the jurisdiction of this formula.

The remaining two occurrences of the formula are found in the sections dealing with the priestly perquisites from two sacrifices, the *minḥāh* and *ḥaṭṭāʾt*. In the latter case, the object is specified as *bᵉśārāh* (Lev. vi 20). The context makes it clear that the reference is to the meat of the *ḥaṭṭāʾt* cooked by the priests (*vv*. 19, 21). The same holds true for the *minḥāh*; the formula follows the notice that it has been baked by the priests (Lev. vi 10). In both instances, the implication is that the contagious power of sacrifices is effective only after the altar (i.e. the deity) receives its due, i.e., when the *ʾazkārāh* of the *minḥāh* is offered up (e.g. Lev. ii 2, 9) and when the blood of the *ḥaṭṭāʾt* is daubed on the altar horns (e.g. Lev. iv 7, 18, 25, 30, 34). It is no accident that the formula does not occur with the *ʿōlāh* since all the flesh is consumed on the altar with no opportunity for making contact with a profane object. One further implication:

[1] The singling out of the altar (Exod. xxix 37) should occasion no surprise. It was the most exposed of the sancta and within reach of the laity. For the significance of this fact see below.

the sancity of the animal is limited to its offerable parts, i.e., the flesh, suet and blood (cf. Lev. vi 20), but not to its skin which, in the *ʿōlāh*, is given to the officiating priest as his wages (Lev. vii 8). Moreover, though the animal is "most sacred" from the time of its dedication,[2] its offerer, though a layman, may handle it and even perform preliminary rites with it inside the sacred precincts (e.g. hand-laying and slaughtering, Lev. i 4-5, iv 29) without fear of contracting its sanctity.[3] The reason seems to be that the power of contagion is not imparted to the sacrificial animal until its blood is sprinkled on the altar, i.e., when it is charged with the altar's sacred force. Similarly the Red Cow, like every burnt *ḥaṭṭāʾt*, does not convey uncleanness to its handlers until the manipulation of its blood (Num. xix 4).

The *minḥāh* citation is even more illuminating: *bāhem*, the object of *nāgaʿ*, is in the plural (Lev. vi 11). At first glance this is surprising since in the entire pericope (*vv.* 7-11) the *minḥāh* is invariably in the singular. However, closer inspection leaves no doubt that the antecedent is *ʾiššē* a plural noun which not only refers to the *minḥāh* but also to the *ḥaṭṭāʾt* and *ʾāšām* offerings mentioned in the immediately preceding verse (*v.* 10b). The formula here is, then, an attempt to generalize all the sacrifices subject to its ruling. This deduction is comfirmed by a verse in Ezekiel: "This is the place where the priests shall boil the *ʾāšām* and *ḥaṭṭāʾt* and where they shall bake the *minḥāh* in order not to bring *them* out into the outer court and so communicate holiness to the people" (Ezek. xlvi 20).[4] Without further ado, one may deduce that the formula applies only to *qodᵉšē qᵒdāšīm*, "most sacred offerings" (and so specified in each pericope, Lev. vi 10, 18), implying that the meat of the *šᵉlāmīm*, which does not

---

[2] Cf. J. Milgrom, *Cult and Conscience* (Leiden, 1976) p. 39, n. 147; idem, *Studies in Levitical Terminology* (Berkeley, 1970), p. 96, n. 17; idem, "*Šôq hattᵉrūmāh*: A Chapter in Cultic History", *Tarbiẓ* 42 (1973/4), n. 16.

[3] It is striking that the rabbis hold that the *minḥāh* is subject to two sanctifications: when it is dedicated by oral declaration and again when it is placed in a sacred vessel after which its sacred status is irreversible (T. Men. i 16-17; B. Soṭ. 14b [ber.]; cf. M. Men. xii 1). However, it seems to me that the original reason for the second dedication was to set the time for the onset of contagion. For when the *minḥāh* comes into contact with the sacred vessel it absorbs its holiness. The equivalent moment in a flesh sacrifice is when it comes into contact with the altar.

[4] The verbal form *nāgaʿ b-* is absent but implied: so also in Ezek. xliv 19. Ezekiel also serves as corroboration for the rule that sacred flesh is contagious only after it is sacrificed.

fall into the category of "most sacred", would not be affected by the formula.[5]

For the sake of completeness, it should be noted here that the book of Ezekiel applies the formula to a fifth case: the priestly garments (Ezek. xliv 19; cf. xlii 14), which will be discussed anon.[6] Our attention can now turn to the formula itself. Each term will be analysed separately.[7]

§2. *yiqdāš*. The qal of *qādaš* means "become holy". This is its unquestioned meaning elsewhere in Scripture (e.g. Exod. xxix 21; Num. xvii 2, 3; Deut. xxii 9; 1 Sam. xxi 6).[8] Yet in our formula this meaning has been disputed:

(1) The Targums consistently render it *yitqaddaš*, "will purify himself", as Pseudo-Jonathan (on Exod. xxix 37) makes clear: "whoever of the sons of Aaron touches the altar must purify himself; however, it is not possible for the rest of the people to touch (it)

[5] The implication for the meaning of "sacred flesh" (Hag. ii 12) is discussed below, § 5.

[6] This category is missing in P and, as will be shown in § 4, is opposed by it.

[7] Two additional applications of the formula are alleged for 1 Sam. xxi 6 and Isa. lxv 5. In Samuel the enigmatic phrase is *ʾap kī hayyōm yiqdaš bakkeli*. According to one interpretation, David argues that since his men have remained holy by abstaining from women on ordinary campaigns "how much more will they be holy today?" (*NEB*). However, the claim that *k^{e}lī* can refer to the human body is unwarranted. The second interpretation, "how much more today will their vessels be holy?" (*RSV*), is open to the dual objection that the preposition *b-* is ignored and that *yiqdaš* must mean to remain in a holy state. The third rendering, "All the more may consecrated food be put into their vessels today" (*NJPS*), has no basis in the text. The LXX's διὰ τὰ σκεύη μου, "because of my weapons", requires the plural *yiqd^{e}šu* and *kēlay*. It leads S. R. Driver, *Notes on the Hebrew Text of the Books of Samuel* (Oxford, 1913), to conjecture "will they be consecrated with (their) gear?" In any case, at issue is the ancient doctrine of the holiness of the war camp (Deut. xxiii 10-11) whose soldiers must refrain from all defilement including sexual congress (cf. 2 Sam. xi 11). It has, however, nothing to do with the transfer of holiness.

kī q^{e}daštīkā (Isa. lxv 5) is rendered "for I am set apart from you (RSV); "for I am too sacred for you" (*NEB*); "for I am purer/holier than you" (Targum, Rashi, Ibn Ezra, Ibn Janaḥ, Abarbanel). Common to all these interpretations is the notion that the idolater, by dint of his ritual, feels holier than his fellows and keeps them at arm's length lest they defile him. In any case, this is no transfer of holiness, but, on the contrary, the fear of defilement. As far as I know, only J. Pedersen, *Israel III-IV* (London and Copenhagen, 1940), p. 281, and J. L. McKenzie, *Second Isaiah* (Garden City, New York, 1968), preceded by Malbim, translate: "I will sanctify you", requiring, however, that the verb be pointed as a piel. See now J. A. Emerton, "Notes on the text and translation of Isaiah xxii 8-11 and lxv 5", *VT* 30 (1980), pp. 446-50.

[8] On 1 Sam. xxi 6 and Isa. lxv 5 see the preceding note; on Hag. ii 12 see § 5; and on Deut. xxii 9 see § 4.

lest they be consumed by the flashing fire that emanates from the sancta".[9] This interpretation for *yiqdāš*, however, cannot be correct since it is limited to the piel and hithpael stems (e.g., Exod. xix 10, 14; Num. xi 18; Josh. vii 13; 1 Sam. xvi 5; 2 Sam. xi 4; Isa. lxvi 17) but is never found in the qal.

(2) The LXX consistently uses the future passive ἁγιασθήσεται, "shall be holy", which also may be rendered "shall be pure/purify oneself".[10] The first rendering, "shall be holy", would mean that the person touching the sancta must himself be holy, i.e. he need be a priest. However, it is objectionable on philological grounds: only the adjective *qādōš* expresses the state of holiness whereas the qal (and other verb forms) indicates the process of becoming holy. The second rendering, "shall be pure/purify oneself", is rejected for the reason given in (1), above.

(3) Of passing interest is A. B. Ehrlich's rendering, "absorb lethal taboo",[11] in support of which he cites Num. iv 15 where the Kohathites touching sancta are liable to death. The analogy, however, does not hold since the sancta alluded to in this verse are restricted to the most sacred furniture and exclude the most sacred offerings. Also, the death penalty is always indicated by the roots *mwt*[12] and *krt*[13] but never by *qdš*.[14]

The meaning of (*kol-hannōgēaʿ b-*) *yiqdāš* is clarified beyond doubt

---

[9] Since the Targums apply the formula only to priests, *yitqaddaš* cannot mean "sanctify oneself", for priests are holy by virtue of their consecration (Exod. xxix; Lev. viii). The verb can only refer to the ritual ablutions required of the priesthood before they may officiate (Exod. xxx 20). Abraham Maimuni, ad loc., states this position clearly: "(this verb) is similar to 'also the priests (*yitqaddāšū*) shall purify themselves'" (Exod. xix 22, cf. *vv.* 10,14). This interpretation is given by most of the medieval exegetes; cf. Ibn Ezra (Short Commentary), Rashbam, Ḥizkuni, Bechor Shor, Abravanel, and also by the Karaites.

[10] It should be noted that the LXX always renders the root *qdš* as ἁγιάζω, including its occurrences in Bath-Sheba's ablutions from her impurity (*mitqaddešet*, 2 Sam. xi 4) and in the purification of the laity and the priesthood at Mt Sinai (Exod. xix 10, 14, and esp. *v.* 22, *yitqaddāšū*). Thus the LXX could have had in mind that the one who touched the altar had to be in a state of purity.

[11] *Randglossen zur hebräischen Bibel* 1 (Leipzig, 1909) on Exod. xxix 37.

[12] Milgrom, *Studies* (n. 2), pp. 5-8.

[13] Cf. W. Zimmerli, "Die Eigenart der prophetischen Rede des Ezechiel", *ZAW* 66 (1954), pp. 1-26, esp. 13-19; M. Tsevat, "Studies in the Book of Samuel, I", *HUCA* 32 (1961), pp. 191-216; D. Wold, *The Biblical Penalty of Kareth* (University of California Dissertation, 1978).

[14] *yiqdāš* in Hag. ii 12 is rendered by the rabbis as *yiṭmāʾ* (B. Pes. 17a; cf. Radak, and Ibn Janaḥ, *Seper Hasharashim*, s.v. *qdš*) but this is due to their unique interpretation of this verse.

when it is compared to its antonymic formulation (*kol-hannōgēaʿ b-*) *yiṭmāʾ* (e.g., Lev. xi 24, 26, 27, 31, 36, 39, xv 10, 11, 21, 23, 27; cf. Hag. ii 12-13). Just as *yiṭmāʾ* can only mean "shall become impure", so *yiqdāš* must be rendered "shall become holy". The formula, then, must signify that contact with a most sacred object brings about the absorption of its holiness.

§3. *nōgēaʿ*. There is almost no dispute that *nōgēaʿ b-* means "touch, come into contact with".[15] However, the nature of the contact is uncertain. Does it make a difference, for example, if the altar is touched deliberately or accidentally? The question of intention, essential though it be, must await the analysis of the final term *kol*.

§4. *kol*: *whoever or whatever*? Surprisingly it is the simple particle *kol* rather than the other terms of the formula that is difficult to render. Does *kol* include persons or is it restricted to inanimate objects, i.e. shall it be rendered "whoever" or "whatever"? As will be shown, the answer to this question will open a new chapter of Israel's cultic history.

The rabbis are unanimous in opting for "whatever" and eliminating the human factor completely. Indeed, they even reduce the compass of "whatever". The contagious sancta, as noted in § 1, above, are of two kinds: the most sacred furniture and the most sacred offerings. Neither kind, aver the rabbis, is contagious to all objects. The most sacred furniture, such as the altar and its vessels (Exod. xxix 37, xxx 29), *meqaddēš ʾet-hārāʾūy lō*, only "sanctifies that which befits it",[16] e.g. that which qualifies to be placed on the altar or

---

[15] This is contested, as far as I know, only by D. Hoffmann, *Das Buch Leviticus* 1 (Berlin, 1905), on vi 20, where he renders *nāgaʿ b-* as "be penetrated" i.e., holiness transferred by absorption. Hoffmann, however, is influenced by the rabbinic reduction of the sancta's powers of contagion and is thereby forced to give *nāgaʿ b-* a passive connotation it never has and an interpretation which the verses he cites fail to support. The Karaite, Daniel Al-Qumisi (on Hag. ii 12), distinguishes between *nāgaʿ ʾel* and *nāgaʿ b-*, rendering the former "touch indirectly (through a medium)". His rendering works for Num. iv 15 but not for 1 Kgs vi 27, Jonah iii 6, or Job ii 5.

[16] M. Zeb. ix 1 ff.; T. Zeb. ix 4; Sifra Zav 1:1 ff.; cf. *qādešū bakkelī*, "sanctify by (contact with) a holy vessel", M. Soṭ. iii 6; M. Men. xii 1; M. Meil. ii 8-9. Whereas Scripture probably means by "sanctify" that the object belongs to the sanctuary, the rabbis restrict its meaning further that it is only eligible for sacrifice. Hence their rule is that only substances eligible for sacrifice to begin with are affected by the formula.

into a sacred vessel.[17] In other words, whatever is eligible *a priori* as an offering, only that is susceptible to sancta contagion.[18] And as for the most sacred offerings (Lev. vi 11, 20), their contagion is communicable only to articles of food *miššeyibla'*, by absorption.[19]

Poles apart from the restricted contagion posited by the rabbis stands the cultic system of Ezekiel who holds that most sacred offerings consecrate persons and not just food: "This is the place where the priests shall boil the *'āšām* and *ḥaṭṭā't* and where they shall bake the *minḥāh*, in order not to bring them into the outer court and so communicate holiness to the people" (Ezek. xlvi 20).[20] Moreover, Ezekiel adds a category of contagious sancta not included in the rabbis' system (nor in the Pentateuch, see § 1, above), i.e., the priestly garments: "When they go out into the outer court (into the outer court) [21] to the people, they shall take off the garments in which they have been officiating and lay them in the sanctuary's chambers; and they shall put on other garments, lest they communicate holiness to the people with their garments" (xliv 19; cf. xlii 14).[22]

It is germane to enquire: is Ezekiel's ruling his own innovation or does it reflect an older law? An answer is at hand if we examine P's position on this matter. To be sure P contains no explicit law con-

---

[17] For cultic vessels which contain the offering, the rabbis impose further restrictions: (1) The contact takes place inside the sacred precincts (M. Zeb. ix 7; T. Zeb. ix 11); (2) *rā'ûy lō*, "befits it", means either wet or dry measure, not both (ibid.; but R. Samuel disagrees, cf. B. Zeb. 98a); (3) the offering must be inside the vessel (T. Zeb. ix 11, not outside, B. Zeb. 98a); (4) According to R. Yohanan (B. Men. 7a), intention is also required.

[18] So in fact it is repeated that sacrificial animals bearing defects were removed from the altar of the Herodian Temple (M. Zeb. ix 3). However, if the defect occurred after the offering was brought into the Temple court, it was acceptable on the altar (according to T. Zeb. ix 5). On this point there is disagreement whether the offering had to "befit the altar or the altar's hearth", the distinction manifesting itself in sacrificial blood or a libation which is offered on the altar but not consumed upon it (M. Zeb. ix 1; T. Zeb. ix 1, 6, 10; cf. B. Pes. 86a; Zeb. 83b, and Rashi on Exod. xxix 37). Indeed, the rabbis restrict the power of the altar even further when they state that the power of the altar to sanctify lasts only as long as the eligible substance remains in contact with it; but once it is removed, the altar cannot sanctify it a second time (M. Zeb. ix 4; T. Zeb. ix 8; S. Lieberman, *Tosefet Rishonim* 2 [Jerusalem, 1938], pp. 210-11).

[19] Sifra Zav 3:6; ibid., par. 3:6; M. Zeb. xi 8; B. Zeb. 98a (ber.); Men. 83a; cf. Rashi and Ibn Ezra, ad loc. The Karaites maintain that vessels as well as food are infected by most sacred offerings, *Sefer Hamivḥar* on Lev. vi 11.

[20] The ideological basis for Ezekiel's ruling will be discussed below, § 7.

[21] Dittograph. Delete with LXX and many Heb. mss.

[22] So LXX and Targ. The conflict is admitted by Radak and the Gaon of Vilna, *Aderet Elijah*; Abravanel states explicitly: "it is an innovation".

cerning the contagion of the priestly garments but its very omission from P's prescription on the contagion of sancta in Exod. xxx 26-30 betrays P's position in a striking way. These verses warrant close examination:

> 26 With it (the sacred anointing oil) anoint the Tent of Meeting, the Ark of the Pact, 27 the table and all its utensils, the lampstand and all its fittings, the altar of incense, 28 the altar of whole offering and all its utensils, and the laver and its stand. 29 Thus you shall consecrate them so that they may be most sacred; *kol-hannōgēaʿ bāhem yiqdāš.* 30 You shall anoint Aaron and his sons, consecrating them to serve me as priests.

That this principle ends with *v.* 30 is shown by the next verse which begins a new subject, the ways of misusing the anointing oil, and by its formulaic opening: "And speak to the Israelite people as follows". Moreover, the unity of *vv.* 26-30 is proven by the other passages dealing with the anointing oil (prescriptive, Exod. xxix 1-37,[23] xl 1-15; descriptive, Lev. viii 1-30) in which both the priestly garments and the cult objects are anointed during the same ceremonial.

Now it should be noticed that in the above-cited pericope, our formula does not come at its end but in its penultimate verse, after the roster of cult objects and before the anointing of the priests (*v.* 29b). Thus the conclusion is unavoidable that the legislator intentionally excludes the priestly garments from the application of the formula because, in his system, the priestly garments do not communicate holiness. That the priestly garments are not subject to the law of sancta contagion is further underscored by a major omission. By itself, *v.* 30 would lead to the deduction that only the persons of Aaron and his sons are anointed, despite the expressed inclusion of the priestly garments among the anointed articles in all the other accounts (Exod. xxix 21, xl 13-15; Lev. viii 30). Again, the reason for the omission here of the priestly garments must be attributed to an overt attempt to dissociate them from the notion

---

[23] Exod. xxix 36 mentions the anointing of the altar to the exclusion of the rest of the sanctuary. Hoffmann's explanation (n. 15, p. 192) is that the altar was anointed in a manner similar to the priests in that both were sprinkled with the sacred oil (Lev. viii 11, 30). The reason, I aver, is simpler: Exod. xxix focuses only on the seven day consecration service and therefore includes only those rites which were repeated each day, i.e., the altar and priestly consecration (*vv.* 35, 37), and omits the anointing of the rest of the sanctuary which took place on the first day alone. Lev. viii, on the other hand, focuses on the ceremonials of the first day—it says nothing about the following days (except by implication, *vv.* 33)—hence it enumerates all the cult objects.

of contagious holiness. This can mean only one thing: P is engaged in a polemic; it is deliberately opposing a variant tradition such as is found in the book of Ezekiel.[24]

What is the basis for the polemic? It is to be found, I submit, in the taboo concerning clothing made of more than one material, *šaʿaṭnēz* (Lev. xix 19). In the Deuteronomic version of the taboo, the materials are specified as linen and wool (Deut. xxii 11) where it falls among several other taboos against mixtures, *kilʾayim* (*vv.* 9-11), one of which is particularly instructive: "You shall not sow your vineyard with a second kind of seed, else the full crop will become consecrated, both the seed you have sown and all the yield of the vineyard" (*v.* 9).[28] The import of this verse is that mixed seed—again a sacred mixture—will transmit its holiness to its total yield.[26] Thus this context allows us to conclude that a garment of mixed fabrics is also taboo because it is contagiously sacred.

It is therefore hardly an accident that the inner Tabernacle curtains and the outer garments of the high priest—who alone among the priests is permitted to officiate inside the Tabernacle—also consist of a mixture of wool and linen.[27] These fabrics are sacred *per se* and their aspersion with sacred oil (Exod. xxix 21, xl 9) serves only to underscore their inherent sanctity. However, is their sanctity also contagious? P's instructions concerning the transport of the Tabernacle point to the answer. Whereas the sacred furniture is dismantled and covered by the priests before it can be carried away by the Kohathite Levites (Num. iv 3-15), it is the task of the Gershonite

[24] I had already noted this conflict between P and Ezekiel in *Studies* (n. 2), n. 124.

[25] The meaning of *tiqdaš* is "become taboo" (AT) as proposed by the LXX ἵνα μὴ ἁγιασθῇ τὸ γέννημα, "lest the yield be devoted". It is difficult to determine whether the crop is actually forfeit to the sanctuary (*NEB*) or merely prohibited from use (JPS). Rabbinic tradition sides with the latter (Sifre, Deut. 230). Targ. Onk. "lest it be impure" and Targ. Yer. "lest it be liable to burning" also correspond to views held by some rabbis (Y. Kil. viii 1; cf. B. Ked. 56a).

[26] The prohibition of mixed seeds is not unique to Israel. It is found in the Hittite code §§ 166-7, where the older law prescribes the death penalty for both men and women engaged in sowing "seeds upon seeds". E. Neufeld, *The Hittite Laws* (London, 1959), conjectures that since "seed" is often regarded as the body of the gods, this Hittite law ultimately derives from an incest taboo, p. 180 and cf. n. 32.

[27] Recognized by rabbinic tradition, cf. M. Kil. ix 1; B. Yoma 69a; cf. also Josephus, *Ant.*, iv:8, 11. For the significance see M. Haran, "The complex of ritual acts performed inside the Tabernacle", *Scripta Hierosolymitana* 8 (1961), pp. 279-85; idem, "The Priestly Image of the Tabernacle", *HUCA* 36 (1965), pp. 191-226, esp. p. 202.

Levites to dismantle and cart away the Tabernacle curtains (with the exception of the *pārōket*-veil, *v.* 5) and to install them in the reassembled Tabernacle when camp is made (Num. iv 24-28).[28] Thus the Levites who, like the laity, are not holy and, hence, are theoretically ineligible to handle sancta are explicitly charged with the responsibility of handling the sacred curtains. Clearly, these curtains, though of a sacred mixture and anointed with sacred oil, do not communicate holiness. By the same token, it is reasonable to conclude that the outer garments of the high priest compounded of the same sacred mixture, also do not possess contagious holiness. Unfortunately, there is no comparable evidence to prove this point, but the fact that there is neither prohibition nor concern in P lest the high priest make contact with the people with his garments indicates that such contact is of no consequence and need not be avoided.[29]

If, then, P allows lay contact with the sacred mixture comprising the officiating garments of the high priest and the Tabernacle curtains, all the more so would it have no reservations on touching the garments of the ordinary priest made solely of linen and containing no sacred mixture. This reasoning is supported by an incident cited in P. When Nadab and Abihu are struck down at the sanctuary altar,[30]

---

[28] Pace Haran, *HUCA*, p. 220 (n. 27), where he claims that the need to transport the Tabernacle "abolishes" the sanctity of the inner curtains. This ostensible exception irreparably flaws his argument that all the sancta are contagious to persons; cf. also n. 56 below.

[29] Haran, *Scripta* (n. 27), pp. 280-3, argues that the high priest wore his outer garments only when he officiated inside the Tabernacle but not at the outer altar. There are two objections to his view: (1) on the Day of Atonement the high priest wears his special linen robes (Lev. xvi 4) throughout the entire purification ritual, even when he purges the sacrificial altar and dispatches the scapegoat, acts which take place in the outer court outside the tent (*vv.* 17-23). This means that at least for the purification rite of the sanctuary, there is absolutely no distinction between the sanctity of the adytum and that of the outer altar *in respect to his clothing*. Indeed the garments into which he changes to offer up the *ʿōlāh* (*v.* 24) may very well be his full regalia. (2) In the Second Temple the high priest officiated at the daily *tāmīd* wearing his resplendent robes (Ecclus l 11 ff.; M. Tam. vii 2). That he did not fear to bloody them "when the priests were handing him the portions of the sacrifice" (Ecclus l 12; cf. M. Tam. vii 3) is good enough cause for believing that his predecessors in the First Temple were of the same disposition. Besides, where is the scriptural warrant that would have allowed, nay forced, this alleged change?

[30] As noted by *Sefer Hamivḥar*, if they had fallen inside the Tent, the text would have used the verb *bōʾū*, not *qirᵉbū* (Lev. x 4); also the divine fire "came out from in front of the sanctuary" (*v.* 2), indicating that they fell in the court; so Ibn Ezra. Finally, Levites would not have been permitted to enter the sanctuary itself, according to R. Eliezer in Sifra, Milluim, 35.

Moses calls upon their Levitic cousins to carry them out "by their tunics" (Lev. x 5). One would have thought that the divine fire which had consumed their bodies would only have intensified the holiness of their garments, making it essential to drag them out by some other means.[31] The only possible deduction from this case is that in P priestly garments neither are inherently holy nor transmit holiness.[32]

In any event, this view is not shared by Ezekiel. Since the priestly garments have been aspersed with sacred oil he holds that they are imbued with sacred holiness.[33] Now, it can hardly be that Ezekiel originated his ruling. The more likely prospect is that P is the innovator, restricting the power of sancta contagion to the most sacred furniture and offerings but denying it to sacred mixtures of fabrics, not to speak of ordinary priestly clothing. Indeed, as we shall now demonstrate, it even places limits upon the degree of contagion it allots to the altar and to the other cult furniture.

§ 5. *The contagion of sacred offerings.* We are now in a position to assault the question: does *kol* of our formula mean "whatever" or "whoever"? As has been shown, P denies Ezekiel's claim that the priestly garments transmit holiness to persons. However, what is P's position on the contagious power of the other sancta? In particular, what is the extent of the contagious power of the sacrifices? That is, both P and Ezekiel expressly admit that most sacred offerings can transmit holiness (Lev. vi 11, 20; Ezek. xlvi 20); but does P agree

[31] R. Akiba, ibid., indeed posits that the Levites speared the tunics and thereby dragged out the corpses, but the text does not warrant such an interpretation. The term *bekuttonōtām* also permits the interpretation "their (the Levites') tunics", i.e., the Levites used their own garments to drag out the corpses in order to avoid direct contact. In either case, the meaning would be the same: clothing does not transfer holiness.

[32] This latter point is indeed the teaching of Hag. ii 12, see below.

[33] According to the Priestly source, the consecration service was repeated for each high priest (Exod. xxix 29-30) but the consecration of the ordinary priest took place only the first time (cf. Exod. xl 15). How then could Ezekiel regard the garments of the ordinary priest as sacred? The possibility exists that he followed a variant tradition which required the consecration ritual for every new priest. That such a tradition once existed is attested at Qumran where a special day for consecrating new priests was inserted into the calendar (11Q Temple XV 3-XVII 5).

A second question regarding Ezekiel's position: did he also hold *šaʿaṭnēz* a sacred mixture? Since Ezekiel's visionary temple has no high priest this question cannot be resolved. His injunction that ordinary priests may not wear wool is based on pragmatic grounds: "they shall not gird themselves with anything that causes sweat" (xliv 18b). The taboo is retained, but rationalized.

with Ezekiel that sacrifices consecrate persons, or does P differ with Ezekiel on this issue even as it does concerning the priestly garments? Unfortunately, P is silent on this question; it is not even meaningfully silent as in the case of the priestly garments. However, four lines of indirect evidence can be brought to bear on this question and they converge with telling force.

(1) *Leviticus v 14-16*

> The Lord spoke to Moses saying: when a person commits a trespass by being inadvertently remiss with any of the Lord's sancta he shall bring as his penalty to the Lord a ram without blemish from the flock, convertible into payment in silver, by sanctuary weight, as a reparation offering, and he shall make restitution for that of the sancta wherever he was remiss and shall add a fifth to it. When he gives it to the priest, the priest shall make expiation on his behalf with the ram of the reparation offering so that he may be forgiven.[34]

Is the trespasser upon the sancta affected by his sacrilege? The above text states only that the trespasser must restore the sanctum twenty per cent beyond its original value and bring an *'āšām* offering to atone for his desecration. Nothing in the ritual procedure indicates that by desecrating a sanctum the trespasser has absorbed any of its sanctity; otherwise he would be required to undergo a purification ritual to desanctify himself. Moreover, the two verbs which mean "desecrate", *mā'al* and *ḥillēl* are used exclusively in regard to sacred objects but never in regard to man.[35] Therefore, the absence of any desanctification ritual for the trespasser on sancta points to the probability that, in P's system, sancta are not contagious to persons and the formula does not apply.[36]

---

[34] For this translation see *Cult and Conscience* (n. 2), p. 13.

[35] It cannot be argued that the legislator of Lev. v 14-16 takes the formula of sancta contagion for granted and that he is concerned only with the desecration of the sanctum rather than its effect upon the person who contracted it. If there were a desanctification ritual for the offender, the law would have stipulated it along with the *'āšām* sacrifice as an essential prerequisite for entering the sanctuary, just as those who have contracted severe impurity are required to cleanse themselves by ablutions before they may bring their purification offering (e.g. Lev. xiv 9-10, xv 13-14).

[36] In my discussion of *mā'al*, *Cult and Conscience* (n. 2), pp. 16-44, I neglected to discuss the obvious question concerning the fate of the desecrated sanctum. Was it restored to the sanctuary? Lev. v 14-16 answers in the negative: it must be replaced (*šillēm*), presumably even if it is undamaged. The principle is: once desecrated it cannot be reconsecrated. This is confirmed by Josh. vii 24—the desecrated *ḥērem* which should have been devoted to the sanctuary (cf. vi 19-24) must now be destroyed by fire. Perhaps ordinary sancta, being of lesser holiness than *ḥērem*, might be sold rather than destroyed.

(2) *Haggai ii 12*

> If a man is carrying sacrificial flesh in a fold of his garment, and with that touches bread, stew, wine, oil, or any other food, will the latter become holy? In reply, the priests said, "No".

That Haggai puts his question to priests indicates that his question is a cultic matter. Two inferences can be drawn from its formulation relevant to sancta contagion. The first is that the sacred meat has transferred its holiness to the garment but not to its bearer. Thus the question takes for granted that the person handling the sacred meat is not infected with its holiness. Here then is another indication that our formula applies to objects and not to persons. The second inference is that if the sacred meat would itself have come into direct contact with the same objects touched by the garment they assuredly would have been sanctified. But what precisely are these objects? They are "bread, stew, wine, oil or any other food". Thus only foodstuffs would have been affected. However, is it not just as likely that the man's garment would have brushed by a table, a chair or some other furniture? Thus the omission of household utensils and goods from Haggai's question can only imply that these objects cannot become sanctified by contact with sacred meat. In sum, the prophet's question indicates that the Jerusalemite priesthood at the end of the sixth century not only had limited the formula of sancta contagion to objects but had further narrowed its application just to articles of food.

(3) *Exodus xxx 26-29* (cited above)

Our formula concluded the list of consecrated objects and, therefore, applies to all of them. If, however, the effect of touching not just the altar but also the inner sancta is to contract holiness then it would clash with another basic formula in P's system, *hazzār haqqārēb yūmāt*, i.e., death is meted out to the unauthorized encroacher.[37] We would do well to ask: how can encroachers on sancta simultaneously become holy and incur death? The reconciliation of these two formulae is obvious: encroachers are indeed put to death and sancta contagion does not apply to persons.

---

[37] Kohathite Levites are expressly warned "lest they touch (*yigg*^{e}*ʿū*) the sancta and thereby die" (Num. iv 15). Even the disqualified priest is warned that he enters the sanctuary at the risk of his life (Exod. xxviii 43, xxx 20; Lev. x 9, xxi 23 and see *Studies* [n. 2], pp. 38-41). Obviously, the same injunctions apply to laymen (cf. Neh. vi 10 and the discussion above).

(4) *Numbers iv 15*

> When Aaron and his sons have finished covering the sacred objects and all the utensils of the sacred objects at the breaking of the camp, only then shall the Kohathites come and lift them so that they do not come in contact with the sacred objects and die.

Thus the sancta would appear to transmit both holiness and death to those who touch them. How can that be? [38] Moreover, how is it possible for the Gershonite Levites to carry the inner curtains of the Tabernacle (Num. iv 25) since, according to P, they are most sacred (Exod. xxx 20) and hence lethal (Num. iv 15)? Would not the Gershonites incur death? M. Haran, *Temples and Temple Service in Ancient Israel* (Oxford, 1978), p. 179, tries to resolve this problem by hypothesizing that P temporarily suspended the contagion of the Tabernacle structure in order to allow for the Levites to dismantle and transport it. However, as soon as we render *kol* as "whatever" and thereby deprive the sancta of the power to communicate holiness to persons, the paradox is resolved. The Tabernacle curtains, like the rest of the sancta, sanctify objects, not persons. The Levites, then, need have no fear in this regard. But is not the sanctity of the curtains lethal? Again, the answer is No. Only the cult objects specified in the Levitic labors (Num. iv 4-14) are fatal to the unauthorized who touch them. The Tabernacle curtains, however, are not in this list and, hence, may be carried by the Levites with impunity.[39] In sum, the alleged paradox of the sancta is chimerical. The sancta transmit death only to persons and holiness only to objects.

In aggregate the four texts cited above (Lev. v 14-16; Hag. ii 10-12; Exod. xxx 26-29; Num. iv 15) provide indirect but unanimous evidence that sancta are not contagious to persons. Thus the rabbis are probably right. *kol* in P's formula means "whatever" not "whoever". Ezekiel, then, in insisting that sacred food is contagious to persons harbors a variant tradition. Indeed, that Ezekiel is at odds with the prevailing opinion of his time can be extrapolated from the testimony of Haggai who cannot have been removed from Ezekiel's time by more than one generation. From Haggai's question to the priests we have concluded that the Jerusalem priesthood which returned from the Babylonian exile maintained that the contagion

[38] Perhaps that is why the Versions render *yiqdaš* as implying death.

[39] The rabbis reduce the power of all the sancta by claiming that touching them incurs no penalties, Sifre Zuṭa on Num. xviii 3; cf. *Studies* (n. 2), n. 162.

of sacred food is restricted solely to other food but can on no account affect persons. How can we account for Ezekiel's polaric opposition to the priestly establishment of this time? That opposition, I submit, is thrown into clear relief by our formula.

§ 6. *Ezekiel's opposition.* Ezekiel—rather, the tradition he transmits—vehemently opposes the compromise with the laity proposed by P. His blueprint for the temple unequivocally excludes the laity from the inner court and even from the gates to that court (xlvi 3).[40] Sacrificial slaughter is, in his plan, to be performed within the northern gate (xl 39-42) [41]—but by the Levites, not the laity (xliv 11).[42] Even the cooking of the *šᵉlāmīm*, though they may be eaten by the lay offerer, is also to be done by the Levites in the outer court (xlvi 24).[43] Thus the blueprint of Ezekiel's temple reveals a different gradation of holiness from P's Tabernacle. Both hold in common that the shrine *per se* is the domain of the priest. They differ, however, in regard to the sanctity of the outer area. P holds that the layman has access to the forecourt up to the altar so that he can participate in the preparations of the sacrifice. Ezekiel, however, bars the layman entirely from the inner court, even from the northern gate where, in his scheme, the slaughtering takes place, and even from touching the *šᵉlāmīm* meat until it is cooked in the outer court. The slaughtering and cooking are, instead, to be performed by the Levites. The gradation of holiness in each scheme is illustrated in the following diagrams:

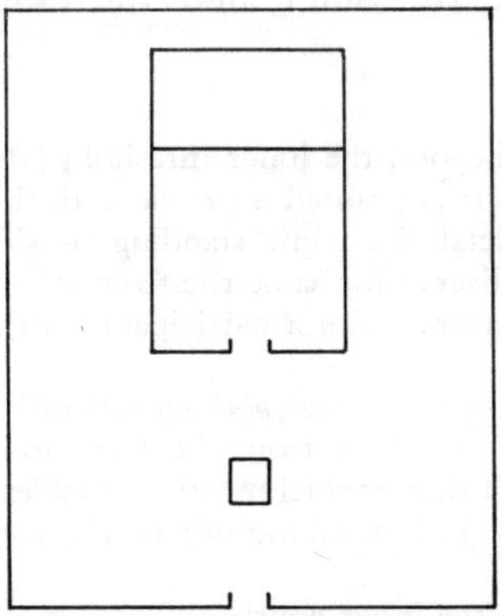

The tabernacle

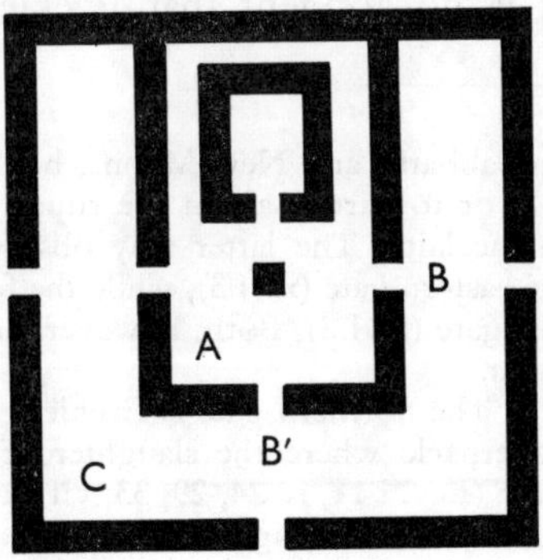

Ezekiel's temple

[40] Even the *nāśī'*, the king's counterpart in Ezekiel, has no access to the inner court. He is conceded only the right to enter the eastern gate, and then only

§ 7. *Ezekiel's principle.* Ezekiel's temple is divided into three concentric domains of holiness which correspond to the three classes in Israel: priests, Levites, and laity. The geometric center of the temple complex is the altar. The innermost area comprising the inner court (A) and its structures, the altar and the temple buildings, are the priestly domain. The northern gate of the inner court (B) where the sacrificial slaughter is performed is accessible to the Levites. The eastern gate (B′) is open to the *nāśīʾ*. The outer court (C) is the only area available to the laity. The priestly Tabernacle is also constructed according to the notion of concentric domains of decreasing holiness but the gradations are more subtle and the boundaries allow for blurring. The center is the adytum (in principle, the Ark). The domain of the priests comprises the Tabernacle tent, the sacrificial altar, and the courtyard between them. But this priestly area is not homogeneous; its sanctity is graded. The adytum is accessible to the high priest alone under limited circumstances (Lev. xvi); [44] the high priest officiates in the Tent and priests on the altar; the altar marks the boundary line between the priestly and lay domains but only the priests have access to it.

Is there an underlying principle that can account for the differences between the two sanctuary blueprints? I believe there is, and it finds expression in our formula. Ezekiel does not accept P's ruling that persons are not subject to the jurisdiction of the formula. According to this priest-prophet, *sancta are contagious to persons*. The proof is to be found, I submit, in the different centers of each sanctuary. It is no accident that Ezekiel has made the outer altar the exact

---

on Sabbaths and New Moons, but not to step beyond the inner threshold (xlvi 1-2) or to participate in the ritual. Thus the *nāśīʾ* is granted a privilege denied to the laity. The latter may observe the sacrificial rite while standing outside the eastern gate (xlvi 3), while the former may observe the same rite from within this gate (xlvi 2). Both, however, are only spectators and not participants in the ritual.

[41] The northern gate is Ezekiel's equivalent to *yerek hammizbēaḥ ṣāpōnāh* of P's Tabernacle where the slaughter of most sacred offerings from the flock took place (Lev. i 11, iv 24, 29, 33, vii 1). Does the fact that Ezekiel mentions "tables" at the place of slaughter indicate that he too (like P) is speaking of animals from the flock and not from the herd?

[42] However, the Levites are also barred from the inner court.

[43] "The ministers of the house" (Ezek. xlvi 24) are the Levites (cf. xliv 11).

[44] Only once a year on the Day of Atonement, according to *v.* 29; in emergencies, according to *vv.* 2 ff. For the distinction, see provisionally *IDB Supp.* (1976), s.v. "Atonement, Day of".

geometric center of his temple complex. In P, the altar is the least holy of the sancta, as exemplified by its covering during transit which is of inferior material to the coverings of the other sancta (Num. iv 3-14). By moving the focus of holiness to the altar, Ezekiel stakes his claim that the altar is of equal sanctity to the inner sancta and hence qualifies for the same degree of contagion which bars lay access.[45] The rest of his plan is of a piece with this premise. It is so conceived that the priests never come into contact with the laity while they are officiating because the entire inner court including its gates—in contradiction to that of P—is off limits to the laity.[46] Moreover, since the sacrifices are as contagious to persons as the cult objects, all lay duties in connection with them, such as slaughtering, are transferred to the Levites. Thus, whereas in P's scheme Levites are indistinguishable from laymen in regard to their access to sancta, Ezekiel in effect *elevates* the Levites by granting them special functions (e.g. slaughtering) and space (the inner gates) which set them apart from the laity.[47] Thus it is Ezekiel's postulate of sancta

---

[45] The ark is missing along with the tables and lampstands from Ezekiel's description of the inner sanctuary (chs. xl-xli). Especially significant is its absence from the temple during the days of Jeremiah (Jer. iii 16). For the discussion, see M. Haran, "The disappearance of the Ark", *IEJ* 13 (1963), pp. 46-58 = *BIES* 25 (1961), pp. 211-23.

[46] In P, only the inner area of the court known as "between the porch and the altar" was off limits to the layman; the forecourt, i.e., before the altar, known as "the entrance to the tent of meeting", was accessible to him (cf. *Studies* [n. 2], n. 166). However, it seems that on the Festival of Tabernacles the entire court was open to the laity, as theoretically implied by P (ibid., n. 211) and explicitly by rabbinic sources (e.g. M. Suk. iv 5). For Ezekiel, however, the entry of any Israelite into any part of the court constituted a sacrilege and hence in his visionary temple he is kept out.

[47] In *Studies* (n. 2), n. 316, I agreed with Wellhausen that Ezekiel's Levites were the former *bāmāh* priests displaced by the Josianic reform for whom Ezekiel found employment in his projected temple. I still believe that it is the most likely historical setting for Ezekiel's enactment, but I am now inclined to the view that it rests on more theoretical and religious grounds. For Ezekiel, the Levites are a buffer between the priests and the laymen. Originally, he admits, they shared the priestly right to officiate at the altar and with the other sancta (xliv 13; cf. *v.* 15). Moreover, if priests and Levites mingle with each other in the northern gate where the slaughtering and other sacrificial preparations take place, then there is apparently no danger that the Levites would be infected by the priestly garments. This view would be corroborated by Ezekiel's use of *ʿam* (xliv 19, xlvi 20, 24), which seems restricted to the laity and excludes the Levites.

On the other hand, the possibility of no mingling must also be considered since the slaughtering table was set up at the *entrance* to the inner gate and thus the Levites may not have been allowed to penetrate farther, a fact that corresponds with the guard duty of the Tabernacle and the Second Temple where the priests

contagion to persons that accounts for the unique floor-plan of his temple and the distribution of the priests, Levites, and laymen within it.[48]

Furthermore, Ezekiel's rule on sancta contagion is the key which explains his differences from P. For example, his list of prohibitions for the priesthood (xliv 17-27) are with only one exception in direct conflict with P, as follows: (1) priests may not wear wool (*vv.* 17-18); P's high priest, however, wears woolen materials (see § 4, above), and the belts worn by ordinary priests probably contain wool (Exod. xxxix 29; B. Yoma 12a); (2) the priestly garments are contagious to persons (*v.* 19), a view opposed by P (above); (3) priests are required to trim their hair (*v.* 20), a rule unknown to P (cf. Lev. x 6); (4) the prohibition to enter the inner court while intoxicated (*v.* 21) agrees with P (Lev. x 9); (5) the prohibition of marrying the widow of a non-priest (*v.* 22) is unknown to P which forbids a priest only to marry a divorcee (Lev. xxi 7); (6) the purification rites for the corpse-contaminated priests are of two weeks duration with a purification offering as the climax (*vv.* 25-27), while in P priests and laymen alike undergo the same week-long purification rite and require no sacrifice (Num. xix 11-12, 16-19).

It should be noted that in each case Ezekiel takes the stricter point of view. This fact in itself should indicate that Ezekiel is no innovator but, on the contrary, is a standard bearer of an older tradition which has been rejected by P. As shown, Ezekiel invokes the viewpoint posited by the oldest biblical narratives that the sancta are contagious to persons. This simple postulate is all that is needed to explain Ezekiel's severer code for the priests whereby he both elevates their holy status and distances them more from the laity,

---

guarded the inside of the gate and the Levites the outside (*Studies* [n. 2], pp. 9-10, esp. nn. 33-4).

In any event Ezekiel's reformulation of the duties of the Levites arises more from an attempt to bar the laity from the inner court than from the customary allegation that he demoted the Levites (provisionally, see *Studies*, nn. 226, 316). Possibly, Ezekiel has conferred a quasi-holy status on the Levites in contradistinction to P which sees no difference at all between the laymen and Levites in regard to their inherent non-sacred character (note too that for Ezekiel the Levites' land is also "holy to the Lord", xlviii 14). Were the Qumranites basing themselves on Ezekiel when they granted the Levites a higher status? Cf. J. Milgrom, "Studies in the Temple Scroll", *JBL* 97 (1978), pp. 501-4.

[48] Is the parapet around the altar of the Herodian temple a reflection of Ezekiel's ruling on the contagion of the altar? So it would be inferred from Josephus, *Wars* V, 5:6-7. However, see *Studies* (n. 2), n. 161.

even to the point of preventing the laity from direct contact with the priestly clothing and the sacrifices.

Another indication of the antiquity of Ezekiel's code is his requirement of a purification sacrifice for the corpse-contaminated priest. The only other person who is subject to this same requirement is P's nazirite (Num. vi 9-11). It can be shown that the naziritic ritual reflected in P contains many ancient elements. For example, the requirements that the *šelāmīm* offering be cooked in the sanctuary premises and that the priest receive his portion from the boiled meat (*v.* 19) are attested in the sanctuary of Shiloh (1 Sam. ii 13-14). Also, the priestly portion is designated as the shoulder, a perquisite which is never again attested in P but which has hallowed precedents throughout the ancient Near East.[49] Thus it can be safely concluded that the requirement for the corpse-contaminated nazirite to bring a purification offering also rests on ancient precedent and that there was a similar tradition for the priest, who, sharing with the nazirite the designation "holy to the Lord" (Lev. xxi 7; Num. vi 8), also would bring a purification offering as his decontamination ritual. Ezekiel's stringent provisions for the priesthood can reflect only an older tradition which had been scuttled by the Jerusalem priesthood in favor of the regulations now found in P. Thus Ezekiel is a religious conservative whose view represents a continuing polemic against the prevailing practice of the Jerusalem Temple.

§ 8. *The reduction of sancta contagion.* The question of *kol* can now be answered. The answer, however, is not univalent. It is a coefficient of time and, hence, variable. In the earlier period, whenever the formula originated, the range of *kol* was unrestricted: even persons were included and intention was not a factor. Indeed, that the word *kol* was chosen for the formula probably indicates that initially no exceptions were intended. The early sources corroborate this assumption: sancta are lethally contagious to persons even when their contact with them is unintentional, e.g. Uzzah's touching the Ark (2 Sam. vi 6-7) and the Beth-Shemeshites' viewing it (1 Sam. vi 19). The theophany at Sinai provides a particularly illuminating example. Whoever trespasses on the mountain must be slain but his slayers must heed that "no hand shall touch him; he shall either be stoned or pierced through" (Exod. xix 13). The implication is clear: the

[49] Cf. J. Milgrom, "The shoulder of the Levites", in Y. Yadin (ed.), *The Temple Scroll* (Jerusalem, 1978), pp. 131-6 (Heb.).

holiness communicated to the offender is of such power that it can be transmitted through a medium. Hence the instrument of death must not allow contact between the offender and his executioner.[50] The Priestly source also provides a telling example: the death of Nadab and Abihu (Lev. x 1-5). The divine fire has executed them for their cultic offense but their bodies may not be touched directly; they must be wrapped in other garments before being removed from the sanctuary (*v.* 5). Again, the holiness contracted by persons can be imparted to a party once removed with fatal results.[51] This second degree holiness is attributed to the sancta associated with the very presence of God (e.g. the Ark, Mt Sinai, the divine fire). The high voltage of the super-sancta is also evidenced by their power to communicate not only by contact but by sight. This already has been noted in the story of the Ark at Beth-Shemesh (1 Sam. vi 19). But even in P which, as will be shown, strives for a reduction in the contagious power of the sancta, the sancta still possess the power to kill their viewers when they are being dismantled (Num. iv 20).[52]

---

[50] In *Studies* (n. 2), pp. 44-6, I have attempted to demontrate that Sinai is the Tabernacle archetype and in the Priestly Source, into which the Sinai pericope is incorporated (note that its framework, Exod. xix 1, xxiv 15a-18, is P), the equivalent to Sinai is the Tabernacle tent into which non-priests are not permitted (see Neh. vi 11 and *Studies* [n. 2], n. 173, for the discussion).

[51] Sancta with second degree contagion may account for the provision, attested in all the old sources, that the property of a proscribed individual or community (*ḥērem*) must be destroyed (Josh. vii 24; Deut. xiii 16-17). Since *ḥērem* is the highest form of dedication (see *Cult and Conscience* [n. 2], pp. 52-4), it therefore resembles the most sacred sancta whose lethal power is communicated to all who come into contact with it. Therefore all the property of the condemned person is destroyed on the presumption that his *ḥērem* status was transmitted to it by contact. M. Greenberg, in M. Haran (ed.), *Yeheẓkel Kaufmann Jubilee Volume* (Jerusalem, 1960), pp. 23-4, has suggested that in the Achan story the condemnation of the property is due to the contagion of the tent, a principle which operates in the impurity laws (Num. xix 14). However, a goodly part of Achan's property such as his beasts would not have entered his tent (note that the tent is mentioned separately from the animals; Josh. vii 24). Therefore it may be that the violator of the *ḥērem* himself, having absorbed the full power of the *ḥērem*, is considered to have transmitted it to his property and is liable to blight his entire community unless he is put to death (so Josh. vi 18, vii 12; cf. Deut. vii 26). Like the one who touches Mt Sinai and can transmit its holiness to others by contact (Exod. xix 12-13), so Achan would have infected all objects, animate and inanimate within his circle with lethal holiness. That is to say, *ḥērem*, like Mt Sinai, can communicate second degree contagion by contact.

[52] This is the view of R. Judah in the name of Rab, B. Yoma 54a (discussed in *Studies* [n. 2], n. 162). This means that when the sancta are stationary they are lethal only to touch, but while they are dismantled their latent power is released and can infect from afar.

Thus even in the early sources a gradation may be detected in the most sacred sancta; the super-sancta—those considered to be the earthly manifestation of the deity—are fatally contagious to those who view them directly and to those who contact them through a medium.

The salient point in the Priestly Code is that it has reduced the range and power of the sancta. First, as has already been demonstrated, P defuses the altar, rendering it non-contagious to persons. Furthermore, as will be shown, whereas in all early sources the altar proves its contagious power by providing asylum, in P, this power is denied. However, P is not consistent in this respect. In the account of the Levites' labors in the Tabernacle (Num. iv) all the sancta bear a deadly contagion upon contact (*v.* 15) [53] and when dismantled, even upon sight (*v.* 20) (cf. n. 52). On the other hand, as demonstrated, the sancta list in Exod. xxx 26-29 allows no other inference but that the sancta are not contagious to persons.

Haggai attests a further reduction. Uncovered sacred food transmits its holiness to food only but not to other objects. Ezekiel, however, records a variant tradition. Holding that sacred food and garments communicate holiness to persons, he espouses the older view that sancta are contagious to persons and opposes the innovative view, championed by P and Haggai, which denies that persons can be infected by sancta. The final reduction in sancta contagion is posited in the Tannaitic sources whereby the altar and its vessels (but not the inner sancta) communicate holiness only to those foodstuffs which qualify as offerings.

§ 9. *The stages of reduction recapitulated.* The following stages in the reduction of *kol* in the formula *kol-hannōgēaʿ yiqdāš* can be discerned:

1. In the pre-biblical stage all sancta communicate holiness to persons, the inner sancta directly by sight and indirectly by touch. This contagion is lethal even if the contact is accidental. The early biblical narratives exemplify this deadly power of the sancta in the Ark, Mt Sinai and the divine fire.[54]

---

[53] It must be remembered that Levites have the same status as the laity in regard to sancta. There is still a gradation in P between the Ark and the other sancta. The Ark is not only covered triply (the only other sanctum with three coverings is the Table of Presence); its immediate cover is the holy veil (see Num. iv 5-15).

[54] The ritual for consecration to the priesthood may also reflect this earlier stage since it calls for the besprinkling of the priests with blood taken from the altar (Exod. xxix 21; cf. Lev. viii 30). As was recognized by Ḥizkuni, this meant

2. The Priestly account of the Levites' work assignment in the Tabernacle (Num. iv) reveals the sancta unchanged from the previous stage only for the brief and rare moment when they are dismantled but otherwise, as shown by the list of the sancta to be anointed (Exod. xxx 26-29), the sancta have lost their power to infect persons even by touch. Ezekiel, however, opts for the older view that sancta are contagious to persons.

3. Haggai restricts the contagion of sancta to foodstuffs.

4. The Tannaim follow Haggai and reduce the contagion of the altar to those foods which qualify as offerings. This change, it should be noted, is minuscule. Both Haggai and the rabbis agree that the sancta transmit their holiness only to foods. Thus the rabbinic ruling on sancta contagion remains the same *all through the Second Commonwealth*, and the major innovation, first detected in Haggai, is traceable back, at the latest, to exilic times.[55]

Thus there is evidence of a progressive reduction in the contagious power of sancta over the entire span of the biblical period.[56] The question automatically raises itself: what forces have brought about this change? That such a question must be asked can be seen when the history of the term *qādōš*, "holy", is compared to the history of its correspondingly opposite force *ṭāmēʾ*, "impure". The fact is that impurity retains its lethal potency all during the biblical period and into rabbinic times. Indeed, the fear of corpse-contamination almost

---

"the blood which was sanctified by the altar". If the blood in turn sanctified the priests it would then be another case of second-degree sancta contagion. The same would be true, I believe, for the power of the *ḥaṭṭāʾt* blood which sanctifies as well as purges the outer altar on the Day of Atonement (Lev. xvi 19); it has been previously brought into the adytum and sprinkled on and before the Ark. The blood is thus sanctified and now able to transfer its holiness to the altar—a second degree contagion.

[55] J. Neusner, "From Scripture to Mishnah: the origins of the Mishnah's Fifth Division", *JBL* 98 (1979), pp. 269-83, claims that the fifth division of the Mishnah contains two innovations: the principle of intention and the neutralization of the altar's power. However, both are rooted in Scripture. The reduction of the altar's power of sanctification to foodstuffs alone, as noted, took place at least as early as Haggai. Intention operates as the principle in a whole battery of cultic laws, e.g. (1) the repentant sinner is assumed to have been remorseful at the time of his crime (Lev. v 20-26; cf. *Cult and Conscience* [n. 2], pp. 84-126). (2) Intention spells the difference between a purification offering and the *kārēt* penalty (Num. xv 22-31). (3) The slaying of the encroacher presumes that his act is intentional (*Studies*, pp. 20-1). There are many other examples.

[56] The view of Haran, (n. 28), that P's system of graded taboos is based on the postulate that sancta are contagious to persons, must accordingly be abandoned.

prevents the city of Tiberias from being built.[57] Why then does the power of impurity remain undiminished whereas the power of holiness is successively reduced? The answer, I submit, lies in specific historic circumstances that forced a change in the contagious power of the one sanctum which was both visible and accessible to all the people—the sacrificial altar.

§ 10. *Asylum altars or asylum cities?* That the altar grants asylum to those who grasp it is a postulate of the early biblical stories (Exod. xxi 13-14; 1 Kgs i 50-51, ii 28-34). It is also attested in the classical world and, therefore, represents a widespread phenomenon.[58] Its basic premise is that those who touch the altar absorb its sanctity and are removed from and immune to the jurisdiction of the profane world. Asylum, then, is a specific application of the formula *kol-hannōgēaʿ yiqdāš*.[59]

P and D, however, attribute the power of asylum not to the altar but to certain cities (Num. xxxv 9-15; Deut. iv 41-43, xix 1-9).[60] What is the relationship between the asylum altar and the asylum cities? Most critics hold that asylum cities were designated by Israelite rulers to replace the anarchic power of the altar to grant asylum, but they are divided on when the change took place. Some opt for the reign of David and Solomon,[61] and some for Josiah; [62] still

[57] Cf. L. Levine, "R. Simeon b. Yoḥai and the purification of Tiberias", *HUCA* 49 (1978), pp. 143-85.

[58] Cf. E. Schlesinger, *Die griechische Asylie* (Göttingen, 1933), and *The Encyclopedia of Religion and Ethics*, s.v. "Asylum", for other cultures as well.

[59] The anomalous nature of this altar contact should not be overlooked. In all other cases it is assumed that the altar conveys a permanent sanctity even when the object affected is removed. But the homicide differs in this respect: his immunity lasts only as long as he remains in contact with the altar.

[60] The question whether JE also recognizes the asylum city is discussed below.

[61] So M. Loehr, *Das Asylwesen im Alten Testament* (Halle, 1930), pp. 171-217, esp. 209-10; S. Klein, "The Cities of the Priests and the Levites", *Meḥqarim 'Arẓiyisraelim* 3:4 (1934), pp. 17-18 (Heb.); W. F. Albright, *Archaeology and the Religion of Israel* (Baltimore, 1946), p. 146; B. Z. Dinur, "The religious character of the Cities of Refuge and the ceremony of admission into them", *EI* 3 (1954), pp. 135-46 (Heb.); E. Nielsen, *Shechem* (Copenhagen, 1955), pp. 208 ff.; M. Greenberg, "The biblical conception of asylum", *JBL* 78 (1959), pp. 125-32; R. de Vaux, *Ancient Israel* (London and New York, 1961), pp. 160-3 = *Les instutions de l'Ancien Testament* 1 (Paris, 1958), pp. 247-50; J. Bright, "Joshua", *IB* 2 (New York and Nashville, 1953), on Josh. xx; A. Soggin, *Joshua* (London, 1972) = *Le livre de Josué* (Neuchâtel, 1970), on Josh. xx;

[62] J. Wellhausen, *Prolegomena to the History of Israel* (Edinburgh, 1885), p. 162 = *Prolegomena zur Geschichte Israels* (Berlin, 1883, 2nd edn of *Geschichte Israels* I, 1878), p. 168; W. R. Smith, *Lectures on the Religion of the Semites* (3rd

others maintain that the asylum cities co-existed with the asylum altar from earliest times.[63] The common denominator of all these theories is that the asylum city was built around a sanctuary, of necessity an important one, whose widely recognized powers of asylum were then extended to the entire city. On the other hand, those who hold that the altars and city asylums sprang up simultaneously maintain that the purpose of the city was to provide permanent quarters for the refugee who sought protection at its altar.[64] According to the first theory, that city asylum replaced altar asylum, those cities were chosen which contained hallowed sanctuaries so that the continuity of asylum would be uninterrupted when the asylum powers of the sanctuaries were revoked. In either case, the underlying assumption remains that asylum cities were sanctuary cities.[65] Our new understanding of P's formula *kol-hannōgēaʿ yiqdāš* throws this assumption into question.

For P, the assumption that asylum cities contain sanctuaries is not only unlikely but inconceivable. Three of the six asylum cities are designated for Transjordan (cf. Deut. iv 43). In P's view, however, Transjordan lies outside the Promised Land (Num. xxxiv 12). In consonance with other ancient traditions P holds that any territory

---

edn, London, 1927), p. 148, n. 1; C. Steuernagel, *Das Deuteronomium* (2nd edn, Göttingen, 1923), p. 123; N. M. Nicolsky, "Das Asylrecht in Israel", *ZAW* 48 (1930), pp. 146-75; J. Morgenstern, "The Book of the Covenant, Part II", *HUCA* 7 (1930), p. 130; M. David, "Die Bestimmung ueber die Asylstaedte", *OTS* 9 (1951), pp. 30-48; M. Noth, *Numbers* (London, 1968), p. 254 = *Das vierte Buch Mose, Numeri* (Göttingen, 1966), p. 219; F. Horst, "Recht und Religion im Bereich des Alten Testaments", *EvTh* 16 (1956), pp. 49-75 (= *Gottes Recht* [Munich, 1961], pp. 260-91), esp. p. 59/273.

[63] A. P. Bissell, *The Law of Asylum in Israel* (Leipzig, 1884), pp. 50 ff., and Y. Kaufmann, *Joshua* (Jerusalem, 1959), pp. 259-70 (Heb.), traced the asylum city to the days of Moses and Joshua; Loehr, (n. 61), to the Canaanites from whom the institution was borrowed. J. Weismann, *Talion und öffentliche Strafe im Mosaischen Rechte* (Leipzig, 1913), p. 71, also rejects the Josianic hypothesis and instead proposes that the asylum city was instituted because the avenger could also avail himself of the law of Exod. xxi 14, thereby taking the law in his own hands and rendering the altar asylum ineffectual. For proof he cites Solomon's slaying of Joab. It is no proof: Solomon acts not as avenger but as king, i.e. as the supreme judge, by which authority he can declare Joab a murderer and subject to the law of Exod. xxi 14.

[64] So in classical antiquity; cf. Tacitus, *Annals* III, chs. 60-3. For discussion see Schlesinger (n. 63); H. Seyrig, "Le Rois Séleucides et la concession de l'asylie", *Syria* 20 (1939), pp. 35 ff.; J. Hempel, "Asylrecht", *RGG* (3rd edn), cols. 1957 ff.

[65] Cf. nn. 61-2, including Weismann (n. 63) and Weinfeld (n. 69); cf. also L. Delekat, "Die Asylstaedte", *Asylie und Schutzorakel am Zionheiligtum* (Leiden, 1967), pp. 290-320.

outside YHWH's land is "impure" (Josh. xxii 19; cf. 1 Sam. xxvi 19; Hos. ix 3; Amos vii 17) and the mere erection of an altar within it is tantamount to treason (Josh. xxii 16 ff.). It is no accident that when the P strand in Joshua specifies the asylum cities it switches verbs so that those in Cisjordan are "sanctified" *wayyaqdīšū* whereas those in Transjordan are described by the neutral *nātenū* (Josh. xx 7-8).[66] Thus P's Transjordan asylums *ipso facto* could not be sanctuary cities. Besides, is it conceivable that P would have ordained asylums in cities where murderers could reside in the proximity of, if not within, the sacred precincts and under extremity (e.g. when extradited) could even grab the horns of the altar? From P's vantage point, the sanctuary would stand under constant threat of pollution. Finally, the legitimacy of multiple sanctuaries is clearly denied by P which posits a single authorized sanctuary.[67] Thus the very existence of a network of sanctuary asylums is precluded in P.

Once the nexus of asylum altar and asylum city is severed it is no longer possible to say that in P the asylum city is the extension or replacement of the sanctuary. What then is the *raison d'être* of P's asylum city? Our formula suggests an answer. As has been demonstrated, P deliberately excludes persons from the contagion of sancta. The altar, in particular, cannot sanctify persons. Thus it is obvious that from the beginning P would have looked with alarm at the entrenched right of altar asylum to attract murderers, thieves, assorted criminals and their pollution to the sanctuary. If anything, P is obsessed with a concern to protect the sancta from defilement lest God vent his anger upon the nation. It thus adopted a simple if radical expedient: it declared that the altar does not give asylum and that *kol-hannōgēaʿ yiqdāš* does not apply to persons. At the same

---

[66] The naming of the cities is postponed till after the conquest (Num. xxxv 9). Hence they are not specified until Josh. xx (cf. Num. xxxv 13-14). W. H. Bennett, *The Book of Joshua* (Leipzig, Baltimore and London, 1895), p. 31, citing J. Hollenberg and followed by nearly every scholar since, believes that the LXX's καὶ διέστειλε which in Num. xxxv 11 translates *hiqrāh* indicates that *wayyaqrū* is the original reading. However, he did not notice that the LXX also uses διαστέλλειν for *hibdīl*, D's term for the establishment of the asylum cities (Deut. xix 2-7). Should one therefore conclude that the LXX's *Vorlage* also read *hiqrāh*? Rather, the LXX might well have indicated that all three Masoretic verbs—*hiqrāh*, *hibdīl*, and *hiqdīš*—are synonymous. Besides, the juxtaposition of the verbs *nātan* and *hiqdīš* in Josh. xx 7-8 is paralleled precisely in Jer. i 5. Thus the case for *wayyaqrū* as the *Vorlage* for the LXX in Josh. xx 7 is in doubt.

[67] Cf. M. Haran, "The idea of centralization of the cult in the Priestly apprehension", *Beer-Sheva* 1 (1973), pp. 114-21 (Heb.).

time it recognized that the accidental homicide needed an asylum to escape the revenge of the blood redeemer. Therefore it devised a solution of establishing six asylum cities equitably distributed throughout the land so that one at least could be reached by the homicide before the avenger overtook him. Thus P's radical reduction of the formula is part and parcel of its establishment of asylum cities. The altar, devitalized of its contagion to persons to prevent its pollution by criminal elements, is henceforth replaced by the asylum cities for the safety of the accidental homicide. Indeed, the fact that P maintains that the altar transmits not holiness but death (Num. iv 15) provides further evidence that P strove to prevent criminals from seeking asylum at the sanctuary; the criminal not only gains no immunity by grasping the altar's horns but makes himself liable to death by divine agency. He now has a double reason to shy away from the sanctuary.[68]

§ 11. *When was the altar asylum abolished*? What are the historical circumstances that account for P's innovation? Clearly, such circumstances must be related to the historic events which brought an end to the institution of altar asylum. When this happened, however, is still debated. According to many critics the altar continued to provide asylum until the Deuteronomic reform under Josiah when the asylum was "secularized" by the replacement of sanctuaries with asylum cities.[69] However, just as a similar theory was refuted for the origin of P's asylum cities, it can be shown that D's asylum cities also were not sanctuaries, albeit on different grounds.

(1) There is common agreement that D's major innovation is its abolition of the local sanctuaries. Thus it is not surprising that invariably when D prescribes a sanctuary ritual it states explicitly, emphatically, and repetitively that henceforth it must be observed only at the one chosen sanctuary.[70] However, D's section on asylum

[68] That P was determined to declare the altar off limits to non-priests may be derived from Josh. ix 27, "That day Joshua made them (the Gibeonites) hewers of wood and drawers of water for the whole community [and for the altar of the Lord, until this day in the place that he would choose]". As can be seen from verse 21 of that chapter, the bracketed ending is an addition which by its content, is clearly attributable to the Deuteronomist. However, in the original P version, the Gibeonites were made serfs of the community, not the Temple, and certainly not for service at the altar.

[69] Cf. esp. Nicolsky and David (n. 62), and M. Weinfeld, *Deuteronomy and the Deuteronomic School* (Oxford, 1972), p. 236, n. 4.

[70] E.g. the pilgrimage festivals (ch. xvi), sacrifices, and sacred gifts (e.g. xii 5-6, 11, 13-14, 17-18, 26-27, xiv 22-27, xv 19-20).

cities (xix 1-13) contains no reference whatsoever to centralization. Surely, if the asylum city supplanted the asylum altar some mention of the uprooting of the latter through centralization would be expected. Moreover as Kaufmann has shown ([n. 63] p. 41), D predicates the establishment of city asylums immediately upon entry into the land (xix 1) and the Transjordanian ones even beforehand (iv 41) whereas centralization is to be effected only after the conquest is complete and the land is settled and tranquil (xii 9). Asylum therefore must be severed from the centralization issue.

(2) Though D uses the term *māqōm* as a holy place [71] both for the central sanctuary which the Lord will choose (*bāḥar*; Deut. xii 5, 11, 14, 18, 21, 26, xiv 23, 25, xv 20, xvi 2, 6, 7, 11, 15, 16, xvii 8, 10, xviii 6, xxvi 2, xxxi 11) and for designating a heathen sanctuary (sing. xii 3, 13; pl. xii 2), it avoids its use in connection with the city asylums and resorts instead to the neutral *ʿārīm* "cities" (Deut. iv 41-43, xix 1-13).

(3) This hypothesis leaves unexplained why Jerusalem was not chosen as an asylum city. Since D does not evidence any objection *per se* to the concept of altar asylum, it could have continued this institution at the central sanctuary where, moreover, a high court was called into existence by D for the express purpose of judging difficult capital crimes (xvii 8).

(4) D also had a precedent in JE for making Jerusalem the asylum city: "I will assign you a *māqōm* to which he can flee" (Exod. xxi 13), to which D could have added, as it did elsewhere, "at the place (*bammāqōm*) which the Lord has chosen".[72] That D does not attach its centralizing formula to JE's single asylum can only mean that the tradition of *multiple* asylum cities pre-existed D. Indeed, D not only assumes their existence but even specifies their names in Transjordan (Deut. iv 41-43).[73]

---

[71] D does not know the term *bāmāh*, as noted by N. Raban, "The Law of the Bamot", *Sēper Biram* (Jerusalem, 1956), pp. 243 ff. (Heb.); instead it uses *māqōm*; cf. also S. Talmon, *Scripta Hierosolymitana* 8 (1961), pp. 351-2; Y. M. Grintz, ""Some observations on the high place in the history of Israel", *VT* 27 (1977), pp. 111-13.

[72] Whether *māqōm* refers here to a sanctuary or city asylum is neither answerable nor relevant. But one thing is sure: it is a single *māqōm*.

[73] Finally, that D could not have innovated the city asylums can be deduced from its prescription for its establishment (Deut. xix 1-13). There are too many lacunae to allow for its successful implementation. Left unspecified, for example, are such essential features as the nature of the refugee's trial and the length of his enforced residence in the asylum city. P's criteria of the *ʿēdāh* judiciary (Num.

(5) D ordains that "when the Lord your God enlarges your territory, as he swore to your fathers, and gives you all the land that he promised to give to your fathers . . . then you shall add three more towns to those three" (Deut. xix 8-9). Now the unconquered land cannot be Transjordan since in the Deuteronomic view it already has been conquered and allocated. Moreover D, no less than P, believes that the land sworn to the fathers does not include Transjordan (iv 26, vii 1, viii 1, ix 1-5). Indeed when D chronicles the conquest of Transjordan it avoids any mention of an oath to the fathers (Deut. ii 24-iii 15) in contrast to every place where it mentions the conquest of Cisjordan (e.g. Deut. vi 23, ix 5, 28, x 11, xxx 20). Thus the land yet to be conquered can only be the territory to the north of the tribal settlement from the sources of the Jordan to the Euphrates (Deut. i 7) or Lebo-Hamath (Num. xxxiv 8; Josh. xiii 5). In effect, D is saying when the full extent of the promised land is annexed an additional three asylum cities are to be situated there. Thus D contemplates the eventual existence of nine asylum cities, three in Transjordan and six in Cisjordan.[74] D, then, cannot have invented the asylum city. It presumes the present existence of six cities just as promulgated by P and it projects the addition of three more.

The sole conclusion which these considerations permit is that D no longer knew of the institution of the asylum altar. If the altar was replaced by the city, it happened long before D. D therefore did not invent the city asylum but inherited it from an older source.

The only attested altar asylum in the Bible is that of David's tent-shrine in Jerusalem (1 Kgs i 51, ii 28). It was not the first since it is inconceivable that David would have invented an institution that held a veto power over his judicial authority. That asylum existed in David's tent-shrine is *eo ipso* evidence that it was hallowed tradition which David did not dare to oppose.

It is to Solomon, however, that we must look as the most likely

---

xxxv 12, 19-20) and the death of the high priest (Num. xxxv 28) or some other unknown system must be presumed. Regarding the trial, D presumes that the Supreme Court is called into session for cases which the lower courts cannot resolve (Deut. xvii 8). D further presumes the existence of a judiciary in every walled city (*v*. 18). Would the trial take place where the homicide occurred, where the murderer or murdered resided, or at the asylum? Deut. xix 11-12 implies the trial at the asylum city; Num. xxxv 20 excludes this possibility; Josh. xx is ambiguous. The matter cannot be decided.

[74] So correctly T. Mak. iii 10; Sifre Deut. 185; Mid. Tan. 114; cf. Y. Mak. ii 6; Maimonides, Homicide 8:4.

candidate for the title of the abolitionist of altar asylum. First, Solomon was of different temperament from his father. His redistricting of Israel for tax purposes in defiance of tribal boundaries and authority is a parade example of his determination not to let tradition stand in the way of his administrative goals. Second, two instances whose historicity is not disputed relate that at the onset of Solomon's reign two of his personal enemies sought asylum at the altar.[75] Thus Solomon must have recognized that the throne was threatened by the immunity of the altar. It would have been to his personal as well as to the national interest to abolish this anarchic institution. Third, if the Chronicler is correct in attributing the beginning of a judicial system to David (1 Chron. xxiii 4, xxvi 29-32)—despite the inflated numbers—then Solomon was already equipped with a system of courts throughout the land capable of handling capital crimes. Fourth, an even more significant factor pinpoints Solomon as the one who annulled altar asylum, a factor that would have prevented his father from doing it—Solomon no longer had to abide by the Tabernacle tradition. He built the Temple, and, though it followed the main architectural plan and cultic appointments of the Tabernacle,[76] it bore the imprint of many an innovation. Above all, it is to be remembered that Solomon installed a new sacrificial altar, one of different dimensions and functions from its Tabernacle predecessor.[77] In any event, the fact remains that henceforth the Temple altar never afforded asylum and was declared off-limits to any non-priest.

Clearly, altar asylum had ceased by the time of the Second Temple. This *terminus ad quem* can be ascertained from Nehemiah's memoirs.

---

[75] Joab was Adonijah's champion. The testament of David regarding Joab's murders (1 Kgs ii 5) may have provided Solomon an additional motive, but it was hardly primary in his thinking. It may, however, account for the fact that Joab was slain at the altar, a literal fulfillment of the law of Exod. xxi 14.

[76] I assume that the Tabernacle of Exodus was David's Tabernacle—cf. F. M. Cross, "The Priestly Tabernacle", *BA* 10 (1947), pp. 45-68 (= *BA Reader* 1 [Garden City, N.Y., 1961], pp. 201-28)—based on an old architectural tradition as evidenced by its similarity to the tenth century Arad sanctuary and adjusted to correspond to the floor plan of the Solomonic temple. See Y. Aharoni, *Beer-Sheva* 1 (1973), pp. 79-86; cf. A. Busink, *Der Tempel von Jerusalem* 1 (Leiden, 1970), p. 603.

[77] Cf. 2 Chron. iv 1. The bronze altar is missing in the building account of Kings, but its presence is assumed (1 Kgs viii 64; 2 Kgs xvi 14) and so is its construction (1 Kgs ix 25); cf. W. Rudolph, *Chronikbücher* (Tübingen, 1955), p. 207; for a complete analysis of the construction of Solomon's temple, see Busink, pp. 162-352.

When Shemaiah informs Nehemiah that his life is in danger and he should lock himself in the Temple, Nehemiah rejects the device on the grounds that his entry into the Temple would make him subject to the death penalty (Neh. vi 6-7). However, since neither Shemaiah's advice nor Nehemiah's reply mentions the more obvious means of seeking the safety of the altar, it must be assumed that such a recourse was not available since the altar no longer afforded asylum.

Furthermore, that the laity was permanently barred from the First Temple may be derived from 2 Kgs xii 10, "And the priest Jehoiada took a chest and bored a hole in its lid. He placed it at the right side of the altar as one entered the House of the Lord, and the priestly guards of the threshold deposited there all the money that was brought into the House of the Lord". The logistics are clear. The layman could cross the threshold and enter the temple court but he could not personally deposit his contribution in the collection box which was "at the right side of the altar". The threshold guards, being priests, alone had access to the altar and they would carry out that task.

In the Second Temple as well, the laity could not come within reach of the altar. Even on the Feast of Tabernacles when many regulations were relaxed and the laity was permitted to circumambulate the altar with their willow branches, only priests (though blemished) were assigned the responsibility of depositing the willows on the altar.[78]

Finally, the asylum cities cannot be divorced from the issue of the Levitic cities. The asylum cities are Levitic cities (Num. xxxv 6; Josh. xxi) and their assignment to the Levites means that they are controlled by the central government. The complexity of this subject puts it beyond the bounds of this paper. But with Klein, Albright, Mazar, Kallai,[79] and others it seems probable that the only time at

[78] Y. Suk. iv 54d; B. Sukk. 43b; Ps. xxvi 6. Cf. S. Safrai, *Pilgrimage at the Time of the Second Temple* (Tel-Aviv, 1965), p. 191, and nn. 164, 166, 167 (Heb.).

[79] Cf. S. Klein, "Priestly and Levitic cities and cities of refuge" (Heb.), *Qobeṣ of the JPES* (Jerusalem, 1935), pp. 81-94; W. F. Albright, "The list of Levitic cities", *Louis Ginzberg Jubilee Volume* (New York, 1945), pp. 49 ff.; B. Mazar, "The cities of the priests and the Levites", *SVT* 7 (1960), pp. 193-205; Z. Kallai, *The Tribes of Israel* (Jerusalem, 1967), pp. 379-403 (Heb.). Doubts concerning a Davidic or Solomonic provenance have been raised by J. L. Peterson, *A Topographical Surface Survey of the Levitical "Cities" of Joshua 21 and 1 Chronicles 6* (unpublished Th. D. dissertation, Seabury-Western Theological Seminary, 1977), who shows that 30 out of 48 Levitic cities bear no trace of a tenth-century occupation. Yet the surface sherds collected during ten person-hours per site (p. 18) can hardly be called conclusive evidence, par-

which all the Levitic cities were in Israelite hands was during the reign of Solomon. Moreover, the clearly archival note of 1 Chron. xxvi 29-32 (adduced by Mazar) pointedly demonstrates that the Levites were assigned administrative functions in Transjordan at the end of David's reign. The Chronicler applies additionally significant information when he affixes the high priestly genealogy (1 Chron. vi 35-38) as the introduction to his list of the Levitic cities, a genealogy which is cut off abruptly with Ahimaaz the son of Zadok and which concludes with: "These are the dwelling places according to their settlement within their borders" (1 Chron. vi 39a; Eng. *v.* 54a). As recently shown by S. Japhet,[80] this can mean only that according to the Chronicler the Levitic cities were not just allocated but actually settled during the time of Ahimaaz the son of Zadok—a contemporary of Solomon.

Yet the radical changes in government and worship notwithstanding, it is hard to believe that Solomon could have uprooted a cultic practice as implanted and hallowed as the altar asylum had he not found powerful allies in the priestly hierarchy of Jerusalem under the high priest Zadok who would have championed the doctrine that sancta do not sanctify persons and hence the altar cannot provide asylum. It must be conceded that any other monarch could also have found sufficient warrant to institute this change, but the unique cluster of motives, both personal and royal, plus the propitious timing of many other simultaneous cultic changes that attended the building of the Temple favors Solomon over all his successors.

One objection to this dating must be met. It might be argued that the city asylum rather than being created by the monarchy would have been abolished by it because an absolute king would not have tolerated the institution of the blood redeemer and would have stamped it out, thereby providing no reason for the existence of asylum of any kind. However, the account of David's reign is all too rife with blood revenge to allow for a quick death to this visceral institution; one need but note its role in the slaying of Abner (2 Sam. iii 29-30), Saul's sons (2 Sam. xxi 1-6), and the son in the Tekoite's fable (2 Sam. xiv 7; comp. *MAL* B, § 2).[81] Indeed the Tekoite's

ticularly when, as a result, it is claimed that Hebron, the city where David ruled and Absalom was crowned, was unoccupied during the tenth century.

[80] "Conquest and settlement in Chronicles", *JBL* 98 (1979), pp. 210-12.

[81] The latter story, it is true, shows that the asylum guaranteed by the king was more effective than any other. I might even agree with F. C. Fensham, "A few aspects of legal practices in Samuel in comparison with legal material

story clearly demonstrates that the asylum city was not in existence during the reign of David else her plea for the king's immediate intervention would have been superflous. Moreover the slaying of Saul's sons proves, as S. E. Loewenstamm has argued,[82] that, when David did not execute Saul's sons by his royal order but surrendered them to the Gibeonites, the institution of the blood redeemer was very much alive in David's time which even the power of the throne could not overrule. Finally, since D not only espouses the asylum city but concedes the redeemer's right to act as the state executioner (Deut. xix 12), this can mean only that the state was forced to make concessions to the clan privilege of blood redemption down to the very end of the monarchy.[83] Thus P's laws of homicide are no utopia but a series of concessions to the social reality precisely as one would expect it at the beginning of the monarchy before the central government could effectively usurp tribal and local jurisdiction. In sum, Solomon's innovation lies in the implementation, not the authorship, of the asylum city. It is in his reign that the interests of the crown and the clergy would have coincided to abolish the asylum of the altar and to replace it with cities of asylum.

§ 12. *The transition from altar to city asylum*: *a conjectural development.*

Analysis of the biblical sources on the law of asylum leads to the following diachronic scheme:

(1) Exod. xxi 13-14 is the earliest known stage of altar asylum

in the ancient Near East", *Die Ou Testamentiese Werkgemeenskap in Suid Afrika* (Pretoria, 1960), pp. 25-7, that David thereby demonstrated his opposition to the institution of blood revenge. One is led, however, to ask: was the machinery of royal justice so efficient that it could always intercede in time to thwart the avenger? Admittedly, this is possible (despite the persistence of blood vengeance in civilized societies until modern times), but it would have taken a long time before the central authorities could have been effectively distributed among the people, and more importantly, before the people themselves would have submitted to the justice of the court instead of exercising what they regarded as their uncompromisable duty to avenge the blood of their slain kinsman. The absence of altar asylum from the Tekoite's story may be due to the ineffectiveness of this institution during David's time. But this could hardly be the case for the asylum city which would have been under the direct control of the monarchy and its judiciary.

[82] *Encyclopaedia Biblica* 5 (Jerusalem, 1968), p. 630, s.v. *mišpāṭ* (Heb.).

[83] Cf. a point made by H. McKeating, "The development of the law on homicide in ancient Israel", *VT* 25 (1975), p. 54. D's law of homicide, Deut. xix 1-13, extended state control even further by prescribing that the murderer would be tried by a state-appointed judiciary (*šōpᵉṭîm*) that convened in his asylum city; cf. J. Milgrom, "The ideological importance of the office of judge in Deuteronomy", *I. Seeligmann Jubilee Volume* (forthcoming).

and it already manifests a curtailment of its contagious power: it is not available to murderers.[84]

(2) Shortly after the Temple was built, most likely during the lifetime of Solomon, the institution of the asylum altar was abolished in every sanctuary (and forbidden in the Temple) and was replaced with six asylum cities in the land, in keeping with the teaching of the Jerusalem priesthood, as incorporated in the Priestly Code.

(3) P's system of asylum cities is adopted by D except for two minor changes: their number, and the date of their inauguration. In fact, D is historically more accurate than P when it specifies that the city asylum should be instituted after the conquest is completed (Deut. xix 1; contrast Num. xxxv 9-11; Josh. xxi). The completion of the conquest is also the time designated by D for the centralization of worship (Deut. xii 9) which the Deuteronomist expressly identifies with the reign of Solomon (1 Kgs iii 2).[85]

(4) Ezekiel's constitution for the restored Israel does not call for asylum cities. This omission may be due to accident [86] or to the virtual elimination of incidences of blood revenge by the end of First Temple times which rendered the institution of asylum obsolete.

In sum, the reduction of sancta contagion discernible in the history of the formula *kol-hannōgēaʿ yiqdāš* provides the key to the understanding of how the institution of the asylum altar was replaced by the asylum city. The process had already begun with JE's exclusion of the murderer from the jurisdiction of the altar. However, it achieves

---

[84] This principle is a radical innovation for, to my knowledge, the sanctuary in antiquity gave asylum indiscriminately, cf. W. R. Smith (n. 62), pp. 148, n. 2, and p. 543. It leads directly to the abolition of altar asylum: "the strong command: 'you shall take him from my very altar to be put to death' (Exod. xxi 14) echoes the protest against the ancient image of sacred immunity: justice is mine, and the altar—my altar. However, religious feeling demanded more. Should the deliberate homicide be granted any asylum whatsoever at the altar? Does not the sanctity of the altar demand that the altar's protection be abolished entirely?" Kaufmann (n. 63), p. 265. The restriction to involuntary manslaughter constituted a revolutionary change since sanctuaries throughout the ancient world did not discriminate.

[85] That P's scheme is earlier than that of D is indicated by Josh. xx where the two are conflated but where D is clearly the later stratum; see provisionally M. David (n. 62). However, this argument cannot be conclusive until it is shown that the Deuteronomist editor of Joshua is of the same vintage as D.

[86] Ezekiel omits many other vitals of the cultic life (e.g. among the festivals: the Feast of Weeks (cf. Deut. xvi 10), the first of the seventh month (Lev. xxiii 24), and the Day of Atonement (Lev. xxiii 27-32); among the sacrificial gifts: the firstborn of pure animals, the redemption of human firstborn and impure animals (Num. xviii 15-18), the Levitic tithe (Num. xviii 21), etc.

its revolutionary transformation in P which so interprets the formula that the altar (together with rest of the sancta) is denied the power to transmit its holiness to persons. P then institutes the asylum cities to compensate for the neutralized altar. D adopts P's innovations with slight quantitative modifications.

PSALMS AND INSCRIPTIONS

BY

PATRICK D. MILLER, Jr.
Richmond, Virginia

The biblical psalms have been studied extensively in the light of extra-biblical materials from the ancient Near East, especially those from Mesopotamia (the works of H. Gunkel, G. Widengren, F. Stummer, C. G. Cumming, S. Mowinckel, G. R. Castellino, etc.) and Canaan (the works of I. Engnell, J. H. Patton, M. J. Dahood, and numerous others). Less attention—for understandable reasons—has been given to the relationship of the Psalms to the growing corpus of Hebrew inscriptions and those from neighboring areas (Phoenicia, Moab, Ammon, Aram) during the Iron Age. Early periods of major inscriptional discovery in the years before and after the turn of the century and in the 1930s did not produce finds demonstrating significant relationships with the Psalms. But the discoveries of more recent times—since about 1960—have presented us with inscriptions demonstrating more and greater affinities with the Psalms. André Lemaire at the last Congress in Göttingen signaled the importance of these materials for the religion of Israel,[1] and I want to follow up his inquiries by focusing particularly or primarily on the potential conversation that may be heard between the canonical psalms and the occasional, individual, and long-lost utterances of those who carved and penned their words on the walls, steles, sherds, and caves of ancient Palestine.

While there have been several major epigraphic finds since 1960, some of these inscriptions demonstrate closer relationships with the language and content of the Psalter than do others. These are the inscriptions from Khirbet el Qôm, Khirbet Beit Lei, and Kuntillet Ajrud. The texts from the former two sites will be the object of attention in these pages.[2] They come from the same social, historical,

---

[1] "L'épigraphie paléo-hébraique et la bible", *Congress Volume*: *Göttingen 1977*, *SVT*, 29 (Leiden, 1978), pp. 165-76.

[2] Reasons of space and the incomplete publication of the texts from Kuntillet Ajrud lead me to omit them from consideration here. They show among other things theophanic language having affinities with the Psalms as well as blessing

and geographical setting out of which came many of the Psalms, i.e., Judah during the time of the Divided Monarchy and the Exile. It should prove both useful and interesting to place the biblical Psalms and contemporary inscriptions alongside each other to see their inter-relationships, to let them reflect off one another as a way of seeking to understand both Psalms and inscriptions more clearly and to demonstrate the continuity of these non-biblical archaic texts with the biblical tradition as it is carried down to the present.[3]

One caveat should be given at the beginning. These inscriptions like all inscriptions are not self evident with regard to either their reading or their meaning. Some of them are exceedingly difficult to read. Some can be read, but the meanings or allusions may be difficult to grasp. The associations and conclusions given here inevitably depend upon the accuracy of the reading and interpretation of these inscriptions—and to a lesser degree the Psalms themselves. Improvements in our understanding of the inscriptions may alter the following analysis at points. The readings proposed here rest upon careful examination of photographs, study of the primary literature, consultation with some of the scholars who have published or studied these inscriptions, and a first-hand examination of some of the more problematic inscriptions in June and July, 1980.

Thirty-five years ago H. L. Ginsberg published an important article entitled "Psalms and Inscriptions of Petition and Acknowledgment".[4] His starting point and primary focus was the then recently published Ben-Hadad stele with its concluding expression indicating the reason for the stele: *zy nzr lh wšmʿ. lqlh* "to whom he prayed and who heard his voice". His interpretation of *nzr* as "he prayed" was based on the context and on Ps. lxi 6. He compared this expression to similar sentences in Phoenician, Palmyrene, and neo-Punic in-

formulae that may be associated with the Aaronic Benediction and the Psalms of Ascents. The writer is indebted to Dr Z. Meshel for showing and discussing with him photographs and facsimiles of the inscriptions from Kuntillet Ajrud. Other inscriptions found in the last two decades will be found to share language and formulae with the Psalms, e.g., the rare word pair *ymt* // *šnt*, which appears in Ugaritic (RS 24. 252, verse 10-13) and on the Tell Siran bottle inscription from Amman as well as in Ps. xc 15 and Deut. xxxii 7, or the line from the Tell Deir Alla texts *wlkw . rʾw . pʿlt ʾlhn*, which is to be compared with Pss. xlvi 9 and lxvi 5.

[3] The biblical connections of these inscriptions are not, of course, only with the Psalter, and while the primary interest of this article is the Psalter I shall not ignore some of the linguistic and material resonances with other parts of the Bible.

[4] A. Marx (ed.), *Louis Ginzberg Jubilee Volume* (New York, 1945), pp. 159-71.

scriptions generally of a votive sort which speak of the petitioner calling the deity and the deity hearing or answering. Ginsberg pointed to the *public* character of the words of thanksgiving and acknowledgment in the Psalms (cf. xxii 23 ff., xxx 5, xxxiv 4 ff., cvii 32, etc.) and then suggested that despite the lack of primary evidence the *verbal* as over against *epigraphic* distinction between the Israelite and non-Israelite forms of public acknowledgement (e.g., Egyptian thanksgiving inscriptions) is more apparent than real. Citing Isa. xxxviii 9 where Hezekiah's prayer is called a *miktāb*, he inferred (following a view going back at least as far as J. D. Michaelis) that it was published by being engraved in stone. The *miktām* of the superscriptions of Pss. xvi and lvi-lx may also refer to these psalms being inscribed. At least the ancient versions seem to have so interpreted it.[5] These psalms of petition like those of acknowledgement would have been inscribed in some fashion.

Ginsberg also took note of the three occasions where superscriptions with *miktām* also have the injunction *'al tašḥēt* (lvii 1, lviii 1, and lix 1), which he suggested "may indeed be a further reflex of the habit of committing Psalms to epigraphy" (p. 171, n. 49). Ginsberg's case is strengthened when one notes that the Phoenician Kilamuwa inscription uses just this verb to refer to the destruction of the inscription: "Whoever destroys (*šḥt*) this inscription may Baal Samad destroy (*šḥt*) his head." The fact, therefore, that three of the four uses of *'al tašḥēt* are related to *miktām* suggests rather strongly that the composers of these superscriptions, whether early or late, were familiar with the practice of recording psalms as inscriptions.[6]

In his study of individual laments against an enemy L. Delekat has set forth rather vigorously the thesis—based partly on some of

---

[5] LXX and Theodotion = στηλογραφία; Gallican Psalter = *in tituli inscriptione* (based on xii); Targum—*gelîpā' terîṣā'* (xvi 1) and *paršegen* (lx 1). More recently Dahood, *Psalms* I (Garden City, 1966), p. 87, has expressed agreement with Ginsberg's interpretation.

[6] One might add to that the clear indication that *sēper* can mean "inscription" as it appears to mean in Job xix 23-24 and elsewhere. Job's wish that his words might be written with "pen of iron" on a *sēper* appears to be a wish that his lament might be inscribed on a rock as perhaps on the walls of a tomb or cave or on a stone stele. The inscription would be his complaint, like the laments of the Psalter. See H. S. Gehman, "Sēpher, an Inscription, in the Book of Job", *JBL* 63 (1944), pp. 303-7; Cf. K. Galling, "Die Grabinschrift Hiobs", *WO* 2 (1954), pp. 3-6; and D. Hillers, *Treaty Curses and the Old Testament Prophets* (Rome, 1964), pp. 45-8.

the evidence cited above as well as North Arabic examples—that these individual psalms were inscribed:

> Der Beter schrieb ursprünglich, etwa am Abend seiner Ankunft, einen kurzen Gebetsruf an die Tempelmauer und fügte, nachdem er die Gewissheit seiner Erhörung erhalten hatte, eine entsprechende Notiz hinzu. Mit der Zeit wurden dann die Gebete länger und kunstvoller. Man liess sie jetzt auf einer Stele eingravieren. Zuweilen war vielleicht auch der Beter nicht mehr selbst der Dichter.[7]

Delekat assumes this *Sitz im Leben* for Pss. lvi, lvii, and lix where the superscriptions discussed above appear above prayers for deliverance from personal enemies. But he goes on to propose that the same may have been true of a large number of laments which include acknowledgements of a hearing (p. 18).

Whether or not Delekat's thesis in all its parts can or should be substantiated, the new epigraphic data indicate that Ginsberg (and those before and after him who have raised the possibility of inscribed psalms) made some brilliant inferences. One of the purposes of this article is to build on his work in relation to the newer inscriptional evidence. When Ginsberg wrote, there was no clearly Israelite or Hebrew inscriptional evidence to support his conclusions.[8] He was

---

[7] *Asylie und Schutzorakel am Zionheiligtum* (Leiden, 1967), p. 18.

[8] Ginsberg said nothing about the Zakir inscription in his discussion, but it represents another Aramaic example of an inscribed report by a king to the effect that his god heard his prayer. The inscription describes in detail the plight of Zakir when Bar Hadad came against him with a coalition. He reports that "I lifted my hands" (*wʾśʾ ydy*) to Baal Shamayn and the god "heard me" (*wyʿnny*) "and spoke to me by seers (*ḥzyn*) and *ʿddyn*". The response of the deity to the plea for help in a prayer was an explicit oracle of salvation, just what one assumes for the response to the laments of the psalms. The terminology of lifting the hands is, of course, common in the Psalter in these terms as well as with *pāras* and *kap* (Pss. xxviii 2, xliv 21, lxiii 5, cxxxiv 2, cxli 2, cxliii 6. Cf. Job xi 13; Lam. i 17, ii 19; and Ps. lxxxviii 10). The response *wyʿnny* gives the vocabulary used frequently in the Psalms as a part of the petition (Pss. iv 2. xiii 4, xxvii 7, lv 3, lxix 17, 18, etc.) as well as the acknowledgement of the deity's hearing (Pss. xxii 22, xxxiv 5, xxxviii 16). The verb *ḥṣl* (l. 14) in the deity's answer to Zakir "I will deliver you" is the Canaanite-Hebrew verb *ḥlṣ*, which is used only poetically and almost exclusively in the Psalms (Pss. vi 5, vii 5, xviii 20, xxxiv 8, 15, lxxxi 8, xci 15, cxvi 8, cxix 153, cxl 2). The associations of this inscription with Psalms and other biblical literature have been pointed out in detail in the following articles: J. C. Greenfield, "The Zakir Inscription and the Danklied", *Proceedings of the Fifth World Congress of Jewish Studies* 1 (Jerusalem, 1969), pp. 174-91; J. F. Ross, "Prophecy in Hamath, Israel, and Mari", *HTR* 63 (1970), pp. 1-28; H. J. Zobel, "Das Gebet um Abwendung der Not und seine Erhörung in den Klagelieder des Alten Testaments und in der Inschrift des Königs Zakir von Hamath", *VT* 21 (1971), pp. 91-9. Cf. W. W. Hallo, "The Royal Correspondence of Larsa: A

entirely dependent upon Egyptian, Aramaic, and Phoenician sources, generally late, i.e. post-biblical (except for the Ben-Hadad stele). Now we have a growing corpus of pre-exilic Hebrew inscriptions (as well as Aramaic and Ammonite) containing forms, formulae, vocabulary, and content relating to the psalms and even providing examples of inscribed prayers. In one case, Khirbet el Qôm, No. 3, we have a superscription that compares with that above Hezekiah's prayer and the superscriptions of the Psalms which have the intention and the effect of personalizing what are otherwise quite general petitions or thanksgivings. The superscription at Khirbet el Qôm is:

ʾryhw. hʿšr [9] *ktbh* [10]
Uriyahu the rich; his inscription.
(or: has written it)

Then at the end there is a colophon referring to the scribe or author of the inscription *lʾnyhw*. That this is the scribe or author is indicated not only by the reference to *ʾryhw* at the beginning but by the reference to Uriyahu in the body of the inscription. The descriptive word *hʿšr* (= *heʿāšīr*) is not unlike the descriptive modifiers in the titles of some of the psalms, such as lxxxviii 1 (*lᵉhêmān hāʾezrāḥî*); lxxxix 1 (*lᵉʾêtān hāʾezrāḥî*); xc 1 (*lᵉmōšeh ʾîš hāʾᵉlōhîm*); and the prayer of Hezehiah (*lᵉḥizkîyāhû melek yᵉhûdāh*).[11] It is possible also, as Dever has suggested, that a *lamed* stood at the beginning of the first line (the text is broken just before the *ʾalef*). If that were the case, the parallel to the psalms would be even greater. The first line would read: "For Uriyahu the rich. His inscription." Finally then, to see how far this inscription confirms Ginsberg's suppositions, the inscription is carved on a stone pillar in the tomb. The fact that the

Sumerian Prototype for the Prayer of Hezekiah?", *Kramer Anniversary Volume* (Neukirchen-Vluyn, 1976), pp. 209-24.

[9] The *ʿayin* in this word is not entirely certain. The writer doubts that the long line going out from it diagonally is meant to be a part of the letter as Dever suggested, reading *qof* here and the whole word as *hqšb*: "Pay attention to". The fourth letter is clearly a *reš* and can not be a *bet* as one can tell by the *bet* further on in this line. The only alternative would be to follow Avigad and Cross and ignore the second letter to read *hśr*, "the prince". But such an approach seems to fly in the face of what is there in the text. While the letter is more triangular than other *ʿayin*s in the Khirbet el Qôm inscription, that seems to be the most plausible reading of this letter.

[10] On this noun as a late Hebrew word see W. G. Dever, "Iron Age Epigraphic Material from the Area of Khirbet el-Kôm", *HUCA* 40-41 (1969-70), p. 159.

[11] If the second word is *haśśār*, it would function in the same way.

inscription is in a tomb does not mean it is not a public acknowledgement. Its inscribed character indicates its public character. Further, the full inscription is not, as Dever put it, "the common sepulchral type". Over against his notion that the Beit Lei Inscription A is "the only pre-exilic Hebrew inscription known thus far which does not belong to the common sepulchral type" (p. 166), most of the pre-exilic Hebrew inscriptions, lapidary or otherwise, are not sepulchral inscriptions guarding tombs. Only the Royal Steward Inscription and Inscription no. 7 at Khirbet el Qôm and the broken Reifenberg inscriptions are true sepulchral inscriptions (and they do not neatly fit the form that Dever outlined, which is more applicable to the Phoenician and Aramaic inscriptions than to the Hebrew). The main inscriptions from such sites as Kh. el Qôm, Kh. Beit Lei, and Kuntillet Ajrud and Nahal Yishai are of a quite different order. It should be noted that the curse formula which appears in these inscriptions (Kh. el Qôm, Kh. Beit Lei, and Nahal Yishai) is not to be identified with the form or formulae of sepulchral or burial Inscriptions. It is a formula for guarding an inscription (see Karatepe and Sefire).[12]

The inscription from Khirbet el Qôm, alluded to above, though it poses some problems in reading and interpretation,[13] shows affinities with psalmody in form, language, and theme. It is capable of being understood either as a prayer by Uriyahu hiding in these tombs and asking Yahweh's deliverance from the external threat,[14] or more

---

[12] For a catalog of West Semitic curses up to 1961 see S. Gevirtz, "West Semitic Curses and the Problem of the Origins of Hebrew Law", *VT* 11 (1961), pp. 137-58. Gevirtz divided them into three categories: commemorative, funerary, and votive. The Hebrew inscriptions mentioned here belong to the first category. With regard to the form *ʾārûr* Gevirtz wrote: "In view of its frequency in the Old Testament, and of its restriction to Hebrew sources, this curse form may be recognized as characteristically and specifically Hebrew" (p. 151, n. 2). The appearance of *ʾārûr* now four times at Khirbet Beit Lei and once at Nahal Ishai serves to provide significant new evidence to support Gevirtz's conclusion.

[13] See A. Lemaire, "Les Inscriptions de Khirbet el-Qôm et l'Ashérah de YHWH", *RB* 84 (1977), pp. 595-608. His reading of the inscription is, in my judgement, correct.

[14] Most recently J. Naveh has adopted this interpretation translating the inscription: "1) Uriyahu the governor wrote it. 2) May Uriyahu be blessed by Yahweh 3) my guardian and by his Asherah, Save him. 4) (save) Uriyahu. ["Graffiti and Dedications" to be published in *BASOR* 235 (1980). I am grateful to Professor Naveh for putting a copy of this article in my hands prior to publication.] Attractive as it is, there are several problems with this reading. While there are clear signs of double writing in the text, there is little justification for regarding several letters that are clearly written as mistakes. Naveh, however, disregards the *ʿayin* before the letters *ś/šr* in line 1 (thus "the governor" instead of "the rich"),

likely as an inscribed prayer or psalm of thanksgiving for the deceased Uriyahu buried—or expected to be—in the tomb. It is to be read and translated as follows:

1. *(l)ʾryhw.hʿšr.ktbh*
2. *brk.ʾryhw.lyhwh*
3. *wmṣryh.lʾšrth | hwšʿ | lh*
4. *lʾnyhw*
5. *ẘlʾ̊šrth*
6. *r h*

1. (For) Uriyahu the rich: his inscription.
   (Or: has written it)
2. Blessed is Uriyahu by Yahweh;
3. Yea from his adversaries by his asherah he has saved him.
4. (Written) by Oniyahu
5. (. . .?) and by his asherah

It is quite possible, as Lemaire has suggested, that the phrase "by his asherah" is out of place and should be at the beginning of line 3. This could be signaled by the repeat of the word in line 5 (see Lemaire) though there may have been more writing in that line. The formula *lyhwh wlʾšrth* or *lyhwh* (epithet) *wlʾšrth* appears several times now at Kuntillet Ajrud. One should assume, however, that the writer wrote what he or she meant to write. If so,—and this is also the case even if there is a displacement—we have two essentially poetic lines creating a psalm of thanksgiving. The *lyhwh* in line 2 is paralleled by *lʾšrth* in line 3 in a way analogous to similar parallelisms in the Psalms where "Yahweh" is the A word and some characteristic of the deity, "his hand", "his soul", "his heart", "his name", "his word", is the B word (e.g. Pss. xi 5, xxviii 5, xxxiii 11, xxxiv 4, cxxx 5).[15]

---

the *waw* at the beginning of line 3, and the *he* after the letters which he reads *nṣry* "my guardian". In addition he reads *nun* for the *mem* that is the second letter of line 3 and is forced to emend line 4 to read "Uriyahu" instead of the very clearly written "Oniyahu". Nor can one regard line 4 as a second object to the final verb of line 3. There is considerable space separating it from the three lines above, and it must be regarded as a colophon.

[15] The use of the *l* in an instrumental sense is unusual except that it is influenced by the *brk* + *l* + *GN* formula of which it is a part. The formulaic character of these expressions would probably have caused the use of *lamed* even if it should be the case that the formula *brk lyhwh* should be understood as "blessed to Yahweh" as recently argued by T. Muraoka, "Hebrew Philological Notes", *Annual*

A further parallelism is present between the verbs *brk* and *hwš*ʿ. The particular formula *brk lyhwh* is less common in the Bible than it is in inscriptions in the light of recent discoveries. It occurs in the Psalms in Ps. cxv 15, though it does also occur a few other times elsewhere (Judg. xvii 2; 1 Sam. xv 13, xxiii 21; 2 Sam. ii 5; Ruth ii 20, and iii 10; cf. Gen. xiv 19). The notion of God's blessing individuals and community with prosperity, life, and posterity is familiar in the Psalms (e.g. xxix 11, lxvii 2, 7, 8, cxv 12-25, cix 28). Even more common is the prayer for deliverance (*hwš*ʿ) from enemies (*ṣārîm* and *ṣōrᵉrîm*). These terms are among the primary designations of the enemies of the individual and of the community (as well as Yahweh himself) in the Psalms, appearing there as here more often in plurality than a single enemy (*ṣārîm*—Pss. iii 2, xiii 5, xxvii 2, 12, xliv 6, 8, lx 14 = cviii 14, lxxviii 66, lxxxi 15, lxxxix 24, 43, xcvii 3, cv 24, cvi 11, cxii 8, cxix 139, 157, cxxxvi 24; *ṣōrᵉrîm*—Pss. vi 8, vii 7, viii 3, x 5, xxiii 5, xxxi 12, xlii 11, lxix 20, lxxiv 4, 23). The common plea of the lamenter(s) is for Yahweh's deliverance (e.g. Ps. iii 8, vii 2, xii 2, xxii 22, xxvii 9, etc.) even as the praying one affirms the salvation that comes from Yahweh (Ps. iii 9, lxviii 20, cxlix 4, etc.). The explicit idiom *hwš*ʿ + object + *min* + *ṣārîm* + suffix is found in Ps. xliv 8 (cf. xxxiv 7). There are, of course, many semantic equivalents for this particular prayer or thanksgiving in the Psalms.

The parallelism of *brk* and *hwš*ʿ as the activity of God occurs in the Psalter and primarily there. Ps. iii is an individual lament that arises out of a situation where many *ṣārîm* oppose the Psalmist (vs. 2) and say there is no *yᵉšûʿātāh* for him from God (vs. 3). It reaches its climax in the petition to God to rise up and "save me" (*hôšîʿēnî*, vs. 8) and concludes in the affirmation:

> *lyhwh hayšûʿāh*
> *ʿal-ʿammᵉkā birkātekā* (vs. 9)
> Salvation belongs to Yahweh;
> your blessing be upon your people.

Psalm xxviii, another lament which concludes with thanksgiving for the deliverance that is assured, ends with a prayer of confidence:

---

of the Japanese Biblical Institute 5 (1979), pp. 92-4; and D. Pardee, "Letters from Tel Arad", *UF* 10 (1973), p. 311. In this latter interpretation the reading would be smoother on the assumption that *lʾšrth* belonged at the beginning of the line after the *waw*.

hôšîʿāh ʾet-ʿammekā
ûbārēk ʾet-naḥᵃlātekā (vs. 9)
Save your people;
bless your heritage.

Similar associations of Yahweh's blessing and his salvation are seen in Pss. xxiv 5 and cix 26-28 (cf. Zech. viii 13).

This relationship between blessing and salvation that is found in the laments and thanksgivings of the Psalms and Khirbet el Qôm is not simply a poetic collocation. It also carries theological weight. Claus Westermann has underscored the actions of blessing and salvation as the primary poles around which the activity of God revolves in the Old Testament, salvation in the sense of Yahweh's deliverance of the community and individuals from particular crises, oppressions, need of various sorts, and blessing in the sense of Yahweh's ongoing provision of the needs and possibilities for life—birth, food, general care, divine protection in the daily experiences of life, the provision for the continuities of life—work, space, food, family.[16] This distinction is a useful and viable one, especially as it guards against an overemphasis on saving activity and historical events as the character and locus of the divine work. But, as Westermann himself has recognized clearly, the activity of God is ultimately one and it is not possible finally to separate the forms and modes of that activity. The Psalms cited here, as well as the prayer of Uriyahu, hold together these two dimensions as one whole. In parallel with one another the two are closely identified. At the same time, as parallelism often indicates, the ones praying these psalms acknowledge God *not only* as the God of salvation *but also* the provider of blessing.[17] For Uriyahu the inscribed thanksgiving attests his life-long experience of being sustained and kept by Yahweh (and his *ʾᵃšērāh*).[18] Indeed his self-definition "Uriyahu the rich" reflects the conviction that he has been

[16] See among other places his Sprunt Lectures at Union Theological Seminary in Virginia, *What Does the Old Testament Say About God* (Atlanta, 1979), chs. 2 and 3.

[17] In an important study of parallelism in Hebrew poetry to be published by Yale University Press, James Kugel has aptly characterized the two parts of a parallel line as indicating in effect "A is so, and *what's more,* B". The two lines of Uriyahu's prayer may be understood in just such a manner.

[18] At this point it is not necessary to go into the question of the possible nature of the *ʾᵃšērāh* of Yahweh in this context. The singular verb *hwšʿ* attests to the fact that the agent of the verbs is Yahweh whatever the relationship of the *ʾᵃšērāh* to Yahweh may be.

blessed by God, for wealth and riches are aspects of Yahweh's blessing (Ps. xxxvii 11, 22, cvii 37-38, cxii 5; 1 Sam. ii 7; 1 Chron. xxix 12, 28). As is typical of the Psalms, the adversaries from whom Yahweh has saved him are not described in any particularity, but one assumes that he experienced,as did others who sang the laments of Israel, occasions when he was treated unjustly, oppressed, derided, or condemned, Now at the end of life he inscribes a prayer of thanksgiving for the blessing and salvation of God in the form and language of the biblical Psalms.[19]

The cave inscriptions and drawings from Khirbet Beit Lei present a number of affinities with the biblical Psalms. While they are found in an antechamber of a tomb, Frank Cross is certainly correct in concluding the main inscriptions are not funerary inscriptions.[20] They are not easy to read or interpret but they are sufficiently clear to confirm Lemaire's characterization of them as "prayers in time of crisis". While they vary in type, three of the main inscriptions are addressed to God and are accompanied by drawings of figures with hands up-raised in prayer. Another appears to be a divine response to prayer. Together they provide our most extensive assemblage of Psalmodic materials prior to the Restoration period, in this case probably the sixth century B.C.[21]

The longest of the Beit Lei Inscriptions (Inscription A) is also the most problematic. Naveh and Lemaire have read the inscription as a hymnic or confessional declaration of the universality of Yahweh's rule and his lordship over Judah and Jerusalem. Cross sees here a

[19] Note particularly the similarity to the summary thanksgiving of Ps. xxxiv 7:

zeh ʿānî qārāʾ wayhwh šāmēaʿ
ûmikkol-ṣārôtāyw hôšîʿô

Greenfield, p. 179, has noted the similarity of this verse to the language and form of the Zakir Inscription.

[20] We would extend that judgement to include also at least most of the *ʾārūr* inscriptions on the walls which are either curses against the enemy or protection of the inscriptions. See F. M. Cross, "The Cave Inscriptions from Khirbet Beit Lei", *Near Eastern Archaeology in the Twentieth Century* (Garden City, New York, 1970), pp. 299-306. The original publication is by Joseph Naveh, "Old Hebrew Inscriptions in a Burial Cave", *IEJ* 13 (1963), pp. 74-92. The most important study in addition to that of Cross is A. Lemaire, "Prières en temps de crise: les inscriptions de Khirbet Beit Lei", *RB* 83 (1976), pp. 558-68.

[21] This follows the dating of Cross (and Naveh, according to a private communication). In terms of their character and content they would be understandable during the time of either the Assyrian crisis in Judah in the late eighth century or the Neo-Babylonia invasion in the early sixth century. Palaeographically, however, the latter circumstance is the more likely occasion.

divine address, in effect an oracle of salvation. The writer had assumed on the basis of photographs as well as the character of the other inscriptions that the reading of Lemaire was correct. The opportunity of spending a prolonged period of time examining the inscription in the summer of 1980 has called that assumption into question and convinced us that Cross is probably on the right track even though part of his reading is conjecture, and any reading will still have some problems. We would read as follows:

> [*ʾn(k)y*] [22] *yhwh ʾlhykh* [23]. *ʾrṣh* [24]
> [25] *ʿ̊ry* / *yhd̊h̊ ẘg̊* [26] *ʾlt̊y* [27] *yršlm*

---

[22] Cross maintains that traces of the *nun* and the *yod* are barely visible, and that there is a word divider after this word. All of that is very questionable in my judgement. I can find no traces of any of these letters and the presumed word divider is a part of the middle stroke of a *kaf* breaking through. This is characteristic of the numerous extra *kafs* that appear on these inscriptions. I am proposing, however, that *ʾny* or *ʾnky* (there may be room for four letters) was incised on the stone at one time and is now obliterated. There are several good reasons for that assumption:

a) Although it is not clear from the photographs, considerable erosion seems to have taken place on the upper right hand side of the stone. The first three letters of the second line though definitely incised are almost worn away.
b) The line down the right hand side of the inscription is carefully incised as a right hand margin. The second line and the second inscription begin at the line. Compare a similar marginal line on one of the pithoi at Kuntillet Ajrud where all the lines begin at the margin.
c) The words *ʾrṣh* and *gʾlty* as first person verbs virtually compel the divine self-predication "I am Yahweh your God" at the beginning.

[23] There are various marks between the *k* and the *h*. It is possible to read a *lamed* there. Its size and depth of incision are in our judgement not a problem (contra Cross). But the stance does not fit *lamed*. More important is the presence under the *he* of a word divider which is ignored by Naveh and Lemaire. One would expect it to be more to the left, but it is clearly incised and like the word divider before *yršlm* in the second line. Further, the tails of *kaf* and *he* come together indicating they are successive letters. The second person masculine singular suffix, as Cross indicates, is the long form, a literary form. It is unprecedented in pre-Exilic inscriptions. "Your God" in the Lachish letters is *ʾlhyk*, and the suffix is the short form elsewhere in the epigraphic material. But this is clearly a poetic and literary piece, so that the first appearance of the long form is not altogether surprising.

[24] While there are other inscriptions that break up words at the end of lines, there is no reason why one would expect that in this case.

[25] The triangular shaped *ʿayin* is not altogether certain because of the problem of erosion, but the traces of it are visible on the stone and in photographs.

[26] The preceding sequence of four letters is the most difficult in the inscription. Cross has indicated the reasons for reading them as *dalet*, *he*, *waw*, *gimel*. The first letter is only partially preserved. It could be a *waw*. The second letter is either a triangular headed *he* or a *dalet*. The *waw* is one of the most crucial letters for

[ʾānōkî]
[ʾanî] yahweh ʾelōhekāh
ʾerṣeh ʿārê yehûdāh
wegāʾaltî yerûšālēm
[I am] Yahweh your God.
I will accept the cities of Judah;
I will redeem Jerusalem.

The lines are good poetry balanced in meter, length, and sense. As Cross has observed, the language is reminiscent of Jeremiah and Second Isaiah, not surprisingly in the light of the time of writing. In form the inscription is more like Second Isaiah than the Psalms, as one would expect for a prophetic oracle of salvation. But the close associations between Psalms and Isa. xl-lxvi are reflected in this inscription also. In form it is clearly a response to the laments and petitions such as one finds in abundance in the Psalter, Psalms such as xliv, lxix, lxxiv, and lxxix, all of which in one way or another can be related to these inscriptions. The oracle assumes threats or hostile forces against Jerusalem and the cities of Judah and answers the prayer and hope of those who have taken refuge in the cave that Yahweh will deliver them from the enemy. The expression *ʿārê yehûdāh* is most common in Jeremiah and the historical books. But it appears also in the Psalms in the *tôdāh* at the conclusion of the lament in Ps. lxix:

kî ʾelōhîm yôšîaʿ ṣiyyôn
weyibneh ʿārê yehûdāh (vs. 36)

This Psalmist, who cries out for Yahweh to redeem him (*gāʾal*, vs. 19) and claims to have borne the reproach (*ḥerpāh*) of those who reproach Yahweh (see below on *ḥrp* at Beit Lei), offers praise and thanksgiving out of the assurance received that God will save Jerusalem and

interpretation. Naveh and Cross read the letter as *waw*. Lemaire reads *he* and says "dont on verrait mal les deux barres inférieures et qui serait en quelque sorts 'coiffé' par un trait de séparation placé un peu haut" (pp. 559-60). But while the diagonal cross stroke is a little long for a *waw* (though not when compared to other letters incised by this scribe) the head is clearly incised above the diagonal stroke but connected to the vertical, a good *waw*. In context it must be seen as a conjunction beginning a new clause. The *gimel* identified by Cross is partially eroded away but sufficiently visible and in accord with the Judaean script of this period. The presumed *lamed* (Naveh and Lemaire) may be made up of a slash that comes down from above the inscription and the horizontal stroke of the *gimel*.

[27] The *taw* is uncertain but possible. The *he* read by Lemaire and Naveh is also possible.

rebuild the cities of Judah, a word of assurance that is essentially the same as this inscription. Like the conclusion of Ps. lxix, Inscription A may be seen as an answer to the short prayer inscribed on the walls of the antechamber of Kh. Beit Lei (Inscription C):

hwšʿ (*y*) *hwḥ*
"Save, O Yahweh"

Ps. lxix begins with the same prayer:

hôšîʿēnî ʾelōhîm (vs. 2) [28]

and ends with the saving word about Jerusalem and the cities of Judah. The parallelism *ṣiyyôn*// *ʿārê yehûdāh* is equivalent to the word pair *ʿry yhdh*// *yršlm*, which occurs in Second Isaiah and Jeremiah as well as Kh. Beit Lei.
The expression *ʾrṣh ʿry yhdh* has its closest parallel in Ps lxxxv 2 (Cross, p. 302):

rāṣîtā yhwh ʾarṣekā
You have accepted, O Yahweh, your land.

That psalm is a communal lament that begins out of the recollection of God's acceptance of his land in the past. Like Khirbet Beit Lei A, the psalm may have in mind the return from Exile. Similarly Ps. lxxvii as a lament asks if God will ever again accept or look with favor (*rṣh*, vs. 8) and ends up in assurance out of the recollection of God's having redeemed (*gʾl*, vs. 16) his people in the past.

The ideology and context of these Psalms and the Khirbet Beit Lei inscriptions are, therefore, very similar, a point that is reinforced when one brings into account another brief inscription found on the walls of the tomb at Beit Lei and deciphered by Lemaire:

ʾrr ḥ
rpk
ʾārūr ḥō
repāk [29]
Cursed be the one who re-
proaches you.

---

[28] See lxxxvi 2 and the grounding of the cry *hôšaʿ* in the claim *ʾattāh ʾelōhay*, "you are my God", the same as the divine word of assurance in Khirbet Beit Lei A; so also cvi 47. Cf. the imperative cry to Yahweh to save in iii 8, xii 2, xx 10, xxviii 9, cxviii 25, etc.

[29] In this brief execration which is not as poetic as Inscription A the more common short form of the suffix is used.

Lemaire has correctly recognized that this brief inscription is a prayer to the deity. The context, i.e. Inscriptions A, B, and C which are either divine address or address to God, makes that clear. It is further confirmed, however, by the uses of *ḥrp* (vb.) + second masculine singular suffix in the Old Testament. There are only two cases where the object of this verb is identified by a second masculine singular pronoun. Both instances are in the Psalms (lxix 10 and lxxix 12) and are addressed to God, the suffix referring to him. It is to be noted that the curse here has nothing to do with opening the tomb. In fact none of the several *ʾārūr* examples at Khirbet Beit Lei is a warning to protect a tomb. This particular inscription is a prayer curse against the common enemies of Yahweh and the petitioner.

The expression *ʾārūr* is not itself common in the Psalms. It appears only in Ps. cxix 21 in a somewhat different usage, but one that in its context has affinities with the Beit Lei text. In Ps. cxix 21-22 the *ʾᵃrûrîm*, "cursed ones", appear to be those who utter *ḥerpāh* against the righteous Psalmist. But whether or not the technical term *ʾārûr* is used in the Psalms, prayers against an enemy that are in effect curses against him or them do appear in the Psalter.[30] An excellent and important example is Psalm lxix already alluded to in regard to Inscription A. Not only are vss. 23-29 imprecations against the enemies of the Psalmist, but the primary characteristic of these enemies is *ḥerpāh* (vss. 8, 10 (2 ×), 11, 20, and 21). Furthermore, the *ḥerpāh* which the singer laments is that of "those who taunt you (*ḥôrᵉpekā*)". The appropriate way to respond to those who continually cast taunts against the Psalmist and against God is to pray (jussive) that they may be destroyed by Yahweh. It is just this move that is made in the prayers of Beit Lei.

The question remains, however, for both the inscription and the Psalms: what is the action against God and his righteous ones that is described by the verb *ḥārap* and the noun *ḥerpāh*? Both forms are exceedingly common in the Psalms,[31] occurring almost entirely in laments and referring to the activity of the enemies.[32] One cannot

---

[30] See Gunkel, *Einleitung in die Psalmen* (Gottingen, 1933), para. 4.8 and 6.15.

[31] Verb: xlii 11, xliv 17, lv 13, lvii 4, lxix 10, lxxiv 10, 18, lxxix 12, lxxxix 52 (2x), cii 9, cxix 42.
Noun: xv 3, xxii 7, xxxi 12, xxxix 9, xliv 14, lxix 8, 10, 11, 20, 21, lxxi 13, lxxiv 22, lxxviii 66, lxxix 4, 12, lxxxix 42, 51, cix 25, cxix 22, 39.

[32] Frequently against the Psalmist but also against Yahweh (lxix 10, lxxiv 10, 18, 22, lxxix 4, 12) and against his anointed (lxxxix 51, 52).

always discern the nature of the *ḥerpāh* in the laments, but the narrative uses of this word offer some clues as to the content of the accusations or complaints of the Psalmists.

Judges viii 15: The men of Succoth and Penuel *ḥrp* Gideon by asking the question: "Are Zebah and Zalmuna already in your hand that we should give you bread?" It is a question that scoffs at Gideon's power. He has not got the enemy and they do not think he will, and so why should they feed him?

Nehemiah iii 33-34: Sanballat and Tobiah taunt (*ḥrp*) the Jews by a series of questions, all of which imply the ineffectuality of the Jews. In vss. 36-37 Nehemiah responds to this with a typical lament and petition.

Nehemiah vi 13: A prophet sent by Sanballat and Tobiah tries to persuade Nehemiah that he should hide in the temple because people are coming to kill him. Nehemiah sees this as a ruse by his enemies to make him seem afraid so that they may then taunt (*ḥrp*) him. No question is included because the taunt is not given, but the issue of the taunt is seen as Nehemiah's potential powerlessness and fear.

1 Samuel xxv 39: When David sends messengers to Nabal requesting food for his men, Nabal replies with a series of questions: "Who is David? Who is the son of Jesse? There are many servants breaking away from their master. Shall I take my bread and my water and my meat that I have killed for my shearers, and give it to men who come from I do not know where?" David calls this response *ḥerpāh*.

1 Samuel xvii 10, 25, 26, 36, 45: Goliath says: "*ʾanî ḥēraptî* the ranks of Israel today." In other words he is challenging or taunting them for their powerlessness against his strength. He begins his taunt with questions: "Why have you come out to draw up for battle? Am I not a Philistine, and are you servants of Saul?" David is told of the taunt of Israel by Goliath, and receives himself the taunt: "Am I a dog that you come to me with sticks?" But David addresses Goliath as having taunted (*ḥrp*) the armies of the living God (vss. 26, 36), the God of the armies of Israel (vs. 45). He correctly perceives the taunt as a challenge to the power of Yahweh, and the defeat of Goliath as the removal of the *ḥerpāh* (vs. 26).

2 Kings xix 4, 16, 22, 23 (cf. 2 Chr. xxxii 17; Isa. xxxvii 17, 23, 24): Hezekiah twice refers to the words of the Rabshakeh as taunting

(*ḥrp*) the living God (the same term as in the David narrative). Then in Isaiah's oracle Yahweh twice says that Sennacherib has taunted (*ḥrp*) the Holy One of Israel, Yahweh. What is it that is so characterized? One finds out from the Rabshakeh's speech in chapter xviii. He tells the people not to listen to Hezekiah when he says the Lord will deliver us. Then he asks the questions: "Has any of the gods of the nations ever delivered his land out of the hands of the king of Assyria? Where are the gods of Hamath and Arpad? Where are the gods of Sepharvaim, Hena, and Ivvah? Have they delivered Samaria out of my hand? Who among all the gods of the countries have delivered their countries out of my hand that the Lord should deliver Jerusalem out of my hand?" (vss. 33-35).

Joel ii 17-19: The *ḥerpāh* of the nations is defined as the question: "Where is their God?" Yahweh's positive response to the petition is his taking away the *ḥerpāh* of the people among the nations.

In all these instances it is clear the *ḥerpāh* is a taunt against someone's power and status. It is characterized by questions of the enemy challenging the power of the one being taunted or of his god. When we look at the Psalms a number of uses accord with this picture. In Ps. xlii 14 the Psalmist says: "My adversaries taunt me when they say to me all day long: 'Where is your God?' " That is exactly the question of the Rabshakeh and indeed what *ḥerpāh* is—the taunt of an enemy about one's plight and assumptions of the powerlessness of the person in his or her situation. But it is also a challenge against God's power. The lamenter of Ps. lxix waits for God (vs. 4), over and over referring to the *ḥerpāh*, the taunts, he receives (vss. 8, 10 (2 ×), 11, 20, 21) and identifying these taunts as also "taunting you" (vs. 10). And as we have noted, the Psalm includes a series of imprecations against the *ḥôrᵉpekā*. The situation of the Psalm is not spelled out, but it may well have been similar to that of Nehemiah described above.

The communal lament of Ps. lxxiv addresses a situation not unlike the occasion of the Rabshakeh's speech. Only its setting is probably roughly contemporaneous with the Beit Lei inscriptions—the period after the Babylonian destruction of Jerusalem and the temple.[33] The

---

[33] Cf. J. J. M. Roberts, "Of Signs, Prophets, and Time Limits: A Note on Ps. 74:9", *CBQ* 39 (1977), pp. 474-81.

enemy has invaded the sanctuary and destroyed it. The community three times describes this as taunt (*ḥrp*) against Yahweh, a challenge to his power (vss. 10, 18, 22). A similar situation may be presupposed for Ps. lxxix. The destruction of Jerusalem and the temple means the people have become *ḥerpāh* to their neighbors (vs. 4). But that is also *ḥerpāh* against Yahweh (vs. 12). The only content given to the taunt is the question: "Where is their God?" (vs. 10). So in a prayer curse like the one at Beit Lei (vs. 12) the lamenters call to Yahweh to demonstrate his power against the taunters by showing that even in the destruction he was the one in charge and will turn their taunts back against them.

One could cite other examples (xxii 7, xliv 12, lxxxix 51-52, etc.), but they do not add significantly to our understanding. The brief prayer-curse of Khirbet Beit Lei must be seen as belonging to the mode of speech and understanding represented in these Psalms and other texts. It is a curse against one who has challenged or questioned the power of Yahweh because of the powerlessness of his servants or people. That challenge or taunt is embodied especially in rhetorical questions and most particularly the question: "Where is your God?"[34] Lemaire relates this and the other inscriptions to the invasion of Sennacherib. In the light of the frequency of reference to Sennacherib's *ḥerpāh* against Yahweh the suggestion is most attractive. But, on the basis of palaeographical analysis, it is more likely that the enemy is Nebuchadnezzar or the Neo-Babylonian Empire, though one can only conjecture. In many instances *ḥerpāh* is a taunt of one nation or its representative against another nation and its god. The stories of Sennacherib and Hezekiah, David and Goliath, and Nehemiah and his foes give us suggestions of the kind of context that would have elicited these words.

This curse inscription also serves to demonstrate the inter-connections of these inscriptions as well as the relationships with the various Psalms such as lxix, lxxiv, and lxxix mentioned earlier. While one can only speculate about the intention of those who carved these inscriptions to relate them to one another, functionally and in terms of their associations with the biblical Psalms, Inscription A serves as a response to the petition of Inscription C: "Save, Yahweh!" (cf.

[34] The explicit content of *ḥerpāh* is given in a different form in Ps. xxii 7 but is still a clear challenge to the power of Yahweh. Cf. 2 Chron. xxxii 17. There are, of course, other forms of *ḥerpāh*, but the passages discussed here seem to provide the best clues to the nature of *ḥerpāh* in the laments of the Psalms and the Beit Lei text.

Ps. xxxv 3). But it also addresses the *ḥerpāh* of the one against whom the prayer curse inscription speaks. If the *ḥerpāh* is embodied in the taunt "Where is your God?" and the skepticism about God's power to deliver, then Inscription A both answers the question in the self predication "I am your God" and then declares Yahweh's power and intention to save.[35]

If the reading of Inscription A given here is correct, then not only does it use language reminiscent of Second Isaiah as well as the Psalms, but in form and structure it is markedly similar, albeit abbreviated, to the oracle of salvation genre in Second Isaiah and elsewhere. The assurance "fear not" does not appear, but the bases for that assurance in the oracle of salvation are given in usual form, i.e. a nominal sentence describing the relationship and an indication in verbal sentences of what God will do to help. The declaration "I am your God" appears more than once as the basis in Second Isaiah, and in xli 13 is the precise form of Inscription A, i.e. *ʾanî yhwh ʾelōhekā.* The verb *gāʾal* appears frequently in Isaiah xl-lv to describe God's activity in behalf of exiled Judah. In xliii 2 it is used in a verbal sentence as a basis of assurance very much like the final colon of Inscription A:

ʾal-tîrāʾ kî geʾaltîkā

There is yet another prayer inscription at Khirbet Beit Lei, Inscription B according to Naveh's order, inscribed below Inscription A. While there are some difficulties in reading it, the basic thrust of it is fairly clear. I would read and translate it as follows:

p [36]*qd yh* ʾ [37]*l* [38]*ḥ̊n̊n̊ nqh yh yhwh*
peqōd yāh ʾēl ḥannūn
naqqēh yāh yahweh
Be mindful, Yah Gracious God;
Absolve, Yah Yahweh.

[35] Cf. Is. li 7-8 where Yahweh sets "my salvation" (*yešûʿātî*) against "human taunting" (*ḥerpat ʾenôš*).

[36] As Lemaire has noted, this letter may be *mem*, *nun*, or *pe*. I think it unlikely that it is *mem*, and the presumed hook at the top of the posited *nun* appears to be somewhat separated from the main cross stroke. The best reading is *pe* reinforced by what clearly appears to be *dalet* rather than *he* in third position.

[37] The *alef* is very clear and characteristic of the *ʾalefs* of this inscription. It has a double flourish as the final stroke, distinguishing it from the so-called "Avigad Alef" of other inscriptions having a single final flourish.

[38] A *he* appears above the *lamed* and seems to be a mistake or false start. Cf. Cross.

The inscription is a poetic petition comprising a balanced bicolon. There are three aspects of the text that are of primary interest in this context: (a) the word *yāh*; (b) the divine name and title *ʾēl ḥannūn*; and (c) the verbs *pāqad* and *niqqāh*. The word *yāh* has been explained by Cross as a particle of entreaty already familiar from Ugaritic, Aramaic, Arabic, and New Hebrew. Such an explanation fits the context and may be correct. It should be noted, however, that the existence of such a particle elsewhere in Classical Hebrew is very uncertain, though some have proposed to find examples. Furthermore, the divine name *Yāh* is quite familiar, especially in the Psalms. Indeed it appears more than once prefacing another divine name as it does here:

Ps. lxviii 19 —*yāh ʾᵉlōhîm*
Ps. cxxx 3 —*yāh ʾᵃdōnāy* (Some MSS have *yāh yahweh*)
Isa. xii 2 —*yāh yahweh*
Isa. xxvi 4 —*yāh yahweh*
Isa. xxxviii 8 —*yāh yāh*

All these double names are suspect, and usually one of the elements is eliminated in the text critical process. S. Talmon has given a very plausible interpretation of the development of Isa. xii 2 out of Ex. xv 2, which would have had originally only one divine name.[39] But the texts from Khirbet Beit Lei now caution against a quick dismissal of one of these elements. The *yāh* form by itself is not simply a late phenomenon. It appears in early poems such as Ex. xv 2,[40] xvii 16; Ps. lxviii 19, and lxxxix 9. Furthermore, the repetition of *Yahweh* as a name appears also in Ex. xxxiv 6-7 [41] a passage that has a number of important affinities with this inscription. The repetition of the divine name is not extraordinary. It occurs elsewhere in the Psalms (e.g. l 1) and is certainly appropriate for a vocative in an impassioned lament, as for example, in Ps. xxii 1. So while other explanations are possible, the use of *yāh* in the Psalms and along with other names now has an analogue in the Khirbet Beit Lei Inscription B.

The expression *yāh ʾēl ḥannūn*—and possibly *yāh yahweh*—arises out of the ancient Yahwistic revelation in Ex. xxxiv 6-7 alluded to above:

yhwh yhwh ʾēl raḥûm wᵉḥannûn

[39] "Double Readings", *VT* 4 (1954), pp. 206-7.
[40] But see Talmon for the argument that *yāh* is not original here.
[41] There is, of course, the possibility that the first *yahweh* is the subject of *wayyiqrāʾ* (cf. Num. xiv 18), but that is less likely.

The similarities can hardly be ignored from the repetition of divine names to the actual epithets that are used. Here the Beit Lei inscriptions stand in close continuity with the traditions and modes of Hebrew psalmody. The word *ḥannûn* is used only as an attribute of Yahweh and half of the occurrences outside Ex. xxxiv 6 are in the Psalms. We find in Inscription B the same phenomenon that occurs frequently in the Psalms. An ancient liturgical formula, which describes the primal nature or character of God, becomes the basis for trusting in Yahweh and praising him (ciii 8, cxlv 8) and for calling on his help (lxxxvi 15).[42] Free variations or shortened forms of the formula appear also as hymnic elements in cxi 4, cxii 4, and cxvi 5. In li 3, lxix 14, and lxxvii 9-10 the formula is modified and used as a basis for pleas for help. In the parenetic elaboration of the legal traditions (Ex. xxii 26) Yahweh explicitly declares that when the victim of injustice cries to him he will listen "for I am gracious" (*kî ḥannûn ʾānî*). The inscribed prayer in the cave at Beit Lei is an example of just such a cry invoking the graciousness of Yahweh as a basis for help.

The verbs of this petition, *pāqad* and *niqqāh* are not common to the vocabulary of prayer in the Psalter. The imperative *naqqēnî* appears in the petition at the conclusion of Psalm xix followed by the expected result *weniqqêtî* (vss. 13 and 14). The imperative of *pāqad* appears in Ps. lxxx 15 and cvi 4; both times as calls to Yahweh for help. In both cases the Psalmist prays for Yahweh's favorable attention in the midst of communal sin and distress, which may be the same sort of context in which this inscribed prayer was set down. There are few other uses of the verb in the Psalms although it occurs with a similar positive force in Ps. viii 5. Both verbs are appropriate for the language of prayer or petition, and the occurrences in Inscription B now add to our knowledge of such prayer usage.

When, however, one asks why these two verbs of such infrequent use in prayer occur together in this one-line prayer, more needs to be said. For what is taking place here is an important extension of the process described above, i.e. the use of traditional credal or liturgical formulae as a basis for praise or petition. In this case, however, we have an instance of a creative re-use or reformulation of the traditional

[42] Cf. K. Sakenfeld, *The Meaning of Hesed in the Hebrew Bible* (Missoula, Montana, 1978), pp. 111 ff. The formulations of this Inscription may be added to Sakenfeld's argument against the frequent view that Ex. xxxiv 6-7 is late and secondary. Its use here and in the Psalms assumes a sufficiently long history of tradition to establish it as a fundamental liturgical formula on which Israel would draw with some frequency.

material to serve a new purpose, indeed one almost counter to the original use of the language. Michael Fishbane has recently described this sort of dynamic inner-biblical reinterpretation and offered several examples.[43] Now we have an excellent illustration from extra-biblical literature. We have already shown the dependence of this inscription on Ex. xxxiv 6-7 as far as the divine names or epithets are concerned. But that dependence extends throughout the whole inscription. The only place in the Hebrew Bible where the two verbs *pāqad* and *niqqāh* appear together in any sort of correlation is Ex. xxxiv 6-7 and its variant Num. xiv 18.[44] The one or ones responsible for the prayer of Inscription B are wholly dependent upon this confessional formula but exercise a significant freedom in drawing upon it. The verbs *niqqāh* and *pāqad* appear in the final clauses of this description of the characteristics of Yahweh: *weⁿaqqēh lōʾ yeⁿaqqeh pōqēd ʿᵃwôn ʾābôt ʿal-bānîm weʿal-bᵉnê bānîm ʿal-šillēšîm weʿal-ribbēʿîm*. But in Ex. xxxiv 6-7 (= Num. xiv 18) these verbs express the *negative*, judging activity of God alongside the mercy expressed in the rest of the formula. In a creative and somewhat audacious way the writer of Inscription B now turns those negative statements of God's judging activity into appeals for God's gracious attention and deliverance,[45] a move that is made possible by the fact that both verbs are capable of expressing either God's mercy or God's judgement.[46] While the attributes of God in the Exodus-Numbers formula are his unwillingness to hold innocent the guilty and his visiting to punish, the inscriptional prayer uses the same verbs to appeal to God's character as one who acquits the innocent or absolves from guilt and as one who visits to care for and protect. Like others who uttered laments the one praying in this tomb utters his or her

[43] "Torah and Tradition", in D. A. Knight (ed.), *Tradition and Theology in the Old Testament* (Philadelphia, 1977), pp. 275-300.

[44] One should perhaps also include Ex. xx 4-7 = Deut. v 7-11 where the negative uses of *pāqad* and *niqqāh* serve to bind together the paranesis and thus the commandments themselves that forbid making graven images or using Yahweh's name emptily.

[45] Fishbane, pp. 280-1, notes another example of a transformation of the language of Ex. xxiv 6-7: "In this reuse of the 'attribute-formula' (Exod. 34:6-7) in Nah 1:2-3 terms of compassion are transformed into terms of war". It should be noted that the Nahum verses are also dependent upon Num. xiv 17-18 as indicated by the comparison of *gdl kḥ* in Nah. i 3 with *yigdal-nāʾ kōaḥ* and *kᵉgōdel ḥasdekā* in Num. xiv 17-18.

[46] It is, of course, possible that *pqd* in Inscription B means "Visit (our enemies)" or that the expression is ambiguous, but the positive use of *niqqāh* makes those possibilities less likely.

petition in the conviction of innocence and confidence in Yahweh's mercy.

The last of the inscriptions from the cave at Khirbet Beit Lei should be brought into the picture and forms an appropriate conclusion to this study. It is difficult to interpret and appears to contain mistakes and some attempt at correction. The sequence of letters is ʾ ʾ*rr yšrmḥrh*, a sequence that makes little sense. In the light of his discovery of the cave inscriptions at Nahal Yishai which begins ʾ*rr* ʾ*šr ymḥh.*[47] P. Bar Adon proposes to read ʾ*rr* ʾ*šr* (*y*)*mḥh* at Khirbet Beit Lei and translates, "Cursed be he who will efface".[48] In this he is followed by Naveh [49] and Lemaire, the latter on the basis of a somewhat different analysis that assumes the first ʾ*alef* and the *yod* are misplaced.

While the reading of this inscription of necessity must remain tentative, the interpretation proposed above does make sense of an otherwise senseless group of consonants. It also provides a kind of superscription for the Khirbet Beit Lei inscriptions analogous to the ʾ*al-tašḥēt lᵉdāwīd miktām* of Pss. lvii, lviii, and lix. Such an injunction or malediction against one disturbing the text often comes at the end of an inscription, but the Nahal Yishai inscription shows us a case of its appearing as a kind of superscription to an extended series of blessings. Whether the Khirbet Beit Lei malediction is the first or last word, it seems to have been heeded, intentionally or unintentionally, and thus preserved for the readers of Israel's psalms in later millennia the prayers and cries of those whose circumstances are no less veiled than are the historical and life settings of those who composed the canonical Psalms but who also shared with the biblical psalmists a common language of prayer and a sure confidence in the saving power of Yahweh.[50]

[The research for this article was made possible by a grant from the National Endowment for the Humanities.]

---

[47] This reading assumes the final letter is a triangular headed *he* as elsewhere at Kh. Beit Lei. That assumption may be correct, but it is far from certain.

[48] "An Early Hebrew Inscription in a Judean Desert Cave", *IEJ* 25 (1975), p. 231.

[49] Bar Adon says: "This suggestion is considered possible by Naveh".

[50] While little can be said of the setting in life of the inscriptions from Khirbet el Qôm or Khirbet Beit Lei, it is hardly likely that they were inscribed in a cultic setting, though they may represent uses of forms that were remembered from a cultic setting. The assumption that the writer—and any persons with him—of the Khirbet Beit Lei inscriptions were hiding in this tomb and possibly fleeing national oppressors is most likely and consistent with the Psalmodic relationships discussed here.

WEISHEITLICHE BEARBEITUNG VON PSALMEN

Ein Beitrag zum Verständnis der Sammlung des Psalters

VON

JOSEPH REINDL

Erfurt

Der Psalter in seiner uns vorliegenden Gestalt steht am Ende eines langen Traditionsprozesses, der nicht nur die einzelnen Psalmen, sondern auch ihre Sammlung betrifft. Dem Psalter gingen Teilsammlungen voraus, deren Existenz sich auf Grund äußerer Kriterien wie der Psalmenüberschriften, aber auch aus inneren Gründen wie der Zusammenstellung thematisch verwandter Psalmen ergibt. Die Gestalt dieser Vorläufer des heutigen Psalters und den Vorgang ihrer Vereinigung bis zur daraus resultierenden Endgestalt hat man zu rekonstruieren versucht.[1] H.-J. Kraus urteilt allerdings auch in der Neubearbeitung seines Psalmenkommentars über das Ergebnis dieser Bemühungen noch recht skeptisch: "Die allmählich sich bildenden Teilsammlungen und kleineren Liederrollen ... sind wahrscheinlich um 300 v.Chr. zu dem in seiner Entstehungsgeschichte nicht genauer erklärbaren Kanon zusammengewachsen".[2] Über einen Punkt der Entstehungsgeschichte des Psalters scheint allerdings fast allgemeine Übereinstimmung zu bestehen: Der Traditionsort sowohl der Psalmen, wie auch ihrer Sammlungen und damit auch der Ort, an dem der Psalter seine endgültige Gestalt gefunden hat, ist im jerusalemer Tempel zu suchen;[3] denn der Psalter gilt ziemlich

---

[1] Neben den entsprechenden Einleitungsparagraphen der Psalmenkommentare sind besonders zu nennen: C. Westermann, "Zur Sammlung des Psalters" *ThViat* 8 (1962), S. 278-84 (= *Forschung am Alten Testament* [München, 1964], S. 336-43); H. Gese, "Zur Geschichte der Kultsänger am zweiten Tempel", in *Abraham unser Vater*, FS O. Michel (Leiden, 1963), S. 222-34; ders., "Die Entstehung der Büchereinteilung des Psalters", in *Wort, Lied und Gottesspruch*, FS J. Ziegler (Würzburg, 1972), S. 57-64—beides jetzt in H. Gese, *Vom Sinai zum Zion. Alttestamentliche Beiträge zur biblischen Theologie* (München, 1974), S. 147-58, 159-67.

[2] *Die Psalmen* (Neukirchen-Vluyn, [5]1978), S. 77 (Wo nicht anders ausdrücklich vermerkt, wird unter Kraus, *Psalmen*, stets diese Auflage zitiert).

[3] "Mittelpunkt der Entstehungs-, Traditions- und Sammlungsgeschichte ist der Tempel von Jerusalem gewesen", Kraus, S. 77.

allgemein als das "Gesangbuch des zweiten Tempels" oder—etwas differenzierter—als das "Lieder- und Gebetbuch der nachexilischen Gemeinde" (Kraus). Seiner Meinung über die Überlieferung und Sammlung der Psalmen hat Kraus dadurch noch eine besonders einleuchtende Fassung gegeben, daß er nunmehr für die Entstehung, Tradierung und Sammlung der Psalmen nur noch einen einzigen Sitz im Leben angibt. Denn während er in den früheren Auflagen seines Kommentars für die Entstehung der Psalmen neben der Tätigkeit der priesterlichen (und prophetischen) Kultbediensteten noch mit "Dichtungen einzelner Glieder des alttestamentlichen Volkes" rechnet (1.-4. Aufl., S. LXI) lehnt er nun die Annahme von "Privatdichtungen" dezidiert ab. Priester und Tempelsänger waren in jedem Fall die "vermittelnden Instanzen", auch dort, wo die persönlichen Erfahrungen Einzelner ihren Ausdruck finden sollten (S. 73 f.). Unter dieser Voraussetzung, daß ausschließlich der Kult als Bestimmung und der Kultort als Traditionsort gesehen wird, erscheint auch seine schon früher geäußerte Meinung verständlich, daß die Frage, zu welchem Zweck der Psalter zusammengestellt worden sei, gar nicht richtig gestellt werde, da "die Überlieferung und Sammlung einzelner Psalmen mit einer gewissen Zwangsläufigkeit zur Zusammenfassung und Ordnung aller Teilsammlungen und Liedergruppen drängte" (S. 13). Nun ist die Tendenz zur Ordnung und Sichtung eines vorhandenen Bestandes zweifellos unbestreitbar ein wichtiger Faktor für die Entstehung von Sammlungen. Aber vermag sie zu erklären, warum die Sammlung gerade so und nicht anders erfolgt, wie es zur Rezeption einer bestimmten Anzahl von überlieferten Liedern kommt und warum diese so oder anders geordnet wurden? Das Sammeln ist immer ein zielgerichteter Vorgang; hinter jeder Sammlung steht eine bestimmte Motivation und eine Absicht. Es lohnt sich, danach zu fragen—auch für die Sammlung des Psalters.

1. Schon die Entstehung der Teilsammlungen wird nicht nur durch die Absicht zur Zusammenstellung des Überkommenen, sondern durch wenigstens teilweise erschließbare Motivationen bestimmt. Die frühesten Sammlungen, die für uns greifbar werden, sind wohl jene, die durch die Überschrift einer bestimmten Sängergruppe (Asaf, Bᵉnê Qorach, Heman usw.) zugeschrieben werden.[4] Setzen wir

[4] Den Versuch einer zeitlichen Einordnung unternimmt Gese, "Zur Geschichte der Kultsänger am zweiten Tempel", s. Anm. 1.

voraus, daß diese Angaben nicht frei erfunden sind, dann stellt sich die Frage, warum diese Psalmen gerade mit den betreffenden Gruppen in Verbindung gebracht wurden. Wollten die einzelnen, anscheinend rivalisierenden Gruppen (Gese, S. 224 ff.) damit Anspruch auf die Urheberschaft an den betreffenden Psalmen erheben? Oder bedeutet die Zuschreibung, daß jede Sängergilde ihr eigenes Repertoire besaß, das vor fremden Ansprüchen eifersüchtig gehütet wurde? Auf jeden Fall sind solche Zuschreibungen Ausdruck des Interesses, das eine bestimmte Gruppe an den jeweiligen Psalmen hatte. Ihre Sammlung ist demnach von den Sonderinteressen einer Gemeinschaft motiviert worden und nicht einfachhin dem Bedürfnis nach Systematisierung zu verdanken. Da es sich bei der Gemeinschaft um eine Gilde von Kultsängern handelte, darf man voraussetzen, daß der Ort, an dem dies geschah, der Tempel war; allerdings ist der Sitz im Leben der Sammlung dann genauer zu bestimmen: Es ist nicht der Bereich des Kultes, sondern das "Berufsinteresse" der Kultsänger.

Ein beträchtlicher Teil der Psalmen, die den Sängergruppen zugeschrieben werden, ist in den elohistischen Psalter (Ps. xlii-lxxxiii [5]) eingegangen. Kann man voraussetzen, daß für seinen Redaktor, der auf bereits bestehende Sammlungen zurückgreift und aus ihnen auswählt, die gleiche Motivation maßgebend war wie bei den älteren Teilsammlungen? Die planmäßige Anlage der Sammlung läßt hier auf ein vorwiegend an der Systematisierung orientiertes Interesse schließen. Zudem weist die theologische Bearbeitung der Psalmen, der Ersatz des Gottesnamens Jahwe durch Elohim, darauf hin, daß der Redaktor dieser Sammlung oder die Kreise, die hinter ihm zu suchen sind, einem bestimmten theologischen Programm verpflichtet waren. Mögen also auch für den elohistischen Psalter dem Tempelkult verpflichtete Kreise verantwortlich sein,[6] diese Sammlung läßt jedenfalls auf ganz andere Motive, vielleicht auch auf eine andere Zweckbestimmung schließen.

Eine dritte größere Einheit bildet der erste Davidspsalter (Ps. iii-xli). Kraus vermißt in ihr im Gegensatz zum elohistischen Psalter die planvolle Anordnung (S. 10). Immerhin hat C. Westermann beobachtet, daß in dieser Sammlung fast nur Psalmen des Einzelnen enthalten sind; [7] C. Barth verweist auf die "concatenatio" als ein

[5] Gese zählt auch Ps. lxxxiv noch dazu, "Die Entstehung der Büchereinteilung des Psalters", S. 58 f., s. Anm. 1.

[6] H. Gunkel-J. Begrich, *Einleitung in die Psalmen* (Göttingen, ^{2}1966), S. 451.

[7] "Zur Sammlung des Psalters", S. 281, s. Anm. 1.

mögliches Anordnungsprinzip.[8] Wenn seine Ansicht zutrifft, könnte sich hier schon eine andere als nur liturgische Verwendung der Psalmen andeuten: sie wären nicht mehr als einzelne Psalmen nach einem mehr oder weniger äußerlichen Prinzip zusammengestellt, sondern jeweils in eine besondere Beziehung zu den benachbarten Psalmen gesetzt worden.

2. Die bisher an den Vorläufern des endgültigen Psalters gesammelten Beobachtungen sollen hier nicht weiter verfolgt werden. Sie ermuntern uns aber, mit gewecktem Problembewußtsein nunmehr an den kanonischen Psalter heranzutreten. Auch er ist nicht als organisch gewachsenes Gebilde am Ende einer Entwicklung einfach "da gewesen". Er ist aus bestimmten Motiven heraus und mit einer bestimmten Absicht in die Form gebracht worden, die er heute besitzt. Es ist nicht ohne weiteres vorauszusetzen, daß diese die gleichen waren wie bei der Enstehung der Einzelsammlungen. Bereits Gunkel-Begrich haben darauf verwiesen, daß ein Schluß von den Einzelsammlungen, die kultischen Zwecken dienten, auf das Ganze des Psalters nicht zwingend sei (S. 443 f.). Wenn wir nach Antworten auf unsere Fragen suchen, haben wir hier sogar festeren Boden unter den Füßen, als bei den Teilsammlungen. Dort mußten die Sammlungen erst auf Grund unterschiedlich zu wertender Kriterien wiedergewonnen werden, wobei es auch noch offen bleiben muß, ob die Teilsammlungen bei ihrer redaktionellen Vereinigung wirklich im Originalzustand belassen wurden. Der Psalter liegt uns dagegen als Ganzes in der Gestalt vor, die ihm sein Redaktor gab; wir können daher hier zuverlässigere und weniger spekulative Ergebnisse hinsichtlich der Intentionen des Redaktors erwarten.

Zunächst ist die Meinung auszuschließen, die Endgestalt des Psalters sei mehr oder weniger ein Zufallsprodukt. Dem Redaktor mögen bereits weitgehend vereinigte Teilsammlungen vorgelegen haben; er läßt aber deutlich erkennen, daß er den Psalter nicht als Ansammlung von einzelnen Liedern, sondern als eine Einheit ansieht. Unverkennbares Zeichen dafür ist die Art und Weise, wie er Anfang und Schluß der Sammlung gestaltet hat. Die Ps. i und cl gelten vielen wohl mit Recht als redaktionelle Zutaten.[9]

---

[8] "Concatenatio im ersten Buch des Psalters", in *Wort und Wirklichkeit*, FS E. L. Rapp (Meisenheim am Glan, 1976), S. 30-40.

[9] Vgl. G. Fohrer, *Einleitung in das Alte Testament* (Heidelberg, [10]1965), S. 320.

2.1 Der imperativische Hymnus Ps. cl muß nicht vom Redaktor geschaffen worden sein; er ist vielmehr auch als selbständiges liturgisches Lied denkbar (Kraus, S. 1149). Er steht aber kaum zufällig am Ende des Psalters. Für diesen Platz dürfte ihn nicht nur seine imposante formale Gestalt aus gleichgebauten Imperativsätzen [10] empfohlen haben, sondern vor allem sein Inhalt als universaler Aufruf zum Lobpreis, der in V. 6, metrisch wie stilistisch deutlich vom übrigen Text abgehoben,[11] seinen Höhepunkt erreicht. Mit dem Aufruf *kål-hann*^{e}*šāmāh t*^{e}*hallel yāh*, der kein geschaffenes Lebewesen ausläßt, erreicht aber nicht nur der Ps. cl selbst sein Ziel; er gibt zugleich dem ganzen Psalter eine letzte Sinngebung im alles umfassenden Gotteslob. Man darf auch nicht übersehen, daß Ps. cl nicht isoliert am Ende des Psalters steht: Er bildet mit den unmittelbar vorausgehenden Psalmen (cxlvi-cxlxix) eine Gruppe, die durch das redaktionell als Überschrift und Abschluß zugefügte *hall*^{e}*lû-yāh* zusammengefaßt wird und der Tradition als "Letztes Hallel" bekannt ist.[12] Diese Hallelujah-Psalmen zeigen aber eine Reihe von formalen und inhaltlichen Übereinstimmungen: Sie alle sind Lobpsalmen (allerdings aus unterschiedlichen Gattungen); als vorherrschendes formales Element tritt—mit Ausnahme des Ps. cxlvi [13]—der hymnische Imperativ in Erscheinung; zwischen den Psalmen bestehen teilweise enge und auffällige Stichwortbeziehungen.[14] Ein Unterschied läßt sich allerdings hinsichtlich der unmittelbar zum Lobpreis Aufgerufenen feststellen: in Ps. cxlvi fordert der Psalmist sich selbst zum Gotteslob auf; Ps. cxlvii 12 wird Jerusalem/Zion angesprochen; der Ps. cxlviii richtet seine Aufforderung an die himmlische und irdische Welt; der Ps. cxlxix spricht dagegen die "Gemeinde der Frommen", die "Söhne Zions" an (V. 2); Ps. cl endlich ist in seiner Universalität nicht mehr zu überbieten. Man wird wohl nicht fehlgehen, wenn man in dieser Anordnung eine beabsichtigte Ausweitung des

---

[10] F. Crüsemann, *Studien zur Formgeschichte von Hymnus und Danklied in Israel* (Neukirchen-Vluyn, 1969), S. 79.

[11] Der V. 6 bildet im sonst durchgehend im Metrum 3 + 3 gestalteten Psalm einen alleinstehenden Dreier. Während die Imperativsätze in V. 1-5 ganz regelmäßig die Wortfolge Imperativ + Suff. — mit *b*^{e} konstruierte Näherbestimmung aufweisen, bringt der V. 6 eine invertierte Wortfolge Subjekt—Jussiv—Objekt.

[12] H. Gunkel, *Die Psalmen* (Göttingen, ^{5}1968), S. 613.

[13] Ps. cxlvi beginnt formal als Hymnus eines Einzelnen mit einer Selbstaufforderung; Näheres s.u. S. 346 ff.

[14] Vgl. Ps. cxlvi 10 mit cxlvii 12 (nur hier *ʾ*^{e}*lohayik ṣiyyôn*); Ps. cxlvii 4 mit cxlviii 3; Ps. cxlvii 20 mit cxlviii 14; Ps. cxlviii 14 mit cxlxix 1, 9.

Aufrufes zum Gotteslob erblickt, innerhalb deren Ps. cl mit seinem V. 6 wiederum Höhepunkt und Schlußakkord ist. Die Psalmen des Schlußteiles stehen somit in einer inneren Beziehung und bilden eine gedankliche Einheit, die auf das gemeinsame Ziel des universalen Gotteslobes hingeordnet ist.

2.2. Der den Psalter eröffnende Ps. i richtet sich als eine Art Vorrede (Prooemium) an den Leser und Beter der Psalmen.[15] Er fällt in mehrfacher Hinsicht aus dem Rahmen des Üblichen: Nicht nur, daß er keiner der dem jetzigen Psalter vorausgehenden Teilsammlungen zuzuordnen ist,[16] auch seiner literarischen Art nach [17] ist er, wie bereits R. Kittel treffend gesagt hat, "kein Psalm im eigentlichen Sinn".[18] Seine formale Gestaltung wie seine inhaltliche Aussage weist den Ps. i als ein Stück weisheitlicher Lehrdichtung aus. Ein "Weisheitslehrer" spricht seinen Schüler an, um ihn in seiner Entscheidung für den gewählten Weg der weisheitlichen Lebensführung zu bestärken. Er warnt vor dem "Weg der Frevler" (V. 6b), der zum Scheitern verurteilt ist, und preist den *ṣaddîq*, der den Umgang mit den Frevlern meidet und sich statt dessen dem Studium der Torah widmet (V. 1, 2). Der Weisheitslehrer gibt damit zu erkennen, daß sein Ideal nicht das des traditionellen *ḥākām* ist, sondern von jener Richtung der Weisheit Israels geprägt ist, die sich nach dem Exil durchzusetzen begann: Die Torah erscheint jetzt als Quelle und Summe aller Weisheit; das Studium der schriftlichen Überlieferung (V. 2b *ûbᵉtôrātô yähgäh yômām wālāylāh* meint das meditierende Lesen

[15] Zum Folgenden vgl. die ausführliche Begründung bei J. Reindl, "Psalm 1 und der Sitz im Leben des Psalters", *ThJb*(L) 1979 (Leipzig, 1979), S. 39-50.

[16] Westermann (s. Anm. 1), S. 280 f., äußert die Vermutung, Ps. i habe bereits für eine Vorstufe des jetzigen Psalters zusammen mit Ps. cxix den Rahmen abgegeben. Er kann sich dafür allerdings nur auf die "entfernte Entsprechung" zwischen den beiden Psalmen stützen. Ps. cxix ist aber mit seinem voluminösen Umfang nur schwer als Abschluß einer Sammlung vorzustellen. Dort, wo Psalmen (oder Psalmteile) als Abschluß einer Sammlung fungieren, handelt es sich fast immer um Hymnen oder hymnische Stücke (Doxologien), vgl. Ps. cl, lxxxii 18 f.; Sir. li 1-12.—Die Folgerungen Westermanns weisen indes in ähnliche Richtung wie sie hier vorgetragen wird, s.u. Anm. 27.—Als Einleitung zur Teilsammlung Ps. i-xci faßt R. E. Murphy den Ps. i auf, "The Classification of 'Wisdom Psalms' ", *SVT* 9 (1963), S. 162.

[17] Es ist eine in der Form des Makarismus vorgetragene Weisheitslehre; nur Ps. cxii hält in vergleichbarer Weise die Form der Seligpreisung bis zum Ende durch, ohne in Gebetsform überzugehen.

[18] *Die Psalmen* (Leipzig, $^{3.4}$1922), S. 1.

der Schriften) [19] ist daher die vorrangige Aufgabe des Weisen, der damit zunehmend die Gestalt des "Schriftgelehrten" annimmt. Der Redaktor der Psalmensammlung muß nicht der Schöpfer dieses Lehrgedichtes sein; [20] er hat ihn aber offenbar als geeignet befunden, als Vorrede für den Psalter zu dienen und damit seine eigene Auffassung von diesem Buch auszudrücken. Das hier geschilderte Idealbild des *ṣaddîq* ist in seinen Augen auch das Ideal dessen, der dieses Buch zur Hand nimmt; die Torah, zu deren Studium und Meditation er auffordert, ist, nicht anders als im sapientiellen Verständnis des gleichen Textes, der Inbegriff der Offenbarung Jahwes, die in den überkommennen Schriften niedergelegt ist. In unserem Kontext "schließt der Begriff *twrh* auf jeden Fall, und zwar sogar in erster Linie die Schriftrolle der Psalmen in sich" (Kraus, S. 136). Damit aber zeigt sich ein neues Verständnis der Psalmen an, das sie nicht mehr oder jedenfalls nicht mehr ausschließlich als Kultgesänge begreift.[21]

3. Durch die dem Buch gegebene Rahmung läßt der Redaktor des Psalters also recht deutlich seine Auffassung von den Psalmen erkennen. An ihr ist zunächst bemerkenswert, daß der Psalter nun nicht länger als eine mehr oder weniger geordnete Ansammlung von einzelnen Psalmen erscheint, sondern als *ein Buch*, ein Ganzes vorgestellt wird. Selbstverständlich wird dadurch die Qualität der Psalmen als Einzeltexte, die jeder für sich seine Aussage und seine Aufgabe haben, nicht beeinträchtigt; aber sie erhalten die neue Qualität, nunmehr Teil eines größeren Ganzen und damit einer übergeordneten Einheit zu sein. Denn in *dieser* Hinsicht will der Redaktor des Psalters sie als Torah verstanden wissen; auch ist nicht mehr nur der einzelne Psalm Lobpreisung (was ja nur von einem kleinen Teil der Psalmen unmittelbar gesagt werden könnte), sondern als Aufgabe des ganzen Buches erscheint es nunmehr, *kål-hannᵉšāmāh* zum Lobpreis Jahwes zu führen.[22] Der einzelne Psalm

---

[19] Das Verbum *hāgāh* meint das "besinnliche Lesen . . ., das sich das Wort mit leiser Unterstützung der Stimme einprägt . . ." (H. W. Wolff, "Psalm 1", *Ev Th* [1949/50], S. 391).

[20] "Von seiner literarischen Art her ist allerdings zu vermuten, daß dieser Text ursprünglich einer anderen Bestimmung gedient hat als der, das 'Prooemium' des Psalters zu bilden", J. Reindl (s. Anm. 15.), S. 44.

[21] R. E. Murphy, *SVT* 9 (1963), S. 162: "its intention is to present the psalter as a study-book".

[22] Vielleicht hat die gleiche Auffassung auch dazu geführt, dem Buch den Titel *tᵉhillîm* zu geben; damit ist sicher nicht eine "Gesamtbezeichnung des Inhalts der 150 Psalmen" gemeint (gegen Kraus, S. 1).

tritt damit aus seiner gewissermaßen natürlichen Isolation heraus und will im Kontext der anderen Psalmen, ja des ganzen Psalters gelesen und verstanden werden. Das war schon an der redaktionellen Komposition des Schlußteiles des Psalters zu beobachten.

Damit ist aber unmittelbar ein weiteres Phänomen verbunden. Die Psalmen sind ihrer jeweiligen Gattung entsprechend für einen ganz bestimmten Anlaß oder jedenfalls eine genauer beschreibbare Situation gedachte Dichtungen. Jede Psalmengattung hat ihren unverwechselbaren Sitz im Leben und ist von daher in ihren Verwendungsmöglichkeiten beschränkt; der Sitz im Leben ist nicht ohne weiteres austauschbar, der Psalm eignet sich nicht für jede beliebige Gelegenheit.[23] Wird der Psalm nun aber—der Intention des Redaktors entsprechend—nicht mehr bei einer bestimmten kultischen Gelegenheit gesungen, sondern vom Frommen als Jahwes Torah gelesen, mit Eifer studiert und im Kontext der Torah betrachtet, dann ist er seiner Situationsgebundenheit enthoben. Das *ûbᵉtôrātô yähgäh yômām wālāylāh* von Ps. i 2b ist durchaus wörtlich gemeint: Weil die Psalmen für ihn Jahwes Weisung sind, ist der Fromme "Tag und Nacht" bereit, in ihnen zu lesen und aus ihnen zu lernen, d.h. ohne Rücksicht auf die Situation, für die sie ursprünglich bestimmt waren. Der ursprüngliche Sitz im Leben verblaßt (nicht: verschwindet!) vor dem neuen Sitz im Leben, den der Psalter erhalten hat.

Ein solcher Umgang mit den Psalmen, wie er sich hier abzeichnet, läßt nicht vermuten, daß der Redaktor des Psalters im Kreis der Tempelsänger beheimatet ist.[24] Er ist vielmehr in jenem Milieu verwurzelt, von dem uns der von ihm offenbar so geliebte Ps. i ein recht anschauliches Bild entwirft. Er gehört selbst zu jenen aus der Torahfrömmigkeit lebenden, schriftkundigen Männern, die an die Stelle der "Weisen" der alten Zeit getreten sind und deren

---

[23] Die alttestamentliche Literatur kennt allerdings die Verwendung einer literarischen Gattung außerhalb ihres ursprünglichen Sitzes im Leben (z.B. die Verwendung von Psalmengattungen in prophetischer Rede), wie auch das Phänomen der Verfremdung einer Gattung (z.B. Am. v 1-3). So können auch Psalmen im Verlauf ihrer Überlieferungsgeschichte ihrem ursprünglichen Sitz im Leben entfremdet werden (z.B. Königspsalmen im nachexilischen Gottesdienst; Verwendung von Psalmen einzelner durch die "Gemeinde"; doch sind dem Grenzen gesetzt: Hymnen und Klagelieder sind von ihrer Funktion her in kultischer Verwendung nicht austauschbar.

[24] Es ist zwar nicht auszuschließen, daß zwischen Weisheitslehrern und Kultpersonal teilweise Personalunion bestand (Mowinckel, *SVT* 3, S. 206), hier geht es aber um das "milieu sapientiel" in dem der Redaktor des Psalters beheimatet ist.

Idealbild Jesus Sirach nachzeichnet.[25] Zu deren Charakteristika gehört es allerdings auch, daß sie sich in bewußtem und gewolltem Gegensatz zu anderen Volksgenossen befinden, die sich mit Worten und Taten über die Torah Jahwes hinwegsetzen (vgl. Ps. i 1).

Wenn der Psalter nun als Gegenstand des Studiums und der Meditation des gesetzesfrommen Schriftgelehrten einen neuen Sitz im Leben gefunden hat, bedeutet das freilich nicht, daß damit seine bisherige Verwendung aufgegeben würde. Der Psalter wird auch in seiner Endgestalt im Gottesdienst Israels verwendet.[26] Der neue Sitz im Leben kommt zum traditionellen hinzu. Die Psalmen sind und bleiben Gebetsformulare; aber sie dienen nun auch der Unterweisung und Belehrung und erhalten damit eine Funktion, die eigentlich weisheitlichen Literaturformen zukam.

4. Die hier vorgetragene Schlußfolgerung aus der Verwendung von Ps. i als Prooemium des Psalters ist schon mehrfach gezogen, aber bisher kaum weiter verfolgt worden.[27] Sie steht bisher aber nur auf unserer Interpretation von Ps. i; wir müssen daher fragen, inwieweit sie durch andere Fakten abgesichert werden kann.

Zunächst wäre darauf zu verweisen, daß die "neue Verwendung" der Psalmen nicht erst mit der Redaktion des Psalters aufkommt. Bestimmte Psalmengattungen zeigen schon von ihrer Struktur her eine Neigung zur Aufnahme lehrhafter Tendenzen.[28] Sie waren mit und durch ihren liturgischen Vollzug für die Beteiligten nicht nur Gebet, sondern auch "Weisung", der es zu folgen galt. Darüber hinaus

---

[25] Sir. xxxix 1-11, vgl. G. von Rad, *Weisheit in Israel* (Neukirchen-Vluyn, 1970), S. 37.

[26] Jedenfalls gilt das für den Gottesdienst der Synagogen; daß in der Tempelliturgie Psalmen verwendet wurden, steht außer Frage, es gibt jedoch kein ausdrückliches Zeugnis dafür, daß der Psalter als solcher dabei eine Rolle spielte, auch nicht, daß er Exklusivrechte im gottesdienstlichen Gebrauch gehabt hätte. Vgl. A. Arens, *Die Psalmen im Gottesdienst des Alten Bundes* (Trier, 1961). Der Nachweis, daß die angenommene Verwendung im synagogalen Lesegottesdienst die Sammlung des Psalters veranlaßt oder auch nur beeinflußt hätte, ist bisher nicht gelungen.

[27] Außer den Hinweisen bei Kittel, *Die Psalmen*, S. 1 f.; Westermann (s. Anm. 1), S. 281; G. Fohrer, *Einleitung in das Alte Testament* (Heidelberg, [10]1965), vgl. besonders S. Mowinckel, "Psalms and Wisdom", *SVT* 3 (1955), S. 216, und *Offersang og Sangoffer* (Oslo, 1951), S. 466 ff.

[28] Zum Danklied des Einzelnen gehört als Anrede an die Mitfeiernden von vornherein auch die lehrhafte Weitergabe der vom Dankenden gemachten Heilserfahrung und die Mahnung, aus dem, was dem Beter widerfahren ist, Konsequenzen für das eigene Verhalten zu ziehen; vgl. Gunkel-Begrich, *Einleitung*, S. 277; Kraus, *Psalmen*, S. 54.

sind sapientielle Formen und Motive auch in solche Gattungen eingedrungen, in denen sie eigentlich nicht zu erwarten sind, nämlich in Hymnen und Klagelieder (Gunkel-Begrich, S. 387 f.). Dieses Phänomen mit dem Hinweis abzutun, es handele sich um Aufweichung oder Auflösung der Formen, ist keine hinreichende Erklärung. Abweichung von den Form "gesetzen" ist immer ein Zeichen für ein gewandeltes Verständnis. Wir können darin einen Hinweis sehen, daß die betreffenden Psalmen trotz ihrer Verwendung im Kult nicht mehr ausschließlich als Agenden und Formulare angesehen wurden. Schließlich bleibt festzuhalten, daß sich auch schon in den Vorstufen des jetzigen Psalters Texte finden, die keine Beziehung zum Kult mehr erkennen lassen und rein meditativen oder lehrhaften Charakter haben.[29] Auch wenn sie, wie ihre Aufnahme in diese Sammlungen zeigt, dann doch im Gottesdienst verwendet wurden, kann man sich schwer vorstellen, daß sie damit ihrer ursprünglichen Funktion als Weisheitsdichtungen entfremdet worden wären. Das Neue ist demnach nicht die außerliturgische Verwendung der Psalmen als "Meditationstexte" an sich, sondern die Tatsache, daß der Psalter als Ganzes diesem Sitz im Leben zugeordnet wird. Denn das hat zur Folge, daß nun auch Psalmen unter den Aspekt "weisheitlicher" Lehre gestellt werden, deren kultische Herkunft und deren gottesdienstliche Verwendung unbestreitbar ist.

Man darf vermuten, daß die veränderte Art des Umganges mit den Psalmen, die der redaktionelle Rahmen des Psalters bezeugt, auch im Text des Psalters selbst ihre Spuren hinterlassen hat: als "weisheitliche" Bearbeitung älterer, d.h. dem Sammler und Redaktor bereits vorgegebener Psalmen. Natürlich ist nicht vorauszusetzen, daß Spuren solcher vom Interesse der torahfrommen und schriftgelehrten Weisheit geleiteten Bearbeitung sich durchgehend bemerkbar machen. Mancher Text war auch ohne Abänderung für den veränderten Gebrauch geeignet. Ein Text wie Ps. xv, zweifellos liturgischer Herkunft, konnte ohne weiteres auch als Weisung über das rechte Verhalten des *pōʿel ṣädäq* verstanden werden.[30] Aber nicht

---

[29] Z.B. ist Ps. xlix eine reine Lehrdichtung, er gehört zur Gruppe der Korachitenpsalmen; Ps. lxxiii scheint zwar im Kult gemachte Erfahrungen wiederzugeben (Kraus, *Psalmen*, S. 666), ist jedoch selbst kein Kultlied; er trägt die Zuordnung *leʾāsāp*.

[30] Kraus, S. 254: "Später wird der Psalm als Gebetslied dem Betenden die *notae* des *ṣdjq* vergegenwärtigt haben und ein Bestandteil der *twrh*-Frömmigkeit des Judentums geworden sein".

immer ist eine Adaptation ohne weiteres möglich; dem Leser müssen Hilfen und Anweisungen gegeben werden, damit er einen vorgegebenen Text als Torah Jahwes verstehen kann. Gelegentlich muß die Aussage eines Psalmes auch korrigiert oder ergänzt werden. Die Art und Weise, wie vorgegebene Texte bearbeitet werden, ist uns aus der prophetischen Textüberlieferung bekannt. Auch im Psalter selbst gibt es genügend Beispiele.[31] Da wird ein ursprünglich für die Rezitation eines Einzelnen bestimmter Psalm zum Lied der Kultgemeinde "umfunktioniert": In Ps. xxviii wird das Klagelied eines Einzelnen durch V. 8 f um die Fürbitte für Volk und König erweitert; die Ps. cxxviii (V. 6b) und cxxxi (V. 3) bedürfen nur eines angehängten Friedenswunsches bzw. Mahnwortes, um für den Gebrauch der Gemeinde geeignet zu sein. Bei Ps. xxix dagegen wird durch den angefügten V. 11 auch die inhaltliche Aussage verändert: Aus dem Lied über die kosmische Herrschaft des höchsten Gottes, wird ein Hymnus auf die segensreiche Herrschaft Jahwes über Israel. In allen diesen Fällen ist offenbar der gewandelte Sitz im Leben des Psalms für die Erweiterung bzw. Ergänzung des ursprünglichen Textes verantwortlich.

Ehe wir nun Beispiele für die Bearbeitung älterer Psalmen im Sinne der torahgebundenen Weisheit behandeln, seien einige methodische Hinweise erlaubt. Da es sich um eine redaktionelle Bearbeitung handelt, ist damit zurechnen, daß sie den überlieferten Textbestand weitgehend geschont hat. Wir sahen schon an den angeführten Beispielen, daß solche Zusätze vornehmlich am Ende des Textes zu finden waren. Außer durch Texterweiterungen könnte auch durch interpretierende Glossen das Verständnis eines Psalms in die vom Bearbeiter gewünschte Richtung gelenkt worden sein. Zur Auffindung derartiger Eingriffe in den Text ist auf die bekannten Regeln der Text- und Literarkritik zurückzugreifen. Wir haben indes noch mit einer weiteren Möglichkeit zu rechnen wie sich die Intention des Bearbeiters im redigierten Text bemerkbar macht; sie hängt damit zusammen, daß hier der Sonderfall der Zusammenstellung ursprünglich selbständiger Texteinheiten vorliegt. Soweit der Bearbeiter dabei nicht an vorgegebene Anordnungen gebunden ist, kann er seine Auffassung

[31] Kraus, S. 76 f., deutet ganz allgemein die Möglichkeit an, daß "im Traditionsprozeß Rezeptionen, Erweiterungen und Aktualisierungen durchgeführt wurden". Er verweist auf Beispiele, wo sich die Veränderung der historischen Situation in Zusätzen zum ursprünglichen Text niederschlägt. S. auch S. Mowinckel, *Psalmenstudien* VI (Kristiania, 1924; reprint Amsterdam, 1961), S. 36.

auch durch die von ihm gewählte Abfolge und damit Zuordnung der Texte zueinander deutlich machen. Der Schlußteil des Psalters (Ps. cxlvi-cl) hat dafür schon ein Beispiel geliefert.

5. Als erstes Beispiel soll die Glosse in Ps. l 16a unsere These illustrieren. Daß V. 16a (*w^e lārāšā' 'āmar 'ălohîm*) eine Glosse ist, wird kaum bestritten.[32] Die Worte erwecken den Eindruck, als beginne hier eine neue Gottesrede; sie unterbrechen jedoch die von V. 7-23 durchgehende Gottesrede. Das ganze Stück ist durchgehend als Anrede in der 2.m.sg. konzipiert, ein Wechsel in der Person des Angeredeten (V. 7 nennt ausdrücklich "mein Volk" und "Israel") ist nirgendwo angedeutet. Die drei Worte stehen außerhalb des gleichmäßigen Metrums 3 + 3, das nach der Redeeröffnung (V. 7: 3 + 3 + 3) vorherrscht. Als prosaischer Einschub unterbricht die Glosse den Rhythmus des Textes. Es ist also nur zu fragen, was die Glosse erreichen will. Offensichtlich soll der danach folgende Text nicht mehr als Anrede an Israel, sondern als gegen "den Frevler" gerichtete Scheltrede verstanden werden. Interpretiert der Glossator damit nur die Intention des Verfassers?[33] Man wird das verneinen müssen. Der Text ist vielmehr durchgehend als *eine* Rede konzipiert. Seine Einheitlichkeit läßt sich formkritisch absichern: Nur in V. 7 steht eine "Eröffnung der Anklage" und in V. 23 werden beide Anklagepunkte noch einmal in einer Art Schlußwort zusammengefaßt. Allerdings ist die Anklage in zwei Gedankengänge gegliedert, die in V. 8 bzw. V. 16 jeweils mit einer Art Abgrenzung des Streitpunktes beginnen und in V. 14 f. und V. 22 mit einer Mahnung bzw. Warnung enden. Es ist die Absicht der Glosse, die Anklagepunkte auf zwei Adressaten zu verteilen: Die Belehrung über die rechte Todah richte sich an Israel, die Warnung vor dem mißbräuchlichen Umgang mit Gottes Gebot und Bund aber werde dem "Frevler" vorgehalten. Ein einzelner, vielleicht sogar ein inmitten der Versammlung als Frevler Entlarvter sei hier angesprochen.[34] A. Weiser meint sogar, eine Scheidung zwischen *ṣaddîqîm* und *r^e šā'îm* innerhalb der

---

[32] H. Schmidt, *Die Psalmen* (Tübingen, 1934), der in Ps. l zwei ursprünglich selbständige Gedichte erkennen will, nimmt allerdings den V. 16a als Kriterium für die literarkritische Scheidung, S. 97.

[33] So versteht Kraus, *Psalmen*, S. 535, die Glosse: "Die einleitende Formel . . . in 16 führt als sekundärer Einschub in das Verständnis der zweiten Redephase (16 ff) ein".

[34] Schmidt, S. 97, und Kraus, S. 535, folgen hierin dem von der Glosse vorgezeichneten Verständnis.

Kultgemeinde müsse "seit alter Zeit Bestandteil des Bundeskultes gewesen" sein.[35] Dem ist jedoch entgegenzuhalten, daß es geradezu als Charakteristikum prophetischer Scheltrede[36] gelten kann, ihre Anklage undifferenziert an alle Zuhörer zu richten (vgl. Am. v 21-23; Jes. i 10-17; Jer. vii 1-15 u.ö.). So gilt auch hier ursprünglich die Warnung vor einer nur mit den Lippen praktizierten Torahfrömmigkeit allen, "die den Bund beim Opfer geschlossen haben",[37] ebenso wie die Mahnung zur rechten Opferpraxis allen gegolten hat. Gerade die undifferenzierte Anrede aber hat beim Glossator Anstoß erregt. Er trägt deshalb nachträglich die Unterscheidung ein, die der prophetische Redestil um der Wirksamkeit der Warnung willen vermeidet. Der Grund dafür ist nicht schwer zu finden. Er liegt darin, daß bei der Herausnahme des Psalms aus dem gottesdienstlichen Zusammenhang der Leser oder Beter des Psalms sich selbst direkt und nicht mehr nur als Teil der Gemeinschaft angesprochen fühlen muß. Dann aber ist der hier enthaltene Vorwurf ungerechtfertigt bei einem, der davon überzeugt ist, nicht zu den "Gottvergessenen" (V. 22) zu gehören, der sich vielmehr von der Gemeinschaft mit den *r^ešā^cîm* ausdrücklich distanziert, wie es Ps. i 1 beschrieben ist. Ist er zudem noch, wie Ps. i 2 sagt, Tag und Nacht mit dem Studium der Torah befaßt, dann muß es ihm vollends unmöglich sein, die Worte von V. 16 f auf sich zu beziehen; denn für ihn ist das Zitieren und Rezitieren der Gesetze ja nichts anderes als die wortgetreue Erfüllung dessen, was die Torah selbst vorschreibt (Dtn. vi 7 ff.). Die Glosse ist demnach aus der Haltung eines Mannes wie des *ṣaddîq* von Ps. i und damit auch des Redaktors des Psalters voll verständlich.[38] Sie ist zudem ein Zeichen dafür, daß der Glossator den Psalm nicht mehr im Kontext des liturgischen Geschehens sieht.

---

[35] *Die Psalmen* (Göttingen, [8]1973), S. 257.

[36] Die Gattung der prophetischen Schelt- oder Gerichtsrede ist für die Formgebung der Gottesrede jedenfalls bestimmend gewesen, auch wenn man darüber im Zweifel sein kann, ob nicht doch ein priesterlicher Sprecher vorauszusetzen ist (vgl. Kraus, S. 527 bzw. 529).

[37] Ob diese Anrede auf einen gerade vollzogenen Bundesschluß oder eine Bundeserneuerung zurückzuführen ist, kann dahingestellt bleiben. Für eine Bundeserneuerungsfeier hat sich Kraus auch in der neuesten Auflage seines Kommentars wieder ausgesprochen (S. 530).

[38] An Ps. i 2 und seine Schilderung des die Torah studierenden Schriftgelehrten fühlt sich auch Kittel erinnert, *Psalmen*, S. 186; er glaubt allerdings, daß die Schelte unseres Psalms sich gerade gegen die "äußere Gesetzlichkeit" der Schriftgelehrten richte.

6. Auch in Ps. cxlvi läßt sich ein glossenartiger Textzusatz entdecken. Allerdings ist die Ausgangsposition hier schon anders als bei Ps. l. Der Ps. cxlvi stammt nicht aus der Liturgie.[39] Er gehört nicht nur zu den Spätlingen des Psalters, sondern ist auch von seinem Verfasser bereits als "didaktischer Psalm" konzipiert worden, für den die Form des "Hymnus einen Einzelnen" [40] nur noch die äußere Hülle ist. Der Verfasser von Ps. cxlvi gehört wohl selbst schon zu den schriftkundigen und toraheifrigen Weisen der Spätzeit. Er hat den Psalm für die betende und meditierende Lesung durch einen Gleichgesinnten oder "Schüler" bestimmt. Die Glossierung läßt sich in diesem Fall also nicht mit einem Wechsel des Sitzes im Leben begründen.

Der beanstandete Vers ist V. 9. Er bildet das Ende einer Reihe von hymnischen Partizipien (V. 6b-9a; V. 6a ist eine formelhafte Gottesprädikation und gehört nicht dazu). Die Partizipien beziehen sich zurück auf die im Makarismus V. 5 (der eigentlichen Mitte des Psalms) genannte Gottesbezeichnung *yhwh ʾälohāyw*, ohne syntaktisch von ihr abzuhängen. Zwei Reihen von Partizipialsätzen sind zu unterscheiden: Zunächst echte "hymnische Partizipien",[41] die den Gottesnamen selbst nicht nennen, aber auf seine Nennung abzielen. Dies geschieht dann in einer zweiten Reihe (V. 7b-9aα), die in auffälliger Weise jedesmal den Jahwenamen voranstellt und somit regelrechte Partizipialsätze bildet:

Der die Treue wahrt in Ewigkeit,
Recht schafft den Unterdrückten,
Brot gibt den Hungernden:

Jahwe ist's, der die Gefesselten befreit,
Jahwe ist's, der die Blinden sehend macht,
Jahwe ist's, der die Gebeugten aufrichtet,
Jahwe ist's, der die Gerechten liebt,
Jahwe ist's, der die Fremden behütet,
Waise und Witwe richtet er auf;
Aber den Weg der Frevler macht er krumm.

---

[39] Zu Ps. cxlvi vgl. meinen Aufsatz "Gotteslob als Weisheitslehre", in *Dein Wort beachten. Alttestamentliche Aufsätze*, hrg. von J. Reindl unter Mitarbeit von G. Hentschel (Leipzig, 1981), S. 116-35; dort wird eine ausführliche Untersuchung der Form und des Sitzes im Leben von Ps. cxlvi geboten. Die hier zugrunde gelegten Auffassungen finden sich dort eingehender begründet.

[40] Zu dieser Gattung und ihrer Problematik vgl. Crüsemann (S. Anm. 10), S. 285-306.

[41] A.a.O., S. 81-152, bes. S. 95 f.

Am Ende der Reihe fällt eine Unstimmigkeit auf: der gedankliche Sprung von Jahwes Tun an Fremden, Waisen und Witwen zum Gericht an den Frevlern. Nach einem Vorschlag von G. Bickell, den B. Duhm aufgegriffen hat,[42] soll eine Umstellung hier Ordnung schaffen: V. 8b gehöre vor V. 9b und ergebe mit ihm zusammen einen antithetischen Parallelismus:

> Jahwe liebt die Gerechten,
> aber den Weg der Frevler macht er krumm.

Der Vorschlag ist bestechend, muß aber dennoch Bedenken erwecken. Er hat keinerlei Stütze in der Textüberlieferung; es handelt sich um eine freie Konjektur. Zum andern wird durch die Umstellung die stilistisch durch die Reihung gleichgebauter Sätze aufgebaute Spannung, die sich am Ende im invertierten Verbalsatz löst, unschön zerstört. In der Konsequenz führt das dazu, den ganzen rekonstruierten Vers als Glosse auszuscheiden.[43]

Die Störung der Textharmonie geht vielmehr nur auf V. 9b zurück.[44] Der stilistische Aufbau der Reihe weist V. 9a als deren eigentlichen Abschluß aus.[45] Die "überzählige" Sonderstellung von V. 9b wird auch bei der metrischen Gliederung des Abschnittes deutlich, wenn diese nur die durch das Stilmittel des Parallelismus gegebene Ordnung innerhalb des Textes beachtet.[46] Schließlich ist darauf zu verweisen, daß V. 9b auch mit seiner Aussage innerhalb des Ps. cxlvi isoliert dasteht. Dieser Psalm hat es nicht thematisch mit dem Gegensatz zwischen *ṣaddîqîm* und *r^e šā ͑îm* zu tun.[47] Sein Thema ist vielmehr die Verläßlichkeit Jahwes als Helfer derer, die der

---

[42] B. Duhm, *Die Psalmen* (Freiburg, 1899), S. 297.

[43] Eine solche Operation ist nicht nur unnötig (s.u.); es wäre auch nur schwer zu erklären, warum die Glosse nachträglich auseinandergerissen wurde.

[44] Dies hat C. A. Briggs richtig erkannt, *Psalms* II (Edinburgh, 1907, reprint 1951), S. 532.

[45] Die Reihung von Partizipialsätzen, an deren Ende ein invertierter Verbalsatz als Klimax steht, wird als Stilmittel auch 1 Sam. ii 7 f.; Ps. cxiii 5b-7 gebraucht. Auch Briggs erklärt V. 9a für "a proper conclusion", S. 531.

[46] Wenn man den synthetischen Parallelismus in V. 9a respektiert, wird man hier einen Doppeldreier (3 + 3) zählen; es ergibt sich dann, daß auch 7aα + β. 7b + 8aα. 8aβ + b jeweils einen Doppeldreier bilden; dadurch bleibt auch der Parallelismus in V. 7a unangetastet. Es bleiben als einzelne Dreier übrig 6b (vgl. dazu J. Reindl [s. Anm. 39], S. 121 f.) und 9b.

[47] Ps. cxlvi unterscheidet sich dadurch von den gerade zur Begründung der Textumstellung in V. 8 und 9 herangezogenen "Parallelen" 1 Sam. ii 9 f. und Ps. i 6; in beiden Psalmen spielt der Gegensätz zwischen *ṣaddîqîm* und *r^e šā ͑îm* thematisch die Hauptrolle.

Hilfe entbehren. Ähnlich wie in Ps. cxiii 6-9 kommt das Schicksal der Frevler dabei nicht in sein Blickfeld. Die Kongruenz der verschiedenen Argumente läßt somit den Schluß zu, daß V. 9b nicht zum ursprünglichen Bestand gehört. Er ist als Glosse zu erklären, die den Gedankengang erweitert. Sie ergänzt einerseits allgemein zu den Aussagen über den Helfergott diejenige über den den Frevler strafenden Gott (Gunkel, *Die Psalmen*, S. 613). Speziell zielt sie aber auf die Aussage *yhwh ʾoheb ṣaddîqîm* in V. 8b. Im Kontext der Jahwes hilfreiches Tun an den Schwachen beschreibenden Partizipialsätze sind die *ṣaddîqîm* aber im juridischen Sinn als die unschuldig Angeklagten zu verstehen, auf deren Seite sich Jahwe im Gottesurteil stellt.[48] Der Glossator hat das Wort offenbar nicht in diesem speziellen Sinn verstanden, sondern im Sinne sowohl der weisheitlichen Sprache, wie auch der häufigen Verwendung in den Psalmen als Terminus für den torahtreuen Frommen; dessen unfehlbar sich assoziierendes Gegenbild aber sind die *rᵉšāʿîm*. Sie mußten sich ihm bei seinem Verständnis der *ṣaddîqîm* auch hier aufdrängen. Er mag dabei durchaus die Formulierungen von Ps. i 6 im Auge gehabt haben; der Anklang an sie ist unverkennbar (vgl. Briggs, Gunkel and Kraus z.St.). Demnach ist auch diese erweiternde Glosse ein Hinweis auf eine Bearbeitung des Psalters aus der in Ps. i gegebenen Grundtendenz heraus.[49]

7. Auch der Abschluß des Ps. civ ist m.E. ähnlich zu beurteilen. Es ist wieder ein Psalm, der der Grundform des "Hymnus eines Einzelnen" folgt.[50] Der Psalmist tritt als Individuum allerdings nur am Anfang (V. 1a) und am Ende (V. 33, 34)[51] deutlich hervor. Der Schlußteil beginnt bereits in V. 31 mit einem "Segenswunsch" für Jahwe,[52] dem das Lobversprechen (wie Ps. cxlvi 2) und der Wunsch des Sängers für sich selbst folgt: "Möge ihm mein Dichten gefal-

---

[48] Man beachte die Konsoziierung mit den Termini *ʿᵃšûqîm*, *ʾᵃsûrîm* und *kᵉpûpîm*, zu denen Kraus bemerkt: "7aα und 7b bezieht sich wohl auf das befreiende Gottesurteil, durch das unschuldig angeklagte und inhaftierte Menschen gerettet werden", *Psalmen* S. 1133.

[49] Daß die Glosse nicht nach V. 8b wo sie zu erwarten wäre, sondern an ihren jetzigen Platz gekommen ist, liegt wohl einerseits an der gleichen Struktur des Satzbaues mit V. 9aβ, andererseits sollte sie sicher den wirkungsvollen Abschluß der Reihe bilden.

[50] Crüsemann (s. Anm. 10), S. 287 und 295.

[51] Die Wiederholung des Introitusverses am Ende (V. 35b) ist jedenfalls sekundär, vgl. Crüsemann, S. 290.

[52] Gunkel-Begrich, *Einleitung*, S. 56 (Nr. 35).

len, möge ich mich an Jahwe erfreuen!" (V. 34) Dabei korrespondiert die Freude des Dichters an Jahwe der Freude Jahwes an seiner Schöpfung (V. 31). Damit ist der Gedankengang in sich geschlossen. Es folgt indessen noch ein weiterer Wunschsatz—eine Verwünschung der "Sünder" und "Frevler". So geläufig solche Verwünschungen oder Feindbitten in den Klageliedern sind, so ungewöhnlich ist es, sie am Ende eines Hymnus vorzufinden.[53] Das Auftauchen dieses Elementes ist also aus der Formensprache des Hymnus nicht zu erklären. Ohne darauf allzu großes Gewicht zu legen, kann man noch die Beobachtung hinzufügen, daß im hymnischen Abgesang VV. 31-34 allein viermal der Jahwename genannt wird, während V. 35 ihn vermeidet. Stärker fällt ins Gewicht, daß wiederum ein inhaltlich dem ganzen Psalm sonst fremder Gedanke zur Sprache kommt. Der Psalmist hat bis hierhin keinen Gedanken an die *ḥaṭṭā'îm* und *r^ešā'îm* verschwendet. Sein Thema ist vielmehr die unbeschränkte und unbestrittene Herrschaft des Schöpfers Jahwe in seiner Schöpfung. Ein Hinweis auf eine mögliche Störung der Schöpfungsharmonie ist höchstens in V. 9 zu finden: dort aber wird gesagt, daß dem Meer als potentieller Chaosmacht für immer feste Grenzen gezogen sind. Der ganze Psalm ist ein einziger Preis der *kābôd* des Schöpfergottes. Die "Sünder" und "Frevler" werden nicht ins Visier genommen. Daß sie nun, nach dem formgerechten Abschluß des Psalms, in V. 35 doch noch in den Blick kommen, legt die Vermutung nahe, daß dieser Vers eine nachträgliche Erweiterung ist.[54]

Was kann diese Erweiterung des Textes veranlaßt haben? Vielleicht kann man den Glossator einen Realisten nennen, der weiß, daß eine solche Harmonie, wie sie unser Psalm besingt, noch nicht verwirklicht ist. Man kann dann wohl sicher sein, daß dieser Realitätssinn daher rührt, daß dem Bearbeiter des Psalms die *r^ešā'îm* selbst ein Problem sind, mit dem er sich auseinandersetzen muß. Das würde dem entsprechen, was wir über das Milieu sagten, aus dem der Redaktor des Psalters kommt—eine Situation der Auseinandersetzung zwischen gesetzestreuen Juden und Menschen, denen Jahwes Torah

---

[53] Gunkel-Begrich, S. 56 f. (Nr. 36), zählen sie zwar zu den Formelementen des Hymnusschlusses; doch besteht der dort wie im Kommentar gemachte Hinweis auf Ps. cxxxix 19 zu Unrecht: Der Psalm ist kein Hymnus; er enthält zwar hymnische Elemente, aber gerade die V. 9-22. (23, 24) sind formkritisch anders zu bestimmen. Auch der Verweis auf Ri. v 31 bei Gunkel und Crüsemann (S. 295) ist ohne Beweiskraft, da es sich bei Ri. v um die Sonderform eines Siegesliedes handelt, bei der das Motiv der Feindverwünschung unbedingt dazugehört.

[54] Dies ist von Briggs, *Psalms II*, schon richtig erkannt worden (S. 337, 339).

nicht unbedingt mit der Weltordnung identisch ist. Auf jeden Fall bezeugt die Texterweiterung, daß der Bearbeiter den Psalm überdacht und in das Licht seiner Erfahrungen gestellt hat. Der Psalm hat offenbar seinen ursprünglichen Haftpunkt im Kult (Kraus, S. 881) mit einer Verwendung als Lesetext vertauscht.

8. Ein viertes und letztes Beispiel soll die Methode des Bearbeiters aufzeigen, durch redaktionelle Zusammenstellung ursprünglich nicht aufeinander bezogener Psalmen dem Leser des Psalters eine bestimmte Deutung nahezulegen. Bei solchem Verfahren sind dem Belieben des Redaktors freilich gewisse Grenzen gesteckt, vor allem dann, wenn er ihm bereits vorliegende, vielleicht schon über längere Zeit tradierte und dadurch verfestigte Sammlungen übernimmt. Das ist besonders für den ersten Teil des Psalters, bis zum Ende des sog. Dritten Buches der Fall (1. Davidspsalter, Elohistischer Psalter mit Nachtrag); der zweite Teil, von Ps. xc an, ist weit weniger deutlich durch vorgegebene Sammlungen geprägt, jedenfalls sind die darin auftauchenden Sammlungen nicht so umfangreich und eher nach inhaltlichen Gesichtspunkten ausgewählt (Jahwe-Königs-Lieder, *maʿalôt*-Psalmen, Halleluja-Psalmen). Dazwischen stehen Psalmen, die anscheinend als "Einzelgänger" ihren Platz gefunden haben (z.B. Ps. cxix, cxxxvii); andere wieder sind als "Zwillingspsalmen" anzusehen, z.B. Ps. cv und cvi, cxi und cxii.[55] Gleich am Anfang des sogenannten Vierten Buches stehen drei Psalmen, die nach der Meinung Westermanns "keinen Zusammenhang erkennen" lassen:[56] Die Ps. xc, xci und xcii. Ihnen folgt mit den Jahwe-Malak-Liedern eine offenbar nach inhaltlichen Gesichtspunkten zusammengestelle Gruppe. Sollten die drei ersten Psalmen ganz zufällig an ihren Platz gekommen sein?

Zunächst muß freilich gesagt werden, daß die drei Psalmen von ihrer Gattung her keine Gemeinsamkeit aufweisen: Ps. xc wird durch Elememte des Volksklageliedes wie durch ein Gerüst zusammengehalten; Ps. xci läßt Anlehnungen an einen liturgischen Vorgang erkennen;[57] der Ps. xcii schließlich folgt dem Schema eines Dankliedes

[55] W. Zimmerli, "Zwillingspsalmen", in *Wort, Lied und Gottesspruch*, FS J. Ziegler (Würzburg, 1972), S. 105-13, bes. 109; = *Studien zur alttestamentlichen Theologie und Prophetie* (München, 1974), S. 261-70, bes. 267 f.

[56] Westermann (s. Anm. 1), S. 282.

[57] Die konkrete kultische Situation wird meist als Aufnahme eines Asylanten in den Schutzbereich des Tempels gedeutet, vgl. Kraus, *Psalmen*, S. 803 f. P. Hugger, *Jahwe meine Zuflucht, Gestalt und Theologie des 91. Psalms* (Münsterschwarz-

eines Einzelnen. Dennoch haben die drei Psalmen schon in ihrer Formensprache etwas Gemeinsames—bei jedem von ihnen treten weisheitliche Redeformen und eine didaktische Tendenz deutlich in Erscheinung. Bei Ps. xc ist der konkrete Anlaß der Klage der Gemeinschaft deshalb nicht mehr zu erkennen, weil an die Stelle konkreter Notschilderungen Klagen über die Vergänglichkeit des Menschenlebens getreten sind.[58] Ps. xci läßt in seinem Hauptteil, einer "Belehrung" über den Schutz, den das Verweilen im Haus Jahwes gewährt, ebenfalls eine ausgeprägte didaktische Absicht erkennen: der Angesprochene soll dazu bewegt werden, sich zu Jahwe als "seiner Zuflucht" zu bekennen (V. 2, 9). Das Danklied von Ps. xcii ist dadurch gekennzeichnet, daß die Erfahrung, auf die der Dankende sich stützt, hier eine "Erkenntnis" ist (V. 7 ff.); die weisheitlichen Formen und Themen sind dadurch so dominant geworden, daß Crüsemann urteilt: "So ist ein Psalm entstanden, dessen Grundschema das Danklied des Einzelnen darstellt, der aber durch hymnische und weisheitliche Motive und Formen zu einem neuen Ganzen umgeformt wurde" (Crüsemann [s. Anm. 10], S. 283, Anm. 1).

Die weisheitlich-didaktische Prägung ist jedoch nicht das einzige, was die drei Psalmen miteinander verbindet. Es bestehen auch auffällige Stichwortzusammenhänge zwischen jeweils zwei der drei. Die wichtigsten seien hier aufgeführt:

Sowohl Ps. xc 1, wie auch xci 9 wird Jahwe als der *mā'ôn* des Beters angesprochen; das Wort findet sich in dieser Verwendung nur noch Ps. lxxi 3.[59]

Die Psalmen xci und xcii benutzen beide gleich im ersten Vers die Gottesbezeichnung *'älyôn*.

Mehrfach sind die Fäden, die sich zwischen Ps. xc und xcii spannen; wir werden gleich noch darauf zurückkommen. Hier sei zunächst nur erwähnt, daß für Jahwes Wirken der in dieser Bedeutung seltene Terminus *på'ᵃläkā* xc 16 und xcii 5 vorkommt; auch der Vergleich

---

ach, 1971), interpretiert die Situation wesentlich anders: ein Verehrer des Gottes der Väter wird aufgefordert, "nunmehr auch in Jerusalem (seinen Gott Jahwe) zu verehren"; in der Analyse der Form geht er jedoch von der gleichen Struktur aus, S. 18.

[58] C. Westermann, "Der 90. Psalm", *Forschung am Alten Testament* (München 1964), S. 344.

[59] Die Korrektur in *mā'ôz*, die die LXX vorauszusetzen scheint, wird von Hugger, S. 45, mit Recht abgelehnt.

mit sprossendem (*ṣûṣ hif.*) Gras sowohl in xc 6 wie in xcii 8 ist jedenfalls auffällig.

Die hier registrierten Wortanklänge sind freilich noch nicht viel mehr als ein Beweis für eine assoziative Zusammenstellung. Doch bieten sie den Anlaß danach zu fragen, inwieweit für die Anordnung der drei Psalmen etwa eine gedankliche Verbindung maßgebend war, die dem Redaktor wichtig erschien.

Zunächst muß festgestellt werden, daß alle drei Psalmen—und zwar gerade in den Stücken, die weisheitlich-lehrhaft beeinflußt sind,—unter allerdings jeweils anderem Aspekt vom Ergehen des Menschen handeln: der Ps. xc vom allgemeinen Menschenlos, der Ps. xci vom Menschen, der sich unter Jahwes Schutz begeben hat, Ps. xcii schließlich vom unterschiedlichen Los des Frevlers und des Gerechten. Am eindeutigsten ist der Ps. xcii auf dieses Thema hin ausgerichtet.[60] Er beginnt formgerecht als Danklied, wenn auch "in einer Mischung von Toda-Formel . . . und der Einleitung zu einem Hymnus eines Einzelnen",[61] indem der Psalmist seine Absicht kundtut, für eine ihm zuteil gewordene Gnade (*ḥasdäkā wä'ᵃmûnātᵉkā*) zu danken. Der Anlaß dazu besteht freilich nicht—wie üblicherweise im individuellen Danklied—in einer Rettungserfahrung, sondern in einer Erkenntnis, die ihm—im Gegensatz zum *'îš-baʿar*—zuteil geworden ist (V. 6 f.). Die gewonnene Einsicht betrifft das Schicksal von *rᵉšāʿîm* und *ṣaddîqîm*. Offenbar war das scheinbare Wohlergehen der Frevler das Problem, das den Beter des Psalms in besonderer Weise gequält hat. Die Lösung liegt ganz auf der Linie weisheitlicher Lehre über den Tun-Ergehens-Zusammenhang; sie wird allerdings als eigene Erfahrung (V. 11 f.)[62] des Psalmisten mitgeteilt: Die Frevler sind trotz ihres scheinbaren Wohlergehns dem Untergang geweiht, der Gerechte dagegen kann bis ins hohe Alter an der Fülle des Lebens partizipieren. So wird das Geschick des *ṣaddîq* zum Argument für Jahwes "Rechtschaffenheit".

Was der Psalmist von xcii hier als seine aus Erfahrung gewonnene Erkenntnis beschreibt, ist nun aber genau das, was in Ps. xci dem-

---

[60] N. M. Sarna, "The Psalm for the Sabbath Day (Psalm 92)", *JBL* 81 (1962), S. 155-68.

[61] Crüsemann (s. Anm. 10), S. 238 Anm. 1.

[62] Der V. 11 ist wohl in diesem Sinne zu verstehen, läßt aber trotz der plastischen Ausdrucksweise keinen Rückschluß auf die Art der "Rettungserfahrung" zu (gegen Schmidt, *Die Psalmen*, S. 173 f., der an Heilung in Krankheit denkt).

jenigen, der sich zu Jahwe bekennt,[63] zugesagt wird. Die "Belehrung", die in V. 3-13 an die Aufforderung, die Bekenntnisformel zu sprechen, angefügt wird, verheißt ein Doppeltes: den Schutz Jahwes in allen drohenden tödlichen Gefahren und die Vergeltung an den "Frevlern": *raq b^{e}ʿênâkā tabbîṭ wešillumat r^{e}šāʿîm tirʾäh* (V. 8). Ps. xcii bestätigt als "Erfahrung", was der Verfasser von Ps. xci als "Lehre" vorgetragen hat. Die beiden Psalmen entsprechen einander inhaltlich also in diesem einen Punkt; man könnte sie in die Kategorie Zusage (Verheißung)-Erfüllung einordnen; und dies scheint mit ihrer Nebeneinanderordnung beabsichtigt zu sein.

Der Ps. xcii läßt aber auch einen Rückblick auf Ps. xc zu. Beide sind einander bereits durch ihre Form komplementär zugeordnet: als Klagelied und Danklied (freilich unter der Einschränkung, daß es sich im einen Fall um ein Klagelied der Gemeinschaft, im anderen um ein individuelles Danklied handelt; doch scheint dies von den Sammlern der Psalmen weniger als gravierend empfunden worden zu sein als von unserer alles eindeutig klassifizierenden Auslegung). Als Klagelied hat Ps. xc eine doppelte Funktion: Gott die Not der Bedrängten Klage erhebend vor Augen zu stellen und zugleich um Abhilfe zu bitten.

Was die Bitten betrifft, so zeigt sich, daß sie in V. 13-17 [64] zum Teil wörtlich dem entsprechen, was Ps. xcii als bereits empfangene Gabe dankbar bekennt:

Ps. xc	Ps. xcii
V. 14a: Sättige uns am Morgen mit deiner Huld (*babboqär b^{e}ḥaṣdäkā*)	V. 3: Ich will verkünden am Morgen deine Huld (*babboqär ḥasdäkā*)
V. 14b: . . .damit wir uns freuen und jubeln (*ûn^{e}rann^{e}nāh w^{e}niśm^{e}ḥāh*)	V. 5: Du hast mich erfreut (*śimmaḥtanî*) . . . und ich kann jubeln (*ʾ^{a}rannen*)
V. 16: Laß offenbar werden deinen Knechten dein Wirken (*påʿ^{å}läkā*)	(Du hast mich erfreut) an deinem Wirken (*b^{e}påʿ^{å}läkā*)

Wenn man dazu noch die Bitte in V. 12 um ein *l^{e}bab ḥåkmāh* mit der triumphierenden Feststellung von Ps. xcii 6 f. vergleicht, wird die offensichtlich beabsichtigte Beziehung des einen auf den anderen

[63] In welcher Weise dieses Bekenntnis zu Jahwe zu interpretieren ist, kann in diesem Zusammenhang auf sich beruhen.

[64] Die V. 13-17 werden von Gunkel, *Die Psalmen*, S. 399, nach dem Vorgang von Duhm u.a. für eine nachträgliche Erweiterung gehalten; dagegen mit Recht Westermann, "Der 90. Psalm", S. 348.

Psalm unübersehbar. Zwischen den beiden Psalmen soll das Verhältnis von Klage (Bitte) und gewährter Hilfe (Rettung) erkannt werden.

Wir müssen aber noch auf die "Klagen" des Ps. xc zurückkommen. Sie benennen keine konkrete Notlage, sondern beklagen im Kontrast zur Ewigkeit des Schöpfergottes (V. 2) das Los der geschaffenen Menschen (*b^e^nê ʾādām*): Sie gleichen dem immer wieder nachwachsenden Gras—"am Morgen sprießt es und blüht—am Abend wird es geschnitten und welkt" (V. 6). "Klagepunkt" ist also das gemeinsame und unabwendbare Todesschicksal aller Menschen ohne Unterschied. Das Problem verschärft sich, weil der Psalmist Tod und Sünde in einem unlösbaren Zusammenhang sieht (V. 8).[65]

Das gleiche Motiv, das hier als Klage verwendet wird, benutzt der Ps. xcii auch; aber er macht ein sorgfältiges "distinguo": *biproaḥ r^e^šāʿîm k^e^mô ʿeśāb wayyāṣîṣû kål-poʿ^a^lê ʾāwän l^e^hašmîdām ʿ^a^dê-ʿad*—für den *ṣaddîq* dagegen hat er das Bild des üppig und fruchtbar gedeihenden Baumes parat.[66] Ihm geht es also nicht um das gemeinsame Todeslos aller Menschen, sondern um das sich im Leben bereits unterschiedlich gestaltende Schicksal von Frevler und Gerechtem. Die von uns vorhin aufgezeigten Verbindungen zwischen den beiden Psalmen deuten an, daß der Redaktor sie bei ihrer Zusammenstellung dennoch aufeinander bezogen wissen wollte. Für ihn ist Ps. xcii die Antwort auf die in Ps. xc aufgeworfenen Fragen. Es ist freilich die Antwort der traditionellen Weisheitslehre; sie rückt in ihrem Sinn das Problem von Ps. xc "zurecht", indem sie aus dem anthropologischen Anliegen eine Frage nach der "Gerechtigkeit" Gottes heraushört und im Sinne der Theodizee beantwortet. Es wird überraschend deutlich, wie sehr dem Redaktor daran gelegen ist, die überlieferte Lehre zu wahren; er deutet—auch gegen den ursprünglichen Sinn des Psalmes—als echter "Hüter der Tradition".[67] Die auffällige Nähe zum Gedankengang von Ps. i zeigt, daß unser Interpret genau aus dem dort dokumentierten geistigen Milieu heraus ans Werk gegangen ist, als er die drei Psalmen xc bis xcii einander zuordnete.

---

[65] C. Westermann, S. 347 f.

[66] Die V. 13-15 gebrauchen für die Schilderung des Ergehens des *ṣaddîq* das gleiche Bild wie Ps. i 3; der Ps. i steht aber auch in seiner Theologie vom *rāšāʿ* und *ṣaddîq* dem Ps. xcii nahe.

[67] Die Rolle, "guardians of law tradition and law interpretation" zusein, hat S. Mowinckel den Weisheitslehrern der nachexilischen Zeit mit Recht zugeschrieben, s. *SVT* 3, S. 208.

9. Unsere Untersuchung der drei Psalmstellen und der Dreiergruppe hat das erhoffte Ergebnis gebracht: Die vermuteten Spuren einer "weisheitlichen" Bearbeitung konnten gefunden werden. Es läßt sich zwar nicht zwingend beweisen, daß die Bearbeitung an allen drei bzw. vier Stellen auf die gleiche Hand zurückgeht. Immerhin zeigten alle Bearbeitungen sowohl in ihrer theologischen Grundtendenz (Hervorhebung des Unterschiedes von *ṣaddîq* und *rešāʿîm*; Versuch eines Ausgleichs mit der traditionellen Lehre) wie auch in der Art ihres Umgangs mit den Psalmen (im Kontext der "Schrift" zu meditierendes, weisunggebendes Wort) eine weitgehende Übereinstimmung. Es ergibt sich somit eine hohe Wahrscheinlichkeit dafür, daß alle Bearbeitungen der gleichen redaktionellen Phase zuzuschreiben sind. Die immer wieder feststellbaren Beziehungen auf Ps. i lassen erkennen, daß dies die Phase der abschließenden Redaktion des Psalters war.

Damit bestätigt sich aber auch das vorläufige Bild, das wir uns von der Redaktion des Psalters gemacht haben. Sie war mehr als eine bloße Zusammenstellung bereits vorliegender Sammlungen. Sie gab der Sammlung nicht nur einen Rahmen, der aus der Ansammlung von Einzeltexten *ein* Buch machte, sondern trug auch eine bestimmte Deutung an die Psalmen heran. Damit wurde ein Buch geschaffen, daß dafür bestimmt war, in bestimmten Kreisen als "Lehre" gelesen, meditiert und angenommen zu werden. Redaktion wie der zu erschließende Adressatenkreis gehören offensichtlich dem gleichen Milieu der aus dem Geiste der Torah lebenden, der bereits schriftlich vorliegenden Tradition verpflichteten und um ihre Wahrung bemühten schriftgelehrten Weisen an.

10. Das Ergebnis scheint für die Auslegung der Psalmen nicht ohne Belang zu sein. Einige denkbare Konsequenzen seien zum Schluß noch angedeutet:

(1) Es konnte eine "weisheitliche" Bearbeitung des Psalters bei seiner Endredaktion nachgewiesen werden. Damit ergibt sich die Möglichkeit, mit solcher Bearbeitung auch an weiteren Stellen zu rechnen. Es sollte daher nachgeprüft werden, ob nicht in mancher Glosse oder Texterweiterung die Hand des Redaktors erkannt werden könnte.[68]

---

[68] Die Erweiterung, die der Ps. li in V. 20 f. gefunden hat, muß z.B. nicht Ausdruck einer kultisch-rituell orientierten Frömmigkeit sein, sondern kann auch damit erklärt werden, daß der Bearbeiter den Psalm im Gesamtkontext der Torah mitsamt der zu ihr gehörenden Kultgesetzgebung verstehen wollte.

(2) Wenigstens an zwei Stellen (Ps. xc-xcii und Ps. cxlvi-cl) konnte die Bezugnahme mehrerer Psalmen aufeinander als Ordnungsprinzip des Redaktors wahrscheinlich gemacht werden. Das ermutigt dazu, der redaktionsgeschichtlichen Fragestellung noch mehr Aufmerksamkeit zu schenken.[69] Auch wenn von vornherein mit zahlreichen Fehlanzeigen gerechnet werden muß, sollte dennoch bei der Exegese eines Einzelpsalms die Frage nach seiner Einordnung in den redaktionellen Zusammenhang nicht vernachlässigt werden.

(3) Für den Psalter in seiner redigierten Endgestalt konnte ein gegenüber dem liturgischen Gebrauch veränderter Sitz im Leben ausgemacht werden. Er war für das Verständnis der Psalmen in den Kreisen von Belang, die Lehre und Leben der Spätzeit des Alten Testamentes bzw. der Frühzeit des Judentums maßgeblich geprägt haben. Auch der Umgang mit den Psalmen, wie ihn die neutestamentlichen Schriftsteller selbstverständlich voraussetzen, zeichnet sich hier bereits ab. Dieser Verständniswandel sollte aber auch bei der Psalmenauslegung berücksichtigt werden; die Auslegung darf sich nicht einseitig auf eine—oft nur hypothetisch zu erschließende—Urgestalt stützen. Die Überlieferungs- und Interpretationsgeschichte der Psalmen bis hin zu ihrem Platz im kanonischen Psalter ist als innerbiblischer Vorgang zu werten und zu beachten. Keiner Phase des Überlieferungsgeschehens kann von vornherein die allein maßgebliche Bedeutung zugesprochen werden.

(4) Möglicherweise kann im Ergebnis unserer Untersuchung auch ein Beitrag zur Erhellung der Kanongeschichte gefunden werden. Wenn die Kreise, in denen die Redaktion des Psalters entstand, in ihm bereits Jahwes Torah suchten und fanden und darum den Psalter als "Gotteswort" als Gegenstand des Studiums und der Meditation empfahlen, dann bezeugt dies das "kanonische" Ansehen, das die Psalmen zu dieser Zeit bereits besaßen. Andererseits hat der Aspekt des Gotteswortes, den die Redaktoren dem Psalter gaben, für die Rezeption des nunmehr entstandenen Buches in den werdenden Kanon vielleicht ebenso große Bedeutung gehabt, wie die Verwendung der Psalmen im Kult.

---

[69] Vgl. die Hinweise von Zimmerli (s. Anm. 55), S. 105 f.

PRIESTERTHEOLOGIE UND PRIESTERSCHRIFT

Zur Eigenart der priesterlichen Schicht im Pentateuch

von

MAGNE SAEBØ

Oslo

I

Seit dem vorigen Kongress — in Göttingen — hat Julius Wellhausens epochemachende Darstellung *Prolegomena zur Geschichte Israels*, die im Jahr 1878 unter dem Namen *Geschichte Israels*, *I* erschienen ist, ihr hundertjähriges Jubiläum feiern können.[1] Dies ist nun kein beliebiges Jubiläum. Denn der lange Schatten dieses Gelehrten, der — nach den Worten von Rudolf Smend — der "grösste deutsche Alttestamentler der Vergangenheit" ist,[2] und die nachhaltige Auswirkung seines Grosswerks der *Prolegomena* reichen bis in unsere Mitte hinein. Doch gewiss, zwischen ihm und uns steht eine Reihe namhafter Gelehrten, die auf je ihre Weise die Erforschung des Alten Testaments um grosse Schritte vorwärts gebracht haben; was die Arbeit am Pentateuch betrifft, sind besonders andere deutsche Alttestamentler wie Hermann Gunkel und Hugo Gressman, Gerhard von Rad und Martin Noth zu nennen. Es dürfte aber weder müssig noch unsachgemäss sein, nun über diese — und noch andere — hinaus auf Wellhausen zurückzugreifen; denn neben ihnen allen steht er. Zudem wird wohl das Werk Wellhausens als der wichtigste Treffpunkt jüdischer und christlicher Bibelforscher gelten können; denn sowohl ältere jüdische Exegeten wie David Hoffmann, Benno Jacob, Umberto Cassuto und Yehezkel Kaufmann als auch heutige Kollegen wie Menahem Haran und Moshe Weinfeld haben sich vor

---

[1] Mit der 2. Ausgabe (Berlin, 1883) wurde der Titel zu *Prolegomena* etc. geändert. Vgl. noch Wellhausens skizzenhafte Darstellung *Geschichte Israels*, die im Jahr 1880 als Privatdruck erschien, und die nun von Rudolf Smend in Julius Wellhausen, *Grundrisse zum Alten Testament* (München, 1965), pp. 13-64, herausgegeben worden ist.

[2] P. 5. Zu einer Würdigung Wellhausens vgl. u.a. O. Eissfeldt, "Julius Wellhausen" (aus dem Jahr 1920, nun in) *Kl. Schr.* I (Tübingen, 1962), pp. 56-71; ders., *RGG*³ VI (1962), Sp. 1594 f. (mit Lit.); dazu L. Perlitt, *Vatke und Wellhausen*, *BZAW* 94 (Berlin, 1965).

allen mit ihm auseinandergesetzt[3]. Für eine erneute Beschäftigung mit Wellhausen — vielleicht sollte man nun in noch grösserem Ausmass seine Werke wieder lesen — ist jedoch die sachliche Begründung am wichtigsten; und dazu lädt die gegenwärtige Situation ein.

In der Forschung am Pentateuch heute, wo sich so Vieles in Veränderung und Gärung befindet, so dass "der neue Wein" die alten Methoden-Schläuche zu zerreissen droht, hat man das Augenmerk insonderheit auf den Jahwisten gerichtet. Mit dem Elohisten war es sowieso oft eine unsichere Sache.[4] Der Deuteronomist hat sich nunmehr verselbständigt und hat eine dominierende Stellung erreicht, die wohl vor einiger Zeit noch völlig undenkbar war.[5] Für den restlichen Tetrateuch Gen.-Num. (und vielleicht Teile von Josua) scheint dann der Jahwist "die feste Burg" geworden zu sein, in dessen Schatten die sog. Priesterschrift weithin stehen geblieben ist. Im Zusammenhang mit den schweren Attacken, die neuerdings Hans Heinrich Schmid und besonders Rolf Rendtorff gegen den Jahwisten geritten haben, scheint man ausserdem der Meinung zu sein, dass wenn nun der Jahwist als die "Hauptquelle" fallen sollte, dann die gesamte Urkundenhypothese auch noch fallen würde.[6]

[3] Vgl. nun M. Haran, *Biblical Research in Hebrew. A Discussion of its Character and Trends* (Jerusalem, 1970); ders., *Temples and Temple-Service in Ancient Israel. An Inquiry into the Character of Cult Phenomena and the Historical Setting of the Priestly School* (Oxford, 1978); M. Weinfeld, *Deuteronomy and the Deuteronomic School* (Oxford, 1972); ders., *Getting at the Roots of Wellhausen's Understanding of the Law of Israel. On the 100th Anniversary of the Prolegomena* (The Inst. for Adv. Studies. The Hebrew Univ. of Jerus., Report No. 14/79, Jerusalem, 1979). S. auch K.-J. Illman, "Modern judisk bibelforskning", *Nordisk Judaistik / Scandinavian Jewish Studies* 1 (1975), pp. 3-14.

[4] Vgl. etwa P. Volz / W. Rudolph, *Der Elohist als Erzähler. Ein Irrweg der Pentateuchkritik?*, *BZAW* 63 (Giessen, 1933), bes. pp. 135-42; S. Mowinckel, *Erwägungen zur Pentateuchquellenfrage* (Oslo, 1964, = *NTT* 65, [1964], pp. 1-138), pp. 59-118.

[5] Die Zahl der Untersuchungen zum Dtn/Dtr/Dtr.Geschichtswerk und besonders zur dtr. Theologie ist fast unüberschaubar geworden; viele segeln in Fahrwasser der Forschungen von Rads; als exempla instar omnium seien erwähnt L. Perlitt, *Bundestheologie im Alten Testament* (Neukirchen-Vluyn, 1969), sowie die Beiträge von F. Crüsemann, S. Herrmann, N. Lohfink, R. Rendtorff und R. Smend in H. W. Wolff (Hrsg.), *Probleme biblischer Theologie. Gerhard von Rad zum 70. Geburtstag* (München, 1971).

[6] R. Rendtorff, "Der 'Jahwist' als Theologe? Zum Dilemma der Pentateuchkritik", *Congress Volume: Edinburgh 1974*, *SVT* 28 (Leiden, 1975), pp. 158-66; ders., *Das überlieferungsgeschichtliche Problem des Pentateuch*, *BZAW* 147 (Berlin, 1976); H. H. Schmid, *Der sogenannte Jahwist. Beobachtungen und Fragen zur Pentateuchforschung*, (Zürich, 1976). Als Reaktion darauf sind u.a. zu erwähnen: E.

Dabei hat Rendtorff anhand sehr beachtlicher Gründe gegen die neuere oder "klassische" und bis heute weithin angenommene Urkundenhypothese (bzw. Vierquellen-theorie) sich vor allem mit von Rad und Noth auseinandergesetzt; in erster Linie ist ihnen vorgeworfen worden, dass sie trotz ihrer überlieferungsgeschichtlichen Methode an der Urkundenhypothese festgehalten haben. Mit dem "Vater" der klassischen Urkundenhypothese hat Rendtorff sich aber nicht direkt ins Gefecht eingelassen; und das braucht nicht eine Zufälligkeit zu sein. Bei Wellhausen ging es um weit mehr als nur die literarkritische Arbeitsweise, die übrigens auch Rendtorff nicht hat aufgeben wollen (*BZAW* 147, pp. 148 f.). Wellhausens Ausarbeitung bzw. Anwendung der Urkundenhypothese, bei der er — wie andere grosse Theologen einschliesslich der des Alten Testaments — sich als Sammler und Deuter zugleich erwies,[7] war in einer historischen Gesamtdeutung des Alten Testaments, seiner Religion wie seiner Geschichte, fest eingeordnet. "Wellhausen war Historiker", sagt Otto Eissfeldt treffend und fährt fort: "Er hat Blick gehabt für Einzelheiten, für die 'Antiquitäten'. Die einzelnen Perioden des Geschichtsverlaufs haben ihm in lebendigster Anschaulichkeit vor Augen gestanden... Aber das Ziel seines Forschens war immer dies, die grossen Linien der Entwicklung zu erschauen, die Hauptkräfte des Werdens zu erfassen ... Erfassung und Darstellung des inneren Kräftespiels eines Geschichtsverlaufs — das hat er immer erstrebt und immer erreicht. Geschichte ist ihm nicht Nebeneinander und Nacheinander von Ereignissen und Personen, Geschichte ist ihm ein Miteinander und Gegeneinander von Kräften und Ideen" (*Kl. Schr.* I, p. 69).

Nun ist Wellhausen öfter — und nicht ohne Grund — im Hinblick auf die philosophischen Voraussetzungen seiner Darstellung der historisch-religiösen Entwicklung in Israel eingeschätzt worden. Er war aber im höheren Ausmass Exeget und Historiker als Philosoph.[8]

Otto, "Stehen wir vor einem Umbruch in der Pentateuchkritik?", *VuF* 22 (1977), pp. 82-97; W. McKane's Besprechung von *BZAW* 147 in *VT* 28 (1978), pp. 371-82; mehrere Beiträge in *JSOT* 3 (1977), pp. 2-60; vgl. auch noch L. Schmidt, "Überlegungen zum Jahwisten", *EvTh* 37 (1977), pp. 230-47.

[7] Vgl. etwa H.-J. Kraus, *Geschichte der historisch-kritischen Erforschung des Alten Testaments* (Neukirchen Kr. Moers, 1956), p. 240: "Man wird nicht sagen dürfen, dass Wellhausen der geniale Entdecker neuer Fragestellungen, Methoden und Geschichtsaspekte ist. . . Die geniale Tat Wellhausens aber war die meisterhafte Verknüpfung verschiedenster Vorarbeiten zu einem scharfen und in sich geschlossenen Gesamtbild".

[8] Vgl. dazu nun v.a. L. Perlitt, *Vatke und Wellhausen. Geschichtsphilosophische*

Wenn auch philosophische Elemente verschiedener Art da sind, liegen jedoch die Schwerpunkte seiner Auffassung in seiner Deutung der alttestamentlichen Texte selbst. Wenn er bei seiner Deutung der Texte, deren Grundproblem ihm in der dominierenden Vorrangstellung des Gesetzes im Pentateuch lag, überdies noch mit einer schroffen Kontrastierung des älteren Israel zum jüngeren Judentum und mit einer Abwertung des Judentums und des in ihm siegenden Gesetzes endete, dann ist es aber durchaus verständlich, dass dies als eine radikale Herausforderung empfunden wurde, und zwar insonderheit bei jüdischen Lesern und Gelehrten. Die grundsätzliche Frage wird dabei eben die sein, ob oder inwieweit sich seine Sicht an den Texten wirklich bewahrheiten lässt. Nun hat neuerdings Weinfeld zur Erklärung der negativen Beurteilung des Gesetzes in den *Prolegomena* auf Ausführungen in Wellhausens frühere Buch über *Die Pharisäer und die Sadducäer* (Greifswald, 1874) hingewiesen.[9] Da gibt es gewiss Zusammenhänge, die zu beachten sind, doch reichen sie zu einer Begründung des Gesetzesverständnisses Wellhausens nicht aus. Wellhausen gründet seine Ansichten in den *Prolegomena* nicht auf spätere Phänomene, sondern — wiederum lässt sich das sagen — sie wurzeln in seiner Deutung alttestamentlicher Texte, und zwar nun solcher Texte, die sich in der sog. Priesterschrift befinden, oder die nahe mit ihr verbunden sind; und von denen wird gleich die Rede sein. Denn, wie er selbst in der Inhaltsangabe der *Prolegomena* sagt: "Um den Priesterkodex und seine geschichtliche Stellung handelt es sich" (*Prolegomena zur Geschichte Israels* [3. Ausg., Berlin, 1886], p. V). Will man nun in diesen — etwas vernachlässigten — Fragen um den Priesterkodex noch vorwärts kommen, scheint der Weg zunächst rückwärts zu führen, zurück in die Vergangenheit, um eben mit Wellhausens *Prolegomena* anzufangen — obwohl das alles einem Kreis wie diesem wohlbekannt erscheint; doch darf es dabei auch Unbeachtetes geben. So darf das Ereignis der *Prolegomena*-Feier dazu Anlass geben, einige wichtige Positionen innerhalb der modernen Priesterschriftforschung unter Bezugnahme auf die ältere bei Wellhausen kritisch zu überprüfen.

II

Für die sog. Priesterschrift hat es in der modernen Forschung

Voraussetzungen und historiographische Motive für die Darstellung der Religion und Geschichte Israels durch Wilhelm Vatke und Julius Wellhausen, *BZAW* 94 (Berlin, 1965), bes. pp. 153 ff.

[9] *Getting at the Roots* (s. Anm. 3 oben), pp. 3 ff.

eigentlich nur einen Wendepunkt gegeben, und der liegt in den *Prolegomena* von Wellhausen. Er ist von der älteren These einer elohistischen "Grundschrift" ausgegangen, die in "Leviticus nebst den verwandten Teilen der angrenzenden Bücher, Exod. 25-40 mit Ausnahme von Kap. 32-34, und Num. 1-10. 15-19. 25-36 mit geringen Ausnahmen" ihren "Grundstock" hat, und die darum — wie er später sagt — "nach ihrem Inhalt und Ursprung der Priesterkodex zu heissen verdient" (pp. 7 u. 9). In bezug auf Wellhausens Umdatierung des Priesterkodex in nachexilische Zeit, also auf seinen Anschluss an die These der *lex post prophetas*, werden gewöhnlich seine Vorgänger Eduard Reuss und Karl Heinrich Graf genannt, wie auch Wellhausen selber tut (p. 4); doch ist sein weiterer Fingerzeig auf Vorgänger weithin unbeachtet geblieben, und zwar sein Hinweis auf Wilhelm Martin Leberecht de Wette und seine zweibändige *Beiträge zur Einleitung in das Alte Testament*.[10] Will man die *Prolegomena* recht einschätzen können, soll man sie nur an die Seite der *Beiträge* von de Wette legen. Da bekommt das Chronik-Kapitel der *Prolegomena* geradezu eine Schlüsselposition für Wellhausens kritische Auffassung und Darstellung der Geschichte Israels, so wie sie aus der durch das Gesetz beherrschten "mosaischen Geschichte" zu erheben ist. Denn wie de Wette zu seiner "Kritik der Bücher Mose als Quelle der Geschichte" — wie der Hauptteil des zweiten Bandes seiner *Beiträge* betitelt ist — durch eine kritische Untersuchung der Chronik und ihrer besonderen Geschichtsschreibung — im ersten Band der *Beiträge* — geführt worden ist, so scheint Wellhausen denselben Weg gegangen zu sein, zumal er im Jahr 1870 seine akademische Laufbahn mit einer Dissertation über die Juda-Genealogie in 1 Chr. ii und iv angetreten hat.[11] Denn bei den beiden Forschern "bildet die Chronik das Einfallstor zu einer historischen Kritik der Geschichte Israels", wie Thomas Willi in seinem beachtenswerten Buch über die Chronik mit Recht ausge-

---

[10] Von den *Beiträgen* umfasst Bd 1 (Halle, 1806) zunächst eine "Historisch-kritische Untersuchung über die Bücher der Chronik", pp. 1-132, darauf folgen "Resultate für die Geschichte der Mosaischen Bücher und Gesetzgebung", pp. 133-299; und Bd 2, *Kritik der Israelitischen Geschichte* (Halle, 1807), identisch mit dessen *Erster Theil. Kritik der Mosaischen Geschichte*, umfasst zunächst "Maximen" (in bezug auf seine Hermeneutik und Geschichtsschreibung, pp. 1-18), sodann den Hauptteil "Kritik der Bücher Mose als Quelle der Geschichte" (pp. 19-408), der ein fortlaufender Durchgang des ganzen Pentateuch ist, und der durch "Resultate und Bemerkungen" (pp. 396-408) abgeschlossen ist. Repr. Nachdruck beider Bände Darmstadt 1970. Vgl. sonst *Prolegomena*, p. 4.

[11] *De gentibus et familiis Judaeis quae I Chr. 2.4. enumerantur*, Diss. lic. theol. (Göttingen, 1870). Vgl. *Prolegomena*, p. 223.

führt hat und dabei ein Wort Wellhausens über seine Abhängigkeit von de Wette auch noch erwähnt, und zwar dieses: "Was ich im alten Testament gemacht habe, steht ja alles schon bei ihm".[12] Nun, anders als sein grosses Vorbild hat Wellhausen für die Spätdatierung des Priesterkodex Anerkennung erstrebt — und gewonnen.

Was sich dann für diese Forscher aus der Nähe des Priesterkodex zur Chronik — oder eher umgekehrt — klar ergibt, ist vor allem die späte geschichtliche Konstruktion in beiden Werken. "Von einer Tradition aus vorexilischer Zeit kann also in der Chronik nicht die Rede sein", sagt etwa Wellhausen, "weder in I. 1-9 noch in I. 10 — II. 36", also in der gesamten Chronik nicht (*Prolegomena*, p. 229). "In dem Gesamtbilde, welches sie malt, spiegelt sich ihre eigene Gegenwart, nicht das Altertum wieder" (p. 217). Dieser generelle Satz Wellhausens wurde fast zu einem Dogma in der literarkritischen Schule, was die Geschichtlichkeit der Chronik betrifft.[13] Denn auf der Grundlage des Gesetzes dichtet die Chronik die Tatsachen der Vergangenheit um "und denkt sich das alte hebräische Volk genau nach dem Muster der späteren jüdischen Gemeinde" (p. 195). Und "der Unterschied im Geist der Zeiten beruht auf dem inzwischen eingetretenen Einfluss des Priesterkodex" (p. 176, vgl. auch p. 378). Also, dem Gang der Entwicklung nach: so wie der Priesterkodex, so auch die Chronik. Wellhausen hatte aber den methodologischen Griff vorgenommen, mit der späteren, der Chronik, anzufangen, um so — die Entwicklung zurückrollend — durch sie den Ort des Priesterkodex historisch einpeilen zu können.

Damit ist auch schon etwas zum innern Verhältnis zwischen den geschichtlich/erzählerischen und den direkt legislativen Elementen im Priesterkodex selbst gesagt worden, das ist eine um so wichtigere Frage, als Wellhausen die Endredaktion des Hexateuchs auf den Priesterkodex zurückführt (pp. 393 ff.). In der schon anvisierten Perspektive scheint allerdings die Möglichkeit wahrer Geschichtserzählung hier nicht allzu gross zu sein. "Scheidet man nun ausser dem Deuteronomium auch diese Grundschrift [also: den Priesterkodex] aus", sagt Wellhausen, "so bleibt das jehovistische Geschichtsbuch übrig, welches im Gegensatz zu jenen beiden wesentlich erzäh-

---

[12] *Die Chronik als Auslegung. Untersuchungen zur literarischen Gestaltung der historischen Überlieferung Israels* (Göttingen, 1972), p. 44, vgl. pp. 33 ff.

[13] Nähere Nachweise in dem Art.: M. Saebø, "Chronistische Theologie/ Chronistisches Geschichtswerk", in der *Theol. Realenzyklopädie* VIII, pp. 74-87.

lender Natur ist und den Überlieferungsstoff recht mit Behagen ausbreitet". Legislative Elemente gibt es da nur an einer Stelle, und zwar in Ex. xx-xxiii und in xxxiv (p. 7). Der Priesterkodex dagegen "erdrückt alsbald die Erzählung durch die Last des legislativen Stoffes" (p. 357), der in ihm das dominierende Element ist. "*Historisch ist nur die Form, sie dient dem gesetzlichen Stoff als Rahmen um ihn anzuordnen, oder als Maske um ihn zu verkleiden. Gewöhnlich ist der Faden der Erzählung sehr dünn*" (p. 7). "Es ist als ob P der rote Faden sei, an dem die Perlen von JE aufgereiht werden" (p. 345). So umfasst also der Priesterkodex sowohl einen dünnen Erzählungsfaden, der aber als Verbindungselement noch für den JE und den gesamten Hexateuch Bedeutung erhält, als auch, andererseits, eine grosse Anhäufung gesetzlichen Materials in der Mitte des Pentateuchs, oder — wie Wellhausen und andere sagen — des Hexateuchs. In einer seiner späteren Darstellungen kann Wellhausen den Sachverhalt auch so formulieren: "Der Priesterkodex in seiner gegenwärtigen Form und Grösse weist nicht die planvolle Gliederung und strenge Construktion auf, wodurch sich Q [= quatuor, als Abkürzung für das erzählende "Vierbundesbuch"] auszeichnet, es ist ein Conglomerat, worin sich an einen ursprünglichen Kern (= Q) andere Schichten in gleichartiger Krystallisation angesetzt haben".[14]

An der letzten Stelle scheint Wellhausen einen ergänzenden Wachstumsprozess anzunehmen. Aber auch so ist ihm offenbar sehr daran gelegen, bei der geradezu überwältigenden Dominanz des legislativen Materials im Priesterkodex ihm doch noch einen Erzählungsfaden nachweisen zu können. So hat es den Anschein, dass sich diese besondere Quelle nur auf diese Weise — also als eine geschichtliche Quelle — neben den übrigen Quellen recht einordnen lässt. Wellhausen — der sonst öfter eine beissende Feder haben konnte — drückt sich aber in diesem Punkt bemerkenswert vorsichtig aus, was wohl als ein Anzeichen der grossen Schwierigkeit dieser Sache aufgefasst werden darf. Seit Theodor Nöldekes *Untersuchungen*[15] aus dem Jahr 1869 ist man im grossen ganzen über die Ausscheidung der Texte, also über den grösseren Umfang des Priesterkodex, einig gewesen. Das eigentliche — und heikle — Problem ist aber das der Sonderung und der näheren Bestimmung des Materials innerhalb des

---

[14] *Die Composition des Hexateuchs und der historischen Bücher des Alten Testaments* (Berlin, [2]1889), p. 137; vgl. p. 3.

[15] *Untersuchungen zur Kritik des Alten Testaments* (Kiel, 1869); Teil 1: "Die s.g. Grundschrift des Pentateuchs", pp. 1-144; hier bes. pp. 143 f.

Priesterkodex; oder auch noch anders ausgedrückt, es ist die Frage — die wirkliche Kernfrage des Sachfeldes — was nun eigentlich die Grösse "Priesterkodex", oder wie es nunmehr heisst: "Priesterschrift", sei bzw. sein darf.

Wenn man sich sodann im Blick auf diese Spitzenfrage von Wellhausen her an vielen anderen Literarkritikern vorbei zu neueren Forschern auf dem Gebiet des Pentateuch/Hexateuch bewegt, wird man sowohl die lange Nachwirkung der einschlägigen Ansätze bei Wellhausen als auch neuere und recht bemerkenswerte Akzent-Verschiebungen, und insofern eine gewisse neue Tendenz, wahrnehmen können. Dabei kann man übrigens eine terminologische Zwischenbemerkung machen, und zwar die, dass schon der Wechsel von der Bezeichnung "Priesterkodex", die Wellhausen — wie schon erwähnt wurde — im Blick auf den legislativen "Grundstock" vorgeschlagen hat, zu der neutraleren Bezeichnung "Priesterschrift" — vielleicht etwas überraschend — eben ein Ausdruck dieser neuen Tendenz sein kann. Nun, während bei Wellhausen zwischen den erzählerischen und den legislativen Elementen im Priesterkodex noch ein gewisses Gleichgewicht bestand, *ist die neue Tendenz vor allem darin erkennbar, dass das Hauptgewicht jetzt mehr oder weniger einseitig auf den erzählerisch/geschichtlichen Teil gelegt wird*; und in diesem Fall würde ja die alte Bezeichnung "Priesterkodex" nicht gut passen.[16]

Wenn man sich nun zunächst an Otto Eissfeldts *Hexateuch-Synopse* (1922) wendet, findet man, dass er sie nur auf die Erzählungsfäden der Quellen konzentriert hat, während alle Abschnitte gesetzlichen Inhalts beiseite gelassen sind.[17] Das könnte allerdings etwa aus Raumgründen praktisch begründet sein. Ganz anders ist aber der Sachverhalt in den wichtigen Arbeiten von Martin Noth aus den Jahren 1943 und 1948 [18] und in Karl Elligers bekannter Studie "Sinn und Ursprung der priesterlichen Geschichtserzählung" (1952) sowie in seinem sehr beachtenswerten Kommentar zu Leviticus aus dem Jahr 1966.[19] Richtungsweisend ist wohl dabei vor allem Noth gewesen, aber auf andere Weise auch Elliger.

[16] Vgl. M. Noth, *Überlieferungsgeschichte des Pentateuch* (Stuttgart, 1948; Stuttgart und Darmstadt, ²1960), p. 9: "Man sollte sie [d.h. die von Noth sonst sogenannte "P-Erzählung"] mit irgendeiner neutralen Bezeichnung versehen".

[17] *Hexateuch-Synopse. Die Erzählung der fünf Bücher Mose und des Buches Josua mit dem Anfange des Richterbuches*. . . (Leipzig, 1922; Darmstadt, ²1962), p. xi.

[18] *Überlieferungsgeschichtliche Studien* (Halle, 1943; Tübingen und Darmstadt, ²1957); s. sonst Anm. 16 oben.

[19] "Sinn. . .", *ZThK* 49 (1952), pp. 121-43, nun in ders., *Kleine Schriften zum Alten Testament* (München, 1966), pp. 174-98; ders., *Leviticus* (Tübingen, 1966).

In seinen *Überlieferungsgeschichtliche Studien* (1943) hat Noth im Anhang den Umfang der P-Erzählung, die sonst die literarische Grundlage des Pentateuch bildet, auf Gen.-Num. (samt Dtn. xxxiv *1, 7-9) beschränkt und ihr damit eine fortsetzende Landnahme-Erzählung in Josua abgeschnitten (pp. 180-211 — darin anders etwa S. Mowinckel,[20] was aber hier auf sich beruhen muss). Sodann hat er in seiner *Überlieferungsgeschichte des Pentateuch* (1948) nachzuweisen versucht, dass "P seiner Gesamtanlage nach ein *Erzählungswerk* ist", und dass dies "noch ausschliesslicher, als gemeinhin angenommen zu werden pflegt", aufzufassen sei (p. 7; die Heraushebung von Noth). Denn mit diesem Erzählungswerk haben die "gesetzlichen Partien ... die zwar das ausgesprochen kultisch-rituelle Interesse und daher auch eine bestimmte, in jerusalemisch-priesterlichen Kreisen beheimatete Sprache und Terminologie mit der P-Erzählung teilen, aber *literarisch mit dieser von Hause aus nichts zu tun*" (ebd.; die Heraushebung von mir). Wenn Noth sodann folgert, dass sich die P "damit viel entschiedener und eindeutiger eben als eine *Erzählung*" erweist (p. 9; die Heraushebung von Noth), charakterisiert Rendtorff diese Schlussfolgerung — mit vollem Recht — als "einen erstaunlichen Zirkelschluss" (*Das überlieferungsgeschichtliche Problem*, p. 112).

Noth scheint allerdings gewisse Schwierigkeiten gespürt zu haben, vor allem wenn es um eine genauere Bestimmung der Theologie der P-Erzählung geht, er hat aber seine Sicht konsequent durchgeführt. Trotz ihrer Bezeichnung ist die "Priesterschrift" kein "ausgesprochenes Priesterwerk"; wenn ihr Verfasser ein Priester sein sollte, "so ist doch der Geist seines Werkes nicht eben unbedingt priesterlich" (*Überlieferungsgeschichte*, p. 260). Ihren Schwerpunkt hat die Theologie der P in der Sinai-*Erzählung*, die über "die Eröffnung des legitimen Kultes" und "damit die Konstitution der zwölf israelitischen Stämme als Kultgemeinde" berichtet. Dabei ist es aber unzweifelhaft, "dass sich darin die allgemeine und nicht etwa nur speziell priesterliche Vorstellung vom rechten Gottesdienst in der Spätzeit, aus der die P-Erzählung stammt, ausspricht" (pp. 262-3). Es ist doch sehr erstaunlich, wie Noth bei dieser theologischen Deutung der P-Erzählung in einem weiten Bogen um alles Kultische und Priesterliche herumgeht; sollte auch an dieser Stelle vielleicht das Erbe von Wellhausens *Prolegomena* sich ausgewirkt haben? Denn gegen Ende seiner

---

[20] *Tetrateuch - Pentateuch - Hexateuch. Die Berichte über die Landnahme in den drei altisraelitischen Geschichtswerken, BZAW* 90 (Berlin, 1964); vgl. sonst Anm. 4 oben.

Ausführungen bezeichnet Wellhausen den Kultus als "das heidnische Element in der israelitischen Religion... Wenn er nun im Priesterkodex zur Hauptsache gemacht wird, so scheint das einem systematischen Rückfall in das Heidentum gleichzukommen" (p. 442). So scharf und abwertend würde bestimmt kein neuerer Forscher den Kultus beurteilen, zumal die Arbeit von Sigmund Mowinckel und anderen eine gewaltige Gegenwirkung ausgeübt hat, — doch die *vestigia terrent*. Im Grunde handelt es sich wohl um die Macht des Systems der Urkundenhypothese, demzufolge die Priesterschrift ihre Existenzberechtigung grundsätzlich darin besitzt, sich als Erzählung und Geschichtswerk neben den anderen alten Geschichtswerken bzw. Erzählungsfäden erweisen zu können.

Die erwähnte Studie von Elliger über "Sinn und Ursprung der priesterlichen Geschichtserzählung" hat diesen Aspekt eigentlich nur noch gesteigert, indem er das Augenmerk schärfer auf die geschichtliche Situation des priesterlichen Geschichtserzählers, des Verfassers, gerichtet hat. Im grossen ganzen stimmt Elliger mit Noth in der Abgrenzung der priesterlichen Grundschrift, der sog. Pg, überein, auch darin, dass er die Landnahme-Erzählung in Josua ausscheidet (*Kl. Schr.*, pp. 174-5). Doch zieht Elliger ganz andere Konsequenzen daraus, und zwar sieht er das Thema der Landnahme in Kanaan auf dem Hintergrund der Exilsituation des priesterlichen Verfassers und seiner Adressaten in seiner Geschichtserzählung *transparent* vorhanden (pp. 184-9). "Noch im Exil befindet sich unser Zeuge. Von daher erklärt sich seine Zurückhaltung in kultischen Dingen", sagt Elliger, während er sonst mehrfach den Einschlag von "Verheissung" und "Erfüllung" in der priesterlichen Geschichtserzählung hervorhebt. So rückt Elliger die Priesterschrift einigermassen in die Nähe der Erzählungsweise des J bzw. JE und in die Nähe der späteren Propheten. Zur abschliessenden Charakteristik der priesterlichen Geschichtserzählung sagt Elliger: "Sie ist im babylonischen Exil entstanden als tröstendes und mahnendes Zeugnis von dem wundermächtig-überlegenen, herrlich-huldvollen Gott der Verheissung, dem Herrn der Weltgeschichte und in Sonderheit der Geschichte Israels, deren Ziel unverrückbar bleibt: ein grosses Volk, befreit zu ewigem Besitz des Landes Kanaan, und Gott der Gott dieses Volkes" (p. 198). Dazu könnte man eigentlich nur noch die schlichte Bemerkung machen: Und das soll besonders Priesterliches sein? Es scheint vielmehr die Stimme eines Propheten zu sein.

Nichtsdestoweniger hat Elliger keinen geringen Nachhall erhalten.

Man hat nun etwa von der "Hoffnung auf Heimkehr in der Priesterschrift" geredet.[21] Vor allem hat Walter Brueggemann in einem Versuch, das Kerygma des priesterlichen Verfassers näher zu bestimmen, Gen. i 28 auf dem Hintergrund der Exilsituation verstehen wollen,[22] während Sean E. McEvenue seinen besonderen Erzählungsstil untersucht hat.[23] Sehr beachtenswert war das Referat von Norbert Lohfink beim vorigen Kongress, wobei er dem Begriff der "Geschichte" in Verbindung mit der Priesterschrift sorgfältig nachgegangen ist.[24]

Immerhin, bei alledem wächst allmählich ein tiefer Zweifel heran. Und wer Ohren hat, hört schon bei namhaften Verfechtern des priesterlichen Geschichtswerkes selbst Äusserungen, die von einem schlechten Gewissen zeugen können. Es ist Einiges daran, das nicht ganz stimmt. Die Schwierigkeit Noths, die Theologie der P-Erzählung zu bestimmen, wurde schon erwähnt. Man wundert sich bei Elliger etwas über das viele Reden von "Transparenz" und "Hintergründigkeit" der priesterlichen Geschichtserzählung; und am Ende sagt er doch schlicht und einfach: "hier handelt es sich gar nicht um eigentliche Geschichtsschreibung... Vor allem hat sich herausgestellt, dass des Erzählers Interesse im Grunde nicht auf die geschichtlichen Vorgänge als solche, sondern auf die Glaubenswahrheiten geht, die er aus ihnen abliest" (p. 195). In seiner vorzüglichen Einführung in *Die Entstehung des Alten Testaments* sagt allerletzt Rudolf Smend, der offenbar nach einem gewissen Gleichgewicht der besprochenen Elemente strebt: "*Trotz allem* ist P ein *Erzählungswerk*, das, *in welcher Weise auch immer*, eine lange Folge von Ereignissen und Personen zum Gegenstand hat".[25] Der Abschnitt, der mit diesen Worten anfängt, endet mit dem folgenden Satz: "das Werk als ein Erzählungswerk droht aus den Fugen zu geraten" (p. 51). Gleichzeitig warnt Smend — mit Recht — vor "einer groben Alternative": "hier Erzählung, dort Gesetz", und fährt fort: "P will fraglos beides bieten, beides steht für ihn in einem engen und notwendigen Zusammenhang, beides färbt auch stark aufeinander ab" (p. 51). Darin ist Smend gewiss zuzu-

---

[21] R. Kilian, "Die Hoffnung auf Heimkehr in der Priesterschrift", *BiLeb* 7 (1966), pp. 39-51.

[22] "The Kerygma of the Priestly Writers", *ZAW* 84 (1972), pp. 397-414.

[23] *The Narrative Style of the Priestly Writer* (Roma, 1971).

[24] "Die Priesterschrift und die Geschichte", *Congress Volume: Göttingen 1977*, *SVT* 29 (Leiden, 1978), pp. 189-225.

[25] *Die Entstehung des Alten Testaments* (Stuttgart, 1978), pp. 49 f, (die mittlere Heraushebung vom Verf. selbst).

stimmen. Die weit schwierigere Frage ist aber die, welcher der beiden Teile der ursprüngliche und typische "Priesterliche" sei, ob also P "grundsätzlich" ein Geschichtswerk sei, in das das Gesetzliche und Kultische sekundär (als Ps) eingefügt ist, oder aber ob das Kultische und Gesetzliche — auch hier sollte noch präziser unterschieden werden — das besonders "Priesterliche" sei, das allmählich durch die Überlieferung ergänzt und erweitert, dabei auch geschichtlich eingeordnet und umrahmt worden ist. Beides gehört ohne Zweifel mit hinzu; es handelt sich aber hier um eine Frage der *Priorität. Diese Grundfrage haben die Literarkritiker durch die Urkundenhypothese sehr zugunsten des Geschichtlichen beantwortet*; ihre Lösung ist bis heute allgemein anerkannt worden und hat fast einen axiomatischen Wert erhalten. Die Frage drängt sich aber nun auf, ob nicht die Urkundenhypothese — von den älteren Geschichtswerken ausgehend — der kultischen Priestertradition etwas ihr Fremdes, sozusagen eine Zwangsjacke, aufgezwungen habe.

In diesem Zusammenhang ist die Behandlung der Priesterschrift in Gerhard von Rads *Theologie des Alten Testaments*[26] noch bemerkenswerter, als es beim ersten Anblick scheinen mag. Zunächst behandelt er, als ersten Punkt auf knappen drei Seiten, "Die Priesterschrift als Geschichtswerk"; er hält daran fest, betont aber den Unterschied sowohl zu D als auch zu JE. Das "echte theologische Anliegen der Geschichte" in P ist aber "sehr anderer Art als die der jehovistischen Geschichtsdarstellung. Der Gegenstand der Darstellung ist nicht... die verborgene Führung der Menschen..., sondern das Herauswachsen bestimmter kultischer Institutionen aus der Geschichte ... Wir haben es mit spezifisch preisterlichen Literatur zu tun, deren Wachstumsgesetze wir noch weniger kennen" (p. 246). Darauf folgt eine breit ausladende, fast 50 Seiten umfassende, Darstellung der *Theologie* der Priesterschrift, die mit dem Punkt über "Zelt, Lade und Herrlichkeit Gottes" anfängt, und die mit "Sünde und Sühne" sowie mit "Rein — unrein. Krankheit und Tod" endet (pp. 247-93).

In dieser Darstellung spürt man weithin dieselben Proportionen und dieselbe sachliche Konzentration wie im mittleren Pentateuch selbst; das Hauptgewicht hat *die priesterliche Kulttheologie*. Dabei besteht aber eigentlich die Möglichkeit einer ganz anderen Denkweise, einer anderen methodologischen Annäherungsweise zum

---

[26] I (München, [4]1962), pp. 245-93; vgl. auch ders., *Die Priesterschrift im Hexateuch* (Stuttgart, 1934).

Stoff als die der wellhausenschen Urkundenhypothese; denn man braucht nicht so sehr linear geschichtlich und entwicklungsmässig zu denken und den angenommenen Endpunkt so stark zu betonen, wie es bei Wellhausen der Fall war, sondern man kann *von einer Mitte her* den Stoff in dem Griff bekommen und ihn von da her entfalten, und zwar von der priesterlichen Kulttheologie her, deren innerster Kern *die Präsenz des — segnenden und sühnenden — heiligen Gottes* zu sein scheint. Der Stoff ist überaus vielgestaltig und hat eine mehrschichtige Geschichte durchgemacht, der in ihren Schichtungen und Stadien nachzugehen ist. Dazu gehören schliesslich auch die Verzahnungen mit den heilsgeschichtlichen Überlieferungen. Wie sich das ausgewirkt hat, lässt sich bei dieser Gelegenheit beispielsweise an den Festkalendern kurz zeigen.

III

Wendet man sich nun an die sog. Festkalender, und zwar in Ex. xxiii 14-17, xxxiv 18, 22-23; Dtn. xvi 1-17; Lev. xxiii 4-44 samt Num. xxviii-xxix, wozu noch Ez. xlv 18-25 hinzukommen kann, greift man einen Themenkreis auf, dem zwar Wellhausen in seinen *Prolegomena* grosse Aufmerksamkeit gewidmet hat (pp. 84-121), der aber auf dem Hintergrund der neueren form- und traditionsgeschichtlichen Forschung aufs neue hätte untersucht werden müssen. Denn die Kalender sind nicht als eine besondere formelle und überlieferungsgeschichtliche Grösse, sozusagen als eine eigene Gattung, sondern fast nur in ihrem jeweiligen Kontext sowie in Verbindung mit einzelnen Festen erörtert worden;[27] eine monographische Behandlung würde eine beklagenswürdige Lücke ausfüllen können. Bei dieser Gelegenheit kann es sich nur um einige wenige und kurze Bemerkungen handeln.

Die Kalender sind so aufgezählt worden, wie sie traditionell den Quellen bzw. Traditionsschichten zugeschrieben werden, und zwar der erste und kürzeste in Ex. xxiii dem Bundesbuch — oder bei einigen dem E, dann Ex. xxxiv dem J, weiter Dtn. xvi dem D, Lev. xxiii dem H sowie Num. xxviii f. dem P. In dieser Weise werden sie aber isoliert, und das ihnen Gemeinsame, ihre Kontinuität, geht verloren. Sieht man sie dagegen in *synoptischer* Darstellung als eine beson-

---

[27] Wichtige Ansätze finden sich bei R. de Vaux, *Les institutions de l'Ancien Testament* II (Paris, 1960), pp. 366-70; H.-J. Kraus, *Gottesdienst in Israel* (München, ²1962), pp. 40-50; vgl. auch G. B. Gray, *Sacrifice in the Old Testament* (Oxford, 1925; New York, ²1971), pp. 271-84.

dere Grösse an, treten sowohl Gemeinsamkeiten wie Unterschiede klarer hervor; und eine recht kurze und einfache Basisform scheint ihnen zugrundezuliegen. Dieser Grundform kommt man in Ex. xxiii 14-17 am nächsten, wo es heisst:

> 14 Dreimal im Jahr sollst du mir ein Fest feiern (*tāḥōg*):
> 15 Das Massot-Fest (*ḥag hammaṣṣôt*) sollst du halten; sieben Tage lang sollst du ungesäuerte Brote essen, wie ich dir geboten habe, zur bestimmten Zeit im Monat Abib; denn in diesem Monat bist du aus Ägypten ausgezogen.
> Man soll nicht mit leeren Händen vor mir erscheinen.
> 16 Sodann das Fest der Kornernte (*w*^{e}*ḥag haqqāṣîr*), der Erstlinge deines Ertrages von der Aussaat, mit der du das Feld bestelltest,
> und das Fest der Lese (*w*^{e}*ḥag hāʾāsip*) beim Herausgehen des Jahres, wenn du deinen Ertrag vom Felde einsammelst.
> 17 Dreimal im Jahr sollen alle deine männlichen Personen vor dem Herrn Jahwe erscheinen.[28]

Dieser Kalender — wie die übrigen — ist fast an jeder Ecke mit Problemen beladen. In diesem Zusammenhang ist es in formeller Hinsicht zunächst interessant, dass die Bestimmungen in V. 14 und 17 einen Rahmen in positiv-apodiktischer Anrede haben, sodann dass die Bestimmungen über die Feste listenmässig aufgezählt sind, was sich daran zeigt, das die Nennung des zweiten Festes in V. 16a über die verschiedenen Elemente in 15aβb hinweg einfach mit *w*^{e}*ḥag* anfängt; so auch betreffs des dritten Festes in V. 16bα. Sachlich interessant ist die heilsgeschichtliche Begründung in V. 15b; ferner ist das Fehlen einer Erwähnung des Passah-Festes bemerkenswert. Trotz der vielen Einschübe in Ex. xxxiv 19-21 ist die in Ex. xxiii beobachtete Form auch im nächsten Kalender klar ersichtlich; hier liegen zudem noch einige terminologische Änderungen vor (wie etwa die Bezeichnung *ḥag šābūʿōt* für das zweite Fest, V. 22, wobei doch die Aufzählungsform durch *w*^{e}*ḥag* beibehalten ist). Diesen beiden gegenüber ist der dritte Kalender in Dtn. xvi sehr wortreich und hat den typisch ermahnenden Stil des Dtn. Auffallend ist hier vor allem, dass das Passah-Fest dominierend im Vordergrund steht; und nichtsdestoweniger endet der Kalender in V. 16 f., durch typisch dtn.

---

[28] Textliche und literarische Probleme können an dieser Stelle nicht erörtert werden.

Stoff erweitert, mit der Rahmen-Formel des "dreimal im Jahr" und nennt dabei das Passah-Fest nicht. Der vierte Kalender in Lev. xxiii und besonders der fünfte in Num. xxviii-xxix sind noch wortreicher, nun aber aufgrund vieler, ganz präziser Opferbestimmungen samt möglichst genauen kalendarischen Bestimmungen. Hier ist sonst die Form der Gottesrede an Mose vorherrschend. Anhand mehrerer Einleitungen sowie Abschlüsse in Lev. xxiii lässt sich ein allmähliches Wachsen im Kalender beobachten. — Und vieles mehr könnte noch erwähnt werden.

Nun aber einige grundsätzliche Erwägungen in bezug auf das oben kurz Behandelte. Wellhausen hat mit Recht in seinen *Prolegomena* eine Entwicklung im Stoff gesehen. Wenn er aber die Stoffe auf eine ganz bestimmte Entwicklungslinie im Rahmen einer Reihe von Quellenschriften fest eingeordnet hat, erheben sich aber Fragen, inwieweit dieses Verfahren dem Stoff sachgemäss ist. Man könnte dabei etwa fragen: Sind nicht die kultischen Bestimmungen in Ex. xxiii oder gar in Dtn. xvi ebenso "priesterlich" wie die in Lev. und Num.? Handelt es sich nicht vielmehr auf dem ganzen Weg um ein durchaus *priesterliches* Überlieferungsmaterial, das aber zu verschiedenen Zeiten und bei verschiedenen Gelegenheiten — sogar in einem prophetischen Kontext wie Ez. xlv — auch verschiedene Gestalten gewinnen konnte? Ein entwickeltes Opfersystem braucht auch nicht spät datiert zu werden; denn ein solches hat es gewiss auch im Tempeldienst der Königszeit gegeben. Die verschiedenen Kalender mögen dabei verschiedenen Absichten gedient haben. Die kürzeren Kalender in Ex. sowie der predigtartige im Dtn. scheinen mehr dem Volk, den Laien, zugewandt zu sein, während die längeren und komplizierten in Lev. und besonders Num. im höheren Mass von einem besonderen priesterlichen Berufswissen zeugen; sie sind — wenn man will — "gelehrter".[29] Aber sie nur aus diesem Grunde einer eigenen "Priesterschrift" zuerkennen zu wollen, leuchtet nicht ohne weiteres ein, eher im Gegenteil.

Einige haben sich denn auch gegen die Sicht der vielen zitierten Literarkritiker geäussert. Man darf dabei das Ohr den Worten eines namhaften Repräsentanten der kritischen AT-Forschung wie Johannes Hempel leihen, der in seinem Pauly-Wissowa-Artikel zum "Priesterkodex" sagt: "Wir haben es bei P nicht mit einem schrift-

---

[29] Vgl. dazu noch R. Rendtorff, *Die Gesetze in der Priesterschrift* (Göttingen, [2]1963), etwa p. 77, sowie K. Koch, *Die Priesterschrift von Exodus 25 bis Leviticus 16* (Göttingen, 1959).

lichen Erzählungswerk zu tun, das selbst aus durchlaufenden Quellsträngen zusammengefügt und durch sekundäre Einsätze erweitert worden wäre. Vielmehr ist P in mehreren Stufen aus der mündlichen Unterweisung der Laien oder auch der Novizen durch eine Priesterschaft zu verstehen, welche die rechte 'Erkenntnis' Jahwes und seines Willens zu ihrem Ziele hat und in einzelnen 'Lektionen' verläuft".[30] Auf mehr oder weniger ähnliche Weise haben sich früher Johs. Pedersen [31] und Ivan Engnell,[32] später etwa Artur Weiser [33] sowie neuerdings Haran und Weinfeld (s. Anm. 3 oben), Rolf Rendtorff und auch Ronald E. Clements [34] geäussert; hier werden die Altertümlichkeit des Stoffes oder die Existenz einer längeren, besonderen Priestertradition bzw. Priesterschule betont.

Ohne dass man notwendigerweise die Existenz eines Priesterkodex bzw. einer Priesterschrift direkt bestreiten muss, lässt sich also Einiges — und viel mehr könnte noch erwähnt werden — aufzeigen, das für eine Akzent-Verschiebung in entgegengesetzter Richtung als der heute üblichen spricht, und zwar *eine Akzent-Verschiebung weg von der nun lange beliebten Betonung des Erzählerischen und Geschichtlichen in der Priestertradition, wonach die Priesterschrift grundsätzlich als ein Geschichtswerk verstanden wird, zum Kultisch-Rituellen und Gesetzlichen der Priestertraditionen als ihrem Proprium*. Das führt nun weiter auf die besondere *Priestertheologie* als ihre Mitte, die das alles trägt; von ihr soll nun abschliessend — zur Ausfüllung und Abrundung zugleich kurz die Rede sein.

IV

Lange Zeit schon hat es eine lebhafte Debatte über Grundlage und Gestalt, Sinn und Ziel einer alttestamentlichen Theologie gegeben. Auch bei dieser Debatte hat die "Geschichte" bzw. haben geschichtliche Gesichtspunkte eine erhebliche Rolle gespielt. Das habe ich bei anderer Gelegenheit diskutiert und dabei auch neue Gesichtspunkte

---

[30] *PRE* XXII, col. 1943-67; das Zitat col. 1965.

[31] "Die Auffassung vom Alten Textament", *ZAW* 49 (1931), pp. 161-81; ders., "Passahfest und Passahlegende", *ZAW* 52 (1934), pp. 161-75.

[32] *Gamla Testamentet. En traditionshistorisk inledning* I (Stockholm, 1945), pp. 168-259; ders., *Critical Essays on the Old Testament* (London, 1970), bes. pp. 3-11 u. 50-67, sowie Artikel in *SBU* (bes. 2. Aufl., 1962-3).

[33] *Einleitung in das Alte Testament* (Göttingen, [5]1963), pp. 124-30.

[34] Zu R. Rendtorff s. oben Anm. 6. Sonst R. E. Clements, "Pentateuchal Problems", in G. W. Anderson (Hrsg.), *Tradition and Interpretation* (Oxford, 1979), pp. 96-124. — Zur früheren Kritik s. etwa Volz (Anm. 4 oben).

einzuführen versucht, und zwar milieugeschichtliche, indem nach den Beziehungen der wichtigsten Haupttypen alttestamentlicher Theologie zu entsprechenden Kreisen von Theologen im alten Israel gefragt wurde; das alles kann aber hier nicht entfaltet werden.[35] Es sei jedoch erwähnt, dass in erster Linie zwischen drei Haupttypen alttestamentlicher Theologie unterschieden werden darf, und zwar zwischen einer *geschichtsbezogenen Heilstheologie*, die vor allem in einmaligen Grosstaten Gottes ihren Gegenstand hatte, und sodann einer *Ordnungsthologie* bzw. Schöpfungstheologie der Weisen sowie endlich einer *Kulttheologie* (bzw. kultbezogenen Heilstheologie) der Priester, die hier von besonderem Interesse ist.[36]

Auch eine weitere Erörterung der besonderen Kulttheologie der Priester, die auch über historischen Bücher hinausreicht — man denke etwa an die Psalmen — kann bei dieser Gelegenheit nicht vorgenommen werden. Immerhin, die Hauptsache oder das Proprium der priesterlichen Kulttheologie lässt sich doch festlegen; ihre Hauptsache — da wo ihr Herz am stärksten schlägt — ist *die Gegenwart, die Präsenz, der göttlichen Herrlichkeit, in welcher Form sie auch geschieht, das heilbringende Licht des heiligen und gnädigen, segnenden Gottes, und zwar am heiligen Ort, wo die heiligen Riten des Kultus ausgeführt werden.*[37] Von der Mitte der priesterlichen Kulttheologie her relativieren sich einigermassen die gegenwärtigen literarkritischen Positionen, was den Priesterkodex bzw. der Priesterschrift betrifft. Es lässt sich auch sagen, dass, wer den Wald des religiösen Hintergrundes im Kultus vor den vielen Bäumen der mancherlei kultischen Bestimmungen und

[35] "Hvem var Israels teologer? Om struktureringen av 'den gammeltestamentlige teologi' ", *SEÅ* 41-2 (1976-77), pp. 189-205 (Ringgren-FS), nun in Saebø, *Ordene og Ordet. Gammeltestamentlige studier* (Oslo, 1979), pp. 25-41. Die hier nur angedeuteten Gesichtspunkte, die ich seit Jahren in Vorlesungen vorgeführt habe, und die ich im April 1978 in drei Gastvorlesungen in der Divinity School der Universität Cambridge einigermassen entfalten durfte, gedenke ich in einer eigenen Veröffentlichung näher zu begründen.

[36] Zur letzteren vgl. etwa Haran; s. Anm. 3 oben.

[37] Vgl. oben Abschnitt II, Ende. Eine ausführlichere Begründung kann aus Raumgründen hier nicht geschehen. Die priesterliche Theologie hat man sonst sehr unterschiedlich beschrieben; vgl. etwa C. Westermann, "Die Herrlichkeit Gottes in der Priesterschrift", *AThANT* 59 (Zürich, 1971), pp. 227-49 (Eichrodt-FS), nun in Westermann, *Forschung am Alten Testament. Ges. Stud.* II (München, 1974), pp. 115-37; W. Zimmerli, "Sinaibund und Abrahambund. Ein Beitrag zum Verständnis der Priesterschrift", *EvTh* 16 (1960), pp. 268-80, nun in Zimmerli, *Gottes Offenbarung* (München, 1969), pp. 205-16; E. Cortese, "La teologia del Documento Sacerdotale", *Rivista Biblica* 26 (1978), pp. 113-37, der die Theologie von Pg und von Ps gesondert behandelt.

Gesetze nicht sieht, weder den israelitischen Kultus noch die alttestamentliche Religion und Theologie recht verstanden oder eingeschätzt hat — so wie es im gewissen Ausmass in den *Prolegomena* von Julius Wellhausen doch der Fall war. Bei ihm hat ja — wie schon erwähnt — das Kultisch/Rituelle die "wahre Religion" des Alten Testaments, so wie er sie verstanden hat, in den Untergang gebracht (p. 442).

V

Es wurde mit dem hundertjährigen Jubiläum von Wellhausens *Prolegomena zur Geschichte Israels* angefangen; und nun sind wir am Ende bei ihnen auch gelandet. Mehrfach war in dem Obigen von der immensen Auswirkung dieses Werkes die Rede. Man lässt sich dabei gerne an die Schlussworte von Eissfeldts Wellhausen-Artikel aus dem Jahre 1920 erinnern, wo er sagt: "Wellhausen gehört nicht der Vergangenheit an. Er wirkt in der Gegenwart, und er hat auch dem kommenden Geschlechte viel zu geben" ([s. Anm. 2 oben] p. 71).

Und doch möchte man die Frage noch hinzufügen: Ist es nun nicht an der Zeit, von dem Hundertjährigen aufzubrechen? Es würde dem alten Wahrheits-Sucher Wellhausen gewiss eine hohe Ehre sein, nun weiter und in neuen Formen die Wahrheit der biblischen Texte zu suchen.

AUF DER SUCHE NACH NEUEN PERSPEKTIVEN FÜR DIE PENTATEUCHFORSCHUNG

VON

HANS HEINRICH SCHMID

Zürich

I. Der gegenwärtige Neuaufbruch in der Pentateuchforschung

Seit mehr als hundert Jahren gehört die Quellentheorie—weitgehend unbestritten—zu den Grundlagen der Pentateuchforschung. Es scheint, dass diese Aera ihrem Ende entgegengeht. In jüngster Zeit ist jedenfalls eine bereits beträchtliche Anzahl von Aufsätzen und Monographien erschienen, die nicht mehr nur bisherige Forschungsarbeit verfeinern und Einzelfragen weiter klären, sondern auf eine Überprüfung der Grundlagen der Pentateuchforschung insgesamt zielen. In aller Regel münden sie aus in eine mehr oder weniger explizite Kritik der Quellentheorie.

"Re-examining the foundations" [1]—das war die Parole, mit der im Dezember 1964 F. V. Winnett vor die Society of Biblical Literature trat—und "Re-examining the foundations"—das ist der Anspruch, den diese neueren Publikationen gemeinsam erheben.

Wie ist es zu diesem Neuaufbruch in der Pentateuchforschung gekommen? Er hat sehr wohl seine Gründe: Die Pentateuchforschung hat—gerade in ihrem Umgang mit der Quellentheorie—in zahlreiche Spannungen geführt.

Es ergaben sich Spannungen innerhalb der Quellentheorie selbst. Zwar war man sich einig: Es ist mit Quellen, mit J, E, D und P, zu rechnen. Doch in der Beschreibung dieser Quellen geriet man in Kontradiktionen. Sind sie Zulieferer von "Stoffen" oder Sammlungen geprägter Überlieferung? Bieten sie Sage, Geschichtsschreibung oder theologische Reflexion? Stehen hinter ihnen einzelne Schriftstellerpersönlichkeiten oder Erzählerschulen? Sind ihre Verfasser Sammler, Redaktoren oder Autoren? Sind sie getreue Tradenten der Überlieferung oder Schöpfer originaler Werke? Wo enden die Quellen? Mit der Wüstenwanderung, mit der Landnahme oder

---

[1] *JBL* 84 (1965), S. 1-19.

noch später? Hat der Elohist überhaupt einen Anfang und der Jahwist einen Schluss? Die unterschiedlichsten Thesen und Thesenkombinationen wurden vertreten—und sie fügten sich erstaunlicherweise alle in den vorgegebenen Rahmen der vier Symbole J, E, D und P.

Es ergaben sich Spannungen zwischen der Quellentheorie und den zu behandelnden Texten. Zwar war man sich einig: Der Text ist auf Quellen zu verteilen. Doch was in der Genesis vielleicht noch möglich war, führte in Exodus und Numeri in erhebliche Schwierigkeiten. In vielen Fällen blieb die Zuweisung der Texte ungewiss und umstritten. Meist fehlten auch nur einigermassen sichere Beurteilungskriterien. Andere Texte sperrten sich gegen jede Quellenzuweisung. Man bemühte Elemente der Ergänzungshypothese, man erfand neue Quellen und schied "Zusätze" aus. Und über allem wölbte sich—davon unberührt—wie ein ehernes Dach die überkommene Quellentheorie.

Es ergaben sich Spannungen aufgrund der Ausweitung des methodischen Instrumentariums. Zur Literarkritik der Quellentheorie trat die formgeschichtliche Fragestellung. Zunächst war die Zuständigkeit der beiden Methoden eindeutig geregelt: Die Literarkritik hatte die literarischen Texte zum Gegenstand, die Formgeschichte die mündliche Tradition. Doch die Wege der Methoden überschnitten sich: Die Literarkritik wurde auch zur Differenzierung innerhalb der mündlichen Tradition beigezogen, und mittels der Formgeschichte begann man auch nach literarischen Gattungen zu fragen. Hinzu traten Überlieferungs- und Redaktionsgeschichte. Hier wurden die beiden Begriffe promiscue verwendet, dort fein säuberlich auf mündliche und schriftliche Überlieferungsstufe verteilt—auch wenn die Frage nach den Übergängen zwischen den Stufen umstritten blieb. Es entstand ein komplexes Methodengeflecht—doch die Quellentheorie blieb von diesen Vorgängen unberührt. Sie war so resistent, dass sie sogar von den sonst z.T. so missionarisch auftretenden Text- und Sprachtheoretikern als a priori gegeben hingenommen wurde.

Es ergaben sich schliesslich Spannungen zwischen der Datierung der Quellen und den historischen Voraussetzungen der für sie in Anspruch genommenen Zeiten. Texte mit prophetischer Prägung sollten aus einer Zeit stammen, in der es eine formenprägende Prophetie noch gar nicht gab. Texte, die Elemente der Jerusalemer Königsideologie übernehmen, sollten in der vorstaatlichen Zeit wurzeln. Mehrfach wurden Beziehungen zwischen Jahwist und Deuteronomist beobachtet, doch die beiden Überlieferungs- und Textkomplexe blieben um Jahrhunderte voneinander getrennt. Und vor allem: Auf der einen Seite wird mit der Quellentheorie vertreten, dass die alten Einzeltraditionen in einer langen Geschichte in vorstaatlicher Zeit zusammengewachsen seien. Auf der anderen Seite aber haben wir in der Zwischenzeit die für diesen Vorgang nötigen geistigen und institutionellen Voraussetzungen aus unserem Bild der Frühgeschichte Israels weitgehend gestrichen (Stichwort Amphiktyonie; Stichwort: Kleines geschichtliches Credo; Stichwort: Gehörte Juda zum vorstaatlichen Israel?).

Die Spannungen haben ein beunruhigendes Mass angenommen. Der Punkt ist erreicht, an welchem die Spannung zur Aporie wird und die Beunruhigung umschlägt in die Frage: Stimmen unsere Voraussetzungen noch? Hat sich nicht vielleicht die Quellentheorie selbst als unzureichend erwiesen?

Nicht wenige Forscher sind heute der Meinung, dass diese Konsequenz zu ziehen sei, und sie sind auf der Suche nach einem neuen Bild für das Werden des Pentateuchs.

Bestritten wird insbesondere die Existenz eines alten, in die salomonische Zeit zu datierenden Jahwisten—an Autoren nenne ich etwa F. V. Winnett,[2] N. E. Wagner,[3] J. Van Seters,[4] R. Rendtorff,[5] H. Vorländer,[6] H. C. Schmitt,[7] M. Rose,[8] und auch ich selbst habe mich in diese Richtung geäussert.[9] Stattdessen ist nun oft die Rede von einem "Late J", einem "späten Jahwisten", der in den Umkreis der

---

[2] Vgl. Anm. 1.

[3] *A Literary Analysis of Genesis 12-36* (Diss. Toronto, 1965); "Abraham and David?", *Studies on the Ancient Palestinian World, presented to Professor F. V. Winnett* (Toronto, 1972), S. 117-40; "A Response to Professor Rolf Rendtorff", *JSOT* 3 (1977), S. 20-7.

[4] *Abraham in History and Tradition* (New Haven-London, 1975); "Confessional Reformulations in the Exilic Period", *VT* 22 (1972), S. 448-59; "The Yahwist as Theologian? A Response", *JSOT* 3 (1977), S. 15-20.

[5] "Der 'Jahwist' als Theologe? Zum Dilemma der Pentateuchkritik", *SVT* 28 (1975), S. 158-66 = "The 'Yahwist' as Theologian? The Dilemma of Pentateuchal Criticism", *JSOT* 3 (1977), S. 2-9; *Das überlieferungsgeschichtliche Problem des Pentateuchs* (Berlin, 1976) = *BZAW* 147.

[6] *Die Entstehungszeit des jehowistischen Geschichtswerkes* (Frankfurt, 1978) = *Europäische Hochschulschriften XIII/109.*

[7] *Die nichtpriesterliche Josephsgeschichte. Ein Beitrag zur neuesten Pentateuchkritik* (Berlin, 1980) = *BZAW* 154.

[8] *Deuteronomist und Jahwist. Untersuchungen zum Verhältnis der beiden Geschichtswerke* (Zürich, 1981).

[9] *Der sogenannte Jahwist* (Zürich, 1976).

Exilszeit und in die Nähe des deuteronomisch-deuteronomistischen Denkens gerückt wird. Andere Autoren wie L. Perlitt,[10] A. Reichert,[11] E. Zenger [12] oder R. Smend [13] gehen nicht so weit. Doch auch was sie uns als Jahwisten präsentieren, bedeutet gemessen am überkommenen Bild eine erhebliche Destruktion. Auch bei ihnen schrumpfen die alten Quellen zusammen—zugunsten literarisch und theologisch gewichtiger protodeuteronomischer oder deuteronomistischer Schichten und Redaktionen.[14]

Was sich hier vollzieht, sind nicht nur Umdatierungen; hier verändert sich das Gesamtgefüge—nicht zuletzt im Hinblick auf das Verhältnis von Tradition und Interpretation.

Dieser Umschichtungsprozess hat natürlich Konsequenzen auch für den Elohisten. Er verliert seinen bisherigen Ort und seine bisherige Funktion. Die einen ordnen jetzt das elohistische Material dem spätdatierten Jahwisten vor und sehen in ihm eine erste Bearbeitungsstufe des alten Traditionsmaterials (so etwa F. V. Winnett, N. E. Wagner, J. Van Seters, H. C. Schmitt).[15] Andere verzichten auf ihn völlig; was bisher als elohistisch galt, verstehen sie als eine Stufe des vor- oder innerjahwistischen Überlieferungsprozesses (so etwa R. Rendtorff oder meine eigenen Äusserungen, vgl. Anm. 5 und 9).

---

[10] *Bundestheologie im Alten Testament* (Neukirchen, 1969).

[11] *Der Jehowist und die sogenannten deuteronomistischen Erweiterungen im Buch Exodus* (Diss. Tübingen, 1972).

[12] *Die Sinaitheophanie—Untersuchungen zum jahwistischen und elohistischen Geschichtswerk* (Würzburg, 1971), vgl. P. Weimar-E. Zenger, *Exodus—Geschichten und Geschichte der Befreiung Israels* (Stuttgart, 1975).

[13] *Die Entstehung des Alten Testaments* (Stuttgart, 1978).

[14] Vgl. auch die bei Van Seters, *Abraham*, S. 130, Anm. 16, und Schmid, *Jahwist*, S. 10, Anm. 3 f., genannten Autoren und Titel. Zwar hatte schon J. Wellhausen auf die Nähe des Jehowisten zum deuteronomistischen Denken aufmerksam gemacht, z.B. *Die Composition des Hexateuchs* (Berlin, ⁴1963), S. 94, wo er zum Stichwort "Jehovist" die Fussnote anfügt: "Dessen Geistesverwandtschaft mit dem Deuteronomium tritt wiederum auffallend hervor—wenn nicht ausser ihm noch ein Deuteronomist anzunehmen ist." Doch dieser Hinweis wurde in der Folgezeit weitgehend übersehen. So konnte R. Smend in seinem Nachruf auf M. Noth formulieren: Es "fehlt den Büchern Genesis—Numeri gänzlich eine deuteronomistische Redaktion" (M. Noth, *Gesammelte Studien zum Alten Testament II* [München, 1969], S. 156). Ähnlich klingt es bei G. Fohrer: "In die Bücher Genesis—Numeri hat die deuteronomistische Schule wenig eingegriffen" (*Geschichte der israelitischen Religion* [Berlin, 1969], S. 309; vgl. ds., *Einleitung in das Alte Testament* [Heidelberg, ¹⁰1965], S. 181). M. Noth selbst hatte immerhin für Exodus und Numeri von deuteronomistischen Zusätzen gesprochen (*Überlieferungsgeschichte des Pentateuch* [Stuttgart, 1948, ²1960], S. 32, Anm. 106; S. 35, Anm. 125).

[15] Vgl. o. Anm. 1-4, 7, vgl. auch 11.

Die Ausgrenzung der Priesterschrift ist bisher nicht ernsthaft angefochten worden, doch werden im Zuge der Umstrukturierung des Ganzen wieder neu Stimmen laut, die in ihr nicht eine selbständige Quelle, sondern lediglich eine späte Bearbeitung des jehowistischen Pentateuchs sehen möchten.

Ingesamt scheint sich bei den meisten der bisher genannten Autoren an die Stelle der Quellentheorie ein Bild der Entstehung des Pentateuchs zu schieben, das der Struktur nach seine nächste Parallele im Bereich der deuteronomistischen Traditions- und Literaturwerdung hat.

Nicht nur an den Ergebnissen der bisherigen Pentateuchforschung hat sich die Kritik entzündet, sondern auch an der Art ihres Zugriffs. Die Pentateuchforschung der letzten hundert Jahre hat methodisch "von vorn" angesetzt: Sie hat ihre Kriterien an der Genesis gewonnen und von da auf den übrigen Pentateuch übertragen. Dass dieser Einsatz in Exodus und Numeri zu praktisch unüberwindlichen Schwierigkeiten geführt hat, ist bekannt.[16] So werden heute in zunehmenden Masse Analysen zu Exodus und Numeri vorgelegt, die von den an der Genesis gewonnenen Ergebnissen zunächst einmal abstrahieren; die entsprechenden Arbeiten von L. Perlitt, E. Zenger oder A. Reichert sowie meine eigene Untersuchung (vgl. Anm. 9-12) wären hier etwa zu nennen. Die Resultate dieses Ansatzes rechtfertigen zweifellos den Versuch. Noch zugespitzter schlägt M. Rose (vgl. Anm. 8) vor, die Arbeit am Pentateuch ganz hinten, d.h. im Bereich der Übergänge zum deuteronomistischen Geschichtswerk anzusetzen und dann zurückzugreifen. Dabei erweist sich sogar als denkbar, dass der sogenannte Jahwist als immer weiter zurückgreifende Fortschreibung des (bereits vorliegenden) ältesten deuteronomistischen Geschichtswerks zu begreifen sein könnte.[17]

Noch in anderer Weise hat die bisherige Pentateuchforschung ihren

---

[16] Vgl. etwa M. Noth, *Das vierte Buch Mose. Numeri* (Göttingen, 1966), S. 8: "Nimmt man das 4. Mosebuch für sich, so käme man nicht leicht auf den Gedanken an 'durchlaufende Quellen', sondern eher auf den Gedanken an eine unsystematische Zusammenstellung von zahllosen Überlieferungsstücken sehr verschiedenen Inhalts, Alters und Charakters ('Fragmentenhypothese')". Nur von der inhaltlichen Zugehörigkeit zum Pentateuch her lässt sich sagen: "Es ist daher gerechtfertigt, mit den anderwärts gewonnenen Ergebnissen der Pentateuchanalyse . . . an das 4. Mosebuch heranzutreten und die durchlaufenden Pentateuch-'Quellen' auch in diesem Buche zu erwarten, selbst wenn, wie gesagt, der Sachverhalt im 4. Mosebuch von sich aus nicht gerade auf diese Ergebnisse hinführt."

[17] Vgl. auch J. Van Seters, "Recent Studies on the Pentateuch: A Crisis in Method", erscheint in *JAOS* 99 (1979), S. 663-73.

Ausgang methodisch "von vorn" genommen: in ihrer überlieferungsgeschichtlichen Fragestellung. In aller Regel galt die erste Frage den mutmasslich ältesten Überlieferungen und Schichten. Die jüngeren traten dann als deren Weiterentwicklung in Blick. Auch an diesem Punkt wird heute der Ruf nach einer methodischen Umkehrung laut. So setzt z.B. R. Smend in seiner *Entstehung des Alten Testaments* (vgl. Anm. 13) hinten, bei der Endredaktion des Pentateuchs ein und geht dann schrittweise bis zur vorliterarischen Überlieferung zurück. Noch konsequenter verfährt darin eine Gruppe jüngerer Kollegen (B. Diebner und H. Schult,[18] B. Zuber[19]). Für sie ist Traditionskritik prinzipiell nicht mehr als Überlieferungsgeschichte ("von vorn"), sondern als Rezeptionskritik ("von hinten") zu betreiben. Dabei erweist sich allerdings der Rückgriff hinter die Schwelle des Exils als äusserst schwierig, und es entsteht das Bild eines Pentateuchs, der im wesentlichen als Produkt der persisch-hellenistischen Zeit zu betrachten ist. Noch einmal anders konkretisiert sich schliesslich der Ansatz "von hinten" bei D. J. A. Clines (*The Theme of the Pentateuch* [Sheffield, 1978]), der die lange vernachlässigte Frage nach Sinn und Funktion der Pentateucherzählung als ganzer stellt, auf der Stufe ihrer Endredaktion.

Was besagt das alles? Viele, sehr viele Selbstverständlichkeiten der Pentateuchforschung sind fraglich geworden. Ebenso deutlich ist allerdings, dass eine allgemein verbindliche neue Sicht vom Werden des Pentateuchs noch nicht gewonnen ist. Vielleicht sind im Vergleich mit der bisherigen Pentateuchforschung die Divergenzen und Kontradiktionen sogar eher noch zahlreicher geworden.

Wollen wir weiterkommen, reicht es nicht aus, nur einzelne Versatzstücke des Pentateuchs noch einmal anders zu arrangieren.[20] Es reicht nicht aus, ohne Überprüfung der foundations die Denkbarkeit eines alten Jahwisten zu beteuern[21] oder vom Jahwisten bisheriger Prägung nur zu retten, was noch zu retten ist.[22] Es reicht auch nicht aus, der der Quellentheorie zugrundeliegenden Problem-

---

[18] Zusammenfassend: B. Diebner, "Neue Ansätze in der Pentateuch-Forschung", *DBAT* 13 (1978), S. 2-13.

[19] "Marginalien zur Quellentheorie", *DBAT* 12 (1977), S. 14-29.

[20] Als Beispiel sei genannt: H. Seebass, "Num. XI, XII und die Hypothese des Jahwisten", *VT* 28 (1978), S. 214-23.

[21] So etwa L. Schmidt, "Überlegungen zum Jahwisten", *EvTh* 37 (1977), S. 230-47.

[22] Dies scheint mir der Fall zu sein bei E. Zenger (o. Anm. 12); vgl. auch E. Otto, *Das Mazzotfest in Gilgal* (Stuttgart, 1975).

lage auszuweichen, wie es etwa im Genesiskommentar von C. Westermann [23] in zunehmendem Masse zu beobachten ist.

Wollen wir weiterkommen, müssen wir grundsätzlicher ansetzen. Wir stehen vor der Aufgabe, neue—und wenn möglich gemeinsame—Perspektiven für die Pentateuchforschung zu gewinnen.

Diese Frage nach neuen Perspektiven wird an sehr verschiedenen Punkten ansetzen können und müssen. So werden Sie von mir nicht erwarten, dass ich heute fertige Lösungen vorlege. Dennoch möchte ich zu ihrer Behandlung einen Beitrag liefern. Ich greife einen Teilaspekt heraus und stelle einige Überlegungen dazu an, welches die *Rahmenbedingungen* sind, unter welchen solche Perspektiven überhaupt zu gewinnen sind. Darin geht es tatsächlich um die foundations unseres Forschungszweiges. Allerdings bezweifle ich, dass die Frage nach den foundations in den bisher vorgelegten Entwürfen schon grundsätzlich genug gestellt worden ist.

Wo lassen wir diese Überlegungen am besten beginnen? Ich greife dazu einen Rat des Alten Testamentes auf. Perspektiven für die Zukunft hat das Alte Testament—gerade auch im Pentateuch—zu wesentlichen Stücken aus der kritischen Aufarbeitung der Vergangenheit gewonnen. Kritische Aufarbeitung der Vergangenheit heisst in unserem Zusammenhang zunächst die Frage zu stellen: Welches sind denn die entscheidenden Grundlagen und Perspektiven der bisherigen Pentateuchforschung? Aus ihrer Beantwortung wird sich ergeben, in welche Richtung wir weiterzuschreiten hätten.

II. Die grundlagen der bisherigen Pentateuchforschung

Wo liegen die entscheidenden Grundlagen der bisherigen Pentateuchforschung?

Das erste Standbein der Forschung am Pentateuch ist seit ihren Anfängen die konkrete Einzelbeobachtung am Text. Die Forschung war herausgefordert durch die bekannten formalen, stilistischen, inhaltlichen, historischen und theologischen Spannungen im Pentateuch selbst. Diese Spannungen wollen erklärt sein. An ihnen wird auch die Pentateuchforschung der Zukunft nicht vorbeisehen können. Die Einzelbeobachtung war—und bleibt—die erste und wichtigste Grundlage der Pentateuchforschung.

Diese Feststellung mag auf den ersten Blick besehen banal erscheinen. Sie verliert jedoch sogleich an Banalität, wenn auch die Grenzen der

[23] Besonders ab Kap. xii: *Genesis*, 2. Teilband (Neukirchen, ab 1977) = *BK* I/2.

Einzelbeobachtung in Rechnung gestellt werden. Die Einzelbeobachtung kann differenzieren, sie kann unterscheiden, sie kann Relationen aufweisen. Doch das Beziehungsnetz, das sie zu knüpfen vermag, bleibt relativ, begrenzt, ohne Kontext. Sinn und Evidenz erhält es erst aus dem Blick über den Einzeltext, ja über den Pentateuch hinaus auf das gesamte Leben und Denken Israels. Darum stand in der bisherigen Pentateuchforschung—jedenfalls bei den richtungsweisenden Forschern—die Einzelexegese immer in engem Zusammenhang mit einem Gesamtbild der Geschichte Israels und seiner Religion.

So ist bei J. Wellhausen die Unterscheidung der Priesterschrift vom jehowistischen Geschichtswerk und die Spätdatierung von P essentieller Teil seines völlig neuen Entwurfs der Geschichte Israels. H. Gunkels Analysen zum Pentateuch haben ihren Gesamtkontext in seinem Bild der Literaturgeschichte Israels gefunden. Das Werden des Pentateuchs, wie es sich M. Noth vorgestellt hat, ist nicht denkbar ohne den Hintergrund seines Aufrisses der Geschichte Israels, insbesondere nicht ohne den seiner Hypothese der vorstaatlichen Zwölfstämmeamphiktyonie. G. von Rads Konzeption des Jahwisten als eines Theologen schliesslich ist fest verknüpft mit von Rads Gesamtsicht, wonach der alttestamentliche Glaube von allem Anfang an theologisch spezifischer Geschichtsglaube gewesen sei.

Einzelexegetische Arbeit und das, was J. Wellhausen (*Geschichte Israels* I [Berlin, 1878], S. 174) einst "Gesamtanschauung" genannt hat, hängen aufs engste zusammen. Der Konnex zwischen beiden vollzog sich dabei durchaus wechselseitig: Die Einzelbeobachtung lieferte die Bausteine für die Gesamtsicht wie gleichzeitig die Gesamtsicht die Beobachtung leitete. Dieser Zusammenhang ist bei der Würdigung der Ergebnisse der bisherigen Pentateuchforschung immer mit zu berücksichtigen, und auch die künftige Arbeit am Pentateuch wird sich ihm nicht entziehen können. Ja mehr: Es ist sogar zu fordern, dass auch wir unsere Einzelarbeit auf solche Integration in ein Gesamtbild ausrichten—wie andrerseits unsere Gesamtentwürfe den einzelexegetischen Befunden standhalten müssen.

Doch mit den Stichworten "Einzelbeobachtung" und "Gesamtanschauung" sind die Grundbedingungen der bisherigen Pentateuchforschung noch nicht zureichend bestimmt. Ein dritter Aspekt tritt hinzu: einer, der Einzelbeobachtung und Gesamtbild weit mehr mitbestimmt, als uns in der Regel bewusst ist. Ich meine die Prägung der einzelnen Forscher durch die übergreifenden Fragestellungen und Perspektiven ihrer je eigenen geistesgeschichtlichen Situation.

Dieser Aspekt scheint mir für unsere Fragestellung besonders wichtig zu sein.

So ist z.B. die Arbeit Wellhausens und Gunkels nicht denkbar ohne den Kontakt zum Geschichtsdenken des ausgehenden 19. Jahrhunderts, dem Historismus.[24] Es ist die Perspektive des Historismus, aus der Wellhausen und Gunkel nach Geschichte fragen und aus der sie *kritisch* nach Geschichte fragen. Aus der Perspektive des Historismus fragen sie kritisch nach den *Quellen* der Geschichte, darum treiben sie—wie die Historiker—Quellenkritik. Mit gewichtigen Vertretern des Historismus [25] teilen sie—unter dem Einfluss Herders und der Romantik—die Hochschätzung der historischen Frühzeit und die Abwertung der Spätzeit. Dieser Hintergrund ist sowohl dafür bestimmend, dass ihr Herz in erster Linie bei den alten und ältesten Überlieferungen schlug, als auch dafür, dass die Spätdatierung der Priesterschrift erst jetzt wirklich evident wurde.

Bei Wellhausen dominiert die historiographische Fragestellung. In ihr gründet sein Interesse an der Unterscheidung zwischen dem Jehowisten und der Priesterschrift. Beide Werke sind ihm daher in erster Linie Geschichtsquellen, je für die vor- und nachexilische Zeit. Gegenüber dem Geschichtsbuch des Jehowisten treten Jahwist und Elohist als blosse Zulieferer der "Stoffe" in den Hintergrund. Dabei ist für Wellhausen Geschichte im wesentlichen Geschichte der Nation (Belege bei Perlitt, S. 176 f.). Wenn man bedenkt, welch grosse Bedeutung dem Nationalen gerade um 1870 zukam, werden auch hier Beziehungen deutlich. Doch diese Ausrichtung auf das Nationale hatte bei Wellhausen Konsequenzen: Sie bewirkte, dass bei ihm nicht nur die Spätzeit, sondern auch die Vorgeschichte Israels ausserhalb seines eigentlichen Interesses stand, hier war Israel eben noch nicht, bzw. nicht mehr Nation.

Bei Gunkel steht nicht die historiographische Frage im Vordergrund, sondern die nach der konkreten Anschauung ursprünglichen religiösen Lebens und deren unmittelbaren sprachlichen Äusserungen. Hier wirken anerkanntermassen Impulse der Romantik und vor allem der ästhetischen Betrachtungsweise Herders nach. Darin liegt der Ansatzpunkt für Gunkels Rückfrage hinter die literarische Gestalt der

[24] Für Wellhausen ist dies besonders nachdrücklich herausgearbeitet bei L. Perlitt, *Vatke und Wellhausen* (Berlin, 1965) = *BZAW* 94. Für die geistesgeschichtlichen Hintergründe der Arbeit H. Gunkels vgl. W. Klatt, *Hermann Gunkel* (Göttingen, 1969).

[25] Etwa B. G. Niebuhr, L. v Ranke oder Th. Mommsen, vgl. Perlitt, S. 57-71.

Pentateuchquellen zurück in die mündliche Tradition und damit für die Entdeckung der Gattungen mündlicher Rede. Damit verändert sich gegenüber Wellhausen z.B. das Bild des Jahwisten. Der Jahwist erscheint nicht mehr als Vorstufe des Jehowisten, sondern als Endstufe mündlicher Tradition. Er vermittelt nicht mehr nur "Stoffe", sondern ist zum "Sammler" bereits geprägter Überlieferungen geworden.[26] Auch dies hat Konsequenzen. Aufgrund der postulierten Nähe zur mündlichen Tradition, die in besonderer Weise in die Frühzeit weist, wird nun der Jahwist gegenüber der Ansetzung durch Wellhausen um rund hundert Jahre älter.[27] Gleichzeitig spricht ihm Gunkel alle theoretisierenden Passagen ab—so etwa die als unvermittelte Gottesreden stilisierten Verheissungsreden der Genesis (*Genesis*, S. XCII). Denn diese Sammler erzählen—nach Gunkel—"Geschichten" und formulieren noch keine "Gedanken". Diese "Gedanken" gehören schon zum Übergang in die Spätzeit, die Gunkel später in seiner Literaturgeschichte unter dem Titel "Die Epigonen" abhandelt. Wo nicht mehr das Geschehen im Vordergrund steht, sondern nur noch die Beurteilung, da ist nach Gunkel der bewundernswerte Geist der Vorzeit verflogen.[28] So ist auch Gunkels Sicht des Pentateuchs entscheidend geprägt von den Denkvoraussetzungen seiner eigenen Zeit.

So viele bleibende Erkenntnisse der Historismus auch hervorgebracht hat—an sich wie in seinen Auswirkungen auf die alttestament-

---

[26] *Genesis* (Göttingen, [6]1964), S. LXXX ff. Vgl. dazu die berühmte Formulierung: "Diese Sammler sind zu denken als treue, fromme Männer, voller ehrfürchtiger Liebe zu den alten schönen Erzählungen ihres Volkes" (*Geschichte der israelitischen Literatur* [Sonderdruck Darmstadt, 1963], S. 22).

[27] Vor Wellhausen war der Jahwist als "prophetische Quelle" meist dem 8. Jahrhundert zugewiesen worden (Nachweise bei Schmid, *Jahwist*, S. 13, Anm. 12). Wellhausen hat diese Ansetzung übernommen mit dem Hinweis, dass schon bei ihm "die Einwirkung jenes specifischen Prophetismus, den wir von Amos ab verfolgen können" nachweisbar sei (*Prolegomena zur Geschichte Israels* [Berlin, [3]1886], S. 377). Nach Gunkel gehört nun der Jahwist ins 9. Jahrhundert (*Genesis*, S. XCI). Die Berührungen mit dem Prophetismus sind ihm Hinweis darauf, "wie die Gedanken der Propheten in manchem schon lange vor Amos umgingen" (*ebda*).

[28] Vgl. die Formulierung bezüglich der Deuteronomistik, der Priesterschrift und der Chronik: "Alle diese Erzählwerke stellen einen immer tieferen Sturz in der Kunst der Geschichtserzählung dar: nicht das Geschehen interessiert diese Späteren und Spätesten mehr, sondern nur noch die Beurteilung; und ihre Beurteilung vermag sich in den Geist der Vorzeit nicht zu finden" (*Geschichte der israelitischen Literatur*, S. 46). Wäre nicht das prophetische Erbe geblieben—wie bei Wellhausen das individuelle Bewusstsein—, wäre von hier aus eine Brücke zum Neuen Testament völlig undenkbar.

liche Wissenschaft—, so wurden mit dem Beginn unseres Jahrhunderts doch auch dessen Aporien deutlich. Aus der Einsicht in die historische Bedingtheit (und Relativität) allen Geschehens liess sich die Frage nach dem Absoluten, nach der Wahrheit in der Geschichte nicht mehr beantworten. Die alttestamentliche Theologie war zur Religionsgeschichte Israels geworden, und Wellhausen war von der Theologischen zur Philosophischen Fakultät übergewechselt. Auf breiter Ebene setzten Bewegungen zur Überwindung des Historismus ein, Namen wie Dilthey, Croce, Troeltsch mögen für viele stehen. Dieser Umbruch gehört zu den Voraussetzungen der Arbeit G. von Rads.

Bei B. Croce (*Theorie und Geschichte der Historiographie* [Tübingen, 1930], S. 244) steht einmal der (ironische) Satz zu lesen: "Die Kühnheit, die Einmischung des Gedankens in die Geschichte zu verwerfen ..., hatten ... die völlig unschuldigen Philologen". Als er diesen Satz schrieb, dachte Croce nicht an die alttestamentliche Wissenschaft. Und doch kennzeichnet die Formulierung einen wichtigen Punkt des Unterschieds von Rads zu Wellhausen und Gunkel: Geschichte ist für von Rad nicht mehr nur Geschichte der Fakten und Lebensäusserungen, sondern ebensosehr, wenn nicht sogar in erster Linie, Geschichte der Gedanken—oder mit einem Zentralbegriff von Rads formuliert: Geschichte ist in erster Linie als Überlieferungsgeschichte zu begreifen.[29]

Ein zweites Beispiel für diesen Hintergrund des Ansatzes bei von Rad: Nach den Erkenntnissen des Historismus muss angesichts der Individualität des Historischen auf die Deduktion oder Konstruktion eines allgemeinen, zeitlosen Wertsystems verzichtet werden. Wenn die Frage nach Wertmassstäben dennoch nicht aufgegeben werden kann—und darf—, dann können Massstäbe nur aus dem Begreifen der Entwicklung selbst gewonnen werden. So stellen sich die Dinge etwa bei E. Troeltsch[30] dar, der dann formuliert: "Immer erst in der Berührung zwischen Vergangenem und Gegenwärtigem bildet sich der eigentliche letzte entscheidende Massstab, der zugleich die Zukunftsgestaltung in die unbekannte endlose Zukunft hineintreibt" (S. 178). Darin liegt fast eine Vorwegnahme der Geschichts-

[29] Vgl. zusammenfassend: R. Rendtorff, "Die alttestamentlichen Überlieferungen als Grundthema der Lebensarbeit Gerhard von Rads", in *Gerhard von Rad. Seine Bedeutung für die Theologie* (München, 1973).

[30] *Der Historismus und seine Probleme. Erstes Buch: Das logische Problem der Geschichtsphilosophie* (Tübingen, 1922) = *Gesammelte Schriften* 3, bes. S. 164-79.

theologie von Rads. Von Rad verzichtet ja dezidiert auf die Bestimmung einer allgemeinen, zeitlosen Mitte des Alten Testamentes und setzt an deren Stelle nichts anderes als den überlieferungsgeschichtlichen Prozess selbst.[31] In dessen Rahmen ergeben sich die entscheidenden Werte aus eben jener "Berührung zwischen Vergangenem und Gegenwärtigem", welche gleichzeitig die Geschichte in eine immer weiter gehende Zukunft treibt.

Vor dem Hintergrund dieses zwar historisch orientierten, aber dennoch antihistoristischen Ansatzes werden die Pentateuchquellen nun Stationen des überlieferungsgeschichtlichen Prozesses. Sie sind aus ihrer jeweiligen Gegenwart herausgewachsene Auslegung der erstmals im kleinen geschichtlichen Credo fixierten Vergangenheit und gleichzeitig Ausgangspunkt immer weiter in die Zukunft drängender überlieferungsgeschichtlicher Transformationen und Ausweitungen.

Schon bei Troeltsch war der Vorgang dieser Wertsetzung ein auf eigener Entscheidung und Verantwortung beruhender Sprung, "eine Sache des Glaubens in dem tiefen und vollen Sinne des Wortes" (S. 175, vgl. 178). Dem entspricht bei von Rad, welche zentrale Stelle dem "Glauben" im Umgang mit der Geschichte zugewiesen wird.[32] Auch das hat seine Konsequenzen: So wird z.B. der Jahwist zum Theologen.[33] Ist der Jahwist aber Theologe, dann brauchen ihm die "Gedanken", etwa diejenigen der Väterverheissungen, nicht mehr abgesprochen zu werden; im Gegenteil: In nicht wenigen Fällen werden nun gerade solche Texte, die Gunkel aufgrund seiner Voraussetzungen als späte Zufügung ansah, bei von Rad zum hermeneutischen Schlüssel für das Verständnis des jahwistischen Werkes (Beispiele bei Schmid, *Jahwist*, S. 147-51).

---

[31] *Theologie des Alten Testaments* II (München, 1960), S. 376.

[32] Zur Rückweisung selbst der Aussage, Jahwe sei die Mitte des Alten Testamentes (durch von Rad (*Theologie des Alten Testaments* II, S. 376) vgl. E. Troeltsch, S. 184: "Geht man aber mit Heraklit und mit der prophetisch-christlichen Ideenwelt von der nie begrifflich erschöpfbaren, schaffenden Lebendigkeit des göttlichen Willens aus . . ., dann entschwindet freilich jede Möglichkeit einer Konstruktion des Gesamtgeschehens der Welt und unserer demgegenüber winzigen planetarischen Geschichte, aber wir gewinnen die Lebenstiefe, aus der heraus mit der inneren Beweglichkeit und Wandlung Gottes selber auch die Wandlung und Beweglichkeit der Wahrheit und des Ideals verständlich wird zusammen mit einer trotzdem verbleibenden Einstellung auf eine letzte Wahrheit und Einheit, die aber nur Gott selber weiß, wenn man sein Wissen Wissen nennen darf."

[33] Vgl. vor allem "Das formgeschichtliche Problem des Hexateuch", in *Gesammelte Studien zum Alten Testament* I (München, 1958), S. 9-86.

Aufgrund dieses Ansatzes, der schon dem Jahwisten ein erhebliches Mass an Reflexion zugestand, hätte es sich eigentlich nahegelegt, diesen Jahwisten in eine nicht allzu frühe Zeit der Geschichte Israels zu datieren. Faktisch ist jedoch bei von Rad das Gegenteil der Fall: Der Jahwist rückt gegenüber der Ansetzung Gunkels um noch einmal rund hundert Jahre hinauf.[34] Auch dafür dürften nicht nur exegetische Gründe massgebend gewesen sein. Auf der einen Seite wird man darin trotz der sonst zu beobachtenden Abkehr vom Historismus eine Nachwirkung der Hochschätzung der Frühzeit im 19. Jahrhundert sehen müssen. Noch gewichtiger aber scheint mir ein zweiter Aspekt zu sein. G. von Rad zeichnet nicht nur seinen Jahwisten als Theologen, sondern auch er selbst befragt das Alte Testament aus einem dezidiert theologischen Interesse heraus. Darin fusst er auf jener theologiegeschichtlichen Wende der 20er und 30er Jahre, die etwa in der Form der dialektischen Theologie, aber auch in zahlreichen theologischen Neuansätzen innerhalb unseres Faches [35] zur Überwindung des Historismus beitrug. In diesem Kontext ist für von Rad nun die Frage nach dem theologischen Spezifikum Israels unausweichlich—dies aber in ganz bestimmter Ausrichtung. Dass sich die israelitische Religion erst allmählich aus dem Heidentum emporgearbeitet habe, wie es Wellhausen dargestellt hatte,[36] konnte von Rad nicht mehr nachvollziehen. Für ihn trug der Jahweglaube von allem Anfang [37] an die spezifisch israelitischen Züge eines Geschichtsglaubens, der sich von den Religionsformen der Umwelt, insbesondere von der Naturreligion Kanaans, im Ansatz unterschied.

---

[34] Nach von Rad soll er aus der "freigeistigen Ära" der "salomonischen Aufklärung" stammen, vgl. *Gesammelte Studien* I, S. 76, 80; *Das erste Buch Mose. Genesis* (Göttingen, 1953), S. 10 u.ö.

[35] Vgl. etwa R. Kittel, "Die Zukunft der alttestamentlichen Wissenschaft", *ZAW* 39 (1921), S. 84-99; W. Staerk, "Religionsgeschichte und Religionsphilosophie in ihrer Bedeutung für die biblische Theologie des Alten Testaments", *ZThK* 4 (1923/24), S. 289-300; O. Eissfeldt, "Israelitisch-jüdische Religionsgeschichte und alttestamentliche Theologie", *ZAW* 44 (1926), S. 1-12 = *Kleine Schriften* 1 (Tübingen, 1962), S. 105-14, wie auch die Tatsache, dass nun wieder Theologien des Alten Testamentes erschienen (beginnend mit W. Eichrodt und L. Köhler).

[36] Vgl. *Israelitische und jüdische Geschichte* (Berlin, ³1897), S. 21 im Kapitel "Die Anfänge des Volkes": "Die Israeliten waren eine Nation wie andere Nationen" und *ebda*, S. 34: "Die israelitische Religion hat sich aus dem Heidentum erst allmählich emporgearbeitet; das eben ist der Inhalt ihrer Geschichte."

[37] Dieser Anfang liegt nach von Rad noch erheblich hinter dem Jahwisten: in den vom kleinen geschichtlichen Credo überlieferten "Hauptdaten der Heilsgeschichte" (*Gesammelte Studien* I, S. 12).

Die Beziehung zum Offenbarungsverständnis K. Barths liegt auf der Hand: Offenbarung vollzieht sich totaliter aliter, sie hat mit der Religion und den Religionen nichts zu tun. Vor diesem Hintergrund musste für von Rad das jahwistische Werk als das erste umfassende Dokument des spezifisch alttestamentlichen Geschichtsglaubens qualitativ von der kanaanäischen Religiosität abgehoben werden, und es konnte nicht ein Ergebnis der Geschichte israelitischer Religion sein, sondern musste zu deren Anfängen gehören. Auch bei von Rad greifen so die historische Arbeit und die Voraussetzungen seiner eigenen geistesgeschichtlichen Situation eng ineinander.

Damit breche ich den Rückblick auf die bisherige Pentateuchforschung ab. Er erwies den engen Konnex von Einzelexegese, Gesamtanschauung und—hier besonders unterstrichen—den jeweiligen geistesgeschichtlichen Voraussetzungen der einzelnen Forscher. Es ging mir nicht darum, den genannten Forschern etwa den Vorwurf zu machen, nur Perspektiven und Erwartungen ihrer eigenen Zeit auf die Texte projiziert zu haben. Ziel des Rückblicks war vielmehr, Ansatz und Ergebnisse bisheriger Forschungsarbeit besser zu verstehen. Denn was mit dem aufgewiesenen Konnex beschrieben ist, ist nichts anderes als der (sachnotwendige und unentrinnbare) hermeneutische Zirkel, in dem sich die bisherige Pentateuchforschung vollzog. Aus diesem Zirkel ergaben sich den einzelnen Forschern die Fragestellungen und die Möglichkeiten, Beobachtungen zu machen und Zusammenhänge zu sehen—gerade auch neue Beobachtungen zu machen und neue Zusammenhänge zu sehen. Doch es war der gleiche Zirkel, der auf der anderen Seite gewisse Ergebnisse schon vorausbestimmte und andere Perspektiven ausblendete. Erst wenn wir diesen Zirkel zu Gesicht bekommen, sind wir bei den eigentlichen Grundlagen der Pentateuchforschung.

Gleichzeitig ergibt der Rückblick gerade auf dieser Ebene, dass wir tatsächlich allen Anlass zu einer Überprüfung der foundations unseres Forschungszweiges haben: Eine ganze Reihe von Voraussetzungen der bisherigen Pentateuchforschung hat ihre Verbindlichkeit eingebüsst—und dies gilt es in seinen Konsequenzen zu bedenken.

Das allerdings heisst—und auch dies zeigt der Rückblick—: Die Überprüfung der Grundlagen kann sich nicht auf die Überprüfung der grundlegenden Ergebnisse der bisherigen Pentateuchforschung beschränken. Sie hat vielmehr den gesamten Verstehenskonnex unseres Forschungszweiges mit seinen facheigenen und fachfremden

Implikationen aufzuarbeiten. Denn wir müssen uns dessen bewusst sein, dass sich auch unsere Arbeit am Pentateuch in einem ähnlichen Zirkel vollzieht—und vollziehen *muss*. Auf der Suche nach neuen Perspektiven für die Pentateuchforschung haben wir uns daher Rechenschaft darüber abzulegen, an welchen Punkten sich die Bedingungen dieses Zirkels auf dem Weg von unseren Vätern zu uns verändert haben.[38]

III. Auf der Suche nach neuen Perspektiven für die Pentateuchforschung

Aus der Fülle der Aspekte des hermeneutischen Zirkels greife ich nochmals den heraus, dem eben schon im Rückblick das Hauptinteresse gegolten hat: den der eigenen geistesgeschichtlichen Situation der einzelnen Forscher. Obwohl es natürlich unmöglich ist, in den wenigen verbleibenden Minuten unsere eigene geistesgeschichtliche Situation auch nur annähernd zu charakterisieren, möchte ich doch einen kleinen Versuch in diese Richtung wagen. Ich frage: Mit welchen geistesgeschichtlichen Verschiebungen auf dem Weg von unseren Vätern und Grossvätern zu uns stehen die eingangs skizzierten Neuansätze in Zusammenhang? Wodurch sind sie herausgefordert, wodurch sind sie ermöglicht, und welche Perspektiven für die weitere Forschung ergeben sich daraus?

Wie eingangs angedeutet, vertreten mehrere Autoren heute—in dieser oder jener Form—eine Art der Spätansetzung des sogenannten Jahwisten. Der Nachweis dafür wird in aller Regel einzelexegetisch geführt. Doch dass entsprechende Beobachtungen möglich wurden—und in dieser Form erst jetzt möglich wurden, hängt zweifellos mit bestimmten Denkvoraussetzungen unserer Zeit zusammen.

Insgesamt teilen wir die romantische Hochschätzung der Frühzeit nicht mehr. Es fällt auf, dass nicht nur in der alttestamentlichen Wissenschaft, sondern auch in der allgemeinen Geschichtswissen-

---

[38] Aufs Grundsätzliche gesehen hat J. Wellhausen heute noch recht mit seiner Formulierung: "Konstruiren muß man bekanntlich die Geschichte immer; die Reihe Priesterkodex Jehovist Deuteronomium (oder wir könnten heute allgemein sagen: die Ergebnisse der bisherigen Pentateuchforschung) ist (sind) auch nichts durch die Überlieferung oder durch die Natur der Dinge Gegebenes, sondern nur eine wenige Decennien alte Hypothese, von der man jedoch die freilich etwas unfaßbaren Gründe vergessen hat und die dadurch in den Augen ihrer Anhänger den Schein des Objektiven, d.h. den Charakter des Dogmas bekommt. Der Unterschied ist nur, ob man gut oder schlecht konstruirt" (*Prolegomena zur Geschichte Israels* [Berlin und Leipzig, ^{6}1927], S. 365).

schaft die Spätzeiten neues Interesse gefunden haben, und wir können heute auch den Spätzeiten positive Seiten abgewinnen. Hängt dies damit zusammen, dass wir selbst in gewissem Sinne in einer Spätzeit leben? Jedenfalls sind wir—im Gegensatz zur bisherigen Pentateuchforschung—schon von da her nicht mehr gezwungen, eine so originale Leistung wie die des "Jahwisten" unbedingt so früh wie möglich anzusetzen. Nicht nur in der alttestamentlichen Wissenschaft, sondern auch etwa in der Ägyptologie und in der Assyriologie werden heute manche bisher als alt angesehene Texte in eine spätere Zeit datiert!

Gerade in diesem Zusammenhang spielt in den heutigen Geisteswissenschaften der Begriff der Erfahrung eine zentrale Rolle. Hier ist historisches Bewusstsein erst denkbar vor dem Hintergrund eines in sich vielfältigen und auch strittigen Erfahrungsschatzes. Dass der Geschichtsentwurf des sogenannten Jahwisten nicht nur die Erfahrungen der vorstaatlichen Zeit, sondern auch—und vielleicht sogar in erster Linie—die der Königszeit und insbesondere diejenigen der Prophetie bereits voraussetzt und verarbeitet, ist von daher heute durchaus denkbar geworden. Ja mehr: Erst diese neuen Fragestellungen unserer Zeit haben *die* Beobachtungen am Text ermöglicht, die nun bei manchen von uns zu einer Spätdatierung des Jahwisten führen.

Gewichtige Vertreter heutiger Geschichtswissenschaft messen insbesondere der Erfahrung der Krise eine gewichtige Funktion für die Entstehung historischen Denkens zu. Dieser Zusammenhang ist uns ja im Hinblick auf das deuteronomistische Denken schon seit längerem bekannt. Eine Verbindung auch des sogenannten Jahwisten mit der Krise des Exils und dem deuteronomistischen Denken ist von da her durchaus plausibel.[39] Es ist von da her nicht ausgeschlossen, dass der gegenwärtige Neuaufbruch in der Pentateuchforschung eine ebenso einschneidende Neuorientierung innerhalb der alttestamentlichen Wissenschaft einleiten könnte wie die einst von Wellhausen in Gang gebrachte: Es könnte sich erweisen, dass nicht nur das Priestergesetz jünger ist als die Prophetie, sondern auch das Denken in den Kategorien der Geschichte.[40]

---

[39] Schon G. von Rad hat den Jahwisten vor dem Hintergrund einer Krise verstanden, allerdings der mit dem Verfall der Amphiktyonie und der Staatenbildung einhergehenden (*Das erste Buch Mose*, S. 11)—im Unterschied zu M. Noth, der die entscheidende Gestaltung des Pentateuchs (in der von ihm angenommenen Grundschrift G) der Blütezeit des Stämmebundes zuschrieb (*Überlieferungsgeschichte des Pentateuch*, S. 46-8).

[40] Wie sich mir diese Zusammenhänge darbieten, habe ich dargelegt in

Allerdings: Dass es diese Krise war, die zum Werden des Pentateuchs geführt hat und nicht etwa, wie von Rad (*Das erste Buch Mose*, S. 11) annahm, die mit dem Untergang der Amphiktyonie und der Staatenbildung verbundene, muss begründet werden. Doch dafür spricht tatsächlich eine ganze Reihe von Hinweisen. Auch unser Bild der Frühzeit Israels hat sich ja in den letzten Jahren erheblich verändert. Die Amphiktyoniehypothese wird aufgegeben werden müssen, die Existenz eines Gottesbundes als alte Institution wird bestritten, das kleine geschichtliche Credo ist als spät erwiesen, die Frühansetzung der Väterüberlieferung und der Josephsgeschichte wird angefochten. Ob das Königtum wirklich eine alte Einheit zerstört hat, ist nicht mehr so ganz sicher. Im Gegenteil: Wir müssen damit rechnen, dass die geistige Situation Israels auch nach der Staatenbildung noch sehr komplex war und dass auch für die Königszeit mit sehr unterschiedlichen Traditionslinien im Nordreich, in Jerusalem und im Landjudäertum zu rechnen ist, wie auch mit einem Nebeneinander von Sesshaftigkeit und Nomadismus. Unsere "Gesamtanschauung" hat sich in einem Masse verändert, dass sie die Last jedenfalls der von M. Noth und G. von Rad vertretenen Pentateuchhypothesen kaum mehr zu tragen vermag.

Auch methodisch ist uns einiges fraglich geworden, so etwa die von Wellhausen vorausgesetzte Linearität der historischen Entwicklung oder die unmittelbare chronologische Aufreihung des Weges von einfachen zu komplexen Gattungen und von der mündlichen zur schriftlichen Überlieferung, wie sie Gunkel gezeichnet hat.

Auch diese Veränderungen im Bild der Frühgeschichte Israels spiegeln Verschiebungen in unserem eigenen Denken: Problematisch geworden sind uns alle historisch und methodisch vorschnell vereinheitlichenden Tendenzen. Wir haben—auch ausserhalb der alttestamentlichen Wissenschaft—erkannt, dass historische Entwicklungen in aller Regel von einer bunten Vielfalt und nicht von Einheitskonzeptionen ausgehen. Uniformierungen sind fast durchgehend Kennzeichen eines rückblickenden Gestaltungswillens, dem die Pluriformität zum Problem geworden ist. Die Spätansetzung des im Pentateuch entwickelten Bildes einer einheitlichen Geschichte von

---

"Das alttestamentliche Verständnis von Geschichte in seinem Verhältnis zum gemeinorientalischen Denken", *WuD* 13 (1975), S. 9-21; *Jahwist*, S. 174-84; vgl. auch "Altorientalisch-alttestamentliche Weisheit und ihr Verhältnis zur Geschichte" in *Altorientalische Welt in der alttestamentlichen Theologie* (Zürich, 1974), S. 64-90.

der Schöpfung bis zur Landnahme ist auch von da her in besonderem Masse denkbar geworden.

Der Zerfall des bisher relativ einheitlichen Bildes der Frühgeschichte Israels hängt noch in anderer Hinsicht mit dem Wandel unseres eigenen Bewusstseins zusammen. Wir erfahren unsere eigene Zeit als äusserst komplex. Das Bild einer relativ einheitlichen Vergangenheit hat für unsere eigene Situation keine klärende, keine wirklichkeitserschliessende Funktion mehr. Im Gegenteil: Gerade unsere eigene komplexe Situation lässt uns erkennen, dass auch die Vergangenheit um einiges komplexer war, als wir dies bisher annahmen.

Verändert haben sich im weiteren die Bedingungen, unter denen die Frage nach dem Verhältnis von biblischem Glauben und altorientalischer Religionsgeschichte zu stellen ist. Die nicht nur, aber besonders bei von Rad zu beobachtende Zurückhaltung gegenüber religionsgeschichtlichen Fragestellungen wird heute von vielen aufgegeben. Dazu zwingt nicht nur das fast erdrückende religionsgeschichtliche Material, das der Auswertung harrt. Dazu befreit und ermutigt auch, dass heute gesamttheologisch dem Phänomen der Religion eine weit grössere, auch positive Bedeutsamkeit zugemessen wird, als dies im Ausstrahlungsbereich der dialektischen Theologie der Fall war. So können wir heute nicht nur historisch, sondern auch theologisch offen die Frage stellen, wie gross denn wirklich der Unterschied der Religiosität Israels etwa zur Zeit Salomos zu vergleichbaren Religionsformen der Umwelt war, wo die Unterschiede wirklich liegen und ob die Frühansetzung des Jahwisten nicht gerade auch religionsgeschichtlich zu einem eklatanten Anachronismus führt. Denn der Gedanke, dass das Spezifische des Alten Testamentes nicht von allem Anfang an da gewesen ist, sondern erst in einer langen Geschichte der Erfahrung allmählich gewachsen sein könnte, ist heute—in Abkehr von den Voraussetzungen der dialektischen Theologie—auch gesamttheologisch verantwortbar. Vielleicht hätten wir gerade vom Pentateuch her zu dieser gesamttheologischen Debatte sogar einiges beizutragen.

Ist mit der Möglichkeit zu rechnen, dass der sogenannte Jahwist spät zu datieren ist, stellt sich die überlieferungsgeschichtliche Frage nach seiner Vorgeschichte neu. Es ist davor zu warnen, diese Rückfrage als irrelevant zu betrachten und die Erzählungen des Pentateuchs als insgesamt spät "produziert" zu betrachten, zur Selbstdefinition bestimmter Gruppen des Judentums gegenüber den damaligen Mächten—wie es heute auch vorgeschlagen wird.[41] Zwar hat auch diese Sichtweise heute ihren weiteren Kontext: in der materialistischen Geschichtsauffassung, die Geschichtsentwürfe ihrem Wesen nach als ideologische Bewältigung vorgegebener gesellschaftlicher und politischer Machtstrukturen interpretiert. Sosehr von dieser Seite her zu Recht die Beziehung auch biblischer Texte zu gesellschaftlichen und politischen Vorgegebenheiten betont wird, so lässt sich dennoch schon heute sagen, dass eine Verabsolutierung dieses Ansatzes zu mindestens ebenso grossen Einseitigkeiten führt wie die romantische Dekadenztheorie oder der idealistische Fortschrittsglaube.

Ist die Aufgabe der überlieferungsgeschichtlichen Rückfrage anerkannt, wird sich aber gerade diese ohne eine "Gesamtanschauung" nicht lösen lassen. Wer einen alten Jahwisten—etwa als "Nationalepos" (Smend, *Entstehung*, S. 87)—annehmen will, muss exegetisch und historisch nachweisen, dass es in der Frühzeit Israels tatsächlich ein solches Einheitsbewusstsein gegeben hat, oder sich fragen, ob in diesem Postulat nicht vielleicht doch noch zu viele Voraussetzungen Wellhausens und Gunkels nachwirken. Wer einen vorjahwistischen Elohisten postuliert,[42] muss im Rahmen einer solchen Gesamtanschauung exegetisch und historisch seinen Ort angeben können, auch den Ort, an dem er hätte literarisch werden können. Wer andrerseits die Verschriftung älterer Traditionen erst im Rahmen eines späten Jahwisten sehen will,[43] muss darüber Auskunft geben, wo und mit welcher Funktion sie dann vorher lebendig gewesen sind, warum sie damals nur mündlich tradiert wurden und noch ohne Einfluss auf die sonst erhaltene vorexilische Literatur gewesen sind.[44]

Damit wir dabei gerade angesichts unserer heutigen Forschungslage nicht zu unkontrollierbarer Willkür verleitet werden, scheint mir unabdingbar nötig, dass wir den Pentateuch wieder bewusst in den Kontext des gesamten Alten Testamentes stellen. Das geringe Interesse, das bei Gunkel die Prophetie fand, und die bis ins Editionstechnische hineinreichende Trennung der historischen von den pro-

[41] Vgl. die oben Anm. 18 und 19 genannten Autoren und Titel.
[42] Vgl. die Verweise oben Anm. 15.
[43] Vgl. die Verweise oben Anm. 5 und 9.
[44] Persönlich meine ich, daß dazu tatsächlich einiges gesagt werden kann. Vgl. oben Anm. und die Ausführungen in *Altorientalische Welt in der alttestamentlichen Theologie* insgesamt.

phetischen Überlieferungen bei von Rad wirken noch immer nach. Noch mehr als bisher haben wir die Prophetie, die Deuteronomistik, die Psalmen auszuwerten—gerade auch in ihrer Polemik—, um den faktischen Gang der israelitischen Religionsgeschichte und damit den historischen und geistigen Rahmen älterer Überlieferungen erkennen zu können. Ein halbes Buch über die Überlieferungsgeschichte der Väterverheissungen zu schreiben, ohne je einen Blick auf das übrige Alte Testament zu werfen, kann daher m.E. nur aus Zufall das Richtige treffen. Auch hier gehören Einzelbeobachtung und "Gesamtanschauung" untrennbar zusammen.

Stellen wir in Rechnung, dass sich alle unsere Arbeit im beschriebenen hermeneutischen Zirkel bewegt, hat dies Konsequenzen nach beiden Seiten: Wer die Ergebnisse der bisherigen Pentateuchforschung weiterhin vertreten will, muss zur Kenntnis nehmen, dass zahlreiche ihrer Voraussetzungen dahingefallen sind. Er wird sie neu begründen müssen. In der heutigen Forschungslage liegt die Beweislast nicht nur bei denen, die nach Neuansätzen suchen, sondern ebensosehr bei denen, die am Überkommenen festhalten. Wer andrerseits unterwegs ist nach neuen Horizonten, wird darauf zu achten haben, dass er nun nicht einfach Denkvoraussetzungen unserer Zeit in die Texte hineinprojiziert—gerade *weil* es legitim und nötig ist, aufgrund neuer Voraussetzungen neue Fragen zu stellen und neue Beobachtungen zu machen. Vielleicht finden wir so wieder neu zu gemeinsamen Perspektiven für die Pentateuchforschung.

DER SINN DER SOGENNANTEN NOACHITISCHEN GEBOTE (GENESIS IX 1-7)

VON

L. STACHOWIAK
Lublin

Es gehört zu den bekanntesten Ergebnissen der Urgeschichte der Genesis, dass die Fluterzählung der Priesterschrift von der des Jahwisten in vielen Punkten abweicht. In der gegenwärtigen Form der Erzählung von Gen. vi-ix scheint die Priesterschrift vorzuherrschen, jedenfalls sind deren grössere literarische Einheiten in die Sintfluterzählung der Genesis eingearbeitet worden. Die literarische Struktur der beiden Traditionen weist auf eine lange Vorgeschichte hin, die in die mündlichen Überlieferungen der Frühkulturen führt und möglicherweise auch eine Kenntnis der literarischen Fassung des Themas "Sintflut" in den Hochkulturen voraussetzt. Es ist nicht unsere Aufgabe, den Entwicklungswegen des weltverbreiteten Themas nachzugehen bzw. zu entscheiden, welcher Entwicklungsstufe die biblische Darstellung einzuordnen ist. Es steht aber fest, dass diese nicht ganz einheitlich ist und dass mit intensiver Umarbeitung des traditionellen Stoffes innerhalb der religiösen und theologischen Strömungen Israels gerechnet werden muss. Freilich erlaubt uns die form- und redaktionsgeschichtliche Untersuchung der vorliegenden Berichte über die Sintflut keine sichere Schichtung. Wenn auch die Scheidung der Quellen in Gen. vi-ix als gesichert gelten kann, geht die Reflexion über die Entstehung der Traditionskomplexe oft über Vermutungen nicht hinaus. Auch die gegenseitige Beziehung zwischen der jahwistischen Überlieferung über die Sintflut und jener der Priesterschrift ist kaum eindeutig zu klären; die Abhängigkeit der Priesterschrift von der älteren, jahwistischen Fassung der Sintflut lässt sich nicht nachweisen. Sollte die Priesterschrift die jahwistische Fassung gekannt haben, was durchaus wahrscheinlich ist, so wäre diese nicht die einzige, ja nicht einmal die Hauptquelle gewesen. Ausser dem gemeinsamen fünfgliedrigen Schema der Erzählung und einigen Wiederholungen der Motive oder gar Wendungen sind in beiden Fassungen beträchtliche Unterschiede festzustellen, auf die hier nicht näher eingegangen werden kann. Die beiden in grossen Zügen erhaltenen biblischen Traditionen über die Flut stimmen zwar in der theologischen Grundtendenz überein: sie suchen das allgemeinmenschliche Kulturgut, nämlich das Bewusstsein des Erschaffenseins und zugleich der Gefährdung des Seins durch einen Untergang, das in manchen Kulturkreisen zum Ausdruck gelangt, im Lichte des Gottesverhältnisses darzulegen. Es ist daher selbstverständlich, dass sowohl beim Jahwisten wie auch in der Priesterschrift die Fluterzählung mit dem Schöpfungsvorgang eng verbunden ist. Der Zusammenhang ist ja in der grossen Sintfluttradition fest verankert.

Doch wirkt sich dabei die verschiedene Auffassung von Menschen in seiner Erhöhung und in seinem Fall aus. Die Wege der Übertragung des Urgeschehens in den Zeitraum der Geschichte waren in beiden biblischen Traditionen verschieden. Der rettende Eingriff Gottes nach der Sintflut, der den geschichtlichen Lauf der neuen Menschheit ermöglicht, trägt in der Priesterschrift ein ganz besonderes Merkmal.

Die Aufstellung der sog. "noachitischen Gebote" gehört bekanntlich zum Schlussteil der Sintfluterzählung, nämlich zum Bericht vom Wiedererstehen der Menschheit nach der Katastrophe. Die meisten ausserbiblischen Überlieferungen über die Flut führen diesen Schlussteil weiter aus, indem sie damit den Übergang zur historisch feststellbaren Weltordnung herstellen bzw. die Auswirkung der Flut auf die damalige Menschheit betonen möchten. Neben den ätiologischen Aussagen [1] über die Herkunft der Völker, deren Zerstreuung und Sprachverwirrung kommen auch religiöse oder gar theologische Motive zur Sprache. Es geht zumeist darum, dass die Götter ihren Vernichtungswillen zurücknehmen, und die Davongekommenen Opfer darbringen. Den älteren Traditionen entstammen solche Gedankenkomplexe wie die Verheissung des Nichtwiederkehrens der Flut, die Bewahrung der Menschheit und die Zusicherung des Lebensrhythmus. In rein formeller Hinsicht dürfte die zweigliedrige Gestaltung des Schlussteiles vorgegeben sein, wie dies aus der Parallelität zwischen jahwistischem Text von Gen. viii 21a-22 und priesterschriftlichem Abschluss der Sintfluterzählung (Gen. ix 1-17) hervorgeht. Doch der Vergleich zwischen der negativen und positiven Fassung des göttlichen Beschlusses im jahwistischen Text (Gen. ix 21a-22) und dem Bericht vom Segen und Bund in Gen. ix 1-17 führt

---

[1] Man vgl. F. W. Golka, "The Aetiologies in the Old Testament. Part II", *VT* 27 (1977), SS. 44-6.

zu keinem Aufweis eines vorgegebenen Zusammenhanges. Bei aller Neigung der Priesterschrift zur Interpretation und Auslegung [2] lassen sich die bestehenden Ähnlichkeiten in einzelnen ursprünglichen Motiven der Sintfluterzählung nicht auflösen, worauf wir noch zurückkommen werden.

Die von der Priesterschrift in Gen. ix 1-17 verwendete Stilform verbietet es jedenfalls, den priesterschriftlichen Schlussteil auf die Vorlagen zurückzuführen.[3] Dies bedeutet zwar nicht, dass dieser vom Verfasser der Grundschrift der P bzw. von späteren Redaktoren völlig frei geschaffen wurde. Zudem liegt hier keine übliche ätiologische Auslegung vor sondern ein grundsätzlicher Ausspruch, in dem das Ziel der ganzen Sintfluterzählung dargelegt wird. Man kann aber mit Recht fragen, ob und inwiefern die Reihenfolge Segen-Berit ursprünglich ist, ferner ob die innerhalb des Segens dargestellten Beschränkungen des menschlichen Verfügungsrechtes über die Tierwelt derselben Traditionsschicht wie die Grundsatzerklärung zuzuweisen sind. Endlich wird zu fragen sein, ob bzw. in welchem Sinne der herkömmliche Bundesgedanke für die Gestaltung der Abschlussperikope in Frage kommt.

Da Gen. ix 1-6 unmissverständlich auf den Schöpfungssegen Gottes von Gen. i 28-29 bezug nimmt, scheint die Aussage klar zu sein. Durch die Sintflutkatastrophe ist die Zuneigung Gottes des Schöpfers nicht in Frage gestellt worden. Ist aber dann die feierliche Zusicherung der Fortdauer der Lebensordnung in Form einer *b^erît* zufällig oder wird sie irgendwie vom Bundeserneuerungsgedanken bestimmt?

Es ist mehrmals darauf hingewiesen worden, dass das Bundesverständnis der Priesterschrift von jenem der anderen Traditionen wesentlich abweicht.[4] Eine *b^erît* im Sinne von P kommt nah an eine Verheissung oder feierliche Zusicherung heran, wobei die Bundesinitiative stets von Gott ergriffen wird. Man muss gestehen, dass das heutige Bundesverständnis in der Exegese stark von den zwischenmenschlichen Beziehungen oder gar vom Rechtswesen bestimmt ist. Die form- und literarkritische Forschung hat den Eindruck verstärkt, dass eine alttestamentliche *b^erît* notwendigerweise auf gegenseitigen

---

[2] Vgl. J. G. Vink, *The Date and Origin of the Priestly Code in the Old Testament* (Leiden, 1969).

[3] C. Westermann, *Genesis 1-11* (Neukirchen-Vluyn, 1974), S. 617, betont, dass "die Zweigliederung des abschliessenden Gotteswortes bei P ihm von der Tradition vorgegeben war".

[4] Man vgl. G. von Rad, *Theologie des A.T.* 1 (Berlin, [4]1969), S. 148 f.

Verpflichtungen beruht. Es ist demgegenüber zu betonen, dass das einzigartige Verhältnis, in das Gott in der Genesis zu seiner Schöpfung tritt, nicht unbedingt im Sinne von Leistung und Gegenleistung zu verstehen ist. Es ist nämlich ein Gemeinschaftsverhältnis, das der Gnade Gottes entstammt und die gesammte Menschheit umfasst. Freilich werden damit die Menschen zur Anerkennung der göttlichen Hoheitsrechte verpflichtet, ohne dass dies in einer Reihe von Einzelbestimmungen ausgeführt wird. Ein so verstandener "Bund" hebt sich sicher in einigen Punkten vom Abraham- und Sinaibund ab. Man muss überhaupt fragen, ob der Bundesbegriff im Alten Testament als univok angesehen werden kann, wie das zumeist geschieht. Das Bundesverständnis erfuhr im Laufe der Zeit und im Zusammenhang mit dem wechselnden Schicksal des Gottesvolkes mannigfache Akzentverschiebungen. In den späteren Schriften wird er immer allgemeiner aufgefasst und die Darstellung des sog. Noahbundes ist ein wichtiges wenn auch wenig beachtetes Zeugnis dieser Entwicklung. Freilich ist J. J. P. Valetons These,[5] im Priesterkodex sei das Wort *b^e^rît* ein theologischer Kunstausdruck, längst überwunden, wirkt aber doch in vielen Abhandlungen noch nach.

Ohne in die Diskussion über die Entstehung und Geschichte der Priesterschrift [6] eingreifen zu wollen, soll hier betont werden, dass die Verheissung Gottes an Noah im Sinne einer *b^e^rît* zum Grundbestand dieser Tradition gehört. Dieser Text scheint das Selbstverständnis der priesterlichen Kreise der mittelpersischen Zeit wiederzugeben, wonach das Heilshandeln Gottes nicht nur Israel, sondern allen Menschen, ja der ganzen Schöpfung gilt. Der Erweis der göttlichen Huld in der Schöpfung ist für P eine Art von Vorgeschichte des Bundes, wie etwa die Exodus-Wunder in den Sinai-Traditionen. Die Sonderstellung Israels vor Gott wird dabei weder verneint noch übersehen, darf aber keineswegs zur radikalen Abschliessung und Absonderung von anderen Völkern führen, die beispielsweise in den Aussagen von Joel iv 12 und Maleachi i 2-5 nachklingen. Man darf nicht ausser Acht lassen, dass die als *b^e^rît* dargestellte Verheissung an alle Menschen eine negative Form hat und somit keinesfalls mit dem Sinaibund vergliechen werden kann.

Wenn auf den ersten Seiten der Bibel der mit dem Segen bekräftigte

---

[5] "Bedeutung und Stellung des Wortes *bryt* im Priestercodex", *ZAW* 12 (1892), SS. 1-22.
[6] Vgl. Vink, SS. 8-63.

Fortpflanzungsauftrag und die Herrschaft über alle Lebewesen ausgesagt und mit dem Wort *b^{e}rît* umschrieben wird, so scheint damit eine Deutung des Bundesverhältnisses zwischen Jahwe und seinem Volk vorzuliegen. Zuerst ist diese Deutung negativ. Die im Judentum übliche Überzeugung, dass das göttliche Heil für die Völker [7] nur im Zusammenhang der Erwählung Israels möglich ist, wird indirekt zur Diskussion gestellt. Die priesterliche Fassung des Abrahambundes (Gen. xvii) sagt zwar weiter nichts über die Beteiligung der Völker an den Verheissungen, doch ist die Zusage an Sara, dass sie "zu Völkern werden" soll und Könige von Nationen aus ihr hervorgehen, in diesem Zusammenhang bemerkenswert. Positiv bedeutet es, dass die Völker in einer gottgegebenen Ordnung leben und göttlicher Verheissung teilhaftig werden ohne darin auf das auserwählte Volk angewiesen zu sein. Die allen Menschen ohne Ausnahme zugute kommende Beständigkeit der Welt und ihrer Lebensordnung will nicht nur Ätiologie der gegenwärtigen Welt werden. Zweifellos meint die Priesterschrift nicht eine ideale, Gottes Satzungen befolgende Welt, aber auch nicht eine unter göttlichem Fluch stehende Völkerwelt. Die Sicht der Priesterschrift ist weniger optimistisch als realistisch: sie weiss wohl um die Verderblichkeit allen Fleisches (Gen. vi 12). Wie auch der Umfang des Begriffs *kol-bāśār* zu bestimmen sein mag, ist damit vor allem eine grosse, näher unbestimmte Menschengruppe gemeint, die Subjekt der Verderbnis ist.[8] Diese Verderbnis bleibt nach der Sintflut weiter bestehen, wird aber von göttlicher Langmut und Grossherzigkeit überwunden, indem Gott dem Walten der verhängnisvollen Chaosmächte in der Sintflut ein Ende setzt.

Das bis jetzt Gesagte verbietet es, die sog. noachitischen Gebote als Vorbedingung der *b^{e}rît* zu verstehen. Damit erhebt sich aber die Frage nach ihrer Rolle im priesterschriftlichen Bundesdenken, das beiden Teilen von Gen. ix 1-17 zugrunde liegt. Es besteht kein Grund das der P sonst geläufige Bundesverständnis unserem Text abzusprechen und das Wort *b^{e}rît* lediglich als theologisches Interpretament der Fluttradition hinzustellen. Es ist wahr, dass die lange Vorgeschichte der Fluttradition einen Bundesschluss nicht kennt. Indessen muss

---

[7] Man vgl. A. Rétif-P. Lamarche, *Das Heil der Völker* (Düsseldorf, 1960), und H. Gross, "Der Universalismus des Heils nach der Urgeschichte", *Trier-Theol.Z.* 73 (1964), SS. 145-53.

[8] Ausführlich darüber handelt A. R. Hulst, "*Kol bāśār* in der priesterlichen Fluterzählung", *OTS* 12 (1958), SS. 28-68.

die Frage offen bleiben, inwiefern die Grundschrift von P bzw. ihre späteren Bearbeiter sich durch diese Vorgeschichte verpflichtet wussten. Jedenfalls lässt sich in der Priesterschrift ein zielbewusstes theologisches Denken nachweisen und für dieses Denken ist die Bundesidee konstitutiv. Dazu kommt noch ein anderer Umstand. Sicher ist die Priesterschrift irgendwie an die Fluttradition gebunden, sie scheint aber vor allem die Menschen ihrer Gegenwart anzusprechen und sich mit deren Problemen auseinanderzusetzen. Mit dem Bundesbegriff werden "bestimmte Aussagen über die Beschaffenheit einer Zeit des Gottesvolkes vor seinem Gott zum Ausdruck gebracht",[9] und gerade die priesterschriftliche *b*e*rît* trägt die Merkmale der politischen Lage des Bundesvolkes. Dass die Beziehungen der jüdischen Gemeinde zu andern Volksgruppen in der persischen Zeit akut wurde, braucht nicht lange ausgeführt zu werden. Gleichwohl wäre es ein überaus kühner Gedanke, die fremden Völker in den Israelbund einzubeziehen, und er ist der Priesterschrift kaum zuzumuten. Doch der Umstand, dass der Segen Gottes den Völkern nicht vorenthalten ist, führt dazu, ihre gottgegebene Lebensordnung analog als Bund zu bezeichnen und in manchen Punkten nach dem Vorbild des Israel-Bundes darzustellen.

Ein fernes Echo der Bundesformel mag die Entsprechung von *w*e*'attem* und *wa'*a*nî* in Gen. ix 7, 9 sein; merkwürdigerweise tritt sie auch im Abrahambund hervor (Gen. xvii 4, 9). Dies fällt umso mehr auf, als es im Noah-Text um eine Schlussformel des ersten Teils und die Einführung zum zweiten geht. Die Bundespartner werden in V. 9 ausdrücklich genannt und nochmals im abschliessenden Teil (V. 17) mit *kol-bāśār* umschrieben; ein Bundeszeichen wird festgesetzt. Man muss natürlich mit Nachdruck betonen, dass darüber hinaus Gen. ix 1-17 eine Stilform aufweist, die sich von den meisten Berichten über eine Bundesschliessung unterscheidet. Die augenscheinliche Form der "göttlichen Rede", die schon Gunkel an unserem Text so stark betonte, ist für unsere Reflexion wenig relevant. Dieser Stil entspricht den übrigen Aussagen der Fluterzählung und vor allem dem Schöpfungssegen, auf den hier bezug genommen wird. Wichtiger ist der sorgfältige Aufbau beider Abschlussreden. Die Stilform der Inklusion, die die beiden Reden umrahmt, weist auf einen progressiven Aufbau hin, der jedoch nicht ohne weiteres ersichtlich ist. Von einer *b*e*rît* wird direkt erst ab V. 9 geredet. In

[9] W. Zimmerli, *Grundriss der alttestamentlichen Theologie* (Stuttgart, 1972), S. 47.

V. 8 geht eine Einleitungsformel voraus, die im wesentlichen mit den Einführungsworten von ix 1b übereinstimmt.

Der priesterschriftliche Bundesbegriff gehört entschieden zum verheissenden Typ [10] im Gegensatz zum verpflichtenden mosaischen Bund. Wird dieser in der heute greifbaren Priesterschrift eher vorausgesetzt ohne ausführlich dargestellt zu werden, so hängt dies mit den Sinai-Satzungen zusammen. Da das vorexilische Volk an ihnen scheiterte, galt es auf die Bundesverheissungen an Abraham zurückzugreifen. Sie enthielten keinerlei Verpflichtungen noch Satzungen, von denen die Gültigkeit und Wirkung des Bundes abhängig wäre. Somit scheint es unangebracht zu sein, die noachitischen Gebote – wenigstens in der Absicht der priesterschriftlichen Grundschrift – als Einzelbestimmungen des Bundes zu verstehen. Übrigens war ein auf menschliche Gegenleistung gestützter Gottesbund der Priesterschrift völlig fremd: er war die Frucht der Gnade. Vielleicht ist es kein Zufall, dass die Priesterschrift die übliche Redenwendung *kārat b^e^rît* meidet und dafür *hēqîm* oder *nātan b^e^rît* verwendet. Es geht darum, die Gratuität des göttlichen Bundes zu betonen.

Umso dringender wird die Frage nach dem Sinn der in Gen. ix 4, 6 aufgestellten Satzungen und nach deren Verhältnis zu der *b^e^rît* von ix 10-16. Bereits die Reihenfolge Verpflichtung – Bund wäre nicht evident im Rahmen der üblichen Bundesschliessung. Man kann die Parallelität des Segens mit dem Bund in Betracht ziehen, doch kaum einen sichtbaren Zusammenhang zwischen den Satzungen und der Zusicherung Gottes über das Nichtwiedereintreffen der Flut. Die Wiederaufnahme des Schöpfersegens ist in rein formaler Hinsicht mit der Vorgeschichte im üblichen Bundesformular vergleichbar, obwohl eigentlich erst mit dem Bund das Urgeschehen zur Geschichte wird. Die Priesterschrift hat die *b^e^rît*-Vorstellung zu einem System ausgebaut, das die ganze Geschichte umfasst.[11] Es wäre wohl besser von einer paränetischen Einleitung zum folgenden Bund zu reden. Im Deuteronomium ist es stets eine Paränese historischen Inhalts; in der priesterschriftlichen Darstellung des Urgeschehens knüpfte sie notwendigerweise an den Schöpfungssegen an. Es ist also alles andere als eine Gebots- oder Gesetzesparänese, wie sie im späteren Schrifttum anzutreffen ist. Die Kompositionstechnik entspricht den

[10] Vgl. M. Weinfeld, *b^e^rît*, *ThWAT* 1, Sp. 799.

[11] G. Fohrer, "Altes Testament—'Amphiktyonie' und 'Bund'?", *ThLZ* 91 (1966), Sp. 900. Überdies s. P. Buis, *La notion d'alliance dans l'Ancien Testament* (Paris, 1976).

Gesetzen der paränetischen Literatur: freie, ungezwungene, allgemeingültige Hinweise, die nur lose mit der theologischen Argumentation zusammenhängen. Es liegt hier eine Stichwortkomposition vor, die um die Worte "Blut" und "Leben" gruppiert wird.

Die Ausdehnung der Herrschaft des Menschen über die Tierwelt wird im Hinblick auf die weitere Argumentation hervorgehoben; in der Tat lag sie schon der Schöpfungserzählung (Gen. i 29) zugrunde ohne jedoch an dieser Stelle erwähnt zu werden. Hier wurden bekanntlich zwei verschiedene Traditionen eingearbeitet. Ausser der Vorstellung von der Herrschaft der Menschen über die Tiere, die wahrscheinlich auch deren Töten umfasste, weiss der priesterschriftliche Verfasser um einen allgemeinen Frieden der Urzeit, wo Vegetabilien die einzige Nahrung des Menschen gewesen waren. Die in Gen. i 29-30 bestehende Spannung wird hier nicht in dem Sinne überwunden, dass alle Lebewesen in die Schuld des Menschen verwickelt waren und somit eine Neuregelung der Beziehungen zwischen Mensch und Tier notwendig geworden ist. Die Zusammenfügung beider Traditionen in dem Sinne, dass mit der Bestimmung der vegetarischen Nahrung das Töten der Tiere der Verfügungsgewalt des Menschen vorenthalten wäre, mag vom geschichtlichen Denken bestimmt worden sein. Der Gedanke an eine ursprüngliche Harmonie der Schöpfung passte wohl zur Vorstellung von einer Schöpfung die "gut" war. Doch bei einem Schritt vom Urgeschehen zur Geschichte, also zu einem gegenwartsnahen Zustand, verlangte dies nach einer weiteren Erklärung. Dieses Denken war aber zugleich von der politischen Lage des Gottesvolkes bestimmt. Das religiöse Klima der letzten Exilsjahre, das bei Deuterojesaja zum Ausdruck kommt und in den ersten Jahrzehnten nach dem Exil immer wieder zum Vorschein tritt – man denke nur an die *b^erît* mit den Völkern bei Zacharia xi 10 – förderte die pazifistischen Tendenzen.[12] Man war geneigt, angesichts der religiösen und politischen Toleranz der persischen Behörde im Nahen Osten zu betonen, dass die Oberherrschaft der Menschen nur der Tierwelt gilt und die zwischenmenschlichen Beziehungen als Echo des Schöpfungssegens zu gestalten sind. Der Segen Gottes für die Menschen behält auch nach der grossen Exilkatastrophe seine Wirkung, gerade wie nach der Sintflut; der Gedanke wird in das Urgeschehen zurückprojiziert. Die im Schöpfungsbericht festgesetzte Grenze zwischen Mensch und Tier muss jetzt eindeutiger gezogen

[12] Vgl. Vink, S. 84.

werden, nicht weil die übrigen Lebenwesen in die Schuld des Menschen verwickelt worden wären, sondern damit das Verfügungsrecht über das Leben genau umschrieben werden kann. Dieses Recht liegt eben in Gottes Hand und kann selbst im Hinblick auf die der menschlichen Gewalt übergebenen Tiere nicht überfordert werden.

Einzelne sog. "noachitische Gebote" sollen hier auf ihre Herkunft und Begriffsinhalt nicht geprüft werden. Es ist jedoch zu bemerken, dass die Vorstellung vom Leben, das mit dem Blut identisch ist bzw. dem pulsierenden Blut innewohnt, ein relativ spätes Theologumenon der priesterlichen Kreise bildet und kaum über das sechste Jahrhundert hinausreicht.[13] Ursprünglich in der Opfertheologie beheimatet, wird der Gedanke wohl in den Exilsjahren in die Anthropologie übertragen. Zur Weiterführung einer paränetischen Reflexion genügt an sich, dass die beiden Begriffe "Blut" und "Leben" aufeinander bezogen werden. Allerdings lässt der komplizierte Aufbau der Aussage vermuten, dass es dem Verfasser auch um eine exakte Bestimmung des theologischen Inhalts ging.

Die Form der eingeführten Einschränkungen im Verfügungsrecht des Menschen über das Leben erinnert an die apodiktischen Sätze. Diese Form hat auch die spätere Tradition verleitet, darin Einzelgebote für die Heiden zu sehen.[14] Das mehrdeutige *'ak* pflegt in der Priesterschrift eine Einschränkung einzuführen, kaum aber ein selbstständiges Gebot. Die paränetische Begründung zielt auf Gewährleistung und Sicherung des menschlichen Lebens, das durch die Gewalttat und die Urwildheit gefährdet werden kann.[15] Gott setzt darin keine zu befolgenden Gebote ein, sondern erinnert an die Grundvoraussetzung des von ihm gesegneten menschlichen Lebens. Durch eine Gewalttat des Menschen wird nicht nur eine bestimmte, gottgegebene Ordnung in Frage gestellt sondern das Vorbild Gottes im Menschen getroffen. Dieser Hinweis entstammt der priesterschriftlichen Auslegung des göttlichen Anspruchs auf das menschliche Leben. Die Formulierung des Anspruchs mag eine sehr alte Überlieferung wiedergeben, wie dies aus der Solidaritätshaftung von Mensch und Tier hervorgeht, die übrigens dem Bundesbuch (Ex. xxi 28-32) wohlbekannt ist. Das Problem der Verantwortlichkeit des Täters wird nicht gestellt.

---

[13] Vgl. H. Christ, *Blutvergiessen im A.T.* (Basel, 1977), S. 140.

[14] Vgl. H. Revel, "Noahide Laws", *Univ. Jewish Encyclopaedia* 8, SS. 227 f.

[15] Man vgl. K. H. Kaspar, *Die priesterliche Bericht vom 'Noahbund'. Eine exegetisch-theologische Untersuchung zu Gen 9, 1-17* (Diss. lic., Münster i. W., 1969, Maschinenschr.), S. 176.

Wichtig ist die Tatsache, dass das gottgeschenkte Leben angetastet worden ist. Der Abschluss der Bundes-Vorgeschichte ist eher an den Folgen des Tatbestandes interessiert: wie nämlich gegen einen Mörder vorzugehen ist. Ob der chiastisch dargestellte Grundsatz von 6a, wonach der Strafvollzug durch den Menschen zu erfolgen hat, apodiktischer Rechtssatz ist, muss dahingestellt bleiben. Der kunstvolle Aufbau und das Wortspiel *dam – 'ādām* führt eher in ein weisheitliches Milieu, das an den Vergeltungsmassnahmen interessiert war. Im Rahmen der Paränese werden gern Sprüche verschiedener Herkunft und verschiedenen Inhalts unvermittelt zusammengefügt und einem Grundgedanken untergeordnet. Dieser ist aber klar: der Mensch richtet den Mörder lediglich als bevollmächtigter Vollstrecker der göttlichen Forderung, da letztlich Gott und nur Gott der einzig legitime Bluträcher aller Menschen ist (Kaspar, S. 85).

Die Weiterentwicklung des Themas der "noachitischen Gebote" hängt mit der Entwicklung des Bundesbegriffs zusammen. Man war immer mehr geneigt, den Bundesinhalt in den Einzelbestimmungen zu sehen, die wieder gern mit dem Gesetz identifiziert wurden. Als Ansatz zu dieser Deutung griff die spätere Forschung gern nach den besprochenen Grundsätzen des Noahbundes. Die in der Bundesparänese dargestellten Richtlinien des menschlichen Zusammenlebens und vor allem die Unantastbarkeit des Lebens überhaupt wurden zu einem kleinen codex der Mindestforderungen für die Heiden, die sich einer gottgegebenen Ordnung einfügen wollten. Selbst innerhalb der nachbiblischen Literatur wurde z.B. der Menschenmord nur ein Verbot unter anderen; diese Auffassung scheint auch im Aposteldekret von Apg. xv 29 (vgl. 20) nachzuwirken. Dabei gingen aber einige wichtige kulturgeschichtliche und theologische Inhalte verloren. In der heutigen Erforschung der Bibel, wo der Heilsuniversalismus so sehr betont wird, sollten diese Inhalte wieder neu geprüft und ans Licht gestellt werden.

MOSES UND ARON

Der biblische Stoff und seine Interpretation in der gleichnamigen Oper von Arnold Schönberg *

VON

ODIL HANNES STECK

Zürich

Es mag manchen wundernehmen, auf diesem Kongreß inmitten historischer Studien zum Alten Testament auch den Vortrag über eine Oper zu finden—gewiß für jeden, der sie kennt, eines der großen und faszinierenden Bühnenwerke unseres Jahrhunderts: die Oper "Moses und Aron" von Arnold Schönberg.[1] Aus zwei Gründen jedoch steht dieses Werk unserem Wiener Kongreß weniger fern, als es auf den ersten Blick scheinen möchte.

Der eine Grund: Wien. Arnold Schönberg, 1874 hier geboren, bildet zusammen mit seinen Schülern Alban Berg und Anton von Webern musikgeschichtlich den Kern der sogenannten "Zweiten Wiener Schule", die in den Jahren nach dem Ersten Weltkrieg in ihrem musikalischen Profil voll hervortritt; Schönbergs erste Studien zu "Moses und Aron" fallen noch in diese Zeit. Neben Joseph Haydns Oratorium "Die Schöpfung", 1798 im Palais des Fürsten Schwarzenberg in Wien uraufgeführt, ist Schönbergs "Moses und Aron" dasjenige Werk, in dem sich das musikalische Wien und das Alte Testament am meisten nahekommen, auch wenn die maßgeblichen Gestaltungsvorgänge biographisch gesehen bereits jenseits der Wiener Jahre Schönbergs liegen: die erste Textfassung dieses Stoffes 1928, die endgültige Niederschrift von Text, Komposition und szenischen Vorstellungen für die ersten beiden Akte in den Jahren 1930-32 sowie die Weiterarbeit an Text, Szene und Komposition des im wesentlichen unvertont gebliebenen dritten Aktes

---

* Im folgenden wird das Manuskript des Kongreßvortrags wiedergegeben. Eine erheblich erweitere Fassung, die zusätzlich ausführliche Nachweise und Stellungnahmen im Rahmen der Schönberg-Forschung bietet, ist mit gleichem Titel als Kaiser Traktat Nr 56 (München, 1981) erschienen.

[1] Zur Erleichterung für den interessierten Leser werden Textzitate nach dem Textbuch zur Oper mit Angabe von Akt, Szene und Seitenzahl gegeben: Arnold Schoenberg, *Moses und Aron, Oper in drei Akten. Textbuch* (Mainz, 1957).

bis etwa 1937; auch die Uraufführung der Oper fand nicht in Wien, sondern Jahre nach Schönbergs Tod in Hamburg und Zürich statt.

Aber wir wollen mit unserem Vortrag nicht nur einem Wiener Genius auf diesem Kongreß unsere Reverenz erweisen. Der zweite Grund, in diesem Rahmen über Schönberg zu sprechen, ist ein sachlicher. Der bedeutende Schönberg-Kenner und -Biograph Hans Heinz Stuckenschmidt hat 1957 anläßlich der Zürcher szenischen Uraufführung der Oper geschrieben: "Schönberg hat mit diesem genialen Werk abermals der Bühne Anregungen gegeben, die weit über seine Zeit hinauswirken werden. Die biblische Größe seiner Konzeption spottet aller Einwände".[2] Eine Textprobe aus dem dritten Akt mag solche Wertung illustrieren; dort sagt Moses zu seinem Bruder Aron:

Dienen, dem Gottesgedanken zu dienen,
ist die Freiheit, zu der dieses Volk
auserwählt ist.
Du aber unterwarfst es fremden Göttern,
unterwarfst es dem Kalb und der
Feuer- und der Wolkensäule.
Denn du tust wie das Volk,
weil du fühlst wie es
und so denkst.
Und der Gott, den du zeigst,
ist ein Bild der Ohnmacht,
ist abhängig von einem Gesetz über
sich; muß erfüllen, was er versprochen hat; muß tun, um was er
gebeten wird,
ist gebunden an sein Wort.
Wie die Menschen handeln—gut
oder böse—so muß er:
strafen ihr Böses, belohnen ihr Gutes.
Aber der Mensch ist unabhängig und tut,
was ihm beliebt aus freiem Willen.
Hier beherrschen die Bilder bereits
den Gedanken, statt ihn auszudrücken.
Ein Allmächtiger—was
immer er auch halte—ist zu nichts
verpflichtet
durch nichts gebunden.
Ihn bindet nicht die Tat des Frevlers,
nicht das Gebet des Guten,
nicht das Opfer des Reuigen.[3]

[2] *Neue Zürcher Zeitung* Nr. 1685/1 vom 9.6.1957.
[3] III/1 (S. 31 f.).

Dieses Zitat läßt ahnen, daß bereits der Text von "Moses und Aron", den sich Schönberg unbeschadet biblischer Grundlagen in völlig eigenständiger Sprachgestalt selbst geschrieben hat, nicht irgendein beliebiges Libretto darstellt. Dieser Text ist ein von Schönberg bereits sprachlich höchst überlegt und präzise gestaltetes Sinnganzes, das in seinem sachlichen Gewicht auch uns zu Verstehen und Vergleich mit dem biblischen Stoff herausfordert.

Dieser Herausforderung wollen wir uns unter folgenden Voraussetzungen stellen. Erstens: Wir konzentrieren unsere Ausführungen ganz auf Schönbergs *Text* der Oper; von den Sinnaspekten Schönbergs, die sich aus seinen genauen szenischen Vorstellungen und vor allem aus der Anlage der musikalischen Komposition der ersten beiden Akte ergeben, kann in unserem Rahmen jetzt nur indirekt die Rede sein. Zweitens: Auch *der Text des* nicht mehr komponierten *dritten Aktes* wird von uns als integraler Bestandteil des von Schönberg in dieser Oper erstellten Sinnganzen angesehen; verbreitete Mutmaßungen der Art, Schönberg habe "Moses und Aron" selbst für nicht vollendbar gehalten oder sei gar von der Substanz seines Werkes in späteren Jahren abgerückt, sind völlig gegenstandslos, anderslautende Spekulationen müßig. Drittens: Wie "Moses und Aron" zu verstehen ist, ist ausweislich der Schönberg-Forschung und der Regiekonzepte zahlreicher Bühneninszenierungen überaus umstritten; nur darin scheint seltsame Einmütigkeit zu herrschen, daß das Religiöse dieser Oper nur als Einkleidung säkularer Realitäten anzusehen ist. Der von uns vorgelegte Versuch, "Moses und Aron" zu verstehen, richtet sich streng auf die *Aussageintention*, die *Schönberg selbst* vorhatte. Als solcher basiert er auf einer genauen, Wort für Wort im Ganzen bedenkenden Untersuchung des Textes im Sinne seines Verfassers und auf einer Auswertung der erreichbaren Selbstzeugnisse Schönbergs.

Wenn wir uns heute morgen dem Reiz überlassen, den Text von Schönbergs "Moses und Aron" und seinen biblischen Stoff ineinander zu spiegeln, dann sollen uns *drei Fragestellungen* leiten. Zuerst die eher noch vordergründige Frage nach dem *Stoff*: Welches Bild ergibt sich, wenn man den biblischen Stoff, wie er sich dem Alttestamentler darstellt, mit Handlungsgefüge und Wortgestalt der Oper vergleicht? Die zweite, nun allerdings zentrale Frage richtet sich auf die *Interpretation* des Stoffes: Welchen Sinn hat Schönberg in dem biblischen Stoff gesehen und wie verhält sich Schönbergs Sinngebung zum Alten Testament? Dieser Vergleich muß ergeben, ob und in welcher

Weise die Sache des Alten Testaments selbst von Schönberg zur Gestaltung gebracht wurde und hier zurecht von "biblischer Größe" gesprochen werden kann. Drittens schließlich wird nach *Folgerungen* aus den gewonnenen Einsichten zu fragen sein.

I. *Der Stoff*

Das äußere Handlungsgefüge der Oper "Moses und Aron" geht mit der biblischen Erzählungsfolge im großen wie in wichtigen Einzelzügen auf den ersten Blick durchaus *konform*—Zeichen eingehender und nachdenklicher Bibellektüre Schönbergs, die der Textgestaltung sicher zugrundeliegt. Der *erste Akt* hat seine stoffliche Grundlage in Ex. iii und iv: Die Oper beginnt in der Wüste mit Moses Berufung durch Gott aus dem brennenden Dornbusch, dann wird sein Bruder Aaron unterwiesen als Moses Mund und Mittler für Israel, und schließlich—Höhepunkt des ersten Aktes—das Auftreten beider vor dem Volk: Aaron gibt Israel die Gottesworte Moses weiter und führt die drei Beglaubigungswunder aus, die Moses angekündigt waren—der Stab Moses, der zur Schlange wird und wieder zum Stab, die aussätzige und wieder gesundete Hand Moses, schließlich das ausgegossene Nilwasser, das zu Blut wird—, und das Volk kommt zum Glauben. Nicht anders der *zweite Akt*. Das Aufbegehren des aus Ägypten inzwischen befreiten Volkes, als Mose vierzig Tage fern auf dem Gottesberg weilt, das Goldene, auf Betreiben des Volkes von Aaron gefertigte Kalb, vor dem das Volk opfert, tafelt und sich belustigt, die Rückkehr Moses, das Zertrümmern der Gesetzestafeln und Aarons Zurechtweisung durch Mose, all das hat seine Basis in der berühmten biblischen Erzählung vom Goldenen Kalb Ex. xxxii. Auch der nur im Text gegebene *dritte Akt* gründet sich auf ein biblisches Kapitel, nun aus dem 4. Mosebuch, Num. xx: der Tod Aarons im Anschluß an das Wasserwunder für das dürstende Volk, das der Stab dem Felsen in der Wüste entlockt hat. Hinzu kommen zahlreiche Einzelzüge wie zum Beispiel das erste und zweite Gebot des Dekalogs oder die Israel geleitende Wolken- und Feuersäule, die im biblischen Text an anderer Stelle ihren Anhalt haben.

Sieht man nun aber näher zu, dann treten neben solchen Übereinstimmungen im äußeren Handlungsgefüge für den Alttestamentler freilich stärker die *Unterschiede* in den Vordergrund; sie betreffen Auswahl und Perspektive des Stoffes ebenso wie die Akzentuierung der Einzelzüge.

Zunächst zur *Auswahl.* Schönberg baut die Handlung der Oper auf drei im Alten Testament weiter auseinanderliegende Texte: Ex. iii und iv, Ex. xxxii und Num. xx. Als Alttestamentler können wir diese Texte jedoch nicht so isolieren; sie gehören in der Bibel ja in einen großen Erzählungszusammenhang von der Schöpfung bis zum Eintritt Israels in das gelobte Land; erst aus diesem Zusammenhang empfangen sie ihren Sinn. Moseberufung und Aaronbeauftragung zielen auf die Freilassung des Volkes durch den Pharao, auf Auszug aus Ägypten und Landnahme. Das Goldene Kalb wie das Wasserwunder aus dem Felsen sind in der biblischen Geschichtsdarstellung nur gravierend-retardierende Einzelepisoden auf diesem Wege, und die gelegentlich erwähnte Spannung zwischen Mose und Aaron ist in der Bibel nirgends prinzipiell und vor allem keineswegs dominierend.—Schönberg hingegen wählt so aus, daß das wirklich Dominierende des biblischen Berichtes verschwindet: Die Plagenwunder vor Pharao, der endlich erwirkte Auszug aus Ägypten, die für Israel grundlegende Rettung am Schilfmeer liegen in der Oper zwischen dem ersten und zweiten Akt,[4] werden also szenisch völlig übergangen und nur in der Rückblende matt gestreift; das fundamentale Geschehen der Gesetzgebung am Sinai, in der Bibel immerhin über fünfzig Kapitel, kommt ebensowenig zur Darstellung [5] wie der beherrschende Zug Aarons als Urbild des Priesters Gottes; und das Ziel, der Einzug Israels in das gelobte Land, liegt bereits weit jenseits des Handlungsrahmens der Oper.[6] Schönberg verfährt so nicht zufällig oder aus dramaturgischen Überlegungen, sondern in voller Absicht: Sein Moses sieht in der Befreiung des Volkes aus Ägypten dezidiert das Werk Arons, das Israel in Wahrheit nur in tiefere Knechtschaft geführt hat;[7] seinem Moses ist das Sinaigesetz mit Lohn-, Strafe- und Opferbestimmungen im Unterschied zu Aron

[4] Das Ende des ersten Aktes entspricht im biblischen Bericht Ex. iv 31; das Zwischenspiel und der Beginn des zweiten Aktes basieren auf der in Ex. xxxii 1 erzählten Situation.

[5] Schönberg übergeht nicht nur die Gesetzgebung in Ex. xx-xxiii, xxv-xxxi, die handlungsmäßig vor den zweiten Akt gehörte, sondern auch Ex. xxxiv und die großen Passagen priesterlicher Gesetze in Ex. xxxv—Num. x, die in das Handlungsgeschehen zwischen dem zweiten und dritten Akt fallen. Der dritte Akt selbst spielt in einer von Schönberg frei geschaffenen Szene, die in dem biblischen Bericht zwischen dem erfolgten Wasserwunder (Num. xx 11) und dem Tod Aarons (Num. xx 28), der als letztes biblisches Handlungsgeschehen auch in die Oper aufgenommen ist, zu situieren wäre.

[6] Bei Schönberg bleibt Israel in der Situation von Num. xx, in der Wüste.

[7] Vgl. vor allem III/1 (S. 32).

gerade nicht ein wesentlicher Zugang Israels zu Gott;[8] und daß das Land, wo Milch und Honig fließt, ein wirkliches Land wäre, ist in der Oper wieder Mißverständnis Arons für ein anderes Ziel.[9]

Eine zweite Differenz betrifft die *unterschiedliche Perspektive des biblischen Stoffes*. Schönberg sieht die verwendeten, sehr eigenständig ausgewählten Texte alle auf einer Ebene, so wie sie jetzt in der Bibel gegeben sind. Infolgedessen muß er mit einer Fülle von Aspekten, ja auch Spannungen der biblischen Gesamterzählung fertigwerden, um deren Verstehen er, wie wir wissen, hart gerungen hat—Aspekte und Spannungen in Einzelheiten der Handlung, in der Zeichnung Moses und vor allem in der schillernden Zeichnung Aarons. Der alttestamentlichen Forschung hingegen stellt sich derselbe Stoff in seinem biblisch-erzählenden Rahmen ganz anders dar—nicht auf einer Ebene, sondern in geschichtlicher Tiefendimension. Für unsere alttestamentliche Perspektive ist der Stoff ja nicht Endstadium einer sklavischen, sondern einer produktiven, fortschreibenden Überlieferung, in der mehrere Jahrhunderte ihre Spuren hinterlassen haben—übereinandergelagerte und verschränkte Wachstumsschichten, durch die unterschiedliche und spannungsvolle Akzente im überlieferten Bild der Frühgeschichte Israels zueinander kamen. Dieser Vorgang produktiver Weiterüberlieferung der eigenen Frühgeschichte aufgrund einer sich wandelnden Gotteserfahrung späterer Zeiten ist es, weswegen das Bild Moses wechselt — der machtvolle, wunderkräftige Führer des Volkes oder der Künder des Gesetzes, der Bringer und Wahrer des Verbotes anderer Götter und ihrer Bilder. Deshalb aber wechselt auch das Bild des Volkes, eines glaubenden, wankelmütigen, abfallenden, gehorsamen, murrenden Volkes. Und deshalb wechselt vor allem das Bild Aarons—als Volksführer, als Urbild des wahren Priesters, aber auch als problematische Gestalt, rebellisch gegen Mose, ungehorsam wie Mose, eine Gestalt, die dem Abfall des Volkes von Gott nachgibt und das Wirken Moses desavouiert. In Moses und Aaron der biblischen Erzählung kommen vorwiegend Autoritäts- und Lehrprobleme einer viel späteren Zeit zur Klärung durch produktive Weitergestaltung der gründenden Frühgeschichte Israels. Wie ja auch in der Geschichte vom Goldenen Kalb nicht ein Ereignis aus der Wüstenzeit selbst aufgegriffen wird, sondern das viel spätere Staatsheiligtum des frühköniglichen Nordreiches, einbezogen in das Bild der Frühzeit und aus ihm kritisiert.

---

[8] Vgl. vor allem II/5 (S. 28).

[9] Vgl. vor allem III/1 (S. 30).

Aus dieser historischen Tiefendimension eines langzeitigen Überlieferungswerdens der Texte also resultiert ihre komplex-spannungsvoll vorliegende Gestalt in der Bibel; aus ihr wird sie für alttestamentliche Forschung verständlich. Schönberg kennt diese Perspektive nicht; er hat ganz flächig, wie er selbst schreibt, "... aus dem mächtigen Stoff vor allem diese Elemente in den Vordergrund gerückt: Der Gedanke des unvorstellbaren Gottes, des auserwählten Volkes und des Volksführers".[10]

Dieses Briefzitat führt uns nun zur dritten Differenz, der *unterschiedlichen Akzentuierung der Einzelzüge* in der Bibel und bei Schönberg im Dienste jener drei exponierten Elemente. Schönbergs Eingriffe in die biblische Vorlage sind in dieser Hinsicht besonders tief.

Schon *die grundlegende Berufung des Moses aus dem Dornbusch* zu Beginn der Oper ist völlig umgestaltet.[11] Moses wird hier mitnichten zum Befreier aus Ägypten und Führer in das Verheißungsland berufen; sein Auftrag lautet nur: "Verkünde!" Bei Schönberg hat Gott Moses nämlich einzig und allein eine Erkenntnis gewährt, er hat den Gottesgedanken der Väter in ihm wiedererweckt; und dieser Gedanke, diese gemäße Wahrnehmung Gottes lautet in den ersten Worten der Oper: "Einziger, ewiger, allgegenwärtiger, unsichtbarer und unvorstellbarer Gott ...!" Moses Auftrag bei Schönberg ist es allein, diesen Gottesgedanken Israel zu verkünden, weil Gott dieses Volk befreien will, nicht aus Ägypten, sondern "daß es nicht mehr Vergänglichem diene!" Entsprechend sind die biblischen Zusagen Gottes an Moses bei Schönberg nicht auf das gelobte Land gerichtet, sondern wieder verändert: "... das gelobe ich dir: Dieses Volk ist auserwählt vor allen Völkern, das Volk des einzigen Gottes zu sein, daß es ihn erkenne und sich ihm allein ganz widme; daß es alle Prüfungen bestehe, denen—in Jahrtausenden—der Gedanke ausgesetzt ist. Und das verheiße ich dir: Ich will euch dorthin führen, wo ihr mit dem Ewigen einig und allen Völkern ein Vorbild werdet." Am Ende des dritten Aktes wird dieses gottgesetzte Ziel Israels ausdrücklich aufgenommen und präzisiert: "... in (der Wunschlosigkeit) der Wüste seid ihr unüberwindlich und werdet das Ziel erreichen: Vereinigt mit Gott".[12] So lauten die letzten Worte des Operntextes, ein Ring schließt sich, die These kehrt in der Synthese wieder. Doch

[10] Vgl. A. Schoenberg, *Briefe*, ausgewählt und hrsg. von E. Stein (Mainz, 1958), S. 188.
[11] Vgl. I/1 (S. 5-6).
[12] Vgl. III/1 (S. 32).

zurück zum Anfang der Oper. Gegen den biblischen Text mit seinen konkret-einmaligen Auszugsereignissen akzentuiert Schönberg die Anfangsszene der Berufung also auf eine Erkenntnis, gerichtet auf das geoffenbarte Wesen Gottes, nicht allein jetzt beim Auszug, sondern wie es immer ist, wie es denkend als Gedanke von Moses wahrgenommen wird und vom Volk bewahrend aufgenommen werden soll. Die veränderte Verheißung, die Führung zur Vereinigung mit Gott, entspricht dieser allzeitigen Wesensperspektive.

Konsequent wird auch *im Fortgang der Oper* nach dieser Berufungsszene der biblische Stoff mit seinem dramatischen Hin und Her in diesem Sinne von Schönberg ganz neu akzentuiert, und zwar bis zu Beginn des letzten Aktes zu einer einzigen Kette nicht bestandener "Prüfungen" [13] dieses Gottesgedankens in Israel—die große Antithese in der Sicht Schönbergs. Das von Moses wahrgenommene Wesen Gottes drängt zu Verkündigung und Aufnahme, aber, so läßt die Opernhandlung nun erleben, es ereignet sich auf verschiedene Weise ein einziges Scheitern—bei Aron, der der Mittler sein sollte, und beim Volk, ja am Ende des zweiten Aktes zeitweilig sogar im Zweifel von Moses.

Schönberg exponiert drei Modi dieses Scheiterns. Auf höchst subtile Weise wird das Scheitern der Vermittlung des Wesens Gottes an Israel vorgeführt in den beiden Lehrdialogen zwischen Moses und Aron allein—zu Anfang bei der Beauftragung Arons [14] und am Ende bei seiner Zurechtweisung durch Moses nach dem Goldenen Kalb.[15] Moses will im Sinne seines Auftrags, daß Aron dem Volk das allzeitige Wesen Gottes vermittelt, den freien und darum unvorstellbaren Gott, frei auch gegenüber seinen jeweiligen Handlungen für Israel in einzelnen, greifbaren Verheißungen, Wundern, Geboten und Verboten. Aron hingegen orientiert sich nicht an Gott und seinem Wesen, sondern allein am Volk und seinen Möglichkeiten, Gott aufzunehmen—der Weg des Volkes zu Gott ist sein Leitbild. Deshalb verkürzt Aron das Wesen Gottes und nimmt nur den je und je dem Volk anschaulich-vorstellbaren Gott auf—Gottes partielle, jeweilige Einzelmanifestationen, an denen geliebt, geopfert, gehorcht, gehofft werden kann; der Gottesgedanke Moses, das allzeitig freie Wesen Gottes, so meint er, vermittle sich darin indirekt, tatsächlich aber geht es in der Vermittlung verloten—eine Position

---

[13] Vgl. I/1 (S. 6).
[14] Vgl. I/2 (S. 6-8).
[15] Vgl. II/5 (S. 26-9).

handlicher Theologie, am Ende des zweiten Aktes voll verzweifelter Anfechtung auch für Moses selbst: Ist das wahr, "So war alles Wahnsinn, was ich gedacht habe, und kann und darf nicht gesagt werden! O Wort, du Wort, das mir fehlt!"[16]

Massiver mißlingt in einem zweiten Modus des Scheiterns die Vermittlung des Gottesgedankens, als Moses in den Hintergrund gerät und Aron mit seiner Sendung allein vor das Volk tritt am Ende des ersten Aktes [17]—im biblischen Grundtext Ex. iv ein problemlos vollkommen Glauben weckender Vorgang.[18] Anders Schönberg—nachgerade im Widerspruch zur Bibel. Stand im ersten Modus des Scheiterns noch der partiell-manifeste Gott, den Aron protegiert, der Vermittlung des Wesens Gottes an Israel im Wege, so sind es nun die Erwartungen des Volkes. In dieser vierten Szene des ersten Aktes wird der Gottesgedanke Moses von Aron angepaßt an die maßgeblichen Erwartungen des Volkes an das Göttliche und diesen Erwartungen völlig unterworfen. Aron führt die drei Wunder aus und handhabt in ihnen Gott vorstellbar-hoffnungserweckend als den, der menschliches Vermögen zu übersteigen vermag—Gott demonstrabel als der Stärkere, Größere, wie ihn das Volk jetzt braucht.[19] Gott in seinem Wesen also verloren und ersetzt durch Gott, wie er den Wünschen und Bedürfnissen des Volkes rational genügt; der Glaube an den Auszugsgott ist dadurch geweckt;[20] Vergeistigtes mag später, im Alter kommen.[21]

Aber selbst mit dieser Verfälschung, die den allzeit unvorstellbaren Gott durch den jeweilig anschaulich-gebrauchten Gott ersetzt, scheitert Aron schließlich—in der grandiosen Szene des Goldenen Kalbs, als Gott das Volk warten läßt und schweigt.[22] Hier, in völliger Lösung von Moses, führt Arons Position beim Volk nicht mehr zur Verfälschung des Gottesgedankens, sondern in einem dritten Modus des Scheiterns zur totalen Antithese. Was hier am Kalb als Gott gefeiert wird, ist nurmehr der Mensch selbst: "Verehrt euch selbst in diesem Sinnbild!",[23] sagt Aron. Religion ist hier nurmehr

---

[16] II/5 (S. 29).

[17] Vgl. den zweiten Teil von I/4 (S. 13-17).

[18] Vgl. Ex. iv 30 f.

[19] Vgl. die theologische Funktion der drei Beglaubigungswunder gemäß der Gottesstimme in I/1 (S. 5) mit der Funktion, die sie in Arons Ausführung in I/4 gewinnen (S. 13 ff.).

[20] Vgl. die Chorstücke in I/4.

[21] I/4 (S. 16).

[22] II/3 (S. 22-5) und schon II/2 (S. 20 f.).

[23] II/3 (S. 22) und schon II/2 (S. 21).

pure Projektion, produziert aus dem Inneren des Menschen. Gegenüber dem scheinbar "seelenlosen Glauben" Moses [24] ist Gott nurmehr Bedürfnis aus alltagsnaher Lebensgegenwart [25] — Scheingöttlichkeit, gebraucht, überschaubar, fühlbar, ordnend, begreiflich, mächtig; Göttliches erlebt als Aufopferung, Suggestion und Unterwerfung, erlebt als Humanität, Sozialmenschlichkeit,[26] Hingabe, erlebt als Verwüstung, Rausch, sexuelle Orgiastik. Hier ist die größte Distanz zum Gottesgedanken Moses erreicht. Die Orientierung am Volk führt hier nicht nur zu Verengungen Gottes, insofern sich seine partiellen Manifestationen als Bilder vor sein Wesen schieben; hier am Goldenen Kalb ist sich nun der Mensch selbst Gottesbild, der religiöse Mensch und sonst absolut nichts!

Der dritte Akt mit seinem großen, Aron decouvrierenden Monolog Moses [27] bringt bei Schönberg die Synthese, die Klärung, die Lösung des Problems, wie sich der Gottesgedanke Moses Israel ungetrübt vermitteln läßt; wir haben die entscheidenden Formulierungen bereits eingangs zitiert. In den drei von Schönberg exponierten Elementen: unvorstellbarer Gott—auserwähltes Volk—Volksführer ist, so zeigt sich jetzt, Problem nicht die Vermittlung des Gottesgedankens als solche und auch nicht die Gott vermittelnden Vorstellungen, Bilder, Zeichen, Wunder an sich. In dieser Richtung wird die Oper allermeist verstanden—mißverstanden. Problem ist vielmehr einzig und allein der gemäße Ausgangspunkt und seine bleibend-unverfälschte Präsenz in aller Vermittlung. Arons Höchstes ist das auserwählte Volk, unabhängig-willensfreie Menschen mit Vorstellungen von Gott, denen Gott entsprechen muß, um Gott zu sein—ein Bild der Ohnmacht, an das Aron das Wesen Gottes verrät. Für Moses hingegen muß ständig und überall vom offenbaren, allzeitigen Wesen Gottes ausgegangen werden, wenn Gott Gott sein soll. Von seiner absoluten Freiheit, Unabhängigkeit, von seinem stets vorgängigen, überlegenen Subjektsein gegenüber Gefühl, Sehnsucht, Ratio des Menschen, aber auch gegenüber Gottes eigenen, jeweiligen Worten, Geboten, Wundern und Manifestationen. Nicht einer scheinbaren Willensfreiheit und Unabhängigkeit, sondern diesem Gottesgedanken zu dienen, das ist die Freiheit, zu der dieses Volk erwählt ist.

[24] *Briefe*, S. 188.

[25] II/2 (S. 21), vgl. II/3 (S. 23).

[26] Vgl. die Anweisung zur szenischen Gestaltung innerhalb von II/3 unmittelbar vor der Orgie (S. 23).

[27] III/1 (S. 31 f.).

Wo stehen diese Reflexionen in den biblischen Grundkapiteln von "Moses und Aron"?

Wir sehen: bis in den letzten Akt hinein zeigt sich der biblische Stoff völlig überformt von einer textfern-eigenständigen Thematik Schönbergs. Ein Rückblick auf die Stoffbehandlung in der Oper im ganzen bestätigt im einzelnen, was Schönberg selbst gesagt hat, daß er sich nämlich in "Moses und Aron" "nur in wenigem streng an die Bibel halte".[28] "Moses und Aron" also eine biblisch-unbiblische Oper, über die wir leichthin hinweggehen können, um sie ganz der Theaterwelt zu überlassen? So einfach kommen wir nicht davon; doch dies muß die Interpretation zeigen.

II. *Interpretation*

Wie ist die Oper im Sinne Schönbergs zu verstehen?

Die neuen Akzente, die wir im Unterschied zum biblischen Stoff wahrgenommen haben, lassen darüber keinen Zweifel. "Moses und Aron" ist kein Handlungsdrama, auch kein Psychodrama, sondern wie man treffender gesagt hat, ein "Ideendrama",[29] ursprünglich ja als Oratorium geplant, eine "Bekenntnisdichtung".[30] Ihr *Thema* ist nicht weniger als der alttestamentliche Gott, dessen Bezeugung allein Israel zu Israel macht, und Sendung und Aufgabe des Gottesvolkes, um derentwillen allein es erwählt ist. *Problem* und *Handlung der Oper* sind die Bedingungen der Übermittlung dieses alttestamentlich offenbarten Gottes an das Volk durch seine Führer und die Gefahr allseitiger Verfälschung und Prüfung, die der Wahrnehmung Gottes in dieser Vermittlung drohen und die Sendung des Volkes zunichte machen. Schönberg exponiert gerade dieses Problem, weil ihm seit den zwanziger Jahren leidenschaftlich an der Substanz des Gottesvolkes in seiner—durchaus auch politischen—Identität gelegen ist. Nicht die psychologisch-genetische Frage, wie Glaube in Israel entsteht—doch immer an konkret-jeweiligen Gotteserfahrungen—, bewegt ihn, sondern die Frage, was Israel bleibend zu Israel macht, was ihm in allem bleibt, wie es wesentlich wird. Kern dieses Problems ist für Schönberg deshalb Israels Bewahrung des "reinen, wahren mosaischen Monotheismus", wie er sagt.

---

[28] *Briefe*, S. 188.

[29] So K. H. Wörner, *Gotteswort und Magie. Die Oper "Moses und Aron" von Arnold Schönberg* (Heidelberg, 1959), S. 30.

[30] So H. H. Stuckenschmidt, *Schönberg. Leben, Umwelt, Werk* (Zürich, 1974), S. 320.

Einfach ausgedrückt: Kern dieses Problems ist die Weitergabe und Aufnahme in Israel, daß der eine Gott des Alten Testaments alles betrifft und doch von nichts abhängig ist, nicht einmal von dem, was er selbst gesagt und getan hat.

Darum die Leidenschaft von Schönbergs Moses für das uneinholbare, immerwährende Prae Gottes, für Gottes absolute Handlungsfreiheit und Unabhängigkeit gegenüber allem, für seine bleibende Unvorstellbarkeit und Unsichtbarkeit. In Sprache fassen dies die tragenden *Gottesepitheta* der Oper schon in ihren ersten Worten: "Einziger, ewiger, allgegenwärtiger, unsichtbarer und unvorstellbarer Gott!" Sie sind nichts anderes als Schönbergs Sprachgestalt der alttestamentlichen Gotteswahrnehmung im ersten und zweiten Gebot.

Ihnen korrespondieren auf der menschlichen Seite "*Gedanke*", "*Denken*". Nicht weil Gott ein Erdachtes wäre oder nur in einer subjektiv intelligiblen Welt existierte und sich allein an den Intellekt wendet. Gedanke und Denken sind für Schönberg vielmehr das Medium, um das unvorstellbare Subjektsein Gottes aufzunehmen vor allen begrenzenden Vorstellungen Gottes aus den Bedürfnissen und Sehnsüchten der Menschen. Gedanke und Denken sind das gemäße Medium, die Freiheit Gottes aber auch in Gottes eigenen Worten und Taten wahrzunehmen und ihn jeder Überschaubarkeit, Kalkulierbarkeit, jedem Genügenmüssen gegenüber menschlichen Anforderungen zu entwinden.[31] Im großen *antithetischen Mittelteil der Oper* hat Schönberg diese Verfälschungen und Surrogate gezeigt, die Aron und das Volk subtil oder massiv der Gottheit Gottes beilegen, wie wir in der Akzentuierung der Einzelzüge gesehen haben.

Was muß nach Schönberg statt dessen geschehen, damit das auserwählte Volk seine Sendung wahrnimmt und sein Ziel erreicht? Moses sagt es in dem entscheidenden, zu Aron und zum Volk gewandten *Schlußmonolog des dritten Aktes*: In der Begegnung Israels mit Gott kommt es auf den Ausgangspunkt der Gotteswahrnehmung

[31] Daß der Gottesgedanke, das allzeitige Wesen des absolut freien Gottes gerade auch nicht in den jeweiligen Manifestationen Gottes selbst aufgehen darf, arbeitet Schönberg vor allem an dem Mißverstehen Arons in I/2, an dessen Ausführung der in I/1 zugesagten Beglaubigungswunder in I/4 und an der klärenden Zurechtweisung Arons in III/1 (S. 31 f.) heraus. Den Grund für diese Sicht bringt Schönberg wieder in dem entscheidenden Schlußmonolog Moses in III/1 (S. 31) auf den Begriff, wo Moses zu Aron sagt: "Und der Gott, den du zeigst, ist ein Bild der Ohnmacht, ist abhängig von einem Gesetz über sich; muß (!) erfüllen, was er (!) versprochen hat; muß (!) tun, um was er gebeten wird, ist gebunden (!) an sein (!) Wort".

an. Der aller menschlichen Religiosität entgegengesetzte, andere Ausgangspunkt beim offenbaren, freien, unvorstellbaren Gott muß stetig zur Geltung kommen, um das Wesen Gottes in all seinem Wirken und in allen Gotteswahrnehmungen aufzunehmen. Und entsprechend auf Seiten des Volkes: Der Ausgangspunkt der eigenen Wünsche, Bedürfnisse, der Gott durch Projektionen des Menschen beherrscht, muß sich wandeln in Wunschlosigkeit, die sich ganz der Gottesbeziehung widmet. Gott muß Israel so vermittelt werden, daß sich das absolute Subjektsein des offenbaren Gottes in Israels Denken spiegelt und in der Lebensganzheit bewahrt bleibt—nicht ohne Bilder, Vorstellungen, Erfahrungen und Zeichen, aber so, daß all dies Ausdruck des stetig beherrschenden Gottesgedankens bleibt, statt ihn begrenzend-verfälschend selbst zu beherrschen. Eine rein theoretische Lösung? Dramatisierte Lehre vom Glauben Israels an das abstrakte Wesen Gottes? Israel auf Gedeih und Verderb einem unberechenbaren, de facto willkürlichen Übergott ausgeliefert? Ist das die Aussage Schönbergs in seiner Oper?

Zwei Aspekte dürfen nicht vergessen werden. Einmal: Schönberg richtet seine Aussage an das konkrete Gottesvolk seiner Zeit, das immer auch schon in einer konkreten Gottesbeziehung steht; er redet nicht an den jeweiligen Manifestationen, Bildern und Erfahrungen Gottes vorbei. Aber Schönberg fragt, was das Wesentliche, Bleibende an Gott und Israel in dieser Gottesbegegnung ausmacht. Ferner: Schönberg unterscheidet in diesem die Oper klärenden Schlußmonolog Moses zwischen den Bildern, sofern sie das Wesen Gottes beherrschen und sofern sie es ausdrücken. Israel bewahrt das Wesen Gottes und damit sein eigenes Wesen, wenn es—nicht neben, sondern—in den jeweiligen Manifestationen, Bildern, Erfahrungen Gottes die Tiefe der absoluten Freiheit Gottes aufnimmt, wenn es darin also nicht sich und seinen Bedürfnissen, sondern Gott begegnet. Und Israel verfälscht das Wesen Gottes und damit sein eigenes Wesen, wenn es den jeweilig manifesten, den gebrauchten, gewünschten, in Bildern vorgestellten Gott für das Wesen Gottes hält und Gottes absolut freies Subjektsein damit Bildern von ihm unterwirft, um seiner habhaft zu werden.

"Moses und Aron" also eine unbiblische Oper, weil sie sich nur in wenigem an die Bibel hält? Man bedenke, was in diesem Werk geschehen ist. Eine Oper, die das absolute Prae Gottes zum *Thema* macht, das Gottsein Gottes, wie es nicht in diesem oder jenem Text manifest wird, sondern wie es im ganzen Alten Testament, in allen

Widerfahrnissen Israels stetig immer dasselbe bleibt, auch wenn Gott Abraham den Sohn der Verheißung wieder zu opfern befiehlt, auch wenn Gott wie ein Rätsel im Leidensschicksal des gerechten Hiob steht. Das Gottsein Gottes, das in allem stetig bleibt, auch wenn Gott Israel das Verheißungsland wieder genommen hat und den Tempel seiner Gegenwart zerstört. Diese wesenhafte Freiheit und Unvorstellbarkeit Gottes, diese Wahrnehmung Gottes als des freien und einzigen Spenders alles Geschehens für Israel in Licht und Dunkel, diese leidenschaftliche Wahrung der Transzendenz Gottes gegenüber der Welt, auch der Welt des Gottesvolkes, ist innerste Substanz des Alten Testaments; hätte das Alte Israel sie nicht aufgenommen, wäre das Alte Testament nie geschrieben. Für Israel und die Völker dieses offenbare, freie, welt-und menschenunabhängige von Außen des einen, einzigen Gottes zu wahren und es unbedingt freizuhalten von Extrapolationen, von Verkleinerungen, Vermessungen, Verkürzungen der Freiheit und Offenbarung Gottes nach dem Maß menschlicher Vorstellbarkeit und welthafter Abbildlichkeit, das ist die *Grundintention Schönbergs* in dieser Oper. Auf daß nicht der Mensch Gott nach seinem Bilde schaffe!

Schönberg kämpft gegen die grassierende Versuchung, von einem Gott zu reden und die besseren Möglichkeiten des Menschen, die Kraft seiner Wünsche und Sehnsüchte zu meinen, und seien sie noch so gefühlstief, liebevoll, berauschend, noch so edel, sozial und noch so human. Die Oper "Moses und Aron" ist ein leidenschaftliches Plädoyer für die Gottheit des biblischen Gottes, für sein striktes Gegenüber zu Israel, zur Welt, zum Menschen. Diese Intention ist zentral biblisch, so biblisch wie das erste und zweite Gebot, und es ist in dieser Hinsicht die Sache des Alten Testaments selbst, die hier in biblischer Größe zur Sprache gebracht wird, in einer Strenge und Entschiedenheit, die praktizierte Theologie vielfach beschämen könnte.

Biblisch ist auch das Vorgehen Schönbergs in der *freien Verwendung des Stoffs*, auch wenn die Differenzen zu einem historisch-exegetischen Wortsinn der alttestamentlichen Texte bleiben. Wie alle der Gotteswahrheit und den Fragen der Gegenwart gleichermaßen verpflichtete Theologie und Predigt, ja wie die biblische Überlieferung selbst, die fortgestaltet wird, um die Gotteswahrnehmung angesichts der Fragen auch späterer Zeit in den Erzählungen der Frühzeit zu klären, so interpretiert auch Schönberg die Stoffe von Moses und Aaron. Er verschränkt sie erstens mit der zentralen Sache des ganzen Alten Testaments, dem ersten und zweiten Gebot nahe bei Deuterojesaja. Und er tut dies zweitens im Lichte eines Problems, das der biblische Stoff selbst noch nicht behandelt, das Schönberg aber der langen Erfahrungsgeschichte seither und den Lebensprägungen und geistigen Auseinandersetzungen seiner Zeit entnimmt. Das Problem der Inhaftierung Gottes in den Erfahrungen von ihm und das Problem der menschlichen Selbstproduktion von Religiösem als in Wahrheit psychologisches Phänomen, als rauschhaft-temporäre Selbsttranszendierung, als Verschleierung sozial-gesellschaftlicher Mängelzustände, als Kreation menschlicher Entlastung. In dieser Dynamik und ihrer gefährlichen Verfälschung des biblischen Gottes reflektiert Schönberg den biblischen Stoff, gestaltet ihn darum neu und zeigt ihn so um die Erfahrungen der Moderne vermittelt auf einer höheren Reflexionsebene wieder gültig. Deshalb müht sich Schönberg um eine neue Sprache in der erklärten Überzeugung, die bis in sein Todesjahr in seinen Briefen und religiösen Dichtungen manifest ist, daß die biblische Sprache zeitbedingt-vergangene Sprache ist und der biblische Gehalt in der Sprach-, Denk- und Ausdrucksweise des Menschen der Moderne neu gefaßt werden muß.

"Moses und Aron" also in bestimmter Hinsicht eine zentral biblische Oper von der unbedingten Gottheit Gottes, darin Judentum und Christentum gleichermaßen ein gewaltiges Zeugnis von Grund und Herkunft ihres Glaubens; von einer künstlerischen und theologischen Gewalt, die nur tiefer Ehrerbietung vor Großem Raum läßt.

Einige Folgerungen mögen unseren Vortrag beschließen.

III. *Folgerungen*

Nach dem ursprünglichen Sinn alttestamentlicher Texte zu fragen, wie es unseres Amtes ist, und nach dem ursprünglichen Sinn Schönbergscher Texte zu fragen, ist für uns Ausdruck derselben wissenschaftlichen Haltung: Anwalt, Wächter zu sein für Größeres, einzutreten für anderes in seiner Eigenständigkeit, ohne das wir nur ärmer wären. So betrachtet, ist "Moses und Aron" ohne eine genaue, den Wortlaut bedenkende Untersuchung des Textes im Sinne Schönbergs nicht zu verstehen.

Bereits der Text verbietet heute verbreitete *Interpretationen* und *Inszenierungen*, die den biblisch-religiösen Inhalt der Oper lediglich als Einkleidung, Verschleierung säkularer Realitäten ansehen. So als sei das Hauptthema von "Moses und Aron" die Spannung zwischen abstraktem Gedanken und anschaulichem Bild. Oder die Dialektik von Idee und Verwirklichung. Oder der Gegensatz von Geist und Materie. Oder Gestaltung einer biographischen Erfahrung, nämlich der Schwierigkeit des Künstlers Schönberg, sich der Gemeinschaft, der Gesellschaft zu vermitteln. Oder, so die aktuellste Deutung, diese Oper als Gleichnis für die heutige Anstrengung um die Verwirklichung des Menschen. In all diesen Deutungen werden bestenfalls Nebenzüge der Oper aus der geistigen und lebensmäßigen Vorprägung Schönbergs unsachgemäß zum Hauptthema erhoben, und schlimmstenfalls wird ein überkommenes Kunstwerk so zum Claqueur für unsere Probleme erniedrigt und um seinen besonderen Impuls gebracht in der Grundüberzeugung, daß es der Interpret natürlich besser weiß und den Transfer in die moderne Aktualität oder die Aufhellung der "objektiven" Wahrheit gegenüber dem bloß subjektiven Selbstverständnis Schönbergs erst selber zu leisten hätte. Man möge dabei aber nur achten, daß das scheinbar gegenwartsgemäße, modernistisch-religionslose Verständnis dieser Oper nicht weit hinter Schönberg zurückbleibt: Er hat schon seit 1912 gemäß einem Brief an Richard Dehmel den Gott findenden Menschen von heute im Auge, der "durch den Materialismus, Sozialismus, Anarchie durchgegangen ist, der Atheist war"; [32] und noch in seinem Todesjahr hat er sich gegen eine Deutung von "Moses und Aron" im Sinne der Geist-Materie-Dialektik oder biographisch der Psychologie des Künstlers entschieden verwahrt: "Das ist Ende des 19ten Jahrhunderts, aber nicht ich. Der Stoff und seine Behandlung sind rein religionsphilosophisch".[33] Was Schönberg meint, resultiert aus einem tiefen Umbruch seiner religiösen Position in den zwanziger Jahren—hinaus über eine rein theosophisch-universale Läuterungs- und Erlösungsmystik, die er in Balzacs "Seraphita" kennengelernt hat, hin zum "biblischen Weg", so der Titel seines Dramas, das er 1922-23 konzipiert und 1927 niedergeschrieben hat, hin zum Judentum und seiner Vorbildfunktion für die Welt, hin zu einem Gegensatz, der an die Stelle eines theosophisch-christlichen Geist-Materie-Dualismus tritt, der Gegensatz: biblisch offenbarter Gott versus Mensch und selbst produzierte Religiosität. In diesem Sinne will Schönberg selbst "Moses und Aron" zugunsten der substantiellen Identität Israels verstanden wissen. Zwei Briefstellen unterstreichen dies unübersehbar: ". . . Gott (hat) Israel als das Volk auserwählt, dessen Aufgabe es ist, trotz aller Verfolgungen, trotz aller Leiden den reinen, wahren

[32] *Briefe*, S. 31.
[33] *Briefe*, S. 298.

mosaischen Monotheismus aufrecht zu erhalten ...".[34] Fragt man, wie Israel diese Aufgabe erfüllen kann, so antwortet Schönberg darauf an anderer Stelle: "Im Exil sich zu erhalten, unvermischt und ungebrochen, bis die Stunde der Erlösung kommt!" [35] Daß Schönberg an dieser Position lebenslang festgehalten hat, zeigen Selbstzeugnisse, religiöse Dichtungen und Kompositionen bis in das Todesjahr hinein absolut eindeutig. Dies hat Konsequenzen für den dritten Akt. Da er integraler Bestandteil der Oper ist und im Gang ihrer Sachaussage die unverzichtbare Lösung und Klärung bedeutet, wären verstärkt Überlegungen anzustellen, wie er mit zur Aufführung kommen kann, wenn anders Schönbergs Sinngebung von "Moses und Aron" in Szene gesetzt werden soll.

Eine zweite und letzte Reihe von Folgerungen betrifft *Fragen.* Fragen an die theologische Konzeption von "Moses und Aron". Sie haben aber erst ihr Recht, wenn man in Ehrerbietung den Boden Schönbergs betreten und sich der Gewalt seiner Aussage ausgesetzt hat. Fragen, nicht wie die skeptisch-geistvollen, die Theodor Adorno an das Gesamtkunstwerk "Moses und Aron" gestellt hat,[36] sondern Fragen aus der Bibel an das Wollen Schönbergs im Text der Oper. *Fragen aus dem Alten Testament*, das diesen einen, weltunterschiedenen Gott in Führung und Rätsel, in Gericht und Gnade als den nahen, erfahrbaren, spürbaren, im geschichtlichen Weg Israels wahrnehmbaren Gott bezeugt und doch seine unbedingte Freiheit wahrt, wo Schönberg vielleicht der Abstraktion des Prinzipiellen nahekommt. Und für Christen nicht minder *Fragen aus dem Neuen Testament*, wonach Gott bis zur Menschwerdung im Leben, Leiden und Sterben Jesu in Welt eingeht, ohne in Welt aufzugehen, und sich in letzter Unmittelbarkeit den Menschen nahegibt. Zeichen, daß Gott Welt, Leben, Menschsein, Geschichte, Erfahrung, Gefühl annimmt, mit Sinn tränkt, wo Schönbergs Moses im Nachhall theosophischer Entsagungsmystik absoluter Wunschlosigkeit die Vereinigung mit Gott als Ziel nicht vielleicht doch nur neben dem Leben und an ihm vorbei sehen kann. Aber diese Bereiche sind im dritten Akt eher nur angedeutet und offengelassen; in den Spätwerken finden sich auch wieder andere Züge. In ihrem Kern wird die Aussage

[34] *Briefe*, S. 298.
[35] *Briefe*, S. 95.
[36] Th. W. Adorno, Sakrales Fragment. Über Schönbergs Moses und Aron, in: Th. W. Adorno, *Gesammelte Schriften* Bd 16, *Musikalische Schriften I-III* (Frankfurt, 1978), S. 454-75.

Schönbergs durch biblische Anfragen freilich nicht gemindert. Im Gegenteil. Schönbergs Problem in "Moses und Aron" ist ja der fundamentale und wesenhaft unverzichtbare Rahmen solcher Fragen: Die Gottheit des biblischen Gottes zu wahren in ihrer Freiheit gegenüber allen religiösen Gottesprojektionen. Ohne diese zentrale Thematik von "Moses und Aron" könnte auch die biblische Überlieferung nur zur Religiosität verfälscht werden. Ohne dieses zentral-biblische, seherische Zeugnis in "Moses und Aron" für Juden, Christen, für alle bliebe auch unsere Welt nur Welt, geschunden und zerstört von dem Wahn, der Mensch, *er* sei Gott.

Ich schließe mit Worten Schönbergs, die "Moses und Aron" noch einmal spiegeln, gedichtet und komponiert 1950 kurz vor seinem Tode, der erste der "Modernen Psalmen", op. 50c:

> O du mein Gott: alle Völker preisen dich
> und versichern dich ihrer Ergebenheit.
> Was aber kann es dir bedeuten, ob ich das
> auch tue oder nicht?
> Wer bin ich, daß ich glauben soll, mein
> Gebet sei eine Notwendigkeit?
> Wenn ich Gott sage, weiß ich, daß ich damit
> von dem Einzigen, Ewigen, Allmächtigen, All-
> wissenden und Unvorstellbaren spreche, von dem ich
> mir ein Bild weder machen kann noch soll.
> An den ich keinen Anspruch erheben darf
> oder kann, der mein heißestes Gebet erfüllen oder
> nicht beachten wird. Und trotzdem bete ich, wie alles Lebende
> betet; trotzdem erbitte ich Gnaden und Wunder;
> Erfüllungen.
> Trotzdem bete ich, denn ich will nicht des
> beseligenden Gefühls der Einigkeit, der Ver-
> bindung mit dir verlustig werden.
> O du mein Gott, deine Gnade hat uns das Gebet
> gelassen, als eine Verbindung, eine
> beseligende Verbindung mit dir. Als eine
> Seligkeit, die uns mehr gibt als jede Erfüllung.[37]

---

[37] A. Schoenberg, *Moderne Psalmen*, hrsg. von R. Kolisch (Mainz, 1956). Der Text dieses Psalms findet sich auch in A. Schönberg, *Gesamtausgabe*, *V. Chorwerke*, Reihe A, Band 19 (Mainz und Wien, 1975), S. 151 ff., sowie in *Psalmen vom Expressionismus bis zur Gegenwart*, hrsg. von P. Kurz (Freiburg, 1978), S. 77.

OLD TESTAMENT—THE DISCIPLINE AND ITS GOALS

BY

MOSHE WEINFELD

Jerusalem

The Old Testament should be regarded as one of the most venerable subjects of study in Humanities. It serves as the basis of the three great world religions and of Western culture in general. It is unnecessary to elaborate on this point. However, a feeling of uneasiness has prevailed in the last decade within the ranks of Old Testament scholars. Nothing seems sure in our field of study. Almost everything is under dispute. One should confess that this scepticism has great advantages. Old conventions should always be revised, especially when new data become available and, as I shall try to demonstrate, prejudices and misconceptions could be removed by studying closely the culture of the ancient Near East.

The question, however, is how far we can proceed with our critique and revision of the old principles. It seems that the critique is sometimes far-fetched and borders on nihilism. I have in mind especially some recent attitudes towards the patriarchal narratives on the one hand and to the existence of the sources in the Pentateuch on the other.

The patriarchal stories are dated by some recent scholars [1] to the exilic period: on the other hand, the existence of basic sources of the Tetrateuch is highly questioned.[2] The common view prevailing until now that the Hebrew narratives of the Pentateuch were composed and compiled during the period of the monarchy is now criticized, and there is a tendency to date the basic compositions of the Pentateuch in the period of the Exile.[3] If this view were accepted, it would mean that the classical literature of ancient Israel embodied in the Pentateuch started to acquire its present form in the period of decline, i.e.

---

[1] Cf. J. Van Seters, *Abraham in History and Tradition* (New Haven, Conn., and London, 1975).

[2] Cf. R. Rendtorff, *Das überlieferungsgeschichtliche Problem des Pentateuch*, *BZAW* 147 (1977).

[3] For a late dating of the J source cf. H. H. Schmid, *Der sogenannte Jahwist, Beobachtungen und Fragen zur Pentateuchforschung* (Zürich, 1976).

after the death of Josiah in 609; in other words, the literary creation represented by D, P, and the so-called J and E, did not come into being before the end of the monarchy. This would imply that the great and glorious periods of Israel's history such as the Davidic-Solomonic period, the times of Jeroboam II, Uzziah or Hezekiah did not produce literary works on the national level, which seems astonishing. But the main weakness of this new trend lies in the fact that it disregards elementary factors relevant to the problem:

1. The three main layers of the Pentateuch, the conventional JE, P, D—you may name them A, B, C or the like—are linked to three legal codes: the Covenant Code, the Priestly Code and the Deuteronomic Code. It is justifiably assumed that these codes literally and ideologically suit the narratives to which they are linked. It was indeed this factor which enabled W. M. L. de Wette to develop his epoch-making thesis about the date of Deuteronomy. The code of Deuteronomy with its insistence on the centralization of the cult provided the key for the historical background of the whole book of Deuteronomy, and, as is well known, the date of Deuteronomy served as the point of departure for dating as pre-Josianic the sources which do not demand centralization. This refers not only to the law such as the Covenant Code, but also to the narratives which accept as legitimate the building of altars, and sacrificing anywhere, erecting *maṣṣēbōt* and planting trees in sacred places (Gen. xii 7, xxi 33, xxvi 25, xxviii 18, xxxiii 20, xxxv 14, xlvi 1; Exod. xxiv 4).

The historical setting of each source is thus conditioned by the nature of the legal code which is incorporated in it. The literary body which comprises the Covenant Code must then be older than the corpus which comprises the Deuteronomic Code. The same applies to the Priestly strand of the Pentateuch, the date of which is conditioned by the date of the laws of its corresponding code. In dating the literary sources, one cannot ignore the historical background of the codes incorporated in them.

2. In the narratives of the book of Deuteronomy, one finds quotations from various stories incorporated in the so-called JE source of the Tetrateuch. There is no reason to suppose that the author of Deuteronomy was dependent upon isolated traditions and not upon a continuous source. Passages from various parts of the books of Exodus and Numbers are quoted verbatim in Deuteronomy,[4] which

[4] Especially in chapters i-iii and ix-x; cf. S. R. Driver, *Deuteronomy* (3rd edn, Edinburgh, 1902), pp. 19, 24, 29, 33, 112.

means that the material was taken from a crystallized literary work and not from a fluid oral tradition. If changes and deviations of significance are found in these quotations, they can be explained by the particular view of the author of Deuteronomy. Thus, for example, the burning of the golden calf by Moses and the strewing of its dust upon the water, told in Exod. xxxii 20, is repeated in Deut. ix 21; but there is an important deviation in the description of the use of the dust of the calf. In Exodus the dust spread upon the water is given to the Israelites to drink, which implies some kind of trial by ordeal.[5] The author of Deuteronomy, however, completely omits this detail and reports only that Moses cast the dust of the calf into the stream of water. As I have tried to demonstrate elsewhere, the author of Deuteronomy does not permit the use of magical devices for judicial procedures and therefore ignores the clause about the drinking of the water.[6] The post-exilic writers too quote Pentateuchal scripture verbatim (compare, for example, Ezra ix 12 with Deut. vii 3, xxiii 7; Neh. i 5 with Deut. vii 9, 12; Neh. ix 7 with Gen. xv 7; 2 Ch. xx 17 with Ex. xiv 13), which means that the Pentateuch had already reached its present form before the Exile.

3. The so-called JE source, especially in Genesis, is guided by the idea of a great nation, *gwy gdwl*, expanding and subjugating nations a concept which could hardly be crystallized in times of national decline. Scholars indeed overlooked the fact that in the promises to the patriarchs we find, besides the promises for land and seed, a third element: the promise of national expansion, which is not less prominent than seed and land. This is actually implied in the formula *gwy gdwl* prevailing in the so called J source. It occurs first in the opening pericope of the patriarchal narratives in Gen. xii 2 and is further attested not only in Genesis but also in Exodus (xxxii 10) and in Numbers (xiv 12). That it means physical greatness may be learned from Gen. xxi 18 where it refers to Ishmael, who certainly does not bear a spiritual mission. The "greatness" of Israel is expressed here by territorial expansion (Gen. xv 18-21, xxvi 4, xxviii 14; Ex. xxiii 31) as well as by subjugating nations (Gen. xxv 23, xxvii 29, 40, xlix 10; Num. xxiii 24, xxiv 8, 17 ff.). In fact, the political grandeur reflected in this source comes to expression in the stories which describe the relationship between the patriarchs and their

---

[5] Cf. the ordeal in Num. v 11-31, and see BT Abodah Zarah 44a.

[6] M. Weinfeld, *Deuteronomy and the Deuteronomic School* (Oxford, 1972), p. 234.

neighbours. Transjordan is protected by Abraham (ch. xiv) and actually lies under his control as far as to the north of Damascus (xiv 15). The covenants of the Patriarchs with the Philistines (xxi 22 ff., xxvi 26 ff.) reflect the relations of the United Monarchy with the Philistines, while the treaty of Jacob with Laban (xxxi 44 f.) in Gilead reflects some kind of settlement with the Arameans during the beginning of the monarchy. The superiority of Jacob over Esau in the patriarchal narratives reflects the subjugation of Edom by David. As B. Mazar has shown,[7] all the other politico-ethnic details in Genesis fit perfectly the David-Solomonic period.

The national-political grandeur reflected in the patriarchal narratives is thus not limited to a particular cycle but underlies all the narratives in Genesis, which means that all the stories were composed under the impact of an imperial reality. The national and political background of the patriarchal stories reminds us of Ps. lxxii, ascribed to Solomon. There we find Israel ruling "from sea to sea" (*v.* 8) and Kings and nations bowing to (*wyštḥww lw*) the King of Israel and serving him (*yʿbdwhw*, *v.* 11, cp. Gen. xxvii 29). As in the passages in Genesis about the nations blessing themselves—*nbrk/htbrk*—in Israel (xii 3, xviii 18, xxii 18, xxvi 4, xxviii 14) we find here the nations blessing themselves in the King of Israel (*wytbrkw bw*) (*v.* 17, LXX).[8] This political tendency can be understood only against the background of a flourishing state or empire [9] and to explain its emergence in the Exilic period is absurd.

In comparison with the imperial greatness of Israel expressed in the patriarchal narratives as well as in the Balaam stories (Num. xxiv 17 ff.) the book of Deuteronomy, which repeats the promises about seed and land, omits altogether the theme of physical greatness. Furthermore, Deuteronomy is aware of the fact that Israel is the smallest of all the peoples (vii 7) and that its greatness lies in the wise and righteous laws it observes (iv 5-6). The concept of *gwy gdwl* has undergone a transformation: "great nation", which has a physical and political sense in Genesis, obtains a spiritual and religious sense in Deutero-

---

[7] *JNES* 28 (1969), pp. 73-83.

[8] The parallel colon "all nations will deem him happy" *kl gwym yʾšrwhw* (cf. Gen. xxx 13) proves that *wytbrkw* should be taken as reflexive and not passive. At the beginning of the verse we read "may his name be eternal", which is like Gen. xii 2-3 where "the great name" precedes the blessing.

[9] Cf. M. Weinfeld, "The Awakening of national consciousness in Israel in the seventh century BCE", *ʿOZ le-Davidʾ Biblical Essays in honor of D. Ben Gurion* (Jerusalem, 1964), pp. 396 ff. (Hebrew).

nomy. In this case also we find dependence upon the previous sources (J or JE) by way of reinterpretation and polemic.

In order to evaluate the chronological setting of the sources in the Tetrateuch one has then to take into consideration their legal, historical and ideological aspects, and not just the literary-critical ones. When we take into account all the aspects it turns out that the conventional solution for the nature and date of the J source (10-9th century BCE) stands on a firm basis.

The scepticism raised against old conventions has its merits as far as it concerns the exact division of the material into sources and confidence in the dates of these sources. The distinction between J and E in Exodus-Numbers as well as the exact date of their composition is far from established, and the same applies to the date of the Priestly code. We should check anew Wellhausen's thesis about the lateness of the Priestly code, a revision which is badly needed in the light of the discoveries of the ancient Near East, as we shall indicate below. In fact, even on the pure literary critical level Wellhausen's hypothesis cannot be sustained. A. Dillmann, the giant of 19th century biblical criticism, questioned seriously Wellhausen's theory about P, and his criticism has not got its due consideration. Dillmann's commentary on the Pentateuch [10] is still the best, and it was in the framework of this extensive philological work that he voiced his criticism against Wellhausen. This is important since he did not content himself with general arguments but applied Wellhausen's theory to each pericope and passage in the Priestly source and found it failing. As is well known, criticism of Wellhausen on this point is now raised and elaborated in Israel, but in general scholarship the late date of P is still prevalent and other literary creations are dated on the basis of the lateness of P.

Criticism should be also applied to the problem of Trito-Isaiah which has gone unchallenged since B. Duhm. When we review this problem anew, which has been recently done by Y. Kaufmann,[11] M. Haran [12] and others,[13] it becomes clear that the fixing of the border between Deutero- and Trito-Isaiah has no real basis. The gap between

[10] *Kurzgefasstes Exegetisches Handbuch zum AT*: *Genesis*^{6} (Leipzig, 1892); *Exodus-Leviticus* (1882); *Numeri, Deuteronomium und Josua*^{2} (1886).

[11] *History of Israelite Religion* 4 (Tel-Aviv, 1956) (Hebrew), pp. 51 ff.

[12] *SVT* 9 (1963), pp. 127-55; *Between Rishonot* (*Former Prophecies*) *and Hadashot* (*New Prophecies*) (Jerusalem, 1962) (Hebrew).

[13] Cf. e.g. F. Maass, "Tritojesaja", *Festschrift L. Rost*, *BZAW* 104 (1967), pp. 153-63.

chaps. xlviii and xlix is much bigger than the gap between chaps. lv and lvi.

Until now we have dealt with central problems about which there is a general consensus which has been recently put in question. There are, however, many more problems about which no consensus has been reached. We still do not know the dates of the Psalmodic works, the different collections of proverbs in the book of Proverbs or the work of Job, its framework as well as the poetry. Neither is there agreement about the dates of Deutero-Zechariah and the scrolls of Ruth and the Song of Songs. There is general agreement about the date of the editor of the Former Prophets, the Deuteronomist, but considerable disagreement about the layers of this editorial work and its proper extent. In fact, the discerning of layers or strata in any given text has become almost a fashion in our days, and everyone does it according to his own taste. In a sense this situation of dissent and controversies in OT scholarship invites challenge. The treatment of any subject in biblical scholarship demands a variety of skills and aptitudes: a feeling for history, law and philology, a literary approach, an understanding for religion and anthropology and above all plenty of imagination. However, the outcome is mostly discouraging. In the final stage of the analysis of a chapter or a division in scripture one does not know whether an integrated source or a composite one lies before him; the date of the text under scrutiny is unknown; so too is the identity of its author. It is likewise hard to establish the theological meaning of the text in question if we do not know approximately to which stage in the history and spiritual development of the people the passage belongs. This situation opens vast possibilities for speculation. Every suggestion can be defended, and everyone is free to discern as many layers in the text as he wants. Sometimes he may even find this or that particular school supporting his hypothesis. For young scholars there exists an unlimited range of speculations and theories, and everyone may claim originality, since no consensus prevails. Scholars from other disciplines look upon us with disdain. "What kind of sterile speculative work are you engaged in?" they often ask. "You simply do not have enough documentary evidence in order to establish facts, dates, layers, etc." In fact, everyone of us has the feeling that much time and effort is spent on speculations that do not get us anywhere. A hundred and fifty years of critical research have exhausted our field, and the last fifty years have not advanced us.

It is interesting that Assyriologists and Egyptologists confront a situation which is just the opposite of ours. They work with documents whose date of writing can usually be established beyond any doubt. But the laconic and dry nature of these documents does not leave room for imagination. In contrast to the biblical texts they lack sophistication and the ideological, historical dimension which characterize the O.T. However, their dates and their nature are known.

Unfortunately, Assyriologists and Egyptologists are so absorbed with the discoveries in their fields that they do not care for O.T. scholarship at all. It is the O.T. scholars who should resort to these discoveries in order to enrich the factual basis of O.T. evidence. The various cultural, historical and religious phenomena of Mesopotamia, Ugarit, Egypt, etc. can be easily dated and could be of use for reconstructing the date and nature of similar phenomena in the Bible. Thus, for example, it has been commonly accepted that the story of creation and the story of the flood are separate traditions which existed independently of each other and have been linked together by an editor. This could be allegedly supported by the fact that in Mesopotania too the creation story *enuma eliš* and the flood story in the Gilgamesh epic are separate literary entities which have nothing in common. However, the publication of the Atrahasis epic of the beginning of the second millennium BCE [14] has shown that stories about a flood following creation were prevailing in the ancient Near East hundreds of years before the biblical account. Not less important than epic is the field of law and ritual of the ancient Near East. No serious work could be done today without referring to Mesopotamian law and Hittite ritual. The civil law of the Covenant Code has many affinities with the Mesopotanian codes, and the same applies to ritual.

Ritual ceremonies and detailed cultic prescriptions found in the Priestly Code which were considered by Wellhausen as a late development in Israelite religion turn now out to be one of the basic characteristics of ancient Near-Eastern cult. Thus we find in the lists of Hittite festivals a prescription such as "one bull, seven lambs, one goat, bread and wine" [15] which is to be compared with, for example, Num. xxix 2 f.: "one bull ... seven lambs ... one goat ... meal

---

[14] W. G. Lambert, A. R. Millard, *Atraḫasīs, The Babylonian Story of The Flood* (Oxford, 1969).

[15] Cf. A. M. Dincol, M. Darga, *Anatolica* 3 (1969-70), pp. 99 f.

offering and wine libation". Sin and guilt offerings as well as purification ceremonies by means of birds are well attested in the Hittite-Hurrian rituals, as I have shown elsewhere.[16]

The Hittite substitute rituals [17] seem to be close to the biblical scapegoat ritual. Here we find,[18] as in Lev. xvi 21, that the ram is driven out to the plain and that the hands should be laid upon the animal before it is chased away.

One of the pillars of Wellhausen's structure concerning the P source is the distinction between priests and Levites. The Levites are, according to his view, a particular Israelite development, an outcome of the abolition of the high places in the times of Josiah. However, two types of temple personnel, priests who are in the charge of the inner temple area on the one hand, and non-priests who watch the outside area of the temple on the other, are attested—as shown by J. Milgrom [19]—in the Hittite temple instructions. Like the Levites, so the outside keepers in the Hittite cultic law are bound to assist the priests of the inside in their task.[20]

According to Wellhausen, the law of Jubilee in P was introduced by the Priestly author as a compromise because the people were not ready to liberate their slaves every seven years. As a concession the slaves were permitted to be kept until the fiftieth year. As long as no external evidence of the existence of these institutions was known, Wellhausen's view remained plausible. The external evidence, however, refutes his hypothesis. We now know that at the beginning of the second millennium there existed in Mesopotamia a year of general release, the *mīšarum* or *andurārum* year in which debts were cancelled and slaves released.[21] The *andurārum* or *durārum*, which etymologically equals Hebrew *dĕrōr*, is called in Sumerian ama-ra-gi "return to the mother", i.e. to the bosom of the family, an idea which lies beneath the *dĕrōr* of the Pentateuch: "Each of you (shall return to his holding

---

[16] See my article in *Shnaton. An Annual for Biblical and Ancient Near Eastern Studies* 4 (1980), pp. 82-4.

[17] Cf. H. M. Kümmel, "Ersatzkönig und Sündenbock", *ZAW* 80 (1968), pp. 289-318.

[18] Cf. O. R. Gurney, *Some Aspects of Hittite Religion* (London, 1977), pp. 57 ff.

[19] "The Shared Custody of the Tabernacle and a Hittite Analogy", *JAOS* 90 (1970), pp. 204-9.

[20] Cf. H. Hoffner, "The Hittites and Hurrians", in D. J. Wiseman (ed.), *Peoples of Old Testament Times* (Oxford, 1973), p. 219.

[21] See my article in XXV *Rencontre Assyriologique Internationale* 3-7 July 1978, Berlin (forthcoming).

and each of you) shall return to his family" (Lev. xxv 10). The Hebrew phrase *yṣʾ bybl* "to be freed" in the Jubilee is the precise rendering of the Mesopotamian *ina durāri uṣû*. In striking similarity to Lev. xxv 9, where the Jubilee is proclaimed by the sound of the horn, the *dĕrōr* year in Mesopotamia is proclaimed by the raising of the torch.[22] Both acts were classical ancient methods of publicizing any announcement (cf. Jer. vi 1: "blow the horn in Tekoa, set up a fire signal at Beth-hakkerem").

Wellhausen believed that the New Year and the Day of Atonement, which are attested only in the Priestly Code, were conceived and born in the Exile when confession, purification and fasting replaced joyous festivals. However, a New Year festival associated with purification and removal of sin, etc. was prevalent in the ancient Near East and is most prominent in the Mesopotamian rituals which, as in Israel, are called *kuppuru*.[23] In Israel the New Year purification lasted ten days (cf. Ezek. xl 1) whereas in Mesopotamia the New Year ceremonies lasted for twelve days.[24] The New Year and the Day of Atonement have not been mentioned in the other sources because those sources are not concerned with ritual ceremonies of a technical nature as is the Priestly Code. In fact, Wellhausen's claim that the New Year and Day of Atonement originated in the exile seems most surprising. Whence this notion that an ancient people tends to invent for itself new festivals? Whoever has some knowledge about the culture of ancient Near Eastern peoples will be astonished to hear that a people invented for itself a new religious festival.

Let us consider some other subjects affected by ancient Near Eastern discoveries. Prophetic activity through inspiration and ecstasy and the phenomenon of prophetic messages have been discovered in Mari,[25] which shows that the idea suggested by some scholars [26] that Israel was the first to introduce prophetic message cannot be sustained any more. Psalmodic literature and Wisdom have much in common with the parallel genres in the ancient Near East, and there is no room here for elaboration of this subject. However, Ps. cvii deserves to be mentioned, because a book on the subject has recently

---

[22] Ibid. and references there.

[23] Cf. F. Thureau-Dangin, *Rituels Accadiens* (Paris, 1921), pp. 136 ff., 285 ff.

[24] Cf. M. Tadmor, "Rosh Hashanah", *Enc. Miqraʾit* 7, cols. 305-11.

[25] M. Weinfeld, "The Ancient Near Eastern patterns in prophetic literature", *VT* 27 (1977), pp. 178 ff.

[26] Ibid. and references there.

been published. This psalm speaks about four cases of thanksgiving: the traveller who came back from a dangerous journey, the seafarer who arrived safely at his destination, the prisoner who was released from jail, and the sick man who recovered from his sickness. The nature of this psalm, its *Gattung*, date, *Sitz im Leben*, etc. have caused much concern. W. Beyerlin has recently suggested that the case of the seafarer was added later and was composed by a late scribe working under wisdom influence. Now, these four cases of deliverance are enumerated in the so-called Šamaš Hymn in Mesopotamia,[27] which shows that they represent a common pattern in hymnic literature. The *Sitz im Leben* of this hymnic pattern is actually found in a Jewish tradition preserved until this day. According to this tradition, whose legal basis is attested in the Talmud (B. Ber. 54B), the four groups of people mentioned above are to perform a thanksgiving ceremony in public (in the temple or later in the Synagogue). In this case we find a nice combination of a biblical Psalm, an ancient Near Eastern text and a cultic religious practice.

Another instructive case of ancient Near Eastern discoveries is the so-called Dynastic prophecy published by A. K. Grayson.[28] It is not yet widely known amongst biblical Scholars that this document reveals for the first time an Akkadian text parallel to that of Daniel dealing with the four world empires.

In the last twenty years much work has been done in the comparison of the Covenant in the Bible with treaties of the ancient Near East. Although there is some exaggeration in seeking for parallels in this field, one must admit that we have moved ahead in the understanding of the covenant thanks to the ancient Near Eastern covenantal documents. G. von Rad posed the right question in connection with Deuteronomy: how does one explain the strange combination of history, law, blessings and curses and taking the oath? He explained it by pointing to a ceremony which allegedly contained all these elements: the Levites who recited the history imposed the Law by means of an oath, sanctioned by blessings and curses.[29] The treaties

---

[27] Cf. my article in *Shnaton* 2 (1977), pp. 241, 245.

[28] *Babylonian Historical-Literary Texts* (Toronto, 1975), p. 33, lines 11 ff. See most recently on this problem W. G. Lambert, *The Background of Jewish Apocalyptic*, The Ethel M. Wood Lecture delivered before the University of London on 22 February 1977 (London, 1978).

[29] *The Problem of the Hexateuch and other Essays* (Edinburgh and London, 1966), E. tr. of *Gesammelte Studien zum AT* (Munich, 1958).

that have been discovered, and especially the Hittite treaties, have taught us that such a structure of history, stipulations, blessings and curses, witnesses and oath is characteristic of the covenantal documents in the ancient Near East. The strange thing here is that these documents had been available for the scholarly world since 1923 (published by E. F. Weidner),[30] but had been used only in 1954 by G. E. Mendenhall[31] after 30 years. This shows us how important it is for biblical scholars to stand on the watch for every text discovered in the ancient Near East.

It is true that the constant search for ancient Near Eastern texts means a heavy burden for biblical scholarship, for it is not enough to read the texts in translation. Serious philogical work cannot be done on the basis of translated works alone. Students of the Bible will therefore have to resort to the original texts, which means control of the languages in which they were written. It is more profitable, however, to study ancient languages than to waste time on sterile speculations about strata and layers within a given biblical text on which no two scholars agree. Of course, analysis of the biblical literature, which means distinction of sources and traditions, should not be abandoned, but in order to make real progress we have to search for fallow ground to break, and it could be achieved by using new material which is being discovered and published by our colleagues in the fields of Assyriology and Egyptology.

In the area of textual criticism this has actually happened. Scholars do not tend any more to correct scripture arbitrarily but look for objective evidence which is steadily growing, such as Qumran texts, Targums, and Versions.

The growing dissatisfaction with current biblical criticism has caused the rise of a new trend of biblical scholarship, the so called "Canonical Approach", a phrase coined by B. S. Childs in his Introduction.[32] This represents a sound fresh approach in research, namely, the endeavour mainly to understand the view of the author of the book or the broad composition under discussion. However, although this is a legitimate tendency which should be encouraged, it cannot replace the quest for the history of the smaller literary units

---

[30] *Politische Dokumente aus Kleinasien* (Leipzig, 1923).

[31] "Law and Covenant in Israel and the Ancient Near East", *Biblical Archaeologist* 17 (1954), pp. 26 ff.

[32] *Introduction to the Old Testament as Scripture* (London, 1979).

which reflect the reality as seen by the older generations themselves and not only as understood by the late author or editor. By analysing the sources or the various documents we try to follow up the development of institutions, ideas and literature from their beginning and the way to their crystallization. This can be better understood against the background of similar institutions and literary types in the neighbourhood of ancient Israel.

THE IDENTIFICATION AND USE OF QUOTATIONS IN ECCLESIASTES

BY

R. N. WHYBRAY

Hull

One of the most important aspects of the study of the wisdom of Qoheleth is the problem of its relationship to the earlier wisdom of the Old Testament, particularly as represented in the gnomic or proverbial literature collected in Proverbs x-xxix.[1] The problem may be expressed in the following way: did Qoheleth regard himself as an exponent of "wisdom" in the same sense as the authors of the book of Proverbs? Was it his purpose to oppose the teaching of his predecessors in its entirety, or merely to modify certain aspects of it? Do the occasional apparently contradictory statements in the book show him to have been himself subject to doubts or contradictions, or was he rather quoting older sayings only to refute them? Or are we to follow some of the older critics and regard certain verses as having been added to the original text by interpolators? [2]

Some progress towards the solution of these problems may perhaps be obtained by looking again at the question of the supposed quotations of earlier wisdom sayings in the book of Qoheleth and at the way in which they fit into their contexts. However, the *identification* of such quotations constitutes a problem. Some sayings in the book certainly stand out from their contexts as sayings which are self-contained: they make good sense on their own. But are they in fact quotations from earlier literature, or were they composed in traditional fashion by Qoheleth himself? Can one distinguish between two

---

[1] See especially K. Galling, *Die Krise der Aufklärung in Israel* (Mainz, 1952); H. Gese, "Die Krisis der Weisheit bei Koheleth", *Les sagesses du proche-orient ancien* (Paris, 1963), pp. 139-51 = *Vom Sinai zum Zion* (Munich, 1974), pp. 168-79; H. H. Schmid, *Wesen und Geschichte der Weisheit* (Berlin, 1966), pp. 186 ff.; M. Hengel, *Judentum und Hellenismus* (Tübingen, 1969), pp. 210 ff. = E. tr. *Judaism and Hellenism* (London, 1974) 1, pp. 115 ff.; G. von Rad, *Weisheit in Israel* (Neukirchen, 1970), pp. 292 ff. = E. tr. *Wisdom in Israel* (London, 1972), pp. 226 ff.

[2] As maintained especially by C. Siegfried, *Prediger Salomonis und Hoheslied* (Göttingen, 1898²), and E. Podechard, *L'Ecclésiaste* (Paris, 1912).

kinds of such sayings: quotations, and original compositions by the author of the book?

In this essay it is not possible to attempt any major contributions to the solution of the many unsolved problems of the book. What I wish to undertake is some discussion of these putative quotations. It is to Robert Gordis that we owe most of our insights into the use of quotations in the Old Testament books and particularly in Qoheleth. One question, however, he left open as probably insoluble: in his book *Koheleth—The Man and his World. A Study of Ecclesiastes* [3] he wrote: "Whether Koheleth is quoting proverbs already extant, or composing them himself, is difficult to determine." If in fact there is no way of identifying Qoheleth's quotations, any attempt to draw conclusions about the way in which he used them is obviously doomed from the start. What are the possibilities? The kind of sayings which we are discussing might be quotations from some earlier written or oral collection, or quotations by Qoheleth of sayings composed earlier by himself, or passages in which he dropped the discursive style which he mainly employed in his book, and reverted to that of the more conventional wisdom writer. If they are actual quotations of sayings composed by someone other than himself, they may be from an earlier age—contemporary, for example, with the sayings in Prov. x-xxix, many of which must probably be dated in the period of the monarchy—or they may be sayings composed by Qoheleth's own contemporaries. In view of all these possibilities it is indeed probable that the question of authorship—that is, Qoheleth's or another's—will not be capable of solution in all cases. Nevertheless it may be possible to point to some sayings where Qoheleth's authorship is highly improbable: where we are, in other words, almost certainly dealing with quotations by him of sayings composed by others. If this can be done even in a few cases it will be possible to consider the reason for his employment of them and the use to which he put them.

In order to bring my remarks within the compass of this essay I propose here to confine myself to *one* type of saying: the single

[3] (New York, 1955), p. 100 (repr. 1978). His articles "Quotations in Wisdom Literature", *JQR*, N.S. 30 (1939/40), pp. 123-47 = J. L. Crenshaw (ed.), *Studies in Ancient Israelite Wisdom* (New York, 1976), pp. 220-44, and "Quotations in Biblical, Oriental and Rabbinic Literature", *HUCA* 22 (1949), pp. 157-219 = *Poets, Prophets and Sages* (Bloomington and London, 1971), pp. 104-59, should also be consulted.

poetical verse or distich. I shall also confine my comparative material mainly to Prov. x-xxix, chapters which contain the oldest extant collections of such sayings in the Old Testament, and it will be to these chapters that I refer when I use the term "Proverbs".[4] My purpose is to attempt to identify those sayings which because of their similarity to those in Proverbs and for other reasons appear to be quotations from earlier wisdom literature. These are the only ones which offer to the investigator some measure of objective control. It is not my intention to deny the existence of other quotations in Qoheleth, that is, from a period close to that of Qoheleth himself; but I know of no certain method by which such cases can be distinguished from Qoheleth's own writing.

What are the criteria which, when applied to such sayings, offer a high probability that they are quotations of earlier traditional wisdom sayings? Taking Proverbs as the norm, there are, it seems to me, four such criteria. Such sayings must be

1. sayings which are self-contained: that is, which when considered independently of their contexts express complete thoughts;
2. sayings which in *form* correspond closely to sayings in Proverbs;
3. sayings whose *themes* are characteristic of Proverbs, and at the same time in partial or total disagreement or tension either with their immediate contexts or with Qoheleth's characteristic ideas expressed elsewhere in the book;
4. sayings whose *language* is free from late features such as those of the language of Qoheleth, and is either that of classical Hebrew or more particularly of early wisdom literature.

It is of course possible that Qoheleth himself composed sayings identical in all respects with those in the book of Proverbs. We should then be dealing with examples of *pastiche* of an obsolete style. But in view of the fact that—as we shall see—Qoheleth's normal practice when he composed short wisdom sayings was to compose them in his own contemporary style, this would seem to be improbable.

In Qoheleth there are, according to my investigations, at least forty sayings to which the first two of these criteria apply: that is, which are self-contained, and whose form is paralleled in Proverbs;[5]

[4] Specifically to Prov. x 1-xxii 16, xxv-xxix.

[5] Further study is needed of these. At least the following (some of which may require emendation to restore them to their original form) ought to be considered as possible quotations: i 4, 8b, 15, 18 (omitting *kī*), ii 14a, iv 4, 6 (omitting

but most of these fail to conform to one or other, or both, of the last two criteria: in other words, either their language (vocabulary or grammar) is late, and indeed frequently identical with that of Qoheleth himself, or their theme differs from any of the themes occurring in Proverbs—and again is frequently identical with one of Qoheleth's own characteristic themes.

If we leave aside a number of doubtful cases there are then two groups of potentially independent single-distich sayings in the book. Of these, a study of those which resemble Qoheleth in style or theme would be rewarding, but would require a separate investigation. I intend in what follows to confine myself to the other group: those sayings which are *in every respect* indistinguishable in character from those in Proverbs. Of these there are—at least—eight clear examples: ii 14a, iv 5, iv 6 (omitting the final words, "and a striving after wind"), vii 5, vii 6a (i.e. omitting "This also is *hebel*"), ix 17, x 2, x 12.

Before a detailed investigation of these eight sayings is undertaken, one characteristic of them as a group should be mentioned which may be significant but which will not be pursued here. Although these eight sayings *individually* are indistinguishable from those in Proverbs, there is one respect in which *as a group* they have affinities with Qoheleth rather than with Proverbs: as in the rest of the book of Qoheleth, only *one* word for "fool" is used in them. All these eight passages except iv 6 refer to the fool or fools, and in each case the word *k^{e}sīl* is used. This differs from the usage of Proverbs, which has five words for "fool", of which four (*p^{e}tī*, *k^{e}sīl*, *ʾ^{e}wīl*, *lēṣ*) are used frequently either by themselves or in contrast to *ḥākām*, "wise".

Quotations of older Wisdom Sayings in Qoheleth

Each of the eight sayings referred to above will now be examined in respect of the three criteria of form, theme and language. That they all conform to the fourth criterion of being self-contained sayings will be self-evident.

1. ii 14a The wise man has eyes in his head,
   but the fool walks on in darkness.

ūr^{e}ʿūt rūaḥ), 9, 11 (omitting *gam*), 13 ab$^{\alpha}$ (to *ūk^{e}sīl*), 17a$^{\beta}$ (i.e. *qārōb* . . . *zābaḥ*, with some emendation), v 2 (omitting *kī*), 9a (to *t^{e}būʾāh*, adapted), vi 7, 9a, vii 1, 2a (to *mišteh*, 3, 4, 5, 6a, 7 (omitting *kī*), 8, 9, viii 1b, 4 (omitting *baʾ^{a}šer*), 8a$^{\alpha\beta}$ (to *hammāwet* and omitting *lik^{e}lōʾ ʾet-hārūaḥ*), 8a$^{\gamma}$-b (omitting *w^{e}*), ix 4b (omitting *kī*), 17, 18, x 2, 8, 9, 11, 12, 19, xi 1, 4.

a) *Form*. This is an antithetical saying in which, as in many similar sayings in Proverbs, the subject of each clause is placed first. The structure (nominal clause followed by participial clause) is paralleled in Proverbs, e.g. in xii 15:

> The way of a fool is right in his own eyes,
> but a wise man listens to advice.

b) *Theme*. The theme of the conduct respectively of the wise man and the fool and its consequences (here implied rather than explicitly stated) occurs frequently in Proverbs and is there often expressed through the metaphor of walking: words like walk, way, stumble, path etc. are characteristic.[6] The phrase "to walk in the paths of darkness" itself occurs in Prov. ii 13, though in connection with unrighteousness rather than folly. That this saying is a quotation in its present context is shown by the fact that it is immediately followed by a comment which is characteristic of Qoheleth and challenges it: "And yet I perceived that one and the same fate will befall both".[7]

c) *Language*. All the words used in the saying occur in classical Hebrew. There is no trace of late words or usage. Everything points to the saying's being a quotation.

2. iv 5 The fool folds his hands
and consumes his own flesh.

a) *Form*. This saying has synthetic parallelism consisting of two participial clauses, a form which is found also in Prov. xx 8:

> A king sitting on the throne of judgement
> winnows all evil with his eyes.

The second half is short, but not more so than, for example, Prov. xix 17.

b) *Theme*. The theme that laziness leads to ruin is very frequent

---

[6] E.g. Prov. x 17, xii 15, xiii 20, xiv 8, 12, xv 10, 19, 24, xvi 25, xix 2, 3, xxi 16, xxii 5, xxviii 26.

[7] *ʾet-kullām* means "both" here and in vii 18. So Gordis, *Koheleth*, p. 222; K. Galling, *Prediger* (Tübingen, 1969²), p. 90; A. Lauha, *Kohelet* (Neukirchen, 1978), p. 41; and cf. R. N. Whybray, "Qoheleth the Immoralist? (Qoh 7:16-17)", in J. G. Gammie et al. (ed.), *Israelite Wisdom . . . in Honor of Samuel Terrien* (New York, 1978), pp. 200 f.

in Proverbs.[8] The present context, however, speaks of the frustration caused by toil, a theme which is characteristic of Qoheleth.

c) *Language*. Each word occurs frequently in classical Hebrew or in Proverbs. The expression "fold the hands" (*ḥābaq yādayim*) occurs elsewhere only in Prov. vi 10 and xxiv 33, where as here it is an image of laziness. The expression "consume (literally, "eat") one's own flesh", whose meaning is uncertain,[9] occurs only here and in Isa. xlix 26: its absence from Proverbs is thus not significant. This saying appears to be a clear example of a quotation from earlier wisdom.

3. iv 6 Better is a handful with quiet
than two fistfuls with trouble.[10]

a) *Form*. The omission of the final words *ūreʿūt rūaḥ*, "and striving after wind", a phrase characteristic of and peculiar to Qohelet,[11] improves both metre and parallelism and leaves a so-called *ṭōb*-saying characteristic of Proverbs.[12]

b) *Theme*. Beyond the attainment of a sufficiency, wealth is not worth the toil involved in acquiring it. This is certainly a theme of Qoheleth's and is in fact elaborated in the verses which immediately follow; but similar sayings occur in Proverbs:

---

[8] E.g. Prov. x 4, 5, xii 11, 24, 27, xiii 4, xv 19, xviii 9, xix 15, 24, xx 4, 13, xxviii 19.

[9] The view of several commentators that it refers to starvation consequent upon the fool's failure to provide food for himself may well be right. Cf. L. Koehler-W. Baumgartner, *Lexicon in Veteris Testamenti Libros* (Leiden, 1953), p. 43: "verzehrt (innerlich) sich". Even G. R. Driver, "Problems and Solutions", *VT* 4 (1954), p. 228, had no solution to offer: "Whatever this expression may connote ...". Mic. iii 3 and Ps. xxvii 2, cited by some commentaries in this connection, are irrelevant because they refer to the eating of the flesh of others, not to eating one's own flesh. The idiom is probably a quite different one. Isa. xlix 26, where Israel's oppressors are to be made to eat their own flesh and drink their own blood, is also almost certainly of an entirely different order.

[10] There is no need to follow Galling (*Prediger*, p. 98) and others in emending *naḥat* and *ʿāmāl* by adding the copula. The two nouns are adverbial accusatives (so Gordis, *Koheleth*, p. 241; H. W. Hertzberg, *Der Prediger* (Gütersloh, 1963), p. 102).

[11] i 14, ii 11, 17, 26, iv 4, 6, vi 9. The word *reʿūt* does not occur elsewhere in the Old Testament.

[12] I.e., sayings characterized by the construction *ṭōb ... min-*, "Better (is) ... than ...". There are sixteen examples of this type of saying in Prov. x 1-xxii 16 and xxv-xxix, viz. xii 9, xv 16, 17, xvi 8, 19, 32; xvii 1, xix 1, 22, xxi 9, 19, xxv 24, xxvii 5, 10, xxviii 6.

i. Prov. xiv 30 points out the importance of tranquillity:

A tranquil mind gives life to the flesh,
but envy makes the bones rot.

ii. Prov. xvii 1 also praises the virtue of tranquillity in terms similar to the saying under consideration:

Better is a dry morsel with quiet
than a house full of feasting with strife.

iii. Other sayings in Proverbs (xv 16, 17, xvi 8, 19, xxviii 6) also prefer a modest income with righteousness to wealth accompanied by trouble.

The final words of the verse, however, are clearly Qoheleth's own comment on an older saying: "and striving after wind".

c) *Language*. All the words used are those of classical Hebrew. *m*[e]*lō' kap*, "handful", occurs also in 1 Kings xvii 12. *ḥopnayim*, "two fists", occurs once in Proverbs (xxx 4) and in five other Old Testament passages but not elsewhere in Qoheleth. The whole phrase *m*[e]*lō' ḥopnayim*, "two fistfuls", occurs in Exod. ix 8 and Lev. xvi 12. *naḥat*, "quiet, tranquillity", occurs three times in Qoheleth but also in Prov. xxix 9, twice in Job and once in Isaiah. Only *'āmāl* might suggest that Qoheleth is the author, since this word occurs in the book twenty-two times. But it is by no means peculiar to him, and in the sense in which it is used here ("misery, trouble") it occurs in Prov. xxxi 7 in addition to the many occurrences in the Old Testament in the sense of "wickedness". The saying is thus in every way indistinguishable from the sayings in Proverbs, and although it is not impossible that Qoheleth is the author, the addition of the final words suggests that it is a quotation.

4. vii 5 It is better to listen to a wise man's rebuke
than (is) a man listening to the song of fools.

a) *Form*. The *ṭōb*-saying is of course characteristic of Proverbs. The slight anomaly in which an infinitive ("to listen") is paralleled by a noun ("a man") is also attested in Proverbs, e.g. Prov. xxi 9:

It is better to live in a corner of a roof
than (is) a contentious woman and a brawling household.[13]

[13] So N.E.B. On the difficult phrase *bēt ḥāber* see the commentaries.

b) *Theme.* The themes of the value of listening to the wise and of the contrast between the speech of the wise man and of the fool are both characteristic of Proverbs. Elsewhere in the book of Qoheleth—for example in the story of the wise man whose advice was not sought (ix 14-15)—Qoheleth questions the assumption that the wise man's advice is likely to prevail.

c) *Language.* All the words used here are normal Hebrew vocabulary and have no particular affinities with the language of Qoheleth. *geʿārāh*, "rebuke", occurs nowhere else in Qoheleth but three times in Proverbs and several times elsewhere in the Old Testament. In Prov. xvii 10 it is used in a very similar saying:

> A rebuke goes deeper into a man of understanding
> than a hundred blows into a fool.

There is a similar saying in Prov. xiii 1. The fact that this saying (vii 5) has been joined to the next by *kī*, "for" although the one was clearly not originally the continuation of the other supports the view that it is a quotation by Qoheleth of an earlier saying.

5. vii 6a (omitting the first word *kī* and also omitting 6b, "This also is *hebel*"):

> Like the crackling of thorns under a pot,
> so is the laughter of the fool.

a) *Form.* The comparison of two things expressed as nouns or nominal expressions is very frequent in Proverbs, and the wordplay here (*sīr*, "thorn"; *sīr*, "pot") is reminiscent of pairs such as *zādōn, qālōn* (Prov. xi 2). The second half of the saying is rather short, but we may compare Prov. x 26.

b) *Theme.* The emptiness of fools is revealed in their laughter. Prov. xxix 9 has a similar reference to the laughter of fools, and their speech is compared to a thorn in Prov. xxvi 9. References to their empty babbling are frequent, e.g. Prov. x 14, xiv 3, 7, xv 2, 14, xviii 6, 7. This theme is itself not opposed to the ideas of Qoheleth, but the context shows that the saying is a quotation. In spite of the word *kī*, "for", at the beginning it is clearly not the continuation of verse 5, since there is a change of reference: verse 5 is about the song of fools but verse 6 about their laughter. The two verses are both quotations and were originally independent one of the other. The addition of the final words "This also is vanity (*hebel*)", a characteristic comment of Qoheleth's and not part of the metrical line, suggests that here too he is quoting an older saying.

c) *Language*. The language has no particular affinities with that of Qoheleth. *sîr*, "pot", is frequent in the Old Testament, but does not occur in Proverbs and occurs only here in Qoheleth. *sîr*, "thorn", though rare, is as old as Hos. ii 8 and Amos iv 2. *śāḥaq*, "laugh", a word which occurs frequently in the Old Testament, is found three times in Proverbs but only here in Qoheleth.

6. ix 17 Wise men's words (spoken) in calm are worth hearing
rather than a ruler's shouting among fools.

a) *Form*. If the above rendering is correct [14] this is a comparison-saying of the same kind as Prov. xvii 10:

A rebuke goes deeper into a man of understanding
than a hundred blows into a fool.

b) *Theme*. The superiority of the wise man with his calm speech is a theme which occurs very frequently in Proverbs. The noun *naḥat*, "calm, quiet", is used in a very similar context in Prov. xxix 9:

If a wise man quarrels with a fool
he meets with rage and scorn and there is no quiet.

But the immediately preceding story of the poor man whose advice was not heeded (verses 14-16), which expresses Qoheleth's own view, is clearly different from the tenor of this saying, which again suggests that it is a quotation.

c) *Language*. *naḥat* has already been discussed under iv 6. *mōšēl*, "ruler", frequent in the Old Testament, occurs five times in Proverbs and only twice in Qoheleth (vii 19, x 5) where the word *šallîṭ* is also used for "ruler". There are thus no affinities with the language of Qoheleth.

7. x 2 The wise man's understanding inclines him to the right,
and the fool's to the left.

---

[14] The commentaries differ about the syntactical relationship of *nišmāʿîm* to its context (see Gordis, *Koheleth*, pp. 190, 312; Galling, *Prediger*, p. 115; Hertzberg, *Prediger*, p. 183). Galling translates: "Worte der Weisen in Ruhe gehört, sind mehr als. . .". I have followed Lauha's translation (*Kohelet*, pp. 175, 178).

a) *Form*. This saying in antithetical parallelism consisting of two nominal clauses may be compared with several in Proverbs including Prov. x 16:

The wage of the righteous leads to life,
the gain of the wicked to sin.

b) *Theme*. The theme of the contrast between the respective fates of the wise man and the fool is characteristic of Proverbs. But the optimism of this older saying is negated by the pessimistic comment of Qoheleth in the previous verse: "A little folly outweighs wisdom and honour".[15]

c) *Language*. This is normal classical Hebrew. There are no affinities with the language of Qoheleth.

8. x 12 The speech of a wise man brings him favour,
but the lips of a fool destroy him.

a) *Form*. This pattern of nominal clause followed by verbal clause in antithetic parallelism is also found in Proverbs, e.g. Prov. x 7:

The memory of the righteous is a source of blessing,
but the name of the wicked will rot.

b) *Theme*. The themes of the importance of wise speech and of the consequences of wise and foolish talk are characteristic of Proverbs. As in the cases of vii 5, ix 17 and x 2 the optimism of this saying is in contrast with Qoheleth's views on the improbability of the wise man's words being heeded.

c) *Language*. Again, there are no affinities with the language of Qoheleth. *ḥēn*, "favour", frequent in the Old Testament, occurs also frequently in Proverbs, sometimes in sayings very similar to the present one:

xiii 15 Good sense wins favour,
but the way of the treacherous leads to their destruction.[16]

---

[15] Or "an abundance of wisdom" (Gordis, *Koheleth*, pp. 190, 315).

[16] Reading *ʾēdām* for *ʾētān* with some commentaries and the N.E.B. See L. H. Brockington, *The Hebrew Text of the Old Testament. The Readings Adopted by the Translators of the New English Bible* (Oxford and Cambridge, 1973), p. 161. Cf. LXX.

xxviii 23 He who rebukes a man will win favour [17]
rather than he who flatters with his tongue.

But it occurs in only one other passage in Qoheleth (ix 11). *bālaʿ* (Piel), "swallow up, destroy", occurs frequently in the Old Testament, but this is the only example in the wisdom books of its use in the sense of bringing ruin on a person.

Qoheleth's use of his quotations

The eight sayings discussed above are, then, all examples of sayings whose themes are characteristic of the teaching of Prov. x-xxix. Since their form and language are also those of an earlier period we may conclude that they are older sayings (not necessarily the only ones, but the only really clear examples) which Qoheleth incorporated into his book as quotations. Why did he do this? What use did he make of them? A consideration of these questions may shed light on Qoheleth's relationship to earlier wisdom: that is, on the extent to which he agreed with it and the extent to which he parted from it.

It will be seen as the study proceeds that he used these sayings in two ways. Some of them he quoted with full approval, either making no comment of his own or confirming and elaborating the statements which they make. Others he used in the course of a more complex kind of argument in which he distinguished between absolute and relative truths. It will be observed that in no case did he quote one of these sayings simply in order to contradict or refute it completely.

1. *Sayings to which Qoheleth gave unqualified approval*

x 3 is a saying by Qoheleth himself in which he expresses approval of the older saying x 2. Having quoted the older saying

The wise man's understanding inclines him to the right,
and the fool's to the left,

he added, in prose, his own comment: "Even on a journey, when the fool is travelling, he lacks sense, and says about everyone else, 'He is a fool' " (or perhaps, "He tells everyone else that he himself is a fool"). The late form *kešehassākāl* (Qere *keššessākāl*) and the use of

---

[17] Omitting the difficult *ʾaḥaray*, "after me", which may however be a corruption. One Ms has *ʾaḥarāw*, which is accepted by the N.E.B. (see Brockington, p. 167) and translated by "in the end".

the word *sākāl*, "fool" (five times in Qoheleth and only twice elsewhere in the Old Testament—Jer. iv 22; v 21) suggest that this is a comment made by Qoheleth himself.

x 13 similarly is a comment by Qoheleth, though it purports to be the continuation of the older saying in x 12. The older saying is as follows:

> The speech of a wise man brings him favour,
> but the lips of a fool destroy him.

Qoheleth's comment is:

> The beginning of his speech is folly,
> and the end of his speech wicked madness.

The use of the words *siklūt*, "folly" and *hōlēlūt*, "madness", both of which are peculiar to and characteristic of Qoheleth, shows that this is not the second half of an original double proverb but an addition made by Qoheleth himself. Verse 14 is a further elaboration of the theme by Qoheleth in prose, again—like verse 13—restricting the scope of the discourse to the fool alone.

In vii 5 and vii 6, as has already been pointed out, Qoheleth has joined together two older sayings, the first about the speech of the wise man and the fool and the second about the empty laughter of the fool. He has also added his own comment, "This also is *hebel*", which clearly refers to and approves of these sayings in their contempt for fools.

In all these cases, then, Qoheleth quoted older sayings and gave them his full approval. Why did he do this, and what exactly did he find to approve of in the older wisdom? The usual modern—and, I think, correct—interpretation of these older sayings in which the wise man is contrasted with the fool is that it is possible for a man to achieve success and happiness by imitating the former and avoiding the behaviour of the latter.[18] But is this what Qoheleth understood by these sayings? Did he agree with their essentially optimistic teaching?

If we look more closely at his comments it will be clear that this

[18] In some sayings in Proverbs this is clearly implied, e.g. Prov. xiii 14:
The teaching of the wise man is a fountain of life,
that one may avoid (*lāsūr min-*) the snares of death.

is not the case. In all the instances which we have just considered there is a significant fact to be noticed: whereas the older or the first saying presents two modes of conduct for comparison, those of the wise man and of the fool, Qoheleth's comment refers only to one of these: the foolish one. Thus x 2 contrasts the "understanding" (*lēb*) of the wise man and that of the fool, but verse 3 speaks only of the fool as he walks along calling others fools. Again, x 12 contrasts the speech of the wise man and the fool, but verse 13 only develops the thought about the fool's speech, and verse 14 likewise. Finally the two older sayings in vii 5 and 6 have been selected and arranged so that whereas verse 5 contrasts the wise man's rebuke with the song of fools, verse 6 speaks only of fools and their laughter. The comment "This also is *hebel*" made by Qoheleth at the end betrays his purpose in all this: it is the vanity of life as exemplified by the behaviour of the *fool* which he wishes to emphasize.

Qoheleth valued these older sayings, then, not because they teach, by contrasting two modes of conduct, that one can be happy if one wishes by choosing wise conduct rather than foolish, but because they offer evidence congenial to his own view, that the world is at least as full of fools as it is of wise men. "*This*", he says, "is vanity". In other words, Qoheleth has completely reinterpreted the wise-foolish contrast of the older sayings, seeing in them a meaning quite different from that which we are accustomed to see in them. For him they express not an optimistic teaching but a pessimistic one: the presence of folly in the world is—to use his own imagery—the fly in the ointment (x 1) which makes ineffective the wisdom existing in the world, which if only it existed without the counterweight of folly would make it a good world.

Thus in the cases which we have considered Qoheleth only "approved" the older wisdom because he interpreted it in a sense which fitted his own view of the world; and the way in which he has commented on it shows that he believed that although wisdom and folly co-exist in the world, folly predominates. As he himself said in x 1, "A little folly outweighs wisdom". It is for this reason that he has placed a saying—whether of his own composition or not—which mentions only folly immediately after each saying which mentions wisdom and folly together. In this way he succeeds in each case in concluding his reflection with all the emphasis placed on the tragic, or at least frustrating, existence of folly.

2. *Sayings to which Qoheleth gave relative approval*

The conclusion reached in the foregoing section is confirmed by the use which Qoheleth made of the other older sayings which we have identified. The passages in which these occur belong to the type which Galling called the "gebrochene Sentenz", in which Qoheleth cites a traditional truth and accepts it as far as it goes while also pointing to other facts of life which seriously weaken its effectiveness and so lead to a pessimistic rather than an optimistic conclusion.[19]

ii 12-17 is a passage devoted to a discussion of wisdom and folly in which the quotation from older wisdom, verse 14a, plays a supporting role in an otherwise self-contained argument of this type. It is preceded by verse 13, a verse whose authorship is indicated by the use of the words *yitrōn*, "advantage, profit" and *siklūt*, "folly", both of which are peculiar to and characteristic of Qoheleth: "And I saw that wisdom is more profitable than folly as light is more profitable than darkness". This statement of a traditional truth receives its fatal qualification, again in the words of Qoheleth himself, in verse 15: "But I said to myself, the fate of the fool will befall me also: why have I been so very wise?"

In verses 16 and 17 this pessimistic thought is pursued further. The older saying, verse 14a, is inserted after verse 13 to support the original optimistic proposition:

> The wise man has eyes in his head,
> but the fool walks on in darkness;

and to this Qoheleth, before going on to his further remarks in verses 15-17, has made a direct comment in the same vein: "But I also reflected that one and the same fate will befall both".

There is, then, no question of Qoheleth's quoting an earlier saying simply to refute it. He himself has already expressed his approval of its truth in verse 13. The teaching of the older wisdom, then, is true; but it cannot in the long run overcome the vanity or meaninglessness of life.

The older saying ix 17 is set in a similar context. Throughout the section ix 13-18 the ability of the wise man to achieve what force

---

[19] K. Galling, "Kohelet-Studien", *ZAW* 50 (1932), pp. 277-92; "Stand und Aufgabe der Kohelet-Forschung", *ThR*, N.F. 6 (1934), p. 369; *Die Krise der Aufklärung in Israel*, pp. 14 ff. More detailed analysis of this type of pericope is to be found in F. Ellermeier, *Qohelet* I/1 (Herzberg, 1967).

cannot achieve is accepted, but so also is another fact of life which can entirely negate its value: the wise man's advice is rarely heeded. Verses 14-15, which tell the story of the poor wise man who could have saved the city but whom no-one remembered at the crucial time,[20] already demonstrate both of these truths. Verses 16-18 then make the point again, indeed twice over. Verse 16a, which is probably a quotation of a popular adage, makes an absolute statement about the superiority of wisdom: "Wisdom is better than force". Verse 16b, whose use of the word *miskēn*, "poor", peculiar to Qoheleth, clearly indicates its authorship, states the second truth in a direct comment on the preceding story: "But the poor man's wisdom was despised and his words were not heeded". Verse 17, the older saying, picks up from verse 16b the word *nišmāʿīm*, "heard, heeded", and repeats the first truth:

Wise men's words (spoken) in calm are worth hearing (*nišmāʿīm*)
rather than a ruler's shouting among fools.[21]

This is then qualified in verse 18 in a poetical saying of Qoheleth's own composition (shown by the use of *harbēh*, "much", peculiar to Qoheleth among the wisdom books and used fifteen times by him):

Wisdom is better than weapons of war,
but a single incompetent (*ḥōṭē'*) [22] can destroy much good

(i.e. its good effect). The older saying (verse 17) is, then, quoted to confirm the truth that wisdom is better than force, a truth which Qoheleth himself accepts, though in conjunction with the other, depressing, fact of life.

Finally, in iv 5 and 6 Qoheleth uses two older sayings to express a similar two-part argument, this time on the value of hard work and its corresponding drawbacks. iv 5,

The fool folds his hands
and consumes his own flesh,

expresses the thought that work is indispensable to life, while iv 6,

---

[20] So most modern commentaries. The alternative interpretation, according to which the poor man did save the city but was subsequently forgotten, is less probable in the context.

[21] See note 14 above.

[22] Cf. Prov. xix 2. Gordis, *Koheleth*, p. 310, translates by "fool".

Better is a handful with quiet
than two fistfuls with trouble

makes the point that, while the former statement is true, overwork in order to make a fortune is not worth the candle. Qoheleth's final words "and striving after wind" stress the truth of the second saying.

Concluding Observations

It is now possible to give some tentative answers to the questions posed at the beginning of this article.

1. His use of wisdom sayings from an earlier period shows that Qoheleth regarded himself as a wisdom writer in the Israelite tradition. Whenever possible he made use in the course of his arguments of the insights of the wisdom of the past.

2. His purpose in quoting these sayings was not to demonstrate their falsity. He quoted them because he accepted their truth.

3. His approval of them, however, was of a distinctive and characteristic kind. He saw in the contrast which they make between wisdom and folly not the optimistic doctrine that man is free by choosing wisdom to seek and obtain success and happiness but rather the pessimistic one that folly generally prevails over wisdom, so that life is meaningless.

A further observation may be made about Qoheleth's *selection* of older sayings. Although the examples discussed above may not be the only quotations which he makes from the wisdom of an earlier period—there are a number of other sayings which may belong to this category, though the evidence for this seems to me to be less conclusive[23]—nevertheless the sayings in the book which do not by their theme or language betray a late origin are very few. For the most part Qoheleth seems to have been unable to find sayings which he could use to express or support his radical teaching, and so he mainly went his own way, guided simply by his personal observation of the world.

It may also be noted that all the sayings which he quotes from earlier wisdom are "secular": that is, they deal with themes such as wisdom and folly, work and idleness, the quiet life and the troubled life, success and failure, not with righteousness and wickedness or with piety and impiety. They represent only one side of the teaching of older wisdom represented by Prov. x-xxix.

---

[23] Especially vi 7, vii 7, vii 8, xi 1, xi 4.

Unresolved questions

Finally some questions which remain unsolved may be noted.

1. Study is needed of the fairly numerous sayings in Qoheleth mentioned earlier which have the form of sayings in Proverbs, but whose language shows them to be contemporary with Qoheleth. Some of these express views which are characteristic of Qoheleth himself; others are reminiscent of Proverbs in theme as well as in form. If we are to discover whether these are quotations or the work of Qoheleth himself some examination of their function in their present contexts will be necessary.

2. A further question concerns the possibility that some of the sayings expressed in late language may be older sayings whose language has been "modernized". As has already been pointed out, even in those sayings which are clearly quotations from earlier wisdom the only word used for "fool" is *k*[e]*sīl*, a limitation of vocabulary which corresponds to Qoheleth's own usage but not to that of Proverbs. It is possible that in some of these sayings Qoheleth himself substituted *k*[e]*sīl* for some other word, although it should be noted that Ben Sirach, writing somewhat later, shows no such limitation of vocabulary. But this question requires further thought.

TRADITION UND INTERPRETATION IN EXODUS XV 1-21

VON

ERICH ZENGER

Münster

I.

Der Text Ex. xv 1-21, der sich im überlieferten Textzusammenhang des Buches Exodus, also auf der Ebene der Endredaktion, deutlich als eigener Abschnitt abgrenzen läßt, gilt zwar als einer der Basistexte des Alten Testaments und der Religion Israels, aber er ist zugleich einer der schwierigsten und strittigsten Texte. Über die poetische Struktur, über Aufbau, Gattung und Sitz im Leben, über die Datierung, über die literarische Einheitlichkeit sowie über den traditionsgeschichtlichen und redaktionsgeschichtlichen Ort gehen die Meinungen außerordentlich stark auseinander.[1] Da hier kein differenzierter

[1] Vgl. außer den Kommentaren vor allem: A. Bender, "Das Lied Exodus 15", *ZAW* 23 (1903), pp. 1-48; P. Haupt, "Moses' song of triumph", *AJSL* 20 (1904), pp. 149-72; H. Schmidt, "Das Meerlied. Ex 15, 2-19", *ZAW* 49 (1931), pp. 59-66; M. Rozelaar, "The Song of the Sea", *VT* 2 (1952), pp. 220-8; F. M. Cross - D. N. Freedman, "The Song of Miriam", *JNES* 14 (1955), pp. 237-50; J. D. W. Watts, "The Song of the Sea-Ex. XV", *VT* 7 (1957), pp. 371-80; J. Schreiner, *Sion — Jerusalem Jahwes Königssitz. Theologie der Heiligen Stadt im Alten Testament* (München, 1963), pp. 208-10; N. Lohfink, "De Moysis epinicio (Ex 15, 1-18)", *VD* 41 (1963), pp. 277-89; ders., *Das Siegeslied am Schilfmeer. Christliche Auseinandersetzungen mit dem Alten Testament* (Frankfurt, 1965), pp. 102-8; G. Fohrer, *Überlieferung und Geschichte des Exodus. Eine Analyse von Ex 1-15* (Berlin, 1964), pp. 110-16; J. Muilenburg, "A Liturgy on the Triumphs of Yahweh", in *Studia Biblica et Semitica Th. C. Vriezen dedicata* (Wageningen, 1966), pp. 233-51; F. Crüsemann, *Studien zur Formgeschichte von Hymnus und Danklied in Israel* (Neukirchen, 1969), pp. 19-24, 193-4; G. W. Coats "The Song of the Sea", *CBQ* 31 (1969), pp. 1-17; B. S. Childs, "A Traditio-Historical Study of the Reed Sea Tradition", *VT* 20 (1970), pp. 406-18; F. Stolz, *Jahwes und Israels Kriege. Kriegstheorien und Kriegserfahrungen im Glauben des alten Israel* (Zürich, 1972), pp. 90-4; F. M. Cross, *Canaanite Myth and Hebrew Epic. Essays in the History of the Religion of Israel* (Cambridge, Massachusetts, 1973), pp. 121-44; D. N. Freedman, "Strophe and Meter in Exodus 15", in *A Light unto My Path. O.T. Studies in Honor of Jacob M. Myers* (Philadelphia, 1974), pp. 163-203; G. W. Coats, "History and Theology in the Sea Tradition", *ST* 29 (1975), pp. 53-62; D. Patrick, "Traditio-History of the Reed Sea Account", *VT* 26 (1976), pp. 248-9; S. I. L. Norin, *Er spaltete das Meer. Die Auszugsüberlieferung in Psalmen und Kult des alten Israel* (Lund, 1977), pp. 77-107; G. W. Coats,

und umfassender Forschungsüberblick gegeben werden kann, sollen stattdessen verschiedene Typen von Hypothesen mit ihren entscheidenden Argumenten knapp skizziert werden, um so einen möglichst breiten Problemhorizont für unsere eigene Hypothese zu gewinnen.[2]

Ein *erstes Problem* ist das Verhältnis der beiden Lieder Ex. xv 1b-18 und Ex. xv 21b zueinander, also das *Verhältnis von "Meerlied" und "Mirjamlied"*. Soweit ich sehe, lassen sich in der Forschung vier Ansätze erkennen, um diese Doppelung zu erklären. Ein erstes Modell hält das Meerlied xv 1b-18 für den ursprünglichen Text, während das Mirjamlied xv 21b nur eine Art Refrain dazu war: "Der Kehrvers ist aus dem Hymnus genommen und hat nie eine Sonderexistenz gehabt; er ist immer Introduktion und Kehrvers gewesen".[3] Hier wird der überlieferte literarische Rahmen, insbesondere die einleitende Notiz xv 21a *wăttă'ăn lahèm*, einfach als literaturgeschichtliche Hypothese umgesetzt. Ein zweites Modell sieht im kurzen Mirjamlied den ursprünglichen Text, der dann sekundär zu dem breiten Meerlied ausgestaltet wurde.[4] Ein drittes Modell haben mehrfach F. M. Cross und D. N. Freedman vorgelegt. Nach ihnen ist das Mirjamlied V. 21b "not a different or shorter or the original version of the song, but simply the title of the poem taken from a different cycle of traditions" (*JNES* 14 [1955], p. 237), das Lied habe in der heute in Ex. xv 1-18 überlieferten Gestalt ursprünglich in J gestanden, während E ebenfalls das Lied in dieser umfassenden Gestalt meinte, wenn xv 21b als Titel des Lieds zitiert wurde (man müßte also paraphrasieren: Und Mirjam sang ihnen das Lied "Singt Jahwe, denn gar hoch erhob er sich. . ." zu). Schließlich ist noch als viertes Modell die Hypothese von Hans Schmidt zu nennen, der in Ex. xv 1-21 sogar drei verschiedene Stücke erkennen will, die hier zusammengearbeitet wären: einerseits hebt er V. 2-18 als Dankliturgie ab, in der ein einzelner Mensch seine erfahrene individuelle Rettung in einen heilsgeschichtlichen Kontext einordnet, und andererseits teilt er den verbleibenden Textbestand xv 1 und xv 19-21 so auf zwei Quellen auf, daß er in xv 1, 19 bzw. xv 20, 21

"The Sea Tradition in the Wilderness Theme: A Review", *JSOT* 12 (1979), pp. 2-8.

[2] Der Beitrag präzisiert frühere Arbeiten: P. Weimar - E. Zenger, *Exodus. Geschichten und Geschichte der Befreiung Israels* (Stuttgart, 1975.1979²), pp. 71-87; E. Zenger, *Das Buch Exodus* (Düsseldorf, 1978), pp. 151-60.

[3] S. Mowinckel, *Psalmenstudien II* (Oslo, 1922), p. 111.

[4] Diese Position wird von den meisten Autoren und Kommentaren vertreten.

eine "doppelte Überlieferung über die Siegesfeier" nach der Rettung am Meer erhält, wobei "der Triumphgesang fast gleichlautend mitgeteilt wird, das eine Mal aber als ein Loblied, das Mose singt, das andere Mal in der lebensvolleren Darstellung des Siegesreigens als ein Lied, das die Vorsängerin Mirjam vor ihren Frauen intoniert" (*ZAW* 49 [1931], pp. 59 f.). Den Ansatz für diese Theorie bildet Schmidts Betonung des deutlichen Bruchs zwischen V. 1b und V. 2, insofern in V. 2 nach Schmidt ein individuelles Ich spricht, das persönliche Hilfe erfahren hat, während V. 1b von der Rettung Israels singt.

Der *zweite Problembereich* betrifft die poetische Eigenart von Ex. xv 1b-18. Schon die *stichometrische Einteilung*, die ihrerseits wieder die strophische Struktur weitgehend vorentscheidet, ist kontrovers. Vom Ansatz her lassen sich zwei stichometrische Typen unterscheiden, die verständlicherweise bei einzelnen Stichen noch einmal divergieren: die Mehrzahl der Autoren bildet kurze Stichen und ordnet sie als Bikola und Trikola so zusammen, daß eine syntaktische Einheit bisweilen nur mit Hilfe eines Enjambements möglich wird; eine Minderheit folgt dem bei den Psalmen üblichen Prinzip des Parallelismus Membrorum und bildet längere Stichen.[5]

Wie vielfältig die *Strukturbeschreibungen* sind, belegt am einfachsten die Synopse[6] mit einer Auswahl der vorgelegten Hypothesen.

Diese Synopse zeigt, daß es vereinzelte Strukturversuche wie die von R. Smend[7] und von G. Fohrer gibt, die den Text durchgängig in Strophen gliedern,[8] während die Mehrzahl der Autoren mit der Unterscheidung von Rahmen und Korpus arbeitet, wobei die Abgrenzung des Rahmens und die Aufteilung des Korpus dann wieder sehr unterschiedlich ausfallen. Vom Ansatz her wird das Korpus meist in zwei oder drei Teile aufgegliedert. Bei fast allen Strukturmustern spielen die ähnlich im klimaktischen Parallelismus

[5] Vertreter der kurzen Stichen sind u.a. B. S. Childs (Kommentar), G. W. Coats, F. M. Cross, D. N. Freedman, N. Lohfink, J. Muilenburg, H. Schmidt, J. D. Watts. Die Einteilung in lange Stichen wird vorwiegend in Kommentaren vorgenommen, u.a. von: B. Baentsch, G. Beer, U. Cassuto, A. Dillmann, S. R. Driver, M. Noth; vgl. auch S. I. L. Norin und M. Rozelaar, sowie O. Loretz, *UF* 6 (1974), pp. 245-7.

[6] Vgl. auch die Zusammenstellung bei G. W. Coats, *CBQ* 31 (1969), p. 2.

[7] *Die Erzählung des Hexateuch auf ihre Quellen untersucht* (Berlin 1912), p. 143.

[8] Vgl. dazu M. Noth, *Das zweite Buch Mose. Exodus* (Göttingen, 1965[3]), p. 98: "Eine Strophenbildung in dem verhältnismäßig langen Lied ist nicht sicher nachweisbar ... Man müßte schon eine vom überlieferten Bestand stark abweichende Grundform annehmen, wenn man ein rhythmisch ebenmäßiges Lied als ursprünglich voraussetzen sollte."

Konzentrische Struktur
Freedman
1b
2
3-5
6
7-10
11
12-16ab
16cd
17-18
21b

Durchlaufende Strophen	
Smend	Fohrer
1b-3	1b-3
4-7	4-6
8-10	7-8
	9-10
11-13	11-13
14-16b	14-16a
16c-18	16b-18

Zwei Teile	
Beer	Cross
1b-10	1b-12
11-18	13-18

Rahmen und zweiteiliges Korpus	
Rozelaar	Lohfink
1b	1b.3-5
2-10	6-10
11-17	11-17
18	18

Rahmen und dreiteiliges Korpus	
Baentsch	Muilenburg
1b	1b
2-5	2-6
6-10	7-11
11-17	12-16
18	17-18

gestalteten Verse 6 und 11 eine wichtige Rolle, wobei sie entweder als Anfang oder Abschluß einer Strophe/eines Teils bestimmt werden; in der Strukturbeschreibung von D. N. Freedman werden diese Verse zusammen mit V. 16b als Refrains so ausgegliedert, daß eine konzentrische Struktur entsteht, deren Achse V. 11 ist. Besondere Unsicherheit der Autoren offenbart die Tabelle auch über die Funktion von V. 2-5 und V. 16-18. Bei der Beschreibung der Struktur wird häufig auf den unterschiedlichen Stil (Er-Stil in V. 1b-5, 18 und Du-Stil in V. 6-17) und auf den Wechsel von narrativer und hymnischer Sprache hingewiesen. Bunt wie das Bild der Strukturschemata ist auch die Palette der Bestimmung von *Gattung und Sitz im Leben*: Thronbesteigungshymnus beim Thronbesteigungsfest (S. Mowinckel),[9] Herbstfest (G. W. Coats) oder Bundesfest (A.

[9] Vgl. dazu die kritischen Anfragen von H. Groß, "Läßt sich in den Psalmen ein 'Thronbesteigungsfest Gottes' nachweisen?", *TrThZ* 65 (1956), pp. 24-40; K. G. Rendtorff, "Sejrshymnen i Exodus 15 og dens forhold til tronbestigelsealmerne", *DTT* 22 (1959), pp. 156-71.

Weiser), Paschahymnus (J. Pedersen, N. Lohfink), Siegeslied bei der Feier des "ritual conquest" in Gilgal (F. M. Cross), ein ursprünglich amphiktyonischer Hymnus, der später für den Jerusalemer Tempel adaptiert wurde (J. D. W. Watts), eine litaneiartige Liturgie (G. Beer, J. Muilenburg), eine Mischform aus "Solo-Hymnus" und "Danklied" (M. Noth), ein keineswegs im Kult entstandener oder beheimateter freier dichterischer Lobpreis Jahwes in der Mischform von Hymnus, Siegeslied und Danklied (G. Fohrer) oder homiletische Paraphrase des älteren Mirjamlieds (R. H. Pfeiffer).[10]

Je nach dieser Gattungsbestimmung ergibt sich dann auch die *Datierung des Textes*, die vom 12. bis ins 5. Jh. reicht. Als Beispiel für die jeweiligen Argumentationsfiguren mögen die folgenden vier Autoren genügen. In Fortführung mehrerer Publikationen, zum Teil in Zusammenarbeit mit Frank Moore Cross, kommt David Noel Freedman 1974 erneut zum Schluß: "All the data suggest that the poem in its original form was composed in the twelfth century. Its nearest companion in form and style is the Song of Deborah, universally recognized to be a product of the same period" ("Strophe and Meter", p. 202). Für diese Datierung sprechen, wenn auch nicht zwingend, die teilweise archaische Sprache, die poetische Form und einzelne Bilder. Vor allem aber sind es historische Details, die diese Datierung stützen (bzw. verlangen) sollen. Zunächst setzt das Lied zwar die kriegerische Landnahme voraus, aber das Fehlen der Ammoniter in V. 14 f., wo nur Moabiter und Edomiter als Feinde genannt werden, belegt eine exakte Kenntnis der politischen Situation des 13. und 12. Jahrhunderts, die am ehesten durch zeitliche Nähe des Lieds selbst verstehbar ist, zumal z.B. in der deuteronomistischen Literatur dieses exakte Bild verschwindet. Andererseits verlangt die Erwähnung der Philister in V. 14, daß die Philister bereits im Lande sind und einen beträchtlichen Teil desselben kontrollieren. Der Verfasser des Liedes habe dabei allerdings in einer Art Teleskopeinstellung die nach Freedman historische Reihenfolge Landnahme Israels und (erst danach!) Eindringen der Philister nach Palästina umgestellt. Ein weiterer Vertreter der Frühdatierung, wenn auch in differenzierterer Form, ist S. I. L. Norin mit seiner 1977 publizierten Studie *Er spaltete das Meer*. Norin rekonstruiert darin eine Urform des Meerlieds (sie umfaßt etwa 70% des heutigen Textbestands), die aus sprachlichen wie formgeschichtlichen Gründen mit den von

---

[10] *Introduction to the Old Testament* (New York, 1941), p. 281.

diesem Urlied "geschilderten Ereignissen annähernd gleichzeitig oder höchstens etwa ein Jahrhundert jünger sein dürfte". Seiner Form nach ist dieses Urlied eine Nachbildung des Baal-Anat-Mythos, denn außer einzelnen terminologischen Übereinstimmungen weisen der Mythos und das Meerlied ein gemeinsames Schema auf: "Konflikt, Tempelbau, Königtum". Da nach Norin jenes ungewöhnliche Rettungserlebnis, das die Exodusüberlieferung auslöste, in der Nähe des am Mittelmeer gelegenen Heiligtums Baal Zafon stattfand, war es für diese israelitische Volksgruppe "ganz natürlich, nach der Rettung am Meer ihrem Siegeslied die gleiche äußere Form zu geben, die der Mythos davon hatte, wie Baal seine Machtstellung errang, indem er Jam besiegte, einen Tempel erhielt und zum König proklamiert wurde" (pp. 92 f.). "Die rekonstruierte Urform der Dichtung wäre dann auf irgendeinen Zeitpunkt im 12. Jahrhundert v. Chr. zu datieren, als auch der Konflikt mit Moab auf die Ausgestaltung des Lieds einwirken konnte". Eine "durchgreifende Veränderung zu der heutigen Form machte das Meerlied sicherlich durch, als es zu Josias' Zeit einen Platz in dem Jerusalemer Passahkult erhielt. . . Die Redigierung bedeutet eine stärkere Historisierung, die nicht zuletzt auf Bemühungen zurückzuführen sein dürfte, die Assoziationen zu der kanaanäischen Mythologie abzuschwächen. . . Aus dem alten Lied, das in mythologischer Form Jhwh's Sieg über den Feind am Meer pries, ist in seiner historisierten Gestalt ein poetisches Exposé über die Zeit vom Exodus über den Jodanübergang und die Landnahme bis zum Bau des Tempels in Jerusalem geworden" (pp. 105 f.).

Als Vertreter einer mittleren Datierung, die gewöhnlich mit der in V. 17 anvisierten Tempeltheologie von Jerusalem argumentiert, kann der Exoduskommentar von B. Baentsch angesehen werden, wo es u.a. heißt: "Für die nähere Bestimmung des Zeitalters unseres Liedes würde es von Belang sein, wenn sich die Frage bestimmt beantworten ließe, ob das Lied einem der erzählenden Berichte in Kap. 14 zu Grunde liegt, oder ob nicht vielmehr der Dichter von der Darstellung in Kap. 14 abhängig ist". Da in Ex. xv 1-18 mehrere Vorstellungen, die in Ex. xiv unterschiedlichen Schichten angehören, verbunden sind, müßte sich "für jedes gesunde Urteil wenigstens die Vermutung nahe legen, dass. . . das Meerlied demnach jünger als J und E, ja vielleicht sogar jünger als JE sein muß." Der Text kann "schwerlich aus der vordeuteronomischen Zeit stammen; denn die einzigartige Bedeutung, die hier dem jerusalemischen Tempel als dem Centralpunkte des ganzen heiligen Landes beigemessen wird, v. 17b, und die dieser Bedeutung entsprechende Vorstellung, daß die gnadenvolle Führung des Volkes erst mit der Einpflanzung desselben an diesem Heiligtum zu ihrem Abschluß gekommen sei, läßt sich geschichtlich doch nur bei einem Schriftsteller begreifen, der ganz von deuteronomischem Geiste erfüllt war... Ferner zeigt die Benutzung von v. 5 in Neh 9, 11, daß unser Lied gegen Ende des 5. oder Anfang des 4. Jahrhunderts bereits mit der pentat. Geschichtserzählung verbunden war, und die Stellen Jos 2, 9b. 24, die auf die vv. 15b. 16a deutlich anspielen, lassen sogar schließen, dass unser Lied bereits im Exile bekannt gewesen sein muss... Gegen eine Entstehung unseres Liedes im Exile selbst dürfte der triumphierende Ton, der es vom Anfang bis zum Ende durchzieht, sprechen; eher dürfte es der durch das deuteronomische Gesetz heraufgeführten neuen Zeit zugesprochen werden, in der die Erinnerung an die großen Thaten Jahwes in der Vergangenheit eine Neubelebung und religiöse Vertiefung erfahren hatte. Von den späteren, lediglich auf gelehrtem Studium des Hexateuchs beruhenden geschichtlichen Psalmen hebt sich unser Lied jedenfalls durch Originalität vorteilhaft ab" (*Exodus-Leviticus* [Göttingen, 1900], pp. 128 f.). Auf die Schwierigkeit der Datierung von Ex. xv 1-18 weist Georg Fohrer, der schließlich als Repräsentant der Spätdatierung zu Wort kommen soll, ausdrücklich hin. Am ehesten, so führt er in seiner 1964 erschienenen Studie *Überlieferung und Geschichte des Exodus* aus, läßt sich das Alter des Liedes "aus V. 17 f. bestimmen. Die Vorstellung, daß Jahwe sich in Jerusalem eine Wohnung, den Tempel, bereitet hat, um für immer als König herrschen zu können, ist frühestens von der letzten vorexilischen Zeit an zu erwarten. Eher wird man wegen der den V. 18 einleitenden Worte *jhwh jimlok*, die die von Deuterojesaja beeinflußte Aussage *jhwh malak* einer Reihe von Psalmen abwandeln, an die nachexilische Zeit denken müssen, in der auch das Motiv von der Rettung am Meer sehr beliebt wird" (p. 115). "Tatsächlich nötigt nichts—es sei denn die a priori aufgestellte Behauptung, daß es lediglich kultgebundene Lieder geben könne—zu der Annahme, daß Ex. 15, 1b-18 aus dem Kult entstanden oder für den Kult bestimmt sei. Es ist einfach ein dichterischer Preis Jahwes wegen der Rettung am Meer und der folgenden Heilstaten" (pp. 112 f., Anm. 5). "So zeigt das Lied, wie die Erinnerung an die Rettung durch die Jahrhunderte hindurch lebendig geblieben ist" (p. 115).

Gehen demnach die Meinungen über die formgeschichtliche Beurteilung, über die Datierung von Ex. xv 1-18 und das Verhältnis des Meerliedes zum Mirjamlied weit auseinander, so scheint über die Frage der *literarkritischen Einheitlichkeit* des Textes noch am ehesten ein Konsens möglich zu sein. Für eine Reihe von Autoren ist die ursprüngliche Einheitlichkeit überhaupt keine Frage, andere notieren zwar Probleme wie wechselnden Gebrauch von Präfix- und Suffixkonjugation, unterschiedliche Formen der Suffixe, unterschiedliche Länge der Stichen, wechselnde Sinneinheiten von Bikola und Trikola, Mischung unterschiedlicher Traditions- und Stilelemente, aber sie stellen dann eine Reihe von form- und strukturkritischen Betrachtung an, die den Text als sinnvoll strukturiertes Ganzes erweisen, wovor dann die angemerkten kleineren Störungen als "dichterische Freiheit" verschwinden. Beispiele für ein derartiges Vorgehen, das literarkritische Probleme durch formkritische Beobachtungen auf die Seite schiebt, sind die in sich gewiß eindrucksvollen Analysen unseres Textes von Lohfink, Muilenburg, Coats, und Freedman, denen bei aller Unterschiedlichkeit im Detail gemeinsam ist, daß das von ihnen jeweils vorgelegte kunstvolle Strukturschema zugleich die ursprüngliche Einheitlichkeit des Textes beweisen soll. Daß freilich, wie unsere Synopse zeigt, diese Strukturschemata mehr oder weniger stark voneinander abweichen, scheint mir Beweis genug zu sein, daß formkritische Beobachtungen eine detaillierte literakritische Analyse, auch im Bereich der poetischen Literatur, nicht ersetzen können; die neueren Arbeiten von W. Beyerlin zu einzelnen Psalmen [11] dokumentieren ohnehin die Effektivität des literarkritischen Einstiegs auch bei der biblischen Poesie sehr überzeugend.

Im übrigen gibt es durchaus einige Autoren, die unseren Text literarkritisch angehen. Von nicht wenigen Autoren, die die ursprüngliche Einheitlichkeit betonen, wird z.B. V. 2 als Erweiterung oder Glosse beurteilt. Vor allem der Abschnitt V. 12-17 hat wiederholt literarkritische Diskussionen hervorgerufen. Der Kommentar von Dillmann geht sogar so weit, als Urfassung von Ex. xv 1b-18 nur V. 1b-3 gelten zu lassen; allerdings argumentiert Dillmann vorwiegend mit historischen Argumenten. Mit sukzessiver Bearbeitung einer

---

[11] Vgl. zuletzt die Monographien: *Werden und Wesen des 107. Psalms* (Berlin, 1979); *Der 52. Psalm. Studien zu seiner Einordnung* (Stuttgart, 1980).

Ur-Form des Meerlieds rechnen, je auf ihre Weise, in neuerer Zeit vor allem die Arbeiten von Watts [12] und Norin.[13]

Wir brechen hier unseren kleinen Forschungsüberblick ab. Er hat immerhin gezeigt, wie schwer sich die Exegese mit diesem Text tut und wie notwendig die analytische Arbeit an diesem Text ist. Zugleich freilich zeigt die Vielfalt der Meinungen, daß auch unser Beitrag nur ein Versuch sein kann. Aber auch hier gilt: eine Hypothese ist immer noch besser als gar keine Hypothese!

II.

Eine Analyse von Ex. xv 1-21 muß die gedanklich-logische, syntaktisch-stilistische und semantische Kohärenz überprüfen. Wie bei allen literarkritischen Analysen ist dabei streng zwischen den Beobachtungen selbst und ihrer Auswertung zu unterscheiden. Während über die Beobachtungen selbst ein Konsens möglich ist, beginnt bei der Umsetzung der Beobachtungen in eine Texthypothese in der Regel die Scheidung der Geister, weil hier die Gewichtung der einzelnen Beobachtungen verständlicherweise unterschiedlich ausfällt. Eine besondere Schwierigkeit für die Analyse unseres Textes ist zweifellos die dabei vorauszusetzende stichometrische Einteilung. Hier scheint mir als Ausgangspunkt die Aufteilung in Sinneinheiten nach den Gesetzen des Parallelismus-Membrorum, wie sie sich bei den Psalmen bewährt haben, nach wie vor geboten zu sein—vorgängig vor alle weiteren stichometrischen Theorien.[14] Ich halte es auch nicht für gerechtfertigt, das kurze Mirjamlied zum Ausgangspunkt zu nehmen und dann entsprechend kurze Stichen zu suchen.[15] Vielmehr empfiehlt es sich, die für den Großteil des Textes unschwer erkennbare Parallelismus-Struktur mit meist in

---

[12] Die kultgeschichtlichen Hypothesen von Watts haben freilich im Text keinerlei Anhaltspunkte; ebensowenig scheinen mir seine Textumstellungen gerechtfertigt zu sein.

[13] Norin betreibt freilich weitgehend historische Kritik statt Literarkritik: da er das Lied grundsätzlich als (beinahe) mit dem historischen Exodus zeitgenössisch beurteilt, scheidet er alles aus, was historisch nicht zu dieser Hypothese paßt.

[14] Auch das zuletzt von Freedman vorgelegte "syllable counting system" scheidert schon allein daran, daß es zu unterschiedlich langen Stichen kommt, deren wechselnde Länge nicht erklärt werden kann, und daß es syntaktisch zusammengehörende Elemente mehrmals auseinanderreißt.

[15] Dieses Verfahren wäre nur gerechtfertigt, wenn feststünde, daß Mirjamlied (in der Gestalt von V. 1b) und Meerlied von Anfang an eine Einheit gebildet haben.

sich syntaktisch abgeschlossenen Sinneinheiten als Ansatz einer stichometrischen Einteilung zu wählen und entsprechend zu ordnen. Gegenüber der vor allem von Cross, Freedman und Muilenburg vertretenen Einteilung in ungewöhnlich kurze Stichen, die oft nur mit Hilfe eines schwierigen Enjambements zu einer Sinneinheit zusammengebracht werden können, ergeben sich dabei Stichen von, verglichen mit dem Psalter, durchschnittlicher Länge. Es ist im übrigen die Einteilung, wie sie ähnlich u.a. von Mowinckel, Noth und Cassuto vorgelegt wurde.

Vor der literarkritischen Analyse muß noch die Abgrenzung des zu analysierenden Textes begründet werden:

1. Nach vorne läßt sich der Text deutlich abgrenzen. Die vorangehende Erzählung vom Meerwunder hat in Ex. xiv 31 durch die Konstatierung des zweifachen Glaubens Israels an Jahwe und an seinen Knecht Mose ihren offenkundigen Abschluß. Die in Ex. xv 1a angeschlossene Einleitungsformel unseres Liedes ist in ihrer sprachlichen Gestalt typische Redaktorenarbeit. Dies belegen nicht nur vergleichbare Stellen wie Num. xxi 17; Dtn. xxxi 30; Jos. x 12, sondern vor allem die einleitende allgemeine Zeitangabe "damals" (*'az*), die mit der gleichen Angabe in V. 15a rivalisiert (wo sie gut sitzt, vgl. u.), und die trotz pluralischem Subjekt in der 3. Person Singular Präfixkonjugation stehende Angabe *yašîr*, die wohl ausgelöst ist durch die 1. Person Singular *'ašîrā* in V. 1b; auch das syntaktisch sehr schlecht postierte *lyhwh* dürfte durch *lyhwh* in V. 1b ausgelöst sein.

2. Nach hinten läßt sich das in V. 1b beginnende Lied ebenfalls gut abgrenzen. Nicht nur die erzählende Notiz V. 20, 21a setzt sich deutlich ab, sondern auch V. 19 kann ursprünglich nicht zum Meerlied gehört haben. Der Vers ist unbestreitbar Prosa, ist durch die Partikel *kî* nur sehr gekünstelt an V. 18 angeschlossen und gibt eine Darstellung vom Geschehen am Meer, die semantisch und vorstellungsmäßig nicht durch das Meerlied, sondern nur durch die Erzählung Ex. xiv abgedeckt wird. Die Notiz will also offensichtlich einen Zusammenhang mit Ex. xiv herstellen (vgl. Ex. xiv 16, 22, 23, 29 [P^{G}]). Unsere folgende literarkritische Analyse kann sich also zunächst auf V. 1b-18 beschränken.

Was also sind die literarkritischen Beobachtungen bzw. Probleme, die jede Hypothese, wie immer sie aussehen mag, berücksichtigen muß?

1. Unabhängig davon, ob man in der stichometrischen Einteilung

mit langen oder kurzen Stichen arbeitet, fällt V. 2 aus dem Rahmen, insofern die Stichen zu lang (vgl. z.B. die Zählung bei Cross-Freedman) bzw. (in unserer Einteilung) zu kurz sind. Gedanklich sitzt der Vers mit seiner stark generalisierenden individuellen Vertrauensäußerung, die ganz oder teilweise wortgleich mit Jes. xii 2, 4; Ps. cxviii 14, 21, 28 ist, nicht sehr fest im Kontext, zumal von Rettung und Hilfe im Meerlied sonst nicht mehr die Rede ist. Semantisch fällt der Vers schließlich noch durch die Kurzform des Tetragramms auf, das sonst in Ex. xv immer in Langform auftritt.[16]

2. Die beiden kurzen Nominalsätze in V. 3 unterscheiden sich zunächst dadurch vom übrigen Text, ausgenommen V. 9, daß hier zwei syntaktisch selbständige Einheiten zu einem Stichos zusammengebunden sind, der zudem durch seine Länge auffällt. Inhaltlich überrascht die Formulierung von V. 3a vor allem im Blick auf V. 11; diese Schwierigkeit hat schon die Textüberlieferung selbst verunsichert.[17]

3. Auch V. 4a fällt zunächst durch seine Überlänge auf, was bei einigen Autoren zu Streichungen "metri causa" oder zu textkritischen Hypothesen,[18] die allerdings nicht durch die äußere Textüberlieferung gestützt sind, geführt hat. Der Vers nimmt auch dadurch eine Sonderstellung ein, als nur in ihm der Pharao genannt wird, während im übrigen Lied nur allgemein von *sûs w^e^rok^e^bô*, *'ôyeb* und *qamèka* die Rede ist; in der Nennung des Pharao stimmt unser Vers dagegen mit der oben bereits abgegrenzten Notiz V. 19 zusammen, die in ihrer Formulierung auf Ex. xiv zurückgreift. Die Vermutung, V. 4 zeige ähnliches Interesse wie V. 19 (und gehe damit auf dieselbe Hand zurück), wird dadurch gestützt, daß V. 4 und V. 19 zusammen *alle* Bezeichnungen des ägyptischen Heeres bzw. seiner Teile gebraucht, die in Ex. xiv—dort verteilt auf unterschiedliche Erzählfäden—begegnen.[19] Singulär ist in V. 4b auch die Ortsangabe *b^e^yăm sûp*,

---

[16] Textkritische Hypothesen, meist in der Absicht, den Vers als möglichst alt zu retten, bieten: S. Talmon, "A Case of Abbreviation Resulting in Double Readings", *VT* 4 (1954), pp. 206-8; S. E. Loewenstamm, "The Lord is my strength and my glory", *VT* 19 (1969), pp. 464-70; E. M. Good, "Exodus xv 2", *VT* 20 (1970), pp. 358-9; S. B. Parker, "Exodus xv 2 again", *VT* 21 (1971), pp. 373-9; M. Dahood, "Exodus 15, 2 *'anwēhû* and Ugaritic *šnwt*", *Bibl* 59 (1978), pp. 260-1.

[17] Vgl. Cross, *Canaanite Myth*, p. 127, Anm. 53: "The major versions (Sam G Sy) have the reading *gbr mlḥmh*. Evidently we have a conflation of ancient variants: *yahwē gibbō*r and *'iš milḥāmā*."

[18] Vgl. z.B. N. Lohfink, *VD* 41 (1963), p. 284.

[19] xv 4: *mărk^e^bot* (vgl. xiv 25); *ḥăyil* (vgl. xiv 4, 9, 17, 18); *mibḥăr šališaw* (vgl.

während im übrigen Text nur allgemein von Meer die Rede ist; auch der Parallelismus V. 4a//V. 4b mit seiner wiederholenden Verwendung von *yăm* unterscheidet sich von V. 8 und V. 10, wo stärker variiert wird. Die Angabe *yăm sûp* findet sich vor unserem Lied zuletzt in Ex. xiii 18 und nach unserem Lied gleich in Ex. xv 22, dagegen nicht in der Erzählung Ex. xiv. Geschehensmäßig ist der Vers insgesamt eine Wiederholung bzw. Doppelung von V. 1bβ.5.

4. In V. 8 bilden die drei Stichen zwar eine Sinneinheit, doch ist fraglich, ob die Dreierstruktur ursprünglich ist. Vom Parallelismus her entsprechen sich am ehesten V. 8aα und V. 8b, während V. 8aβ sich dadurch hervortut, daß die hier gebrauchte Wendung *niṣṣ^ebû k^emô-ned* ähnlich in Jos. iii 13, 16 und Ps. lxxviii 13 steht.[20]

5. Das in V. 9 zitierte Kampflied hat literarkritisch gesehen drei Besonderheiten. Einmal ist der sowohl in der einleitenden Formel wie in der zitierten Rede selbst verwendete Singular auffällig. Zwar steht auch in V. 6b *'ôyeb* im Singular, doch verwendet der weiterführende Vers 7a dann pluralisches *qamèka*; entsprechend wird im Blick auf die Feinde immer pluralisch konstruiert. Eine zweite Besonderheit ist der in der Feindesrede zweimal durch Suffix hergestellte Bezug auf eine kollektive Größe,[21] wohl Israel, von der im Lied vorher keine Rede ist. Eine dritte Eigenheit des Kampfliedes ist sein sog. Staccato-Stil; vergleichbare Kurzsätze in einem einzigen Stichos weist nur noch V. 3 auf.

6. Die in V. 14-16 geschilderte Reaktion [22] verschiedener Gruppen auf Jahwes Handeln an seinem Volk ist geschehensmäßig, stilistisch und semantisch schwierig. Während V. 14 unvermittelt mit Suffixkonjugation einsetzt, folgt in V. 15 mit *'az* eine Zeitangabe, deren

---

xiv 7); xv 19: *sûs* (vgl. xiv 9, 23); *rèkèb* (vgl. xiv 6, 7, 9, 17, 18, 23, 26, 28); *paraš* (vgl. xiv 9, 17, 18, 23, 26, 28).

[20] Die literarkritische Frage, wie bzw. ob die drei in V. 8 gebrauchten Bilder zusammenpassen, ist vor allem deshalb schwer zu entscheiden, weil die Bedeutung der beiden Verben von V. 8aα und V. 8b nicht klar ist, da die Basis *qp'* außerhalb unserer Stelle nur noch in Zeph. i 12 und Hi. x 10 belegt ist und die Basis *'rm* Hapaxlegomenon ist.

[21] Die im Anschluß an W. F. Albright wiederholt vorgetragene These, in V. 9b läge mem-encliticum vor und nicht Pronominalsuffix, verkennt den archaisierenden Charakter unseres gesamten Textes (vgl. die gleiche Form des Suffixes in V. 7, 12, 15, 17). Dies gilt generell für die Versuche, durch vorschnelle Vergleiche mit dem Ugaritischen eine Datierung alttestamentlicher Texte beweisen zu wollen. Zur Problematik vgl. nun vor allem O. Loretz, *Die Psalmen. Teil II* (Neukirchen, 1979), pp. 1-12, 503-6.

[22] Vgl. N. Waldman, "A Comparative Note on Exodus 15:14-16", *JQR* N.S. 66 (1975/76), pp. 189-92.

Bezugspunkt kaum der vorangehende Vers 14 sein kann. Die Betroffenen selbst werden semantisch in zwei Gruppen gegliedert: während V. 15a mit zwei Tierbildern nur Stammesfürsten nennt, sprechen V. 14 und V. 15b viel allgemeiner von Völkern, von den Bewohnern Philistäas und von allen Bewohnern Kanaans. Sowohl V. 14b als auch V. 15aβ gebrauchen das Verbum *'ḥz*, ohne daß damit eine poetische Steigerung intendiert zu sein scheint; ähnlich wiederholt V. 15b das Partizip *yošᵉbê*, das auch in V. 14b steht. Schließlich fällt V. 15b aus der poetischen Struktur: der Halbvers ist simple Prosa und läßt sich nicht dem Parallelismusgefüge zuordnen; er steht im übrigen wortgleich in Jos. ii 9 und Jos. ii 24.

7. Eine kurze Diskussion verlangt noch V. 17. Fast alle Autoren weisen darauf hin, daß der überlieferte Text schwer verständlich ist.[23] Von der Parallelismusstruktur her sind am ehesten V. 17aβ. 17b zusammenzunehmen; dann aber bleibt V. 17aα als isolierter Stichos übrig, der allerdings vom Gesamtduktus her nach V. 16 unentbehrlich ist. Freedman sucht dieses Problem so zu lösen, daß er nach *tᵉbi'emô* eine weggefallene Ortsangabe *'èl gᵉbûl qådšᵉka* ergänzt und so zwei parallele Stichen erhält. Da dieser Vorschlag durch die Textüberlieferung selbst nicht gedeckt ist, bleibt er fraglich.

III.

Bei der Auswertung der bisher katalogisierten literarkritischen Beobachtungen könnten wir versuchsweise so vorgehen, daß wir die sperrigen Stichen ausgrenzen, was einen Text ergibt, dessen stichometrische und strophische Struktur wegen ihrer Klarheit und wegen ihrer Kohärenz überrascht. Der nach Ausgrenzung der literarkritisch problematischen Stichen verbleibende Textbestand umfaßt 28 Stichen, die sich mit Hilfe des Parallelismus in 7 Strophen zu je 4 Stichen untergliedern lassen:

1.	1bα	*'šyrh lyhwh ky g'h g'h*
	1bβ	*sws wrkbw rmh bym*
	5a	*thmt yksymw*
	5b	*yrdw bmṣwlt kmw 'bn*

---

[23] Die Diskussion geht einmal um die syntaktische Einbindung von V. 17aβb (entweder Fortführung von V. 17aα, wobei dann *bᵉ* zu ergänzen wäre und die auf die Nomina folgenden Worte als asyndetische Attributivsätze zu verstehen wären, oder Neueinsatz) und zum anderen um die Frage, ob hier (und entsprechend in V. 13) das Israel geschenkte Land oder der Tempel gemeint sei.

2.	6a	*ymynk yhwh nʾdry bkḥ*
	6b	*ymynk yhwh trʿṣ ʾwyb*
	7a	*wbrb gʾwnk thrs qmyk*
	7b	*tšlḥ ḥrnk yʾklmw kqš*
3.	8aα	*wbrwḥ ʾpyk nʿrmw mym*
	8aβ	*qpʾw thmt blb ym*
	10a	*nšpt brwḥk ksmw ym*
	10b	*ṣllw kʿwprt bmym ʾdyrym*
4.	11aα	*my kmkh bʾlm yhwh*
	11aβ	*my kmkh nʾdr bqdš*
	11b	*nwrʾ thlt ʿśh plʾ*
	12	*nṭyt ymynk tblʿmw ʾrṣ*
5.	13a	*nḥyt bḥsdk ʿm zw gʾlt*
	13b	*nhlt bʿzk ʾl nwh qdšk*
	15aα	*ʾz nbhlw ʾlwpy ʾdwm*
	15aβ	*ʾyly mwʾb yʾḥzmw rʿd*
6.	16aα	*tpl ʿlyhm ʾymt wpḥd*
	16aβ	*bgdl zrwʿk ydmw kʾbn*
	16bα	*ʿd yʿbr ʿmk yhwh*
	16bβ	*ʿd yʿbr ʿm zw qnyt*
7.	17aα	*tbʾmw wtṭʿmw bhr nḥltk*
	17aβ	*mkwn lšbtk pʿlt yhwh*
	17b	*mqdš ʾdny kwnnw ydyk*
	18	*yhwh ymlk lʿwlm wʿd*

Formal sind die Strophen 2, 4, 6 jeweils durch einen klimaktischen Parallelismus hervorgehoben, wobei freilich nicht zu übersehen ist, daß dieser Parallelismus in Strophe 6 anders gestaltet ist. Zwar ist allen drei Parallelismen gemeinsam, daß sie Jahwe in der zweiten Person anreden, doch weicht V. 16b von V. 6 und von V. 11a ab:

1. V. 6 und V. 11a setzen als Nominalsatz ein, während V. 16b als Verbalsatz beginnt;

2. V. 6 und V. 11a setzen als selbständiger Hauptsatz ein, während V. 16b durch die Konjunktion "während" bei- bzw. untergeordnet ist;

3. In V. 6 und 11b wird der klimaktische Parallelismus durch zwei weitere Stichen inhaltlich weitergeführt, während nach V. 16b thematisch und strophisch mit V. 17 ein Neueinsatz folgt.

Wir werden auf diese Unterschiede noch zurückkommen müssen, doch dürfte trotz dieser Unterschiede der Strukturbezug der drei Strophen aufeinander beabsichtigt sein; möglicherweise ergibt sich durch die Stellung des klimaktischen Parallelismus am Anfang bzw. am Ende der Strophe sogar eine gewollte spiegelbildliche Entsprechung der Strophen 2 und 6, wobei Strophe 4 als Achse hervorgehoben wäre. Diese von uns vorgenommene Stropheneinteilung könnte ein Problem lösen, das viele Autoren immer wieder notiert haben: Funktion und Bedeutung von V. 12. Schon die Synopse der bisher versuchten Strukturierungen zeigt die Unsicherheit, ob V. 12 Abschluß oder Beginn eines Abschnitts ist. Noch größer aber ist die Unsicherheit über die Interpretation des Verses. Da die Wendung *blʿ* + Subjekt *ʾarèṣ* außerhalb unserer Stelle nur mit Blick auf die Datan-Abiram-Episode verwendet wird (Num. xvi 32, 34, xxvi 10; Dtn. xi 6; Ps. cvi 17), hat man auch V. 12 auf sie bezogen und diese Anspielung unter das größere Thema "Führung durch die Wüste" eingeordnet. Freilich bleibt eigenartig, warum das Thema gerade mit dieser Episode eingeführt wird und vor allem, warum, abweichend von allen (!) übrigen Stellen, "hier die Verschlungenen nicht namentlich genannt sind".[24] So ist verständlich, daß die Mehrzahl der Autoren V. 12 noch einmal auf das Meerwunder bezieht, so z.B. Noth in seinem Exoduskommentar: "Das Verschlungenwerden von der Erde V. 12 meint trotz der Auffälligkeit des Ausdrucks gewiß die Vernichtung der Ägypter im Meer, die damit von der Erdoberfläche verschwanden und in den Todesbereich unter der Erde eingingen" (p. 99). Aber auch dieses Verständnis hat seine Schwierigkeiten: es wäre nicht nur ein für dieses Geschehen völlig singuläres Bild, dies umso mehr, als das Meerlied selbst mehrmals das traditionelle Bild von der Vernichtung im /bzw. durch das Wasser hervorhebt; vor allem ist bei dieser Interpretation störend, daß, wie wieder M. Noth selbst unterstreicht, die Vergleichsfrage von V. 11 doch als zusammenfassendes Fazit das vorher breit entfaltete Thema Meerwunder abschließt.[25] So empfiehlt sich von

[24] Crüsemann, *Studien*, p. 193, Anm. 3.

[25] Für Freedman (und ähnlich schon vor ihm Meilenburg, p. 246), "Strophe and Meter", p. 185, bilden dagegen V. 12 und V. 13 eine planvolle Einheit, die er (entsprechend seiner Stichometrie, vgl. oben Anm. 5) in drei Bikola (was unseren 3 Stichen entspricht) einteilt: "each bicolon begins with a perfect form of the verb (2 m.s.); the verbs form an alliterative sequence—*naṭīta*, *naḥīta*, *nēhalta*—and each verb is followed by a noun with the 2 m.s. suffix: *ymynk*, *bḥsdk*, *bʿzk*." Wie wenig solche Gemeinsamkeiten de facto beweisen, wird

unserer Struktur, inbesondere von der Parallelität der Strophen 2 und 4 her, ein Verständnis dieses Verses, das u.a. schon 1861 Carl Friedrich Keil vorgeschlagen hat: "Mit diesen Worten erweitert sich der Blick des Sängers auf alle Großtaten des Herrn, die in jener Wundertat an den Ägyptern beschlossen liegen... Was Ägypten erfahren hat, das wird allen Feinden des Herrn und seines Volks widerfahren."[26] Vers 12 hat damit strukturell eine ähnliche Funktion wie V. 7b: beide Verse generalisieren in einem von der Wasserszenerie abweichenden Bild das tödliche Wirken Jahwes an seinen Feinden; [27] beide Stichen bilden so einen rhetorisch eindrucksvollen Abschluß ihrer Strophe, wobei V. 12 durch den Gebrauch von *y^e^mîn^e^ka* zugleich Strophe 4 mit Strophe 2 verbindet. Daß V. 12 inhaltlich mit V. 11b im Parallelismus stehen kann, belegt Ps. lxxvii 15, wo das Partizip *'ośeh pèlè'* durch das Offenbarmachen der Macht Jahwes unter den Völkern konkretisiert wird,[28] und vor allem das Vorkommen von *nôra'* in den Zionspsalmen xlvii 3; lxxvi 8, 13 als Attribut

offenkundig, wenn man die Unterschiede bedenkt, die V. 12 und V. 13ab voneinander trennen: (1) V. 12 besteht aus zwei asyndetischen Verbalsätzen mit Suffix- bzw. Präfixkonjugation, die einen Folgezusammenhang ausdrücken; die analoge Konstruktion findet sich in V. 7b (dort allerdings mit zweimaliger Präfixkonjugation!). V. 13ab besteht dagegen aus je einem Verbalsatz, wobei V. 13a das Akkusativobjekt durch einen Relativsatz näher bestimmt. (2) Nur in V. 13ab wird das Verbum jeweils durch *b^e^* + *Nomen* präzisieert, was die beiden Stichen in der Tat eng verbindet, sie aber dadurch von V. 12 absetzt. Wie eng diese Verbindung ist, stellt Freedman, p. 187, selbst fest: "With regard to the two bicola of vs 13, we wish to point to an interesting example of combination or enjambment. To begin with, we have closely parallel first cola: *nḥyt bḥsdk*/ *nhlt b'zk*, though, strictly speaking, *ḥsd* and *'z* complement rather than duplicate each other. A form of hendiadys is indicated here: 'your mighty *ḥesed*' or 'your merciful strength'".

[26] *Biblischer Commentar über die Bücher Mose's. Erster Band: Genesis und Exodus* (Leipzig, 1861), p. 461; vgl. ebda: "Auf den Untergang der Aegypter paßt weder das von der Erde Verschlungenwerden, noch der Gebrauch des Imperf., da diese Gottestat als vollbrachte Tatsache in v. 1. 4. 5. 10. 19 durch Perfecta ausgedrückt ist."

[27] Daß zwischen Ex. xv 7b, 12 und Num. xvi 34 f., wo die Motive von der verschlingenden Erde und vom fressenden Feuer nacheineinander stehen, ein Zusammenhang besteht, ist durchaus möglich, vgl. dazu auch J. D. W. Watts, *VT* 7 (1957), pp. 372-4, wo freilich ein wenig plausibler kultischer Sitz vermutet wird.

[28] In Ps. lxxviii 12 meint das Partizip die ägyptischen Plagen. Die Verbindung *'śh* + *nipla'ôt* bezeichnet in Ex. iii 20 ebenfalls die Plagen als Machterweis Jahwes gegenüber Pharao; in Jos. iii 5 bezieht sich die Wendung auf das Überschreiten des Jordan oder (m.E. wahrscheinlicher!) auf den Gottesschrecken, der nach Jos. iii 10 (also Kontext!) die Völker vertreibt. Daß ein derartiges "Wunderwirken" Jahwes Erweis seiner unvergleichbaren Göttlichkeit ist, wie V. 11 hervorhebt, formuliert ähnlich Ps. lxxxvi 10.

des die Völker niederwerfenden Jahwe.[29] Der Form nach ist die Verbindung Unvergleichlichkeitsfrage + Partizipiale Weiterführung + Weiterführung im Verbalsatz im übrigen nicht singulär: sie findet sich ähnlich in Ps. lxxxix 9 f.[30] und Mi. vii 18.[31]

Neben dieser Strukturierung, die Strophe 4 als Mitte hervorhebt, zeigt sich als weiteres Bauprinzip die paarweise Zusammenordnung der Strophen 2 + 3 bzw. 5 + 6. Die erste Zeile von Strophe 2 und die letzte Zeile von Strophe 3 sind durch die seltene Basis *ʾdr* verbunden, während analog die erste Zeile von Strophe 5 und die letzte Zeile von Strophe 6 durch die ähnliche Wendung *ʿăm-zû gaʾalta* bzw. *ʿăm-zû qanîta* als übergeordnete Einheit ausgewiesen werden. Strophe 5 und 6 bilden ohnehin einen Geschehenszusammenhang; da ein solcher zwischen Strophen 2 und Strophe 3 nicht besteht, erfolgt der Anschluß in V. 8aα betont durch waw-emphaticum. Durch diese paarweise Zuordnung wird Jahwes unterschiedliches Handeln an seinen Feinden bzw. an seinem Volk wirkungsvoll kontrastiert.[32]

Nimmt man unsere bisherigen Beobachtungen zur Struktur dieser 28 Stichen mit den schon von anderen Autoren zusammengestellten Stichwortbezügen und rhetorischen Gestaltungstechniken innerhalb des Meerlieds zusammen,[33] dürfte kein Zweifel bestehen, daß hier eine kunstvoll arbeitende Hand am Werk war. Dennoch stellt sich die Frage, ob diese Struktur eine originäre oder eine sekundäre Komposition ist. Es gibt immerhin einige Gründe, die zur Vermutung führen, diese eben beschriebene Struktur gehe erst auf eine Bearbeitung zurück, die eine ihr vorgegebene Ur-Form des Meerlieds ausgestaltet hat. Diese Gründe sind im einzelnen folgende:

1. Falls V. 1b als Zusammenfassung oder als Überschrift eines dann folgenden Hymnus gedacht ist,[34] kann V. 13-17 kaum ursprüng-

---

[29] Vgl. auch Ps. lxviii 36, lxxxix 8, xcvi 4, xcix 3. Zu *teħillā* in der Bedeutung "Ruhmestat" vgl. besonders Jes. xl 8, 12, xlviii 11, lx 6, lxiii 7; Ps. ix 15, lxxi 14, lxxviii 4, lxxix 13, cvi 2.

[30] In diesem Psalm finden sich im Kontext der Unvergleichlichkeitsfrage auch die gleichen Begriffe wie in Ex. xv 11 f.: *pèlèʾ* (V. 6), *qehăl qedošîm* (V. 6), *benê ʾelîm* (V. 7), *sôd-qedošîm* (V. 8), *nôraʾ* (V. 8).

[31] Zur Konstruktion vgl. auch Ps. cxiii 5-7 (Frage + Partizipien + Präfixkonjugation) sowie Ps. xxxv 10 (Frage + Partizip), zur Sache auch Jes. xl 18, 25; Ps. xviii 32, lxxi 19, lxxvii 14, xcv 3, xcvi 4, xcvii 9.

[32] Von hier aus wären die theologisch bedeutsamen Ausführungen von Lohfink, *Siegeslied*, pp. 125-8, zur "Geschichtstypologie im Innern des Liedes" anders zu akzentuieren.

[33] Vgl. besonders die "rhetorische Analyse" von Muilenburg (s. Anm. 1).

[34] Zur Funktion des *kî*-Satzes vgl. die Diskussion bei Crüsemann, *Studien*,

liche Entfaltung des damit angesprochenen Themas gewesen sein.

2. Der klimaktische Parallelismus in V. 16b wirkt wegen der oben angeführten Differenzen gegenüber V. 6, 11a eher als Nachahmung dieser Stilfigur denn als Werk desselben Autors; ähnlich nachahmend wirkt der Vergleich mit den Steinen in V. 16aβ gegenüber V. 5b.

3. Während V. 6 und V. 12 dreimal von der Rechten Jahwes reden, gebraucht V. 16aβ das Wort "Arm Jahwes".

4. Das Thema "Führung des Volkes durch die Feinde hin zum Land/Heiligtum Jahwes" wird anders als das Thema "Vernichtung der Feinde im Meer" nicht durch eine generalisierende hymnische Strophe, vergleichbar V. 6-7 und V. 11-12, abgeschlossen; der deshalb von einigen Autoren gemachte Vorschlag, V. 11-12 als Einleitung von V. 13 ff. zu verstehen, ist schon allein inhaltlich wegen V. 12 nicht möglich.

Diese vier Gründe zusammen rechtfertigen m.E. die schon mehrfach geäußerte Vermutung, V. 13 ff. seien erst sekundär an V. 1b ff. angefügt worden, d.h. nach unserer Abgrenzung: die Strophen 5-7 gehören nicht zur Ur-Fassung des Meerlieds. Schließlich muß bezweifelt werden, ob zu dieser Ur-Fassung die Strophe 3, also V. 8aα, b, 10 gehört haben kann. Immerhin fällt diese Strophe durch einige sprachliche Eigenheiten gegenüber den Strophen 1, 2 und 4 auf:

1. Während V. 6 und V. 11 das Nifal der Basis *'dr* gebrauchen, verwendet V. 10 das einfache Adjektiv *'ăddîr*.

2. Während V. 10 das Verbum *ksh* als Verbum tertiae *h* konstruiert, ist in V. 5 der dritte Radikal ein *y*; im überlieferten Text steht das Piel in V. 5 mit, in V. 10 ohne Dagesch.

3. Das Suffix in V. 5a ist mit *û*, in V. 10 mit *ô* vokalisiert.

Zu diesen sprachlichen Sonderheiten kommt, daß die Strophe 3 eine andere Vorstellung von der Vernichtung der Ägypter hat als Strophe 1. Dies ist natürlich innerhalb einer Dichtung nicht ausgeschlossen, verwundert jedoch, nachdem die in Strophe 1 angesprochene Vorstellung, daß "Jahwe sich hoch erhoben habe [35]

---

pp. 32-5. Freilich bleibt fraglich, ob *kî* in V. 1b die gleiche Funktion haben muß wie in V. 21b: während die Partikel in V. 21b den "Durchführungsteil" einleitet, kann sie in V. 1b durchaus als Begründung verstanden sein—vor allem wenn V. 21b vom Verfasser der "Ur-Form" des Meerlieds aufgegriffen und in V. 1b entsprechend abgewandelt und einem größeren Kontext eingegliedert wurde.

[35] Das Verbum bezeichnet nicht primär die Erhabenheit Jahwes, sondern sein Sich-Erheben: vgl. Weimar-Zenger, *Exodus* pp. 74-5.

und Roß und Reiter/Wagenfahrer [36] ins Meer geworfen/mit dem Bogen geschossen habe" [37] in Strophe 2 aufgegriffen und generalisierend entfaltet wird. Hält man auch Strophe 3 für eine sekundäre Erweiterung, ergibt sich eine Ur-Form des Meerlieds, dessen Struktur und Entstehungssituation so plausibel sind, daß sie diese Hypothese empfehlen:

1.	1bα	*’šyrh lyhwh ky g’h g’h*
	1bβ	*sws wrkbw rmh bym*
	5a	*thmt yksymw*
	5b	*yrdw bmṣwlt kmw ’bn*
2.	6a	*ymynk yhwh n’dry bkḥ*
	6b	*ymynk yhwh tr‘ṣ ’wyb*
	7a	*wbrb g’wnk thrs qmyk*
	7b	*tšlḥ ḥrnk y’klmw kqš*
3.	11aα	*my kmkh b’lm yhwh*
	11aβ	*my kmkh n’dr bqdš*
	11b	*nwr’ thlt ‘śh pl’*
	12	*nṭyt ymynk tbl‘mw ’rṣ*

[36] Die Bedeutung der Wendung *sûs wᵉrokᵉbô* ist umstritten, da *rokeb* sowohl "Reiter" als auch "Wagenfahrer" bezeichnen kann, wobei das Pronominalsuffix bei *rokᵉbô* freilich besser zur Bedeutung "Roß und seinen Reiter" paßt. In diesem Sinn ist die Wendung sicher in Jer. li 21; Sach. xii 4; Hag. ii 22; Hi. xxxix 18, höchstwahrscheinlich auch in 2 Reg. xviii 23 (= Jes. xxxvi 8) zu verstehen. Was in Ex. vx 1b, 21b gemeint ist, hängt nicht zuletzt von der Datierung der beiden Halbverse ab, da Reitertruppen als mobile Waffengattung in der Lebenswelt Israels erst zu Beginn des 1. Jahrtausends, wahrscheinlich erst ab dem 9. Jh., auftraten, während vorher Streitwagenkorps eingesetzt wurden; vgl. hierzu: W. Mayer, "Gedanken zum Einsatz von Streitwagen und Reitern in neuassyrischer Zeit", *UF* 10 (1978), pp. 175-86; B. A. Mastin, "Was the *šāliš* the third man in the chariot?", in J. A. Emerton (Hrsg.), *Studies in the Historical Books of the Old Testament*, *SVT* 30 (Leiden, 1979), pp. 125-54.

[37] Außer Ex. xv 1b, 21b ist die Basis *rmh* nur noch in Jer. iv 29 und Ps. lxxviii 9 belegt, wo es eindeutig "(Pfeile) werfen, schließen" bedeutet. Falls in Ex. xv 1b, 21b *rokᵉbô* "seinen Reiter" meint, wäre die Bedeutung "schießen" durchaus im gewählten Bildkontext, da die Reitertruppen erst ab der Mitte des 8. Jh. auch als Lanzenreiter operierten, während sie vorher nur mit dem Bogen operierten bzw. ebenso außer Gefecht gesetzt wurden. Die Bedeutung "werfen" wird traditionell aus xv 4 erschlossen, was aber nach unserer literarkritischen Analyse sehr problematisch ist.

Die Ur-Form des Meerliedes ist ein dreistrophiger Hymnus auf die Unvergleichbarkeit Jahwes. Die erste Strophe greift das vorgegebene Mirjamlied auf und erweitert es durch eine Schilderung des totalen Untergangs der Ägypter. Die zweite Strophe gestaltet dann dieses Thema grundsätzlich aus und besingt Jahwes Überlegenheit über jedweden Feind. Die dritte Strophe schließlich zieht den Horizont nochmals weiter aus und proklamiert Jahwes Unvergleichbarkeit gegenüber allen Göttern und Himmelsmächten. Beim Versuch, diesen kurzen Hymnus traditionsgeschichtlich zu orten, fällt auf, daß er Wendungen und Vorstellungen verwendet, die vor allem in den Psalmen beheimatet sind.[38] Da in Ps. cxviii 15 f. ein Abschnitt ausdrücklichals Hymnus zitiert wird, der stark an Ex. xv 6 erinnert, und in Ps. xxxv 10 wiederum als Zitat ein Textstück angeführt wird, das Ex. xv 11 sehr ähnlich ist, scheint mir die Vermutung nahe zu liegen, dieser von uns rekonstruierte dreistrophige Hymnus habe nicht nur mit dem Mirjamlied ein ihm vorgegebenes Lied aufgegriffen, sondern habe auch in V. 6 und V. 11 übliches Liedgut verwendet. Man könnte deshalb sogar von einer Art Anthologie hymnischer Fragmente sprechen.

Eine Datierung dieses kleinen Hymnus ist, wie bei allen Psalmen, außerordentlich schwierig. Da er zunächst einmal das Mirjamlied aufgreift, setzt er dieses in jedem Fall voraus.[39] Das theologische

---

[38] Das gilt zunächst für V. 5: zu *t^{e}hôm* vgl. C. Westermann, *ThHAT* II, p. 1027: "t^{e}hōm kommt überwiegend in der Psalmensprache vor (Ps 12, dazu Ex 15, 5.8; Dtn 33, 13; Jes 51, 10; 63, 13; Jon 2, 6; Hab 3, 10 in Psalmengattungen)", zusammen mit *m^{e}ṣôlā* steht *t^{e}hôm* außer im Meerlied noch in Jon. ii 4, 6; Ps. cvii 24, 26; Hi. xli 23 f.; ebenso steht *m^{e}ṣûlā* außer in Mi. vii 19; Sach. i 8, x 11 nur noch in Ps. lxviii 23, lxix 3, 16, lxxxviii 7. Die Vorstellung, daß Jahwe "die Rosse und ihre Reiter" in die Tiefe hinabsinken läßt (*yarăd*), findet sich noch in Hag. ii 22; Neh. ix 11 dürfte von Ex. xv 5 literarisch abhängen, wobei die dort verwendete Basis *šlk* H-Stamm möglicherweise von Ex. xv 4 beeinflußt ist. Das in V. 6 entfaltete Bild von der Rechten Jahwes als Symbol für die Vernichtung der Feinde findet sich Ps. xxi 9 f., xlviii 11, lxxvii 11, lxxviii 54, lxxxix 14, 43, cxviii 15 f.; auch die Basis *qûm* für Feinde (V. 7) ist Psalmensprache: Ps. iii 2, xviii 40, 49, xliv 6, lxxiv 23, xcii 12. Zur Unvergleichlichkeitsfrage von V. 11 vgl. Ps. xviii 32, xxxv 10, lxxi 19, lxxvii 14, lxxxvi 8, lxxxix 7-9, xcv 3, xcvi 4, xcvii 9, cxiii 5. Zu *nôra'* vgl. Anm. 29, zu *ʿośeh pèlè'* vgl. Anm. 39 sowie Ps. lxxviii 12, lxxxviii 11, lxxxix 6. Allerdings finden sich in unserem Hymnus auch Wendungen, die selten belegt oder gar nur ihm eigen sind. V. 6 *rʿṣ* (nur noch: Jdc. 10, 8), V. 7 *šlḥ ḥarôn* (nur noch: Ps. lxxviii 49; Hi. xx 23; vgl. Ez. vii 3), V. 12 *nṭh y^{e}mîn^{e}ka* Subj. *yhwh* (nur hier).

[39] Das Mirjamlied wird meist als sehr als beurteilt, vgl. die Beurteilung der Forschungslage bei R. Smend, *Jahwekrieg und Stämmebund* (Göttingen, ^{3}1966), pp. 78 f.: "das einzige Dokument im Pentateuch, dem ein den Ereignissen einigermaßen zeitgenössischer Charakter wohl nirgends abgestritten wird, das also so etwas wie einen unmittelbaren Quellenwert hat." Die bei P. Weimar - E. Zenger,

Pathos, in dem er Jahwes vernichtendes Handeln an "Roß und Reiter" als Machterweis gegenüber allen weltlichen Mächten und ihren Göttern preist, könnte man sich gut in der Zeit der assyrischen Bedrohung vorstellen, wo "Roß und Reiter" ja erstmals große strategische Bedeutung erhalten und zum großen Thema der jesajanischen Prophetie werden.[40] Einen terminus ante quem bietet jedenfalls die Ausgestaltung dieses dreistrophigen Hymnus zu dem siebenstrophigen Hymnus, der einerseits das Thema "Führung durch die Völkerwelt hin zu Jahwes heiligem Berg" anfügt und andererseits die in der Ur-Form des Liedes nur angedeutete Vernichtung der Ägypter breiter ausmalt. Diese Ausgestaltung inspiriert sich keineswegs an irgendeiner Erzählschicht von Ex. xiv,[41] sondern ist insgesamt von der Theologie[42] und von mythischen Bildern der Zionstheologie[43] geprägt. In dieser Gestalt des Hymnus sind auch Anklänge an den Baal-Mythos, worauf schon oft hingewiesen wurde,[44] nicht zu übersehen. Wie Baal nach dem Sieg über seinen

---

Exodus, pp. 71-87, versuchte Deutung als polemisches Kampflied aus der Zeit Davids vor dem Hintergrund der Philister- und Kanaanäerbedrohung macht u.a. folgende Schwierigkeiten: 1. An der a.a.O. rekonstruierten vorjahwistischen Exodusgeschichte, die in Ex. xiv 31 einen deutlichen Abschluß hat, wirkt es angehängt; 2. Ein Siegeslied der Frauen fehlt in den alten Jahwekriegserzählungen Jos. x; Jdc. iv (Jdc. v ist sekundär an Jdc. iv angeschlossen!); 1 Sam. vii; 3. Falls *sûs w^{e}rok^{e}bô* mit "Roß und *sein* Reiter" (vgl. Anm. 36) zu übersetzen ist, ist der angenommene historische Kontext nicht möglich; 4. Die betont gebrauchte Basis *g'h* weist nach Jes. ii; 5. Ob man das Lied für "vorjahwistisch" oder "jahwistisch" halten kann, hängt auch davon ab, ob Mirjam überhaupt sonst noch in J vorkommt. Angesichts dieser Schwierigkeiten und in Anbetracht der sprachlichen Eigenart des Liedes gegenüber Ex. xiv J scheint mir eine spätere Datierung wahrscheinlicher: wegen der Bezüge zu Jes. ii, wegen der Betonung von "Roß und Reiter", wegen der Rolle Mirjams (die m.E. in J noch keine Rolle spielt, aber als prophetische Figur von Je herausgestellt wird) scheint mir das 8. Jh. v. Chr. als Entstehungszeit durchaus wahrscheinlich.

[40] Vgl. besonders die jesajanische Polemik. Jes. ii 6-22, xxx 16, xxxi 1-3, die in ihrer Entgötterungstendenz mit unserem kleinen Meerlied auffallend klar übereinstimmt (vgl. besonders Jes. xxxi 3!).

[41] Zu den verschiedenen Vorstellungen in Ex. xiv vgl. Zenger, *Das Buch Exodus*, pp. 142-50. Selbst das in V. 10 gebrauchte Motiv vom Wind/Sturm unterscheidet sich von Ex. xiv, worauf Cross, *Canaanite Myth*, pp. 133 f., aufmerksam macht.

[42] Dies gilt sowohl von V. 10, der sich in der Vorstellung mit dtr Jos. xxiv 6 f. berührt als auch von den Theologumena *ʿăm-zû ga'alta* (V. 13a), Arm Jahwes (V. 16) und *hăr năḥalat^{e}ka* (V. 17: vgl. Dtn. iii 25); vor allem liegt in V. 15a das dt/dtr Geschichtsbild vor (vgl. Dtn. ii 2-13). Zu dtr Vorstellungen in Ex. xv vgl. auch Norin, pp. 101-4.

[43] Vgl. Schreiner, *Sion*, pp. 208-10; F. Stolz, *Strukturen und Figuren im Kult von Jerusalem* (Berlin, 1970), pp. 168 ff.

[44] Vgl. besonders Cross, *Canaanite Myth*, pp. 141-3; Norin, pp. 91-3, 104-6.

Gegner, der ihm das Königtum streitig macht, am "Berg seines Erbbesitzes" in dem ihm erbauten Palast seine Königsherrschaft über die Götter antritt, so wird auf dieser Erweiterungsstufe des Meerlieds das im Mirjamlied besungene Ereignis zu einem einzigen großen Geschehenszusammenhang ausgefaltet, das als Kampf mit dem Anti-Jahwe beginnt und mit dem Triumphzug des siegreichen Gottkönigs hin zu seinem Königspalast auf dem Götterberg Zion endet.[45]

Diesen siebenstrophigen Hymnus interessieren nicht primär die einzelnen konkreten Ereignisse oder Etappen, die man von den Geschichtsüberlieferungen her mit den einzelnen Wendungen und Bildern dieses Liedes verbinden könnte. Das Lied sammelt vielmehr wie in einem Brennpunkt den großen Bogen der Israel gründenden Frühgeschichte Exodus-Landnahme-Tempelbau zu einem engen Ereigniszusammenhang und steigert seine Dimensionen durch mythische Bilder zu einem imposanten Modell des Handelns Jahwes "am Anfang" Israels.[46] Versteht man im Anschluß an Mircea Eliade und Wolfhart Pannenberg [47] Mythos als gründende Urzeiterzählung, durch die der bedrohte Mensch sich der ihn haltenden Lebensmacht zu vergewissern versucht,[48] ist das Meerlied deutlich als Mythisierungsvorgang der Geschichtsüberlieferung Israels zu bestimmen. Ähnlich wie die Priesterschrift, die vor allem Lohfink [49] als Mythos im Sinne einer gründenden und normativen Urzeiterzählung beschrieben hat, versucht dieses siebenstrophige Meerlied den tiefen Bruch, den die

---

[45] Allerdings sind die Unterschiede nicht zu übersehen: Zunächst kämpft hier Jahwe nicht mit dem Meer (!)—doch erweist er seine unvergleichbare Mächtigkeit vor den Göttern (V. 11) durch einen Sieg über seine Feinde (V. 5); zum anderen spielt das Thema "Volk" im Baal-Mythos keine Rolle, während es hier so sehr im Vordergrund steht, daß das Volk am Berg Jahwes selbst eingepflanzt wird.

[46] Von daher wäre der große Unterschied zwischen xv und der dt/dtr Geschichtstheologie, wie sie konzentriert im Credo Dtn. xxvi 5-9 vorliegt, zu entfalten.

[47] Vgl. die Definition des Mythos bei M. Eliade, *Das Heilige und das Profane. Vom Wesen des Religiösen* (Hamburg, 1957), p. 57, sowie W. Pannenberg, "Spāthorizonte des Mythos in biblischer und christlicher Überlieferung", in M. Fuhrmann (Hrsg.), *Terror und Spiel. Probleme der Mythenrezeption. Poetik und Hermeneutik IV* (München, 1971), pp. 473-525.

[48] Zu dieser (positiven!) Funktion des Mythischen auch im AT vgl. die wichtige Studie von H. P. Müller, *Jenseits der Entmythologisierung. Orientierungen am Alten Testament* (Neukirchen, ²1979).

[49] "Die Priesterschrift und die Geschichte", in *Congress Volume: Göttingen 1977, SVT 29* (Leiden, 1978), pp. 189-225.

Geschichte Israels durch die Katastrophe von 586 erfahren hat, mythisch zu bewältigen. Das linearätiologische Modell der vorexilischen Geschichtstheologie, wonach die Geschichte Israels als eine Kontinuität des Heilshandelns Jahwes an seinem Volk verstanden wurde war nun zerbrochen. Als *einer* von mehreren, z.T. völlig unterschiedlich ansetzenden Versuchen, diese Situation zu bewältigen, kann dieses siebenstrophige Meerlied gelten. Es ist der Versuch des exilischen bzw. nachexilischen Israel, seine im Bruch der geschichtlichen Kontinuität verlorene Identität wieder zu gewinnen—freilich auf Kosten der Geschichte. Die hier als gründendes Urzeitgeschehen besungene Erringung der Königsherrschaft Jahwes ist das archetypische Modell des Handelns Jahwes, an dem sich das kleine Israel der nachexilischen Zeit festhält und dessen Wirkmacht es im abschließenden Jahwe-Königs-Ruf beschwört.

Möglicherweise erhält diese mythische Beschwörung der Königsmacht Jahwes angesichts der das kleine Israel verängstigenden Mächte dieser Welt noch eine besondere Brisanz, wenn man von V. 17 her das Meerlied im Blick auf den Jerusalemer Tempel der frühnachexilischen Gemeinde interpretieren kann, was freilich nicht ganz unproblematisch ist. In diesem Fall wäre unser Meerlied der Versuch, das Urgeschehen des Anfangs Israel als *auch* in diesem Tempel, der Abbild des mythischen Jahweheiligtums wäre, gegenwärtig und wirkmächtig zu besingen.

IV.

Unsere Analyse hat bisher die oben literarkritisch ausgegrenzten Stichen nicht berücksichtigt. Wenn sich auch für diese Stichen noch eine plausible Einordnung aufzeigen läßt, sind unsere bisherigen Überlegungen eine mögliche Hypothese zur Lösung der Probleme von Ex. xv.

Einen ersten Hinweis zur Beurteilung dieser Stichen haben wir schon bei der literarkritischen Besprechung von V. 4 und von V. 15b erhalten, die wir als Prosa charakterisiert haben; während V. 4 im Blick auf Ex. xiv formuliert ist, begegnet V. 15b wortgleich in Jos. ii 9, 24. Das führt zu der heuristischen These, daß die ausgegrenzten Stichen von einem Redaktor stammen, der das frühnachexilische Meerlied in seinen jetzigen Erzählzusammenhang einfügte und dabei im Stil gelehrter Schriftauslegung das Lied seinem größeren Kontext anpaßte. Diese Hypothese läßt sich zunächst für die Stichen V. 4, 8aβ, 9, 14, 15b unschwer verifizieren:

1. V. 4 ist offensichtlich eine Zusammenstellung des ägyptischen Militärpotentials, die sich an Ex. xiv inspiriert.

2. V. 8aβ trägt die bisher fehlende Vorstellung von den wie eine Mauer stehenden Wassern ein, gebraucht allerdings nicht die Formulierungen von Ex. xiv, sondern von Ps. lxxviii 13; wahrscheinlich liegt auch eine Anspielung auf Jos. iii 13, 16 [50] vor, da auch, wie gleich ausgeführt wird, noch weitere Anspielungen auf das Josuabuch zu erkennen sind.

3. Das Zitat des Kampflieds in den drei Stichen von V. 9 gleicht Ex. xv in zweifacher Hinsicht an Ex. xiv an: der Vers läßt zum einen die Feinde in direkter Rede sprechen, wie dies auch Ex. xiv mehrfach tut, und zum anderen trägt der Vers den im Meerlied ursprünglich ja nicht gegebenen Bezug zur Exodusgeschichte ein; das Motiv von der Jagd nach Beute könnte dabei auf das in Ex. iii 21 f., xi 2f., xii 35 f. entfalteteMotiv der "Beraubung der Ägypter" bezogen sein.[51] In der Formulierung verwendet der Vers die Topik ähnlicher Kampflieder; die beiden ersten Verben stehen auch in Ex. xiv 9.[52]

4. Die beiden Stichen von V. 14 stehen in offenkundigem Zusammenhang mit Dtn. ii 25b.[53] Beiden Texten und nur ihnen gemeinsam ist die Folge *šmʿ-rgz-ḥyl*, um die Reaktion der Völker auf Israels Hindurchziehen zu beschreiben; das in Ex. xv 16b zweimal gebrauchte Verbum *ʿbr* fungiert in Dtn. ii als Leitwort.[54]

5. Die Notiz über die Bewohner Kanaans in V. 15b entspringt sicher dem Interesse, die Wegesroute bis nach Jerusalem umfassend zu charakterisieren; [55] in der Formulierung stammt sie aus Jos. ii

---

[50] Jos. iii 13, 16 unterscheiden sich von Ex. xv 8aβ nicht nur durch das jeweils gebrauchte Verbum (Jos iii 13: *ʿmd*; iii 16: *qûm*), sondern auch durch das Fehlen der Vergleichspartikel *k*ᵉ sowie durch die Betonung, es habe sich um *einen* Damm (vgl. das Bild des in eine Richtung fließenden Flusses!) gehandelt.

[51] Zur semantischen und redaktionskritischen Analyse der drei Texte vgl. P. Weimar, *Die Berufung des Mose. Literaturwissenschaftliche Analyse von Exodus 2, 23-5, 5* (Freiburg-Göttingen, 1980), pp. 55-9, 347-9.

[52] Zur Topik vgl. besonders Gen. xlix 27; Jos. ii 5; Jdc. v 30; 1 Sam. xxx 8; 2 Sam. xxii 38 = Ps. xviii 38, 43; Ps. lxviii 13, lxxi 10 f.; einen möglichen institutionellen Sitz im Leben zeigt 1 Sam. xxx 8 an.

[53] Auf den Zusammenhang von Ex. xv 14 und Dtn. ii 25b hat vor allem hingewiesen: W. L. Moran, "The End of the Unholy War and the Anti-Exodus", *Bibl* 44 (1963), p. 340; allerdings sitzt der Satz in Dtn. ii 25b besser im Kontext als in Ex. xv 14, was für das oben angenommene Abhängigkeitsverhältnis spricht. Zur Topik vgl. auch Ps. xlviii 7, lxxviii 17.

[54] Vgl. Dtn. ii 4, 8 (2x), 13 (2x), 14 (2x), 18, 24, 27, 28, 29, 30. Der enge Zusammenhang mit Dtn. ii spricht m.E. gegen G. W. Coats, *CBQ* 31 (1969), pp. 11-17, der Ex. xv 14-17 von Jos. iv 23, v 1 her deuten möchte.

[55] Ist dieses Interesse erkannt, wird man V. 14-16 kaum als Ansatz für die

9, 24, wobei möglicherweise auch die Parallelisierung Ex. xv 14, 15b//Jos. ii 9, 10 intendiert ist.

Alle bisher besprochenen Stichen stimmen also darin überein, daß sie einmal das Meerlied stärker an die Geschichtsüberlieferungen angleichen und daß sie dabei vorgegebenes, geprägtes Textmaterial aufgreifen. Diese doppelte Tendenz läßt sich auch, wenngleich weniger offenkundig, für den noch nicht behandelten Block V. 2-3 aufzeigen. Zum einen greifen diese beiden Verse, die sich offensichtlich als Kommentar zu V. 1bα (V. 2!) bzw. zu V. 1bβ (V. 3) verstehen, wichtige Schlüsselbegriffe von Ex. xiv auf, nämlich *y^e^šû^c^ā* (vgl. Ex. xiv 13, 30) und *milḥamā* (vgl. Ex. xiv 14, 25), zum anderen bestehen die beiden Verse wieder weitgehend aus vorgegebenen Sprachklischees, die sich ähnlich in Jes. xii 2, 4; Ps. cxviii 14, 21, 28, sowie in Jes. xlii 13; Ps. xxiv 8 (V. 3a) und Ex. iii 15; Jes. xlii 8; Ps. xx 8 (V. 3b) finden.

Diese Beobachtungen stützen unsere Hypothese, diese Erweiterungen seien Werk eines Redaktors, der das Meerlied in den Pentateuch einbaute, zumal sich die gleiche Tendenz, den Bogen nach Ex. xiv hin zu spannen, auch in der Rahmennotiz Ex. xiv 19 findet. Zugleich löste die Einfügung des Liedes eine abschließende Bearbeitung von Ex. xiv aus. Jedenfalls lassen sich einige Fragmente, die in Ex. xiv locker im Erzählkontext sitzen und sich keiner durchgängigen Erzählschicht zuweisen lassen, gut im Horizont von Ex. xv 1-18 verständlich machen.

Eines dieser Fragmente ist die abschließende Notiz in Ex. xiv 31aβ: "Als Israel die große Hand sah, die Jahwe gegen die Ägypter getan hatte". Diese Notiz rivalisiert in ihrer entscheidenden Wortfolge mit Ex. xiv 30b und bildet zusammen mit Ex. xiv 30a eine dreimalige Folge des Wortpaares "Israel-Ägypten". In ihrer Formulierung und theologischen Tendenz, das Meerwunder als alleinige Machttat Jahwes herauszustellen, stimmt Ex. xiv 31aαβ mit dem Textstück Ex. xiv 31aγb zusammen ("die [scil. die Hilfe, vgl. auch Ex. xv 2!] er euch heute tun wird; denn wie ihr die Ägypter heute gesehen habt, werdet ihr sie nicht mehr sehen auf ewig"), die gleichfalls locker im Kontext sitzt und den engen Zusammenhang Ex. xiv 13aαβ, 14 zerreißt. Beide Notizen zusammen passen aber in den theologischen Horizont von Ex. xv 1-18, der Jahwes ewiges Königtum besingt. Ebenfalls im Blick auf Ex. xv 1-18 dürften vom Pentateuch-

Frage der Datierung unseres Textes heranziehen können, wie dies immer wieder geschieht.

redaktor die Ortsangaben "vor Baal-Zafon" in Ex. xiv 2 bzw. Ex. xiv 9 eingefügt worden sein, die den im Meerlied nur angedeuteten religionspolemischen Bezug unterstreichen wollen. Beide Notizen sitzen literarkritisch sperrig in ihrer Umgebung: die Notiz "vor Baal-Zafon, ihm gegenüber sollt ihr euch lagern zum Meer hin" fällt durch ihre Konstruktion in der 2. Person Plural aus der ansonsten in der 3. Person konstruierten priesterschriftlichen Jahwerede Ex. xiv 1-4 heraus. Die entsprechende Ortsangabe "vor Baal-Zafon" in Ex. xiv 9 steht zusammen mit einer syntaktisch nicht eingebundenen Aufzählung "Roß, Wagen des Pharao und seine Reiter und seine Streitmacht", die stark an die redaktionellen Notizen Ex. xv 4, 19 erinnert, ähnlich sperrig im Erzählkontext, so daß auch sie am ehesten auf das Konto von R^P zurückgeht, der damit Ex. xiv und Ex. xv verklammert.[56] Durch diese Verklammerung wird Ex. xiv 1-xv 21 zu einer zweiteiligen Einheit, die im Gesamtplan der Redaktion des Exodus-Buches einen wichtigen Platz einnimmt. Dies soll abschließend noch angedeutet werden—zugleich als Beitrag zu der anstehenden Frage nach einer Neuorientierung der Pentateuchexegese, die stärker als bisher gerade die Letztgestalt des biblischen Textes berücksichtigen muß.[57]

V.

Auf der Ebene des überlieferten Textes läßt sich das Buch Exodus in sieben Teile gliedern, deren Abgrenzung voneinander durch eine Reihe von Struktursignalen angezeigt ist.[58] Der *erste Teil* (Ex. i 1-vi 27) wird gerahmt von einer Liste der Israel-Söhne (Ex. i 1-5) und der Genealogie von Mose und Aaron (Ex. vi 14-27), womit zugleich der Spannungsbogen dieses Teils angegeben ist, der von der Bedrängnis der Israeliten in Ägypten bis hin zur Errettungszusage Jahwes und der Sendung von Mose und Aaron zum Pharao verläuft. Am Schluß dieses Teils werden—damit zum zweiten Teil überleitend

---

[56] Ob auch Ex. xiv 6 von R^P stammt, kann hier offenbleiben; einen Nachweis könnte nur die Analyse von Ex. xiv insgesamt erbringen.

[57] Vgl. Zenger, "Wo steht die Pentateuchforschung heute? Ein kritischer Bericht über zwei wichtige neuere Publikationen", *BZ*, N.F. 24 (1980), pp. 101-16; H.-Ch. Schmitt, "'Priesterliches' und 'prophetisches' Geschichtsverständnis in der Meerwundererzählung Ex 13, 17-14, 31. Beobachtungen zur Endredaktion des Pentateuch", in *Textgemäß ... Fs. für E. Würthwein* (Göttingen, 1980), pp. 139-55; H. Donner, "Der Redaktor. Überlegungen zum vorkritischen Umgang mit der Heiligen Schrift", *Henoch 2* (1980), pp. 1-30; Weimar, *Die Berufung des Mose*, pp. 16-23, 332-66.

[58] Vgl. Weimar-Zenger, *Exodus*, pp. 11-15.

—Mose und Aaron nochmals betont als diejenigen vorgestellt, "die zum Pharao, dem König von Ägypten redeten, um die Israeliten aus Ägypten herauszuführen" (Ex. vi 27). Auch der *zweite Teil* (Ex. vi 28-xi 10), der die Plagengeschichten erzählt, hat eine Rahmung durch die beiden gerneralisierenden und zusammenfassenden Abschnitte Ex. vi 28-30 und Ex. xi 9-10: beide Abschnitte unterstreichen das Nicht-Hören des Pharao, wobei Ex. xi 9-10 nochmals das in den Plagengeschichten selbst mehrfach angesprochene Motiv der "Stärkung" des Herzens des Pharao durch Jahwe und des Nicht-Entlassens der Israeliten durch den Pharao wiederholt. Den *dritten Teil* bildet Ex. xii 1-xvi 35 (V. 36 ist späte Glosse!). Er wird gerahmt durch die beiden Ortsangaben am Anfang "im Lande Ägypten" (Ex. xii 1) und am Ende "in besiedeltes Land/an die Grenzen des Landes Kanaan" (Ex. xvi 35); die Ortsangabe "im Lande Ägypten" verbindet den Beginn des dritten Teils mit dem Beginn des zweiten Teils, da auch dort die Angabe "im Lande Ägypten" gesetzt ist. Thematisch bildet Ex. xii bzw. Ex. xvi die Bestimmungen über Pascha bzw. Sabbat eine Rahmung dieses Teils. In seinem Zentrum steht die wunderbare Errettung Israels am Meer (Ex. xiv 1-xv 21). Über die detaillierte Struktur dieses Teils aus der Sicht der Schlußredaktion werden wir sogleich sprechen. *Der vierte Teil* (Ex. xvii 1-xxiv 18) ist die kompositionelle und theologische Mitte des Exodusbuches. Die strukturelle Abgrenzung von Ex. xvii-xxiv zu einem zusammengehörenden Block, der zunächst durch das Ende des vorangehenden Teils und den offenkundigen Neueinsatz des folgenden Teils in Ex. xxv 1 literarisch markiert ist, wird durch eine Reihe redaktioneller Verklammerungen unterstrichen, die R^P in die ihm vorgegebenen Erzählungen eingefügt hat. So schafft R^P durch entsprechende Zusätze in Ex. xvii 6 (Horeb); xviii 5b (Gottesberg) und xxiv 13 (Gottesberg) für alle Erzählungen die gleiche Szenerie: es sind nun verschiedene Szenen eines einzigen großen Geschehenszusammenhangs am Horeb/Gottesberg/Sinai. Die beiden Rahmengeschichten Ex. xvii und Ex. xxiv sind darüber hinaus durch die gleichen Akteure aufeinanderbezogen: Mose und Josua, Aaron und Hur sowie die Ältesten (Ex. xvii 5, 6, 9, 10, 12 bzw. xxiv 13-14). Der *fünfte Teil* (Ex. xxv 1-xxxi 18) besteht aus einer einzigen, nur hin und wieder durch Wiederholung der Rede-Einleitungsformel gegliederten Gottesrede, die gerahmt ist durch die Rede-Einleitungsformel zu Beginn (xxv 1) und eine Notiz, die ausdrücklich das Ende des Redens Jahwes mit Mose angibt (xxxi 18). Dieser Teil enthält

Bestimmungen für die Errichtung und Ausstattung des Heiligtums, wobei auffälligerweise als Abschluß der Gottesrede Bestimmungen über den Sabbat (xxxi 12-17) stehen, womit der Pentateuchredaktor, von dem diese Sabbattheologie stammt, auf den analogen Sabbatabschnitt in Ex. xvi zurückverweist.[59] Die Szenerie des Ganzen ist die in Ex. xxiv 15-18 von Jahwe selbst herbeigeführte Gottesbegegnung, wodurch die Rückbindung an den vierten Teil des Exodus-Buches unterstrichen wird. Den *sechsten Teil* (Ex. xxxii 1-xxxiv 35) begrenzen die beiden Aussagen am Anfang und am Ende des Textkomplexes: Die Israeliten sahen, daß Mose seinen Abstieg vom Berge verzögerte bzw. sie sahen, daß die Haut seines Gesichtes glänzte (xxxii 1, xxxiv 35). Beide Notizen geben zugleich das Aussagegefälle des Teiles an, das über drei Stationen verläuft: Abfall und Strafe (Ex. xxxii)—Ringen um Jahwes Gegenwart bei seinem Volk (Ex. xxxiii)—Erneuerung des Bundes (Ex. xxxiv). Der *siebte Teil* (Ex. xxxv 1-xl 38) erzählt die Ausführung der im fünften Teil von Gott gegebenen Bestimmungen, also die Errichtung und Ausstattung des Heiligtums. Eine eigentliche literarische Rahmung dieses Teils ist hier zwar nicht zu erkennen, jedoch bildet der Spannungsbogen zwischen dem "Versammeln" des Volkes durch Mose (xxxv 1), das kontrastierend an Ex. xxxii 1 anknüpft (Beginn des vorangehenden Teils!), und der abschließenden Reflexion über das Aufbrechen bzw. Nichtaufbrechen der Israeliten (xl 36-38) eine thematische Verklammerung. Insofern dieser Schlußabschnitt bereits auf die Fortsetzung der Wüstenwanderung vorausblickt, entsteht eine Entsprechung zum Ende des dritten Teils des Buches, wo sich in xvi 35 ein Vorausblick auf die Landnahme findet. Der Abschnitt xl 36-38 ist von R^P übrigens als Abschluß des Buches ingesamt formuliert, was seine Abhängigkeit von Num. ix 15-23, dem geschehensmäßigen Ende der Sinaigeschichte überhaupt, anzeigt.

Die eben skizzierten sieben Teile des Exodus-Buches bilden in ihrer Abfolge eine planvolle Komposition. Im Zentrum steht der vierte Teil, um den sich die übrigen sechs Teile in zwei Dreiergruppen ordnen. In beiden Dreiergruppen sind die Randteile (I + III/V + VII) geschehensmäßig eng aufeinanderbezogen (Bedrängnis + Befreiung/Bestimmungen für die Errichtung des Heiligtums + Ausführung dieser Bestimmungen), während die dazwischen liegenden Teile (II/VI) jeweils ein retardierendes Element im Erzählablauf

[59] Zur Sabbattheologie von R^P vgl. auch Weimar, *Die Berufung des Mose*, pp. 361 f.

(Plagen/Abfall) bilden. Die einzelnen Teile der Dreiergruppen sind jeweils am Anfang untereinander verklammert (vi 28-xii 1, xxxii 1-xxxv 1), aber auch als Gruppen durch eine analoge Schlußnotiz aufeinander bezogen. (xvi 35-xl 36-38). Die bedeutsamste Querverbindung der ersten drei Teile, die sich im Meerlied findet, ist zum einen die Theologie von Namen Jahwes, die R^p in Ex. iii 14b-15 (1. Teil), ix 16b (2. Teil) und in xv 3 eingetragen hat, und zum anderen das Theologumenon von der Unvergleichbarkeit Jahwes, die R^p in Ex. xv 11 vorfand und in Ex. ix 14b als Interpretament in die Plagenerzählungen einfügte. Daß die Teile I-III und V-VII insgesamt auf Teil IV als auf ihre theologische Mitte bezogen sind, wird auf der Ebene der Struktur vor allem durch die Sabbattheologie unmittelbar vor bzw. unmittelbar nach diesem Teil hervorgehoben. Durch diese planvolle Komposition gibt die Pentateuchredaktion dem Buch insgesamt eine bedeutungsvolle Tiefenstruktur, die als Tiefpunkt das in der Fremde durch den Pharao entfremdete Israel und als Höhepunkt das durch Jahwe am Heiligtum zur Gemeinschaft gewordene Israel zeichnet. Als entscheidenden Wendepunkt dieser grundlegenden Veränderung hebt die Redaktion die Sinaitheophanie mit Dekalog und Sinaiberit heraus.

Auch die einzelnen Teile dieser Komposition sind teils unter Aufnahme vorgegebener Struktursignale, teils unter Einfügung neu formulierter Notizen von der Schlußredaktion kunstvoll gegliedert.[60] Ich möchte dies am Bauplan des dritten Teils, in dem unser Text Ex. xv 1-21 steht, in knappen Strichen verdeutlichen.

Der Teil setzt mit einer betonten Ortsangabe in Ex. xii 1 "im Lande Ägypten" ein, entfaltet in einem *ersten Abschnitt* die Feier des ersten Pascha, wobei eine Zusammenstellung verschiedener Pascha-Ordnungen eingeflochten wird; dieser erste Abschnitt kommt mit der Aufforderung der Ägypter, Israel möge das Land verlassen, und mit der Plünderungsnotiz in xii 36 zu seinem geschehensmäßigen Ende. Der *zweite Abschnitt* setzt in xii 37 wieder mit einer Ortsangabe ein ("die Israeliten brachen auf von Ramses nach Sukkot"), die zugleich den Bogen schlägt zu der den Abschnitt beschließenden Notiz xiii 20-22 "sie brachen auf von Sukkot und lagerten in Etam am Rande der Wüste". Beide Notizen stammen vermutlich erst vom Pentateuchredaktor, der damit dem dazwischen gesammelten uneinheitlichen Material einen Rahmen gab. Der *dritte Abschnitt* wird

[60] Vgl. die Kompositionsstruktur des ersten Teiles bei Weimar, *Die Berufung des Mose*, pp. 16-23.

in Ex. xiv 1 dezidiert mit einer Redeeinleitungsformel eröffnet, die aus P stammt; der Abschnitt erzählt die wunderbare Rettung Israels am Meer und hat in der Notiz über den Glauben Israels an Jahwe und an Mose einen wirkungsvollen Abschluß. Daran schließt sich als *vierter Abschnitt* das Meerlied an, das auf der Ebene der Pentateuchredaktion durch xv 1b und xv 21b als beabsichtigte Einheit ausgewiesen ist. Der *fünfte Abschnitt* beginnt in xv 22 wieder, wie der zweite, mit einer Aufbruchnotiz "Und Mose ließ Israel aufbrechen vom Schilfmeer". Wie weit dieser Abschnitt reicht, ist zumindest auf den ersten Blick schwer zu entscheiden; zwar findet sich in Ex. xvi 1 wieder eine Aufbruchnotiz, aber ein dadurch abgegrenzter Abschnitt Ex. xv 22-27 wäre im Vergleich zu den übrigen Abschnitten unproportioniert kurz. Gegen eine Zäsur zwischen xv 27 und xvi 1 spricht die Notiz xvi 4bβ, die deutlich eine Verklammerung nach Ex. xv 25b schlägt; sowohl xvi 4bβ wie auch xv 25-27 sind nachpriesterschriftlich, vielleicht sogar erst von R^p. Geht damit der Horizont von Ex. xv 22-27 bis nach Ex. xvi, so bieten sich zwei Möglichkeiten der Strukturierung an: entweder man läßt den Abschnitt bis nach xvi 35 (36) reichen, wo ein deutlicher Abschluß markiert ist, der zudem durch die Angabe "Land Kanaan" den Bogen nach Ex. xii 1 zurück schlägt, oder man teilt noch einmal zwischen xvi 15 und xvi 16 ab und läßt mit xvi 16 einen *sechsten Abschnitt* beginnen, da nicht nur mit dem Sabbat ein neues Thema eingeführt wird, sondern weil hier überschriftartig mit dem Nominalsatz "Dies ist die Ordnung, die Jahwe gebietet" ein Abschnitt eingeführt wird, der weitgehend vom Pentateuchredaktor formuliert ist und sich, wie die nachstehende Zusammenstellung zeigt, als Nachahmung von Ex. xii darbietet. Daß dieser Nominalsatz strukturgliedernd ist, belegt seine Wiederholung gegen Ende des Abschnitts in Ex. xvi 32. Zwischen Ex. xii und xvi 16 ff. gibt es mehrere Entsprechungen; vgl. die Tabelle auf der übernächsten Seite.

Der dritte Teil des Buches Exodus xii 1-xvi 35 (36) besteht demnach aus sechs Abschnitten, die durch die Endredaktion planvoll aufeinander bezogen sind. Je zwei aufeinander folgende Abschnitte sind durch Stichwortbezüge bzw. vom Geschehen her paarweise zusammengeordnet, wobei die beiden Abschnitte über die Rettung am Meer betont in der Mitte stehen. Die Hinordnung der übrigen Abschnitte auf diese Mitte wird durch spiegelbildliche Entsprechungen unterstrichen, durch die die Abschnitte I + VI sowie II + V in Beziehung gesetzt sind. Die Stichwortbezüge der thematisch ohnehin korrespondendierenden Rahmenabschnitte über Pascha und Sabbat sowie die von R^P zwischen Ex. xiv und Ex. xv 1-21 hergestellten Bezüge wurden bereits oben zusammengestellt. Die wichtigsten Entsprechungen zwischen den beiden mittleren Abschnitten II + V liegen einmal in den Aufbruchnotizen xii 37, xv 22, sodann in der Hervorhebung der Wüste (xiii 18, 20, xv 22, xvi 2) und schließlich in der gemeinsamen Tora-Theologie (xiii 9 f., xv 26, xvi 4). Schematisch läßt sich diese Struktur vereinfacht so darstellen, wie dies auf der folgenden Seite versucht wird.

Von dieser Komposition her, die betont Pascha und Sabbat, also zwei entscheidende kultische Vollzüge des nachexilischen Israel, als Rahmen um das Meerwunder legt und die als weitere Rahmung Israels Weg zur bzw. durch die Wüste unter das Motto "Ich will sie erproben, ob sie nach meiner Tora wandeln oder nicht" (Ex. xvi 4, vgl. xiii 9 f., xv 26) stellt, erhält die alte Tradition vom Meerwunder eine großartige Neuinterpretation: der unvergleichliche Gott, der "Roß und Reiter ins Meer warf", begegnet Israel in der nachexilischen Zeit im Kult und im Halten der Tora!

Ex. xvi		Ex. xii	
16	*zh hdbr ʾšr ṣwh yhwh*	24	*wšmrtm ʾt hdbr hzh*
32	*zh hdbr ʾšr ṣwh yhwh*		
16	*lqṭw mmnw ʾyš lpy ʾklw*	4	*ʾyš lpy ʾklw tksw ʿl hśh*
16	*ʾyš lʾšr bʾhlw tqḥw*	3	*wyqḥw lhm ʾyš śh lbyt ʾbwt*
17	*wyʿśw kn bny yśrʾl*	28	*wyʿśw bny yśrʾl . . . kn ʿśw*
19	*ʾyš ʾl ywtr mmnw ʿd bqr*	10	*lʾtwtyrw mmnw ʿd bqr*
23	*šbtwn šbt qdš lyhwh*	11	*psḥ hwʾ lyhwh*
26	*ššt ymym tlqṭhw*	15	*šbʿt ymym mṣwt tʾklw*
	wbywm hšbyʿy šbt		*ʾk bywm hrʾšwn . . .*
32	*lmšmrt ldrtykm*	14	*ldrtykm ḥqt ʿwlm*
33	*lmšmrt ldrtykm*	17	*ldrtykm ḥqt ʿwlm*

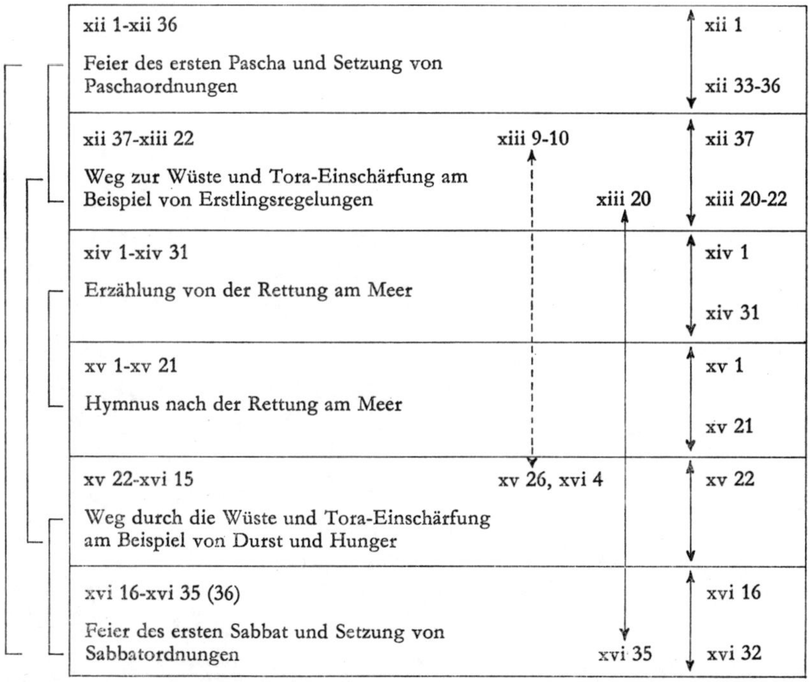